## CHRISTIANITY AND THE LAWS OF CONSCIENCE

This book explores Christian theological, legal, constitutional, historical, and philosophical meanings of *conscience*. It surveys the term in the New Testament text and excavates its meaning for Christian understandings of natural law, the early church Fathers, St. Thomas Aquinas, and the Magisterial Reformers. It explores how conscience has interacted with evangelical political aspirations, rights to sexual expression, and objections to fighting in war. It surveys how the term has been deployed in state and federal constitutional law and how it might be distinguished from related concepts such as religious freedom or religious exercise. It also presents how contemporary Roman Catholic theology and evangelical and Reformed theology understand the term.

**Jeffrey B. Hammond** is an associate professor of law at Faulkner University, Thomas Goode Jones School of Law in Montgomery, Alabama, where he specializes in the intersection of law and Christian theology, constitutional law, and health law.

**Helen M. Alvaré** is a professor of law at the Antonin Scalia Law School, George Mason University in Arlington, Virginia, where she specializes in law and religion and family law. Her books include *Putting Children's Interests First in U.S. Family Law and Policy: With Power Comes Responsibility* (Cambridge University Press, 2018) and *The Conscience of the Institution* (editor).

## LAW AND CHRISTIANITY



The Law and Christianity series publishes cutting-edge work on Catholic, Protestant, and Orthodox Christian contributions to public, private, penal, and procedural law and legal theory. The series aims to promote deep Christian reflection by leading scholars on the fundamentals of law and politics, to build further ecumenical legal understanding across Christian denominations, and to link and amplify the diverse and sometimes isolated Christian legal voices and visions at work in the academy. Works collected by the series include groundbreaking monographs, historical and thematic anthologies, and translations by leading scholars around the globe.

*Books in the Series*

*Christianity and the Laws of Conscience*
edited by Jeffrey B. Hammond and Helen M. Alvaré

*Infidels and Empires in a New World Order: Early Modern Spanish Contributions to International Legal Thought*
David Lantigua

*The Possibility of Religious Freedom: Early Natural Law and the Abrahamic Faiths*
Karen Taliaferro

*Catholic Social Teaching: A Volume of Scholarly Essays*
edited by Gerard Bradley and E. Christian Brugger

*The Immortal Commonwealth: Covenant, Community, and Political Resistance in Early Reformed Thought*
David P. Henreckson

*Great Christian Jurists in American History*
edited by Daniel L. Dreisbach and Mark David Hall

*Great Christian Jurists and Legal Collections in the First Millennium*
edited by Philip L. Reynolds

*English Ecclesiastical Lawyers: A History of Their Life and Work*
R. H. Helmholz

*Law, Love and Freedom: From the Sacred to the Secular*
Joshua Neoh

*Great Christian Jurists in French History*
edited by Olivier Descamps and Rafael Domingo

*Church Law in Modernity: Toward a Theory of Canon Law Between Nature and Culture*
Judith Hahn

*Common Law and Natural Law in America: From the Puritans to the Legal Realists*
Andrew Forsyth

*Care for the World: Laudato Si' and Catholic Social Thought in an Era of Climate Crisis*
edited by Frank Pasquale

*Church, State, and Family: Reconciling Traditional Teachings and Modern Liberties*
John Witte, Jr.

*Great Jurists in Spanish History*
edited by Rafael Domingo and Javier Martínez-Torrón

*Under Caesar's Sword: How Christians Respond to Persecution*
edited by Daniel Philpott and Timothy Samuel Shah

*God and the Illegal Alien*
Robert W. Heimburger

*Christianity and Family Law*
edited by John Witte, Jr. and Gary S. Hauk

*Christianity and Natural Law*
edited by Norman Doe

*Great Christian Jurists in English History*
edited by Mark Hill, QC and R. H. Helmholz

*Agape, Justice, and Law: How Might Christian Love Shape Law?*
edited by Robert F. Cochran, Jr. and Zachary R. Calo

*Calvin's Political Theology and the Public Engagement of the Church*
Matthew J. Tuininga

*God and the Secular Legal System*
Rafael Domingo

*How Marriage Became One of the Sacraments*
Philip L. Reynolds

*Christianity and Freedom (Volume I: Historical Perspectives, Volume II: Contemporary Perspectives)*
edited by Timothy Samuel Shah and Allen D. Hertzke

*The Western Case for Monogamy Over Polygamy*
John Witte, Jr.

*The Distinctiveness of Religion in American Law*
Kathleen A. Brady

*Pope Benedict XVI's Legal Thought: A Dialogue on the Foundation of Law*
edited by Marta Cartabia and Andrea Simoncini

*Introductions to Christianity and Law*

John Witte, Jr. and Frank S. Alexander, eds. *Christianity and Law: An Introduction*. Cambridge University Press, 2008.

John Witte, Jr. and Frank S. Alexander, eds. *Christianity and Human Rights: An Introduction*. Cambridge University Press, 2010.

John Witte, Jr. and Gary Hauk, eds. *Christianity and Family Law: An Introduction*. Cambridge University Press, 2017.

Norman Doe, ed. *Christianity and Natural Law: An Introduction*. Cambridge University Press, 2017.

R. H. Helmholz, ed. *The Profession of Ecclesiastical Lawyers: An Historical Introduction*. Cambridge University Press, 2019.

Rafael Domingo and John Witte, Jr., eds. *Christianity and Global Law*. Routledge and CRC Press, 2020.

Mark Hill, Norman Doe, R. H. Helmholz and John Witte, Jr., eds. *Christianity and Criminal Law*. Routledge and CRC Press, 2020.

*Forthcoming volumes:*

Daniel Crane and Samuel Gregg, eds. *Christianity and Economic Law*. Cambridge University Press, 2021.

Pamela Slotte and John Haskell, eds. *Christianity and International Law*. Cambridge University Press, 2021.

Nicholas Aroney and Ian Leigh, eds. *Christianity and Constitutionalism*. Oxford University Press, 2021.

Silas W. Allard, Kristin E. Heyer and Raj Nadella, eds. *Christianity and the Law of Migration*. Routledge and CRC Press, 2021.

Robert F. CochranJr.Michael P. Moreland, eds. *Christianity and Private Law*. Routledge and CRC Press, 2021.

*We aim to commission other such volumes on Christianity and bankruptcy law, ecclesiastical law, education law, elder law, environmental law, health law, labor law, procedural law, remedies, and other familiar legal topics.*

# Christianity and the Laws of Conscience

AN INTRODUCTION

*Edited by*

**JEFFREY B. HAMMOND**
Faulkner University

**HELEN M. ALVARÉ**
George Mason University

CAMBRIDGE
UNIVERSITY PRESS

**CAMBRIDGE**
**UNIVERSITY PRESS**

University Printing House, Cambridge CB2 8BS, United Kingdom

One Liberty Plaza, 20th Floor, New York, NY 10006, USA

477 Williamstown Road, Port Melbourne, VIC 3207, Australia

314–321, 3rd Floor, Plot 3, Splendor Forum, Jasola District Centre, New Delhi – 110025, India

79 Anson Road, #06–04/06, Singapore 079906

Cambridge University Press is part of the University of Cambridge.

It furthers the University's mission by disseminating knowledge in the pursuit of education, learning, and research at the highest international levels of excellence.

www.cambridge.org
Information on this title: www.cambridge.org/9781108835381
DOI: 10.1017/9781108883856



First published 2021

A catalogue record for this publication is available from the British Library.

*Library of Congress Cataloging-in-Publication Data*
NAMES: Hammond, Jeffrey B., 1975– editor. | Alvaré, Helen, editor.
TITLE: Christianity and the laws of conscience : an introduction / edited by Helen M. Alvaré, George Mason University, Arlington, Virginia; Jeffrey B. Hammond, Faulkner University, Montgomery, Alabama.
DESCRIPTION: Cambridge, United Kingdom ; New York, NY, USA : Cambridge University Press, 2021. | Series: Law and Christianity | Includes bibliographical references and index.
IDENTIFIERS: LCCN 2020012374 (print) | LCCN 2020012375 (ebook) | ISBN 9781108835381 (hardback) | ISBN 9781108793315 (paperback) | ISBN 9781108883856 (epub)
SUBJECTS: LCSH: Liberty of conscience–Philosophy. | Conscience–Religious aspects–Christianity. | Freedom or religion–United States.
CLASSIFICATION: LCC KB2472 .C47 2021 (print) | LCC KB2472 (ebook) | DDC 241/.1–dc23
LC record available at https://lccn.loc.gov/2020012374
LC ebook record available at https://lccn.loc.gov/2020012375

ISBN 978-1-108-83538-1 Hardback

*For Susan*
*and*
*for Catherine, Julian, and Robert Paul*

# Contents

# Contributors

**Helen M. Alvaré** is a professor of law at George Mason University, Antonin Scalia Law School, Arlington, Virginia.

**Edward Andrew** is a professor of political science, *emeritus*, at the University of Toronto, Toronto, Ontario.

**E. Christian Brugger** is a moral theologian and former Dean of the School of Theology and Philosophy at the University of Notre Dame, Sydney, Australia.

**Joseph E. Capizzi** is Ordinary Professor of Moral Theology/Ethics at the Catholic University of America School of Theology and Religious Studies, Washington, DC.

**Peter J. Casarella** is a professor of theology at Duke Divinity School, Durham, North Carolina.

**Nathan S. Chapman** is an associate professor of law at the University of Georgia School of Law, Athens, Georgia.

**Cajetan Cuddy OP** is of the Couvent Saint-Albert-le-Grand (Albertinum), Fribourg, Switzerland.

**Michael J. DeBoer** is an associate professor of law at Faulkner University, Thomas Goode Jones School of Law, Montgomery, Alabama.

**R. Kent Greenawalt** is University Professor at Columbia University Law School, New York, New York.

**Jeffrey B. Hammond** is an associate professor of law at Faulkner University, Thomas Goode Jones School of Law, Montgomery, Alabama.

**David Little** is the T. J. Dermot Dunphy Professor of the Practice in Religion, Ethnicity, and International Conflict, *Emeritus*, at Harvard University Divinity School, Cambridge, Massachusetts.

**Michael McClymond** is a professor of modern Christianity at St. Louis University, St. Louis, Missouri.

**John Anthony McGuckin** is a professor on the Faculty of Theology at the University of Oxford, Oxford, United Kingdom.

**Nathan B. Oman** is the Rollins Professor of Law at The College of William & Mary, Marshall-Wythe School of Law, Williamsburg, Virginia.

**Mark Rienzi** is a professor of law at the Catholic University of America, Columbus School of Law, Washington, DC.

**John L. Thompson** is Senior Professor of Historical Theology and Gaylen and Susan Byker Professor *Emeritus* of Reformed Theology at Fuller Theological Seminary, Pasadena, California.

**Christopher Tollefsen** is the College of Arts and Sciences Distinguished Professor at the University of South Carolina, Columbia, South Carolina.

**Alexis Torrance** is the Archbishop Demetrious Associate Professor of Byzantine Theology at the University of Notre Dame, Notre Dame, Indiana.

**David VanDrunen** is the Robert B. Strimple Professor of Systematic Theology and Christian Ethics at Westminster Seminary California, Escondido, California.

**Micah Watson** is an associate professor of political science at Calvin University, Grand Rapids, Michigan.

**Rosalynde Welch** is an independent scholar, St. Louis, Missouri.

**Wendell Willis** is a retired professor of New Testament at Abilene Christian University, Abilene, Texas.

# Acknowledgments

Jeff Hammond would like to thank his mentor and friend, John Witte, Jr., for commissioning this project and for facilitating the co-editors working together. It has been a joy to work with Professor Alvaré, and I thank her for her wise counsel, keen judgment, and upbeat approach to working on this book. I would also like to thank my colleague, Adam MacLeod, for organizing a conference on the subject of conscience, held in January of 2016 at our home institution in Montgomery, Alabama. That conference was sponsored by the Acton Institute, and the paper I presented there was developed into my chapter in this book. Further, I thank my good friend and colleague, Michael DeBoer, who wrote the excellent chapter on conscience and state constitutions in this collection. Professor DeBoer and I have had many conversations about conscience over the years, and I thank him for his abiding friendship. I dedicate my work on this project to my dear wife, Dr. Susan Hammond. Susan is a busy academic herself, but she has never failed to encourage me in my work, including that on this book.

Helen Alvaré would also like to thank John Witte, Jr. for his encouragement and support at the start and throughout this project. His inspiration to pair with Jeff Hammond proved very fruitful as Professor Hammond is a devoted scholar, a tireless worker, and blessed with kindness and discernment.

Professor Alvaré is also immensely grateful to her research assistant Sarah Christensen, librarians Esther Koblenz and Peter T. Vay, and to her husband and family for their patience during the long drafting and editing process.

Together, the editors would first like to thank Amy Wheeler and Anita Mann of the Emory Center for the Study of Law and Religion for their expert handling of all sorts of details concerning the production, publication, and funding of the book. Second, we thank John Berger, formerly of Cambridge University Press, and now of Fordham University, for his sage shepherding of this project in its early stages. And we also thank Jackie Grant of the Press for providing oversight of the book as it was produced. The editors humbly acknowledge and thank each chapter author for their contributions to this volume. Each author worked through four or more rounds of edits with notable patience, acumen, and good cheer.

The editors thank the University of Notre Dame Press (USA) for allowing Peter Casarella's chapter, "Culture and Conscience in the Thought of Joseph Ratzinger, Pope Benedict XVI," to be reprinted in this volume from a prior University of Notre Dame Press collection, with revisions. The editors also thank Cambridge University Press for allowing David Little's chapter, "Roger Williams and Conscience," to be reprinted in this volume from a prior Cambridge University Press collection, with revisions.

The editors thank Brian Miller for his exceptional technical work on this book. Brian was our expert on all matters having to do with the *Chicago Manual of Style*, and he did his job brilliantly. This book would not have been published without Brian's contribution. Thank you, Brian!

Finally, the editors are profoundly grateful to the McDonald Agape Foundation for its generous funding of this project. In particular, we the thank the late Ambassador Alonzo L. McDonald and Peter McDonald.

# Introduction

HELEN M. ALVARÉ AND JEFFREY B. HAMMOND

A broad array of Christians have wrestled with the subject of conscience from the beginnings of Christianity to the present time. Remarkably – given their differing nationalities, historical circumstances, and religious convictions – leading thinkers have regularly pursued similar questions about conscience. Sometimes they have reached overlapping conclusions. Often, however, concerning both large and small matters, they arrive at different or even radically different answers. But the persistence and correspondence of their inquiries remains a testament to the innate and universal importance of the matter of conscience.

For two millennia, leading scholars and religious figures have asked, for example: Is there such a phenomenon as conscience? What is it? Is it primarily or exclusively a religious matter, possessed by religious people, or does it also pertain to nonreligious people and convictions? What do Old and New Testament sources say about it, if anything? Does Scripture draw from prior religious or philosophical sources that treat conscience? Is conscience more or less, or even exclusively, a subjective or an objective reality? What images and metaphors for conscience are used in Scripture, and which are most helpful?

They have also asked how conscience is formed, wondering whether it is more or less, or even exclusively, the work and voice of God. Is it human beings' own work or voice? Is it the voice of the community? The voice of religious authorities? Can the opinion of a majority or some critical mass of religious adherents constitute such authority? Is conscience in any way sourced in natural law?

They also inquire about where conscience is located. Does it involve the mind, the will, the heart, feelings, and/or the soul? Perhaps some combination of these?

Many religious and academic figures have asked, too, how conscience operates. To what extent does it discern, judge, affirm, accuse, or perhaps simply heighten perceptions of good and evil? Is it more in the nature of a divine judgment or a self-evaluation? Does it have reference more or less or exclusively to the individual or to the community? Can and should a conclusion reached by the conscience be trusted by the individual? If so, to what degree? How great is the influence of sin upon the operation of the human conscience? Is conscience fallible or infallible? What are the human and divine consequences of acting according to an erroneous conscience? If conscience errs, can it be reformed or renewed? If so by whom or what? What is the relationship between conscience and natural law, if any? Should there be one?

As societies became more religiously diverse, there arose more questions concerning conscience in the context of a pluralistic environment. What ought to be the relationship between conscience and positive law? Should the latter accommodate the former, and if so to what extent? Does Scripture or natural law have anything to say on this point? In the legal arena, scholars, lawmakers and judges contest the original and later meanings of legislative and statutory legal protections for religious and nonreligious conscience. They ask about their scope, their limits and the rationales for those limits, their constitutional and political permissibility and wisdom, their coverage of both religious and nonreligious commitments, and their moral and political wisdom and fairness.

Today, legal commentators struggle in particular with questions about accommodating conscience claims asserted by institutions. Which institutions might qualify? Why? In order to protect the individuals who comprise the institution? Because the law commands it? Or because of particular goods and interests possessed by institutions *qua* institutions?

Contemporary legal scholars, judges, and legislators also contend frequently over claims made by individuals in the context of military service, or to resist state laws incorporating ideas about sex, marriage, and parenting increasingly at odds with Christian commitments.

Proposals and common conceptions about conscience have not developed over time in a strictly linear fashion, from one set of ideas toward another set that is in the ascendancy today. Rather, from time to time over the course of the last two millennia, scholars and religious figures have proposed ideas more commonly heard in our own time – about, for example the infallibility or subjective quality of conscience – to significant acclaim. Still, it is broadly true to observe that, as compared with the past, contemporary ideas about conscience tend to value: the individual and individual values over the community and its values, including religious communities and authorities; the subjective over the objective; the nonreligious as much or more than the religious; positive law and majority will over religious conscience; and the political calculus more than the moral calculus.

This book illustrates this trajectory and explores the myriad questions about conscience recited above, during the period from the Old Testament to the present day and across a wide variety of Christian denominations. It treats these from the perspectives of scholars in the disciplines of history, philosophy, law, and theology. Together, the chapters witness to the persistent concern demonstrated by leading Christian intellectuals and religious figures to grasp the meaning and operation and limits of conscience.

While it is impossible to cover every person and text that influenced Christian beliefs about conscience and the rights of conscience respecting law, this book explores those figures and sources arguably exerting the most lasting influence upon the questions and answers about conscience held by a wide variety of Christian communities and sometimes also by society and/or the state. Thus, its chapters examine the Old Testament, the New Testament (especially the Gospels and the writings of St. Paul), the early Church Fathers – both East and West – Thomas Aquinas, Martin Luther, John Calvin, Pierre Bayle, John Edwards, Roger Williams, US federal and state constitutions, The Book of Mormon, the Second Vatican Council, and Pope Benedict XVI. Along the way, chapter authors also engage other important influencers, including but not limited to: Plato, Socrates, the Stoics, Philo, Aristotle, John Locke, René Descartes, Thomas Hobbes, Jean-Jacques Rousseau, James Madison, George Mason, Thomas Jefferson, Cardinal John Henry Newman, Carl Henry, Billy Graham, Harold Berman, Harold Schulweis, John Rawls, and Pope John Paul II.

Given the wide swath of history, personages, religions, sources, and ideas this book covers, the chapters are grouped under three major headings for ease of exploration. The first group of chapters (Part I) treats major themes shaping the understanding of conscience in Christianity: the teachings of the New Testament, the relationship between conscience and natural law in both the Old and the New Testaments, the treatment of conscience in the early years of Christianity, and the meaning and role of the "sensus fidei" and the Magisterium in the formation of conscience according to the Roman Catholic tradition. In Chapter 1, Wendell Willis excavates from within the New Testament (NT) the meanings of what is termed "conscience" in the English language today. Upon surveying all the books of the NT, Willis concludes that *suneidesis* (the word most-often translated in the NT as conscience) does not have a fixed meaning for NT writers. Willis's key contribution is to cleave the reader's understanding of *suneidesis* into two main categories, while also identifying additional shades of meaning across NT texts. For example, in the Pauline corpus, especially in 1 and 2 Corinthians, *suneidesis* seems most often to refer to a person's self-knowledge or internal understandings about himself and his past actions. Here, *suneidesis* should be understood as "consciousness" rather than "conscience". In this sense, *suneidesis* in Corinthians is fundamentally retrospective in nature, while in Romans, *suneidesis* is more often a guide for the believers' future moral choices. Other usages of *suneidesis* in the NT are a variation on the theme first established by Paul: consciousness of past actions or an inner model for one's future actions. In Chapter 2, David VanDrunen ties the natural law concepts found in both the Old and New Testaments to a sense of conscience. The notion of natural law appears early in the Old Testament (OT), in God's covenant with Noah. God instructs Noah that, for example, the killing of an innocent must be recompensed (thereby indicating that innocent people must not be wantonly killed). While there is not one Hebrew word for conscience in the OT, it does identify the "heart" (*leb*) and "kidneys" (*kelayot*) as the mechanisms by which the wise and discerning person applies what he knows to be true about the way the world works. In the New Testament, conscience is the "subjective human faculty that recognizes right and wrong and thus bears witness to a person's standing before the law." The Apostle Paul's discussion of natural law in Romans chapters 2 and 3 reveals that although not all receive God's express law (as did God's people on Mt. Sinai), all people everywhere have an innate sense of moral rectitude to which their consciences testify. All persons everywhere therefore are subject to God's righteous judgment.

In Chapter 3, John McGuckin looks at the earliest writings of Christian theologians about conscience. These relied a great deal upon the Scriptures and upon Plato, Aristotle, Stoics, Cicero, and Seneca and grappled regularly with the positive and negative possibilities of conscience. In the positive account, persons might be assured of certainty in their discernment if conscience is the inner voice of God or an internal compass. Negatively, conscience might be poorly informed and promote delusion. Greek sources concerning conscience were concerned to search out anthropological and cosmological truths, not divine ones. But Christian writers brought the inquiry into the religious domain. St. Paul wrote about conscience in connection with a law "written on the heart," a moral guide to both Christians and pagans, but fallible and in need of the grace and salvation of Christ. The Greek fathers, led by Origen, emphasized conscience as an awareness of divine things, albeit impaired by man's fall, yet still oriented toward union with God and obedience to moral norms. The Latin fathers, led by Augustine, emphasized humanity's corruption after the fall and need for divine grace. Thus, conscience could convict but not necessarily stimulate a person to goodness. Only loving God could accomplish this. In both Latin and Greek Christian wisdom, therefore, conscience was far more than an inner voice instructing about right and wrong. It was a set of reflections on the spiritual identity of human beings.

In Chapter 4, Christian Brugger treats an important contemporary question about conscience in Roman Catholic theology: the role of the *sensus fidei* (the sense of the faith) in relation to the formation and deliberations and correctness of conscience. Some theologians have claimed that when a significant number of the lay faithful come to a conclusion about a matter of faith or morals, they are expressing the *sensus fidei*, which merits recognition as the truth. Consequently, such a conclusion can unfailingly inform the conscience. The much-debated notion of the *sensus fidei* has a long biblical and theological history but was first prominently used by the Catholic Church in the Second Vatican Council's Constitution on the Church, *Lumen Gentium*, as part of the discussion of the work of the laity. There it concerned the idea of a divinely infused capacity of the baptized to understand the truths of, and reject false expressions of, the faith, under the guidance of the Holy Spirit, given their membership in the Mystical Body of Christ with its priestly, prophetic, and kingly roles. It is an intellectual power, though not of a syllogistic nature. Many false conceptions of the meaning and manner of exercise of the *sensus fidei* followed especially in the period after the Council. In these conceptions, it is regularly divorced from the teaching authority of the Church and inappropriately identified as a kind of subjective feeling or sixth sense about good and evil that can be exercised even by those not currently practicing the Catholic faith or engaged with Scripture and the life of Christ-like charity. The *sensus fidei* is rather communal in nature. It is always inclusive of the teachings of Jesus and the Church about right and wrong. It is about the Church as a whole and is witnessed by the universal consent of the whole Church – lay, hierarchy, and religious. It can be blunted by poor liturgy and poor formation. It is limited to matters of faith and morals and attendant to building up the Church. When properly exercised, it is one of the ways the Church can speak infallibly about what is to be believed.

The second group of chapters explores how major religious figures and Christian traditions understood conscience. These chapters cover the Church Fathers, both East and West, St. Thomas Aquinas, the Magisterial Reformers John Calvin and Martin Luther, Pierre Bayle, Roger Williams, Jonathan

Edwards, contemporary Evangelicals, Latter Day Saints, and Joseph Ratzinger who later became Pope Benedict XVI.

In Part II, Chapter 5 by Alexis Torrance considers early Church Fathers' treatment of the origins, natural law associations, roles, limits, and images of conscience. He notes that there is no single, systematic treatment of conscience in the patristic literature, but instead, many treatments that require piecing together. He also advises attention to both the similarities and the differences between contemporary references to conscience and ancient meanings. Contemporary commentators are especially prone to speak of conscience to affirm individually autonomous judgments about subjective thoughts and feelings. Early Church Fathers, however, stressed that conscience is a gift exercised in community presupposing shared convictions. They also stressed the possibility that conscience may become impaired under a variety of influences. The idea and terminology of conscience existed in Greek and Roman culture. Christians, however, especially St. Paul, employed theological reflection in a way crucial to the deliberations of Church Fathers. New Testament letters speak of conscience as a human faculty – an important element of what it means to *be* human. Conscience is given by God, but not God's voice, though it does bring God's voice to bear in our lives. It was a Christian innovation to connect conscience with the idea of a *divinely* inscribed law. Some patristic authors identify conscience with a natural law, generally as distinct from natural law, but bearing witness to it.

Human knowledge of right and wrong will be clouded by sin, though not extinguished. Thus, conscience needs cleansing, first by baptism, but also by following the commandments, and by continual examination of conscience and confession. It also needs "guarding" of different sorts in relation to God, the neighbor, and the material world. It continually requires the grace of the Holy Spirit to govern one's moral action in a way that might lead to God.

Regarding the location of conscience, the fourth and fifth century Macarian Homilies speak of conscience as a "member of the soul," as guiding the heart as a "captain in the mind," and as a judge. It is within the soul but above other faculties of the soul as an arbiter of human activities. It is related to the mind, will, thought, and feelings. It should direct persons toward actions leading to God and away from their opposite. Conscience not only judges but also accuses, causing pain to a transgressor.

In Chapter 6, Cajetan Cuddy OP examines of the nature of conscience according to the intricate categories of St. Thomas Aquinas. Cuddy distinguishes Aquinas's understanding of conscience as an act from a common belief that it is a power of habit. It is an act of ordering knowledge – some universal knowledge, some particular – to a particular act, whether the act is past, present, or future. Conscience directs future acts, and with reference to past acts, can accuse or excuse.

The term "conscience" in Aquinas is distinguishable from the manner in which it is used in contemporary times, to mean an evaluation of whether or not an act is ethical or correct. Aquinas's understanding includes such a judgment, but also includes witnessing to a particular act's being a human (rational, chosen) act, therefore of a moral kind and not an unconscious one.

Aquinas also makes a distinction between conscience and the notion of *synderesis*, which is the habitual, natural, ineradicable, and infallible disposition of the human person that shapes the human power of understanding. *Synderesis* inclines human nature to the good and objects to evil. As a "preamble" to virtue, it provides a habitual awareness of the first principles of morality shaping moral reasoning to be applied to human action and begins with the first principle: do good and avoid evil. While *synderesis* concerns understanding the universal moral principles applicable to all human actions, conscience applies knowledge to a particular act. Thus, conscience proceeds from *synderesis*. But conscience has limits and can be erroneous and in need of correction because of the possibility of limits to or errors about knowledge, or how knowledge applies to the particular situation at hand. An erroneous conscience does not eradicate a human being's orientation to the truth, and error can be removed. Conscience should be distinguished from human free will. Conscience does not compel. It is the cognitional evaluation of whether or not something should be done; but free choice is the application of knowledge to an action and, with a judgment of prudence, the execution of an action. A person may choose to act against a judgment of conscience.

Conscience and the law of God have the same binding force for Aquinas, not because conscience is infallible or human reason is independent of God's law, but because conscience mediates God's moral norms to human beings undertaking a particular action, through the application of *synderesis*, which is always ordered to moral truth, meaning that it is ordered to God. Still, only a correct conscience binds absolutely while an erroneous conscience binds conditionally because our mistaken judgment might be corrected. At the same time, an erroneous judgment might excuse us subjectively if it proceeds from knowledge that is not false by our fault. Still, bad actions proceeding from an erroneous conscience will nevertheless frustrate human flourishing.

In Chapter 7, John Thompson describes how the preeminent figures of the Protestant Reformation, Martin Luther and John Calvin, treated the subject of conscience. For Luther, natural conscience is beset by the weight and ill-ease of knowing that a person can never meet the rigorous requirements of the law. Faith can relieve a human being's downtrodden conscience, which would otherwise accuse and condemn him. In this way, Luther distinguished himself from his teacher, Gabriel Biel, who taught that the Christian should be in a constant state of tension between the peace that comes from contemplating Christ's salvific work on the cross and the disquiet that follows from the thought that one must do "one more thing" to earn God's approval. Instead, once a person accepts the favor of God that flows solely from trusting him, his conscience is liberated. He knows he can do nothing on his own to merit that favor. His conscience is liberated "to trust God's promise of mercy and forgiveness." The highest functioning conscience for Luther, therefore, is the one that does not depend on its own goodness or perfection. To rely upon oneself renders a conscience inherently unreliable.

Calvin teaches that, though a person's conscience is a native-born faculty, it is marred and affected by the fall. Once a person is saved from sin, however, his conscience is transformed so that he desires to obey the essential will of God found in the law. This is true even though adherence to the law will not add in the least to his salvation. For this reason – to assist Geneva's Christians to grow progressively in holiness – Calvin created a catechism to train and chasten the conscience. Calvin also helped to found the Geneva consistory, which was less a disciplinary body, and rather "a school for consciences." Here, religious leaders could address believers' concerns about the Christian life in a loving way, to train hearts and consciences in the ways of God.

In Chapter 8, Jeffrey Hammond sketches the outline of a contemporary biblical theology of conscience. According to Hammond, a sensitive Christian conscience is an ever-growing, constantly recalibrating capacity of the regenerated (converted) person. Then, through the sanctifying work of the Holy Spirit, the Christian truly can seek to fulfill the two great commands of the New Testament: to love God and love your neighbor. The process of working out these commands involves judgment of what to do in any given situation. However, in making any difficult judgment, the converted, sanctified Christian is always aided by the "still, small" voice of the Holy Spirit, wise counselors, prayer, and the certain knowledge that the correct, conscientious decision will always line up with the will of God as revealed in the Word of God.

The redeemed conscience is one that is at the same time bound and freed. The Christian is bound to follow the moral instruction in the New Testament, but at the same time, she is also freed to do it. In this way, the biblically informed, Holy Spirit–led conscience channels the Christian away from decisions and conduct that would displease God, while simultaneously freeing her to both judge and act for the benefit of her neighbor. Baronelle Stutzman, the now famous florist in Washington State, was freed to use her talent to create beautiful floral arrangements for all her customers, no matter their sexual orientation. She was bound, though, to limit that use when asked to use her talent to celebrate something she conscientiously thought to be false – a same-sex wedding. In deploying her conscience, Stutzman reaped significant legal consequences.

The redeemed conscience is one that judges *and* will be judged by the God who perceives the deliberations of all consciences. The Christian, however, sensitive to the Spirit in both deciding and acting, can rest upon her decisions with a sense of equanimity and peace, knowing that she has faithfully exercised her conscience.

In Chapter 9, Edward Andrew discusses Pierre Bayle, an important influence upon the Enlightenment. Bayle held both that conscience was the certain, infallible "voice of God" – a view most often associated with Calvin – and that humans can make errors of judgment. As the Enlightenment progressed, leading thinkers increasingly insisted that social approval, not God's voice, was the guiding force for conscience-based decision-making. Thus, freedom of conscience became less about having an absolute certain inner knowledge of the proper course of action, and more about aligning oneself with social forces that might create harmony, peace, and stability.

Bayle maintained that conscience was a real and identifiable faculty of the human person, although subject to error. This distinguished him from another important Enlightenment thinker, John Locke, who frequently referenced conscience in his political writings. However, in his *Essay concerning Human Understanding*, Locke asserted that conscience was nothing more than one's long-standing beliefs. Bayle, however, proposed that conscience was the careful working out of the practical applications of natural law and Scripture.

Two contemporary figures make fruitful conversation partners for Bayle: Rabbi Harold Schulweis and the jurist Harold Berman. Schulweis views conscience as a force of judgment outside law. Morality is neither fixed nor inherent inside the person; rather, the person with an active conscience constantly calibrates and recalibrates her course of action and judges the right thing to do in particular situations. Berman, however, viewed conscience as a force within or alongside the law, much like a jury. A jury is a legal entity, yet it works *with* the facts and law as the court presents them. In the end, however, it renders its own judgment about the proper decision under the circumstances.

In Chapter 10, David Little presents Roger Williams as a seventeenth-century iconoclast and champion of conscience. Williams was expelled from the Massachusetts Bay colony that ostensibly prized free exercise but in fact recognized it only within narrow bands of religious orthodoxy. Williams thereafter prized freedom of conscience in the charter for the Providence Plantations and Rhode Island. A central guiding principle for Williams is the sharp distinction between the "inward" and "external" fora. The "inward forum" is the conscience, a "spiritual power" changeable by reason and persuasion. The "external forum" is "outward behavior," meaning actions that can be coerced by the governing authority through force, in order to protect life, property, and other tangible interests. Williams provocatively labeled coercive acts against conscience as "soul rape" and "piracy," indicating how deeply and intimately these violated the person.

Williams maintained a fruitful relationship with the Narangansett Indians, having shown them a great deal of respect, as the people who provided him refuge when he was expelled from the Massachusetts Bay colony. He did not attempt to co-opt their government and fully respected their unfettered ability to choose religion (or not), in the quiet of their own internal fora.

In Chapter 11, Michael McClymond summarizes Jonathan Edwards's theology of conscience. Edwards concedes that everyone has a conscience. Everyone's "natural conscience" can perceive right and wrong, but only the converted conscience can fully apprehend God's moral excellence and beauty. Further, the conscience operates on the principle of "reversibility": the empathetic orientation of one's actions considering their effects on others. However, the person with the converted conscience is constantly aware of his propensity to sin and that God's moral demands are forever correct.

Conscience gets stronger and more refined the more it is heeded; conversely, it gets duller the more it is resisted. The faith of true believers removes the stain of a guilty conscience., Even if not redeemed, however, that selfsame natural conscience will agree entirely with the justness of God's righteous punishment for him at the Last Judgment.

In Chapter 12, Micah Watson argues that an active conscience is the natural outgrowth of the evangelical mind. Watson defines evangelicalism as the form of Protestantism that relies on the truths of historical Christianity while navigating between mainline Protestantism and fundamentalism. For evangelicals, the notion of conscience is founded in the Bible, particularly the writings of the Apostle Paul. But the idea also flowered in the period of the post-Reformation world, during which time it was taught that an active conscience was a sign of person's salvation. The notion of conscience also led the evangelical Christian to be active in the world against all forms of unrighteousness. In the United States, this contributed to the proliferation of voluntary societies, where Christians who were "saved for service" could exercise their consciences to spread the Gospel or stamp out perceived evils (like the use of alcohol). As Watson traces the history of evangelical conscience into the twentieth century, he describes voices like Carl F. H. Henry and others who sought a rapprochement between the pious, removed strand of evangelicalism, and adherents who were firmly committed to making the world a better place through social action. Later in the twentieth century, evangelicals sought peaceful existence in society more than society's regeneration. Still, evangelicals continue to conscientiously oppose perceived social evils, including most recently, state recognized same-sex marriage.

In Chapter 13, Rosalynde Welch and Nathan Oman describe how the Church of Jesus Christ of Latter-day Saints (The Church of Jesus Christ) has interacted with conscience. As distinguished from many Protestant accounts of conscience, the Church of Jesus Christ's account does not focus on conscience as internal, subjective choosing by the self. Instead, it relies on externally provided, yet personally received, revelation – whether universally available (the "light of Christ") or more exclusive (the "gift of the Holy Ghost"). And though the church values personal revelation, authoritative interpretations and decisions by the church hierarchy prevail over sincere, conscientiously held beliefs of individual church members.

Though not common, conscientious dissent is not unheard of within the Church of Jesus Christ. Notably, for several decades in the nineteenth century, the church resisted complying with the welter of anti-polygamy laws passed by Congress. Though some resistance appropriated the language of conscience as its basis, others in the church identified outside forces – whether revelation, prophetic oracles, religious persecution, or the Constitution (which the church esteemed as superior to mere laws passed by Congress) – as reasons to resist successive debilitating waves of oppression by the federal government. More recently, in a religious liberty case heard by the Supreme Court (*Bishop* v. *Amos*),[1] the church based its liberty claim on its collective interest in autonomously running its own affairs.

Notwithstanding this, the Church of Jesus Christ generally has prized obedience to government and fealty to law over against idiosyncratic conscientious resistance. Two important documents, including one from Joseph Smith, though not authoritatively revealed, have played a significant role in establishing and maintaining the church's conformity to law and civil government, to the end of the church living peacefully in the community.

1 483 U.S. 327 (1986).

In Chapter 14, Peter Casarella presents the leading themes in Joseph Ratzinger, later Benedict XVI's, reflection on conscience. An important aspect of Benedict XVI's reflections is his discourse on the theology of culture. This is because contemporary ideas about both conscience and culture tend to set aside questions about truth. On the matter of conscience and truth, Benedict emphasizes that conscience is a law written on the heart of every person – available to believers and nonbelievers alike – and not human beings' subjectivity or superficial consciousness. On the matter of truth and culture, Benedict proposes that culture is oriented to the anticipated arrival of a truth orienting persons toward the revelation of a Redeemer, an orientation he calls the "Advent dynamic." Benedict rejects the notion that a culture might be completely irreligious – considering this a quite recent notion. He holds instead that all cultures are in some fashion religious, and also criticizes contemporary thinking that religions are culturally naked. On these bases, Benedict criticizes the contemporary theological notion of "inculturation" as affirming both errors. He proposes instead the notion of "interculturality," the meeting of cultures in which their "Advent dynamic" is preserved. Each culture remains open to encountering the other without sacrificing its own religious foundation or its openness, supported by all cultures' common experience with human nature.

On the matter of the role of truth and conscience, Benedict interacts with the work of Cardinal John Henry Newman and with Socrates' farewell discourse referring to the existence of truth transcending political categories and not of our own making. He concludes that conscience pertains to the perceptible and demanding presence of a voice of truth within the subject. This is distinguished both from the idea that only empirical scientific phenomenon can attain to truth and from the idea of conscience as nothing more than subjective verification. Benedict's general theory of conscience upholds the Thomistic distinction between *synderesis* (an inner ontology rejecting evil and attracting to the good) and conscience as an *act* of recognizing a good, witnessing to it and judging based upon it. This assists Benedict's careful distinction between the necessity of following even an erroneous conscience and blessing subjectivism, given the fact that persons can become deaf to the promptings of truth. Benedict innovates this area in a way that further safeguards against relativism by suggesting that *synderesis* might be better understood according to the Platonic idea of *anamnesis*: an implanted "memory of the origin," or memory of the true and good. This innovation is tied to Benedict's anthropology about human beings' innate dependency upon God and capacity for dialogue with Him. Benedict acknowledges the role of concrete social environments and circumstances as proximate sources of moral knowledge but insists that the person must always consult the will of God, which awakens conscience to its transcendent calling. On the subject of conscience formation, Benedict highlights sources such as Scripture, the Holy Spirit, the witness and advice of others, the magisterium, beauty (which can awaken persons to transcendence), and the identification with the life, death and resurrection of Christ.

The final group of chapters (Part III) looks at the interplay between conscience and US law. These chapters treat both federal and state statutes and constitutions, religious and nonreligious conscience claims, accommodations, legal contests involving sexual expression rights or institutional conscience claims, and conscientious objections to military service. In this last group, in Chapter 15, Nathan Chapman considers the question of the conceptual and doctrinal relationship between the free exercise of religion and the freedom of conscience in the US Constitution and in legislation. He attends to the much- disputed question whether the Constitution might require statutes protecting religion also to protect nonreligious exercises of conscience. Liberal theorists increasingly emphasize the similarity between religion and deep and comprehensive moral or philosophical commitments and insist that there is no good reason to privilege the former over the latter. Chapman concludes that for the founding generation, freedom of conscience *meant* religious freedom, exercised as a response to one's duty to God.

It is not clear what is to be learned about the scope of religious freedom from the founders' declining Madison's proposal that the First Amendment protect rights of conscience. Today, however, courts and legislatures often negotiate different relationships between freedom of religion and of conscience. For example, other portions of the First Amendment, including the rights of speech, press, and of association, have been employed to protect conscience. And some state and federal statutes explicitly extend accommodation not only to religion but also to various other ideas and commitments placed under the heading of conscience. There are a variety of additional means, too, by which the law could extend religious freedom protections to conscience. The Supreme Court could interpret the Free Exercise clause very broadly to include fundamental nonreligious moral commitments; but it has not, even as it has also not defined religion. The Court could hold that privileging religion over nonreligious conscience violates the Establishment or Equal Protection clauses; but it has also declined to do this. Instead, it has held that legislatures can permissibly lift a burden that affects only the free exercise of religion. Sometimes courts have held that – given the tension between the Free Exercise and Establishment clauses – "religion" can include nontheistic beliefs or practices playing a role similar to religion in people's lives. In the case of the federal statute concerning conscientious objection to military service, the Supreme Court has interpreted it to include non-theistic beliefs. Some statutes accommodating religion also explicitly protect similar nonreligious beliefs or practices. This is seen especially in the case of morally grave conduct such as abortion, physician assisted suicide, and capital punishment.

In Chapter 16, Michael DeBoer identifies five historical stages in US state constitutions' attention to protecting religious conscience. In the first and second periods, from roughly 1776 through the 1830s, state constitutions demonstrated the greatest solicitude for religious conscience and generally contained robust free exercise protections. Some states, like Pennsylvania, specifically allowed conscientious objectors to opt out of armed conflict. By the end of the second period, all states had abolished their denominational establishments. In the third period, from the 1830s through the 1920s, several new states were admitted to the Union. Many of these states that adopted new constitutions copied from the first and second periods' constitutions language that was largely protective of religious conscience. During this third period, Congress failed to add to the United States Constitution the so-called Blaine Amendment, which would have completely prohibited public funding or support for any religious body. Several states reacted to this by adding Blaine-like provisions to their own constitutions, thereby signaling a more pronounced break between religion and public life.

During the fourth period, from the 1920s to the 1970s, the United States Supreme Court incorporated to the states the protections of both the Free Exercise and Establishment Clauses of the US Constitution. This largely displaced the practical effect of state constitutional provisions on religion. States that joined the Union or changed their religion provisions in their constitutions adopted language closely reflecting the religion clauses of the First Amendment. Further, during this time, some state supreme courts borrowed federal interpretations of the US Constitution when interpreting their own state constitutions' religion clauses.

In the fifth period, from the 1970s to the present, state constitutional protections respecting religious conscience have not developed in a consistent manner. Some states followed the example set by the 1990 US Supreme Court decision in *Employment Division* v. *Smith*,[2] which relaxed the strict scrutiny standard for free exercise claims. Other states hewed to the more religion-protective line observed in the fourth period. In response to *Smith*,

[2] 494 U.S. 872 (1990).

Congress passed the Religious Freedom Restoration Act of 1993 (RFRA),[3] restoring the strict scrutiny standard to laws burdening religious exercise. The Court later restricted RFRA's application to federal laws. Consequently, some states passed their own RFRAs. Many recent contests involve state non-discrimination laws and same-sex marriage. Religious conscience claimants, especially wedding vendors, regularly fail in their demands for free exercise accommodations under state constitutions.

In Chapter 17, Mark Rienzi highlights the tension in the United States' pluralistic democracy between religious diversity and majority rule. He proposes that the Supreme Court is currently forging a path of accommodation for religion, versus forced conformity, and that this path has not led to anarchy but rather to social benefits. In the past, the Court and legislatures have sometimes pursued quite limited religious toleration or even forced conformity. Today, the accommodationist path is well-illustrated in the Court's second Jehovah's Witness–pledge case and in both legislative and Supreme Court treatment of conscientious objectors to military service. Conscience protections for those opposed to abortion have been strong from the beginnings of constitutionally protected abortion in 1973. They have been extended to both institutions and individuals and often extend to protect not only religious but also non-religious objections. Even following the Supreme Court's 1990 decision significantly curtailing mandatory Free Exercise accommodations, the US Congress and many states quickly adopted religious conscience protections by statute. Many states also interpreted their state constitutions to provide strong protections for religious freedom. This has not resulted in anarchy but has rather effectively preserved the ability of many medical professionals and religious social service institutions to continue serving the public.

In Chapter 18, Helen Alvaré chronicles the rise of conflicts between Christian individuals and institutions and newer laws championing sexual expression rights or interests. Church and state in the recent past shared outlooks on these matters. Today, however, both state and federal laws often mandate facilitation of or cooperation with behaviors opposed to Christian teachings on, for example, abortion or contraception insurance or same-sex relationships. Regularly, both the state and interested civil society groups claim that the new laws are necessary to secure important adult rights and interests such as health, dignity, equality, privacy, or even personal identity. These laws are in dialogue with and reinforced by important cultural

[3] Pub. L. No. 103-141, 107 Stat. 1488 (1993).

movements emphasizing adults' interests in individual autonomy and sexual freedom, among others. Furthermore, leading corporations and media are weighing in to favor sexual expression protections and to discourage exemptions for religious conscience. For Christians, however, religious teachings about sexual expression are closely linked to core articles of faith on matters such as the nature and identity of God, God's relationship to human beings, and how human beings are to treat one another. Christians judge, therefore, that they ought not to cooperate with laws contradicting these commitments. They also point to the close ties between impaired family relationships and increasingly rigid and toxic divides between racial and socioeconomic groups in the United States. In other words, the stakes for both sides of the controversy are high. The future is uncertain and depends upon myriad factors currently in play.

In Chapter 19, Joseph Capizzi lays out the Roman Catholic just war theory and its relationship to the development and sharpening of Catholic teaching on conscience more generally. The scriptural context for the just war teaching is Jesus' farewell discourse to his Apostles in John 14, in which he promises to give peace, but not as world gives, not as a kind of order that an earthly political community might achieve. The world's peace is often tainted with the temptation to sacrifice even neighbors and the innocent for the goals of one group of people, one nation. The just war approach views war within the context of God's granting political authority only for the purpose of promoting legitimate objectives such as order, justice, the common good, and especially peace. War can be a legitimate expression of the conscience but only if ordered toward peace, guided by morality, and open always to the conversion of self and neighbor toward wills joined in communion and ordered toward peace. The just war approach excludes political objectives that could be served only by illicit means, such as vengeance. It prohibits direct harm to noncombatants. Yes, the sword is one possible political means but only because of the reality of sin. Still it is always necessary for the one using the sword to understand that *both* sides, *both* contending parties are potential members of the community for whom peace is a goal, not just the citizens of one state. This follows from the Noahic covenant, from the New Testament, and from the Roman Catholic theory of the state. As against any duty of military service, US law currently protects the conscience of those who oppose *all* wars on the basis of religion or nonreligious morals; these are conscientious objectors (COs). It does not, however, protect those who oppose only *unjust* wars: "selective conscientious objectors" (SCOs). The distinction between COs and SCOs has survived legal challenges that it violates the Establishment Clause on the grounds that it is not denominationally neutral.

But there are strong arguments that an effective military would want to exempt SCOs and that mandatory service harms the SCO in the same manner as the CO. Finally, a consistent application of conscience protection would instruct that soldiers serving in the military retain their moral agency as rational beings with a conscience, generally to refuse to follow orders contravening their conscience and the moral law.

In Chapter 20, Christopher Tollefsen takes up the currently neuralgic question of institutions' claims of conscience rights. He proposes that the Supreme Court's description in *Burwell* v. *Hobby Lobby* of the rights of religious corporations bears on the question. Recently, there is less agreement to respect even individual conscience. Institutional conscience attracts even greater skepticism. Skeptics wonder whether an institution can possess a conscience or demand respect for it. In connection with medical institutions, they ask whether it should be the standard of ethics for doctors to provide patients *all* of the services the law allows, including abortion sterilization, physician assisted suicide, and gender transition. Otherwise, they fear unacceptable costs to clients and employees.

Conscience is predicated of an institution ordinarily by way of analogy to the paradigm case of individual conscience. Nevertheless, institutional conscience can be a valuable reality worthy of protection in its own right. Individuals' conscience claims are regularly linked to the importance of securing personal integrity through keeping commitments. Demands to do evil acts are not honored. Early and later federal laws have protected individual and institutional conscience claims respecting health care. But today there is a more robust debate about institutional conscience in bioethics. It is asserted that institutions, lacking consciousness, can't suffer injury and that any conscience protection will come at the expense of the needs of clients and the consciences of medical professionals. But the value of institutional conscience is implicated in the Supreme Court's consideration of the question of corporate personhood in *Burwell* v. *Hobby Lobby*. This case involved a closely held corporation's refusal to comply with a federal regulation mandating the purchase of health insurance covering drugs and devices that could act to destroy a human embryo. In order to understand its implications for institutional conscience generally, it is helpful to view *Hobby Lobby*'s treatment of corporate religious conscience through the philosophical lenses of agency and intellect. Then it is possible to understand the joint commitment of corporate leaders to act as a "group subject" for purposes of doing business together *and* in a manner consistent with Christian biblical principles. Religion is being exercised by the group-subject's performing or abstaining from physical acts, as a group and for religious reasons. Shielding conscience in the context of group action can be valuable because it is a way of protecting the rights of human beings who need to resort to the corporate form in order to achieve certain ends: the efficiencies that only a group can achieve, business success, and the goods of working together as a family *and* as co-believers (true of the Hobby Lobby corporation). Otherwise the members of the group would be put to the choice between the corporate form and religious freedom. The lessons of *Hobby Lobby* about institutional conscience can be applied to religious hospitals, which are also pursuing joint commitments to health *and* to various religious goals including the goal of building religious community. Because some goods require group action, it is good to have conscience protection for such institutions.

In Chapter 21, Kent Greenawalt discusses the permissibility, the scope, and the rationale for law to provide exemptions to protect religious and nonreligious conscience in the United States. It may be difficult for the law to determine which sentiments amount to "conscience" given differences in individuals' perception and the strength of their convictions. Even the notion of a "religious" conscience is complex. Religious citizens' conclusions even about matters of interest to religion may proceed from religion and reason together or just from reason. It is also not clear what should "count" as religious, given differences between denominations and their ideas over time. How closely does a conviction have to hew to traditional ideas about the nature of religion? There are a host of factors bearing on the permissibility and wisdom of granting exemptions, determining their scope, and deciding whether to extend protections to nonreligious conscience. A first principle is the importance of respect for others and for tolerance in a liberal democracy. The law should also consider the number of persons holding a particular opinion.

All of these questions about exemptions can be considered in the course of looking closely at several often-contested issues. On the matter of the military draft, for example, one should consider the harm possibly caused to colleagues by forcing an objector to serve, whether or not he or she claims a religious or nonreligious objection, and the draft boards' difficulties in assessing whether an objection to a certain war is a matter of conscience. Regarding laws governing the manner of killing animals, because objections will likely be religious, it makes sense to limit exemptions to religious claimants. Regarding ingestion of banned substances, important factors are the degree of importance to the religious claimants and the small likelihood of harm. Concerns about false claims and more intense use of substances indicate that a sensible exemption might be limited to religious gatherings. On abortion, the law should consider the strength, plausibility, and popularity of the view that the embryo or fetus deserves some or a great deal of protection. The objection is strong; it holds that abortion is a kind of murder. Both religious and nonreligious individuals hold it. Exemptions would have to attend, however, to limiting the scope of protection to more direct assistance and to circumstances involving women in dire situations without other alternatives. Regarding contraception prescriptions and insurance, important considerations include the existence of alternative sources and the degree of burden actually visited upon employers. Religions ought not to have exclusive say over what constitutes a burden. On the controversial matter of same-sex marriage, there exists both religious and nonreligious opposition, based upon both religious and plausible nonreligious arguments about the needs of children. Here, it is sensible to distinguish between direct participation in a marriage – for which an exemption is wise – and services that are not direct participation. Same-sex adoption invites consideration of other factors.

PART I

# Themes in Understandings of Conscience in Christianity

1

# Conscience in the New Testament

WENDELL WILLIS

## INTRODUCTION

Today a frequent defense to any challenged moral choice often is: "My conscience is clear!" And some parents may give their children as a basic norm for ethics, "Let your conscience be your guide." These two uses usually imply that a person's conscience can serve as a judge of past actions or a guide for future choices. Both approaches think of conscience as a faculty or universal structure of humans. James Packer, Theology Professor at Regent College, British Columbia, argues that conscience is based on "principles that are in themselves universally valid, and claim everyone's assent."[1] He adds that conscience is God's voice in and to us structurally.[2] This assessment is presented in theological or philosophical terms, although it claims to reflect biblical ideas. Noted Protestant theologian Oliver O'Donovan, summarizing this shift says: "This shift in meaning marks an important, and largely damaging, development in moral psychology, in which the separation of reason and will comes to be treated as normative."[3] When one reflects on how popular the idea of conscience is for people today in connection with ethical questions, it may come as a surprise to learn that it is not a common concept in the Bible and that the meaning of the Greek word is quite different than most contemporary meanings.[4]

[1] James Packer, "Conscience, Choice and Character," in *Law, Morality and the Bible*, eds. Bruce Kaye and Gordon Wenham (Downers Grove, IL: InterVarsity Press, 1978), 176.

[2] Ibid., 177.

[3] Oliver O'Donovan, *Resurrection and Moral Order* (Downers Grove, IL: InterVarsity Press, 1986), 114. He notes this is a change from both non-Christian and biblical meanings of the term.

[4] A very thorough and insightful review of the developments in the use of the word "conscience" in English is provided by C. S. Lewis, "Conscience and Conscious," in *Studies in Words* (Cambridge: Cambridge University Press, 1960), 181–212. Lewis explains that the primary

The translation "conscience" in most English Bibles is an excellent example of how translation is always interpretation. The Greek word often translated "conscience" συνείδησις (*suneidesis*) occurs about thirty times in the New Testament, and it is one of those New Testament words that lacks a synonym in the Hebrew Bible. Some have argued that "heart" in the Old Testament is an equivalent idea, but heart is a different concept having more to do with the emotional center of a human person, while the conscience relates to the mind or reasoning.

As will be discussed below, this word (and its cognates, such as the verb *sunoida* and adjective *sunesis*) has as its root meaning "to know with" (especially with myself).[5] Thus, the most basic meaning is "to be aware" or "conscious" (1 Cor. 4:4, in contrast to the Today's English Version [TEV] translation "My conscience is clear."). In non-biblical Greek usage, the word has primarily a negative connotation – the painful or bad conscience.[6] There are only limited, later uses of the notion of a clear conscience, and even these are highly debatable.

Most of the thirty New Testament references are in Paul's letters. The others are Acts 23:1 and 24:16. It is also used five times in Hebrews (9:9, 14; 10:2, 22; and esp. 13:8 where the clear conscience enables true worship). There are also three uses in 1 Peter: 2:19; 3:16; and 3:21. All these uses will be explored in some detail. It should be emphasized that in the New Testament *suneidesis* is not a widely used idea, it is never developed or elaborated (contrast, for example, other fundamental topics such as Christ's death, the obligation to others, the work of the Spirit).

## GREEK BACKGROUND

Before its use in the New Testament, the Greek word *suneidesis* was commonly, although not frequently, used in philosophical writings. It often occurs with the reflexive personal pronoun, *emauto*, emphasizing self-knowledge.

meaning of *suneidesis* is "to know with" and that normally with one's self – it is awareness of one's own thoughts and actions. He notes how this basic meaning shifted in English, especially in the nineteenth century.

5 O'Donovan, *Resurrection*, 115, says: "But nowhere in the New Testament (nor indeed in the classical world as a whole until a later period) does [*suneidesis*] συνείδησις mean a faculty of *moral direction*." He adds that this shift emerges in the later Greek fathers who speculate on the issue of natural law, for example, Chrysostom.

6 The monograph by C. A. Pierce, *Conscience in the New Testament*, Studies in Biblical Theology, 1st series, vol. 15. (London: SCM, 1955) finds almost all references to the word to be negative and referring to the past.

This self-knowledge is not normally in relationship to a deity but does often carry a value sense about a past choice. In the first century AD, uses of the word and its cognates as neutral and as painful reflection upon past moral decisions continue side by side. In the case of moral evaluation, *suneidesis* is seldom, if ever, concerned about future decisions but only with those of the past.[7] Although authors specializing in non-biblical Greek writings generally agree with these points, several studies find specific exceptions to the consensus interpretations, most often with respect to whether the *suneidesis* has a function related to future decisions.

At one time it was argued that Paul especially, and probably other New Testament writers, took over this term from Stoic philosophy. Because Stoic philosophers emphasized the role of reason in human life, and especially in guiding life choices, such uses do occur.[8] (Although the term was not a technical term only preferred by philosophers, still, in popular philosophical thought of the early Christian era, the connection between *suneidesis* and moral evaluation, particularly of one's past, increased.)[9] It is really more among the Latin Stoics that their term *conscius* (linguistically the Latin equivalent "to know with," usually one's self) acquires greater stress on moral choices, including a positive use. Yet with both Greek and Latin writers, the fundamental sense of personal reflection on past decisions is the most common meaning, and there is not developed the idea of *suneidesis* or *conscius/conscientia* as an independent guide for ethical decisions.[10] Aesthetics scholar Harold Osbourne concludes: "The Greek word is never used of the abstract faculty of Conscience but always of some concrete example of that faculty, directed to personal states or acts of the subject."[11]

7 In addition to Pierce, substantial reviews of the non-biblical use of the word group associated with *suneidesis* can be found in Hans-Joachim Eckstein, *Der Begriff Syneidesis bei Paulus*, Wissenschaftliche Untersuchungen zum Neuen Testament Riehe 2/15 (Tübingen: Mohr, 1983); Christian Maurer, "σuνoίδα, σuνείδησις," in *Theological Dictionary of the New Testament*, vol. 7, ed. Gerhard Friedrich and trans. and ed. Geoffrey W. Bromiley (Grand Rapids, MI: Eerdmans, 1971), 898–919; Harold Osbourne, "σuνείδησις," *Journal of Theological Studies* 32, no. 1 (1931): 167–79. Anthony Thiselton, *The First Epistle to the Corinthians*, New International Greek Testament Commentary (Grand Rapids, MI: Eerdmans, 2000), 640–44, gives a succinct account of the history of interpreting *suneidesis*.

8 For examples, see the thorough chart in Pierce, *Conscience in the New Testament*, 132–47.

9 The arguments against a Stoic background are given in the works cited in n. 7. A detailed study is found in A. Bonhöffer, *Epiket und das Neue Testament* (Giessen: Topelmann, 1964) and more recently in Don Marietta Jr., "Conscience in Greek Stoicism," *Numen* 17, no. 3 (1970): 176–87.

10 Maurer, "σuνoίδα, σuνείδησις," 904.

11 Osbourne, "σuνείδησις," 174. "The primary sense of Consciousness or introspective awareness is much more prominent than in our word." Lewis, "Conscience and Conscious," 197f., does find

A near contemporary to many New Testament authors was the Alexandrian Jewish scholar, Philo, who wrote exclusively in Greek and did use the term *suneidesis*.[12] New Testament professor Richard Horsley shows that Philo has a strong connection to Stoic philosophical concepts. He also gives extensive parallels to Philo with Paul's arguments, but a stronger case can be made with respect to Hebrews having influence on philosophical usage (see "Hebrews"). New Testament scholar Harold Attridge argues that *suneidesis* in Hebrews has both a moral and a non-moral sense of awareness, and the moral sense was specifically the awareness of transgressions and appears in Greco-Jewish literature "precisely in this sense."[13]

## PAULINE USAGES

As noted, Paul is the earliest and most prolific New Testament author using the term *suneidesis*[14] and the earliest Pauline uses are found in his first letter to the Corinthian church (c. AD 51). Because all but three of the occurrences in the undisputed Pauline letters are in his Corinthian letters – the other three are in Romans – it is considered likely that Paul took over this terminology from his encounters with the Corinthian church. This probability is increased because in 1 Corinthians 8 and 10 Paul is in dialogue with arguments made by some Corinthian Christians over their rights/authority to take part in some meals that other Christians thought forbidden, and in places he seems to be quoting from a letter the Corinthians sent to him. However, it still should not be assumed that those with whom Paul argues are using *suneidesis* in a technical sense to refer to a definite source of human moral decision-making. (This means the earlier warning of the danger of a translation bootlegging a modern interpretation of conscience applies to contemporary understandings of the Corinthians' use as well as to Paul's.)

The term occurs in 1 Corinthians 8:7, 10, and 12, in each case referring to a person injured in some way by the eating of meat from a sacrifice to an idol. In each of these three uses that person is described as "weak" (*asthenes*).

in Tatian the idea that "conscience (συνείδησις) is God," but he does not think this is true for the New Testament. Osbourne says the fundamental meaning is to be aware of, conscious of (usually with one's self).

12 Richard Horsley, "Consciousness and Freedom among the Corinthians: 1 Corinthians 8–10," *Catholic Biblical Quarterly* 40, no. 4 (1978): 574–89; on Philo, see esp. 575–77, 580–85.

13 Harold Attridge, *The Epistle to the Hebrews*, Hermeneia, vol. 58 (Philadelphia, PA: Fortress, 1989), 242.

14 A full summary of the history of research of the use of *suneidesis* in Paul is in Paul Jewett, *Paul's Anthropological Terms* (Leiden: Brill, 1971), 402–21.

In two of the verses (7, 10) the problem such eating creates for the weak is explicitly related to their knowledge (*gnosis*). These facts indicate that those who are weak and are injured with respect to their *suneidesis* are such because of their understanding. Inspired by those who defend eating the sacrificial food, they alter their set of values. The problem arises when the weak begin to doubt the truth of the new knowledge they have acted upon, and revert to their prior understanding.[15] In each of these verses the less formal translations of "awareness" or "understanding" are preferable.[16] In spite of this basic Christian confession (8:6) – and the implication that those non-gods are unreal – the weak do not fully understand this when they eat the sacrificial meat (8:7).[17] The fact that the two groups of Christians have different views on what is acceptable and not acceptable food confirms that συνείδησις refers to "understandings" and not to an innate guidance found in all people.[18]

The use of *suneidesis* five times in 1 Corinthians 10:25–29 is very similar.[19] Here too the focus is upon how some understand the significance of meat that

15 There is a strong textual question in v. 7. Several important manuscripts read *suneithia* instead of *suneidesis*. See Thiselton, *The First Epistle to the Corinthians*, 639. In addition to possible assimilation to the other uses of *suneidesis* in the chapter, the alternative reading accords well with the understanding argued in this chapter.

16 Wendell Willis, *Idol Meat in Corinth*, Society of Biblical Literature Dissertations, vol. 68 (Chico, CA: Society of Biblical Literature, 1985), 89–96; Horsley, "Consciousness," 581; and Peter Gardner, *The Gifts of God and the Authentication of a Christian* (Lanham, MA: University Press of America, 1994), 42–54. O'Donovan, *Resurrection*, 115, rightly explains, "Paul is rather concerned with the consciousness which is 'habituated to the idol'; that is to say, the weak brother is really superstitious [in the sense used by the Romans, and this is correct in my opinion], and cannot help taking such beings seriously, so that if he became involved in a pagan feast he would approach it 'as an idol-sacrifice,' i.e. with an idolatrous mind." I differ slightly: the weak would be stressed by their memories of such feasts and prior participation as worship.

17 Paul W. Gooch, "'Conscience' in 1 Corinthians 8 and 10," *New Testament Studies* 31 (1985): 249f., argues that in 1 Corinthians 8:7, 10, and 12, *suneidesis* has only the meaning of consciousness of the self. It is not a moral argument, but "a kind of self-perception, a consciousness of one's guilt or innocence."

18 Bruce Harris, "ΣΥΝΕΙΔΗΣΙΣ (Conscience) in the Pauline Writings," *Westminster Theological Journal* 24, no. 2 (1961–62): 180, discusses this problem and points to a difference between the form of conscience and the content, saying the first is from God and infallible, but the content depends upon how far the individual has learned the will of God. Harris's proposed distinction does not exist if *suneidesis* is understood as "consciousness."

19 Gooch, "'Conscience,'" 247–48, asks if in 1 Corinthians 10 *suneidesis* does have the meaning of "moral conscience"? He also discusses a possible "conflict of consciences" that would require the more robust conscience to give in to the less informed conscience. After his study he concludes, on pp. 249–50: "If we retain the minimal sense of subjective awareness in v. 10 [8:10] this reading is clear and avoids the difficulty of thinking that the weak man's *moral conscience* has somehow been wrongly edified."

has come from a sacrifice (as much domesticated meat did in this culture). The believer who buys meat from the market need not ask about the source or prior history of the meat (10:25). One is not expected to examine his understanding of such meat. Similarly, if a believer is a dinner guest there is no demand for her to make an examination seeking more information about the background of the meat served (10:27). The final use (10:29) is more difficult to explain, largely because the identity (Christian or not?) and the motive of the person who identifies the meat as from sacrifice is unstated (and unknowable). If the informant is also a believer, perhaps one who is "weak," the motive may be to be protective of another Christian.[20] If the informant is a non-believer the motive might be respect (knowing at least some Christians do not wish to eat sacrificial food), or a test of friendship with a Christian. Canadian theologian Paul W. Gooch stresses the possible negative retrospect if someone leads another to eat what becomes a problem for them and suggests the translation "bad feelings."[21] I think in each case "consciousness" or "awareness" is adequate. In 10:28 and 29 the concern is the understandings of the other person, as in chapter 8.

Paul's use of *suneidesis* in 2 Corinthians 1:12 and the verb form *sunoida* in 1 Corinthians 4:4 illustrate the most common use of the term – to refer to a person's self-knowledge. In both cases, Paul is reflecting upon his own integrity and is suggesting his self-knowledge was not giving any evidence that convicts him.[22] This is explicit in 1 Corinthians 4:4, where he says expressly that his self-evaluation does not equal being justified – that is God's work, not Paul's own. In 2 Corinthians 5:11, theologian C. A. Pierce rightly understands "You know as well as we do that we preach in fear of God and do not tamper with the gospel for the sake of human popularity."[23] Thus the *suneidesis* of the Corinthians cannot serve as Paul's ethical judge, but as witnesses to his

[20] Margaret E. Thrall, "The Pauline Use of συνείδησις," *New Testament Studies* 14, no. 1 (1967): 124, argues it is that the weak Christian's conscience would be led to condemn another believer, and that would bring guilt upon himself by his act of judging another.

[21] Gooch, "Conscience," 251–52.

[22] Lewis, "Conscience and Conscious," 187, says "The proper translation is 'I know nothing against myself.'" This self-reflective understanding of *suneidesis* Lewis calls "consciring," and notes, on p. 188: "In the situation within a man, as in the situation between man and man, consciring is presumed to be of evil unless the reverse is explicitly stated."

[23] Pierce, *Conscience in the New Testament*, 87f. The passage, along with 2 Cor 1:12, is among the few that Pierce grants are not negative and referring to a bad conscience. Thrall, "Pauline Use," 123, paraphrases "the sincerity of our motives is made plain to the judgment of your consciences as well [as God's judgment]." But this is interpretive, literally: it is manifest to God, and I hope also is manifest in your *suneidesis*. The simple meaning "understanding" or "awareness" is equally possible. It is not obvious that judgment is involved at all.

ministry. This is not a claim of a conscience always aligning with divine judgment, but specifically with reference to Paul's conduct.

The three uses of the word in Romans are different. There Paul is writing to a church he has no prior connection with; thus, it appears that the Romans are not the source of the terminology (and it is notable that the term *suneidesis* is not used in Romans 14 and 15, which has a discussion about what is acceptable for believers to eat similar to 1 Corinthians 8 and 10).

Romans 9:1 contains an interpretation of *suneidesis* that suggests it has a parallel positive role for the guidance of believers, comparable to that of the Holy Spirit, as a witness to Paul's genuine concern for Israel. However, it is equally possible that he is referring to his awareness of his own understanding of his attitude toward the Jewish people. It is very similar to the phrase he uses in 1 Corinthians 4:4 ("My conscience is clear"); and both set out a positive role for the writer's "conscience." Moreover, in Romans 9:1, Paul has taken an oath based on Christ and has appealed to the Holy Spirit. To appeal to a personal "conscience" therefore seems a weak parallel, but the parallel is to Paul's "speaking the truth in Christ" and "my conscience bears witness in the Holy Spirit." Both are "witnesses" to Paul's oath.

The other two uses of *suneidesis* in Romans are more challenging and present the strongest evidence for *suneidesis* being used as a moral guide for future actions. Taking first Romans 13:5, Paul instructs Christians to submit to the state using three arguments: government is established by God; government has power to punish wrongdoers; and *dia ten suneidesin*. Of the third reason Christian Maurer, author of the standard theological dictionary essay on conscience, suggests three possible interpretations: (1) to avoid a bad conscience that might ensue, (2) out of duty, conviction, or other moral considerations suggested by the conscience, or (3) because of the links seen between the state and God's will.[24] He prefers the third option, that *suneidesis* refers to "responsible awareness that the ultimate foundations both of one's own being and also of the state are in God." Here too the understanding of the word is located in one's knowledge, or awareness of how things are understood. It is notable that in this brief and famous passage the warrants given for obedience are theological (God has caused human government, perhaps just as he has created family structure), civic (the state is authorized to support the good and oppose evil), and personal (the individual believer's awareness of the structure of the world).

[24] Maurer, "συνοίδα, συνείδησις," 915–16. Thrall, "Pauline Use," 120–21, disagreeing with Pierce, *Conscience in New Testament*, 66ff., argues that in this passage the word has a future significance, and might approve some moral duty in advance.

Perhaps the passage that offers the best case for finding in Paul a use of *suneidesis* as a guide in making ethical decisions is Romans 2:15 where *suneidesis* for Gentiles is paralleled to Torah for Jews. The proposed parallel would suggest that *suneidesis* affords Gentiles a guidance also from God. This view has been maintained by several commentators.[25] One important consideration is whether in 2:14 "by nature" (*phusei*) modifies what Gentiles "do" (*poiosin*) or "the law" (*tou nomos*). The former interpretation holds that the ethical actions of Gentiles proves that they have in *suneidesis* a natural version of the Torah. The second view describes the Gentiles as not having "by nature" the law of God. A correct interpretation must also take into account three features. First, the rhetorical function of Romans 2 is to prove that the Jew, even while having the divine Torah, must also be concerned about God's judgment, since God is not a "respecter of persons" (Rom. 2:11). Second, the purpose of chapters 1–3 of Romans is to prove that all humanity, Jews and Gentiles, are in need of God's saving action in Christ. Thus, Paul was not offering a defense for Gentiles. Third, the likelihood of the Gentiles' *suneidesis* justifying their actions is strongly negative – it will *accuse* (*kategorounton* – Paul's only use of this word group), and only possibly *defend* (*apologoumenon*) them.[26] In both cases, the dominant idea is of a witness, either positive or negative, not of a judge who pronounces a verdict. This role, both positive and negative, can be fulfilled by the person's own awareness of their thoughts, or better stated, reason (*logismon*). Without the guidance of Torah, Gentiles are knowledgeable of their reasons for choices, whether good or evil. This accords with Paul's earlier charge in Romans 1:21, 28 that Gentiles repressed an awareness of God, which they possessed (it was obvious, 1:20), but they acted against what they knew about what God's

25 See the summary review by Joseph A. Fitzmyer, *Romans*, Anchor Bible Commentary, vol. 33 (New York, NY: Doubleday, 1992), 309–10. Thrall, "Pauline Use," 123f., says this is a result of Paul regarding the conscience of Gentiles as in some way parallel to the Law for Jews. She finds this equation supported in that both the conscience and the Law are accusatory, see ibid., 124. Harris, "ΣΥΝΕΙΔΗΣΙΣ," 179, concludes: "In the Epistle to the Romans, therefore, we are taught that the conscience is a divine gift to all men, which makes explicit in the moral consciousness the works of the law of God written in the heart." Bo Reicke, "Syneidesis in Röm 2, 15," *Theologische Zeitschrift* 12, no. 2 (1956): 161, suggests that when the pagan enters a Christian worship service and hears the word preached, then responds positively "God really is among you" (1 Cor. 14:24f.), it implies a "conscience" awareness of guilt. However, this still does not mean that Rom, 2:15 is evidence of a "natural law" known by pagans.

26 Terence McGaughey, "Conscience and Decision Making in Some Early Christian Communities," *Irish Biblical Studies* 5, no. 3 (1983): 115–31, notes that the "conscience/ awareness of the Gentiles leads them to an inarticulate and sporadic obedience, but in its positive aspect it proves unreliable." He also notes that Paul is concerned with the "conscience" of groups and their perception of how things are.

judgment would be; nonetheless, they chose to do evil (1:32). Theologian C. K. Barrett argues in respect to this passage that "conscience is not so much the bar at which his conduct is tried, as a major witness, which may be called on either side as the case may be."[27]

In sum, Paul's use of *suneidesis* is best understood if the translation "consciousness" or "awareness" is used instead of "conscience." It appears that he picked up the term from some Christians in Corinth who felt that their better knowledge gave them authority to eat food from pagan sacrifices. They were aware that since there is only one God confessed by Christians, the "so-called gods" in whose honor the sacrifice occurred did not impact the meat – or their authority to eat it. But other Christians, whom these termed weak, did not share this understanding, and when they acted as they did to eat such meat, their prior awareness of the connotations of pagan sacrifice caused them injury.

## DISPUTED PAULINE USAGE

Scholars do not generally regard the three letters referred to as the "Pastorals" (1 and 2 Timothy and Titus) as authentically authored by Paul, so the usage in these letters are not considered when presenting Paul's understanding. However, in these writings, the word *suneidesis* occurs six times (1 Tim. 1:5, 19; 3:9; 4:2; 2 Tim. 1:3; and Titus 1:15). Because of the disputed authorship, some additional questions arise with these uses: (1) Do these uses differ significantly from those of Paul? (2) Do they have a different source or background than Paul's uses? (3) Does *suneidesis* have a different function in these uses?[28] And (4) Why in these four uses is there an adjectival modifier of the word *suneidesis*?

In 1 Timothy 1:5, 19, and 3:9 one finds explicit reference to faith, and in 1 Timothy 1:19, that certain people have "thrust away" the faith. 1 Timothy 4:2, when read with 4:1 is the same, identifying those whose "consciences are seared" as having departed from the faith. This illustrates that the use of *suneidesis* in the letter to Timothy does not mean a general source for guidance but the *suneidesis* is grounded in the faith the author seeks to secure (3:9. See also 2 Tim. 1:3, which follows the creedal statement of 1:2). In Titus 1:15, those

[27] C. K. Barrett, "Paul and the Introspective Conscience," in *The Bible, the Reformation and the Church*, ed. W. P. Stephens, Society of New Testament Supplements, vol. 105 (Sheffield: Sheffield Academic, 1995), 40. He says that in presenting conscience as a witness to inward thoughts, Paul follows Stoic models.

[28] Martin Dibelius and Hans Conzelmann, *The Pastoral Epistles*, Hermenia, trans. Philip Buttolph and Adela Yarbo, (Philadelphia, PA: Fortress, 1972), 18–20, argue that the Pastorals draw the terminology from philosophical usages with the function of showing Christian beliefs as congruous with current popular philosophical ideals, part of presenting "good citizenship."

who are not "sound in the faith" (1:13) but are unbelieving are defiled in both mind (*nous*) and conscience.[29] The conscience has a content: the Christian beliefs held or rejected by a person. Thus, in these letters *suneidesis* is not a neutral guide but its function is dependent upon having Christian faith.

This analysis confirms that the meaning of *suneidesis* in the Pastorals is not fundamentally different from that in the undisputed Pauline letters.[30] There is a difference in the frequent use of qualifiers (such as clean, good, or defiled), which makes explicit what is implied when Paul says (e.g., 1 Cor. 4:4 and 2 Cor. 1:12) that he is "aware" of nothing in his life that condemns him – that is, his conscience is clear. As Marshall summarizes: "We may conclude that there is no great difference between the accepted letters of Paul and the PE [Pastoral Epistles] as regards the place of moral norms in relation to conscience."[31]

## PAUL'S INTROSPECTIVE CONSCIENCE (ROMANS 7)

The reality of conscience as a moral norm or guide for decisions in Paul cannot be restricted to the occurrence of the linguistic group *suneidesis* / *sunioda*. Since the basic meaning is a person's reflection on his or her own attitudes or actions, other ways of expressing this self-reflection must also be considered. One of the most famous Pauline passages related to his own self-reflection on moral matters is Romans 7. In a highly influential article, "St. Paul and the Introspective Conscience of the West,"[32] Krister Stendahl, late New Testament professor, argues that Paul's concept of "justification by faith" was specifically his response to arguments with Jewish believers and not the key to his theology. He thinks both the Protestant emphasis on justification and on believers having an abiding troubled conscience (captured in the Protestant slogan *simul justus et peccator* [at once justified and a sinner]) actually represents the understandings of Augustine and Luther. Stendhal writes:

[29] Ibid., 138. They also say that Titus 1:15 shows that the mind and the conscience are distinct, but the authors also make clear they are connected with the knowledge of God that informs the operation of conscience. That strikes me as a very thin distinction. They add "In each case, the context indicates that the condition of the conscience results in some way from rejection of the apostolic faith."

[30] I. H. Marshall, *The Pastoral Epistles*, NICC (London: T&T Clark, 1999), Excursus 5, 217–27, 224. McGaughey, "Conscience and Decision," 125, says the adjectives used in the Pastorals represent a change with continuity with prior Pauline uses.

[31] Ibid., 224.

[32] Krister Stendahl, "The Apostle Paul and the Introspective Conscience of the West," *Harvard Theological Review* 56, no. 3 (1963): 199–215. Reprinted in Krister Stendahl, *Paul among Jews and Gentiles* (Minneapolis, MN: Fortress, 1976). Page numbers are taken from this reprint.

> Especially in Protestant Christianity – which, however, at this point has its roots in Augustine and in the piety of the Middle Ages – the Pauline awareness of sin has been interpreted in the light of Luther's struggle with his conscience. But it is exactly at that point that we can discern the most drastic difference between Luther and Paul, between the 16th and the 1st century and perhaps, between Eastern and Western Christianity.[33]

Related to the current topic, Stendahl thinks that Paul did not have a troubled conscience arising from his awareness of moral failures in his own actions or practices. The two most important Pauline passages to be considered are Romans 7, especially 7:14–24 and Philippians 3:6. Stendahl emphasizes the Philippians 3:6 passage in which Paul claims his pre-Christian life was "faultless" with respect to the requirements of the Law.

Stendahl's proposal has received mixed reviews. In the work of late divinity professor C. K. Barrett, "Paul and the Introspective Conscience,"[34] he argues that 1 Corinthians 4:4 supports the view that Paul had an introspective conscience, and says "the sentence is properly translated, "'I have nothing on my conscience', that is, I can see in my remembered actions . . . nothing that I now believe to be wrong."[35] With regard to the meaning of conscience, this sentence is somewhat unclear. His translation suggests a formal understanding as a personal moral guide of *suneidesis* as is also suggested later in the paragraph when he says "Paul assumes too that others equally have consciences and may legitimately pass judgment on his (as well as their own) behaviour."[36] But his explanation of his translation seems to understand conscience as "remembered actions." This unclarity continues when he says, "the conscience, though important, is a fallible moral guide," which seems to suggest that conscience is more than past remembrances. It may be his use of the definite article, "the," which leads to confusion about whether he sees in Paul that *suneidesis* means something like a human faculty rather than just an activity (remembering).

When Barrett takes up the controversial and confusing passage, Romans 7:7–25, which is a major text in discussing Paul's "introspective conscience," he says that Paul's conversion – as the apostle notes in Galatians 1 and Philippians 3:6–8 – was connected to his conscience and was "a revolutionary act which belongs to the realm of conscience."[37] He clarifies his

[33] Stendahl, "Introspective Conscience," 79.

[34] C. K. Barrett, "Paul and the Introspective Conscience," in *The Bible, the Reformation and the Church*, ed. W. P. Stephens, Society of New Testament Supplements, vol. 105 (Sheffield: Sheffield Academic, 1995), 36–48.

[35] Ibid., 39.

[36] Ibid.

[37] Ibid., 44.

understanding of Paul's change experience in comparison to Luther and his *Anfechtungen*. "Both Paul and Luther had introspective consciences and each of them found his conscience awakened at the point of the discovery that he stood *corum Deo*" (in the presence of God).[38]

## ACTS OF APOSTLES

The term *suneidesis* is found twice in Acts, both times associated with the Apostle Paul and related to his response to accusations by authorities. In the first, 23:1, Paul tells the Jewish council examining him that he has lived "in all good conscience before God up to this day." His defense is personal; he looks back on his life and is aware of no failure with respect to his religion. This is very similar to 1 Corinthians 4:4, a similar statement about Paul's reflection on his life. The second usage is in Acts 24:16, also a trial scene, in which Paul – having asserted his commitment to the law and the prophets (24:14) and the Pharisaic belief in the resurrection and judgment (24:15) – again says that he has acted with a "blameless conscience" both before God and men. He adds that this has always been the case, which suggests that he is looking back at his past life and actions, not appealing to prior judgments on himself. Both Acts' usages add little to the understanding of *suneidesis* already discussed.

## HEBREWS

In the New Testament, the book of Hebrews has the second largest number of uses of *suneidesis*, after those occurring in Pauline texts (Heb. 9:9, 14; 10:2, 22 "evil" and 13:18 "good"). In Hebrews 9 and 10 a comparison is made between the physical sacrifice on earth and Christ's spiritual sacrifice in heaven. Christ's sacrifice is superior precisely because it is not physical – but unseen in heaven. The thought world of Hebrews is very much shaped by Platonic concepts.[39] The use of categories from Middle Platonism in Hebrews is quite similar to the slightly earlier Jewish author Philo. In summarizing Philo's understanding of *suneidesis*, New Testament scholar James Thompson says that the author uses *pneuma, logikon, psuche* (spirit, reason, and soul) and *suneidesis* almost as synonyms. "All these terms appear to be used in

38 Ibid., 43–48, quote at 47. Barrett explicitly opposes both Stendahl's reading of Romans and of Luther.

39 For the larger issues on Hebrews world view, see James W. Thompson, *The Beginnings of Christian Philosophy*, Catholic Biblical Quarterly Monograph Series, vol. 13 (Washington, DC: Catholic Biblical Association, 1982).

connection with the idea of the divine *logos* whom God has implanted in the human soul."[40] In Hebrews also, *suneidesis* fundamentally means "consciousness."[41]

Because Hebrews assumes and works from a Platonic-shaped worldview in which the visible world is inferior to the invisible world, it is not surprising that this assumption colors how moral concerns are seen. In Hebrews 9 and 10, there is a major contrast between how the heavenly sacrifice cleanses the *suneidesis* of the worshipper, which the fleshly one by definition could not do. Dean William Lane observes that in this argument, *suneidesis* has the sense of "awareness," for even after the sacrifice on the Day of Atonement, the worshippers clearly retained knowledge of sin, because their sacrifice was repeated annually![42] "The rituals of the old covenant could not impinge upon the conscience of the worshipper because they were, by metonymy, 'fleshly ordinances.'"[43] The decisive consideration is that "Σάρξ [*sarx*] and Συνείδησις [*suneidesis*] constitute the two sides of human existence for the author. Σάρξ refers to the earthly sphere of human existence .... But the συνείδησις is the heavenly side .... Συνείδησις refers to the 'consciousness' (10:4) which can be cleansed only by the entrance of Christ into the heavenly tent (cf. 10:22)."[44]

In Hebrews 13:18, the reference to the *suneidesis* is self-referential to the author, given that he requests prayers by the recipients. Literally, the writer says: "You pray concerning us, for we are persuaded that we have a good conscience (*kalan suneidesin*)." Lane says only here does *suneidesis* have a positive meaning in Hebrews. It is an internal witness; it is not engaged in

40 Ibid., 114.

41 Gary Selby, "The Meaning and Function of συνείδησις in Hebrews 9 and 10," *Restoration Quarterly* 28, no. 3 (1985/1986): 144–54.

42 William L. Lane, *Hebrews 9–13*, Word Biblical Commentaries, vol. 47B (Dallas, TX: Word, 1991), 224–25. He says, "In Hebrews the term has deeply religious overtones; the 'conscience' is directed toward God and embraces the whole person in his relation to God .... Apart from 13:18 the term has negative connotations: it is the 'uneasy conscience' with its internal witness that defilement extends to the heart and mind." See also Selby, "Meaning and Function," 150–52. Thus, the annual repetition enforces an awareness of its ultimate ineffectiveness.

43 Attridge, *Hebrews*, 242, 251. Thus, Christ's sacrifice will "cleanse the conscience" (Heb. 9:14). The concept of "cleansing" comes from sacrifice and is frequent in chapters 9 and 10 but only here tied to *suneidesis*.

44 Thompson, *Beginnings*, 108 says that here, "The term for 'conscience' (συνείδησις) appears with its basic meaning for this period." Important, and difficult, here is what is meant by "consciousness." It is not likely that Hebrews shares Philo's belief that *suneidesis* is equivalent to the divine *logos* implanted in the individual. The five uses of *logos* in Hebrews all refer to a message spoken (4:12; 5:11, 13; 13:17). Hebrews does not have a structural concept of "conscience" for each human, as did Stoics.

decision-making but in remembering.[45] Attridge sees here a shift from the earlier emphasis on Christ's sacrifice cleansing "bad consciousness" so that here it is the believer's own desire to behave. Given the variety of uses of the word, the point may be that the author has a "good consciousness" (of his deeds/life) or a "good reputation" if he is thinking about how others feel about him (as noted about Paul in 2 Cor. 5:11, where also it is accompanied by reference to God's positive assessment of the author). In either case, it refers to awareness.

## 1 PETER

Two uses of *suneidesis* occur in 1 Peter, in an ethical list in chapter two instructing Christian slaves on submission to masters. In 2:18–20 the author says that suffering unjustly is a "grace" (*charis*) if done because of "awareness" or "consciousness" of God (2:19, *dia suneidesin theou*).[46] Clearly, here the meaning of the term is thoughtful consideration of God or, in particular, of the selfless conduct and shameful suffering of Christ as an example for his followers (2:21–24). The particular focus for the disciples' awareness is reflection on the conduct of the Lord as worthy of following. In 3:16 and 21 the *suneidesis* is described as "good" (*agathes*). The "awareness" encouraged is not concerned with self-consistency – decisions made in agreement with prior ones – but "awareness of God." This "good conscience" is specifically related to the believer's baptism and the resurrection of Christ (which Christians connected, see Rom. 6:5–11). The believer is urged to keep both these important realities in mind. These connections suggest the translation "consciousness of God."[47]

## SUMMARY

One reason that it is difficult to be clear about the meaning(s) of *suneidesis* in the Bible is often that the statements of scholars are unclear too. When

[45] Lane, *Hebrews 9–13*, 557. Drawing upon his emphasis on the communal nature of the cleansed "consciousness," he finds in this a form of protection against slander and an affirmation of credibility for the community. "It signifies, 'we have a clear conscience' in the specific matter of our conduct toward you."

[46] Lewis, "*Conscience and Conscious*," 192 takes it to be "awareness of," he says, "how the A.V. could get out of it 'for conscience *toward* God,' I am uncertain."

[47] John E. Colwell, "Baptism, Conscience and the Resurrection: A Reappraisal of 1 Peter 3.21," in *Baptism, the New Testament and the Church*, eds. Stanley E. Porter and Anthony R. Cross, Society of New Testament Supplements, vol. 171 (Sheffield: Sheffield Academic, 1999), 214.

someone writes that Paul thinks all people have "a conscience" this can easily be understood to be almost organic (in the same way they have a liver). Yet this may not be what the contemporary writer intends. This is why the suggestion that translating *suneidesis* as "consciousness" is preferable. Theologian and philosopher Paul Gooch proposes three possible definitions of conscience: (1) the moral sense of right and wrong; (2) an inner feeling about the moral status of one's behavior; and (3) a special mode of self-awareness, about "how it is with oneself."[48] The third is the most accurate summary of the biblical usages. The biblical writers do speak of an attentive awareness of beliefs (mostly past beliefs) and practices. If this meaning of *suneidesis* is held in mind, then it is accurate to speak of a person's conscience. In Hebrews, similar to Philo because of its Platonic anthropology, there may be something closer to an organic view of *suneidesis* because the fundamental realities are divided into the seen and the unseen. As a moral guide, however, *suneidesis* in the Bible is shaped by Christian beliefs that guide and assess the way writers understand their lives.

## RECOMMENDED READING


Barrett, C. K. "Paul and the Introspective Conscience." In *The Bible, the Reformation and the Church*. Journal for the Study of the New Testament Supplement Series 105, edited by W. P. Stephens, 36–48. Sheffield: Sheffield Academic, 1995.

Colwell, John E. "Baptism, Conscience and the Resurrection: A Reappraisal of 1 Peter 3:21." In *Baptism, the New Testament and the Church*. Journal for the Study of the New Testament Supplement Series 171, edited by Stanley E. Porter and Anthony R. Cross, 210–27. Sheffield: Sheffield Academic.

Conn, Walter E. *Conscience: Development and Self-Transcendence*. Birmingham, AL: Religious Education Press. 1981.

Gooch, Paul W. "'Conscience' in 1 Corinthians 8 and 10." *New Testament Studies* 33 (1987): 244–54.

"Conscience." In *New Interpreter's Dictionary of the Bible*, vol. 1, edited by Katharine D. Sakenfeld et al., 719–26. Nashville, TN: Abingdon, 2006.

Harris, Bruce F. "SYNEIDHSIS (Conscience) in the Pauline Writings." *Westminster Theological Journal* 24 (1961–62): 173–86.

Jewett, Paul. *Paul's Anthropological Terms*. Leiden: Brill, 1971.

Lewis, C. S. *Studies in Words*. Cambridge: Cambridge University Press, 1960.

McGaughey, Terence. "Conscience and Decision Making in Some Early Christian Communities." *Irish Biblical Studies* 5 (1983): 115–31.

Marshall, I. H. *The Pastoral Epistles*. NICC. London: T&T Clark, 1999.


[48] Paul Gooch, "Conscience," *New Interpreters Dictionary of the Bible*, eds. Katharine D. Sakenfield, et al. (Nashville: Abingdon Press, 2009), 1:720.

Maurer, Christian. "συνοἶδα, συνείδησις." In *Theological Dictionary of the New Testament*, vol. 7, edited by Gerhard Friedrich. Translated and edited by Geoffrey W. Bromiley, 898–919. Grand Rapids, MI: Eerdmans, 1971.
Packer, James. "Situations and Principles: Conscience, Choice and Character." In *Law, Morality and the Bible: A Symposium*, edited by Bruce Kaye and Gordon Wenham. Downers Grove, IL: InterVarsity Press, 1978.
Pierce, C. A. *Conscience in the New Testament*. Studies in Biblical Theology 15. London: SCM, 1955.
Reicke, Bo. "Syneidesis in Rom 2:15." *Theologische Zeitschrift* 12, no. 2 (1956): 157–61.
Selby, Gary. "The Meaning and Function of συνείδησις in Hebrews 9 and 10." *Restoration Quarterly* 29 (1986): 145–54.
Stendahl, Krister. "Paul and the Introspective Conscience of the West." *Harvard Theological Review* 56 (1963): 199–215. Reprinted in Stendahl, Krister. *Paul among Jews and Gentiles*. Minneapolis, MN: Fortress, 1976.
Thrall, Margaret E. "The Pauline Use of SYNDEIDHSIS." *New Testament Studies* 14 (1968): 118–25.
Willis, Wendell Lee. *Idol Meat in Corinth*. Society of Biblical Literature Dissertation Series 68. Chico, CA: Scholars' Press, 1985.

# 2

# Conscience and Natural Law in Scripture

DAVID VANDRUNEN

## INTRODUCTION

While issues of *conscience* and *natural law* are far from identical, Christian thinkers have often believed they overlap. Romans 2:14–15 is an important reason why, for the Apostle Paul speaks about both a law known by nature and the conscience bearing witness. Influential theologians such as Thomas Aquinas and John Calvin, appealing to this text, have explained the concepts of conscience and natural law in relation to each other.

These opening observations may raise more questions than they answer. For one thing, Paul does not define conscience in Romans 2:14–15, but refers to it in passing, suggesting that readers already know what it is. Furthermore, biblical interpreters have never unanimously agreed that this text refers to natural law at all. Thus, in the one text in Scripture that (arguably) mentions both conscience and natural law, the meaning of conscience is largely assumed rather than explained and the notion that Paul even speaks of natural law is controversial. Is the common Christian conviction that conscience and natural law are closely related biblically grounded? If so, where, and how do they in fact relate?

This chapter affirms and explains the biblical relationship of these two ideas. Even where they do not use technical terminology of "conscience" and "natural law," both Old and New Testaments teach the existence of a universally known natural law and of the conscience operative in all human beings – and neither idea is fully comprehensible without the other. We will see in many texts that conscience is the *subjective* human faculty that perceives and responds to the *objective* natural law promulgated in the created order. Biblical material on the relationship of conscience and natural law chiefly establishes that all people, by virtue of being human and living in this world, can and actually do know the true God and his just law, and that all are accountable for how they respond. As creatures with consciences, human beings are obligated to respond *rightly* to natural law as the will of the living God. But I also identify a subcurrent in Scripture indicating that no person has authority to be lord over other people's consciences, and thus that human law properly protects the conscientious decisions of peaceful people.

In order to guide our subsequent study of Scripture, I first describe more specifically what is meant by conscience and natural law. Next, I explore the relationship of conscience and natural law in the Old Testament and New Testament. Finally, I consider what insight Scripture provides concerning the legal protection of conscience.

## CONSCIENCE AND NATURAL LAW: WHAT WE'RE LOOKING FOR

This inquiry could not get far simply by doing a word study or two. The term "natural law" never appears in the Bible, and there is no Old Testament Hebrew equivalent for "conscience." Even in the New Testament, use of the Greek *suneidesis* (conscience) appears only occasionally outside 1 Corinthians. New Testament authors that use the term never define it, but assume readers know what conscience is. Nevertheless, absence of a term does not mean the concept is absent, and failure to define a term does not prevent us from figuring out what it means. I propose that we first consider how the broader Christian tradition has understood conscience and natural law in order to establish what we are talking about. Then we will inquire how Scripture describes and relates these ideas. Of course, Christian theologians have not universally agreed about what conscience or natural law mean precisely. In this section, I look merely at two of the most influential Christian thinkers, Thomas Aquinas and John Calvin, and try to identify what they held in common.

For Thomas, conscience depends upon *synderesis*, a *habit* of the human intellect that understands things naturally, without need of rational investigation. It provides the practical reason with knowledge of the basic principles of morality. Through these principles, "we proceed to discover, and judge of what we have discovered." Conscience does this discovering and judging. It is an *act* (not a habit) of the intellect that applies the basic information *synderesis* provides. It looks back at things done or not done (what Thomas calls "witnessing"), judges what should or should not be done ("inciting" or "binding"), and judges that something was done well or ill ("excusing," "accusing," or "tormenting"). While *synderesis* presents the basic moral principles to the conscience infallibly, conscience applies these principles fallibly.[1]

Calvin sounds similar to Thomas in several respects. For example, Calvin says that all people have "some notions of justice and rectitude . . . implanted by nature" that "dispose" them to make laws. This resembles Thomas's *synderesis*. Calvin also describes "a discrimination and judgment" imprinted on the heart, by which people distinguish "what is just and unjust . . . honest and dishonest." He explains that "heart" refers only to the "understanding," not the will – thus locating conscience in the intellect, as does Thomas. Calvin also, like Thomas, claims that conscience distinguishes just and unjust and proves people guilty by their own testimony.[2] Yet elsewhere Calvin sounds rather different from Thomas. For example, he describes conscience more as a sense of *God's* judgment than as our own moral self-judgment: Conscience is "a sense of the divine justice added as a witness" that stands "as it were between God and man." It drags us before God's bar, exposing our secret sins.[3]

Although the views of Thomas and Calvin were not identical, they held important ideas in common. For both, conscience is a human intellectual faculty that proceeds from foundational notions of right and wrong to make concrete moral judgments. These judgments are reliable and weighty, though fallible. Conscience thus testifies to our accountability before God – this is a major theme for Calvin, but only in the background for Thomas.

This gives us a working conception of conscience. What about natural law? In classical Christian thinking, natural law refers to a universal moral standard that is *natural* rather than *positive*. That is, natural law is not explicitly (or arbitrarily) decreed by a legislator, but implicitly decreed by God through creation itself. It accords with human nature and the broader cosmic order, such that human beings know it naturally, without needing to be told.

Christian theology often associates conscience and natural law closely. For Thomas, the first principles of moral action, understood through *synderesis*,

1 Thomas Aquinas, *Summa Theologiae*, trans. Fathers of the English Dominican Province (Allen, TX: Christian Classics, 1948), 1a 79.12–13. For more detailed discussion of Thomas's views, see Robert J. Smith, *Conscience and Catholicism: The Nature and Function of Conscience in Contemporary Roman Catholic Moral Theology* (Lanham, MD: University Press of America, 1998), ch. 1; Douglas Kries, *The Problem of Natural Law* (Lanham, MD: Lexington Books, 2007), ch. 1.

2 John Calvin, *Commentaries on the Epistle of Paul the Apostle to the Romans*, trans. John Owen (Grand Rapids, MI: Baker, 2003), 96–98; John Calvin, *Institutes of the Christian Religion*, trans. Henry Beveridge (Grand Rapids, MI: Eerdmans, 1953), 2.2.22.

3 Calvin, *Institutes*, 3.19.15. For a more detailed discussion of Calvin on conscience, see Randall C. Zachman, *The Assurance of Faith: Conscience in the Theology of Martin Luther and John Calvin* (Minneapolis, MN: Fortress, 1993), part 2.

are "the precepts of the natural law."[4] This implies that the work of conscience is to apply natural law to concrete circumstances. And Calvin discusses conscience most extensively in his exegesis of Romans 2:14–15 and his description of the "law written on the heart," even speaking as if natural law *is* the apprehension of conscience.[5]

I thus propose the following questions to frame our subsequent investigation: What, if anything, does Scripture say about this human faculty called "conscience" that makes moral judgments about right and wrong and perceives one's standing before God? And does Scripture indicate that this conscience is informed not only by God's positive decrees (particularly, God's law revealed in Scripture) but also by the natural law?

## CONSCIENCE AND NATURAL LAW IN THE OLD TESTAMENT

I begin by exploring how the Old Testament speaks about the concept of conscience, as defined above. Then I broaden the discussion to inquire how it relates conscience to natural law.

### *Conscience*

The first thing Scripture says about human beings is that God created them in his own image (Gen. 1:26–27). Given the perennial importance of this idea for Christian anthropology,[6] we may wonder whether it provides any insight about conscience. Indeed, it does.

Genesis 1:26 (ESV) states: "Then God said, 'Let us make man in our image, after our likeness. And let them have dominion over the fish of the sea and over the birds of the heavens and over the livestock and over all the earth and over every creeping thing that creeps on the earth.'" The image obviously has something to do with ruling over the rest of creation. I believe the most compelling interpretation is that Genesis 1:26 contains a purpose clause: God made humans in his image *in order that* they might exercise dominion. To bear God's image is thoroughly moral. By making them in his image, God granted humans a royal office with a moral commission. God called them to exercise benevolent rule over the world, in likeness to and under the ultimate authority of God's own benevolent rule. Bearing the image, then, also surely

4 Aquinas, *Summa Theologiae*, 1a2ae 94.1 ad.2.

5 Calvin, *Commentaries on Romans*, 96–98; Calvin, *Institutes*, 2.2.22.

6 For description of many views in the history of theology, see John F. Kilner, *Dignity and Destiny: Humanity in the Image of God* (Grand Rapids, MI: Eerdmans, 2015).

Abimelech, they were aware of God's judgment and made their own judgments in accord with it.

## *Natural Wisdom*

The Old Testament wisdom literature – especially Proverbs – also aids our inquiry. Proverbial wisdom demands moral discernment and decision, for both ordinary daily choices and development of virtue over time. I now argue that at the heart of Proverbial wisdom is a well-functioning conscience. I also observe that, for Proverbs, wisdom is acquired primarily through the natural law, thereby illustrating the connection between natural law and conscience.

In Proverbs, wisdom is an intellectual power by which people understand which courses of conduct are good and bad and become able to put this knowledge into skillful practice. This is not the power of memorizing moral rules, or even of applying rules to specific circumstances. Wisdom is rather a *perception* of how the world works and thus of what kinds of behavior are likely to be effective or destructive in concrete cases. Proverbs does not list rules or apply rules, but shows readers how to recognize recurring patterns of how character shapes conduct and how conduct brings blessing or hardship to those around them. Wisdom grasps what is fitting in a particular time and place.[14] Wisdom and conscience must therefore be closely linked. Conscience, as an intellectual faculty that makes prospective moral judgments about courses of action and renders retrospective verdicts on a person's conduct, requires wisdom, and it exhibits wisdom when functioning well.

The frequent use of "heart" in the wisdom literature – ninety-nine times in Proverbs alone – confirms this link between wisdom and conscience.[15] We have seen that judgments of conscience reside in the heart, and in Proverbs the heart is what exercises wisdom. For example, "the heart of him who has understanding seeks knowledge" (Prov. 15:14), and "an intelligent heart acquires knowledge" (18:15). "The wise of heart is called discerning," and "the heart of the wise makes his speech judicious" (16:21, 23). Accordingly, when Solomon asked for a listening heart in order to "discern between good and evil" (1 Kings 3:9), God gave him "a wise and discerning" heart (1 Kings 3:12). The heart is both the seat of conscience and the fount of wisdom.

[14] For more detailed defense of this conception of wisdom and related bibliography, see David VanDrunen, "Learning the Natural Law As Maturation in Wisdom," *In die Skriflig/In Luce Verbi* 50, no. 1 (2016): 1–9.

[15] See Wolff, *Anthropology*, 47; Cf. *NIDOTTE*, 753.

Being wise and having a well-formed conscience are thus inseparable. One might even argue that these two characteristics are one and the same. The fool must therefore be a person with an immature or malfunctioning conscience.

Another consideration strengthens the case. As discussed above, the consciences of Abimelech and the midwives not only judged the moral character of intra-human affairs but also perceived where they stood before God's ultimate judgment. So also with wisdom. Proverbs teems with counsel about mundane affairs: working, choosing a spouse, child-rearing, getting along with neighbors. Yet "the fear of the Lord is the beginning of knowledge" (Prov. 1:7; cf. Job 28:28). Ecclesiastes' wisdom inquiry concludes that people must "fear God and keep his commandments . . . for God will bring every deed into judgment, with every secret thing, whether good or evil" (Eccles. 12:13–14).

Does this link between wisdom and conscience have anything to do with natural law? Since Proverbs was an Israelite document, its context was quite different from that of Abimelech and the midwives: that is, Proverbs was written for those who had the Mosaic law. But while its authors surely assumed that the law of Moses would shape the reader's conscience, Proverbs makes little mention of the written law or of God's redemptive acts toward Israel. Instead, Proverbs describes the wise attaining wisdom primarily through instruction from their elders, observing the world around, and reflecting on their experience within it. They perceive analogies between human conduct, on the one hand, and animal affairs and the cosmic order, on the other hand (see, e.g., Prov. 25–26, 30:18–19, 29–31). The wisdom of Proverbs, to a significant degree, is a *natural* wisdom accessible to all people. This explains why Proverbs incorporates the wisdom literature of pagan nations into its own text (likely in 22:17–24:22) and why two non-Israelites (probably) were among the authors of the book (Agur and Lemuel in Prov. 30–31). Other Old Testament texts also acknowledge the wisdom of non-Israelite peoples (e.g., 1 Kings 4:30; Jer. 49:7; Obad. 8; Ezek. 28:3, 12).[16]

The relation of this natural wisdom to the distinctive wisdom acquired through the law and prophets is a complex subject for another time. I simply note here that, for the Old Testament, having a well-formed conscience required wisdom, and the insight gained through experience, observation, and reflection upon the order of the world was an important aspect of the requisite wisdom – even for an Israelite. That is to say, the wise conscience acquires its understanding, in part, through the natural law.

[16] For further discussion and related bibliography, see VanDrunen, *Divine Covenants*, 375–98.

### *The Prophetic Judgments*

I conclude our study of the Old Testament by turning to several prophetic texts in which the connection of conscience and natural law is prominent. I consider first how the prophets reasoned with Israel and then examine their words to Gentile nations.

The prophets ordinarily addressed the covenant people and often indicted them for violating the Mosaic law. But on occasion, the prophets engaged in a type of natural-law discourse with Israel by speaking as though a natural order permeates the world, which to defy is nonsensical and bizarre. These texts show that as human beings contemplate the natural world, they are capable of understanding fundamental moral and divine truths and responsible for making right judgments about them. The prophets compel them to recognize the foolishness of acting against the grain of the universe.

Isaiah provides poignant examples. At its outset, the prophet calls: "The ox knows its owner, and the donkey its master's crib, but Israel does not know, my people do not understand" (1:3). Dull farm animals recognize their place in the natural order, but the Israelites do not know theirs? It is strange and shameful. Later, Isaiah cries: "Woe to those who call evil good and good evil, who put darkness for light and light for darkness, who put bitter for sweet and sweet for bitter!" (5:20). Darkness is the opposite of light and sweet the opposite of bitter. They are easy to distinguish. To confuse them is to be utterly out of touch with reality. So too for those who cannot differentiate evil and good. In a final example, Isaiah states: "Ah, you who hide deep from the Lord your counsel, whose deeds are in the dark, and who say, 'Who sees us? Who knows us?' You turn things upside down! Shall the potter be regarded as the clay, that the thing made should say of its maker, 'He did not make me'; or the thing formed say of him who formed it, 'He has no understanding'?" (29:15–16). To reject one's creator is to flip reality and rearrange the natural order. It is as bizarre as a pot trying to lord it over the potter.[17] In short, conscience informed by natural law ought to recognize one's obligations under divine authority.

Many Old Testament prophetical books also contain oracles against Gentile nations. Since these nations never received the law of Moses, the prophets address them solely on the basis of natural law, yet they hold these nations fully responsible before God's judgment. Through Amos, for example,

[17] Among other similar examples, see Isaiah 10:15; Amos 3:3–6; 6:12; Psalm 94:8–10. See John Barton, *Understanding Old Testament Ethics: Approaches and Explorations* (Louisville, KY: Westminster John Knox, 2003), chs. 2, 7; and VanDrunen, *Divine Covenants*, 175–77, 187–89.

God calls various peoples to account for slave-trading (1:6), treaty-breaking (1:9), ripping open pregnant women (1:13), and desecration of the dead (2:1). God does not condemn these nations on debatable issues that may justly vary from culture to culture but for committing atrocities that *everybody* should know is wrong.[18]

What had happened to their consciences? The oracles against foreign nations rarely describe the moral reasoning of those they condemn. But when they do, they indicate that these Gentiles had succumbed to *hubris* and acted as though they were "like the Most High" (e.g., Isa. 14:12–15). They exalted themselves and did not fear God. To use the language of Proverbs, they became fools, for they did not cultivate the humility at the center of wisdom (e.g., Prov. 11:2). And without hearts of wisdom, their consciences made heinous moral judgments toward their fellow human beings and despised the ultimate judgment of God.

## CONSCIENCE AND NATURAL LAW IN THE NEW TESTAMENT

The Greek New Testament provides something useful the Hebrew Old Testament does not: a word that means "conscience" (*suneidesis*). Nevertheless, New Testament authors do not define the term or even discuss conscience in any focused or systematic way. And although the New Testament makes clear that Christian faith changes certain things with respect to the believer's conscience and that concerns about conscience should shape behavior within the church, it generally treats the nature and function of conscience as well-known and uncontroversial. I first provide a brief overview of what the New Testament assumes or teaches about conscience and then consider two texts that associate conscience and natural law.

### *General Characteristics of Conscience*

Seven characteristics of conscience in the New Testament stand out. First, conscience is a universal human power. For example, Paul speaks of conscience operating in Gentiles as well as Jews (Rom. 2:15) and he opens his ministry to the judgment of "everyone's conscience" (2 Cor. 4:2). Second, the work of conscience is to bear witness. Its testimony can go in both directions, to acquit or to condemn (Rom. 2:15; 9:1; 2 Cor. 1:12).[19] Third, people's

[18] See VanDrunen, *Divine Covenants*, 167–78, and ch. 4 generally.

[19] See Philip Bosman, *Conscience in Philo and Paul* (Tübingen: Mohr Siebeck, 2003), 198; see contra C. A. Pierce, *Conscience in the New Testament* (London: SCM, 1955), who claims that it

consciences make judgments about others' conduct as well their own.[20] Sometimes people should avoid being judged by another's conscience (1 Cor. 10:28–29), but on other occasions Paul invites it (2 Cor 4:2; 5:11). Fourth, conscience is fallible, but its testimony generally reliable. Paul acknowledges that his judgment of conscience does not settle a matter (1 Cor. 4:4), although he often writes as though conscience witnesses to the truth (e.g., Rom. 2:15; 13:5).[21]

The fifth point qualifies the previous one. In the New Testament, conscience can exist in different spiritual conditions; this confirms Old Testament evidence that conscience can be healthy or ill. Christians' consciences are "good" (Acts 24:1; 1 Tim. 1:5, 19; Heb. 13:18; 1 Pet 3:16, 21) and "pure" or "clear" (Acts 24:16; 1 Tim 3:9; 2 Tim 1:3). In contrast, at least some non-Christians' consciences are "seared" (1 Tim. 4:20), "defiled" (Titus 1:15), and "evil" (Heb. 10:22). Sixth, Christ's sacrifice is what purifies the conscience in need of healing (Heb. 9:9, 14; 10:22). But among Christians, conscience can be either "strong" or "weak," depending upon the degree to which one understands the implications of Christian truth (1 Cor. 8:7, 10, 12).

### *Conscience and Natural Law in the New Testament*

Two of the New Testament texts cited above are especially important for the relation of conscience and natural law: Romans 2:15 and 13:5. Each confirms important conclusions drawn from Old Testament texts above.

Romans 2:14–15 is the *locus classicus* on natural law and conscience: "For when Gentiles, who do not have the law, by nature do what the law requires, they are a law to themselves, even though they do not have the law. They show that the work of the law is written on their hearts, while their conscience also bears witness, and their conflicting thoughts accuse or even excuse them." Most theologians (including Thomas and Calvin) have taken this as a reference to the knowledge of natural law possessed by Gentiles without the law of Moses, whose consciences bear witness on the basis of this natural moral knowledge. Yet dissenters have claimed that Paul refers to *Christian* Gentiles, in whom God has written his law in fulfillment of Jeremiah's promise of the

only condemns; cf. Paul W. Gooch, "'Conscience' in 1 Corinthians 8 and 10," *New Testament Studies* 33 (1987): 244–54, on conscience as awareness of "bad feelings."

[20] See Bosman, *Conscience in Philo and Paul*, 266; contra Pierce, *Conscience in the New Testament*, 16, 42.

[21] See Bosman, *Conscience in Philo and Paul*, 251, 264, 269–73.

new covenant (Jer. 31:33). Opinion is divided among contemporary New Testament scholars.[22]

I believe the natural-law interpretation is the strongest, as I have argued at length elsewhere.[23] In the larger context (Rom. 1:18–3:20), Paul's predominant if not sole focus is to describe the "wrath of God … revealed from heaven against all ungodliness and unrighteousness" (1:18), an unrighteousness leaving Gentile and Jew alike "under sin" (3:9), such that "none is righteous, no, not one" (3:10). Hence, "by works of the law no human being will be justified" (3:20). In light of this, for Paul to muse in 2:14–15 upon the Spirit-infused embrace of God's law prophesied in Jeremiah would not fit the context and would in fact weaken his argument; in contrast, reflecting on Gentiles' knowledge of the natural law bolsters his larger argument that all people are "accountable to God" (3:19), even those without the Mosaic law.

Furthermore, a natural-law interpretation makes sense of the subargument Paul develops in the immediate context, 2:12–16. Paul begins with an uncontroversial principle of justice: "All who have sinned without the law will also perish without the law, and all who have sinned under the law will be judged by the law" (2:12). That is, God will not judge people by a law they neither have nor know. But the next verse complicates matters: "For it is not the hearers of the law who are righteous before God, but the doers of the law who will be justified" (2:13). How is it that only doers of the (Mosaic) law will be justified when many people do not have that law and thus cannot justly be judged by it? Paul's appeal to the natural law in 2:14 provides the answer: although Gentiles do not have the Mosaic law, they know its basic demands through the natural law, and thus God judges Jew and Gentile by the same underlying moral standard.

If this interpretation is correct, it confirms the view that natural law is an objective moral norm, while conscience is a subjective human faculty that recognizes right and wrong and thus bears witness to a person's standing before the law. And it also confirms that this work of conscience has an ultimate divine reference. Paul explains that the doers of the law are righteous "before God" (2:13), and the accusing and excusing thoughts of conscience will extend even to "that day when … God judges the secrets of men by Christ Jesus" (2:16).

22 Among defenders of a natural-law view, see James D. G. Dunn, *Romans 1–8* (Dallas, TX: Word, 1988), 98; and Douglas J. Moo, *The Epistle to the Romans* (Grand Rapids, MI: Eerdmans, 1996), 148–51; Among defenders of a Christian Gentiles view, see C. E. B. Cranfield, *The Epistle to the Romans*, vol. 1 (Edinburgh: T&T Clark, 1975), 155–63; and N. T. Wright, *The Letter to the Romans*, New Interpreter's Bible (Nashville, TN: Abingdon, 2002), 441–43.

23 See VanDrunen, *Divine Covenants*, 233–51.

Romans 13:5 complements 2:14–15. In the midst of broader instruction about civil government (13:1–7), Paul exhorts readers to "be in subjection, not only to avoid . . . wrath but also for the sake of conscience" (13:5). Several things indicate that this appeal takes place in a natural-law context. While the surrounding sections (12:1–21 and 13:8–14) describe the unique character of the Christian life, 13:1–7 omits any reference to Christ, the Spirit, or redemptive grace. Instead, Paul speaks of what "every person" must do: "be subject to the governing authorities" (13:1). Paul does not associate government's work with the rich Christian ethic of surrounding texts, but simply says that magistrates approve "good" conduct and punish the "bad" (13:3).[24] Thus, Paul appeals to conscience as a universal human capacity in 13:5, not to something uniquely Christian. It must be conscience operating on the basis of natural law, as described in 2:15.

As with many texts considered above, Paul says that conscience judges intra-human affairs, but with an ultimate divine reference. On the former front, Paul says the magistrate is a "terror" to those who do evil (13:3) and bears the sword against wrongdoers (13:4). A person might submit to magistrates simply to avoid punishment, but Paul exhorts readers to do so also for conscience's sake, that is, not just for pragmatic reasons but also for moral reasons, not simply to stay out of trouble externally but also to avoid the internal unease of self-condemnation. With respect to the divine dimension, Paul has just written that the magistrate is "the servant of God, an avenger who carries out God's wrath on the wrongdoer" (13:4). By responding to earthly magistrates and their sword, a person responds to God, their magistrates' master. Conscientious accusing or excusing with respect to civil authority will render testimony before the divine judge on the last day.

## NATURAL LAW, CONSCIENCE, AND CIVIL LIBERTY

Our study of conscience and natural law in Scripture has not addressed an important question: What does Scripture say about the protection of conscience as a matter of civil law? In this final section, I reflect briefly on this question. We should be honest about Scripture's relative silence on the subject, although I suggest that there is a compelling, though indirect, biblical argument for the generous legal protection of conscientious judgments.

[24] On the universal rather than distinctively Christian character of this text, see Robert H. Stein, "The Argument of Romans 13:1–7," *Novum Testamentum* 31, no. 4 (1989): 329–30; and Wright, *The Letter to the Romans*, 717, 721.

In the modern West, many people tend to justify the legal protection of conscience on grounds that one person's moral and religious opinions are just as good as anyone else's. But this is not the way Scripture views issues of conscience. In the texts considered above, conscience is good and important because it provides knowledge of the one true God and of his law and judgment – hence, everyone is accountable to him. Scripture never lauds the dignity of people whose consciences choose to worship another god or follow a different moral path but speaks instead of their foolishness and guilt. Also noteworthy is that the only biblical text that explicitly connects conscience and the state, Romans 13:5, speaks of everyone's obligation to submit to the governing authorities, not to the obligation of these authorities to honor everyone's conscientious judgments. Furthermore, biblical stories about civil disobedience – concerning the midwives, Daniel, or the apostles in Acts – describe people justified in conscientious resistance because they are morally right, not people having a civil right to act upon any conscientious judgment whatsoever. The good of respecting other people's consciences, even when wrong, does emerge in 1 Corinthians. Yet Paul wrestles here with how Christians should treat each other and promote their mutual spiritual welfare as members of the church. The text expresses no interest in public policy.

Scripture, therefore, does not support just any rationale for the legal protection of conscience. Nevertheless, I believe a robust view of natural law in Scripture points to an indirect, yet compelling, case for such a policy. This case depends upon an appreciation for the Noahic covenant of Genesis 8:21–9:17. This refers to a covenant that God entered with the entire human race, the animal kingdom, and even the cosmic order after the great flood. The text presents this covenant as foundational for all of God's subsequent dealings with the world, since it is universal in scope and promises the preservation of creation until the end of history. While this covenant does not give any promises of salvation from sin and evil or provide any special instruction about the character of Old Testament Israel or the New Testament church, it does establish the basic terms of God's relationship with the world in general. I have argued elsewhere that this covenant provides theological explanation for natural law. The covenant does not present a detailed moral code but does mention a few basic moral requirements necessary for the survival of the human community and which are incumbent upon its members as image-bearers of God. The Noahic covenant, in short, describes a divinely governed natural order within which human beings must live in certain ways in order to meet their basic needs and maintain their societies. If God sustains and governs the world through the

Noahic covenant, then the Noahic covenant is God's means for promulgating the natural law.[25]

If this argument is sound, then Scripture does provide a natural-law basis for the generous legal protection of conscience. This is because the Noahic covenant implicitly ordains a pluralistic and tolerant civil community. The covenant does not condone worshiping a false god, but neither does it establish any religious test or detailed moral creed that a person must profess in order to participate in human society. The covenant calls for the legal protection of all people against the violence of others (Gen. 9:6), thereby implying that political communities ought to welcome and protect all those who live peacefully with their neighbors, regardless of their moral and religious convictions. In other words, although Scripture never speaks of an ultimate conscientious right *before God* to choose to worship another god or follow another moral path, the Noahic covenant points to a natural-law right *before fellow human beings* not to be excluded from the political community on the basis of one's conscientious convictions and actions – provided one lives in peace. Another way to put it is that no human being has the natural-law authority to try to make the political community narrower than God has ordained it in the Noahic covenant by setting up moral and religious tests for inclusion.[26]

Bolstering this conclusion is that the Noahic covenant refers to human beings as the image of God (Gen. 9:6). This brings us back to where our biblical investigation began. It reminds us of the dignity that all people have as those entrusted with a moral commission to exercise benevolent rule in this world. Even a poor use of conscience is a distinctively human activity that reflects, in however corrupt a way, our likeness to God, the just sovereign of the universe. Although people cannot escape accountability in God's court for their conscientious judgments, according to Scripture, it is a weighty thing for one human being to lord it over the conscience of another.

## RECOMMENDED READING

Barton, John. *Understanding Old Testament Ethics: Approaches and Explorations.* Louisville, KY: Westminster John Knox, 2003.

Berkman, John, and William C. Mattison III, eds. *Searching for a Universal Ethic: Multidisciplinary, Ecumenical, and Interfaith Responses to the Catholic Natural Law Tradition.* Grand Rapids, MI: Eerdmans, 2014.

[25] For a detailed argument, see VanDrunen, *Divine Covenants*, ch. 2.

[26] Ibid., 505–11.

Bockmuehl, Markus. *Jewish Law in Gentile Churches: Halakhah and the Beginning of Christian Public Ethics.* Grand Rapids, MI: Baker Academic, 2003.
Bosman, Philip. *Conscience in Philo and Paul.* Tübingen: Mohr Siebeck, 2003.
Budziszewski, J. *The Line through the Heart: Natural Law As Fact, Theory, and Sign of Contradiction.* Wilmington, DE: ISI, 2009.
Burnside, Jonathan. *God, Justice, and Society: Aspects of Law and Legality in the Bible.* Oxford: Oxford University Press, 2011.
Charles, J. Daryl. *Retrieving the Natural Law: A Return to Moral First Things.* Grand Rapids, MI: Eerdmans, 2008.
Hittinger, Russell. *The First Grace: Rediscovering the Natural Law in a Post-Christian World.* Wilmington, DE: ISI, 2003.
Levering, Matthew. *Biblical Natural Law: A Theocentric and Teleological Approach.* Oxford: Oxford University Press, 2008.
Novak, David. *Natural Law in Judaism.* Cambridge: Cambridge University Press, 1998.
Pierce, C. A. *Conscience in the New Testament.* London: SCM, 1955.
VanDrunen, David. *Divine Covenants and Moral Order: A Biblical Theology of Natural Law.* Grand Rapids, MI: Eerdmans, 2014.

# 3

# Conscience in Early Christian Thought

JOHN ANTHONY MCGUCKIN

The concept of an inner conscious sense of rightness and wrong, often thought of as an inbuilt moral compass set within human awareness by the Creator, is an idea that has been both warmly embraced yet also sternly warned against within the Christian tradition. The earliest writings of the Christian theologians show the roots of this ambivalence. The positive aspect of the notion venerates the inner voice of conscience as a quasi-revelation of the voice of God (or an angel) in the innermost heart or, alternatively, a manifestation of the God-given natural law of rational ethic in a person's life, whatever their stage of development. The negative approach to the idea tends to regard this kind of theological or moral inner certainty as a potentially dangerous spiritual state of discernment that always depends heavily on prior educational, ethical and religious formation and presuppositions (which may themselves be good or bad) but, at worst, is a possible high road to delusion, self-satisfaction and prejudice.[1] The early Christian tradition is full of this ambivalence towards the idea of conscience, both advocating its necessity yet questioning it. Arguably, that foundational dichotomous attitude has not been resolved to this day.

The twin starting points for almost all early Christian thought on the matter were, of course, the scriptures and the writings of the Greek philosophers on ethics and transcendent epistemology: chiefly Plato, Aristotle and the Stoics. Both Plato and the Stoics, in their various ways, stressed the aspects of certain inner knowledge in relation to conscience: the one (at least in the iterations of Platonism in the late antique period) coming at it from the basis of the transcendental ideals mirrored in the spiritual capacity

[1] As in the famous dictum of Jeremy Bentham: 'Fanaticism never sleeps ... it is never stopped by conscience; for it has pressed conscience into its service.' *Introduction to the Principles of Morals and Legislation*, eds. J. H. Burns and H. L. A. Hart (London: Athlone Press, 1970), 156.

of the human (immortal) soul and the others coming at it more concretely in terms of the theory of the universal natural law, to which an articulated human moral sense sought to conform by means of a liberated conscience. Late Platonism's affirmation of transcendentals greatly affected early Christian writers after the time of the New Testament. And, even from the time of the Apostle Paul, Stoic ideas on ethics as a return to a purer natural state of humanity chimed with Christian ideas on the advent of the reforming Kingdom of God. But the early Christian writers, Greek and Latin, were far from simple *repetiteurs*, badly harmonising the ill-meshed thoughts of their ancient predecessors. They were creative synthesists: and their form of synthesis rarely left untouched or untransfigured the raw materials they worked with. In that mix, which was the Patristic reworking of the Greek philosophical and biblical *scholia* that they adopted, the evangelical and apostolic *dicta* took pre-eminence. In this respect, it might be illuminative to briefly review the philosophic and apostolic data they worked from.

Conscience in early Greek semantics begins as a deeply epistemological notion: *synoida*, *syneidesis*, the being aware of something. The pre-Christian Greek thinkers made it an interior and increasingly moral factor by making it reflexive: *synoida emauto* – 'I know within myself'. Used in such a way within the Platonic dialogues, Socrates, for example, ponders on why the Delphic Oracle has called him the 'wisest of men' when he himself is aware only that he knows so little.[2] This crisis of 'awareness' stimulates his entire approach to establishing the 'proper' human life: namely, to seek after wisdom by penetrative reflection teasing out a puzzle or an *aporia*. In the earlier levels of Greek thinking, there is little attempt to connect the terms with any theological determinants: the dominant hope was to establish the standards of reality, whether in terms of cosmology or anthropology. An individual learning to discern true motive and a clear awareness of the standards of his or her personal behaviour was performing a similar function in terms of consciousness, as was a thinker applying acute observation to natural phenomena and from them deducing true cosmic causes and effects in place of mythological ones. In this regard, Aristotle made a lasting impact with his observation that moral behaviour in humans was more an issue of habituation than random insight. Moral *habitus* had both to be educated in a person and practised assiduously, only thus did it become *arête*, virtue or excellence.

[2] Plato, *Apology*, 21.6. This chapter refers to all the works of Plato from J. Burnet, ed., *Platonis Opera* (Oxford: Clarendon Press, 1900–1907). We remember, of course, that for the Delphic Apollonine cult, the great moral goal was self-knowledge: *gnothe seauton*.

By the first century BCE, Greco-Roman and Jewish writers had widely adopted this notion of *syneidesis* as moral awareness and brought it into a more overtly religious domain. Plutarch, for example, writes about the burning force of a bad conscience that constantly reminds us of our sins and calls to mind the possible torments of hell.[3] The very first reference in ancient secular literature to the concept of a 'clear conscience' (*kathara syneidesis*) comes in an Egyptian papyrus of 136 CE, where the author claims to have no awareness of any charge that may be laid against him.[4] The Jewish philosopher, Philo, who was closely read by many of the later Greek Fathers of the Church, was one of the main writers who, using the Greek version of the Hebrew Scriptures known as the Septuagint, brought the idea of *syneidesis* to the fore as the quintessential biblical notion of a pure conscience. In this sense, the concept of a 'pure heart' was frequently found in the Psalms and through them also made its way into the wider Christian consciousness via the monastic movement, which took the Psalter as its daily prayer book. For the Old Testament scribes, however, cleanness of heart was as much a matter of cultic and ritual purity as interior moral standing, though with the later prophets, the moral impetus in the notion began to take the centre stage.

In his late antique exegetical labours, Philo forged the first of the syntheses between Hellenistic moral-philosophical concerns and Hebraic ritual notions of purity in the cause of reinterpreting the demands of the Torah for his now thoroughly Hellenised Jewish readership in Alexandria. The philosopher Christian Maurer calls him 'the first to think through theologically a doctrine of conscience'. For Philo, and for most of the Greek Fathers following after, the primary scriptural authorities for this were the Old Testament passages that spoke of keeping a 'clean heart', largely understood as a pure conscience. This idea of conscience was intimately related to the biblical notion of repentance (*metanoia*), and thus conscience served, for both the Hellenistic Jews and the early Christians, as primarily a mechanism of remembrance of misbehaviour that served, in turn, as a stimulus to return to the right way of living: *orthopraxis*.

In the non-Christian Latin-speaking world, the two main gatekeepers of this concept were Cicero and (more so) Seneca, who both brought Stoic philosophical reflection to bear heavily in their rendering of the key term of moral awareness as *conscientia*. Cicero already uses the argument that it is conscience that largely regulates humankind's behaviour. He describes it as

3 Plutarch, *De Tranquillitate Animi*, 18f. See also Gerhardt Kittel, ed., *Theological Dictionary of the New Testament* (Grand Rapids, MI: Eerdmans, 1978) (hereafter *TDNT*), 2:476a–477a.

4 *Papyrus Osloensis*, 2.17.10; *TDNT*, 2:476.

having a 'great force' and a 'heavy weight' in and of itself.[5] In Latin literature, the turn from the more generic awareness of *syneidesis* meaning 'sensing', to specifically moral and spiritual (soul-centred) or religious reflection, is made more commonly evident. Caesar, for example, speaks of the *animi conscientia* or 'consciousness of the spirit'.[6] This trend was immediately picked up and used by the Latin Apologists among the Christians as a way of showing that the intellectual tradition of the Church was in broad harmony with the best traditions and aspirations of *Romanitas*, rather than (as persecuting authorities argued) a contradiction of classical values that needed to be extirpated. The Christian rhetoricians Tertullian, Cyprian, Minucius Felix and Lactantius all follow this path; and in so doing, they deeply influenced the subsequent ecclesial tradition's approach to conscience from a Neo-Stoic perspective.

The Apostle Paul himself gave no clear definition of what he meant by conscience (*syneidesis*) though he used the term often (fourteen times) and thereby established the word with apostolic authority for later Christianity. More than half of these instances relate to his discussion of whether Christians can legitimately eat meat that was previously offered in the cult of the gods: the custom of most urban butcheries in antiquity. He describes the crisis between the 'weak' of the community, whose conscience forbids them to eat this contaminated food, and that of the more sagacious, who have more fully realised their freedom in a more enlightened awareness of such matters (on the argument that the gods do not exist anyway, and no malign influence can attach itself to a believer in Christ). He ends, however, by appealing to the stronger-minded (whom he has commended) to follow the example of the weaker ones, so that they will not scandalise the weak who believe their conscience has indicated the only right moral path for the Church. So, here from the outset, Paul validates the role of conscience as a moral guide and simultaneously indicates that it is by no means an infallible compass and must be subordinate to the deeper perception of an understanding of salvation (*soteria*), which, for Paul, is led by the overarching sense of how Christ, through his death and resurrection, has set the Church free both from the strictures of Jewish law and pagan religion. This encompassing mystery of salvation in Christ is, for Paul, a transcending *gnosis* that takes precedence over all things and reorientates all things, conscience included.

5 Cicero, *Pro Milone*; cf. 'magna vis est conscientiae' and 'et virtutis et vitiorum grave ipsius conscientiae pondus' (both to the effect of 'how great is the weight of conscience'). P. MacKendrick, ed., *The Speeches of Cicero* (London: Duckworth, 1995), 23.61.

6 Caesar, *Bellum Civile*, ed. C. Damon (Oxford: Oxford Classical Texts, 2015), 3.60.2.

Paul also sent out another warning shot about conscience when he made a marked contrast between his own inner sense of righteousness and the judgement of God, who placed that type of conscience under judgement.[7] This was to affirm his doctrine of salvation by grace: that one's state of moral rectitude did not emanate from self-training (*askesis*) or achievement (*arete*) but from the gift (*charis*) of God alone. Paul believed a person was only righteous if God declared him to be such (through Christ). Peace of heart and mind could thus only be found by trusting in the mercy of a forgiving God, in the knowledge that no human moral achievement would ever suffice, and no self-satisfaction with one's moral achievement could be anything other than sinfulness. For Paul, consciousness of being graced is supplied to the conscience (understood as spiritual sense) by the awareness of a spiritual harmony with the indwelling Spirit.[8] This Pauline trajectory stood in marked contrast with most Hellenistic moral thought and a large amount of Jewish reflection too. It was thus the sign of wisdom and an authentic connection to salvation to be ever uneasy in one's (human) conscience as one assessed one's manner of life and attitudes against the standard of Christ's Gospel. On other occasions, Paul suggests that those who are not 'in Christ' (*en Christo*) will be expected to observe that law, which is 'written on the heart', a duty that falls to Jew and pagan alike and in which the conscience serves as a guiding compass to a high degree.[9]

Paul's complex mystical approach took some time to be absorbed by Christian intellectuals after him. The first generation of the Greek Apostolic Fathers in the century immediately succeeding the New Testament generally fell back to reliance on what had by then become something of a cliché among Stoic and Jewish writers – the conscience as that good voice in the heart commending pure actions by its quietness and frowning on evil tendencies by its agitation. This was never an active dynamic, we might note, but rather a passive form of litmus response. The frequently repeated terms used by the very early second-century Christian writers generally concern inculcating 'a good and blameless conscience' (*syneidesis*).[10] But most of the writing simply echoes the generic moral paranetic discourses of contemporary late Antique Jewish and Stoic thinkers, content with repeating generic forms of the

7 2 Cor. 4:4.
8 Rom. 8:16, 9:1.
9 Rom. 2:15.
10 For the following instances in the Apostolic Fathers, see Bart Ehrman, trans., *The Apostolic Fathers*, 2 vols., Loeb Classical Library (Cambridge, MA: Harvard University Press, 2003–5). See especially *1st Letter of Clement*, 1.3, 41.1, and 45.7; *2nd Letter of Clement*, 16.4; *Epistle of Polycarp*, 5.3; Ignatius, *To the Trallians*, 7.2; *Didache*, 4.14; Hermas, *Mandates*, 3.4.

so-called Roman Household Code to advocate what was good (conformist) citizenship. It was a theme that was found at times in St Paul also.[11]

The Church's first serious, and arguably greatest, exegete of Scripture who could claim a solid philosophical education, was Origen of Alexandria (185–254). His theory of exegesis approached the Scripture as more of a body of oracular literature than any coherent historical evolution of traditions. He taught that the divine Wisdom, or Logos, of God had presented Scriptures across the ages as a treasure that could only be unlocked once one had the proper key to understanding. It was not, in other words, internally logically coherent or self-explanatory in any of its messages. Truth was hidden and clues were given by the Logos to be recognised by the spiritually refined. For those who were not spiritually mature, the literal word often led them astray because they were either unwilling or unable to lift their minds on high. But for those who were attuned to the deeper meanings hidden in the texts by the Divine Logos, it was clear that all things were meant to lead up away from matter and flesh towards an increasing purity of heart that allowed one the possibility of communion with the Logos who hid himself from the crass and the foolish (*Alogoi*). Origen taught consistently that Scripture thus had to be read not historically and sequentially (as if it were a slow linear development) but eschatologically – out of time – and in the realisation that its hidden oracular truths were given in accordance with the mystical profundity of the original messengers who served as vehicles of the Logos and also in the measure of the spiritual profundity of the reader who approaches them for insight. In short, there was a steep hierarchy of value in Scripture.[12]

To begin with, the whole of the Old Testament had to be read in the light of (and subservient to) the New. (Origen was the first to introduce this distinction of Old and New Covenants.) But more so, certain writers were given more weight than others, and they were, so to speak (using a notion borrowed from Rabbi Akiba) 'the first fruits of the first fruits'. This, for him, meant that the two greatest authorities in all of Scripture were the two prophetic seers, John and Paul. After them came the Book of Psalms (seen by Origen as heavily filled with direct, non-historical utterances by the eternal Logos) after that came Isaiah, the synoptic Gospels and the Apostolic epistles, then other New Testament writings and finally the remainder of Old Testament books. This strict hierarchy of interpretive lenses meant that

11 Eph. 3:5; Col. 3:22; Titus 2:9.

12 See further J. A. McGuckin, *The Westminster Handbook to Origen of Alexandria* (Louisville, KY: Westminster John Knox, 2004), 193–97; McGuckin, *Seeing the Glory*, Collected Works, vol. 2 (New York, NY: St Vladimir's Seminary Press, 2017), 159–74.

Pauline literature assumed a very strong dominance on Origen's exegesis. Given that his biblical approach was so heavily used in the Greek Christian world after him, both by his friends and enemies,[13] it meant that the Pauline doctrine on any major topic was pushed to the fore in Christian theological reflection ever after. Following Origen, conscience among the Christians once more assumed the resonances of Paul's mystical teaching riveted to the wider Greek tradition of epistemological awareness. In short, the moral sense became the most acute form of human consciousness and a border point, a liminal space, where refined consciousness (*logos*) merged into divine awareness (*nous*).

Already for some of the more philosophically advanced Greek Christians of the second century onwards, *syneidesis* in the human being was pre-eminently understood as the 'awareness', or consciousness of God and divine things.[14] For Clement of Alexandria, this awareness is one of the pre-eminent energies (*dynameis*) of the soul.[15] It is the force, which, from the soul's knowledge of the exemplar of divine things, gives the moral compass to a believer's life.[16] Clement calls it the best and strongest foundation of the correct life.[17]

However, it was Origen who really elucidated the disconnected ideas present in Paul and who transformed the whole notion into a deeply mystical approach. For Origen, conscience was first and foremost a matter of acute awareness: wisdom (*gnosis*). It was the reflected energy in a human being of the Supreme Wisdom of God (*Logos*). It aroused within a human the realisation that each one was an eternal soul. Moral conscience, therefore, was ultimately the mystical sense of a remembered identity (the origin of the being of souls in eternal bliss with God) in communion with the Logos before the lapse to time and space. This lifted the moral imperative to ontological status: being ethical was not just a return to good behaviours but more so to the springs of immortal being. Origen here was trying to merge aspects of late Platonic epistemology with Christian eschatology. He would get into hot water for this view, both in his lifetime and

[13] Even those who disdained his exegetical theories (such as Theophilus of Alexandria, Jerome, Theodore Mopsuestia or John Chrysostom) have recently been shown to use him extensively and quietly even when castigating him explicitly.

[14] Methodios of Olympus, *Fragment 10 on Job*, in J. P. Migne, ed., *Patrologia Graeca* (Paris: Rue D'Enfer, 1857), 8:408A.

[15] Clement of Alexandria, *Stromata*, 7.7, in Migne, ed., *Patrologia Graeca*, 9:453A and 9:673A; Clement of Alexandria, *Excerpts from Theodotos*, 27, in Migne, ed., *Patrologia Graeca*, 9:673A.

[16] Clement of Alexandria, *Stromata*, 7.8, in Migne, ed., *Patrologia Graeca*, 9:478A, see also 10:423C; Chrysostom, *Homily 1.4 On Second Corinthians*, in Migne, ed., *Patrologia Graeca*, 9:478A, see also 10:423C.

[17] Clement of Alexandria, *Stromata*, 1.1, in Migne, ed., *Patrologia Graeca*, 8.692B.

posthumously; but having purged pre-existence ontology from standard doctrine, the Church took this theological sense of moral conscience as a mystical apprehension of the divine presence to its heart. The idea would rise to great precedence in later tradition, particularly spurred on by the monastic movement and its deep interest in the scrutiny of the inner mind and its motives.

Origen marked a radical return to close attention to the text of Paul. Like the Apostle, he approached the notion of conscience from a mystical perspective – a matter of the sensing of the indwelling power of the grace of God. The Logos is, for Origen, the source of the whole structure and inner meaning and dynamic of the cosmos, especially the 'likeness' to God Himself (*homoiosis*), which, as being the supreme divine Image (*eikon*) in the Cosmos Himself, the Logos has personally located in the human soul, especially rooting it in its higher dynamics of consciousness. For Origen, this close relation of 'the image and the likeness' (divine *Logos* and human spiritual *syneidesis*) fulfills the text in Genesis that defines the original creation of humankind: 'Let us make Man in our own image and likeness.'[18] Using Platonic cosmology, where it suits, Origen explains that this consciousness of God is synonymous with the entrance into all wisdom (*gnosis*) since the soul (the individual considered as a spiritual consciousness) is a-temporal, and indeed the knowledge of God is a remembrance of a time before time when all souls enjoyed a deep ontological union with the Divine Logos, which now (in the fallen material condition) the lapsed soul struggles to rediscover. The return to this former pre-earthly glory (*apokatastasis*) is driven (on earth's moral training ground) by increasingly wise recollection of the glory (*doxa*) and by the force of divine *eros* that transfigures the soul through love. For Origen, here following Paul to a larger degree than Plato, this ascentive love is the force (*dynamis*) that makes moral effort and the ascetical endeavour that underlies it (virtue as *habitus*), synonymous with mystical communion with the Logos. For Origen, conscience is, therefore, an epistemological factor, as it was with Plato; but more than Plato or any of the later Neo-Platonists, the ascentive force is divine *eros* leading to communion. This is why it is, therefore, quintessentially a mystical conception of conscience. Origen's magnificent *Commentary on the Song of Songs* is perhaps the best single work to demonstrate the unfolding of that master-theme; and it was a work that was a major, indeed overwhelmingly dominant, influence on the Latin, Greek and Syriac monastic traditions of the following millennium.

[18] Gen. 1:26.

The Byzantine monastic fathers particularly took up Origen's themes and, in John Klimakos' *Ladder of Divine Ascent*, an early seventh-century book that was used (from its inception to the present day) as the training manual for a monk, *syneidesis* is not merely the moral consciousness of good and evil, but primarily the sense of divine indwelling presence that has to be nurtured and developed as a spiritual faculty in the soul, since it will then provide the full direction of a life well lived.[19] This is the guarding (*phylaxis*) of the heart, which becomes one of the most dominant themes in later spiritual writing. The means of this guarding of the heart are the related attitudes of *nepsis* (focused awareness) and *prosoche* (attentiveness). The later Christian writers who continued Origen's tradition, such as Gregory of Nazianzus (c. 329–90), Gregory of Nyssa (c. 335–94), Maximus the Confessor (c. 580–662) and the later Byzantine monastics who read them closely, also continued to stress the ascentive power of divine *eros* that made the soul of the believer like the lover in the Song of Songs, always seeking restlessly for its Beloved and shaping all its moral and intellectual energies for the goal of loving communion. The strong link between this loving fidelity and obedience to the moral norms had long ago been established in the renowned *mandatum* of 'Maundy' Thursday,[20] when Christ said to his disciples: 'If you love me, keep my commandments.'

The Latin Christian writers generally follow the lead of the Greek tradition in terms of the semantics of conscience. The word's first use (*conscientia*) is again to signify a state of 'common awareness' (*con-scientia*), knowing something along with others, a standard form of social belief.[21] The Christian rhetorician Tertullian adopts and develops this usage when he uses the verb *conscio* to mean to 'know well'.[22] Used as a genitive object, however, the pre-Christian Latin writers used it to signify 'awareness of evil behaviour'.[23] The Stoic use, as demonstrated by Cicero, had spoken extensively about the moral good of a quiet conscience that is to be sought by the wise. This influence tends to predominate among the Latin Fathers, giving a lot of references a certain passive cast. Tertullian, however, uses the idea of

19 John Klimakos, *Ladder of Divine Ascent*, 3.3, in Migne, ed., *Patrologia Graeca*, 88.1656B.

20 John 14:15–21, 'I give you a new commandment' – *mandatum* in Latin.

21 Cicero, *In Catilinam*, 1.1.1; Cicero, *De Finibus*, 2.9.28; Livy, *Historia*, 2.54.7. These writings can be accessed from www.perseus.tufts.edu/hopper/searchresults?q=cicero, and from www.perseus.tufts.edu/hopper/searchresults?q=Livy.

22 "consciens Christus quod esset" (on the soul's knowledge of Christ). Tertullian, *De Carne Christi*, 3, in Migne, ed., *Patrologia Latina*, vols. 1–2 (Paris: Rue D'Enfer, 1844).

23 Cicero, *Pro Cluentio*, 20, 56; Tacitus, *Historia*, 1.25, 1.42; *Digesti (Libri Pandectarum)*, 48.5.29. For the Latin texts, see www.perseus.tufts.edu.

freedom of conscience extensively to argue against the immorality of the Roman penal law, which classified all the acts of a *religio illicita* ('an illegal religion', which Christianity was in his day) as treasonable behaviour demanding the penalty of execution. His argument, that religion is that which quintessentially demands full freedom of choice in order to be practised sincerely, did not hold much water at the time he made it, though it came to have a more dominant resonance in later times and served for subsequent Christian generations (even when they did not observe the principle too well) as the foundational Christian tradition that claimed freedom of worship in a society as an axiomatic right of humankind.

Lactantius (c. 250–325), one of the wittiest and most learned of the Latin Church Apologists, considers the Stoic tradition on conscience carefully before slyly commenting on its defective theological basis:

> And let no one imagine that things go well if there has been no witness to one's misdeed: for all things are known to Him in whose sight we live; and if we are able to conceal anything from all around us, we certainly cannot conceal it from God, from whom nothing can be hidden and nothing kept secret. Seneca closed his exhortations on this subject with an admirable sentiment: 'There is', he says, 'some great deity, and greater than can be imagined; and for him we endeavour to live. Let us make ourselves acceptable to him. What use is it if our conscience is constrained, when we ever lie open to the sight of God.' What can be added with greater truth by him who knew God than has here been said by a man who was ignorant of true religion?[24]

Here Lactantius was affirming the Stoic moral tradition of interiority but contradicting Seneca's theory that the consistently cultivated *habitus* of virtue would accumulate to a coherent guide for living (*ars vivendi*). The Christian theologian insists that morality is not a natural gift within human capacity to fulfill (as evidenced, he says, by the consistent failure of Roman philosophers to achieve the good life either individually or societally).[25] It is rather a divine

[24] Lactantius, *Divine Institutes*, 6.24.11, www.perseus.tufts.edu. In other words, Paul the Apostle could hardly have said it better but did. See Rom. 6:11, 13; Rom. 10:3; Rom. 14:12; 2 Cor. 5:11. The tradition was already in the ether that Paul had some relations with Seneca, although Lactantius implies that he is hardly going to take theological lessons from Seneca when he has the truer source in Paul. Seneca's *Exhortations* are often referred to in Antiquity (here it is fragment 82) but survive only in fragments today. See Marion Lausberg, *Untersuchungen zu Senecas Fragmenten* (Berlin: De Gruyter, 2011).

[25] Augustine would take that theme to much greater lengths in his *De Civitate Dei* where he lamented the iniquity of Rome (and all its moral impotence within its history of violence) as a symbol of the greater moral incapacity (without divine grace) of the whole Earthly City.

grace that lifts humanity out of an animal condition and gives mankind its true nature: *homo erectus*, the transcendent creature.

Observing the use of the term conscience in such later writers as Ambrose (c. 340–97) or Augustine (354–430), however, one notices immediately how much reliance they both give to the doctrine of the Stoics that the whole point of a conscience is to keep it quiet.[26] The heavy reliance of Cyprian, Lactantius, Ambrose and Augustine (and through them the whole subsequent Latin patristic tradition) on Cicero is especially noteworthy. Ambrose's treatises (especially his book *On Duty*) profoundly rely on Cicero's *De Officiis* as a primary source, and Lactantius' *De Opificio Dei*, is evidently an attempt to offer a Christian version of the same. Ambrose attempts the same Christianising plagiarism, but not as effectively as Lactantius. Often Ambrose could more or less be mistaken for Cicero. His concept of conscience is a simple repetition of Tullius: 'Therefore the blessedness of individuals must not be estimated at the value of their known wealth, but according to the voice of their conscience within them. For this, as a true and uncorrupted judge of punishments and rewards, decides between the deserts of the innocent and the guilty.'[27] Nevertheless, Lactantius'[28] and Ambrose's Christianising 'slant' is typical of the other Latin ecclesiastical authors in two ways: firstly, for bringing in more concretely and directly than the Stoics would, the concept of conscience's reliance on the immanent presence of the Divinity. Writing to Eugenius, for example, Ambrose puts it like this: 'Although the imperial power is immense, still consider this O Emperor: how great is God. He sees the hearts of all; He questions the innermost conscience; He knows all things before they happen; He knows the innermost things of your breast. You yourself would never allow yourself to be deceived, so why would you desire to conceal anything from God?'[29] Conscience, for the Christians, thus becomes more than just the effective moral compass within human nature, set there by the Creator, but also, in a real sense, the *oculus dei* searching within the heart.

[26] Ambrose, *On Duty*, 2.1.1: 'So great is the splendour of a virtuous life that a peaceful conscience and a calm innocence make for a happy life.' Commenting on Psalm 39.1, Ambrose concludes: 'For David knew and had read that it was a mark of the divine protection for a man to be hid from the scourge of his own tongue [Job. 5.21] and the witness of his own conscience.' Ambrose, *On Repentance*, 2.6. For the works of Ambrose, see Migne, ed., *Patrologia Latina*, vols. 14–17.

[27] Ambrose, *On Duty*, 1.12.44. (81).

[28] See for example Lactantius, *Divine Institutes*, 4.17; 5.20; 6.13; and 6.24 (reflecting on Cicero's doctrine of conscience).

[29] Ambrose, *Letter* 57.7 *To the Emperor Eugenius*, in Migne, ed., *Patrologia Latina*, 16.875f.

In his more overtly episcopal writings (letters to the faithful and treatises relating to scriptural interpretation), this God-centred (what we may again call mystical) approach is more to the fore in Ambrose. Writing privately to his sister, he speaks of conscience in an evangelical and spiritually Christocentric manner reminiscent of Paul:

> The one who purifies his conscience from the defilement of sin is the one who pours water upon the feet of Christ, for Christ walks within the breast of each one. Take heed, then, never to have your conscience polluted, for then you would begin to defile the feet of Christ. Be careful that He never finds a thorn of wickedness within you, so that when He walks in you His heel may not be wounded.[30]

Augustine had, undoubtedly, the greatest long-term influence on the Latin Christian tradition. In relation to the notion of conscience he does not especially develop significantly further what Lactantius and Ambrose had already prefigured. He does not address the matter directly in any specific treatise, for example. But he did change the overall scenario of moral reflection. His monumental *City of God* best shows his mature thinking in this regard when he considers, from the long perspective, the nature of social ethics.[31] Augustine has been well described as the initiator of 'realism-ethic'. What that means, in short, is that he taught that the human individual conscience was so deeply corrupted by the race's fall into sin from its early origins, that pride and selfishness are engrained in everything that a human does. From such a corrupt matrix nothing purely good can come, except as a result of the gift of divine grace that lifts humanity out from its natural tendency to lapse into evil. In practical terms, social power, even that of masters over slaves, is tolerable in preference to the anarchy that would result if men and women were allowed free rein. It is a deeply pessimistic view of the human condition that the Greek Fathers of the Church never shared or endorsed; but it led Augustine to have a severely skeptical view of the power of the human conscience to move a person towards reformative action. Conscience could convict. It could not necessarily stimulate the good life in practice. For Augustine, only love could so move a human being: and the source of that dynamic energy that could transform was none other than the love of God Himself, who had fashioned the heart and its moral sensibility for

30 Ambrose, *Letter 41.12 To His Sister*, in Migne, ed., *Patrologia Latina*, 16.875f.

31 See further J. A. McGuckin, 'Augustine of Hippo: Architect of Western Christianity's Political Theology', in *Judaic and Christian Visions of the Social Order: Describing, Analyzing and Comparing Systems of the Formative Age*, eds. J. Neusner, B. D. Chilton and A. J. Avery-Peck (New York, NY: University Press of America, 2001), 343–62.

the purposes of calling the heart out of darkness into light. In the following passage he begins by reflecting on the processes involved in a correct (non-literal, but spiritually symbolic) reading of the import of Scripture, and from this basis moves on to what conscience means to him:

> And, therefore, if a man fully understands that 'the goal of the commandment is love, out of a pure heart, and a good conscience, and a faith unfeigned',[32] and is bent upon making all his understanding of Scripture to bear upon these three graces, he may come to the interpretation of these books with an easy mind. For while the apostle says 'love', he adds 'out of a pure heart', to provide against anything being loved but that which is worthy of love. And he joins with this 'a good conscience', in reference to hope; for, if a man has the burden of a bad conscience, he despairs of ever reaching that which he believes in and loves. And in the third place (Paul) says: 'and of faith unfeigned'. For if our faith is free from all hypocrisy, then we both abstain from loving what is unworthy of our love, and by living uprightly we are able to indulge the hope that our hope shall not be in vain.[33]

Here, Love is the energy, conscience again is a compass of sorts and divine grace directs the whole movement, especially through the close and formative study of the divine oracles in Scripture. This is the fourfold system of Augustine: and in this regard it is useful to remember that it would be another millennium before the invention of Christian ethics as a separate intellectual discipline. Even so, this represents some of the earliest form of virtue ethics that elsewhere was reduced down to one of Augustine's most famous moral aphorisms: *Ama et fac quod vis* – namely, love first and then you may do whatever your heart desires – for if one truly loves then the desired result will inevitably be godly and thus good. Conscience for Augustine has value as a compass, but the primary energy in a moral life comes rather from the grace of divine love, as it is confirmed through the twin formative influences of scriptural teaching (about right and wrong) and the call to serve the neighbour selflessly (another form of love). As he puts it in his catechism: 'Purity of life has reference to the love of God and one's neighbor; soundness of doctrine to the knowledge of God and one's neighbor. Every man, moreover, has hope in his own conscience, to the extent that he can perceive that he has attained to the love and knowledge of God and his neighbor.'[34]

This, almost tangential, approach to the nature of spiritual interiority had a deeply formative effect on all later Latin Christian thought. Augustine's

[32] 1 Timothy 1.5 (*Vetus Latina*).
[33] Augustine, *De Doctrina Christiana* (Oxford: Oxford University Press, 1995), 1.40.44.
[34] Ibid., 3.10.14 and 4.21.48.

influence was so dominant in European Christendom that until the high middle ages, there was hardly another theological voice present, and even the earlier Fathers were processed through his theories. In the Greek East, in its classically formative period, from the fourth through to the seventh centuries, Augustine was not read at all. As we have seen, here it was largely Origen's permeating influence that was taken forward in an increasingly ascetical dimension to the Christian understanding of conscience. In both Latin and Greek Christian iterations, conscience, therefore, was never just an inner voice as to the rightness or wrongness of a thing, but rather a more sophisticated scripturally rooted set of reflections on the nature of spiritual identity.

## RECOMMENDED READING

Hausherr, I. *Penthos: The Doctrine of Compunction in the Christian East*. Cistercian Studies Series 53. Kalamazoo, MI: Cistercian Publications, 1982.

Lampe, Geoffrey W. H. *A Patristic Greek Lexicon*. Oxford: Clarendon Press, 1978.

Maurer, Christian. '*Synoida-Syneidesis*'. In *Theological Dictionary of the New Testament*, vol. 7. Edited by Gernard Friedrich. Translated and edited by Geoffrey W. Bromiley, 898–919. Grand Rapids, MI: Eerdmans, 1971.

McGuckin, John A. 'Exegesis and Metaphysics in Origen's Biblical Philosophy'. In *Seeing the Glory, Collected Studies of John A. McGuckin*, vol. 2, 159–74. Yonkers, NY: St Vladimir's Seminary Press, 2017.

*The Westminster Handbook to Origen*. Louisville, KY: Westminster John Knox, 2004.

Pierce, C.A. *Conscience in the New Testament*. Studies in Biblical Theology 15. London: SCM Press, 1955.

Torre, Chiara. 'Seneca and the Christian Tradition'. In *The Cambridge Companion to Seneca*, edited by Shadi Bartsch and Alessandro Schiesaro, 266–76. Cambridge: Cambridge University Press, 2015.

# 4

# *Sensus Fidei*, the Magisterium, and the Formation of Conscience

E. CHRISTIAN BRUGGER

## INTRODUCTION[1]

My purpose in this chapter is to consider how the *sensus fidei* ("sense of the faith") interacts with the Roman Catholic Church's

[1] Biblical quotations are from the Revised Standard Version, *The New Oxford Annotated Bible with the Apocrypha* (New York, NY: Oxford University Press, 1977). Unless otherwise indicated, quotations from the documents of the Second Vatican Council are taken from *Decrees of the Ecumenical Councils*, vol. II, ed. Norman P. Tanner (Washington, DC: Georgetown University Press, 1990). Ecclesiastical documents and texts from Aquinas are abbreviated as follows:

| | |
|---|---|
| AA | *Apostolicam Actuositatem* (1965) (Vatican II Decree on the Apostolate of the Laity) |
| CCC | *Catechism of the Catholic Church* (1997) |
| CL | *Christifideles Laici* (1988) (Apostolic Exhortation of Pope John Paul II on the Vocation and Mission of the Lay Faithful in the Church and in the World) |
| FC | *Familiaris Consortio* (1981) (Apostolic Exhortation of Pope John Paul II on the Role of the Christian Family in the Modern World) |
| FR | *Fides et Ratio* (1998) (Encyclical Letter of Pope John Paul II on the Relationship between Faith and Reason) |
| ID | *Ineffabilis Deus* (1854) (Bull of Pius IX Defining the Dogma of the Immaculate Conception) |
| LG | *Lumen Gentium* (1965) (Vatican II Dogmatic Constitution on the Church) |
| MC | *Mystici Corporis Christi* (1943) (Encyclical Letter of Pope Pius XII on the Mystical Body of Christ) |
| MD | *Munificentissius Deus* (1950) (Apostolic Constitution of Pope Pius XII Defining the Dogma of the Assumption) |
| PA | *Pastor Aeternus* (1870) (Vatican I First Dogmatic Constitution on the Church of Christ) |
| SFLC | The International Theological Commission, *Sensus fidei in the Life of the Church* (2014) |
| ST | *Summa Theologiae* of Thomas Aquinas; trans. Fathers of the English Dominican Province (Westminster, md: Christian Classics, 1981). |
| TT | International Theological Commission, *Theology Today: Perspectives, Principles and Criteria* (2012) |

Magisterium[2] in carrying out the Church's mandate to teach moral doctrines and form the consciences of the faithful. The terms *sensus fidei* and *sensus fidelium* ("sense of the faithful") are both used in the literature to refer to the same reality. They refer to the divinely infused capacity of baptized Christians to understand the truths of divine revelation, to recognize the true voice of the Good Shepherd in preaching, teaching and other forms of pastoral care, as well as to recognize – so as to be able to reject – spurious expressions of the apostolic faith. In some places, the term *sensus fidei* refers to the capacity of individual believers (*sensus fidei fidelis*) and *sensus fidelium* to the capacity of the whole Church to recognize Christian truth (*sensus fidei fidelium*) (SFLC, 3). Given that *sensus fidei* is the term used in Vatican II's important document on the nature of the Church, *Lumen Gentium* (Dogmatic Constitution on the Church) to formally inaugurate the concept in Catholic teaching, I have chosen to use that term to refer to both.

*Sensus fidei* is a relatively new concept in Catholic doctrine and theology. Its meaning is still debated by theologians. For this reason, the first Section ("Sensus Fidei in Theology and Church Teaching"), the longer of the chapter's two sections, is dedicated to a consideration of the *sensus fidei* itself: What is it, what are its manifestations, how can it can be identified, and how can genuine expressions be distinguished from spurious ones? Answers to these will put us in a better position in the second Section ("The Sensus Fidei and the Magisterium") to consider the nature and duties of the Magisterium, especially in relation to the teaching of moral doctrines and the formation of the consciences of believers and to address the specific question of this chapter: How the *sensus fidei* is (or should be) useful to and used by the Magisterium in its task of guarding and transmitting the moral truths of Christ to the faithful? How is the *sensus fidei* an effective principle in guaranteeing the fidelity of Christian truth in the formation of Christian consciences? The latter Section also considers what happens when the pope or bishops teach inconsistently with the apostolic faith and how the *sensus fidei* can be a guide out of such situations.

## *SENSUS FIDEI* IN THEOLOGY AND CHURCH TEACHING

The term *sensus fidei* entered the Catholic Church's formal vocabulary at Vatican II. The idea it represents, however, is much older. It is found in both

| | |
|---|---|
| UUS | *Ut Unum Sint* (1995) (Encyclical Letter of Pope John Paul II on commitment to Ecumenism) |
| VS | *Veritatis Splendor* (1993) (Encyclical Letter of Pope John Paul II Regarding Certain Fundamental Questions of the Church's Moral Teaching) |

[2] The term "Magisterium" is used to refer to the pope and bishops, as the formal body of teachers in the Catholic Church. But more properly, it refers to the *teaching charism* – the authority – vested in them (individually and as a whole body) through their apostolic succession and exercised in union with the bishop of Rome.

the Old and New Testaments and throughout Christian history. It is the idea that God's divine self-communication – referred to in Christian theology as divine revelation – is commended in its entirety to the whole Church in the life and words of Jesus Christ; and it is the whole Church that affirms the faith, is saved by it, reasons over its content, and passes it on in its integrity. This chapter does not consider the historical antecedents to the concept of *sensus fidei* in Catholic theology. For an illuminating account, I direct readers to the document "*Sensus Fidei* in the Life of the Church" published in 2014 by the International Theological Commission (ITC) of the Catholic Church.[3] I begin with the Second Vatican Council's dramatic introduction of the term in *Lumen Gentium*.

The term *sensus fidei* is introduced in chapter 2 entitled "On the People of God." Chapter 1 continued the Pauline teaching elaborated in the encyclical of Pope Pius XII, *Mystici corporis* (1943), that by sending the Holy Spirit, Christ makes all his brothers and sisters "mystically the components of His own Body" (LG, 7). The concept of the Mystical Body of Christ is important for understanding the *sensus fidei*, for it is out of the Christian's unity with Christ that arise both the capacity to recognize the verity of Christian doctrine and the duty it makes incumbent upon him. All members of Christ's body – the baptized – are joined with the Head, who is "entire" in each one (MC, 57). All members of Christ's faithful people, therefore, share in the priestly, prophetic, and kingly office of Christ (see AA, 2); all share the Redeemer's duties of sanctifying, teaching, and ruling in ways proper to their personal vocations. Chapter 2 opens with this in view. Because of their unity with the Head, Christ's members are established as "a chosen race, a royal priesthood, a holy nation . . . who in times past were not a people, but are now the people of God" (no. 9; 1 Pet. 2:9–10). This priestly people are consecrated through baptism to offer spiritual sacrifices, especially through prayer, participation in the sacraments, and a life of holiness. Through all these things, they proclaim the marvelous works of Christ and give ready and perspicuous witness to those who ask them to account for their otherworldly hope (nos. 10–11).

The text then turns to the people of God's participation specifically in the prophetic office of Christ:

[3] See chapter 1, parts 1–2, paragraphs 8–47. The International Theological Commission (ITC) is a body of theologians appointed by the Holy See especially to assist the work of the Congregation for the Doctrine of the Faith. It is an advisory body. As such it holds no ecclesial authority and its documents are not binding on Catholics. See Pope Paul VI's comments at the first plenary session of the newly established ITC (cf. *Acta Apostolica Sedis*, 61 (1969), 713f).

> The holy people of God has a share, too, in the prophetic role of Christ, when it renders him a living witness, especially through a life of faith and charity, and when it offers to God a sacrifice of praise, the tribute of lips that honour his name. The universal body of the faithful, who have received the anointing of the holy one, cannot be mistaken in belief. It displays this particular quality through a supernatural sense of the faith in the whole people when "from the Bishops to the last of the faithful laity," it expresses the consent of all in matters of faith and morals. Through this sense of the faith (*sensu fidei*) which is aroused and sustained by the Spirit of truth, the people of God, under the guidance of the sacred magisterium to which it is faithfully obedient, receives no longer the words of human beings but truly the word of God; it adheres indefectibly to "the faith which was once for all delivered to the saints"; it penetrates more deeply into the same faith through right judgment and applies it more fully to life. (LG, 12)

This passage, the heart of the Council's teaching on the *sensus fidei*, can be summarized in the following ten points, which must be taken as foundational for any post-conciliar consideration of the *sensus fidei*:

(1) The *sensus fidei* is an aspect of the Christian people's *sharing in the prophetic office of Christ.*
(2) This sharing means rendering a living *witness* to Christ through faith and charity.
(3) The subject of the witness – and so the *sensus fidei* – is the *universal body of the faithful*, the whole of the Christian people (including laity, hierarchy, religious).
(4) That to which the people of God give witness are *matters of faith and morals.*
(5) The means of giving witness is *universal consent* in those matters.
(6) The quality of the witness is *infallibility in believing.*
(7) That which makes possible this infallible witness to Christ in matters of faith and morals is a *supernatural sense of the faith.*
(8) Its source is the *Holy Spirit.*
(9) It is active in those who are *faithfully obedient to the Magisterium.*
(10) Because of it the people of God are able *to receive* the word of God, *to adhere* to it indefectibly, *to understanding* it more deeply by making *right judgment* (*recto iudicio*), and *to apply* it more fully to life.

The connection between the prophetic ministry of Christ, which he shares with his faithful people, and the ability of those people to adhere more fully to the salvific message of the Gospel, is the context of the *sensus fidei*. God gives the *sensus fidei* for the sake of *living* the Gospel. This must be kept in mind as we consider these points more deeply.

The exercise of the *sensus fidei* is a prophetic type of act, not in the sense of foreseeing the future, but prophetic in the sense of proclaiming the kingdom of God effectively – making it efficacious – in the world. Jesus continues his prophetic office till the end of time by assisting the Church in the life-giving task of interpreting and handing on the truths of divine revelation. This task is carried out not only through the hierarchy, the formal teachers of the faith, but also through the lay faithful (LG, 35). The elaboration of the apostolate of the laity was one of Vatican II's most important teachings. Here the Council affirms that the prophetic ministry of Christ – of understanding, preserving and transmitting divine revelation – is part of that apostolate (LG, 35; AA, 2; cf. FC, 5).[4] Jesus "commissions" the laity to "witness" to and become a "living instrument" of his salvific mission. This commissioning includes the bestowal of "gifts" by which the power of the Gospel might shine forth more clearly in the world (LG, 33). Among them is the gift of *understanding the faith* – the *sensus fidei* – which belongs to each member of the ecclesial community (LG, 35; FC, 5).

The *sensus fidei* belongs to the whole church (LG, 12). So even expressed by individuals (see LG, 35; FC, 5), it should be understood as ecclesial act. In this sense, the Church bears witness to the integrity of the apostolic deposit through the faithful's participation in the Church's pursuit of understanding and interpreting divine revelation. When it is actually expressed by the universal Church in regard to some doctrine, it can be taken as a sure norm of truth: "The *universitas fidelium* ... cannot be mistaken in belief." The Council places its discussion of the *sensus fidei* in the wider context of the Church's infallibility. It is the Church itself that is infallible. That infallibility can be expressed in the proclamations of the pope alone, or the pope in council with the world's bishops (LG, 25; PA, ch. 4, no. 9). The doctrine of the *sensus fidei* adds to this that infallibility can be expressed through universality in believing. When the whole Church – from the bishops to the laity – affirms some doctrine as true, the very universality of the affirmation guarantees its verity. Infallibility is not *in* the *sensus*; the *sensus* rather witnesses to and indicates that the doctrine is true. This expression of infallibility was frequently affirmed by the Fathers of the Church who appealed to the Church's universal belief as a norm of Christian faith.[5]

4 For a useful consideration of the nature and importance of the Council's teaching on the apostolate of the laity, see Christopher Tollefsen, "Whatever Happened to the Apostolate of the Laity?" in *The Development of Catholic Social Teaching: A Volume of Scholarly Essays*, eds. Gerard Bradley and E. Christian Brugger (Cambridge: Cambridge University Press, 2019), 300–15.

5 The maxim attributed to Vincent of Lérins (d. c. 445) is perhaps the most famous appeal: "We hold that faith which has been believed everywhere, always, by all. For that is truly and in the strictest sense "Catholic," which, as the name itself and the reason of the thing declare,

### But What Is It?

We note that although the Council explains the action of the *sensus fidei*, it tells us relatively little about the nature of the capacity itself. Other than being supernatural, what is it? This is a matter of considerable debate in Catholic theology. It is frequently represented as a kind of "instinct."[6] The concept of instinct is complicated and I do not intend here to engage the philosophical literature on it. But if it is to be used to understand the *sensus fidei*, one common meaning should be dismissed, namely, instinct as a non-intellectual capacity that arrives at knowledge. The ITC seems to hold this understanding in its discussions of the *sensus fidei*: "A form of spontaneous and natural knowledge" (no. 49); "akin … to a natural, immediate and spontaneous reaction, and comparable to a vital instinct or a sort of 'flair' by which the believer clings spontaneously to what conforms to the truth of faith and shuns what is contrary to it" (no. 54); "a sort of perception" (no. 49); "sort of 'sixth sense', 'a kind of spiritual instinct'" (nos. 52–53). Here the *sensus fidei* responds to knowledge but is itself not intellectual, rather, it is perceptual and instinctual; it is able to arrive at true conclusions but from no apparent propositional starting point. This leaves the impression that the *sensus fidei* arrives at true conclusions as if by inspiration, and, in the case of moral judgments, without the assistance of moral principles.

The ITC claims that Aquinas is the source of this understanding of what it refers to as "connatural" knowledge. But Aquinas' account of judgement by "*quandam connaturalitatem*" ("a kind of connaturality") (ST, II-II, q. 45, a. 2c) never says it arises by a faculty other than reason, by some kind of "perception," "sixth sense," "instinct," or "flair." Rather, Aquinas only speaks of right judgments that do not arise after "reason has made its inquiry," that is, after ratiocination; the judgments do not arise from arguments worked out from principles to conclusions.[7] While it is tempting to interpret Aquinas' "connaturality" as a wholly new faculty akin to a sense, it should be resisted.

comprehends all universality." "The Commonitory," in *Nicene and Post-Nicene Fathers of the Christian Church*, series 2, vol. 11, eds. Philip Schaff and Henry Wace (Peabody, MA: Hendrickson, 1995), 132.

6 John J. Burkhard, "*Sensus fidei*: Theological Reflection since Vatican II," *Heythrop Journal* 34 (1993): 41–59, 46; Ormond Rush, "*Sensus Fidei*: Faith 'Making Sense' of Revelation," *Theological Studies* 62 (2001): 231–61, in Charles E. Curran and Lisa A. Fullam, *The Sensu Fidelium and Moral Theology*, Readings in Moral Theology 18 (Mahwah, NJ: Paulist, 2017), 145; International Theological Commission, *The Interpretation of Dogma* (1989), C, II, 1.

7 Rather than Aquinas, the ITC seems to be following Johann A. Möhler's "eminently Christian feeling" from his work *Symbolik oder Darstellung der dogmatischen Gegensätze der Katholiken und Protestanten nach ihren Öffentlichen Bekenntnisschriften* (Mainz: n.p, 1832; English

There is no evidence of a "sixth sense," and neither revelation, nor Church documents, nor Aquinas' account requires the *sensus fidei* to be understood in this way. Moreover, positing such a faculty cuts off the knowledge it generates from reason as its origin.

But it is then fair to ask, if judgments do not arise from *reasoning* or from inspiration, from whence do they arise? And if the form of knowing is not more perceptual than intellectual, why does Vatican II refer to it as a *sensus*?

Vatican II follows certain nineteenth-century theologians in using the term *sensus*, especially John Henry Newman.[8] In the text *On Consulting the Faithful in Matters of Doctrine* that perhaps did more than any other to assist the Church's theological understanding of the *sensus fidei*, Newman uses the term *sensus* in speaking about that force or capacity or tact that steeled the faithful of the fourth century against the falsehoods of the Arians, even when many in the episcopate were sunk in error. Newman uses several terms synonymously: the "the universal conviction of pious Catholics," "the feeling of the faithful," "the sentiments of the people." He contrasts these both to the determinations and definitions of the Magisterium and the testimony of theologians and the learned in general.[9] He is saying that simple Catholics witness to the apostolic deposit, but not in the same way as intellectuals. He clearly means something closer to Aquinas' knowledge-not-arising-from-ratiocination, than knowledge arising from a non-intellectual faculty. Here the activity of the *sensus* should be construed (as from the Latin *sentire* meaning understanding and judging) as a kind of intellectual seeing. Newman's use of the term *sense* in his discussion elsewhere of the "Illative Sense" gets us somewhat closer to his meaning for *sensus fidei*: the Illative Sense is an intellectual faculty that arrives at true judgments without proceeding syllogistically, "parallel to our use of [the term 'sense' as] in 'good sense,' 'common sense,' a 'sense of beauty,' &c."[10]

Vatican II's formal report on LG 12 (the "*Relatio*")[11] can also point us in the direction of an adequate account of the *sensus fidei*. It says the *sensus fidei* "is a

trans. 1843), §38 (quoted in John Henry Newman, *On Consulting the Faithful in Matters of Doctrine* (New York, NY: Sheed & Ward, 1961), 73–74.)

8 The ITC argues that in addition to Newman, Johann Adam Möhler (1796–1838) and Giovanni Perrone (1794–1876) were most influential on Vatican II's conception (see ITC, *The Interpretation of Dogma*, 34ff).

9 Newman, *On Consulting the Faithful in Matters of Doctrine*, 70–73.

10 John Henry Newman, *An Essay in Aid of a Grammar of Assent* (London: Longmans, 1895), 343.

11 A "*relatio*" is a preliminary report distributed to a gathering of bishops prior to formal discussions on a topic to be used as the starting point for preparing an authoritative document; of itself it has no ecclesial authority but can be useful in understanding the "mind" of the bishop at the time.

kind of faculty of the *whole* church (est scilicet quasi facultas totius Ecclesiae), by which the church in faith (*in fide*) sees clearly what has been handed on in revelation, discerns between what is true and false in matters of faith, and at the same time enters more deeply into it and applies it more fully in life."[12]

Sight here is a metaphor for apprehension; discernment means judgment; penetration is insight; and application is moral action. *Sensus* therefore is not principally a sense, or feeling, or instinct. It is a power of the intellect that has a practical aspect.[13]

In Catholic theology, the principle that capacitates true apprehension, judgment, and insight in matters pertaining to divine revelation and that has a practical aspect is the supernatural gift of faith.[14] I propose therefore that the *sensus fidei* should be understood as the sensitivity that arises in a baptized Christian as a result of possessing the gift of faith. Looking more deeply at how this gift is understood in Catholic theology will assist us in understanding the *sensus fidei*.

## *What Is Faith?*

Faith is the human response to God's self-revelation. God reveals himself and then enables people to receive what he reveals. Why must God enable people? The happiness that God promises is both natural and supernatural. The natural capacities of humans by definition are insufficient to direct them to an end beyond their nature. So, they need divine assistance. God's gift of faith assists them to direct themselves to their supernatural end.

Faith can be understood as both something enabling action and as an act. As enabling action, faith is the disposition to receive God's divine communication (ST, 62, I-II, a. 1c; De Ver. 14, a. 2c). In this sense faith is a *habitus*. Since it is a habitus to affirm God's self-communication, it inheres in the mind.[15] As an act, faith expresses itself in affirmation and denial – affirmation of the truths of divine revelation and things consistent with those truths and denial of things contrary (DV, 5). The act consists essentially in knowledge (De Ver. 14, a. 2, ad 10).[16]

[12] *Acta Synodalia Sacrosancti Concilii Oecumenici Vaticani II*, vol. III, part 1 (Vatican City: Typis Polyglottis, 1974), 199; emphasis in text.

[13] Newman, *An Essay in Aid of a Grammar of Assent*, 343.

[14] See Aquinas, ST, II-II, q. 4, a. 2c; I-II, q. 110, a. 4c.

[15] See Aquinas, *De Veritate*, 14, a. 2c.

[16] To make this act, as said, God's grace is necessary. So God gives us grace "moving the heart and turning it to God, opening the eyes of the mind and giving 'joy and ease to everyone in assenting to the truth and believing it'" (DV, 5).

What is the subject matter of faith? It is *that* which God reveals and to which the believer assents; and these are certain propositions concerning his divine plan, especially human salvation (De Ver. 14, a. 2, ad 8; a. 4c, a. 12c), also referred to as articles of faith (14, a. 2, ad 8).[17] These articles include both truths of "faith and morals," morals being distinguished from faith not in that the moral propositions are not revealed but in that they also can be known without the assistance of divine revelation. Through this assent, which requires grace, humans open themselves to God.

I have proposed that the *sensus fidei* is nothing other than the habit of faith. It capacitates one to understand, penetrate, and apply to life the truths of divine revelation and to discern between truth and falsity in their regard. To understand this supernatural virtue, we might compare it to the natural virtue of chastity. Just as the virtue of chastity imparts an inclination of mind, will, and affect to act consistently with the good of marriage and to avoid objects that are contrary to the same good, so too the *sensus fidei* imparts a capacity to affirm what is consistent with divine revelation and to avoid what is contrary to it. Aquinas recognizes this capacity: "By the habit of faith, the human mind is directed to assent to such things as are becoming to a right faith, and not to assent to others" (ST, II-II, q. 1, ad 3). And again, "the habit of faith has this power, that through it the understanding of the believer is withheld from giving assent to things contrary to faith, just as chastity restrains us from acts opposed to chastity" (De Ver. 14, a. 10, ad 10).

We are now closer to the identity of the *sensus fidei*. It is the habit of faith that makes possible the affirmation of God's divine revelation. Where then does the sensitivity to affirm truths and avoid falsehoods arise? Like any habit, the sensitivity is a quality of the capacity in which it inheres. The habit of faith inheres in the intellect. God infuses into the intellect the seminal capacity to receive his divine revelation. The intellect's inclination – its sensitivity – to affirm the truths of divine revelation begins in the form of the divinely infused ability and increases in sensitivity as the intellect acts in accord with the habit. In other words, the act of faith actualizes the habit of faith.

The inclination we call chastity is none other than the inculcation into one's mind, will, and affect of the normative directivity of moral principles (moral truths). Parents, catechists, liturgy, or study might be the sources by which we learn the moral truths. But it is only action in accord with those truths that etches into our characters the virtue of chastity.

[17] We might then ask what is the end or object of the act of faith is God (14, a. 8c)? The object of faith is communion with God. The assent of the believer to truths revealed by God does not end in propositions about God, but in that which the propositions signify (ST, II-II, q. 1, ad 2).

By analogy, after the capacity to affirm divinely revealed truth is infused, the Christian then needs to hear the truths before he can assent to them. Faith comes through hearing; and hearing through preaching; and preaching through the interaction between preachers and listeners (Rom. 10:14–17). To believe something we have to hear it. We are only able to cooperate with God and his salvific plan through acts of faith when we hear the articles of the creed. We strengthen the inclination of the habit of faith by assenting to the truths asserted in the articles. Does this mean we need explicitly to believe all the articles of faith in order to strengthen our *sensus fidei*? Aquinas replies:

> One who does not believe all the articles explicitly can still avoid all errors because the habit of faith keeps him from giving assent to things against the articles which he knows only implicitly. Thus, for instance, if something unusual is proposed, he is suspicious of it and delays assent until he gets instruction from him whose duty it is to decide about doubtful matters of faith. (De Ver. 14, a. 11, ad 2)

One who explicitly believes the primary articles of faith can have implicit understanding of the other articles, since they are logically contained in the former. Which articles are primary? Aquinas' answer seems plausible. Beyond explicitly believing that God exists and exercises providence over human affairs (see Heb. 11:6), believers need to have explicit faith in the Trinity and in the saving incarnation, birth, life, death, and resurrection of Jesus Christ (De Ver. 14, a. 11c). These articles relate to Christian doctrine in the way the self-evident principle of non-contradiction relates to the conclusions of natural reason (ST, II-II, q. 1, a. 7c). They are the premises in which the conclusions are implicitly contained.

The *sensus fidei* then is strengthened in Christians when they believe the foundational articles of faith. The sensitivity we develop from explicitly affirming these primary articles extends to the truths we know only implicitly. The implicit knowledge may not be the result of discursive reasoning, but it does not arise out of nothing. It is still propositionally situated within the primary articles of faith. As the habit of faith grows through prayer, participation in the liturgy, and the directing of one's moral life according to the truths of the Gospel, the believer grows "in the understanding of the realities and words which have been handed down" (DV, 8). This is another way of saying that there is a correlation between growth in the *sensus fidei* and growth in the spiritual life (i.e., in Christian maturity). The *sensus fidei* is the *sensus fidelium* (the understanding of those who are *faithful*). In these, the habit of faith has been shaped by the foundational truths of divine revelation. This may not have been shaped by years of study; most Christians are not scholars. But those

Christians whose *sensus fidei* alerts them to what is true and protects them against what is false must have been catechized in the orthodox faith of the Church. And they must have lived their lives according to their beliefs. This excludes baptized Christians who have adopted patterns of thinking from those who have little regard for the Gospel.

When the faithful arrive at true judgments, it need not be by argument or discursive reasoning. Because the Gospel shapes their habits of thinking, they are able to arrive at true and shun false judgments *as if* by instinct; but only *as if*. It appears instinctual because the process of arriving does not proceed logically. They see the truth but may not be able to explain how they see it. They may not be able to offer arguments or rational grounds other than an appeal to the primacy of the articles of faith. If they were forced to demonstrate how their conclusion derives from these articles, they might founder, become flustered, even set out on irrelevant tangents.[18] And yet they will know that one person's words are consistent with the apostolic faith and another's are not.

Let us consolidate our account thus far. The *sensus fidei* is the habit of Christian faith. The Holy Spirit infuses it at baptism. At first the habit is little more than a capacity to affirm divinely revealed truth. With proper catechesis and cooperating with grace, the habit is strengthened in those who affirm and live the truths they have heard preached. Its subject matter includes truths of faith and morals. By it the faithful are sensitized not only to truths explicitly known but also known implicitly. The habit enables them both to witness *to* them more truly and *against* that which is inconsistent with them more reliably. By it the baptized share in the prophetic office of Christ to cooperate with Jesus in bearing witness to his redemptive plan and so advance that plan in the universe (cf. John 15:26; CT, no. 72).

## *What the* Sensus Fidei *Is Not*

We said the workings, or rather conclusions, of the *sensus fidei* in the minds of believers are propositionally situated within the framework of the primary articles of faith. The believer has real, if only implicit, knowledge of the truths he affirms. This seems to be necessary for a coherent account of the *sensus fidei*. For if it is not itself an orientation inculcated by truths of divine revelation – if it is merely a magical something that somehow, by "divine movements," knows revealed truth and shuns its contrary – then the knowledge it delivers, if knowledge it be, is not normed by anything outside itself.

[18] See Newman's discussion of the Illative Sense at work in the first Protestants. *Grammar*, ch. 9, § 3.2.2.4, 380–81.

This is obviously problematic. The baptized can claim that any conclusion is a legitimate expression of the *sensus fidei* including ones inconsistent with truths of faith and morals; and if many others agree, this is demonstrable evidence of the *sensus* at work.

Thus, the *sensus fidei* as the habit of faith, like any habit, requires activity to grow in strength. For although it is not acquired but infused, its infusion at baptism does not include any propositional knowledge. The baptized infant is capacitated to affirm divine truth. But her mind is still a blank slate. She must still learn the faith. When it is preached, she is attracted by its own inherent attractiveness. This attraction should not be reduced to mentally seeing some kind of inexplicable penumbra surrounding *these* propositions rather than *those*. She is attracted to the Gospel message because in a world of sin, brokenness, and betrayal, the Christians story makes sense – it sounds true – to her. She affirms the truths she hears, and her faith grows stronger.

We might use the image of our muscles. Our muscles are surely given and not acquired; they are endowments that we, as it were, awaken to. But without exercise they will atrophy and so be useless. So too by analogy our faith is a gift, indeed a superabundant gift of God. But it must be exercised to grow strong. Newman writes: "The more devout the faithful grew, the more devoted they showed themselves towards this mystery. And it is the devout who have the surest instinct in discerning the mysteries of which the Holy Spirit breathes the grace through the Church, and who, with as sure a tact, reject what is alien from her teaching."[19]

Some have argued that the opinions of every baptized person should be revered as the possible repository of revealed truth, however disdainful and dismissive the person may be of that truth and of the voice of the Magisterium that proposes it – that the Holy Spirit speaks not only through the faithful, but through the protestations and malignments of the unfaithful.[20] Surely God can use whomever he wills to educate and discipline the Church, just as he used the Assyrians and Babylonians to educate and discipline his chosen people. But because the *sensus fidei* is the *sensus fidelium* – the sensitivity of those with living faith – the voices of those whose faith is dead are by definition not the voices of the faithful. Regarding those who sin mortally without contrition, or who obstinately reject conclusions authoritatively reaffirmed by the Magisterium, when God uses these to teach and discipline

[19] Newman, *On Consulting the Faithful in Matters of Doctrine*, 72 (quoting and affirming the Bishop of Birmingham).

[20] John J. Burkhard, "*Sensus Fidei*: Recent Theological Reflection (1990–2001)," *Heythrop Journal* 46 (2005): 450–75, 464.

the Church, he uses them despite themselves. One point that has been repeated in ecclesial teaching on the *sensus fidei* over the last fifty years is that the opinions of large numbers of Catholics cannot *eo ipso* be equated with the *sensus fidei*.[21]

## THE *SENSUS FIDEI* AND THE MAGISTERIUM

Recall LG's ninth point. Aroused and sustained by Holy Spirit, the *sensus fidei* is alive in those who are faithfully obedient to the Magisterium. The pope and bishops exercise their Magisterium when they teach "authentically" on matters of faith and morals (see LG 25). This means when they teach *as* bishops (i.e., deliberately in their role as successors of the apostles). When they do this their teaching is magisterial (or authoritative). This implies that not all statements of popes and bishops are rightful exercises of their Magisterium. For example, if a pope or bishop were to express an opinion on a scientific issue such as global warming, his opinion, not pertaining to faith or morals, holds no authority. The doctrine of the divine guidance of the Magisterium holds that the assistance of the Holy Spirit does not protect the pope or bishops other than when handing on faithfully the deposit of faith and when teaching in their capacity as teachers of the faithful.

LG's third point above told us that the *witness* to Christ's saving message is a collective work of the Church. This does not mean the manner of witnessing is identical in all believers. Because the pope and bishops enjoy the unique charism to teach, they too enjoy responsibility to formulate authoritatively the truths signified by the collective witness. This reciprocity between the Magisterium and the faithful is essential to guaranteeing that what is held to be part of the deposit of faith is actually so.

The two most outstanding recent examples of this interdependency occurred in 1854 and 1950 respectively in the proclamations of the doctrines of the Immaculate Conception and the bodily Assumption of the Mother of God. In the text where Pope Pius XII declared the doctrine of the Assumption to be dogmatic, the pope wrote:

> This "outstanding agreement of the Catholic prelates and the faithful," affirming that the bodily Assumption of God's Mother into heaven can be defined as a dogma of faith, since it shows us the concordant teaching of the Church's ordinary doctrinal authority and the concordant faith of the Christian people

[21] See Benedict XVI, *Address to the International Theological Commission on the Occasion of Its Annual Plenary Assembly* (December 7, 2012); FC, 5; TT, 34; and especially DV, 35.

> which the same doctrinal authority sustains and directs, thus by itself and in an entirely certain and infallible way, manifests this privilege as a truth revealed by God and contained in that divine deposit which Christ has delivered to his Spouse to be guarded faithfully and to be taught infallibly. (MD, 12)

Pius' teaching is not only a witness to, but an expression of the concord that should exist between the Church as teacher (*Ecclesia docens*) and the Church as faithful disciple (*Ecclesia discens*), helping dispel the caricature of an active hierarchy and passive laity in the mission of handing on the faith (see ITC, 4). Similarly, before the dogma of the Immaculate Conception was proclaimed in 1854, Pope Pius IX petitioned all the world's Catholic bishops to tell him "in writing what the piety and devotion of their faithful was in regard to the Immaculate Conception of the Mother of God" (ID). In this way, he sought assurance from the *sensus fidei* that the dogma he believed pertained to the deposit of faith actually did.

What happens if one who is authorized by apostolic succession to preach the Gospel says something that sounds wrong? Aquinas is confident that the believer's "habit of faith" (*habitus fidei*) will incline him against such preaching, so much so that he presumes the believer has some culpability for recognizing the error: he "is not totally excused by his ignorance." In any case, he "must not give assent" to the teaching.[22] Thus, the *sensus fidei* is not only a defense against the errors of unbelievers. It is a protection against error wherever it is found.

## Sensus Fidei, *Magisterium, and Conscience*

We arrive at the central question of this chapter: How does the *sensus fidei* interact with the Magisterium in the formation of conscience? Specifically, how does the *sensus fidei* affirm moral doctrines and how is that affirmation a resource for the Church's teachers in forming the consciences of the faithful in "matters of morals"?

There are widely differing views of conscience today, some of which are incompatible with each other. Most common is the view that conscience does no more than register disapproval (prospectively or retrospectively) in the form of strong feelings or sentiments of self-reproach and repugnance based on a felt dissonance between some presupposed sense of my own moral uprightness and chosen behavior (either contemplated or committed). Conscience protects this subjective sense. Its judgments stretch no wider than the domain of my subjective sense of myself as a person of my own making.

[22] Thomas Aquinas, *Scriptum super Sententiis* (Commentary on the Sentences of Peter Lombard), book III, distinction 25, ques. 2, art.1D, reply 3.

Contrary to this is the classical understanding of conscience, which I propose for use in this chapter, as an operation of reason in its practical capacity (ST, I, q. 79, a. 13c). The whole domain of practical reason includes reason's grasp of self-evident first practical principles, deliberation over alternatives for action in the light of those principles, the norms derived from them, and moral judgments. Judgments upon what? Upon objective states of affairs, upon living alternatives that require *from me* a conclusion as to whether some contemplated choice before me is permissible, required, or prohibited. My practical conclusion is my judgment here and now that the alternative under consideration is right or wrong, good or evil. These judgments Aquinas and centuries of philosophical tradition call *conscience*. Yes, conscience is the realm of subjectivity insofar as its acts belong to a subject. But conscience judgments are not merely statements that one feels that something is compatible or incompatible with one's sense of self. It is a judgment that something is objectively right or wrong. Conscience looks out upon a world of objective moral truths.

The Magisterium's role then in regard to conscience formation, while rather limited, is critically important. It should teach the faithful what Jesus teaches is morally good and bad, so the faithful's moral knowledge may correspond to Jesus' teaching. It should be specially concerned to ensure that simple and uneducated Christians can easily understand.

The Magisterium does this when it sets forward positive norms, for example, you should do to others whatever you would have them do to you (cf. Matt. 7:12); Christians should seek first God's will for their lives (cf. Matt. 6:33); and all employer-employee relationships should be justly conducted (cf. Deut. 16:20). Although these norms bind always, their precise specification will vary according to time and place. In addition, and more importantly, the Magisterium should teach negative norms and identify the precise conditions for their application, for example, the intentional destruction of innocent human life is always gravely immoral (cf. Exod. 20:13), and any married person who has sexual intercourse with someone other than his or her spouse commits adultery (cf. Mark 10:11–12).

Conscience formation then means informing and forming the moral knowledge of the faithful so that each one can make true judgments about what is right and good. Another term is moral catechesis. The Magisterium should take the catechesis of the faithful with utmost seriousness. For if Christians are not properly catechized, they will not know what Jesus wants them to know; their understanding of divine revelation in "matters of morals" will be partial, shaped in part by sources other than the Gospel; what they believe to be true on moral matters may not conform to the explicit or implicit propositional content of divine revelation; and they will be at a significant disadvantage when they seek to fulfill their Christian duty to choose as Jesus wills them to choose

Conscience formation consists in more than didactic instruction on moral matters. It also importantly entails helping to shape the Christian memory and imagination with biblical images of how Jesus responded to others and how others responded to him. It also involves exposure to the heroes of the Christian faith, the saints, and their stories. These elicit motivation, inspire personal application, and build patterns of prayer. But forming the imagination is not enough. If moral principles are not taught, then the examples of the saints become ambiguous: Did Maximillian Kolbe and Maria Goretti make choices *to* die? Is the self-flagellating asceticism of St. Francis of Assisi a salubrious form of spirituality? Is quiet contemplation something that married persons should strive for? Is celibacy "superior" to marriage? And so on.

### *Lex Orandi, Lex Credenda*

The *sensus fidei* of the faithful is also significantly influenced by and during the liturgy. Churchgoing cradle Catholics attend liturgy weekly for their entire lives, hearing the Scriptures read from beginning to end repeatedly in the lectionary's three-year cycle, hearing homilies on the Scriptures, and attending to the Scriptural formulations of the various forms of the Eucharistic liturgy. In this way, for the majority of believers, the Church's communal prayer in the liturgy shapes their understanding of the deposit of the faith: *lex orandi, lex credendi* ("the way we pray shapes the way we believe").

This maxim is sometimes repeated as if the full richness and truth-content of the Church's liturgy forms the faith of the believing community by a kind of *ex opere operato* (that is, automatically). It is true that *lex orandi, lex credendi* is a law of faith formation for churchgoing Catholics. But in recent decades, many Catholics have not been churchgoing, and many who are have been partially malformed *by their faithful attendance*. Loose biblical translations, liturgical innovations, and homilies expressing the opinions of priests rather than explicating the readings and articles of faith have led to many Catholics both praying and believing superficially. The Church cannot expect the *sensus fidei* of the faithful to be fine-tuned to the meat of the Gospel when it feeds them the bland porridge of insipid liturgy. Referring to the Arian crisis of the fourth century, Newman writes: "Unless [the laity] had been catechized ... in the orthodox faith from the time of their baptism, they never could have had that horror, which they show, of the heterodox Arian doctrine. Their voice, then, is the voice of tradition" (On Consulting the Faithful, 76). So too in moral matters. Unless the laity is catechized in orthodox moral teaching, they cannot possibly be expected to *sentire cum ecclesia* (to think with the Church) on moral matters. The poverty and absence of moral catechesis since the Second Vatican Council is a chief reason why the religious opinions of baptized Catholics today often depart, and sometimes fundamentally, from the truths of divine revelation. It has blunted the sensitivity of the *sensus fidei* of many Catholics making it more likely that putative claims to the *sensus fidei* on moral matters are and have been counterfeit.

## *Identifying the* Sensus Fidei

I end by identifying seven conditions for discerning the *sensus fidei* in the Church on moral matters.[23] Those who offer their opinions to the Church *as if* they are expressions of the *sensus fidei* should:

(1) *Participate in the sacraments.* They should be baptized Catholics who maintain at least minimal participation in the sacramental life of the Church to remain in full communion. They should attend mass at least weekly, be faithful to their annual commitment to participate in sacramental confession, and be in a condition of conscience where they are not aware of any mortal sin.

(2) *Attend to the word of God.* They should nourish themselves on the word of God, minimally in the cycle of readings in the liturgy. Since the chief propositional source of the *sensus fidei* is the word of God attested to in Sacred Scripture, one who offers his opinions *as if* they are the enlightened expressions of the Holy Spirit must be attentive to this primordial source of divine revelation.

(3) *Live by faith.* The author of Hebrews says, "Without faith it is impossible to please him. For whoever would draw near to God must believe that he exists and that he rewards those who seek him" (Heb. 11:6). Since the *sensus fidei* is the habit of faith, it is exercised in those who live by faith. Those who live by faith are being "transformed by the renewal of [their]

[23] These are adapted from ITC, *The Interpretation of Dogma*, nos. 88–104.

minds," which makes them able to "prove what is the will of God, what is good and acceptable and perfect" (Rom. 12:2). The contrary is one who is "conformed to this world," as Peter was when he rebuked Jesus for going to Jerusalem (Matt. 16:22).

(4) *Revere right reason.* One who exercises the *sensus fidei* should believe in the harmony between *fides et ratio*, should see that both open the mind to complementary domains of knowing: faith to "horizons it cannot reach on its own" (FR, 67) and reason to the universe of naturally knowable reality.

(5) *Adhere to the Magisterium.* In the Gospel of Luke, Jesus says to the seventy, "He who hears you hears me, and he who rejects you rejects me, and he who rejects me rejects him who sent me" (Luke 10:16). By divine institution, bishops "have succeeded to the place of the apostles, as shepherds of the Church" (LG, 20). And so, when they teach authentically in continuity with Scripture and tradition, we hear Christ, and when we set ourselves against these teachings, we oppose Christ. "The *sensus fidei* cannot be authentically developed in believers, except to the extent in which they fully participate in the life of the Church, and this demands responsible adherence to the Magisterium."[24]

(6) *Strive for holiness.* Holiness (or Christian perfection) requires that whatever we do, in word or deed, we do in the name of Jesus Christ (Col. 3:17). Perfect holiness means that everything within us capable of being influenced by our own free choices has been made to express and serve Christ-like charity.[25] This can only take place in the life of one with living faith, since only with faith can we be united with God. One whose faith is dead (i.e., one who lives in unrepentant mortal sin) cannot express Christ-like charity (CCC, 1855). None of us has attained Christian perfection. But we must be striving for it to share in the *sensus fidei*. For growth in holiness and growth in the *sensus fidei* are proportional (see ITC, 57).

(7) *Seek the common good of the Church.* The *sensus fidei* is just one expression of the "manifestations of the Spirit for the common good" that St. Paul speaks about in his first letter to the Corinthians (1 Cor. 12:7). It is given for the building up of the body of Christ. Actions that cause "discord" impede the common good (v. 25). Actions that serve charity advance it (ch. 13). The *sensus fidei* therefore must serve charity.

[24] Benedict XVI, *Address to the ITC on the Occasion of Its Annual Plenary Assembly*, December 7, 2012, www.w2.vatican.va/content/benedict-xvi/en/speeches/2012/december/documents/hf_ben-xvi_spe_20121207_cti.html.

[25] Germain Grisez, *Christian Moral Principles* (Chicago, IL: Franciscan Herald Press, 1983), 437.

## RECOMMENDED READING


Alszeghy, Z. "The Sensus Fidei and the Development of Dogma." In *Vatican II: Assessment and Perspectives Twenty-Five Years After (1962–1987)*, vol. 1, edited by René Latourelle, 138–56. New York, NY: Paulist Press, 1988.

Angelini, Giuseppe. "The Sensus Fidelium and Moral Discernment." In *Catholic Theological Ethics in the World Church*, edited by James F. Keenan, 202–9. New York, NY: Continuum, 2007.

Burkhard, John J. "*Sensus fidei*: Meaning, Role and Future of a Teaching of Vatican II," *Louvain Studies* 17 (1992): 18–34.

"*Sensus fidei*: Theological Reflection since Vatican II." *Heythrop Journal* 34 (1993): 41–59, 123–36.

"*Sensus Fidei*: Recent Theological Reflection (1990–2001): Part I." *Heythrop Journal* 46 (2005): 450–75.

"*Sensus Fidei*: Recent Theological Reflection (1990–2001): Part II." *Heythrop Journal* 47 (2006): 38–54.

Congar, OP, Yves. *Lay People in the Church: A Study for a Theology of Laity*. Translated by Donald Attwater. Westminster, MD: The Newman Press, 1967.

Congregation for the Doctrine of the Faith. *Instruction on the Ecclesial Vocation of the Theologian* (Donum Veritatis). 1990.

Curran, Charles E., and Lisa A. Fullam. *The Sensus Fidelium and Moral Theology*. Readings in Moral Theology 18. New York, NY: Paulist Press, 2017.

Ekpo, Anthony. "The Sensus Fidelium and the Threefold Office of Christ: A Reinterpretation of *Lumen Gentium* No. 12." *Theological Studies* 76, no. 2 (2015): 330–46.

International Theological Commission. *Sensus Fidei in the Life of the Church* (2014).

Newman, John Henry. *On Consulting the Faithful in Matters of Doctrine*. New York, NY: Sheed & Ward, 1961.

Rush, Ormond. "Sensus Fidei: Faith 'Making Sense' of Revelation," *Theological Studies* 62 (2001): 231–61.

Second Vatican Council. *Lumen Gentium*. 1965.

Thompson, W. M. "*Sensus Fidelium* and Infallibility." *American Ecclesiastical Review* 167 (1973): 450–86.

Tillard, J. M. R. "*Sensus Fidelium.*" *One in Christ* 11 (1975): 2–29.

PART II

# Conscience According to Major Figures and Traditions

# 5

# Conscience in the Early Church Fathers

ALEXIS TORRANCE

## WHOSE CONSCIENCE?

To approach the topic of conscience in early Christianity from the vantage point of the present might, at first blush, appear rather straightforward. After all, the English word comes straight from the Latin term *conscientia* (literally, "knowing with [oneself]"), which in turn is a direct translation of the Greek term *syneidēsis*, the same term often used by the Apostle Paul (and others) in the New Testament. There is no real linguistic disconnect, in other words, between the early Christian "conscience" and our own. Furthermore, the word is often used by early Christians in ways that generally make intuitive sense to our own understanding of conscience: something that internally guides the person, serving as a witness against some actions (which if committed yield a "bad" conscience connected to remorse) or in favor of others (leading to a "good" or "clear" conscience).

However, care must be exercised to avoid two related pitfalls: the first pitfall is to conflate all the senses in which we now use the word conscience with occurrences of the term in early Christian or patristic texts, and the second pitfall is to allow the real continuity of meaning between ancient and modern to blind us to the real differences, disparities, and distinct nuances that also exist. For example, while both early Christians and moderns can understand the conscience as a person's inner "guide," in the modern context this understanding is usually deployed to help protect individual autonomy and diversity of opinion or approach ("We should all be free to live according to our conscience"). This is quite different from the patristic view, which, in calling conscience our inner "guide," does not presuppose the kind of radical autonomy or moral individualism inherent in our modern conception. If anything, for the early church fathers the conscience presupposes *shared* convictions, and its function is not connected with the language of individual rights. For early Christians, the conscience is considered a gift that is ultimately meant to be a token of *communion* rather than independence, a "knowing with" that guides those who follow its dictates to a relationship of deep peace with God, oneself, one's neighbors, and the world at large.

While the desired destination toward which conscience drives is indeed a lofty one in patristic texts, it is by no means automatically achieved for every bearer of conscience, nor can conscience necessarily even be trusted to take one there. The possibility that the mere presence of conscience might not be enough, and that one's conscience could somehow be impaired or immobilized in the performance of its duty, is a theme of notable importance in the sources and will be treated accordingly. It also happens to be a theme often missing or minimized in modern conceptions of conscience. If it is possible for one's conscience to be dulled, numbed, confused, or darkened, this raises all sorts of interesting questions regarding that great maxim of modern life: simply "follow your conscience." The early church fathers, as we will see, also espouse this maxim but with a far more developed understanding of what counted, and did not count, as one's conscience: it could never mean, for instance, to simply follow the thoughts or feelings you happen to be experiencing in a given moment.

These points have been made at the outset to highlight the fact that dealing with the notion of conscience in early Christianity is indeed more complicated than it might at first seem. We have to be aware that even clear similarities with modern understandings or uses of the term can turn out to require careful unpacking, and sometimes phrases or maxims held in common can prove to be false friends. From a modern perspective, there are likewise glaring omissions in the patristic sources, like the concept of "freedom of conscience."[1] Finally, the early Greek and Latin theological traditions provided no thoroughly systematic treatment of the concepts of *syneidēsis* or *conscientia* that have come down to us. The few extant treatises specifically on the subject are helpful but hardly exhaustive: for a more complete picture we must piece together the evidence that we have as best we can.

Despite all these difficulties – which also serve as caveats for this study – in what follows, an overview of the early Christian understanding of conscience

[1] Although early Christian writers could come close in their arguments for "freedom of religion," on which see Richard Sorabji, *Moral Conscience through the Ages: Fifth Century BCE to the Present* (Oxford: Oxford University Press, 2015), 47–58.

is offered in six sections.[2] The first deals with the conscience as a human faculty, a "part" of what it means to be human. The second looks at the connection made in the sources between conscience and natural law or "the book of nature." The third deals with the role and function(s) of conscience (witness, judge, accuser, scourge, guide, etc.). The fourth treats the issue of a dulled or darkened conscience. The fifth discusses the cleansing of the conscience (including its "examination"). The sixth and concluding section explores the overall "guarding" of the conscience in relation to God, one's neighbor, and the world at large.

## THE FACULTY OF CONSCIENCE

Just as our notion of conscience does not exist in a vacuum, so too the early church fathers did not conjure up the idea themselves but inherited both the term and its basic meaning. Ancient Greek and Roman culture furnished the words *syneidēsis* and *conscientia* together with a definition summarized by Richard Sorabji, one of the leading historians of ancient and early medieval philosophy who has examined the history of conscience in detail, as "sharing knowledge with oneself of a defect."[3] But it was St. Paul and several other New Testament writers who established the term as a given for theological reflection and who supplied the more detailed contours of its meaning for subsequent ecclesiastical writers. The background materials coming from both non-Christian and scriptural sources are examined in more detail elsewhere in this volume and so need not detain us here. The importance of both, especially of the pertinent New Testament texts, will emerge on occasion as the chapter proceeds, but it should always be borne in mind.

When it comes to locating the human conscience, early Christian writers followed the lead of others in considering the conscience part of the inner fabric of the human being. In the New Testament Epistle to Titus, the conscience is paired with, but distinguished from, the mind (Titus 1:15 – "even their mind and conscience is defiled"), while in the Epistle to the Romans the conscience is tied to (but again distinguished from) the heart (cf. Romans 2:15). A popular misconception is that early Christians thought of the conscience as the direct voice of God indwelling every human being, a kind of

2 For the purposes of this chapter, "Early Christian" indicates the period from the second to the eighth centuries. I will limit my remarks to Greek and Latin sources. For a brief discussion of the most common terms for conscience in Syriac and Arabic Christian sources (*tirtå* and *ḍamīr* respectively), see Oddbjørn Leirvik, *Human Conscience and Muslim-Christian Relations: Modern Egyptian Thinkers on al-ḍamīr* (London and New York, NY: Routledge, 2006), 66–78.

3 See Sorabji, *Moral Conscience*, ch. 1.

"oracular" or magical view that would imply that each person can by default "tune in" to God's voice perpetually living inside them. While the conscience and the voice of God have a connection to one another, the two are not direct equivalents (otherwise how could the conscience be described in Titus 1:15 as "defiled"?). In other words, to begin to grasp the patristic approach, this distinction needs to be emphasized: the conscience is understood to be a particular human faculty implanted in the human being and is given by God *but is not itself God or God's voice*.

The text that most clearly delineates the conscience as an inner faculty or "part" of the human being is a collection known as the Macarian Homilies (fourth/fifth century). Traditionally attributed to the early Christian monk Macarius of Egypt, these fifty homilies written for a monastic audience both synthesize a great deal of earlier ascetic theology and were to have a wide-ranging impact on subsequent Christian history, both East and West. Their popularity with Byzantine monks in the East and Spiritual Franciscans, John Wesley, and others in West is in part due to the strong emphasis in the homily collection on concrete and direct experience of God via the human heart. The homilies deal with the faculty of conscience in a number of places. To the question "is the mind different from the soul?" the author replies:

> As the members of the body are many parts, yet they designate one man, so also the members of the soul are many: the mind, the conscience (*syneidēsis*), the will, "thoughts accusing and excusing" (Romans 2:15), yet all these are bound together in one soul even though there are many members. The soul, however, is one, the interior man.[4]

In another homily, the faculty of conscience is described in more detail:

> The heart has a captain in the mind, the conscience, that tests the thoughts that accuse and defend .... You see that our conscience does not approve of thoughts of the kind that lead to sin, but immediately it sets judgment upon them. It does not lie because it witnesses to what it will say before God in the day of judgment like a constant judge .... The whole chariot is under the power of the driver. So also the heart has many natural faculties within itself, but the mind and the conscience admonish and guide the heart. And they wake up the natural faculties that spring up in the heart. For the soul, even though it is one, has many members.[5]

[4] Macarius, *Homily* 7.8 in *Pseudo Macarius: The Fifty Spiritual Homilies and the Great Letter*, trans. George A. Maloney (New York, NY: Paulist Press, 1992), 80.

[5] Macarius, *Homily* 15.33–34, 121 (modified).

Here the function of the conscience as judge is mentioned, which will be looked at again in more detail in "The Functions of Conscience." For now, the significance of these passages lies in identifying the conscience with a faculty of the soul alongside the mind, the will, thoughts, and the heart. It is evidently one of the highest faculties of the soul, serving like a "captain in the mind," and the two together – conscience and mind – constitute the "charioteer" of the heart (the chariot analogy goes back to Plato's *Phaedrus*, in which the chariot represents the human soul and the charioteer intellect or reason, but with no mention there of conscience). At the same time, the faculty of conscience is clearly a part of, and not external to, the "soul" or "inner man." It speaks to God on the day of judgment and so is evidently not identical to God's own voice.

One more passage from the Macarian Homilies dealing with the conscience as a human faculty is worth mentioning. In the first homily, the author discusses the vision of the chariot with four living creatures in Ezekiel 1:4–2:1. He exegetes the four creatures as follows:

> The four animals that bore the chariot were a type of the leading characteristics of the soul. For as the eagle rules over all the other birds and the lion is king of the wild beasts and the bull over the tamed animals and man rules over all creatures, so the soul has certain dominant powers that are superior to others. I am speaking of the faculties of the will, conscience, the mind and the power of loving. For it is through such that the chariot of the soul is directed and it is in these that God resides.[6]

Again, the conscience is described as a leading faculty and characteristic of the soul, this time in company with "the power of loving." What is of interest is that Macarius was not the only one to interpret the four living creatures along these lines. A famous passage in the fourth-century Latin Christian writer Jerome (a passage that was to become critical for medieval scholastic discussions of conscience), also mentions the conscience in this context, comparing it to "the eagle" that does not mix with the other faculties of the soul but oversees and corrects them. Jerome then identifies the conscience with the human "spirit." He is probably drawing on the highly influential third-century Greek Christian writer Origen for these points.[7] What we find in the Macarian Homilies, in other words, is by no means a unique approach.

[6] Macarius, *Homily* 1.3, 38 (modified).

[7] On this, see Douglas Kries, "Origen, Plato, and Conscience (*Synderesis*) in Jerome's Ezekiel Commentary," *Traditio* 57 (2002): 67–83.

The early church fathers saw conscience in the first instance as not only "inside" the human being but an inner *faculty*, a member or part of the soul, and one of the highest faculties at that ("surveying" the others). This might appear to be an obvious point not worth making, but it helps clarify and delineate human conscience as something that is considered together with other human faculties such as mind, will, thought, feeling, etc. *without being the same as them*, just as these other faculties are not considered the same as each other. Moreover, it places or locates the conscience very much *within* the human soul, even if it might soar above the soul's other faculties. For early Christians, the conscience is not itself, to reiterate, the direct voice of God living within us, even if, as we will see, its function is to bring that voice to bear on our lives. It is considered a faculty proper to human nature, a natural capacity of human beings, which precludes it being identified directly with God: God is not a natural human capacity or faculty.

## CONSCIENCE AND NATURAL LAW

That conscience is a constitutive element of human nature is an important claim. It ensures a kind of universality to the concept by attributing a conscience to every member of the human race. If it is inscribed into human beings as a faculty of their nature, and it serves at a basic level as a moral arbiter and "surveyor" of the person's activities, one can see how conscience could easily be connected to the idea of a divinely inscribed law, "written on the heart" (cf. Rom. 2:15). As has been argued by others, this connection is not necessarily obvious and seems to be a specifically Christian innovation in the understanding of conscience. Thus, Sorabji writes that "until St. Paul, sharing knowledge with oneself about wrongdoing and divine law remained separate ideas."[8]

The early church fathers – for whom following St. Paul was a *sine qua non* of theological deliberation – dutifully accepted and expanded on the connection between law and conscience made in Romans 2. If there was a faculty of moral conscience common to all human beings, then there was also a common divine law somehow inscribed within nature itself and to which this moral conscience made reference. Contrary to many assumptions about "natural law," however, the presence of such a law did not mean that knowledge regarding its contents was necessarily obvious or transparently

[8] Sorabji, *Moral Conscience*, 20.

accessible. The clouding of natural law was not only a distinct possibility but was the reality in which humanity as a whole found itself. As the fourth century bishop Ambrose of Milan puts it, although the natural law is "innate" to human beings, because of sin its effects have been greatly diminished. The choking of the natural law through the sin of Adam was, he explains, why the written law eventually had to be given to Moses: "Because the authority of the natural law was corrupted and blotted out by disobedience, the written Law was determined necessary; that man, who had lost all might regain at least a part." The written law "would not have been needed if we had been able to keep the natural law; but, as we did not keep it, the Law of Moses became needful."[9]

Because of the state of sin, natural law can only, taken in itself, go so far and do so much. This is a frequent refrain in early Christian writings. There is little or no effort, for instance, to make appeals to natural law as a potential solution to societal problems or as a basic building block for civilization, and it was certainly not considered an autonomous realm separable from "the law of grace." The reason for this was quite simply that the advent of Christ, both of his person and his teachings (in particular his *commandments*), revealed the whole content of the "natural law" unadulterated and unclouded by the waves of human sin. More than this, Christ was understood to be the only means of keeping that law by means of his grace.

Returning to the connection between natural law and conscience, while generally a distinction is made between the two (as in Paul, where conscience "co-witnesses" to the keeping of the natural law), some patristic authors equate them. Thus, Mark the Ascetic in the fifth century, a highly influential author for the subsequent Byzantine and Eastern Orthodox tradition (as well as finding a sympathetic reader in Martin Luther) calls conscience a "book of nature" (*physikē biblos*) whose words we should put into practice. Similarly, Dorotheus of Gaza in the sixth century, whose popularity extended from East to West through Latin translations undertaken by Benedictine and Jesuit admirers, explicitly calls it "the natural law" (*o physikos nomos*) which, as in Ambrose, is buried through sin.[10]

9 Ambrose of Milan, *Letter* 73 (83), in *Letters*, Fathers of the Church Series 26, trans. Mary Melchior Beyenka (New York, NY: Catholic University of America Press, 1954), 464–68.

10 Mark the Ascetic, *On the Spiritual Law*, in *The Philokalia*, compiled by Nikodemus of the Holy Mountain and Makarios of Corinth, trans. and eds. G. E. H. Palmer, Philip Sherrard, and Kallistos Ware (London: Faber and Faber, 1983), 1, 123; Dorotheus of Gaza, *Instructions* 3.40, in *Discourses and Sayings* trans. Eric Wheeler (Kalamazoo, MI: Cistercian Publications, 1977), 104.

A more developed treatment of this line of thought is given in the eighth century by John of Damascus, whose *Exact Exposition of the Orthodox Faith* is often considered a crowning achievement of the Greek patristic tradition. He sets up a discussion on "the law of God and the law of sin" by defining the law of God as the precept that teaches us God's will. This law is impressed upon our mind, drawing us to itself via the conscience. The willful transgression of this precept results in a second law at work within us, that of sin. What is interesting is that, following Romans 7:22–23, he introduces a third law between that of God and that of sin, namely, the "law of the mind" or "law of the intellect" and identifies this law with the conscience. The law of the intellect (i.e., the conscience) "delights in" the law of God, making the divine precept its will. And yet in the face of the law of sin at work within, the conscience finds itself defeated by the "softness of pleasure," and cannot bring about its desired end of abiding by the law of God. The conscience, in other words, *needs grace* in order to accomplish its task, something made possible by the Incarnation of the Son and the subsequent gift of the Holy Spirit. The coming of the Spirit "affords power to the law of our mind [i.e., our conscience] against the law that is in our members [i.e., the law of sin]."[11] This dynamic will be discussed further when we consider the darkening and cleansing of conscience.

It is clear that natural law and conscience go hand in hand for early Christian writers insofar as both are inscribed into human nature with the purpose of governing and guiding moral action toward God. The relationship was so close that the two could even, on occasion, be identified. If we were to sketch a summary, however, of the patristic definition of conscience with regard to natural law, we might say that the conscience bears favorable witness to what is natural and thus divinely ordained for us: it in a sense *embodies* or *makes present* within us the "natural law," understood as that which our nature is called by God to do and to be. Because of this intimate connection to natural law, by the same token, the conscience serves as a witness in opposition to all that is *against nature*, which is, in effect, the law of sin. However, and crucially for the early fathers, the conscience's act of witnessing in favor of divine precept and against the law of sin is *insufficient* without something more, namely, the grace of the Spirit. Only then can the conscience attain that to which it aspires.

[11] John of Damascus, *An Exact Exposition of the Orthodox Faith* 4.22, in *Writings* (John of Damascus), Fathers of the Church Series 37, trans. Frederic H. Chase Jr. (New York, NY: Catholic University of America Press, 1958), 388–89 (modified).

## THE FUNCTIONS OF CONSCIENCE

The broad task of conscience for the early church fathers has already been described. Insofar as the conscience is a God-given faculty of the soul (indeed, its highest faculty in some authors) wedded to divine precept, it serves as an inner witness and guide, directing the person toward a particular course of action and away from others, and witnessing against the person for acts done in conflict with divine precept and the person's proper end. This role of inner guide and witness designates the basic function of the conscience for early Christians. A great diversity of images and metaphors, however, are deployed in the sources as a way to further describe and illuminate the workings of conscience. It is to some of these images and metaphors that we now turn.

One does not usually associate the terms witness or guide with the infliction of direct pain or damage on someone. Yet in reaction to the person acting in contravention to divine precept, the conscience is often described as inflicting "pangs," "bites," or "pricks," a torment so grievous that several authors can equate such pain with the very fires of hell.[12] We thus also find the stronger terms "accuser," "judge," and "adversary" to describe the functioning of conscience: this is a witness who can also punish. John Chrysostom (fourth century), for instance, describes the conscience as a "tireless accuser" and "incorruptible judge" (i.e., a judge not subject to bribes) who will remain perpetually present to "tear at" and "flay" the guilty even were that person "to escape the notice of all human beings in committing sin."[13]

The conscience as judge is a commonplace in patristic texts, although there is a concern to consider the judiciary role of conscience in a relative and separate sense from that of God himself as the ultimate judge. Diadochus of Photiki (fifth century), another formative figure in the Eastern Christian ascetic tradition, illustrates this when he writes that:

> The judgment of God is far more severe than our conscience. This is what Paul in his wisdom teaches us when he says: "I do not judge myself; for although I am not conscious of anything against myself, yet I am not thereby acquitted. But it is the Lord who judges me." (1 Corinthians 4:3–4)[14]

[12] For instance, Maximus the Confessor, *Epistle* 1.

[13] John Chrysostom, *Homilies on Genesis* 17.4–5, in *Homilies on Genesis 1–17* (St. John Chrysostom), Fathers of the Church Series 74, trans. Robert C. Hill (New York, NY: Catholic University of America Press, 1986), 224.

[14] Diadochus of Photiki, *On Spiritual Knowledge and Discrimination* 100, in *Philokalia*, 1:295.

In addition to being described as accuser and judge, a tradition of biblical interpretation developed that saw the conscience as an inner enemy or adversary, specifically the adversary with whom we are ordered by Jesus to "come to an agreement" (Matt. 5:25). Isaiah the Solitary (fifth century), a noted ascetic from Egypt who settled in Gaza, may have originated this exegesis. He writes:

> If we do not obey our conscience, it will abandon us and we shall fall into the hands of our enemies, who will never let us go. This is what our Lord taught us when He said: "Come to an agreement with your adversary quickly while you are with him in the road, lest he hand you over to the judge, and the judge deliver you to the officer and you are cast into prison" (Matthew 5:25). The conscience is called an "adversary" because it opposes us when we wish to carry out the desires of our flesh; and if we do not listen to our conscience, it delivers us into the hands of our enemies.[15]

We will take up the idea of the conscience "abandoning" a person in the next section. Here what is worth noting is the idea that the conscience functions as our enemy with whom we need to "cut a deal" by giving it whatever it demands.

There is perhaps no more vivid example of these functions of conscience in action than the drama of Augustine's *Confessions*, specifically when he "gives voice" to the faculty of conscience. In Book 8.7.18 he relates having reached a certain crisis point in the postponing of his embrace of Christianity and says,

> the day had now come when I stood naked to myself, and my conscience complained against me: "Where is your tongue? You were saying that, because the truth is uncertain, you do not want to abandon the burden of futility. But look, it is certain now, and the burden still presses on you. Yet wings are won by the freer shoulders of men who have not been exhausted by their searching and have not taken ten years or more to meditate on these matters." This is how I was gnawing at my inner self . . .. What accusations against myself did I not bring? With what verbal rods did I not scourge my soul so that it would follow me in my attempt to go after you [viz. God]![16]

It is worth noticing Augustine's keen sense of the conscience being part of himself (i.e., it is not an external voice talking to him): when conscience speaks, it is Augustine speaking to himself, showing disgust for himself, attacking and scourging himself. To allude to the discussion above on John

[15] Isaiah the Solitary, *On Guarding the Intellect* 3, in *Philokalia*, 1:22–23.

[16] Augustine, *Confessions* 8.7.18, in *Saint Augustine Confessions*, trans. Henry Chadwick (Oxford: Oxford University Press, 1991), 145–46.

of Damascus, what we have is a dramatic performance or playing out of the conflict between "the law of the intellect" and "the law of sin" inside the person. The conscience is considered to be the inner witness, guide, judge, accuser, and adversary, but not in a mere abstract or detached sense: it could be tremendously "vocal," actively and intimately involved in the process of thinking, reasoning, and reflecting.

The metaphors and images for conscience are not limited in the sources to those mentioned, though they are the main ones. There are texts that speak of the conscience as the garment of the soul, a divine spark, a companion, an inner mirror, and more. One rather unique image with which I will end this discussion is one proposed by Gregory of Nyssa (fourth century). In his work *On the Inscriptions of the Psalms*, he muses on the line "for the winepresses" (Psalm 80.inscr LXX) and begins by saying:

> the winepress is the workshop in which wine is made from the crushed grapes. But if the wine flows from grapes which have rotted, or are sour, it immediately becomes sour and undrinkable . . .. But if the grapes which are put in the winepress are good and have been picked at the right time, the wine will flow from the grapes with a pleasant taste and fine bouquet.

He goes on in the same passage to relate this image to the inner life of a human being and writes:

> in the winepress of each soul – now *the conscience is the winepress* – the cluster of grapes of our deeds will stow away for us the wine for the life that follows. And it is absolutely necessary that each of our works be poured in, of whatever sort they happen to be.[17]

The conscience as winepress is an arresting image. Our thoughts and deeds pass through the conscience as through a winepress, which through a careful process of treading, pressing, and sieving yields a wine that is either unmistakably bad or unmistakably good. Unlike the perhaps overly mechanistic implications of the image, the conscience for Gregory is not only a container or "wine vat" here, but is also itself actively treading, pressing, and sieving what comes its way, at the same time bearing witness to the quality of wine produced and "stored up" for the day of judgment. We see then that with Gregory's image of the winepress, the whole diversity of the functions of conscience are brought together in one metaphor.

[17] Gregory of Nyssa, *On the Inscriptions of the Psalms* 2.5, in *Gregory of Nyssa's Treatise on the Inscriptions of the Psalms: Introduction, Translation, and Notes*, trans. Ronald E. Heine (Oxford: Oxford University Press, 1995), 137–38 (emphasis added).

## CONSCIENCE DARKENED

So far, we have discussed the conscience as a natural faculty of the soul, a collaborator with divine precept inscribed within the heart that functions as a person's inner moral witness, accuser, and judge: the "winepress of the soul." We have not yet explored, however, a critical element in early Christian reflection on the conscience, which begins already in the New Testament, namely, that the faculty of conscience could be diminished, darkened, even "evil" (Heb. 10:22). It is a question rarely considered in modern popular views of conscience, though it is arguably one of crucial importance: could our conscience, our inner "winepress," be somehow impaired in the deployment of its duties?

The general assumption of the early church fathers was an emphatic *yes*: if there was a default state of the conscience among human beings, it was one of impairment. The faculty itself might be intact but its functioning was severely hampered by the consequences and reality of sin. We saw Ambrose already tacitly making this point when he speaks of the need for a written law due to humanity having corrupted the authority of the natural law. It is made clearer still by Dorotheus of Gaza, a sixth century theologian mentioned earlier, in his brief treatise on conscience. He begins by describing the conscience as "something divine" sowed into humanity at its creation, "illumining the mind and allowing it to discern good from evil." But he immediately qualifies this by comparing the conscience to "the wells of Jacob" filled up with dirt by the Philistines (cf. Gen. 26:15). The human conscience, in other words, has been buried through sin, becoming functionally useless:

> To this law of conscience adhered the patriarchs and all the holy men of old before the written law .... But when this law was buried and trodden underfoot by men through the onset of sin, we needed a written law, we needed the holy prophets, we needed the instruction of our Master, Jesus Christ, to reveal it and raise it up and bring to life through the observance of the commandments that buried spark.[18]

Dorotheus insists that the conscience itself is never destroyed and that every human being has one. However, the darkening and burial of conscience is a phenomenon all too real and all too tragic. Along with the metaphor of filled-in wells, he compares it to having a lamp adversely affected by impurities, making us see things in a confused and obscured way, or to troubled and muddied water in which we can no longer see our reflection. Little by little,

[18] Dorotheus of Gaza, *Instructions* 3.40, in *Discourses and Sayings*, 104.

he goes on to say, that through sin and heedlessness, we no longer perceive the voice of conscience to the point of thinking we have none at all. This is considered an extremely dangerous state of affairs for Dorotheus and in the tradition as a whole. For although conscience is indestructibly present, the person has now become utterly desensitized to this divine gift (he describes it as arriving at *teleia anaisthesia*, literally, "a complete *anesthesia*"). Such a state of insensibility to the promptings of conscience can only, for Dorotheus, have dire consequences.

We see a similar alarm for this human capacity to dull the conscience in many early Christian texts. Scorning or cheating our conscience begets a sleep in the soul described by Hesychios the Priest (an important early Byzantine ascetic writer flourishing possibly in the eighth century) as "the death of forgetfulness."[19] John Climacus (seventh century), sometime abbot of St. Catherine's monastery on Mt. Sinai and author of the famed spiritual treatise *Ladder of Divine Ascent*, alerts his readers to the grave possibility of entering this state when he writes: "We must be on our guard, in case our conscience has stopped troubling us, not so much because of its being clear but because of its being immersed in sin."[20] A later Byzantine writer simply laments, "what, then, shall we say of those who are enslaved to the passions, and yet think they have a clear conscience?"[21]

For all the apparent pessimism of this position, the sources are agreed that conscience itself cannot ultimately be extinguished. No matter how deeply it is buried, covered over, or obscured, it remains undestroyed and ready for its task. Maximus the Confessor (seventh century), a pivotal theologian for both East and West on the doctrine of Christ as well as sacramental and ascetic theory, fleshes this out:

> He who persuades his conscience to regard the evil he is doing as good by nature reaches out with his moral faculty as with a hand and grasps the tree of life in a reprehensible manner; for he thinks that what is thoroughly evil is by nature immortal. Therefore God, who has implanted in man's conscience a natural hatred of evil, cuts him off from life, for he has now become evil in his will and intention. God acts in this way so that when a man does wrong he cannot persuade his own conscience that what is thoroughly evil is good by nature.[22]

19 Heyschios the Priest, *On Watchfulness and Holiness* 128, in *Philokalia*, 1:184.

20 John Climacus, *Ladder of Divine Ascent* 5.37, in *The Ladder of Divine Ascent*, trans. Colm Luibheid (Mahwah, NJ: Paulist Press, 1982), 130.

21 Peter of Damascus (twelfth century), *A Treasury of Divine Knowledge* 1, in *Philokalia*, 3:102.

22 Maximus the Confessor, *Various Texts on Theology, the Divine Economy, and Virtue and Vice* 2.36, in *Philokalia*, 2:195.

This implies that throughout the process of the darkening or obscuring of the conscience, it nevertheless always remains that "incorruptible judge" praised by John Chrysostom, never wavering from its target, even if a person's freely chosen moral depravity can effectively thwart the conscience from carrying out its duties, yielding a soul "cut off from life."

Such a position helps clarify an issue that recurs in discussions of conscience in early Christianity, namely, the "fallibility" of conscience.[23] The terms "fallible" or "infallible" to describe conscience do not themselves occur in the sources, which makes the discussion particularly prone to difficulties. Viewed from the perspective of the impairment and obscuring of conscience that affects all of fallen humanity, one could certainly sympathize with the idea that the early church fathers viewed the conscience as "fallible," at least in two senses. First, in the sense that the voice of conscience might be stifled or drowned out within us – without us even necessarily being aware that this has happened – thus leading to a state of self-doubt (and so "fallibility") regarding the presence and activity of conscience within. Second, in the sense that even with a readier access to the workings of conscience, the person would not thereby have any "guarantees" of finding their goal since, as intimated by John of Damascus, the conscience is *insufficient* in itself to bring about that goal without the aid of grace.

Yet properly speaking, while access to our conscience might be muffled, and while even with the testimony of a good conscience one was "not thereby justified" (cf. 1 Cor. 4:4), the conscience itself is always considered by early Christians as adamantine in its own commitment to divine precept, unmovable and unshakable in its connection to the law of God. Thus, to call conscience itself "fallible" would be a relativizing move that, while perhaps appealing to modern sensibilities, does not do justice to the way it is approached in the sources. Likewise, however, to call it unqualifiedly "infallible" would confuse the careful delineation made by early Christians of the nuanced role and place of the conscience in a person's life. Although the conscience is certainly considered dependable and correct in itself, because of its complex relationship to the other (often corrupted) faculties of the soul, it was not always clearly or dependably effective in its work. This was what was meant by a "corrupt" or even "evil" conscience: a conscience incapable, because of a person's sin, of fulfilling its task.

This section has attempted to bring to the fore the oft overlooked but vitally important theme of the conscience as obscured or darkened in human beings,

[23] See, e.g., Sorabji, *Moral Conscience*, 33, who argues that with only a small number of exceptions, all the ancients (pagan and Christian) saw the moral conscience as "fallible."

to the point of even being silenced. Rather than an exceptional situation, the darkened conscience was considered the norm for human beings in their fallen state. Conscience was not something, that is to say, which any human being could simply or straightforwardly appeal to or depend on instantaneously without help – the early church fathers were not optimistic humanists in that sense – even if it was always present and always trying to fulfill its duty, however hopelessly. The darkening of conscience, that common lot of human beings, first needed to be reversed: the conscience had to be cleansed.

## THE CLEANSING OF CONSCIENCE

We saw in Dorotheus of Gaza that Christ is presented as the solution to the dilemma of the buried conscience. Christ reveals, raises up, and gives life to this divine spark, something that occurs, Doroethus says, through the keeping of his commandments. His point is rather general, but it provides the basic stance of the early church fathers: we need Christ for the conscience to be healed. More specifically – something presupposed for Dorotheus but explicit already in the New Testament – the conscience first needs to be sacramentally cleansed or washed in the waters of Christian baptism. First Peter 3:21, for instance, identifies "the answer of a good conscience toward God" as the fruit of baptism.

This is an important point for those who might wish to isolate early Christian "insights" regarding conscience from their broader theological framework: the idea of having a clear and good conscience was inextricably bound up with and founded upon initial entrance into the church through Christ's gift of baptism. This was not to deny the reality of conscience to human beings as a whole, but it certainly privileged the Christian with fuller "access" to the benefits of conscience. John Climacus speaks, for example, of the baptized conscience receiving the added benefit of the "words and censure of our guardian angel," which amplify one's conscious perception of sin and the need for repentance, whereas without baptism, the pangs of remorse will be less sharp and more indistinct (and thus less likely to meet with success).[24]

If the initial cleansing of the conscience came through baptism, to be held in that state of good conscience required the keeping of Christ's commandments. The whole of the Christian ascetic tradition, in a sense, is built around this imperative: to abide by the law of Christ and thereby maintain that

[24] John Climacus, *Ladder of Divine Ascent*, 26.sum.64, in *Ladder*, 260.

"answer of a good conscience" first given in baptism. To diverge from Christ's commandments through sin was to "rebury" the conscience. During this process of reburial, especially at the beginning, the conscience would fiercely react, described with the familiar terms of the pangs or pricks or "bites" of conscience. What is significant is that to have pangs or pricks of conscience – what could be termed a "bad" conscience – is not generally discussed in negative terms, as we moderns might expect. To have pangs of conscience was not itself the problem: these pangs and pricks were an opportunity, a call or summons back to the life-giving path of the commandments. The tragedy arose from refusal to act on these pangs, the frenzied attempt to escape them through any means other than the commandments of Christ.

Dealing with the inevitable human failures and frailties that sullied the good conscience and led to its reactionary goading and pricking of the person developed as nothing short of an art form among Christian ascetics. It has been variously studied under the auspices of the *souci de soi* ("care of the self"), the history of introspection, and/or the history of the practice of confession. At stake for early Christians was not simply a "clear conscience" itself but the healing and recovery of an impaired relationship to Christ, as well as the growth and deepening of that relationship. To enable this required that the conscience be unflinchingly observed, an activity usually described in the sources as the *examination* of conscience.

Such examination formed part of the process of the cleansing of conscience. Self-examination was not itself a Christian invention: the Stoic philosophers Seneca and Epictetus, for instance, were known to practice and recommend daily self-examination in the first and second centuries CE. However, its link to confession, not only to God but also to a spiritual guide and/or priest, as well as the sense of a consequent (re-)cleansing of conscience afforded by grace, was developed in Christianity. This is not the place to look at the phenomenon in detail, though it should at least be noted that the fruits of the examination of conscience in confession (whether confession to God alone or before a witness) were not considered to come in an automatic fashion, in the form of a kind of "magical" soothing of the conscience. The gift of a cleansed conscience was always tied to actively abiding or re-abiding in the commandments of Christ. To honestly examine one's conscience, bringing to light and facing the root causes of any pricks or pangs inflicted by it, however small, was considered a key part of Christian life. The danger of leaving the conscience unchecked and unexamined is described by Maximus the Confessor: "Examine your conscience scrupulously . . .. Do not cheat your conscience, for it knows your secrets, and at the hour of your death it will accuse you and in time of prayer it will be a stumbling-block to you."[25] An unexamined conscience had the effect, in other words, of *thwarting* a person in their relationship with God, both when they are about to die (understood as the worst possible moment to be so thwarted), as well as in their regular prayers to God (prayer being the "lifeblood" of one's relationship to God).

We have briefly seen that for the early church fathers, as with every other human faculty, one could not assume that a person's conscience was in an unimpaired and perfect state: in fact, quite the opposite. An initial cleansing of conscience was required through baptism, a cleansing that was maintained through the keeping of Christ's commandments. To stray from these commandments was to betray and rebury the conscience, requiring its careful examination and its re-cleansing, something brought about through frank confession and the inner embrace once again of divine precept (incidentally, such frank confession was itself considered a divine precept, following 1 John 1:9). This drama of the cleansing, examination, and re-cleansing of conscience does not, however, exhaust the early Christian stance toward conscience. One more concern will be mentioned, with which we also conclude, namely, the *guarding* of conscience.

## GUARDING THE CONSCIENCE: A CONCLUSION

If the faculty of conscience must be cleansed, examined, and heeded, it is also, according to the sources, something that needs *guarding*. Stephen Thomas, a philosopher who has written on conscience in Eastern Orthodox Christian thought, is correct, for instance, when he argues that the Greek term *syneidēsis* is for Eastern Christianity "only one term in a whole battery of expressions to convey *nipsis* ['watchfulness']."[26] Not only does the conscience serve as a kind of sentry or watchman in the soul, but a cleansed conscience must itself also be watched and guarded. This theme is developed by Dorotheus of Gaza, a figure discussed above whose approach acts as a fitting summary and capstone for this chapter. He breaks down the guarding of the conscience into three categories: to guard the conscience in relation to God, in relation to one's neighbor, and in relation to the material world more broadly. With respect to God, the guarding of the conscience involves particular attention to what is done or thought by a person secretly and unseen by others: "all that takes place in secret and which no one knows about except God and our conscience,

25 Maximus the Confessor, *Centuries on Love* 4.33, in *Philokalia*, 2:104.

26 Stephen Thomas, "Conscience in Orthodox Thought," in *Conscience in World Religions*, ed. Jayne Hoose (Bodmin: Gracewing and University of Notre Dame Press, 1999), 99–128, 107.

requires guarding. This is what is meant by conscience towards God."[27] Guarding the conscience with respect to one's neighbor means "doing absolutely nothing that we know might afflict or hurt our neighbor, whether by deed, word, gesture, or even a glance."[28] Dorotheus is insistent that a gesture or glance laced with even the slightest hostility toward the other both disturbs our neighbor and wounds our own conscience. Finally, with respect to the broader material world, to guard the conscience means to avoid the misuse and abuse of material things. He gives interestingly mundane examples, such as taking care not to absentmindedly lose things or leave them lying around and not to mistreat one's clothes by over-washing them and thus render them unwearable before their time. To guard the conscience, in short, is for Dorotheus to adopt a watchful, careful, and deliberate approach to every relationship, whether with God himself, the local baker, or the shirt on one's back, ultimately guided in each case by reverence and love.

With this approach, we glimpse a critical impulse in the early Christian understanding of conscience. All while being a faculty of the soul tied up with a person's inner world, the conscience did not represent an independent or individual personal opinion that stood over against the outside world. As a good "winepress," the conscience strove to press out not the bad wine of self-affirmation in tension with the other but the good wine of *communion* with God, neighbor, and the world at large. This was a communion, however, only achievable on the basis of divine precept, concretely revealed in the Gospel of Jesus Christ, to which conscience beckoned. Any inner thought or "voice" that was not directed to this end was not considered to be the voice of conscience but a mark of the mind's confusion and of the burial of conscience through sin. Mark the Ascetic, mentioned above, laments in the fifth century that people in his time did not even know "what it means to live according to our conscience," so the problem is not new.[29] But the contemporary tendency to dismiss the problem altogether and simply affirm whatever someone claims as their conscience, without any regard for what that "conscience" appears to be saying, would be baffling to early Christians. The collapsing of the categories of personal freedom, inner thoughts, emotions, and the voice of conscience is exactly that: an anthropological collapse. To live one's life according to the vagaries and constant flux of one's thoughts and feelings is not, for the early church fathers, to live according to conscience. The human conscience is anchored to the law of God, a law inscribed in nature and

[27] Dorotheus of Gaza, *Instructions* 3.43, in *Discourses*, 106 (modified).
[28] Ibid., 3.44.
[29] Mark the Ascetic, *Letter to Nicholas*, in *Philokalia*, 1:150.

revealed in the commandments of Christ. To live according to conscience, then, was to take hold of those commandments and make them the law of one's own life. This could not occur, moreover, without the action of grace. Only in the grace-filled keeping of Christ's commandments could the conscience – and the person as a whole – find healing, freedom, and rest.

## RECOMMENDED READING

Chadwick, Henry. "Conscience in Ancient Thought." In *Studies on Ancient Christianity*, ch. xx. Farnham, Surrey: Ashgate, 2006.

Chalmers, Stuart P. *Conscience in Context: Historical and Existential Perspectives*. Oxford: Peter Lang AG, 2013.

Clark, Mary. "Augustine on Conscience." In *Studia Patristica*, vol. XXXIII. Papers presented at the Twelfth International Conference of Patristic Studies held in Oxford, 1995: Augustine and his Opponents, edited by E. A. Livingston, 63–67. Leuven: Peeters, 1997.

Dorotheus of Gaza. *Discourses and Sayings*. Translated by Eric Wheeler. Kalamazoo, MI: Cistercian Publications, 1977.

Konvitz, Milton R. "Conscience and Civil Disobedience in Jewish, Christian, and Greek and Roman Thought." *Hastings Law Journal* 29 (1978): 1619–40.

Kries, Douglas. "Origen, Plato, and Conscience (*Synderesis*) in Jerome's Ezekiel Commentary." *Traditio* 57 (2002): 67–83.

Nikodemus of the Holy Mountain and Makarios of Corinth (compilers). *The Philokalia*, 4 vols. Translated by G. E. H. Palmer, Philip Sherrard, and Kallistos Ware. London: Faber and Faber, 1983.

Pierce, Claude Anthony *Conscience in the New Testament*. Canterbury: SCM Press, 1955.

Sorabji, Richard. *Moral Conscience through the Ages*. Chicago, IL: University of Chicago Press, 2014.

Svensson, Manfred. "Augustine on Moral Conscience." *The Heythrop Journal* 54 (2014): 42–54.

Thomas, Stephen. "Conscience in Orthodox Thought." In *Conscience in World Religions*, ed. Jayne Hoose, 99–128. Bodmin: Gracewing and University of Notre Dame Press, 1999.

Torrance, Alexis C. *Repentance in Late Antiquity: Eastern Asceticism and the Framing of the Christian life c. 400–650*. Oxford: Oxford University Press, 2013.

# 6

# St. Thomas Aquinas on Conscience

CAJETAN CUDDY OP

Everyone acknowledges the existence of conscience and defends its importance. Yet, simultaneously, the exact nature of conscience remains a subject of perennial dispute. This presents an intriguing paradox for ethicists and moral theologians. Few other topics can claim such a peculiar blend of unanimity and controversy. All agree *that* it is, but few agree about *what* it is.

This chapter examines the nature of conscience in light of one of history's most influential philosophers and theologians: St. Thomas Aquinas (1225–74). It summarizes the answer Aquinas gave to the question: *What, exactly, is conscience?* Such a task eludes facile realization. Aquinas was a profoundly integrated thinker. His voluminous writings simultaneously manifest complexity and simplicity. These elements find unity within his sapiential search for real truth about true reality. Aristotle's pithy observation that "it belongs to the wise person to order"[1] shaped all of his life and thought. This thirteenth-century priest pursued an ordered consideration of both natural and supernatural being. And within the order of wisdom, things universal and particular, necessary and contingent, each receive their proper place and arrangement. The holistic integration of accurate distinctions within a transcendental unity characterizes his method of inquiry. Although Aquinas never lost sight of the forest for the trees, he always remembered that the trees are an essential part of the forest. There are no shortcuts in Aquinas's tour of the wilderness of reality. Those who choose him as their guide receive a thorough presentation of the forest as it really is – in all of its intricacy.

[1] Aristotle, *Metaphysics* 1.2 (982a18) as cited in Jan A. Aertsen, "Thomas Aquinas on the Good: The Relation between Metaphysics and Ethics," in *Aquinas's Moral Theory: Essays in Honor of Norman Kretzmann*, ed. Scott MacDonald and Eleonore Stump (Ithaca, NY: Cornell University Press, 1999), 235–53, 235.

We will follow Aquinas into one part of the "forest" in this chapter. Indeed, Aquinas will lead us to a very particular tree – a tree representing a subject of much attention and much controversy. To understand the "tree of conscience" we will have to pay attention to the structure of the forest as a whole and even to other greenery that may appear, initially, rather remote. However, if we trust Aquinas to lead us and remain attentive to his analysis, we can arrive at a very satisfying and important destination: the truth about conscience.

## THE SUBJECT OF CONSCIENCE: HUMAN ACTION

Aquinas invites us to reflect on what kind of quest this intellectual journey represents. Everyone intuits that conscience pertains, at least in some way, to judgments about right and wrong, good and evil. Thus, ours is an inquiry into a subject integral to *ethics* and *morals*. Thomas Aquinas observes: "The subject of moral philosophy is human action ordered to an end, or even man, as he is an agent voluntarily acting for an end."[2] The order of human action stands as the primary subject of consideration in formally ethical investigation. This is where our examination of conscience begins.

In a moral discourse, the categories of "right" and "wrong" immediately come to mind. Therefore, we should first note that neither rightness nor wrongness, neither goodness nor evilness, exist as *independent beings*.[3] We do not point to another person – no matter how saintly or how wretched they may be – and exclaim: "She is goodness" or "he is evilness." Moreover, we do not describe particular things or actions as comprehending "evilness" itself. "Murder is evil" resonates with our ethical instincts, but we do not say that "murder is evilness." We recognize that there are other examples of wrongdoing in addition to the unjust taking of human life (e.g., theft, adultery, calumny). Although good and evil are opposed, evil is only real and intelligible in relation to goodness (as the "evil" of blindness is only understood in

[2] Thomas Aquinas, *Sententia libri Ethicorum* bk. 1, lect. 1, no. 3 (p. 2). Unless otherwise noted, all quotations from Aquinas's commentary on Aristotle's *Nicomachean Ethics* (*SLE*) are taken from this English translation: St. Thomas Aquinas, *Commentary on Aristotle's Nicomachean Ethics*, trans. C. I. Litzinger OP (Notre Dame, IN: Dumb Ox Books, 1993).

[3] Of course, this statement is made in reference to contingent and composite beings. God is the only "pure act" being in whom essence and existence are identical. Therefore, God's goodness is essentially different from a creature's goodness. Cf. St. Thomas Aquinas, *Summa Theologiae* I, q. 6; I, q. 13, a. 2. Unless otherwise noted, all quotations from Aquinas's *Summa Theologiae* (*ST*) are taken from the translation of the Fathers of the English Dominican Province (1981; repr., New York, NY: Benziger Brothers, 1947).

relation to the goodness of sight). Hence, as Aquinas demonstrates, "evil" does not exist as a complete and autonomous entity deprived of any and all goodness:

> If it [evil] were complete, it would destroy itself. It would be insupportable – cancelling the subject by which it must be supported if it were to exist. That which is nothing is not able to be called evil since evil is a privation. Any being insofar as it is, is good. Obviously then evil does not take away the total good, but rather some particular good of which it is a privation. Similarly blindness takes away sight but does not take away the animal, without which blindness would not exist. Manifestly, then, evil cannot be complete because in thus taking away the total good [which includes existence], it would even destroy itself.[4]

The existence of pure evil is impossible. Why? Existence is a good thing. It is better to exist than not to exist. And, by definition, a completely evil being would lack all goodness – which means that it would lack even the goodness of existence itself. Therefore, positing the actual existence of a completely evil being is self-contradictory. No such independent being is real or possible.

"Every being, as being, is good" (*ST* 1, q. 5, a. 3), and many different kinds of beings exist. Evil is not a particular kind of independent being but a specific kind of lack and absence in a being. Evil is a *privation*. Privation is really distinct from a simple lack or absence. We would not describe the lack of sight in a stone as a natural "evil." A "good" stone requires many elements (e.g., solidity, density, minerality), but sight is not one of them. A non-seeing stone is not a bad stone (*ST* 1, q. 48, a. 5, ad 1). Furthermore, a rock and a blind person are both real beings – they both enjoy actual existence. Nonetheless, they are not identical. Rocks and persons have essentially different *natures*. And we can only understand the *goodness* of each – their specific kind of fulfillment and perfection – in relation to the ends proper to their given nature. "Every nature desires its own being and its own perfection . . . the being and the perfection of any nature is good" (*ST* 1, q. 48, a. 1). The nature of a stone does not include the power of sight. Therefore, the absence of sight in a stone is not evil. Human nature, by contrast, does include the power of sight. Hence, we must evaluate what is good for a human differently than we evaluate what is good for a rock. Humans and rocks have different natures and, therefore, different ends. The privation of a perfection due to a being on account of its proper nature and purpose constitutes the nature of evil. Evil is a form of nonbeing,

[4] *SLE* bk. 4, lect. 13, no. 808 (pp. 257–58) (translation modified).

yes, but that does not mean that it is not real. A person's blindness is real. However, it is real as a defect in a real person.[5]

With regard to moral evil and moral goodness, Aquinas considers *moral action* – those actions that a human being performs consciously, deliberately, and voluntarily. Moral actions are called "human" because they proceed from what is uniquely human among all bodily creatures: rationality, the spiritual powers of intellect and will (*ST* I-II, q. 1, a. 1). Properly, human acts are those acts that fall under the guidance and control of human reason. Hair-growing and eye-twitching do not qualify as human acts because these types of unconscious activities do not proceed from human reason and will. They just happen. No human act just happens. These latter actions proceed from our proper and characteristic rationality.

Here we pause to observe that "moral" comprises more than simply the ethical categories of "rightness" and "wrongness." Although we commonly speak of "moral" actions and persons in relation to those behaviors and people we find ethically edifying (i.e., a "good deed," a "good person"), all human actions – the ethically good and the ethically bad – are also *moral actions*. Again, they proceed from what Aquinas calls the "proper principle of human actions": the deliberation of reason (*ST* I-II, q. 1, a. 3, ad 3). It is exactly through this broad sense of morality, however, that we are brought to the more specific, *ethical categories* of morality. Because a human action is deliberately willed, its moral quality requires ethical evaluation. A nonhuman act like hair-growing does not invite this type of appraisal. Hair growth occurs (or stops occurring) without rational initiation. Only moral actions elicit *moral judgment*. Indeed, concrete instances of moral action demand it (cf. *ST* I-II, q. 1, a. 4).

A political commentator once remarked in an interview "that to say that the CIA and the KGB engage in similar practices is the equivalent of saying that the man who pushes an old lady into the path of a hurtling bus is not to be distinguished from the man who pushes an old lady out of the path of a hurtling bus ... after all, in both cases someone is pushing old ladies around."[6] This humorous observation effectively illustrates Aquinas's point. There is a real ethical distinction between pushing a woman in front of a moving bus and pushing her out of its path. Both fall within the category of human or moral action, and yet we suspect that the first instance of woman-

5 For more on the nature and various kinds of evil, see William A. Wallace OP, *The Elements of Philosophy: A Compendium for Philosophers and Theologians* (Staten Island, NY: Alba House, 1977), 143–47.

6 William F. Buckley Jr., *Miles Gone By: A Literary Autobiography* (Washington, DC: Regnery Publishing, Inc., 2004), 346.

pushing is morally evil while the second is morally good. But how do we know for sure? This brings us our next topic: human knowledge.

## THE CONTEXT OF CONSCIENCE: HUMAN KNOWLEDGE AND ETHICAL SCIENCE

As the rational soul of the human person enables us to act in a moral way, so it also enables us to understand (1) being, (2) the structure of knowledge itself, and (3) the different kinds of knowledge themselves.[7] Different kinds of beings are known in different kinds of ways. Only found in living things, knowledge is a vital and immanent operation in which a knower is united in an immaterial way to a known object through the act of cognition.[8] Although knowledge also occurs on the level of the senses, our concerns here direct us to focus on intellectual knowledge and its attainment of the truth. "Truth" designates a conformity between the intellect and reality, between knowledge and the thing known. Aquinas consistently and ubiquitously maintains that the end of all knowledge is the attainment of truth. Without the possibility of real truth, a formal pursuit of knowledge would be not only pointless but, ultimately, impossible.

There are three types of knowledge possible for the human intellect: speculative knowledge, practical knowledge, and knowledge that is "partly speculative and partly practical." We can begin to recognize the distinctions between these various kinds of knowledge by considering their *specific objects*. The objects proper to speculative knowledge are *non-operable things* (e.g., divine being, natural beings) – "things that cannot be made or done by us, so that our knowledge of them cannot be directed to activity as to an end." The objects proper to practical knowledge are *operable things* (e.g., shapes, houses, human actions, etc.) – "things that can be made or done by us, so that we can direct the knowledge of them to activity as to an end."[9]

7 Cf. Thomas Aquinas, *De Veritate* q. 1, a. 9 (1:41–42); *ST* I, q. 87. Unless otherwise noted, all quotations from Aquinas's *De Veritate* (*DV*) are taken from this English translation: *The Disputed Questions on Truth*, 3 vols., trans. Robert W. Schmidt SJ (Chicago, IL: Henry Regnery Company, 1952–54). For a detailed analysis of these themes, see Thomas C. O'Brien OP, *Metaphysics and the Existence of God* (Tacoma, WA: Cluny Media, 2017).

8 For two very readable examinations of the nature of knowledge, see Robert Edward Brennan OP, *Thomistic Psychology: A Philosophic Analysis of the Nature of Man* (Tacoma, WA: Cluny Media, 2016), 131–61; Daniel Q. McInerny, *Philosophical Psychology* (Elmhurst Township, PA: The Priestly Fraternity of Saint Peter, 2016), 151–75.

9 Cf. St. Thomas Aquinas, *Super Boethium de Trinitate*, q. 5, a. 1. This passage is available in English: Thomas Aquinas, *The Division and Methods of the Sciences: Questions V and VI of His Commentary on the De Trinitate of Boethius Translated with Introduction and Notes*, trans.

To explain how knowledge can be partially speculative and partially practical, Aquinas identifies two other pertinent elements: (1) the *mode* or *way* of knowledge and (2) the *end* or *intention* of the knower (*ST* I, q. 14, a. 16). Clearly a *line* is an operable object. We can make or draw lines. A carpenter "studies a line insofar as it is useful for his work, in sawing wood or in doing anything else of this nature." However, a "geometrician investigates what a line is – its qualities and its nature by considering the properties and potentialities."[10] Both persons contemplate the same operable object. But the carpenter studies a line in a practical way, while the geometrician studies the line in a speculative way. Their *mode* of knowledge differs. Additionally, we can know operable things for a speculative *end* or for practical purposes. The goal of the speculative does not lie beyond the knowledge of truth itself. The particular end of speculative knowledge is the simple *contemplation of truth*. Conversely, the particular end of practical knowledge is *action*: operation or fabrication. In practical knowledge, contemplating the truth is not the end but the means to a further work. We can learn about a house in order to build a house (practical end). Or we can learn about a house not in order to build one but simply to learn about housebuilding in all of its relevant and related elements (speculative end).

We must note well that Aquinas does not identify two separate intellects in the human person – one speculative and one practical. Rather, our single cognitive power knows things under two aspects and for two different purposes. Put another way, speculative and practical forms of knowledge do not differ essentially insofar as both concern knowledge of the truth. Moreover, practical knowledge presupposes speculative knowledge, while the inverse is not the case. There can be no practical knowledge without prior speculative knowledge. (For example, we cannot build a house unless we already possess some knowledge about houses.) There can be, however, speculative knowledge without practical knowledge. Practical knowledge extends speculative knowledge to a work, and the speculative still remains even if one removes this practical extension.[11]

Finally, the various kinds of knowledge give rise to the variety of *sciences*. Speculative sciences consider those subjects that do not concern doing or making. Practical sciences consider those subjects that do concern doing or making. For example, mathematics is a speculative science because its subject-

Armand Maurer (Toronto: Pontifical Institute of Mediaeval Studies, 1986), 9–24. All quotations in this paragraph are taken from this translation.

10 *SLE* bk. 1, lect. 11, no. 136 (p. 45) (translation modified).

11 Cf. *DV* q. 2, a. 8 (1:97–100). See also S. Edmund Dolan FSC, "Resolution and Composition in Speculative and Practical Discourse," *Laval théologique et philosophique* 6 (1950): 9–62; Steven A. Long, "Speculative Foundations of Moral Theology and the Causality of Grace," *Studies in Christian Ethics* 23 (2010): 398–400.

matter is not something that we do or effect, but only discover. On the other hand, medicine is a practical science because its subject matter (i.e., healing) is something that we do or effect. Speculative science seeks causal knowledge on the level of *universals*. It seeks the *demonstration* of its subject. Practical science seeks causal knowledge of what we can do or make – and this necessarily on the level of the *singular* and the *particular*. It seeks some *construction* of its subject. In light of this, Aquinas concludes that *ethics* is the scientific study of human action that is partly speculative and partly practical. It is practical because it has operable being (i.e., human action, virtue) for its *subject*. Although the *mode* of ethics as a science is primarily speculative, it can also proceed according to a practical mode as well. It is ordered both to the definition and to the construction of good human action and virtue. Nonetheless, the *truth* derived from ethical consideration is speculative. This is evident from the fact that we can know moral truth and yet still act in reprehensible ways. True ethical knowledge can reside in reason alone. Knowing ethical truth, however, is not the same as being a virtuous person. The moral virtue of *prudence* – not the science of ethics – is what actually effects practical truth in human conduct. And the evaluation of human conduct brings us to our next topic of consideration: the act of conscience.

## THE ACT OF CONSCIENCE: THE APPLICATION OF KNOWLEDGE TO A PARTICULAR ACTION

In the writings where he directly addresses conscience, Thomas Aquinas frequently adverts to the meaning of the word itself: "Conscience, according to the very nature of the word, implies the order of knowledge to something."[12] He identifies three elements integral to conscience: knowledge, order, and something else. He then proceeds to clarify that the order referenced here is one of "application." Aquinas explains that "conscience" is not a human power or habit. It is *an act*. And he explains that the "something else" to which knowledge is applied is itself a "particular act."[13] Therefore, conscience is an *act* that comprises the *application* of some sort of *knowledge* to a *particular act*.

The act of conscience takes two general forms. In the first form, we consider whether an act exists or did exist. In the second, we consider

[12] *ST* I, q. 79, a. 13 (translation edited). Cf. *Scriptum super libros Sententiarum* II, d. 24, q. 2, a. 4; *DV* q. 17, a. 1 (2:314–22); *ST* I-II, q. 19, a. 5; *Commentary on the Letter of Saint Paul to the Romans*, trans. F. R. Larcher OP, eds. J. Mortensen and E. Alarcón (Lander, WY: The Aquinas Institute for the Study of Sacred Doctrine, 2012), c. 2, l. 3, no. 219, p. 76.

[13] *DV* q. 17, a. 1 (2:318).

whether an act is correct (*rectus*) or incorrect. In our contemporary usage, "conscience" normally refers to the second form: the ethical or moral consideration of conscience. For Aquinas, however, the act of conscience encompasses more than just questions of ethical judgment or determination. The first use of "conscience" carries with it the connotation of "consciousness" or even an "awareness" of an act's very existence.[14] Through this type of application, we consider a particular act that we *perceive* as occurring (through sense knowledge) or that we *remember* has occurred (through memory). The existential facticity of human action is the object of this first form of conscientious act. Aquinas identifies this mode as "witnessing" to our actions (*ST* I, q. 79, a. 13). This witnessing is important because it identifies whether an action was a truly human action or simply an unconscious act. As we have seen, only human actions receive moral evaluation.

In the second mode of application, we consider whether an action is ethically correct or not. And this second mode admits of two ways. Through the first way, we *discover* something that should be done or should not be done. It references a *future* and a *possible* action. The second way, by contrast, *examines* a *past* action in order to *judge* whether it was ethically right or wrong. When knowledge is applied to a *future act*, conscience directs us and "is said to prod or urge or bind." But when knowledge is applied through an examination of a *past act*, conscience is said either: (1) "to accuse or cause remorse, when that which has been done is found to be out of harmony with the knowledge according to which it is examined" or (2) "to defend or excuse, when that which has been done is found to have proceeded according to the form of the knowledge" we have rightly applied.[15]

In summary, Aquinas explains that conscience, precisely understood, is an act: the application of what we know to a particular action (past, present, or future). He distinguishes conscience from both a power in the human soul and from a habit residing in a power of the human soul. The act of conscience does not stand completely independent from the faculties of the rational soul. An act, after all, is an act of something that has the power of action. Every action depends upon, and proceeds from, a prior power or faculty of acting. The act of sight, for example, presupposes the faculty of sight. The act of sight does not exist as something independent from a seeing

[14] See Ralph M. McInerny, *Ethica Thomistica: The Moral Philosophy of Thomas Aquinas* (Washington, DC: The Catholic University of America Press, 1997), 104–5.

[15] *DV* q. 17, a. 1 (2:319). Cf. *ST* I, q. 79, a. 13.

power. Conscience is an act of human reason. It is an act of evaluation and judgment. Finally, Aquinas explains that conscience proceeds from a habitual disposition that qualifies the human intellect. This habitual disposition is called *synderesis*.

## THE KNOWLEDGE OF CONSCIENCE: *SYNDERESIS* AND HIGHER AND LOWER REASON

Human knowledge requires investigation and the discursive movement of reason. We do not know all truths immediately. On the contrary, we discover truths by reasoning from something that is self-evident or already known to something that is not self-evident and not previously known. With regard to the knowledge of conscience, Aquinas explains that conscience comprises the application of *universal knowledge* to a particular act.[16] Universality is important because it enables the knowledge to extend to a particular action. Evidently, judgments about particular actions also require some form of *particular knowledge* in addition to universal knowledge. The more particular knowledge requisite for the act of conscience is supplied by higher and lower reason. Therefore, through conscience the broad moral awareness of *synderesis* and the more specific ethical judgments of higher reason and lower reason are applied to a particular action.[17]

*Synderesis* is a habitual disposition that shapes the human power of understanding. It is a cognitive principle of action because it encompasses those practical principles from which we reason in moral inquiries.[18] As natural and innate, it serves as a "preamble" to the act of virtue because it objects to evil and inclines the human person to good.[19] *Synderesis* comprises both the power of knowing and the habitual awareness of the universal, first principles of morality that shape this power in relation to human action. The most foundational and universal principle of morality is "good is to be done and pursued, and evil is to be avoided."[20] This principle possesses a general, formal, and universal quality. It does not directly identify particular acts as good or evil but rather tilts the human person toward the practically good in

[16] *Scriptum super libros Sententiarum* II, d. 24, q. 2, a. 4.

[17] *DV* q. 17, a. 2 (2:323–25).

[18] *Scriptum super libros Sententiarum* II, d. 24, q. 2, a. 4; *DV* q. 16, a. 1, ad 4 (2:305); *ST* I, q. 79, a. 12, ad 3.

[19] *DV* q. 16, a. 2, ad 5 (2:310–11).

[20] *ST* I-II, q. 94, a. 2.

general. Hence, it serves as the foundation for any moral determinations about concrete moral norms.

Aquinas explains that our understanding of these first practical principles can suffer no error at any time. *Synderesis* is infallible and unwavering. It represents the natural and ineradicable inclination of human nature to the good in general. *Synderesis* can never undergo a change in which its first principle would become, for example, "evil is to be done and good is to be avoided." Its content is stable and constant. The human person is ordered to the good naturally, and *synderesis* reflects this ordering intellectually. We can recognize the necessity of *synderesis* through reflection on the fact that any act of reasoning requires a movement from one point to another. The ability to deliberate about ethical questions requires and presupposes the presence of a practical "starting point" in the knowing power. Without a point of commencement, no movement is possible. Reasoning of any sort requires some permanent and unchanging starting principles from which the reasoning can begin. Thus, we have an *understanding* of these simple and absolute first principles and we *reason* from them.[21] We possess an instinctive or "connatural" awareness of these first principles – they are "second nature" to us. Conclusions derive their certitude from the stability and certainty of their principles. They depend upon and reflect the character of the principles from which they proceed.

The first practical principles of *synderesis* incline the rational power of the human person to goodness and away from evil. Through these first principles, the human person is able both to discover the truth about moral goodness and to make judgments in the light of this discovery (*ST* 1, q. 79, a. 12). Human reasoning about moral questions often does not invoke these moral first principles in an explicit manner. Nevertheless, they are presupposed in all ethical discursion, and they can be identified upon reflection. Aquinas carefully distinguishes the judgments of conscience from judgments of *synderesis*.[22] The act of conscience applies knowledge to a particular act. It seeks ethical truth in the precise context of a specific human action. The habitual judgments of *synderesis*, by contrast, pertain to universal moral principles applicable to all human actions. The judgment of *synderesis* is one of understanding the principles, while the judgment of conscience is one of reasoning in light of the principles. The particular judgments of conscience are

[21] *DV* q. 15, a. 1 (2:272–75).

[22] Cf. *DV* q. 17, a. 1, ad 4 (2:320–21).

coordinated with the universal judgments of *synderesis*. The habitual knowledge of these latter first moral principles can be applied to any particular action precisely because the principles are not exclusive to one type of action. In a word, *synderesis* makes moral reasoning possible.

Aquinas also emphasizes the role of *higher* and *lower reason* in the act of conscience.[23] Higher and lower reason do not posit two separate powers in the rational soul (*ST* 1, q. 79, a. 9). Rather, the difference between higher and lower reason is found in the different types of *objects* human cognition can consider. The object of higher reason is any reality above the rational human soul in its essence or existence. Higher reason can contemplate a higher nature and truth, or it can receive from them some intelligibility or a "quasi-example of acting." God and the moral norms of his eternal reason (e.g., "God must be obeyed") are examples of higher reason's direct objects. The object of lower reason is any being that lies beneath the human soul in its essence or existence and the moral norms human reason can derive from these beings (e.g., "we must live according to reason"). It can study things of a lower order through contemplation or manage them through action. Any natural thing that we can consider through reason (unaided by faith) can be an object of lower reason.

Finally, Aquinas remarks that higher and lower reason can be both speculative and active.[24] Both reasons refer to truth and human action, and their proper moral norms abide with more *particularity* than the universal norms of *synderesis*. All of these judgments work in harmony. *Synderesis* and the habit of wisdom perfect higher reason. The habit of scientific knowledge perfects lower reason. Moreover, with regard to conscience's application of these judgments to a specific act, he explains that (1) these judgments can all be applied simultaneously or (2) only one of them can be applied. Through these active, "operative habits of reason," conscience *examines* our past actions. And according to these same habits, conscience takes *counsel* about those things that should be done. The examination of conscience, then, concerns both actions of the past and actions of the future. Counsel, on the contrary, relates only to actions of the future.[25]

## THE JUDGMENT OF CONSCIENCE: TRUTH (OR ERROR) ABOUT A HUMAN ACT

The universal understanding of *synderesis* and the more particular knowledge of higher and lower reason intersect in the act of conscience. Their

[23] Cf. *DV* q. 15 (2:267–99).
[24] *DV* q. 15, a. 2, ad 5 (2:284).
[25] *DV* q. 17, a. 1 (2:319).

interplay enables an accurate judgment about an action's goodness. Because *synderesis* is universal and a specific action is quite particular, conscience requires some additional *particular* knowledge in order to evaluate a specific action. Higher reason and lower reason supply this requisite particular knowledge. The dynamic between these various forms of knowledge also accounts for the possibility of an erroneous judgment. Aquinas observes that "the act of conscience is the result of a kind of particular syllogism."[26] He provides an example of the kind of syllogism he has in mind:

> For example, if the judgment of *synderesis* expresses this statement: "I must not do anything which is forbidden by the law of God," and if the knowledge of higher reason presents this minor premise: "Sexual intercourse with this woman is forbidden by the law of God," the application of conscience will be made by concluding: "I must abstain from this intercourse."

In this case, the universal judgment of *synderesis* supplies the major premise. The judgment of higher reason supplies the minor premise. And the conclusion is the dictate of conscience. Formally, this syllogism has no problems. It is structurally sound. We might ask, however: *Is the conclusion true?* Before we can answer this question, we must consider the ways in which error can enter into a particular syllogism of this sort.

Aquinas explains that errors in reasoning (speculatively or practically) can happen because of *errors in the principles* or because we *neglected the proper logical form* when we construct the syllogism. *Synderesis* is "supreme in the judgment of conscience." Its universal and "pure" knowledge does not ever include error. Therefore, we cannot attribute any erroneous conclusion to a problem on the level of *synderesis*. Higher and lower reason, however, do not enjoy such infallibility. Higher reason can err "when one judges something to be licit or illicit which is not." Here Aquinas cites the example of those "who believe that oaths are forbidden by God." Such is not the case. Likewise, error can occur in lower reason, as happens when "one is mistaken about civil norms of what is just or unjust, good or bad." Conscience errs in judgment when errors of higher and lower reason enter into our ethical reasoning. The order of judgments in conscience – from the universal to the more particular – can be diagrammed in the following manner:

[26] *DV* q. 17, a. 2 (2:324). All quotations in this section are taken from this article.

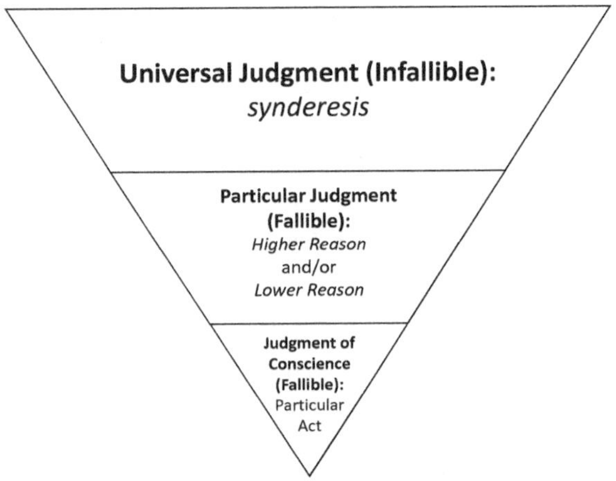


Finally, conscience can also err when it does not correctly apply knowledge to an act or when it makes a false deduction.[27] In sum, it can err because of an error in the *knowledge* applied or in the *application* of knowledge itself. Both the knowledge and the application of knowledge must be correct in order for the judgment of conscience to be correct. Even if only one of these is in error, the act of conscience as a whole is compromised.

In reference to the example cited above, the veracity of this particular syllogism depends upon the minor premise: "Sexual intercourse with this woman is forbidden by the law of God." If this is a true statement, then the syllogism is both valid and true. However, if this statement is not true (because the woman is my wife), it represents an error on the level of higher reasoning (i.e., God's law does not forbid sexual intercourse with one's wife). In this latter case, the syllogism would be valid but false. The conclusion follows from the premises, but the premises do not all reflect the truth and thus neither does the conclusion.

Significantly, Aquinas draws our attention to one particular circumstance in which conscience can never err. "When the particular act to which conscience is applied has a universal judgment about it in *synderesis*" conscience can never be mistaken. "Error does not occur when we are dealing with particular conclusions which are derived directly from universal principles and expressed in the same terms." For example, no one errs speculatively in the particular judgment "*this* whole is greater than its parts" because no one

[27] Cf. *DV* q. 16, a. 2, ad 1 (2:310).

can err in the universal judgment that "*every* whole is greater than its parts." The reason for this is clear: the "every" of the universal judgment includes the "this" of the particular judgment because the latter is a true "whole." "Every whole is greater than its parts. This whole is a whole. Therefore, this whole is greater than its parts." In like manner, Aquinas argues that no one can err in the particular judgments "I should love God" or "some evil should be done," because *synderesis* counts among its universal judgments: "All should love God" and "all evil should be avoided."

## THE LIMITS OF CONSCIENCE: WHAT IT DOES AND WHAT IT DOES NOT DO

In order to understand the effects of conscience, we must remain clear about the exact nature of conscientious judgment. We recall that "conscience is a kind of dictate of the reason (for it is an application of knowledge to action)" (*ST* I-II, q. 19, a. 5). We have briefly examined how reason operates vis-à-vis the understanding of *synderesis* and the knowledge of higher and lower reason. The conscientious dictate of reason emerges from the application of this understanding and these kinds of knowledge to a particular action. Moreover, we observed that knowledge can be speculative, practical, or partly speculative and partly practical. It appears that conscience, for Aquinas, is an instrument of practical knowledge. The proper subject of conscience is human act. Human acts are operable things. The proper object of practical knowledge is operable things. Therefore, the dictates of conscience are a form of practical knowledge. There is also a further distinction within practical knowledge, however, to which we must advert.

All practical knowledge is operational. It is directed to a work. Its end is action. And yet there are two different ways in which knowledge is so directed.[28] First, there is *actual practical knowledge*. Aquinas explains that this kind of practical knowledge is *actually* (not just potentially) directed to operation. For example: an artist conceives a form in his mind (e.g., the form of a horse) that he intends to impart to matter (e.g., marble) in order to make a statue (of a horse). This is actual practical knowledge – knowledge that is actually ordained to some work (in this case, to sculpting).

Secondly, there is *habitual* or *virtual practical knowledge*. This kind of practical knowledge is *order-able* to an act but is *not actually* ordered. For example: an artist conceives a form (e.g., the form of a horse); he knows how

[28] Cf. *DV* q. 3, a. 3 (1:150–56).

he would operate were he to sculpt a horse statue (e.g., how he would apply the form to the marble with the appropriate tools), but he does not actually intend to sculpt a horse. This second kind of practical knowledge never attains the level of action because the artist does not intend to actualize it. However, it is truly practical knowledge *formally* – it is a knowledge that is ordered to action. Here we recognize the *subjective* elements of practical and speculative knowledge. We can know something practical but not intend to practice it. In this instance, we encounter something objectively practical (e.g., housebuilding) that is known speculatively (because of the person's end: to know about housebuilding, not to build a house). Therefore, we must distinguish the end of the *knowledge* itself from the end of the *one who knows* himself or herself.

All of this enables us to understand what conscience does and what conscience does not do. Conscience discovers the moral quality of an action – whether we should do it or should not do it. But Aquinas is very clear that conscience is a purely cognitional evaluation. Neither the will nor any judgments of choice lie within its proper boundaries. Therefore, conscience makes a determination about an action's goodness, but it cannot actually *enact* a good action (because actual human action requires more than knowledge). Conscience considers the *good as true*, but it does not engage the *good as good*.[29] Aquinas explains that the true and the good coincide.[30] The truth is a certain good. Every good is true. Subsequently, the good can be considered *speculatively* when *its truth* is considered. The good, of course, can also be considered practically as well. A *practical* consideration of the good considers the good *as good* – and here the good serves as the goal of an actual operation. A practical consideration of goodness requires that the good be pursued through a work or action. It is always conjoined to an operation. It is an active – indeed, *actional* – consideration that is never merely intellectual. The phrase "the good as good" can be accurately rephrased as "the good *as a concrete end of an appetite*." A practical consideration, therefore, engages the good affectively as well as intellectually. Hence, the purely intellectual judgment of conscience does not require that any actual judgment of choice follow.

Aquinas makes an important comparison and contrast between the judgments of conscience and the judgment of free choice. They are similar insofar as both are concerned with a particular act. They differ insofar as the judgment of conscience takes place in a purely cognitional way, whereas

[29] See Ralph McInerny, "Prudence and Conscience," *The Thomist* 38, no. 2 (1974): 294–305.
[30] Cf. *DV* q. 3, a. 3, ad 9 (1:155).

the judgment of free choice activates what we know – it takes knowledge from the sphere of abstraction and incorporates knowledge into the world of acting. Unlike conscience, the moral virtue of prudence does execute a particular action.[31] In fact, any act of prudence that does not affect a human act is not truly an act of prudence. Prudence employs the general practical science of ethics and the particular practical science of conscience. The essential difference between the judgment of conscience and the free-choice judgment of prudence can be summarized in this way: the judgment of conscience terminates in an understood "ought," and the judgment of prudence terminates in an act of practical truth (i.e., actually doing what ought to be done). Conscience can determine the truth about the practical, but it cannot affect practical truth. Practical truth always includes moral action – it is truth in action.

What does conscience do? It enables us to determine whether an action is truly good. What does conscience not do? It does not compel us to do the good. Conscience pertains to the good as true but not to the good as good.

## THE CORRECTION OF CONSCIENCE

The distinction between the judgment of conscience and the judgment of free choice enables Aquinas to identify two possible sources of error in moral action. Sometimes conscience itself can err (as we have seen). At other times, the judgment of conscience remains free from error while the judgment of free choice suffers perversion. He offers fornication as an example. The judgment of conscience may conclude rightly that it is evil to fornicate with this person. However, the judgment of free choice may fail to attain practical truth because of elements present in the action (for example, the pleasure of fornication). It is possible to act in a way that conscience has identified as truly evil because we desire the pleasure associated with the forbidden act. Aquinas calls this an instance of "evil conscience," insofar as the action was not in accord with the judgment of moral knowledge.[32]

Aquinas teaches that conscience and the law of God share the same binding force. This requires careful consideration in order to avoid misunderstanding his point. He does not say that the judgments of human reason stand autonomous to, or independent from, the law of God. Because God is infinite, nothing can surpass his authority. Rather, conscience only dictates

[31] Cf. *SLE* bk. 6, lect. 7, no. 1200 (p. 382).

[32] *DV* q. 17, a. 1, ad 4 (2:320–21).

that an action ought to be performed (or avoided) *because* it is perceived to be in conformity (or not in conformity) with the law of God. God orients us to truth and goodness through our nature and the innate judgments of *synderesis*. Therefore, conscience mediates God's moral norms to us through the application of this knowledge to human action. The judgment of conscience is always ordered to moral truth. Although it is possible to fail in our search for truth, it is not possible for the human intellect to stop seeking the truth. This order to the truth is, ultimately, an ordering to God – the principle and end of all truth and order. Therefore, any ethical judgment carries with it a connection to the truth and authority of God who established the ethical order.

Conscience – whether true or erroneous – is binding. Aquinas explains that a correct conscience binds *absolutely* and for an *intrinsic* reason. If our conscience correctly concludes that committing an act of fornication is wrong, we cannot reverse this judgment without committing a sin "in the very error of changing such a conscience."[33] Thus, a correct conscience enjoys a certain stability. It binds *intrinsically* because it actually possesses the truth. It binds *absolutely* because it cannot reverse its judgment without sin. An erroneous conscience, by contrast, only binds in a qualified way. It binds *conditionally* and for an *extrinsic* reason. He gives a simple reason for this qualification: an erroneous conscience can be corrected. If our conscience erroneously concludes that we ought to commit an act of fornication, we are only bound to commit an act of fornication as long as the mistaken judgment remains. This erroneous judgment, however, need not continue. Although inverting a correct moral judgment is bad, correcting a mistaken judgment is good. Moreover, only because we believe that our erroneous conscience is correct do we hold on to its mistaken judgment. An objectively erroneous conscience has its binding power under the aspect of truth. The error in an erroneous conscience is not absolute. It binds *conditionally*, because the error can be removed. It binds *extrinsically* because we perpetuate an objective moral error only because we believe it to be the *truth*. Therefore, our fundamental relation to the truth accounts for both correct and incorrect ethical judgments.[34]

An error in judgment can, sometimes, excuse us from moral wrongdoing *subjectively*. Aquinas explains that this is the case when our erroneous

[33] *DV* q. 17, a. 4 (2:331–33).

[34] For more on the binding power of conscience in relation to truth and error, see Tobias Hoffmann, "Conscience and *Synderesis*," in *The Oxford Handbook of Aquinas*, eds. Brian Davies and Eleonore Stump (Oxford: Oxford University Press, 2012), 255–64.

judgment proceeds from knowledge that is false at no fault of our own. Not all ignorance, however, is legitimate ignorance. Sometimes we are to blame for our misinformed state. Furthermore, an erroneous conscience does not have the ability to remove the *objective* effects of bad moral behavior. Even if our conscience – at no fault of our own – concludes that an act of theft is permitted, for example, the act of theft is still wrong and harmful. Only good actions perfect the human person in particular and society in general. Bad actions never perfect – even if we mistakenly believe that they are good. Good actions alone facilitate human flourishing. Bad actions always frustrate the fulfillment of our inclination to the good.[35]

Here we can recognize two significant, big-picture elements present within Aquinas's consideration of erroneous conscience. First, an erroneous conscience may bind but only in a discrete moment and for a discrete act. The intellect is not indifferent to truth. Only the truth perfects the knowing power. Second, an act of erroneous practical judgment does not enslave the human intellect. Although the human intellect can err in a given instance, it is still ordered to the truth absolutely speaking. A mistaken conscience, thus, does not reduce us to a state of perpetual moral error, because the human intellect never forfeits its orientation to the truth. Aquinas makes this very clear: it is always possible to remove error from our consciences and sin from our lives.

## CONCLUSION

St. Thomas Aquinas teaches that conscience comprises an act of speculative judgment that reaches to the intellectual limits of practical science (ethics). Conscience is a valuable thing. It is an extension of moral science to particular moral acts. This is important for the human person. Science pertains to universal truth. Moral action, however, lies within the realm of the concrete and the particular. Through conscience, moral science illuminates human action. But conscience always remains within the limits of moral science. It never escapes the cognitive boundaries from which it proceeds.

Therefore, the value of conscience lies in its relation to particular ethical truth. The limitation of conscience resides in the fact that it cannot, by itself, execute good actions in the concrete. The virtuous person, nonetheless,

[35] For more on this important theme, see Romanus Cessario OP, "On Bad Actions, Good Intentions, and Loving God," in *Theology and Sanctity*, ed. Cajetan Cuddy OP (Ave Maria, FL: Sapientia Press, 2014), 172–95.

requires both: knowledge of ethical truth and the execution of truth in practice. Conscience alone cannot fulfill the deepest longings of the human person. We also need the moral virtue of prudence. Conscience without prudence is insufficient for moral behavior. Brilliant moral philosophy does not equate with happy, virtuous living. Prudence without conscience, however, is also insufficient. Prudence requires the detailed ethical "road map" that moral science provides through conscience. Without conscience, prudence may become disoriented and lose sight of its true end (and forfeit its virtuous identity). Without prudence, human persons cannot fulfill their orientation to the truth through their actions.

Proverbs 23:7 says: "As a man thinketh in his heart, so is he." This wise saying is well-known. Aquinas, certainly, appreciated the truth it expresses. Consequently, it is no surprise that he devoted much of his life to the study of moral science. He wanted to help us understand the truth in our hearts, so that we could act according to the truth in our lives.[36]

## RECOMMENDED READING

Brennan, Robert Edward. *Thomistic Psychology: A Philosophic Analysis of the Nature of Man*, edited by Cajetan Cuddy. Tacoma, WA: Cluny Media, 2016.

Caulfield, Joseph. "Practical Ignorance in Moral Actions." *Laval théologique et philosophique* 7, no. 1 (1951): 69–122.

Cessario, Romanus. "On Bad Actions, Good Intentions, and Loving God." In *Theology and Sanctity*, edited by Cajetan Cuddy, 172–95. Ave Maria, FL: Sapientia Press, 2014.

Doherty, Reginald. *The Judgments of Conscience and Prudence*. River Forest, IL: The Aquinas Library, 1961.

Dolan, S. Edmund, "Resolution and Composition in Speculative and Practical Discourse." *Laval théologique et philosophique* 6, no. 1 (1950): 9–62.

Elders, Leo J. "St. Thomas Aquinas' Doctrine of Conscience." In *Lex et Libertas: Freedom and Law according to St. Thomas Aquinas*, edited by L. J. Elders and K. Hedwig, 125–34. Vatican City: Pontificia Accademia di S. Tommaso e di Religione Cattolica, 1987.

Hoffmann, Tobias. "Conscience and *Synderesis*." In *The Oxford Handbook of Aquinas*, edited by Brian Davies and Eleonore Stump, 255–64. Oxford: Oxford University Press, 2012.

McInerny, Ralph. *Ethica Thomistica: The Moral Philosophy of Thomas Aquinas*, rev. ed. Washington, DC: The Catholic University of America Press, 1997.

"Prudence and Conscience." *The Thomist* 38, no. 2 (1974): 291–305.

[36] I would like to acknowledge the kind assistance of Gregory Pine OP who read an early draft of this chapter and offered helpful comments.

Pinckaers, Servais. "Conscience and the Christian Tradition." In *The Pinckaers Reader: Renewing Thomistic Moral Theology*, edited by John Berkman and Craig Steven Titus, 321–41. Washington, DC: The Catholic University of America Press, 2005.
Potts, Timothy C. *Conscience in Medieval Philosophy*. Cambridge: Cambridge University Press, 1980.
Reese, Philip Neri. "The End of Ethics: A Thomistic Investigation." *New Blackfriars* 95 (2014): 285–94.
Somme, Luc-Thomas. "The Infallibility, Impeccability and Indestructibility of *Synderesis*." *Studies in Christian Ethics* 19, no. 3 (2006): 403–16.

# 7

# Reforming the Conscience

## *Magisterial Reformers on the Theory and Practice of Conscience*

JOHN L. THOMPSON

No words uttered during the Reformation have echoed across the centuries more persistently, nor perhaps more ambiguously, than Luther's final sentence at the Diet of Worms in 1521: "I cannot do otherwise, here I stand, may God help me, Amen." To be sure, no small part of that ambiguity ought to derive from scholarly doubts as to whether Luther actually uttered all of these words, but the better-attested sentences that precede are no less forceful:

> Unless I am convinced by the testimony of the Scriptures or by clear reason (for I do not trust either in the pope or in councils alone, since it is well known that they have often erred and contradicted themselves), I am bound by the Scriptures I have quoted and my conscience is captive to the Word of God. I cannot and I will not retract anything, since it is neither safe nor right to go against conscience.... May God help me, Amen.[1]

Either way, whether cited as a laconic epitaph ("Here I stand") or with Luther's fuller insistence that "it is neither safe nor right to go against conscience," his speech has taken on a life of its own, invoked as a handy precedent for defying authority or sounded as a clarion to defend the autonomy of the modern individual. Unfortunately, Luther's appeal to conscience is less often appreciated for its context and complexity.

Luther, of course, was not the only Reformer in the sixteenth century to struggle with conscience – not just on an existential level but also as a pastor and theologian, charged to care for the consciences of their congregations as

[1] The textual problem of "Here I stand, I can do no other" is treated in passing by the editors of the American Edition in J. J. Pelikan, H. C. Oswald, and H. T. Lehmann, eds., "Luther at the Diet of Worms," in *Luther's Works*, vol. 32, *Career of the Reformer II* (Philadelphia, PA: Fortress, 1960), 112–13; this edition is hereafter cited as LW. See also Martin Brecht, *Martin Luther: His Road to Reformation, 1483–1521*, trans. James L. Schaaf, 3 vols., (Philadelphia, PA: Fortress, 1985–93), 1:460.

well as to teach laity and future pastors how to understand and live with their consciences. This chapter will examine the place of conscience in the teaching and practices of the Magisterial Reformation by focusing on two influential but significantly different figures: Martin Luther and John Calvin. After sketching how these two early Protestants theorized about the conscience in some of their key texts, we will consider how those theories of conscience were diversely applied by early Protestants (whether well or badly) to the public and private controversies that inevitably arose.

## LUTHER: CHASTENING THE UNBELIEVING CONSCIENCE

The Protestant Reformation could be caricatured as sheerly the product of a wounded conscience – if, that is, one were willing to grant such determinative weight to Luther's famous struggle with his restless scruples to find assurance that a wrathful God nonetheless wished, in Christ, to embrace sinners such as he. Without a doubt, Luther's struggles resonated with those of his contemporaries, but those struggles also need to be situated in the context of what late medieval Christians (particularly Luther) would have been taught to think about conscience.

The link between late medieval discussions of conscience and Luther's particular crisis of conscience is strong and direct, for despite having joined a strict Augustinian order, Luther's theological formation was mediated not only by Augustine but also by Gabriel Biel, an influential fifteenth-century theologian who was a Pelagian in all but name. For Biel, sinners still retain a natural capacity to love God purely and "above all," and that is precisely what God, in his grace, requires of us: acts of repentance for sin that are truly contrite, that is, not marred by self-regard or fear of punishment but performed out of love for God. In more popular terms, Biel said, God merely demands that sinners "do their very best" (*facere quod in se est*), and grace will surely follow.[2] Granted, an act of repentance driven by fear (or, technically, by *attrition* rather than *contrition*) would be better than nothing, but Biel, with his strong convictions about the enduring potency of the human will, urged his hearers to consider how generously God rewards us when we exert our innate powers and simply try harder.

2 Biel's penitential and pastoral theology is treated at length by the classic study of Heiko Augustinus Oberman, *The Harvest of Medieval Theology: Gabriel Biel and Late Medieval Nominalism* (Grand Rapids, MI: Eerdmans, 1967), 147–84. For Biel as a Pelagian, see especially 176–77.

Biel thus emphasized, by turns, divine mercy and divine justice: for while God could have ignored human need and brokenness, God instead intervened in Christ. However, no one benefits from God's merciful intervention without "doing one's best." How? By performing works of virtue, which are the means by which love for God is best expressed. Biel's pastoral theology deliberately left Christians in a state of perpetual anxiety, a pious dialectic of hope and fear: we hope in God's mercy as we look back at the cross, but we fear God's righteous judgment as we anticipate our final reckoning. For Biel, the best pastors will keep the consciences of their flock in the anxious middle, neither cocksure of God's mercy nor in despair at God's justice.

The young Luther absorbed what Biel taught, but Luther would eventually number Biel among those smug sophists "who have never struggled with any temptations or true terrors of sin and death."[3] Luther's struggles, however, were legendary. Late in life he recalled how he was shaken to the core whenever the Bible mentioned "the righteousness of God," which he originally took to portend God's holy wrath against unholy sinners.

> Though I lived as a monk without reproach, I felt that I was a sinner before God with an extremely disturbed conscience. I could not believe that he was placated by my [works of] satisfaction. I did not love, yes, I hated the righteous God who punishes sinners, and secretly ... I was angry with God, and said, "As if, indeed, it is not enough, that miserable sinners, eternally lost through original sin, are crushed by every kind of calamity by the law of the decalogue, without having God add pain to pain by the gospel and also by the gospel threatening us with his righteousness and wrath!" Thus I raged with a fierce and troubled conscience.[4]

Luther's breakthrough came when he realized that "the righteousness of God" designated not God's punishing righteousness but the righteousness with which sinners are clothed when freely justified by God – a justification derived not from one's self-generated act of "loving God above all" but from trusting Christ precisely in the context where God's law exposes one's own sin, hypocrisy, and self-deception. In brief, for Luther, nothing insults God more

[3] Martin Luther, *Lectures on Galatians*, 1535 (LW 26:127).

[4] Martin Luther, "Preface to the Complete Edition of Luther's Latin Writings" (1545), LW 34:336–37. Luther typically treats conscience not as an identifiable faculty of judgment or volition but to designate the whole human person as a sinner accused by the law – much like the Pauline use of "flesh." On Luther's innovative and totalizing definition of conscience, see Michael G. Baylor, *Action and Person: Conscience in Late Scholasticism and the Young Luther* (Leiden: Brill, 1977), 157–272.

than a sinner who pretends or even tries to attain a divine standard of love or to fulfill the divine law. Yet nothing delights God more than a sinner who *trusts God's word* – not only where that word brings judgment, but also where that word proclaims a Christ who came not for the righteous but for those sick with sin. Striving to please God with good works dishonors God because such efforts distrust and disregard God's declared judgment that all human beings are sinners.[5] This seeming paradox is typical of Luther: those who receive God's favor are, ironically, those who know themselves as unworthy and destitute.[6]

In speaking of his "fierce and troubled conscience," Luther alludes to the incongruity that he once experienced the gospel as more burdensome than the law. In fact, the distinction between law and gospel is a key to Luther's theology. It also discloses how he understands a sinner's conscience to function – and malfunction:

> Commands, to be sure, teach what is good, but what is taught is not thereby done. For the commands show what we ought to do but do not give the power to do it. They were instead established for this: so that they may reveal individuals to themselves. Through the commands they know their inability to do good, and they despair of their own powers.[7]

God's law thus does less to guide us toward success than to reveal our perennial failures – and the absurdity of self-reliance. And while the conscience functions well when it alerts us to our moral and theological failings, it functions badly when it then impels us to adopt Biel's advice: to try harder, do more works, undertake more rigorous penitence, strive to love God more, and more sincerely. Luther's initial dispute with Roman Catholic teaching was driven by his concern for Christian consciences, which were being misled to place their trust not in Christ alone but in adherence to spurious laws, human traditions, and false teachings.

The faith that justifies, however, manifests in a God-given disposition to trust God's promises of mercy and forgiveness. Faith thus silences the sinful conscience and looks not to personal achievement but to God's gift of forgiveness, freely granted in Christ. In this way, consciences are freed from the unsettling accusations of the law, just as Paul wrote in Romans 5:1:

5 Luther makes this point in one of his most influential treatises, "The Freedom of a Christian" (1520). See the new translation in Timothy J. Wengert, ed., *The Annotated Luther*, vol. 1, *The Roots of Reform* (Philadelphia, PA: Fortress, 2015), 467–538.

6 Luther made many of these points early on and sharpened them (often explicitly) against Gabriel Biel in the 1517 "Disputation against Scholastic Theology" (LW 31:3–16).

7 Luther, "The Freedom of a Christian," in *Roots of Reform*, 494.

"Therefore, since we are justified by faith, we have peace with God through our Lord Jesus Christ."[8]

But just how silent is the conscience of a justified sinner supposed to be? In brief, conscience functions best in the life of a Christian when it has been chastened – when it realizes its own idolatrous propensity to trust itself and not God.[9] The Christian life therefore constantly entails setting aside the accusations of conscience in order to live wholly by faith, trusting in God's merciful promise.

But does the conscience do anything to guide or prompt the good works that follow justification? In fact, Luther was reluctant to grant it such a role. His insistence that Christians are freed from accusations of conscience (perhaps even from conscience altogether) finds an illuminating parallel in what he said about the two principal uses of the law. First, the law exercises *a civil function*, restraining social evil by threatening punishment; then, more importantly, the law also has *an evangelical function*, driving us to Christ by disclosing our own inadequacy. But Luther resisted what Calvin (following the precedent of Philip Melanchthon) would describe as the law's "third use" – as a guide for Christian behavior. To reintroduce the law into the Christian life, Luther worried, turns Christ into a new Moses.[10] Precisely where Luther might have tasked the conscience with prodding Christians to do good works, he preferred to say that these works arise spontaneously, from "a free and merry spirit" (though occasionally from a free and merry conscience) – phrasing that the Lutheran *Formula of Concord* came to favor in 1577.[11]

8 Cited by Luther in his appendix to "The Proceedings at Augsburg (1518)," in *Roots of Reform*, 146.

9 For more on the dynamics of the hypocritical conscience, see Randall C. Zachman, "The Idolatrous Religion of Conscience," in *The Assurance of Faith: Conscience in the Theology of Martin Luther and John Calvin* (Minneapolis, MN: Fortress, 1993), 19–39.

10 See Luther's remarks in his "Preface to the New Testament" (1522, 1545), LW 35:360. On the origins of the law's "third use," see Timothy J. Wengert, *Law and Gospel: Philip Melanchthon's Debate with John Agricola of Eisleben over Poenitentia* (Grand Rapids, MI: Baker Books, 1997), 177–201.

11 *Formula of Concord* § 6.17 states that Christians, who are "born again through the Spirit of God and set free from the Law … do everything … from a free and cheerful spirit. Works of this kind are not, properly speaking, works of the law but works and fruits of the Spirit." See *The Book of Concord: The Confessions of the Evangelical Lutheran Church*, ed. Robert Kolb and Timothy J. Wengert (Minneapolis, MN: Fortress, 2000), 590. Cf. §2 of Luther's 1519 "Sermon on the Sacrament of Penance," in *Roots of Reform*, 188, where true forgiveness "does away with the heart's fear and timidity before God; it makes the conscience lighthearted and merry inwardly." Significantly, *Formula of Concord* §6 was written in response to a series of Lutheran antinomian controversies that eventually led to the affirmation of the law's third use. See

For Luther, a conscience that has found peace with God is a conscience – a person – that is free indeed, because freed from fear of judgment and from the futility of self-reliance. God has supplied everything, asking only for trust. Luther's famous words at the Diet of Worms were not intended, therefore, as a defense of his conscience per se, much less of worldly freedom or individualism. On the contrary, Luther was defending the utter priority of the word of God not only to guide his teachings and writings but also, first and foremost, as the only possible way to know that he, still confessedly a sinner, was loved and saved by God. Granted, there are other forms of freedom in life, but if the conscience's natural tendency to cope with fear by generating more works has been replaced by trust in God's merciful provision, no worldly servitude or persecution can bring harm. Hence, Luther's plea to his interlocutors was not to dispute with his conscience per se but to recognize the preeminent authority of the clear word of God, to which Luther's now-peaceful conscience was merely a witness.[12]

## CALVIN: DISCIPLINING THE CHRISTIAN CONSCIENCE

Luther's teachings on how faith in Christ frees the conscience found an eager audience all across Europe, not least of all with John Calvin, for whom peace of conscience was as much a hallmark of the gospel as it was for Luther, and (per Romans 5:1) just as tied to justification by faith. For Calvin, both the prerequisite and the chief benefit of justification is assurance, a concomitant of faith. But the main impediment to attaining assurance is the conscience: for as long as it is unsure of its standing before God, the conscience "continuously trembles, wavers, tosses, is tormented and vexed, shakes, hates, and flees the sight of God."[13] Writing against Cardinal Sadoleto, Calvin underscored the futility of the Catholic penitential system, which left him "far off from true peace of conscience," even as Sadoleto's theology was "superficial" for never

Timothy J. Wengert, "Antinomianism," in *The Oxford Encyclopedia of the Reformation*, ed. Hans J. Hillerbrand, 4 vols. (New York, NY: Oxford University Press, 1996), 1:51–53.

12 Of course, Luther's plea stands or falls on whether the word of God is, in fact, clear – a point not lost on his interlocutors, who feared that every Christian would become his or her own interpreter. Competing interpretations of Scripture could be resolved only by the univocal authority of the Roman Catholic magisterium, and that explains why the secretary presiding at the Diet of Worms could dismiss Luther's pangs of conscience, because they derived from the wrong authority: "Lay aside your conscience, Martin; you must lay it aside because it is in error; and it will be safe and proper for you to recant." See "Luther at the Diet of Worms," LW 32:130.

13 John Calvin, *Institutes of the Christian Religion* 3.4.2. All references to this work are from the Battles translation of the 1559 Latin version (Philadelphia, PA: Westminster, 1960), cited only by the usual book.chapter.paragraph divisions.

having experienced "serious struggles of conscience."[14] Calvin's identification with Luther's starting point is clear.

But Calvin differed with Luther over how the Christian life should unfold after justification, stressing much more the importance of transformation and holiness in the Christian community. To that end, Calvin was more explicit in extolling the role of the law in its third use, as a guide to the divine character and (thus) to God's design for Christian character as well. A tranquil conscience was still something to seek and treasure, but both conscience and law were more active impulses in Calvin's picture of the Christian life after justification. In this section, we will take for granted much of what Luther said about how the demands of the law drive sinners to despair (and to seek relief outside of themselves) as largely affirmed also by Calvin. Instead, we will focus on how Calvin's desire for a godly and disciplined church intersected and sometimes clashed with the gospel's offer of freedom of conscience.

Traditionally, Christian accounts of how conscience functions as a natural part of human beings and human societies have drawn heavily on Romans 2:14–16:

> When Gentiles who do not have the law do by nature what the law requires, they are a law to themselves, even though they do not have the law. They show that what the law requires is written on their hearts, while their conscience also bears witness and their conflicting thoughts accuse or perhaps excuse them on that day when … God judges the secrets of all by Christ Jesus.

This rich passage has been prized by medievals and moderns no less than by Reformers, Calvin not least. One can hardly miss that whatever the *written law* asked of the people of God in the Old Testament, somehow those commands were also found among the Gentiles – within them *by nature*, imprinted on their hearts and attested by *conflicting thoughts*, all of which are ingredients in a Pauline definition of conscience, albeit in a sense that Paul left unspecified. Romans 2 plays a huge role in Christian doctrines of *natural law* – the notion that what God reveals and commands in the Bible can also be read in the "book of nature." Reformers such as Luther and Calvin also drew the traditional conclusion that the commandments in the Decalogue are attested to every human conscience also by the *law of nature*. Everyone knows that theft and adultery and lying are wrong. Everyone knows parents are to be honored. In their heart of hearts, all know there is a divine Maker who deserves thanks and loyalty. But knowing does not mean obeying.

[14] John Calvin, "Reply to Sadolet (1539)," in *Calvin: Theological Treatises*, ed. J. K. S. Reid (Philadelphia, PA: Westminster, 1954), 251, 243.

These "natural" components and correlates of conscience are prominent in Calvin. Conscience is "a sort of guardian appointed for man to note and spy out his secrets" or "a witness joined to them." It is "a sense of divine judgment" and "a certain mean between God and man." It is a part of our creatureliness over which we do not have full control, for "it does not allow man to suppress within himself what he knows, but pursues him to the point of convicting him."[15] What all people "know" but would "suppress" is precisely the natural law, which itself is practically equivalent to "the law of God which we call the moral law." Indeed, there is scarcely any duty to God or neighbor that we should not have been able to perceive through the natural law, but in our fallen state the natural law – as mediated by conscience – only deprives us of the excuse of ignorance. Natural law is obscured by our dullness. And conscience, though it be "the innermost part of the soul," is itself impaired by the general depravity of our nature. Hence, just as it is possible to disregard the natural law, so may one forsake conscience or even lull it to sleep by disregarding God's judgment.

Though more could be said about Calvin's concept of conscience, especially within the framework of his theological anthropology, it is evident that the proper function of conscience is tied to the law – natural law, moral law, the law of God, the Ten Commandments – which is "written, even engraved, upon the hearts of all." And however much the law is a rebuke and a threat to the consciences of sinners, the solution is not to do away with the law, for the law (in all its forms) is to be commended to believers as a guide to God's will. Indeed, for Calvin, the third use of the law is integral to what he calls the second part of Christian freedom. Specifically, because the justified conscience is *free from perpetual dread of the law*, the conscience is also *free to obey God's will* (as found in the law) with a willing heart.

Calvin's passion for salvation by grace was thus matched or surpassed by his quest for pure worship in the reforming of the church. Christian consciences were urged by every means to grasp Christian freedom in both aspects: in the spiritual relief that derives from free forgiveness but also in transforming sin – whether private sins or public – into holiness. In Calvin's picture of the Christian life, self-examination is a crucial ingredient that depends on one's awareness of conscience and that is thereby related to a host of topics, including knowledge of God and of oneself, repentance,

[15] Calvin focuses on conscience in *Institutes* 3.19.15 and 4.10.3, but the concept permeates his writings; see especially his commentaries on Romans 2:15 and 5:1, and on 1 Thessalonians 3:13. This and the following paragraph also draw (in order) on *Institutes* 4.20.16, 2.2.22, 2.1.8; and 2.8.1, 2.7.12, 3.19.4, 3.11.1.

self-denial, responding to suffering, and participation in the Lord's Supper as an act of acceptable worship.[16] To be sure, Calvin's concern that God be rightly worshiped really meant, broadly, that God be *obeyed*. And Calvin was quick to teach the people of Geneva that God's instructions must be followed, whether found in the natural law or in the laws of the Bible.

Consequently, when Calvin joined Guillaume Farel in 1536 to bolster Geneva's sputtering reform, a high priority was to draw up a catechism and a confession of faith. These instruments would teach the Genevans not only how salvation derives from God's grace, not from works (the first part of Christian freedom), but also how believers' gratitude ought to be expressed through love of God and neighbor in ways helpfully mapped by the Decalogue. But as things turned out, Calvin and Farel had asked for more than many Genevans were ready to concede.

## CONSCIENCE AND CONTROVERSIES AMONG THE MAGISTERIAL REFORMERS

Calvin's first reforms miscarried badly. Dismissed by Geneva in 1538, Calvin served a French congregation in Strasbourg until Geneva invited him back in 1541. Yet his early missteps serve to introduce the first of several more general controversies to be treated here, all of which strained the connections of theory and practice with respect to conscience. These include whether church or state authority may demand confession and conformity in religious matters; the problem of "Nicodemism" or dissimulating one's faith; freedom of conscience in *adiaphora* or "indifferent matters," along with the problem of the weak or erring conscience; and the place of natural law and conscience in regulating social mores as well as in extending pastoral care. During the sixteenth century, each of these issues acquired a degree of notoriety that variously implicated Luther, Calvin, and all their colleagues.

### *Conscience and Confession*

For Calvin, the "double grace" bestowed by Christ yields not only justification, with evident benefits for the oppressed conscience, but also the beginnings of sanctification, which in Geneva had serious implications for

16 "Self-examination is the individual's appropriation of all that Calvin has said about conscience." See David L. Foxgrover, "John Calvin's Understanding of Conscience," PhD diss., Claremont Graduate School, 1978, 311.

regulating church and society. In April 1537, the Geneva council began circulating the new confession to residents, who were expected to subscribe in order to be admitted to the Lord's Supper. Murmuring quickly arose. Many balked not so much over affirming a Reformed understanding of the gospel but at promising to live by God's law. One dissenter professed readiness to swear to the "articles of reformation" but not to the Ten Commandments "because," he apologized, "they're hard to keep."[17] Calvin tried to control the damage early in 1538. In a new preface to the catechism, addressed to international readers, he argued that there is nothing aberrant about demanding a public confession of faith, for Christian beliefs are meaningless if there is no commitment to try to practice them. After all, Calvin fumed, the confession itself plainly says fulfilling the law is impossible and that no one can be justified by the law! But despite downplaying the specter of legalism or works-righteousness, Calvin's ideals drove his defense: the goal of mandatory confession is not only to protect the Lord's Supper from the ungodly and vice versa but also to seek general *edification*, to be manifested "in sober fear of God, sincere piety, and unfeigned holiness of morals."[18]

The Genevan confession thus made two points about conscience: first, that consciences are freed from the burden of the law by faith in Christ; second, the less obvious point that Christian consciences exist in community and are therefore by no means autonomous. Certainly, Calvin was well aware that spurious rules, human traditions, externals, and ceremonies do more to produce "servile conformity" than Christian freedom. And that is why Calvin's preface had to address the tension between a wrong-headed pursuit of legal righteousness and "the lawful use of freedom" that leads to genuine piety and sanctification by a proper use of divine precepts such as the Ten Commandments. Calvin's governing assumption was that now-freed consciences, if truly Christian, would be quick to submit to the word of God – and equally quick to submit to instruction by ministers of the Word, such as himself.

Calvin's campaign for mandatory subscription in Geneva came to a halt when he and Farel were dismissed by the city council in April 1538. When he returned in 1541, he turned instead to the formation of the *consistory* – a body of pastors empowered not to prosecute criminal offenses but to

[17] The anecdote is reported by Amédée Roget, *Histoire du peuple du Genève*, vol. 1, 1536–1542 (Geneva, 1870–87), 43n.

[18] See "John Calvin: Catechism 1538," trans. Ford Lewis Battles, in I. John Hesselink, *Calvin's First Catechism: A Commentary* (Louisville, KY: Westminster John Knox, 1997), 7.

scrutinize the behavior of residents with respect to their beliefs and morality. Though some have denigrated the consistory as inquisitorial, fairer accounts describe it as a "mandatory counseling service."[19] But it could also be depicted as *a school for consciences*, insofar as its interventions routinely addressed malformed beliefs, remnants of Catholic superstitions, marital discord, and even strife between neighbors. Such interventions were intended to prompt Genevans to engage their discipleship more conscientiously, applying God's word to awaken consciences that seemed all too tranquil.

## *Nicodemism and Dissimulation*

Calvin's commitment to public profession of one's faith never faltered: "Scripture has always joined confession with faith; and ... if we truly believe with the heart ... we ought also to confess with the mouth to that salvation which we believe."[20] Yet his exhortations were resisted not only in Geneva but also abroad, particularly among those who lived in Roman Catholic territories and did not want their Reformed sympathies known. Calvin branded such timid believers as *Nicodemites*, after Nicodemus in John 3, who came to Jesus only by night. Obviously, Protestants in France risked persecution if they declared their beliefs openly, but Calvin saw their feigned participation in the "idolatry" of the Mass as an insult to God and a danger to their souls. Calvin was not wholly impractical: believers were free to flee from persecution, a traditional Christian option. But at the very least, such Nicodemites should

> thoroughly examine their consciences .... They should not extenuate their faults, nor seek some lame excuse and comfort and flatter themselves in their weakness. Rather, they ought often to bring to mind the wretchedness and the offense they commit, so as more ardently to desire the remedy and seek the means to obtain it.[21]

[19] This now-common description was coined by Robert M. Kingdon in "Calvin and the Family: The Work of the Consistory of Geneva," *Pacific Theological Review* 17 (1984): 5–18. Jeffrey R. Watt illustrates its application in "Reconciliation and the Confession of Sins: The Evidence from the Consistory in Calvin's Geneva," in *Calvin and Luther: The Continuing Relationship*, ed. R. Ward Holder (Göttingen: Vandenhoeck & Ruprecht, 2013), 105–20.

[20] "Articles Concerning the Organization of the Church and of Worship at Geneva, 1537," in *Calvin: Theological Treatises*, 54.

[21] John Calvin, "A Letter to Some Friends" (1540), in *Come Out from among Them: "Anti-Nicodemite" Writings of John Calvin*, trans. Seth Skolnitsky (Dallas, TX: Protestant Heritage, 2001), 43–44.

Later, Calvin would add yet another traditional but unattractive option: to suffer martyrdom.[22]

Not surprisingly, oppressed Protestants remained critical of a reformer who was safe behind the walls of Geneva, even though Calvin's rigorous stance was supported in 1545 by Philip Melanchthon, Martin Bucer, and Peter Martyr Vermigli, and later still by Heinrich Bullinger and the ministers of Zurich.[23] Yet Calvin's counsel that believers could flee persecution in order to confess their faith openly was not empty advice. Like many Protestant cities, Geneva became a haven for religious refugees, principally from France but from other countries as well.

## *Freedom of Conscience in Things Indifferent*

The driving force of Luther's declamation at the Diet of Worms was that human innovations – whether canon law, papal bull, or ecumenical creed – cannot bind the conscience. Only God's word can do that. God alone is lord of the conscience. But human laws are still necessary, whether civil laws or church polity, and the Bible authorizes such laws and rulers in texts like Romans 13:1–7 and 1 Peter 2:13–17. Calvin's first formal presentation to the Genevan city council was a list of regulations for organizing the church, and while his first catechism and confession defended freedom of conscience against "human traditions," both documents also repeated this line, more or less:

> The ordinances that are *necessary* for the internal discipline of the Church, and belong solely to the maintenance of peace, honesty and good order in the assembly of Christians, *we do not hold to be human traditions at all*, in as much as they are comprised under the general command of Paul, where he desires that all be done among them decently and in order.[24]

In Calvin's eyes, then, the Genevan confession was itself necessary for the church's discipline and therefore not really a human tradition – and, thus, not eligible for conscientious dissent.

Yet Luther and Calvin recognized many things as *not* essential to the faith. In these "indifferent" matters, freedom must be protected even while

[22] John Calvin, "A Short Treatise Setting Forth What the Faithful Man Must Do When He Is among Papists and He Knows the Truth of the Gospel" (1543), in *Come Out from among Them*, 50–51.

[23] Calvin's dealings with Nicodemism are nicely summarized by Wulfurt de Greef, *The Writings of John Calvin: An Introductory Guide* (Louisville, KY: Westminster John Knox, 2008), 120–26.

[24] John Calvin, "Confession of Faith (1536)," in *Calvin: Theological Treatises*, 30 (italics mine).

consciences are trained to use that freedom to serve God and neighbor. Paul's admonishment to "decency and order" guided a good deal of Protestant thought: even where the conscience is not bound by any law, Christians will still obey "the law of love" (Rom. 13:8) that binds them to love their neighbors. Such love often means limiting one's freedom for the sake of a neighbor with a weak conscience – a topic addressed at length in Romans 14–15 and 1 Corinthians 8–10.

Still, Protestants regularly argued over how to define "indifferent" – and over which party or position truly represented the weaker conscience so as to deserve deference from those supposedly stronger in faith. In 1521–22, Luther was hiding in the Wartburg Castle when his Wittenberg colleagues began to purge worship of unbiblical ceremonies and images. Though not dissenting from these changes in principle, Luther returned to preach against *forced* changes as potentially hurtful to weak consciences. Though Roman Catholic practices may be merely human inventions, they may also be tolerated for a time for the sake of the weak.

Catholic liturgy and ceremonies often sparked controversies over adiaphora. Generally, ceremonies were instinctively seen as indifferent matters, not necessarily helpful or harmful and certainly not salvific; but Protestants also saw that what may have begun as an innocent augmentation to worship could become a new law, with the weight of church authority now tyrannizing the consciences of the laity. They also recognized that ceremonies and traditions could be detrimental for their *symbolic* value: though indifferent per se, ceremonies might be stumbling blocks to the weak if made mandatory, especially if they inculcate spurious precepts. Following the 1547 defeat of the Lutheran alliance known as the Schmalkald League, the Diet of Augsburg demanded a return to pre-Reformation ceremonies, sacraments, and polity. Some Lutherans sought to accommodate this arrangement: while still defending Luther's doctrine of justification, they regarded these reinstituted ceremonies as adiaphora, as practices not harmful to faith or conscience. Stricter Lutherans insisted that while externals are indeed indifferent when the church is at peace, religious conflict changes their significance. The resulting strife led to a chapter in the *Formula of Concord* that explained, thirty years later, how only the strict position was correct:

> In a time of persecution that demands confession of the faith – particularly when the opponents are striving either through violence and coercion or through craft and deceit to suppress pure teaching and subtly to slip their false teaching back into our churches – such things, even indifferent

things, may in no way be permitted with a clear conscience and without damaging the divine truth.[25]

In England, under Edward VI, the "vestments controversy" took a similar path. Newly Protestant clergy voiced a conscientious objection to the symbolic significance of vestments that bore too much resemblance to what Catholic priests had recently worn – thereby giving laity a confusing impression but also allowing the Church of England to make an indifferent practice binding on the clergy, regardless of their scruples to the contrary.[26]

## *Conscience, Legislation, and Pastoral Advice*

As the Reformers understood Romans 2, the proper dictates of conscience echo the teachings of the law – whether the divine law or the law of nature. Not surprisingly, assumptions about what nature teaches also influenced the laws and counsels that the Reformers were called on to formulate. Appeals to nature, with conscience an ever-present partner, often supplemented biblical arguments for these ordinances.

One example derives from their reform of matrimonial legislation. Once "Scripture alone" became the touchstone for doctrine and practice, other dominoes soon fell: clerical celibacy was set aside, marriage ceased to be deemed inferior to consecrated chastity, and grounds for divorce and remarriage were newly reconsidered. Luther addressed marriage in several early sermons and treatises, and the ecclesiastical ordinances that Calvin drafted in 1541 were followed by proposals for new matrimonial legislation in 1546.

Calvin's ordinances deal with pressing issues of the day, such as clandestine marriage and parental permission, prohibited degrees of consanguinity, annulment, and divorce.[27] He addresses these issues with thoughtful common sense and rarely appeals to Scripture or other authorities – except in a series of ordinances dealing with incest and prohibited relations. There, the initial prohibition against marriage between parent and child is explained on the grounds that "this contravenes natural decency and is forbidden both by the

[25] Kolb and Wengert, eds., *The Book of Concord*, 636.

[26] On the vestments controversy, see Bernard J. Verkamp, *The Indifferent Mean: Adiaphorism in the English Reformation to 1554* (Athens, OH; Detroit, MI: Ohio University Press; Wayne State University Press, 1977); and J. H. Primus, *The Vestments Controversy: An Historical Study of the Earliest Tensions within the Church of England in the Reigns of Edward VI and Elizabeth* (Kampen: J. H. Kok, 1960).

[27] Translated in John Witte Jr. and Robert M. Kingdon, *Sex, Marriage, and Family Life in John Calvin's Geneva*, vol. 1, *Courtship, Engagement, and Marriage* (Grand Rapids, MI: Eerdmans, 2005), 51–61. See especially § 25 and § 28.

law of God and by the civil law" – successively invoking the law of nature, Scripture, and secular legal tradition. A few paragraphs later, the marriage of first-cousins is also prohibited: yet not because it is forbidden "either by the law of God or Roman civil law," but rather "to avoid scandal, because for a long time this has not been the custom" – though the ordinance also states that this prohibition may change later on. One sees Calvin wrestling here to correlate Scripture, nature, and conscience, trying hard to conform to the Bible on topics that it does not always make clear, while simultaneously recognizing that the Bible gives permission to forms of marriage that the consciences of those in Geneva would find scandalous and, thus, wounding to faith.[28]

Calvin was not alone in finding it hard to derive pastoral guidance from the Bible's general precepts. Luther, too, could drift toward inconsistency in his appeals to conscience. Assessing Tamar's deception of Judah in Genesis 38, Luther was willing to tolerate her lie but not her harlotry: "The Holy Spirit does not move or impel anyone," he declaimed, "to fornication and incest."[29] Nonetheless, perhaps the most infamous appeal to conscience ever made during the Reformation occurred in 1540, when Luther counseled his own prince, Philip of Hesse, to commit bigamy.

Philip ruled from 1519 and embraced Luther's reform in 1524 – the same year he entered into a frigid marriage that he soon violated by acts of adultery. But conscience plagued him. He began pestering Luther for permission to take a second wife, as the Old Testament patriarchs had done. Luther hesitated: though he believed the patriarchs had special divine permission for their behavior, he was less sure of Philip. But if Luther refused, might the Pope grant this dispensation? Philip's threat to realign with the Roman Catholic Emperor was scarcely veiled. Luther capitulated.

Still, the weightiest factor was Luther's perception of Philip's *conscience*. Wracked by guilt for breaking his marriage vows, Philip abstained from communion on most occasions and feared his damnation. We have already noted Luther's compassion for sinners who yearn for righteousness but whose consciences are crushed by their own incapacity. Having known him for eighteen years, Luther seems to have concluded that Philip was incapable of change, however much he yearned for a clear conscience. What should a pastor do?

28 For an instance where Calvin reversed his teachings on the related topic of levirate marriage while claiming nature equally as a warrant for both views (at least while he held them), see John L. Thompson, "Second Thoughts about Conscience: Nature, the Law, and the Law of Nature in Calvin's Pentateuchal Exegesis," in *Calvinus Pastor Ecclesiae*, eds. Herman J. Selderhuis and Arnold Huijgen (Göttingen: Vandenhoeck & Ruprecht, 2016), 123–47.

29 Martin Luther, *Lectures on Genesis* 38:16–18, 20–22 (LW 7:31, 39).

Luther's advice mixes biblical exegesis with his own conscience's worries. He reiterates that marriage ought to be the union of a man and a woman as one flesh. He insists that Old Testament examples are less a warrant for us than a warning. Yet he concedes that if God could allow the patriarchs to take an additional wife (or more), such a deed cannot be damnable in and of itself.[30] And while Luther does not suppose that Philip received such permission directly from God, he explicitly stresses his own authority as Philip's pastor and underscores the rationale: namely, that Philip is in a situation of dire necessity (*notturfft*) – implying that his very soul was at stake – and *necessity*, in fact, is a warrant sufficient to justify an exception to the usual standards of morality according to the classical notion of equity, which tailors justice to fit the circumstances.

Luther went on to generalize, "Not every statement [in the Bible] needs to be observed if the conscience is right."[31] Clearly, Luther believed that his authority as a pastor and minister of the Word authorized him to issue such exceptional counsel to Philip's broken conscience. But some have regarded Luther's advice as "one of the worst mistakes" of his career,[32] and Calvin's vehement rebuke of patriarchal polygamy may well have been a response to Luther's miscalculated compassion.

## *The Limits of Protecting Consciences*

As these cases illustrate, the Magisterial Reformers regarded it as a crucial pastoral task not only to protect weak consciences but also to strengthen them: to wean them from superstitious attachments and to ground them in the teachings of the gospel, which would instill not only peace of conscience but also reformation of character. His allowance for Philip's polygamy shows how much Luther could indulge the "weaker" Christian – but there were limits. Neither Luther nor Calvin gave any quarter to the sort of behavior that could masquerade as a matter of conscience when something else, in their judgment, was surely at play – whether stubbornness or hypocrisy, rebellion or heresy. In an eloquent chapter on Christian freedom in Calvin's *Institutes* (3.19), several long paragraphs target those who abuse their freedom to the

[30] Martin Brecht, *Martin Luther: The Preservation of the Church, 1532–1546*, trans. James L. Schaaf (Minneapolis, MN: Fortress, 1993), 3:205.

[31] Luther and Melanchthon to Landgrave Philip of Hesse, December 10, 1539, #3423 in D. Martin, ed. *Luthers Werke, Kritische Gesamtausgabe: Tischreden*, 6 vols. (Weimar: Hermann Böhlaus Nachfolger, 1912–21), 8:643: "So ist auch nit alle rede zu achten, wenn das gewissen recht stehet."

[32] The opinion of Brecht, in *Martin Luther*, 214.

injury of the weak. Like any pastor, Calvin was well aware that "persons of bitter disposition and pharisaical pride" could be quick to fabricate occasions for taking offense. But such individuals are to be resisted and rebuked, not indulged. No one has the right to invoke claims of conscience in service of self-indulgence, nor in support of any teaching or practice that contradicts either the obligation to love one's neighbor or the still higher obligation to honor God and the precepts delivered by God's word. Stubbornness, hypocrisy, rebellion, and heresy all run afoul of these criteria.[33] And neither Luther nor Calvin wanted to be known as a friend of rebellion or heresy. Accordingly, while Luther or Calvin would have agreed that consciences cannot be compelled, neither of them would have wanted a weak or erring conscience to overturn biblical authority – nor pastoral authority, either. As ministers of the Word, both Reformers saw themselves bound by the authority of their office: called and commissioned to exercise discernment and even to pass judgment on the moral integrity of those who appeared before them. But despite their newly recovered commitments to the authority of "Scripture alone" and to an ostensibly literal reading of the text, their pastoral judgments were necessarily also subjective. So Luther trusted Philip, if warily, and granted him a surprising concession; but the German reformer turned viciously against the supposedly "Christian" peasants in 1525 when violence and insurrection revealed their true character.[34] Similarly, Calvin pleaded for freedom of conscience in many venues, but in demanding that residents subscribe to the new Geneva

33 There is thus no "right of conscience" that can be invoked by even genuinely weak consciences in support of practices or beliefs that contradict what the Protestant Reformers would have regarded as biblical teaching – and there was ample Roman Catholic precedent for such a conclusion, as in Aquinas's discussion of how obstinacy is a chief ingredient in heresy (*Summa Theologiae* II-II.11.1–4). Like Aquinas, the Reformers weighed heresy not in the currency of conscience but against its expression of blasphemy and its capacity to inflict eternal harm on one's neighbor. Calvin's polarizing involvement with Michael Servetus, which led to the latter's execution for heresy in 1553 – the same year in which he had been sentenced to die also by Catholic authorities in Vienne – displays more diffidence toward punishing Servetus than is often acknowledged; see, most recently, the moderating assessment of Gary W. Jenkins, *Calvin's Tormentors: Understanding the Conflicts That Shaped the Reformer* (Grand Rapids, MI: Baker Academic, 2018), 47–61.

34 Luther's indulgence of Philip's *moral* failing is probably to be categorically distinguished, in Luther's eyes, from the peasants' *doctrinal* misconstrual of the gospel. But see David M. Whitford, "'It Is Not Forbidden That a Man May Have More Than One Wife.' Luther's Pastoral Advice on Bigamy and Marriage," in *Mixed Matches: Transgressive Unions in Germany from the Reformation to the Enlightenment*, eds. David M. Luebke and Mary Lindemann (New York, NY: Berghahn, 2014), 14–30, who vigorously argues that Luther's pastoral advice "was not guided by theological principle" but rather embodied "that most common of human frailties, in which one condemns one's enemies and forgives one's friends" (26).

confession, he worried less about the people's consciences than about his own, as a pastor charged to guard the dignity of the Lord's Supper against being polluted by the ungodly, unbelievers, and hypocrites.[35] Luther, to be sure, may well have given himself greater license in resolving conflicts with the moral law in favor of the conscience – and some of Calvin's rigor may have been provoked by such laxity in Luther or other reformers. But Calvin would have preferred to herald as the principle of his moral guidance not rigor or legalism, but freedom: because, as he concluded in his chapter on Christian freedom, the freedom of conscience that God intends for us, properly understood, is never at odds with the laws that God also enjoins, however much those laws may bind our outward actions.[36]

## THE REFORMATION LEGACY: CASES OF CONSCIENCE AS PASTORAL CARE

As exemplified by Luther and Calvin – in sermons and commentaries, in legislation and pastoral advice – the early Reformers had high ideals for how Christians might find peace of conscience through the forgiveness mediated by Christ. They also modeled the uncertainties of forsaking the authority of the Roman Catholic magisterium and substituting Scripture alone – an authority that they nonetheless sought to correlate and integrate with their understandings and experiences of conscience as an inner law of nature, as well as with appeals to the principles of equity and necessity, and occasionally with corroborating testimonies from Roman civil law and even the *ius gentium* or law of nations.

If seeds of the Magisterial Reformation lay in relieving the anguish of sinners' consciences by sweeping aside contrived ecclesiastical traditions and laws that bound sinners and their consciences to obligations never warranted by Scripture, the fruit of reform would mature as an equal concern for the transformation of sinners' lives. This was always Calvin's agenda, but the Lutheran antinomian controversies eventually brought the third use of the law into the *Formula of Concord*. Even Luther came to accommodate something of Melanchthon's views. Writing in 1539, he warned that "[these antinomians] may be fine Easter preachers, but they are very poor Pentecost preachers," because while they boldly proclaim justification by faith, they

[35] I discuss how Calvin favors his own (pastoral) conscience in "Confessions, Conscience, and Coercion in the Early Calvin," in *Calvin and the Early Reformation*, ed. Brian C. Brewer and David M. Whitford (Leiden: Brill, 2020), 155–79.

[36] Calvin, *Institutes* 3.19.16.

omit the Holy Spirit's sanctifying and vivifying work in the life of the Christian.[37]

Perhaps the most striking testimony to the trajectory that saw the evangelical use of the law (as an inducement to self-despair and thus to faith in Christ) carefully juxtaposed with the law's third use is the development of a formal literature of casuistry as a form of pastoral care among the Reformed, particularly in England, followed not long after by Lutheran casuistry. Among the Reformed, a pattern was set, arguably, by William Perkins's *Cases of Conscience* (1606), and he had many successors – William Ames, Richard Baxter, Joseph Hall, Jeremy Taylor, among others – through the later seventeenth century.[38] But Lutherans also produced a robust literature of conscience, signaled by the appearance of Georg Dedeken's *Treasury of Councils and Decisions* in 1623 and Friedrich Balduin's *On Cases of Conscience* in 1628.[39]

But this literature of conscience had significant and continuous precedents in earlier writings – in Luther's collected letters and his table talk, in treatises on marriage penned by many Lutherans and Reformed, and in the many loci or "common places" wherein Protestant commentaries often addressed both theological and practical questions. The later literature of conscience thus explicated the trajectory of the earliest Reformation writings, in which the theological insights that aimed to restore Christians' spiritual freedom and peace of conscience quickly led to significant social changes, impelling Christians of all stations to seek help and instruction for ethical decisions.

Historically, conscience has been a malleable notion, yet an inevitable component of Christian theology and practice. It lies at the heart of Christian spirituality and practical theology. It was the forum for all of Luther's struggles. It is the key to what Calvin memorably described in his *Institutes*' opening sentence as theology's subject matter, namely, "the knowledge of God and the knowledge of ourselves." If the Magisterial Reformation began as a *cri de coeur* from fearful consciences in thrall of the law and enslaved by sin, it quickly became also a movement for social change and personal transformation, variously embraced and resisted by the

37 Martin Luther, "On Councils and the Church" (1539), LW 41:114.

38 William Perkins, *The Whole Treatise of the Cases of Conscience* (STC 19669; Cambridge, 1606).

39 For an introduction to post-Reformation Lutheran casuistry and to the work of Dedeken and Balduin in particular, see the excellent study of Benjamin T. G. Mayes, *Counsel and Conscience: Lutheran Casuistry and Moral Reasoning after the Reformation* (Göttingen: Vandenhoeck & Ruprecht, 2011).

men and women of sixteenth-century Europe. A good part of the Reformers' response came by way of the legislation and pastoral theology that explicitly addressed conscience and cases and thus fulfilled the Reformation's original twofold quest: to bring peace to the sinner's conscience as well as to fulfill the law of love.

## RECOMMENDED READING


Althaus, Paul. *The Ethics of Martin Luther*. Translated by Robert C. Schultz. Philadelphia, PA: Fortress, 1972.

Andrew, Edward G. "Christian Conscience and the Protestant Reformation." In *Conscience and Its Critics: Protestant Conscience, Enlightenment Reason, and Modern Subjectivity*, 12–33. Toronto: University of Toronto Press, 2012.

Baylor, Michael G. *Action and Person: Conscience in Late Scholasticism and the Young Luther*. Leiden: Brill, 1977.

Foxgrover, David L. "John Calvin's Understanding of Conscience." PhD diss., Claremont Graduate School, 1978.

Grabill, Stephen J. *Rediscovering the Natural Law in Reformed Theological Ethics*. Grand Rapids, MI: Eerdmans, 2006.

Haas, Guenther H. *The Concept of Equity in Calvin's Ethics*. Waterloo: Wilfrid Laurier University Press, 1997.

Hains, Todd R. "Luther and Bound Conscience in His German Church Postils." MA thesis, Trinity Evangelical Divinity School, 2007. www.tren.com/edocs/search.cfm?p0061690.

Mayes, Benjamin T. G. *Counsel and Conscience: Lutheran Casuistry and Moral Reasoning after the Reformation*. Göttingen: Vandenhoeck & Ruprecht, 2011.

Primus, J. H. *The Vestments Controversy: An Historical Study of the Earliest Tensions within the Church of England in the Reigns of Edward VI and Elizabeth*. Kampen: J. H. Kok, 1960.

Thompson, John L. "The Immoralities of the Patriarchs in the History of Exegesis: A Reassessment of Calvin's Position." *Calvin Theological Journal* 26 (1991): 9–46.

"Patriarchs, Polygamy, and Private Resistance: John Calvin and Others on Breaking God's Rules." *Sixteenth Century Journal* 25 (1994): 3–27.

"Second Thoughts about Conscience: Nature, the Law, and the Law of Nature in Calvin's Pentateuchal Exegesis." In *Calvinus Pastor Ecclesiae*, edited by Herman J. Selderhuis and Arnold Huijgen, 123–47. Göttingen: Vandenhoeck & Ruprecht, 2016.

Verkamp, Bernard J. *The Indifferent Mean: Adiaphorism in the English Reformation to 1554*. Athens, OH; Detroit, MI: Ohio University Press; Wayne State University Press, 1977.

Wengert, Timothy J. *Reading the Bible with Martin Luther: An Introductory Guide*. Grand Rapids, MI: Baker Academic, 2013.

Zachman, Randall C. *The Assurance of Faith: Conscience in the Theology of Martin Luther and John Calvin*. Minneapolis, MN: Fortress, 1993.

# 8

# Toward a Theology of a Redeemed Conscience

JEFFREY B. HAMMOND

## INTRODUCTION

Conscience, like love, "is a many splendored thing."[1] Appeals to conscience are made in different situations. One man, for example, has no problem in taking up arms to fight in a war prosecuted by his country, while another man thinks that the war is not just or that to fire any shot, regardless of whether it is fired dispassionately or in anger or in self-defense, would vitiate his most cherished principles about the inviolability of human life. The latter might say that it was his conscience that forbade him from registering for the draft or reporting for active duty. Likewise, and perhaps equally important, the former man's willingness to come to the aid of his country might not be borne out of reflex but rather a considered, reasoned judgment about the justness of his country's cause and the perceived duties of citizenship that compel him to answer the call of duty. In other words, his conscience told him to answer the call.

Contemporarily, applications of conscience have transformed from the traditional categories of conscientious objection to war fighting and refusal to do an act – like a physician refusing to assist in a suicide – to requests to be sprung from the normal obligations of a freely chosen vocation. Take, for example, state laws liberating pharmacists and other health care workers from dispensing prescription drugs, like abortifacients, which violate their conscientious scruples.[2] Or take, as another example, the now (in)famous Kentucky

[1] "Love is a many splendored thing" is a famous line found in many pieces of art including *Love Is a Many-Splendored Thing* (1955), directed by Henry King (Beverly Hills, ca: Twentieth Century Fox Home Entertainment, 2013), Blu-ray, DVD.

[2] See, e.g., South Dakota Codified Laws §36-11-70(a)(1). That provision states, "No pharmacist may be required to dispense medication if there is reason to believe that medication would be used to: (1) Cause an abortion."

County Clerk, Kim Davis, who refused to dispense a clean marriage certificate to same-sex couples looking for legal sanction in her office. Appeals to conscience were made on her behalf for her refusal to grant the exact certificates the same-sex applicants requested.[3]

Given that people are appealing to conscience and are being freed, or not, from job requirements, business transactions, and discharging the duties of their elected office, etc., it is important to do a bit of foundational work to determine what in fact conscience is and how it functions. However, it is impossible to describe how conscience works at all times for all people. Rather, it is more profitable to describe how conscience works in particular conscientious people. Therefore, as a religious person – more specifically, as an evangelical Protestant sympathetic toward Reformed Protestantism – I have taken up the charge of describing conscience from that position.[4]

It is important to note that conscience is not the exclusive domain of religious people. Thus, it should go without saying that conscience is not the exclusive domain of Christians – whether Orthodox or Catholic. And it is certainly not the exclusive domain of Protestant Christians, whether evangelical, Reformed, fundamentalist, or mainline. Nor is it the exclusive prerogative of other monotheists, such as Jews or Muslims, or other religious people. Conscience, rightly defined and deployed, is available to anyone – whether atheist or agnostic, merely "spiritual," or even deeply and traditionally religious. There is a pith, a core essence of conscience that is possessed by all people of goodwill that involves acting in accordance with truth, as one understands it, and no matter the consequences that follow from those actions.[5]

Having said that, it is impossible to uncouple oneself from one's situation. Therefore, this chapter describes the phenomenon of conscience from the

[3] "Kentucky Clerk Has a 'Clean Conscience' in Jail, Attorney Says," cbsnews.com, www.cbsnews.com/news/kentucky-clerk-kim-davis-has-a-clean-conscience-in-jail-attorney-says/.

[4] Instead of using the descriptors "evangelical" or "Reformed" throughout this chapter, I have chosen, for convenience's sake, to primarily use the adjective "Christian" to describe conscience, fully realizing that mine is not the only evangelical, Reformed, fundamentalist, or otherwise Protestant position on conscience. Furthermore, mine emphatically is not the exclusive Christian position. This book has a variety of positions on conscience from multiple confessions.

[5] But cf., Claudia I. Emerson and Abdallah S. Daar, "Defining Conscience and Acting Conscientiously," *American Journal of Bioethics* 7, no. 12 (2007): 19–21, www.dx.doi.org/10.1080/15265160701709974. "We argue, indeed, that it is possible to distinguish between the conscience and acting conscientiously," especially in the context of physicians invoking their consciences when faced with the possibility of performing morally problematic medical services. Ibid., 19.

author's perspective as an evangelical who takes his faith seriously. Though there is an understanding of conscience that is available to all people of goodwill, it is impossible to fully describe conscience apart from one's most closely held moral, philosophical, and theological commitments. Discerning the demands of conscience and then acting in a manner consistent with those demands often leads the conscientious person to suffer in some way: whether imprisonment, or financial penalty, or loss of reputation, or some other deprivation. It is hard to square with experience that a person would be willing to suffer for a reason unless that reason was important to him or her.

Let us first, then, consider a working definition of conscience, which will be unpacked in the remainder of this chapter: Conscience is a capacity of the heart, the mind, and the will, that leads the person to act or refrain from acting, in accordance with the truth, as best as she knows it, when confronted with a demand for her action. As a capacity, Christian conscience is informed by the Bible and the Holy Spirit, along with reason, experience, and wise counselors, to be discerning as to when to invoke its prerogatives. Once exercised, conscience orients the person to a posture of peace and equanimity despite the outward consequences and judgments of her action or refusal to act.

Over the remainder of this chapter, the Christian conscience will be described as a capacity of the redeemed heart, mind, and will, leading one to act, or not, as the case may be. I will then describe the role that biblical theology and the Holy Spirit play in working with and activating the Christian conscience. Finally, I will describe the results that attend to the Christian after having exercised her conscience.

## CONSCIENCE AS A CAPACITY OF THE REDEEMED HEART, MIND, AND WILL

### *The Struggles of the Natural Man*

It is traditional in any theology to begin with theology is – the study of God and his attributes and actions in the world that he created. This step must be adumbrated for reasons of space. Suffice it say, however, that all of God's attributes, but particularly his holiness, indict all humans, including me. I fail to live up to God's exquisite goodness, his moral perfection, and his ability to love and regard human beings made in his image. God is truly set apart in the splendor of his beauty. And I am not. I am, rather, mired in the depravity of my sin. I intentionally describe myself wallowing in the "depravity of my sin" rather than the "depravity of my sins" because "sin" bespeaks the constitution of my natural state as a sinner who is an enemy of God, whereas "sins" represent something that I do, not necessarily who I am. Nevertheless, I am stuck in the hatred of my neighbor. I am puzzled by my inability to follow God, as I perceive he is leading me through his Word, through the counsel of those wiser than I, through prayer, and through the combination of all of the above through the testimony of the Holy Spirit in the inner chamber of my heart.

Of my own will, I cannot match God's holiness. Thus, for our purposes here, we will shift the orientation of this contemplation about God's attributes to his relationship with humankind, for, at least as far as the evangelical is concerned, the living out of conscience is an attribute of sanctified anthropology more than it is a reflection of theology proper. Notwithstanding this, the Petrine instruction that I "be holy, for I [God] am holy" (1 Pet. 1:16 NIV) mocks me because I am constitutionally unable to fulfill it. My will is entirely set on my desires, my prerogatives, and my estimation of my own goodness.

That is not to say that my natural man is unable to discern *some* of what God desires of me. For example, Martin Luther and his close friend, Philip Melanchthon, taught that the Ten Commandments are a deposit of the moral duties of all humankind regardless of the status of their relationship with God.[6] This foundation of the moral law was and is available to all people.

Sometimes, the natural law immediately informs me of its implications. At other times, I must catch up to its demands. For example, Hobby Lobby and related companies have always excluded, "consistent with their religious beliefs," the abortifacient drug RU-486 from their companies' insurance plans.[7] Further, the Green family (the owners of Hobby Lobby and a related company) came to the decision to remove two abortifacients that were already in their companies' insurance plans before the issuance of the so-called contraception mandate, after realizing the drugs'/devices' destructive power and realizing that paying for their use was not consonant with their (the Greens' and their companies') hard won, time-tested, and *religiously based* values.[8]

For the Christian to more fully live and act according to truth, as she understands it, her conscience needs to be redeemed and refined, changed so that it is sensitive to the gaps between the demands of God's moral law – which

6 John Witte Jr., *Law and Protestantism: The Legal Teachings of the Lutheran Reformation* (Cambridge: Cambridge University Press, 2002), 113–15, 125–27.

7 *Hobby Lobby, Inc., et. al.* v. *Sebelius, et. al.*, Case #: 5:12-cv-01000-HE (Verified Complaint), ¶54. (W.D., Okla., 2012).

8 Ibid., ¶55.

is a reflection of God's holiness to which every Christian should aspire – and the positive law with its sometimes inconsistent demands.

### *Changing Hearts, Minds, and Wills through Regeneration and Sanctification*

In the Reformed account of Christian initiation and soteriology, this sensitivity would be impossible without God taking the initiative in his relationship with me. Of his own initiative, God reaches down and begins to change my heart, mind, and will. He takes the initiative in saving me, "not because of righteous things [I have] done, but because of his mercy" (Titus 3:5). God exchanges my flinty heart of stone with its pride, arrogance, and insolence, and replaces it with a soft "heart of flesh," pliable to the end of being responsive to both God's leading and the needs of my fellows (see Ezek. 36:26). In this work of regeneration (which, again, is wholly God's work, and not my own; Titus 3:5), God is entirely responsible for operating on my heart so that I can respond to him in faith. I cannot do anything to bring about God's work of regeneration; yet the work is so marvelous and unique that I am fundamentally different after it has sought me out and changed me.[9]

Regeneration is a point in time that the believer can point to and say that God has claimed the new believer for himself. However, sanctification is a more gradual process in which the Holy Spirit consistently works on my dispositions and affections, so that my heart and mind, once turned toward God in regeneration, maintain their orientation and direction. After regeneration, God calls the believer by name, and there is no doubt in her mind when God says, "you are mine" (Isa. 43:1). There is no doubt that she is God's, and she is secure in his eternal plans, purposes, and promises. However, this side of eternity she cannot fully shake the vestiges of her sin nature. She cannot trust either her heart or mind to always respond to life's situations and conundrums in a way that pleases God.[10]

In sanctification, the believer's affections and will are gradually reoriented toward God. Though regeneration may happen over a period of time, sanctification by the Holy Spirit takes a lifetime, as all that one is and has – one's thoughts, feelings, inclinations, decisions, and judgments – must forever be captured and recaptured and be brought under the sovereign control of God.

[9] See, e.g., J. I. Packer, "Regeneration," Monergism.com, www.monergism.com/thethreshold/articles/onsite/packer_regen.html (for an authoritative statement on regeneration written by a renowned twentieth-century evangelical theologian).

[10] See, e.g., *Westminster Confession of Faith* (1643), ch. 13, Christian Classics Ethereal Library, www.ccel.org/ccel/anonymous/westminster3.pdf (for a well-known early Reformed creedal statement about sanctification).

But, importantly, once recreated, the Christian's heart is now capable of truly loving and serving God and neighbor, as she continues to grow in both grace and truth (see 2 Pet. 3:17–18). Thus, once the believer begins to walk along the path of sanctification, her conscience becomes active and alive – searching her thoughts, actions, and responses to others, and correspondingly, shuffling off its dormancy and laziness (see, e.g., Heb. 12:14). This conscientious vibrancy is attributable to the work of the Holy Spirit, through the Bible, on the believer's heart and mind.

Thus, in a very real sense, the conscience of the Christian is a "capacity." By capacity, I mean the regenerated and sanctified ability of the Christian to live and act according to the truth, as she knows it. Though it is accurate that the non-Protestant or even the non-religious person can have an active conscience, it is not true, I think, that that person can have a conscience as well-developed as the person whose heart and mind have been redeemed. In drawing the mind toward himself, God graciously unbinds the chains that sin has shackled upon the heart and mind of the new believer. It is in this state as a free believer that the Christian can more clearly see her obligations to live, move, and act in God's world.

It is through the life-long process of sanctification that God continually calibrates and re-orders the believer's mind, heart, and desires so that they are set upon him. Let us pause for just a moment to affirm that God, through the agency of the Holy Spirit acting through Scripture, does indeed continually press upon my reason and will, because they have not escaped unscathed from the Fall. There is a continual need for the Christian to have his mind renewed as he seeks an ever-closer relationship with God (see Rom. 12:2). While my reason and your reason might eventually arrive at the same conclusion regarding a course of action (regarding something to be done, such as, say, what our consciences dictate), what they cannot do is provide us with the same *motivations* for arriving at that end. While the reasonable person might act (exercise his conscience) for reason's sake, the conscientious Christian exercises her conscience because she has been changed and sanctified and wants to obey and please the God who has done the changing and sanctifying.

## *Law, Love, and the Foundation of Conscience*

Once the believer determines to partner with the Holy Spirit in the process of sanctification, the Christian's conscience becomes active and searching and seeks to latch upon and act according to truth as best as she can discern it. Of course, sometimes she fails in this quest (see Rom. 7:14–25). The foundation of her conscientious quest to live and act according to truth will be Jesus' two main legal injunctions: first to love God with all of her heart, soul, mind, and strength, and secondly, to love her neighbor as herself (Luke 10:27, cf. Deut. 6:5 and Lev. 19:18).

It is instructive that these two "greatest commands" from the Gospels and the Tanakh are legal injunctions. The Jews who heard Jesus preach this exposition of the Deuteronomy and Leviticus texts would have certainly taken Jesus' preaching as something that *bound* them to love God by obeying his revealed will and by serving and preferring their neighbor.

At this point, we have a real conundrum. What might have been binding on the careful Jew of Jesus' time (or before, for that matter) is not true of the careful Christian (evangelical, Catholic, or fundamentalist) of today. Were he alive today, I suspect that the Apostle Paul would look askance at any claim that to follow the way of Jesus means to keep the civil and ceremonial law found in the Old Testament (see Rom. 6:14). Please, therefore, do not understand my prior discussion of love and law that way. To be clear, I deny any thought or suggestion that conscience, much less the plain teaching of the Bible, demands adherence to the Old Testament's ceremonial and civil law. If robotic, even slavish, adherence to the law as found in the Old Testament is what is meant by theonomy, then that is something to be forthrightly rejected.

Let me be plain, however, about what I do mean. It is a consistent, even central, tenet of evangelical and Reformed thought that the Bible holds great sway over the life and daily practice of the believer. Historically, this has been borne out: one of the five traditional *solas* of Reformed Protestantism is, of course *sola scriptura*.[11] For the contemporary believer, *sola scriptura* means, at least, a firm commitment to take what is profitable for today from the Old Testament – its narrative, its theology, its poetry, its wisdom, its history, and moral law, and ask of God to use those raw materials to become a better, more sensitive, and more faithful Christian.[12] "All Scripture is

[11] For a contemporary account of *sola scriptura*, see Matthew Barrett, *God's Word Alone – The Authority of Scripture: What the Reformers Taught . . . and Why It Still Matters* (Grand Rapids, MI: Zondervan Academic, 2016).

[12] Jesus himself quoted and interpreted Scripture in a variety of ministry and personal situations. One of the more well-known of such instances involved him quoting Deuteronomy 8:3 in his temptation by Satan: "It is written: 'Man shall not live on bread alone but by every word that comes from the mouth of God'" (Matt. 4:4). Matthew Barrett notes the phenomenon of Jesus quoting and relying on Scripture. He writes:

> In countless ways, Jesus leans on that authority as he combats the religious leaders of his day, quoting the Old Testament as the inspired, God-breathed word that they are accountable to. Jesus also replies to Satan in the wilderness temptation by citing the Scriptures as his authority, and not just as his authority but as the inerrant word of God,

God-breathed . . ." said the Apostle Paul to his protégé Timothy (2 Tim. 3:16), and of course, when he wrote that, he was referring to what we now know as the Old Testament.

But a commitment to *sola scriptura* also means an equally firm commitment to the New Testament and its narrative of incarnation, cross, and resurrection, its theology of mission and evangelization, and its ethical instruction. Thus, because evangelical Protestants hold to Paul's Timothean instruction that "all Scripture is God breathed" as applicable to the New Testament as well as the Old, in matters of conscience (roughly speaking, disputed matters where there are two or more plausible positions to take), the evangelical looks with a keen eye to the New Testament's ethical instruction as the grist to be poured through the filter of prayer and the Holy Spirit's "still small" (1 Kings 19:12 KJV) promptings in the conscience's inner reaches.

How does this work? Taken as a whole, the New Testament is a relatively brief volume, comprising but a few hundred pages. Written two thousand years ago, it cannot possibly speak to every situation in which modern Christians find themselves. It therefore takes something of an interpretive heuristic to understand how the Bible and conscience work together. First, some account of the text's plain meaning should be made. When the Apostle Paul wrote to the Ephesian church for "husbands [to] love your wives," we are left with a fairly wide gap to know exactly what that instruction means (Eph. 5:25). However, this is where conscience kicks in. Take, for example, disputes between husbands and wives. Though my wife and I might have a heated argument, one in which sharp positions are taken and in which unkind words are spoken (words which, frankly, if we were reading our Bibles more, we would not say to each other), my conscience reminds me that my argument can never lead to violence. In other words, my conscience tells me that, as I keep the ethical instruction to love my wife at the top of my mind (even as we are arguing), it reminds me that the love I am called to display to my wife means that I would never hit her. In other words, hitting her is never a loving act and could never be justified as such. Thus, in this sense, conscience has a *negative function* – telling me what I should not do if I want to live as the Bible describes I should live.

> the word that is trustworthy and reliable and clear and sufficient, in order to counter Satan's deceptive ways. (Matt. 4:1–11)

Matthew Barrett, "*What Is Sola Scriptura?*," ZA *(Zondervan Academic) Blog*, August 2, 2018, zondervanacademic.com/blog/what-is-sola-scriptura.

### *The Work of the Holy Spirit in the Believer's Conscience*

For the Christian, the Bible is not a wooden book of rules to be slavishly applied, as an empirical scientist would apply the laws of chemistry or physics to a besetting scientific problem. For conscience to be rightly engaged, there must be an ongoing conversation between the Bible and considered interpretations of the Bible over the centuries, wise counsel from fellow Christians, and the gentle leading of the Holy Spirit. In his last night before his crucifixion, Jesus promised his disciples a counselor that would "teach you all things and will remind you of everything I have said to you" (John 14:26). As an undivided, eternally co-existing person of God himself, the indwelling Holy Spirit does not and indeed cannot work at cross-purposes with God's will revealed in the Bible. In the disciples' preaching ministries, the Spirit would remind them of the words and actions of Jesus. For contemporary Christians outside of the apostolic period, the Spirit reminds, directs, and points to the words of Jesus and others as preserved in the Bible. The Spirit speaks a word to the believer tailored to the believer's circumstances and situation that is, at all times, entirely consistent with the Bible. Indeed, the substance of the Spirit's promptings and guidance comes from the Bible itself. In sum, what I call the Christian conscience is the active work of the Holy Spirit in leading, guiding, nudging, and prompting the believer to act consistently with what she knows to be true as revealed in the Bible.

### *Tying the Threads of the Redeemed Conscience Together*

And now, how should we tie all the disparate threads together regarding the capacity of conscience? Jesus' immediate hearers are not the only ones who should understand his injunction of God and neighbor love as binding as law. Traditional theological acknowledgments of Jesus' divinity give weight, heft, and yes, *bindingness* to his words. It is bindingness that is borne out of humility. This is a humility that, when one reads about him, realizes that he was conceived and born under unbelievable circumstances, worked miracles among thousands of people that defied all natural understandings of belief, and once executed, was brought to life again – itself unbelievable to "eyes [that] fail to see" (see Mark 8:18). Instead of being an unsophisticated path of moral knowledge, Christians who are determined to obey Jesus because it is Jesus speaking the words – believable despite his unbelievable circumstances – themselves display a theological plainness and trust that leads them to believe, "trust, and obey."[13]

The bindingness of Christ's two laws of love are not, essentially, binding because of any consequences that I fear if I abrogate them. I find it very instructive in this regard that David Green and his family (of Hobby Lobby) were willing to fight the contraception mandate, even when acquiescence to it would have meant certain escape from its retrograde penalties.[14] They did not let their apprehension of what might befall their collective position, namely, their wealth, limit what their consciences were instructing them to do. In the same way, Christ's laws of love and the apostolic instruction found elsewhere in the New Testament are binding on me, because, like Hart's quintessential (civil) law-abiding person, I find that, as a regenerated, sanctified believer in Jesus, I now share in Christ's own "internal point of view."[15] My heart, my emotions, my dispositions, my judgments, my all, have been fundamentally changed so that, in the core of my very being, "[he] is mine, and I am his" (Song of Sol. 2:16, paraphrase). Really, I can do no other than prioritize these foundational mechanisms in my conscience.

To conclude this section: for the Christian, conscience is a capacity of the regenerated and sanctified heart, mind, and will, conditioned by the believer's desire to love God and love neighbor, by obeying what she reads in the Bible (especially the New Testament), as conditioned by the guidance of the Holy Spirit and wise counsel of other, mature Christians.

## BEING BOUND AND BEING FREED

To reemphasize, for the evangelical, conscience is a manifestation of the redeemed/regenerated person who has been saved by grace and who has begun the process of sanctification through the inner working of the Holy Spirit. Importantly, the grist for her conscience is not keeping the labyrinthine maze of ceremonial and civil law found in the Old Testament, which she could never do, even if she tried. Rather, she is bound to the law of love – the

[13] Indeed, this author grew up in a denomination that frequently sang the hymn "Trust and Obey" in worship services. See "Trust and Obey," lyrics by John Henry Sammis and music by Daniel Brink Towner (1877) in *Songs of Faith and Praise*, ed. Alton H. Howard (West Monroe, LA: Howard Publishing Co., 1994), 915.

[14] See *Hobby Lobby*, Complaint, ¶144.

[15] See, e.g., Scott J. Shapiro, "What Is the Internal Point of View?" *Fordham Law Review* 75 (2006): 1157 and H. L. A. Hart, *The Concept of Law*, 2nd ed. (Oxford: Oxford University Press, 1994), 89.

heart of the moral law in both the Old and New Testaments – which, when kept, always manifests itself in love of both God and neighbor.

The sanctified conscience continues to find manifestations of God's moral law in the Old Testament, yet his attention is focused on ethical instruction as it is revealed in the New Testament. And here we have two important theological points to make. First, keeping the moral precepts, instructions, and even commands found in the New Testament does not, indeed, it cannot, affect the Christian's forensic position with God (see Eph. 2:8, 9). If salvation and reorientation are manifestations of grace that are God's alone to grant, then my acts or omissions can neither add nor detract from that grace. Second, the moral precepts, instructions, and commands found in the New Testament function in that way for those who have "eyes because they see" and "ears because they hear" (see Matt. 13:16). That is, the precepts, instructions, and commands of the New Testament are binding on those who have been saved. While they do provide warning for those who are not part of the Christian community, they are not binding on them. The New Testament is the church's book, and those who find themselves loyal first to the church will find themselves heeding moral instruction and reproof in the church's book. And that is why this perspective on conscience is just that – one perspective on conscience. To be sure, it is a perspective that should be honored and given space to act, but it is just one perspective.

The bindingness of the New Testament and its provision of substantive content for the Christian conscience is reflective of how the Christian processes and orders the "overlapping jurisdictions" to which he is subject.[16] In practically every case of conscientious objection to some positive law of the state – whether it is the Green and Hahn families' objections to subsidizing abortifacients or other examples, the objector has never demanded a wholesale exemption from all laws of the community. The evangelical can live, indeed desires to live, in both the earthly kingdom of law and the heavenly kingdom of grace. But when there is a conflict between these two jurisdictions, he always chooses the obligations of the kingdom in which he will live eternally (see, generally, Acts 4). This, I think, is one of the most convincing reasons why conscience should be given wide berth and acceptance within the political community: its demands are relatively mild, all things considered.

The Christian finds herself irresistibly bound to the internal perspective of Christ's rule, reign, and manifestations of his will (namely, the Bible). It is this reign to which she gives the primary loyalty of her life. But she also finds

[16] See, e.g., Michael J. DeBoer, "Forward: Overlapping Jurisdictions, Religion, Conscience, and Fundamental Questions," *Faulkner Law Review* 4 (Spring) (2013): 299–320.

herself bound in the internal perspective of the civil legal system to which she must give a (large) measure of respect and loyalty. She obeys the law because it exists and can be accepted as law.[17] As with her obedience to the "easy yoke" of Christ, she willingly obeys the civil law not because she fears the consequences of not obeying the law, but rather, she fundamentally seeks to be a law-abiding person (see Matt. 11:30 and Rom. 13:1–6). She knows that what it means to be a citizen or American is wrapped up, in large part, with acquiescing to the rule of law in her life. But, because she has these divided loyalties, she has, in a very real sense, a divided mind. The contemporary Christian is very much caught up in the traditional Lutheran conundrum of one foot in the kingdom of this world and one foot in the kingdom of heaven.[18]

Exercising conscience should be a troubling concept for the evangelical Christian because of her divided loyalties between the earthly and heavenly realms. Theologically speaking, the Christian is fully committed to proclaiming and living in the goodness of God's creation and everything that is derivative from creation, including human law. However, Reformation luminaries acknowledge that law serves more than one purpose. Law, in Luther and Melanchthon's estimation, restrains, reproves, and teaches.[19] It provides a modicum of order for an earthly realm that is beset by sin and sinful people. This is a key insight from Luther. Though it is descriptively true that humans would still need law even if "[all] men were angels," Luther was not necessarily considering the coordinating function of law.[20] For Luther, but especially for Melanchthon, law is multivalent – in its human form, law teaches the Christian to be a good citizen and obedient follower of the prince. Earthly iterations of civil law can model the best of God's law found in the Bible. But law also warns and punishes. It follows with severe sanctions after disobedience. Law manifests with consequences to punish those who cannot restrain themselves. So, for Luther, human law is both/and not either/or.[21]

Importantly, one of the problems of holding up a historical figure – even foundational ones like Luther and Melanchthon as examples for contemporary praxis – is that the exemplar's situation is likely to be much different than our own. For example, even though Luther thought of the civil law as having a coercive element, he did not see civil law and divine law as found in the Bible, as working at cross-purposes. There are at least a few reasons for this: (1)

17 See Shapiro, "What Is the Internal Point of View?," 1160.

18 See Witte, *Law and Protestantism*, 87–117.

19 Ibid., 101–5; 127–29.

20 James Madison, *Federalist* 51, in *The Founders Constitution*, vol. 1, eds. Philip B. Kurland and Ralph Lerner (Chicago, IL: University of Chicago Press, 1987): 330.

21 See Witte, *Law and Protestantism*, 101–5, 127–38.

the temporal jurisdictions in Reformation Germany were smaller and less diverse than contemporary America; (2) the civil law was less developed in Reformation Germany than in contemporary America; there was less law with which to be concerned; and (3) there was an emphasis in Reformation Germany upon making the civil law consonant with natural law norms, even though the state and church were thought of as separate jurisdictions.

Thus, the principle to be gleaned from a Lutheran understanding of both law and anthropology is the tension between competing realms. Though in Luther and Melanchthon's day, the principles and precepts of the civil law might have mostly lined up with what the prince could glean from the natural law as articulated in the Ten Commandments, there might be times when the prince's law might diverge from what he found there.[22] However, in contemporary America, the sheer magnitude, scope, and amount of law(s) and the many different motivations that go into their making oftentimes work against what Christians can read of God's revealed will in the Bible.

Luther's insight into conscience is that it has both a restraining and liberating function for the Christian. If the Christian is *bound* to follow the moral precepts, instructions, and commands of the New Testament, he is also *freed* to do so as well.[23] The Christian is always and forever *coram Deo* ("in the presence of God"). Thus, as Matt Ley argues, "the conscience is our standing before God, coram deo. As such it always searching for that which it can be made subject to, the god to which it can bow."[24] The *coram Deo* aspect of Reformation theology is sobering, because it forces the Christian to realize that all of her life, but especially her conscience, is continually in the knowledge and judgment of God. She is therefore obligated to choose wisely when exercising her conscience.

The Apostle Paul summarized it thusly: "In the same way, count yourselves dead to sin but alive to God in Christ Jesus" (Rom. 6:11). The moral law within the New Testament not only constrains the Christian's actions but it also provides the road signs of moral and spiritual excellence, without which she self-thwarts her journey of sanctification. This is the paradox of conscience. Conscience may seem to be prohibiting or restricting a certain course of action, reminding me that God's moral law is to be obeyed when faced with a countervailing direction from human law. God's moral law is not

[22] Ibid., 137, 138.

[23] Matt Ley, "Luther's Understanding of the Bound Conscience," *Journal of Lutheran Ethics* 10, no. 11, (2010), elca.org/JLE/Articles/246.

[24] Ibid.

prohibition for prohibition's sake. It also frees the Christian to fulfill that which is best about God's moral law.

Conscience, for Luther, is not only a negative function. It not only binds, but it also frees the Christian. The Apostle Paul says it thusly: "The love of Christ compels us . . ." (2 Cor. 5:14 NKJV). Though there are many present examples of this, the best one I can find is, again, the Green family of the *Hobby Lobby* case. This family has always seen it as their duty to provide competitive wages and fringe benefits, like health insurance for their employees, even before the 2010 passage of the large employer mandate in the Affordable Care Act (ACA).[25] To be sure, before the passage of the ACA, the duties that the Greens sensed about providing health insurance were not legal duties. Instead, they perceived that the dignity of those working for them required care, provision, and maintenance. They perceived that one of the inherent obligations of employers was to provide, not only a paycheck but also other forms of compensation that would allow employees to care for their whole persons. They perceived that, to live according to the full counsel of the Bible, loving one's neighbor as oneself required care for the neighbor's (in this case their employees') health needs.[26] In short, they perceived that a just relationship between employer and employee required them to provide health insurance for their store employees *even though the law did not require it*. The Greens' consciences were *freed* to act, not because of what the law compelled them to do, but because of what their consciences instructed them to do. And importantly, after receiving that instruction, they acted upon it.

Another example is striking. In Ryan Anderson's book, *Truth Overruled: The Future of Marriage and Religious Freedom*, he tells the story of Barronelle Stutzman, the Washington state florist who refused to provide flowers for the wedding of long-time customer Robert Ingersoll and his gay partner. Word of Ms. Stutzman's refusal to provide the wedding flowers made its way back to the Washington Attorney General. Once a judge got a hold of her, she was found liable under Washington's anti-discrimination and consumer protection laws and was slapped with massive fines that threatened her shop as a going concern. The Washington Attorney General offered Ms. Stutzman a Faustian bargain: pay a $2,001 fine and promise to provide floral arrangements for gay weddings, and the crushing fine would be rescinded. Ms. Stutzman refused, and in her touching letter to the Attorney General, she latched onto the striking words of the Washington Constitution, which promised all

[25] See *Hobby Lobby*, Complaint, ¶50–52.

[26] Ibid., ¶52: "As part of their religious obligations, the Green family also provides excellent health insurance coverage to Hobby Lobby's and Mardel's employees through a self-insured plan."

Washingtonians: "Freedom of conscience in all matters of religious sentiment."[27]

This Washington constitutional provision (and similar provisions in other state constitutions) beautifully illustrates in the positive law what I mean by being both bound and freed to act in conscience. Anderson reports that Ms. Stutzman served Mr. Ingersoll on a number of occasions and considered him to be a friend. She refused to provide floral arrangements for Ingersoll's wedding after a caring yet frank conversation that it was her religious scruples that prevented her from celebrating his wedding with the product of her work.[28]

In my estimation, this anecdote signals four important conclusions about conscience:(1) Barronelle Stutzman refused to provide flowers for Robert Ingersoll's wedding because her conscience instructed her not to. (2) She believed that, under her state's constitution, her conscience had the capacity or prerogative to refuse to provide those flowers. (3) That primary law recognized that conscience was free to act (or refuse to act, as the case may be), because of her religious convictions, thereby signaling that conscience and religion (or "religious sentiment" or religious instruction) are in fact different things, yet they are very intimately related. (4) Stutzman's general work as a florist was animated by her religious beliefs. In other words, Stutzman believed that providing flowers for a wedding ceremony meant mixing her work with the truth claims of what is proclaimed in that wedding ceremony. It would violate something at the core of her very being to lend her approval and participate through her creative work in a truth claim that she did not believe was, in fact, true. So, in one sense, Stutzman was free to offer her services as a florist as a gift of love to God and her neighbors; yet she was bound to refuse her services when those services would be seen as her approbation of something at its core that was false.[29]

[27] Ryan T. Anderson, *Truth Overruled: The Future of Marriage and Religious Freedom* (Washington, DC: Regnery, 2015), 96–97. Since Anderson penned his account of Stutzman's ordeal, she lost her appeal in the state of Washington's court system. See *State* v. *Arlene's Flowers, Inc.*, 389 P.3d 543 (2017). This ruling was appealed to the United States Supreme Court, which remanded the case to the Washington Supreme Court and ordered it to reconsider its judgment in light of the US Supreme Court's decision in the *Masterpiece Cakeshop* case. 138 S.Ct. 2671 (2018). Upon remand, the Washington Supreme Court again ruled against Stutzman, holding, among other things, that she did violate Washington's anti-discrimination law. *State* v. *Arlene's Flowers, Inc.*, 441 P.3d 1203 (2019).

[28] Anderson, *Truth Overruled*, 97.

[29] Ibid., 96–98.

## LIVING UNDER THE JUDGMENT OF GOD

The other great and foundational Protestant reformer, John Calvin, described conscience as opening up the Christian to the judgment of God. Part of Calvin's understanding of conscience was that it was a faculty of knowledge – "to note and spy out all his secrets that nothing may remain buried in the darkness. Whence the ancient proverb: 'Conscience is a thousand witnesses.'"[30] Clearly, for Calvin, conscience was (again, in part) the openness of the person before God to be accused, sanctioned, or approved. Conscience, therefore, has much to do with God's judgment over the person.[31]

Contrast Calvin's understanding of conscience as the judge with the broader Reformation mantra of *coram Deo*, which speaks of the entire person – affections, mind, and will – that is, the Christian, living her life entirely before the watchful eye of God. This makes sense, as the New Testament clearly witnesses that God will judge the human heart, thoughts, and actions (see 1 Cor. 4:5, Rom. 2:16, and Rom. 2:6). Because of God's holiness and righteous standards, all human beings will be judged. This judgment is ultimately a part of God's nature and goodness. Because God created the world and see that it was good (though later ontologically affected by the Fall), that means that God retains a full measure of ownership and stewardship over his creation. God superintends that which he creates. God will judge that which he has created (humankind) according to his own perfect standards. For those who have not "cloth[ed] [themselves] with Christ" (Rom. 13:14; see also Gal. 3:27), this judgment will be a forensic reckoning into eternity. For those who know and are known by God, the judgment will reckon, not so much the believer's eternal security but rather her relative status within the eternal kingdom of God. For everyone, part of the judgment will consist of how the person handled matters of conscience when presented to her.

This makes it all the more imperative for the Christian, then, to prime the pump of her conscience so that it acts in ways that are consonant with the arc of the Bible and the Holy Spirit's leading. It is therefore not so much an impending fear of doom that rouses the Christian into making sure that her

[30] John Calvin, *Institutes of the Christian Religion*, 2 vols., ed. John T. McNeil, trans. and indexed by Ford Lewis Battles, 3.19.15 (Philadelphia, PA: Westminster Press, 1960), 1:848, quoting ("Conscience is a thousand witnesses"), Quintilian, *Institutes of Oratory* v.xi.41 (LCL Quintilian II., 294f.). See also, Matthew Lee Anderson, "Our Neutered Consciences: Calvin and the Awareness of God's Judgment," *Mere Orthodoxy Blog*, December 10, 2009, mereorthodoxy.com/our-neutered-consciences-calvin-and-the-awareness-of-gods-judgment/ (discussing, among other things, this passage from Calvin).

[31] Anderson, "Our Neutered Consciences."

conscience is properly formed, but it is rather anticipation – an eager expectation that a test is coming – and a desire to have the proper tools to pass the test once it comes.

But the judgment of God is also about the here and now as much as it is about the hereafter. Discerning and then acting properly in the moment when conscience is deployed leads to peace of mind and heart. Discerning and then acting against the promptings of conscience leads to disquiet, unease, and ill feelings. In this case, the Christian knows that she has truly *violated* something important to her.

### *Peace after Judgment*

Take two contemporary examples. The Kentucky clerk, Kim Davis, is a bit of an outlier when it comes to God's judgment because she publicly claimed that, in her estimation, she would be condemned to Hell were she to facilitate same-sex marriages in her office.[32] Nevertheless, Davis's conscience-based resistance led her to peacefully go to jail, because she defied a federal judge's order to issue marriage licenses to same-sex couples under her name.[33]

Again, I come back to the Green family. If the Greens weren't going to lose all of their fortune, were they to lose *Burwell* v. *Hobby Lobby*, their company would have stood to pay astronomical, nine-figure fines for refusing to provide proper health insurance to their employees (without the mandated abortifacients). Yet, what did they do? Well, it is clear what they did not do. They did not take the easy way out. It would have been much easier, I suspect, to bow out of the fight with the Department of Health and Human Services even before litigation began and meekly acquiesce to putting the four controversial drugs and devices back into their insurance plans. But that is not what they did. They fought, and not for the sake of fighting or for notoriety. Rather, they fought based on a principle that the money they controlled would not subsidize the taking of innocent human life. And in the end, the Greens were at peace no matter how the Supreme Court ruled.[34]

[32] Abby Ohlheiser, "Kentucky Clerk Kim Davis on Gay Marriage Licenses: 'It Is a Heaven or Hell Decision,'" Acts of Faith newsletter, *Washington Post*, September 1, 2015, www.washingtonpost.com/news/acts-of-faith/wp/2015/09/01/kentucky-clerk-kim-davis-on-gay-marriage-licenses-it-is-a-heaven-or-hell-decision/.

[33] "Kentucky Clerk Kim Davis Released from Jail," *CBS News*, September 8, 2015, cbsnews.com, www.cbsnews.com/news/kentucky-clerk-kim-davis-released-from-jail/.

[34] Cathy Lynn Grossman, "Hobby Lobby's Steve Green Stands on Faith against Obamacare Mandate," Religion News Service, March 17, 2014, www.washingtonpost.com/national/religion/hobby-lobbys-steve-green-stands-on-faith-against-obamacare-mandate/2014/03/17/d17d0960-ae18-11e3-b8b3-44b1d1cd4c1f_story.html.

## CONCLUSION

Though conscience, like love, might be a "many splendored thing," for the Christian, conscience's essence is relatively straightforward. It is the capacity of the transformed heart and mind to perceive truth, as announced in the Bible and as taught and reinforced by the Holy Spirit, and finally as acted upon by the believer's changed will. Sometimes conscience tells the believer to stop and go no further, and sometimes it tells the believer to "go" in service to the neighbor. But whether it signals to the believer to bid or stay, the action taken at the direction of conscience is always borne out of love for the God who redeemed and transformed the believer and the neighbor who God also created and loves.

## RECOMMENDED READING


Bavinck, Herman. *Reformed Ethics*, vol. 1: *Created, Fallen, and Converted Humanity*, edited by John Bolt. Grand Rapids, MI: Baker Academic, 2019.

Chapman, Nathan S. "Disentangling Conscience and Religion" *University of Illinois Law Review* 2013, no. 4 (2013): 1457–1501.

Dreisbach, Daniel L., and Mark David Hall, eds. *The Sacred Rights of Conscience: Selected Readings on Religious Liberty and Church-State Relations in the American Founding*. Indianapolis, IN: Liberty Fund, 2009.

Foxgrover, David. "Conscience." In *The Westminster Handbook to Reformed Theology*, edited by Donald K. McKim. Louisville, KY: Westminster John Knox Press, 2001: 41–42.

Hopgood, Miles. "Consciences Bound and Liberated," *Dialog* 58, no. 2 (June 2019): 131–39.

*Masterpiece Cakeshop, Ltd.* v. *Colorado Civil Rights Comm'n*, 138 S.Ct. 1719 (2018).

Ojakangas, Mika. *The Voice of Conscience: A Political Genealogy of Western Ethical Experience*. New York, NY: Bloomsbury Academic, 2013.

Sorabji, Richard. *Moral Conscience through the Ages: Fifth Century BCE to the Present*. Oxford: Oxford University Press, 2014.

Strohm, Paul. *Conscience: A Very Short Introduction*. Oxford: Oxford University Press, 2011.

Zachman, Randall C. *The Assurance of Faith: Conscience in the Theology of Martin Luther and John Calvin*. Minneapolis, MN: Fortress Press, 1993.

# 9

# Pierre Bayle

## *An Enlightened Alternative to John Locke*

EDWARD ANDREW

### INTRODUCTION: BAYLE BETWEEN REFORMATION AND ENLIGHTENMENT

Pierre Bayle has been widely admired as one of the fathers of Enlightenment, more a follower of the tradition of Montaigne's skepticism than an adherent of Calvin's moral certainty. Voltaire, Hume, and Gibbon proclaimed Bayle as one of their own. Gibbon enthusiastically repeated Bayle's principle: "I am most truly a Protestant, for I protest indifferently against all systems and all sects."[1] Bayle has been recognized as a central figure in the European Enlightenment, whether as part of a Protestant,[2] or a secular, anti-Christian[3] Enlightenment. This chapter will examine the combination of tolerant skepticism and Calvinist certitude, of scholarly openness and resolute commitment, in Bayle's bold and original justification of erroneous conscience.

Bayle's originality consisted in upholding views of conscience both as the infallible voice of God within human beings but also as subject to errors of judgment. He combined a traditional Calvinist teaching on the certitude of the call of conscience with a novel argument about why human conscientious

[1] *The Miscellaneous Works of Edward Gibbon, Esq. in 5 Volumes*, ed. John Lord Sheffield (London: John Murray, 1814), 1:69–70.

[2] See Élizabeth Labrousse, *Pierre Bayle* (The Hague: Martinus Nijhoff, 1963); John Kilcullen, *Sincerity and Truth: Essays on Arnauld, Bayle and Toleration* (Oxford: Clarendon Press, 1988); J. B. Schneewind, *The Invention of Autonomy: A History of Moral Philosophy* (Cambridge: Cambridge University Press, 1998); Charles Griswold Jr., *Adam Smith and the Virtues of Enlightenment* (Cambridge: Cambridge University Press, 1999); Edward G. Andrew, *Patrons of Enlightenment* (Toronto: University of Toronto Press, 2006).

[3] See H. T. Mason, *Pierre Bayle and Voltaire* (Oxford: Oxford University Press, 1963); Craig C. Brush, *Montaigne and Bayle: Variations on the Theme of Skepticism* (The Hague: Martinus Nijhoff, 1966); Robert C. Bartlett, *The Idea of Enlightenment: A Post-Mortem Study* (Toronto: University of Toronto Press, 2001); Ronald Beiner, *Civil Religion: A Dialogue in the History of Political Philosophy* (Cambridge: Cambridge University Press, 2011).

judgments could err, an argument that was congenial to eighteenth-century Enlightenment thinkers. This chapter explores Bayle's conception of conscience and erroneous conscience and demonstrates how Bayle differed not only from Roman Catholic conceptions of conscience but also from an emergent empirical understanding of consciousness that was espoused by the eighteenth-century Enlightenment. In doing so, Bayle's conception of conscience will be contrasted with his contemporary John Locke's ideas about conscience and consciousness, and while indicating how their differences pertain to questions about religious toleration and heresy and also to the right of revolution against oppressive governments.

The issue dividing Bayle, who thought lawless sedition was to be avoided, and Locke, who justified the right of revolution against Catholic monarchs and arbitrary governments, turns on the relationship of conscience and law. Two contemporary thinkers, Harold M. Schulweis and Harold J. Berman, present contrasting accounts of conscience that clarify aspects of Bayle's and Locke's understanding of conscience. Schulweis sees conscience as standing in opposition to law, whereas Berman finds conscience also embedded in law. The chapter will conclude with an assessment of the reason why Bayle's understanding of conscience is pertinent to contemporary self-understanding, particularly with respect to the question of human equality.

The issue of erroneous conscience was dramatically raised at the Diet of Worms when Johann von Eck entreated the schismatic Luther: "Lay aside your conscience, Martin; you must lay it aside because it is in error." Luther famously replied: "My conscience is captive to the Word of God. I cannot and will not retract anything, since it is neither safe nor right to go against conscience. I cannot do otherwise, here I stand, may God help me. Amen."[4] Neither von Eck nor Luther thought that their judgments were possibly mistaken. The central question is: How can conscience err if it is the inner voice of God?

Some Catholic theologians claim that St. Thomas Aquinas supported the right of erroneous conscience insofar as he thought that pagans who converted to Christianity expediently but against their beliefs were morally wrong, but Pope St. John Paul II, in *Veritatis Splendor* (1993), also citing St. Thomas, declared: "It is never acceptable to confuse a 'subjective' error about the moral good with the 'objective' truth rationally proposed to men in virtue of his end, or to make the moral value of an act performed with a true and correct conscience equivalent to the moral value of an act performed by following

[4] Martin Luther, *Works*, ed. Jaroslav Pelikan (St. Louis, MO: Concordia Publishing House, 1958), 32:112, 130.

the judgment of an erroneous conscience." *Veritatis Splendor* maintained that "the Catholic Church is by the will of Christ the teacher of truth." *The Catechism of the Catholic Church* (2000) declared the duty of Catholics "to correct the errors of moral conscience."[5]

Bayle's justification of erroneous conscience challenges the notion of "objective" truth or transforms it into "subjective" truthfulness. The diligence of one's search for salvation matters more than the path one has taken, and the sincerity of one's convictions counts more than their correctness. Two centuries after Bayle, Cardinal Newman knew he was walking on eggshells when he wrote: "Certainly, if I am obliged to bring religion into after-dinner toasts (which indeed does not seem quite the thing) I shall drink – to the Pope, if you please – still, to Conscience first, and to the Pope afterwards."[6] Is conscience anchored in the tradition of the fathers of the Catholic Church, or bound by the Bible, with each person their own interpreter of the Bible, as Luther thought, or free-floating, guided by an inner gyroscope and compass? The European Enlightenment rejected conscience as church doctrine, as biblical revelation, and as inner monitor of conduct.

The German noun *Gewissen* (conscience) is related to the adjective *gewiss* (certain, sure) and the noun *Gewissheit* (certainty). The European Enlightenment constituted a concerted assault on unwarranted certainty. Locke's *Essay concerning Human Understanding* reconceived certainty as a kind of probability;[7] moral certainty is "the highest degree of probability."[8] Locke's *Essay* denounced the idea of conscience as a certain innate guide to moral conduct; conscience is not "written on their Hearts" but is the product of their upbringing, education, and environment. Conscience, Locke wrote "is nothing else, but our own Opinion or Judgment of the Moral Rectitude or Pravity of our own Actions."[9]

5 Germain Grisez and Russell Shaw, "Conscience: Knowledge of Moral Truth," and Richard M. Gula, "The Moral Conscience" in *Conscience*, ed. Charles E. Curran (New York, NY: Paulist Press, 2004), 39–50 and 51–64. This volume also contains *Veritas Splendor* and *The Catechism of the Catholic Church* at 75, 77, and 81.

6 John Henry Newman, *A Letter to the Duke of Norfolk on the Occasion of Mr. Gladstone's Recent Expostulation* (London: Pickering, 1875), 66. One wonders if some of the contributors to Curran's *Conscience* would drink to Newman's toast.

7 John Locke, *An Essay concerning Human Understanding* (London: Thomas Basett, 1690), IV. XVI.6–7.

8 See Barbara J. Shapiro, *Probability and Certainty in Seventeenth-Century England: A Study of the Relationships between Natural Science, Religion, History, Law and Literature* (Princeton, NJ: Princeton University Press, 1983); Barbara J. Shapiro, *"Beyond Reasonable Doubt" and "Probable Cause": Historical Perspectives on the Anglo-American Law of Evidence* (Berkeley, CA: University of California Press, 1991).

9 Locke, *Essay*, I.iii.8.

Locke made a distinction between conscience and consciousness. The latter word was coined in 1678 by Ralph Cudworth in *The True Intellectual System of the Universe*.[10] Until then, awareness and self-awareness were merged with the capacity for moral judgment in the French and English word *conscience* and the German word, *Gewissen*. Locke's *Essay concerning Human Understanding* not only dismissed conscience as an innate practical principle but also established consciousness as constitutive of personal identity or the existence of the self.[11] Christian Wolff's translation of Locke's *Essay* created the German word denoting consciousness (*Bewusstsein*), which was previously contained in, and undistinguished from, *Gewissen* (conscience). The French rejected Leibniz's suggestion of *consciosité* for the English *consciousness*, and Locke's French translators, Pierre Coste and Jean Leclerc, had difficulties making the distinction between consciousness and conscience, since the French *conscience* means both self-awareness and moral discernment.[12] In the entry for conscience in Diderot's and D'Alembert's *Encyclopédie*, a sigh of lament is evident when the old-fashioned theological sense of conscience is undifferentiated from the philosophic sense: "What the English express by the word *consciousness* can only be rendered in French by periphrasis."[13] Locke's distinction between conscience and consciousness might be said to culminate in Freud's distinction between the unconscious superego and the conscious ego.

Opposition to conscience as an innate practical principle, or indeed to the conception of innate ideas, might well be definitive of Enlightenment. In his *Discours Préliminaire à L'Encyclopédie*, D'Alembert wanted to put his compatriot, Descartes, on the pedestal with the revered fathers of Enlightenment (Bacon, Locke, and Newton) but, since Descartes was a proponent of innate ideas, his approach to philosophy was antithetical to the expanding, empirical knowledge promoted by *L'Encyclopédie*.

The enlightened notion of policing by social approbation and disapprobation replaced sixteenth and seventeenth century ideas of conscience as the divine cop within human beings. Locke thought that "esteem and disgrace are ... the most powerful incentives of the mind." Social censure and

[10] Ralph Cudworth, *The True Intellectual System of the Universe* (London: Richard Royston, 1678).

[11] Locke, *Essay*, II.i.11; II.xxvii.16–17.

[12] Catherine Glyn Davies, "Conviction and Sentiment Interieur," in *Conscience As Consciousness: The Idea of Self-Awareness in French Philosophic Writing from Descartes to Diderot* (Oxford: The Voltaire Society, 1990).

[13] Denis Diderot and Jean D'Alembert, *L'Encyclopédieou Dictionnaire raisonné des sciences, des arts and des métiers* (1751) (New York, NY: Microprint Corporation, 1969), t. 3, 902.

approbation are the most powerful motivating factors in human nature and history, generally more powerful than divine law and civil law in shaping human conduct.[14] Hutcheson, Hume, Smith, Voltaire, La Mettrie, Helvétius, Holbach, Diderot, and D'Alembert agreed with Locke that moral conduct is the product of the desire for praise or approbation and the fear of social censure and disgrace and is more effectively regulated by love of social approbation and fear of social censure than by love of God and fear of His punishment for sin. Character and reputation become synonymous in the eighteenth century; the inner compass became a radar to meet, or nor clash with, social expectations. Freedom *of* conscience ceased to mean freedom *for* the inner certainty of conscience; rather, it signified a tolerant skepticism of all religious claims and a preference for institutional arrangements fostering civic peace, rather than doctrinal truth.

## PIERRE BAYLE'S PHILOSOPHIC COMMENTARY ON THE GOSPEL

Bayle's *A Philosophical Commentary on These Words of the Gospel, Luke XIV.23 "Compel Them to Come in, That My House May Be Full"* is a magnificent argument for religious toleration but, despite its title, is not biblical hermeneutics or interpretation. Bayle did not rely on biblical exegesis to conclude that compulsion in religion is a violation of the soul, that forcing people into the church is driving them out, and that "Non-Toleration is the sole cause of all the Disorders which are falsely imputed to Toleration."[15] The light of natural reason or "the Conscience of Right and Wrong imprinted in the Souls of all Men," not the tradition of canonical interpretation of Scripture, is the rule by which the Bible is to be interpreted.[16] Bayle's view that natural reason is sufficient to interpret Scripture was one of the grounds upon which Voltaire, Hume, and Gibbon held Bayle up as one of their own. But Bayle's view of conscience as "the eternal Law and Rule antecedent to all Religions of positive Institution" and "the primary, original, and infallible rule of Rectitude" imprinted by God on human minds was contrary to the Enlightenment's rejection of innate ideas and its espousal of the mind as originally a blank sheet of paper, subsequently printed by one's upbringing and the experience of one's surroundings. With respect to conscience,

[14] Locke, *Essay*, II.xxvii.10–12.

[15] Pierre Bayle, *A Philosophical Commentary on These Words of the Gospel, Luke XIV.13 Compel Them to Come in, That My House May Be Full*, eds. John Kilcullen and Chandran Kukathas (Indianapolis, IN: Liberty Fund, 2003), 57.

[16] Ibid., 66, 70.

Elisabeth Labrousse is undoubtedly correct in asserting that Bayle was not just a skeptic in the tradition from Montaigne to Voltaire but a religious thinker on a path between Calvin and Rousseau.[17]

In his interpretation of Luke 14:23, Bayle asserted that since compulsion is directly contrary to the spirit of the Gospels – and he did not provide any biblical warrant for his premise – "the literal sense therefore of these words must needs be false."[18] He did not examine the Bible for other senses of the Greek word *anagkazô* than physical force, such as a pressing invitation or an urgent entreaty. Nor did Bayle examine the context of Luke14:23: "And the lord said unto the servant, Go out unto the highways and hedges, and compel them to come in, that my house may be filled." Luke 14:13 bears the message of exalting the humble – "the poor, the maimed, the lame and the blind" – and those lurking in the highways and hedges seem lower on the social scale than the poor and disabled. Since those who are normally scorned might well be reluctant to accept an invitation to a rich man's feast, the rich man or lord might have said to his servant, "don't take no for an answer," or "I insist," without the intention that the servant should drag the reluctant into the feast. Rather than challenging St. Augustine's construction that those in the highways and hedges are heretics, Bayle took the Augustinian interpretation as a historical fact justifying the Catholic Church's persecution of Donatists in Augustine's time and the Catholic Church's persecution of Huguenots in his own time.[19] In countering St. Augustine on heresy and schism, Bayle occasionally referred to the Bible indicating that St. Paul was "the only inspir'd Writer" to allude to schisms in the church. But Bayle provided no biblical warrant for his certainty that compulsion is both wicked and stupid or counterproductive. Conscience, not Scripture, provides us all with "the eternal Laws of Just and Honest" and thus "the reveal'd Truth was subordinate to the natural light in him."[20]

All human beings, not just Christians, are guided by conscience. Bayle, in his *Dictionnaire Historique et Critique*, wrote that reputed atheists, such as Hobbes and Spinoza, lived virtuous lives. In that work, Bayle also described a

[17] Elisabeth Labrousse, *Bayle* (Oxford: Oxford University Press, 1983), 5.

[18] Bayle, *Philosophical Commentary*, 80.

[19] Bayle had much at stake with respect to Catholic views of heresy. Raised a Protestant, he converted to Catholicism in his early twenties but reverted back to Protestantism a year later and qualified as a heretic in Catholic doctrine. When the Protestant academy in Sedan was closed down, Bayle fled to Rotterdam where he published works offensive to clerical authorities in France. His brother Jacob was imprisoned in Pierre's stead, and after being tortured, died in prison. See Labrousse, *Bayle*, 26–33; Hubert Bost, *Pierre Bayle* (Paris: Fayard, 2006), ch. 8.

[20] Bayle, *Philosophical Commentary*, 70.

sect of atheists, founded by Matthias Knuzen in 1673, called the Conscienciaries, who asserted "that there is no other God, no other Religion, no other lawful Magistracy, but *Conscience*, which teaches every man the three fundamental Principles of the Law, *to hurt no body, to live honestly, and to give every one his due*." Bayle wrote that the Consciencaries were "horribly impious", even "stark mad." However, he added, "the impertincies of this German [Matthias Knuzen] shew us that the notions of natural religion, the Ideas of the *honestum*, the impressions of reason, in a word the inward light of conscience, may continue in the mind of a man, even when the notion of the being of God, and the belief of another world are intirely rooted out."[21]

While Locke's *Letters concerning Toleration* denied toleration to Catholics and atheists, and his *Reasonableness of Christianity* denied toleration to Jews and Muslims as well as Catholics and atheists, Bayle advocated universal toleration – to atheists, Socinians (followers of sixteenth-century Italian theologians Laelius and Faustus Socinus whose doctrines are similar to modern Unitarians), Jews, Muslims, as well as Christians. To be sure, in the wake of the Revocation of the Edict of Nantes and the torturing to death of his brother Jacob for publishing Bayle's works, Bayle thought toleration of Catholics should be conditional on Catholic toleration of Protestants and could be limited on pragmatic grounds insofar as Catholic subjects of Protestant rulers retain their civil rights to life and property.[22] In subsequent years, repelled by Protestant intolerance of his former friend, Pierre Jurieu, and Calvinist expatriates in Holland, as well as by anti-Catholicism in Britain, Bayle ceased to qualify his advocacy of universal toleration. In addition, Bayle argued against prevailing practices in both France and England of bringing nonconformists into the national churches by reserving governmental, military, civil service, university, and professional posts to Catholics and Anglicans respectively. Bayle wrote: "I should be for a Law excluding new Converts from all the Privileges and Favors of which they were incapable by their former Religion; because thus we might be assur'd, that their Conversion proceeded purely from Conviction, and that they did not play the Hypocrites."[23] In contrast to Locke's implausible claim that religious conviction cannot be coerced by the state, Bayle recognized that the suppression of Calvinist dissent in seventeenth-century France and England had been effective by excluding dissenters from professional and governmental careers. Locke's view is

[21] Pierre Bayle, A *General Dictionary* (London: James Bettenham, 1738), 6:554–55.
[22] Bayle, *Philosophical Commentary*, 191–93, 572–74.
[23] Ibid., 192.

implausible because, as Hume indicated, the children of converts would hardly be told of the hypocrisy of their fathers' and grandfathers' conversions.

The difference between Locke's and Bayle's views on religious toleration was not simply that the latter lacked the former's anti-Catholic bigotry but that Locke did not think conscience an innate practical principle and Bayle did. Locke made a lot of use of the word *conscience* in his political writings, his *Letters concerning Toleration* and his *Two Treatises of Government*, but, in his philosophic *Essay concerning Human Understanding*, he dismissed conscience as nothing more than opinion based on one's upbringing and social environment. One's conscience is what one has been brought up to believe is right and what those around one believe. One's conscience is just one's conviction of right and wrong, a conviction sanctified as conscience because it is *one's own* belief.

How could Bayle hold that conscience, innate in all human beings, is infallible in its judgments of right and wrong, and also hold that "an erroneous Conscience has the same Rights as an enlighten'd Conscience."[24] To illustrate the right of erroneous conscience, Bayle cited the case of the wife of Martin Guerre and an imposter who claimed to be the husband and was accepted as such by Madame Guerre. The tale has been well told by Natalie Zemon Davis in *The Return of Martin Guerre*. Michel de Montaigne, with whom Bayle has been compared, was at the trial of the imposter and thought the verdict – that the imposter be put to death – uncertain. Davis wrote that Montaigne overlooked the confession of the imposter (Arnaud du Tilh, known as Pansette) before he was hanged. Davis, however, indicated that the trial judge, who later wrote up his account of the trial, "believed he had found out who the imposter was, but at the heart of his *Arrest Memorable* is an uncertainty as unsettling as Montaigne's." Davis concluded her book with a note of Montaigne's skepticism: "I think I have uncovered the true face of the past – or has Pansette done it once again?"[25]

Davis did not assess Bayle's interpretation of Bertrande Guerre. The trial was set in the time of religious wars between Huguenots and Catholics, but Davis did not consider Bayle's view that the two Martins Guerre – the real one and the imposter – symbolized Protestantism and Catholicism. A skeptic might think there is nothing much to distinguish the imposter from the true Martin Guerre since the wife, and many of his and her kin, accepted the imposter as Martin Guerre (a man who left his family to fight in the wars and

[24] Ibid., 219.

[25] Natalie Zemon Davis, *The Return of Martin Guerre* (Cambridge, MA: Harvard University Press, 1983), 119–25. The movie of the same name was based on Davis's research.

returned home after the imposter Arnaud had lived with his wife and had a child with her). Bayle considered the wife innocent, not for the reason that Davis does – women have to do whatever they must when their husbands desert them – but, insofar as Madame Guerre "sincerely believed him to be her Husband, and deceiv'd by the resemblance," she was not guilty of adultery or bigamy.[26] The "objective" truth of who was her real husband did not matter; her sincerity or truthfulness mattered. We might contrast Bayle's view with the aforementioned *Veritatis Splendor*'s declaration that "it is never acceptable to confuse a 'subjective' error about the moral good with the 'objective' truth." Madame Guerre's conscience was clear to the extent that she was deceived and was sincerely in error about taking an imposter for her husband. The Protestant judge, Jean de Coras, who sentenced the imposter to death, ruled that the imposter's daughter, Bernarde, was legitimate because her mother thought she was having intercourse with Martin Guerre.[27]

The moral of this story, for Bayle, is that conscience is the test of moral conduct: "This Touchstone is Conscience, and that the interior Perception of this Conscience, and its full and intire Conviction, is the final Criterion of that Conduct which everyone ought to keep."[28] Just as different bodies require different nourishment to achieve optimal health, so different souls may flourish best as Protestants, others as Catholics, others as Jews, others as Muslims, and so forth.[29] "God requires no more than a sincere and diligent search after Truth."[30] Bayle thought his position was far from moral relativism. Conscience obliges one to engage in a diligent search for truth, not accept the beliefs of one's parents or peers; it is the personalization of the natural and divine laws to love God and your fellow human beings. Conscience is the particular application of natural law and scriptural revelation, which requires diligence and intelligence. Bayle's conscience does not produce Montaigne's skepticism but rather moral certainty. By conscience, "we give the Lye, who without it might tell us there was no certainty in any thing."[31]

Enlightened skeptics found the certainties of Protestant conscience lawless and dangerous. Bayle's prime concern was to decriminalize heresy and to leave heretics to the judgment of God alone "so long as they disturb not the publick Peace; I mean, so long as they obey the Laws." Magistrates may legitimately suppress those "who endanger the public Peace by Doctrines

[26] Bayle, *Philosophical Commentary*, 273.
[27] Davis, *Return of Martin Guerre*, 88.
[28] Bayle, *Philosophical Commentary*, 270–71.
[29] Ibid.
[30] Ibid.
[31] Ibid., 277.

tending to Sedition, Rapine, Murder, Perjury, etc." Religious sects are to be tolerated to the extent that they obey the laws, respect the property rights of others, and pay their fair share of taxes.[32] Conscience can, but should not, be used as an excuse for lawless or seditious conduct: "Conspiracies against the state are the greatest crimes men can commit, and yet some persons suffer themselves to be drawn into conspiracies by such motives as they think morally good: so true is it, that man's conscience is liable to the most monstrous errors!"[33]

Bayle seemed to follow Calvin's view of the duty of citizens to obey the law and civil authority, although the latter came to think that lawless or tyrannical rulers forfeit the allegiance of their citizens. His successor, Theodore Beza, developed a doctrine of justified resistance to lawless magistrates by subordinate magistrates, a moderate doctrine that became more radical in Scotland and in France after the Saint Bartholomew's Day Massacre of 1572. Locke extended Beza's moderate right of resistance into an extreme right of armed revolution in his *Second Treatise of Government*. Locke declared: "And when the Body of the People, or any single Man, is deprived of their Right, or is under the Exercise of a power without right, and have no Appeal on Earth, they have a liberty to appeal to Heaven, whenever they judge the Cause of sufficient moment."[34] That judgment call is based on conscience: "Of that I my self can only be Judge in my own Conscience, as I will answer it at the great Day, to the Supreme Judge of all Men."[35] Despite his skepticism about conscience in his philosophic *Essay concerning Human Understanding*, Locke deployed conscience as the court of last resort with respect to the right of revolution against Catholic kings. Locke's *Two Treatises of Government* was written during the Exclusion Crisis, the attempt by Whigs to exclude the Catholic James II from the crown, and was published after the Glorious Revolution when William of Orange replaced James II as the king of England. Bayle did not assent to the right of revolution; his blend of philosophic skepticism and Calvinist certainty was the converse of Locke's.

Bayle's opposition to the right of revolution arose in response to the Protestant triumphalism of his compatriot, Pierre Jurieu, who hailed William of Orange as a white knight crusading against Catholicism and who deprecated Bayle's advocacy of universal toleration. Whereas Bayle and

32 Ibid., 183, 190.

33 Bayle, *General Dictionary*, 4:437.

34 John Locke, *Two Treatises of Government*, ed. Peter Laslett (Cambridge: Cambridge University Press, 1963), II.168.

35 Ibid., II.21.

many of Locke's fellow Whigs welcomed James II's Declaration of Indulgence removing the requirement that only adherents of the Church of England are eligible for civil and military posts, which had barred Catholics, Protestant Dissenters, Unitarians, Jews, Muslims, and unbelievers from public office, Jurieu and Locke thought that James was attempting to bring in Catholic officers to bolster absolute government and endanger property and liberty.[36] Bayle feared the emergence of a Protestant Inquisition; "better Leviathan than Torquemada."[37] Bayle's apprehension pertained more to Ireland, where Protestant Orangemen oppressed Irish Catholics, than to England; England's "Glorious Revolution" was not, for Ireland, the "Bloodless Revolution." For Scotland, the Glorious Revolution brought in its wake the Jacobite rebellions of those loyal to the Stuart monarchy and the bloody suppression of Jacobitism.

Most of the Enlightenment thinkers espoused Locke's skepticism about the claims of conscience in his *Essay concerning Human Understanding* and thought that providing sanctity to individual judgment of right and wrong is anarchic and antinomian. On the other hand, the "radical Enlightenment" (Price, Priestley, Paine) and the romantic reaction to Enlightenment (Rousseau, Wollstonecraft, Blake) affirmed conscience as the basis of the right of revolution from Locke's *Second Treatise on Government* without the skepticism of Locke's *Essay*.

## CONSCIENCE AND LAW

Bayle's view of the relationship of law and conscience might be clarified through a consideration of two thoughtful contemporary thinkers, Harold M. Schulweis and Harold J. Berman. Schulweis's position is that conscience stands in opposition to law, whereas Berman's position is that conscience is embedded in the practice of common law. Schulweis asserts: "Conscience without law is capricious. Law without conscience is heartless."[38] Rabbi Schulweis is aware that his championship of conscience appears heterodox to many Jewish scholars. Indeed, there is no Hebrew word for conscience in the Old Testament; the equivalent for the New Testament *conscience* is *leb*

36 Mark Goldie, "John Locke's Circle and James II," *The Historical Journal*, 35 (1992): 578–86; Labrousse, *Bayle*, 34.

37 Cited in Labrousse, *Pierre Bayle*, 2:517. See also Labrousse, *Bayle*, 33–39; Jonathan Israel, "General Introduction," in *The Anglo-Dutch Moment: Essays on the Glorious Revolution and Its World Impact*, ed. J. Israel (Cambridge: Cambridge University Press, 1991), 34–36.

38 Harold M. Schulweis, *Conscience: The Duty to Obey and the Duty to Disobey* (Woodstock, VT: Jewish Lights, 2008), 34.

(heart). Schulweis cited other Jewish scholars and thinkers asserting that "The Torah and the prophets never appeal to moral conscience, for such an appeal is always suspect as a possible expression of idolatry." Since the word is not found in the Torah, conscience may be considered "an atheistic, indeed an idolatrous concept." Conscience may presuppose that God's will and commands may be judged by a merely human sense of morality.[39] Against the more orthodox interpretations of Judaism, Schulweis pointed out that Abraham argued, bargained, and fought with God when He seemed unjust – citing Genesis 18:20–33 with respect to the destruction of Sodom and Gomorrah – and Moses checked God's wrath with the idolaters of the golden calf (Exod. 32:9–11). Schulweis also indicated that Moses nullified God's command that the iniquity of the father shall be visited upon the children to the third or fourth generation (Exod. 20:5) with Moses' proclamation: "The fathers shall not be put to death for the children, neither shall the children be put to death for the fathers" (Deut. 24:16). Schulweis's message is that conscience does not submit blindly to divine command. Piety is not blind submission to divine command.[40]

Schulweis points out that the modern Hebrew word for conscience *matzpun* derives from *tzafun* (the hidden matzoh at Passover seders) and *matzpen* (compass). Conscience is the inner compass from which we get our bearings. A compass is not a detailed map to direct our conduct, as the Torah is to orthodox Jews. Above all, neither compasses nor maps are global positioning systems; they are instruments that require intelligent application to the terrain on which one is traveling to determine the direction one wants to follow. Compass users and map readers become more accomplished the more they use them, the more they err and discover how they erred; the more they exercise their judgment, the fitter their consciences will be. Reliance on global positioning systems, however false their presumed infallibility, will allow one's sense of direction to atrophy. Schulweis does not think humans have an innate sense of moral direction, as the atrocities of the twentieth century attest. However, he does think conscience can be cultivated and it is the duty of all religions "to instill in its adherents the sanctity of conscience," to obey laws binding equally on all human beings and to disobey those laws that are discriminatory, inequitable, or unjust. Conscience is akin to Aristotle's *epeikeia* (equity), in *Nicomachean Ethics*, where law as a general rule must be adapted to particular circumstances "like the leaden rule in the Lesbian style

39 Ibid., 23–24.
40 Ibid., 20.

of masonry" and is flexible or "has no fixed shape but adapts itself to the outlines of each stone."[41]

Schulweis is not clear when conscience demands that we obey and when conscience demands that we disobey law; our culture, he says, reinforces the propriety of obeying law, rather than resisting unjust laws. The conscienceless behavior of concentration camp guards at Auschwitz and Abu Ghraib exemplify cultures of obedience. Schulweis insists that no law is sacrosanct in the sense that it is immune from criticism and dissent, and conscience is that which prompts us to disobey inequitable rules or unjust laws. One might question whether Schulweis's understanding of the development of conscience might be seen as relativist or historicist, contrary to natural and divine law, or what Bayle called "the eternal Law and Rule" or "the eternal Laws of Just and Honest" inscribed in conscience.

Here Schulweis is joined by Harold J. Berman, who thought living traditions require change as well as continuity or traditions become lifeless traditionalisms.[42] Tradition is the selective repetition of the past, which grows, like English common law, on the basis of precedent and judicial decisions. Yet the growth of common law does not conflict with the stability of the Ten Commandments; the common law and Bayle's inner light are the particular or personal specifications of an unchanging bedrock. Berman thinks all law is graven in human conscience: the little girl who says "that toy is mine" is the basis of property law; the boy who whines "you promised" is the foundation of contract law; the "you hit me first" grounds tort law: and "Daddy said I could" is the basis of constitutional law.[43] Berman indicated that tradition is not necessarily in conflict with natural right and its inscription in conscience. Yet Berman would hardly want children, equipped only with their sense of natural right or conscience, as trial judges, or even as jurors in common law trials.

Berman defended the notion of "artificial reason" of the common lawyers, Sir Edward Coke and Sir Matthew Hale, against the natural right jurisprudence of Thomas Hobbes.[44] The flaw in Berman's account is that he assumes that Hobbes was just a legal positivist, one who believes law is the command of the sovereign (whether a monarch, or a few of the people or of a majority of

[41] Aristotle, *Nicomachean Ethics*, trans. Christopher Rowe (Oxford: Oxford University Press, 2002), 1137a–38a.

[42] Harold J. Berman, *Law and Revolution II: The Impact of the Protestant Reformation on the Western Legal Tradition* (Cambridge, MA: Harvard University Press, 2006), 3, 244–45.

[43] Harold J. Berman, *Law and Language: Effective Symbols of Community*, eds. John Witte Jr. and Christopher J. Manzer (New York, NY: Cambridge University Press, 2013), 29.

[44] Berman, *Law and Revolution II*, 257–63.

the people). Berman neglects the fact that Hobbes championed the common law practice of trial by jury and that jury verdicts according to conscience decide the law, not just the fact, as Sir Edward Coke declared. That is, Coke would confine jurors to the question of whether or not the accused were present at a meeting place on a particular date, whereas Hobbes insisted that juries decide whether a meeting of Quakers constituted seditious assembly. Jury verdicts according to conscience are independent of the instructions of crown-appointed judges. Those accused of crimes have the right of self-defense, a right not to be tortured, and a right to select and reject jurors. Hobbes's insistence that jurors have the right to decide the law, not just the facts of the case, indicates that juries have a central role in Hobbesian legal theory mediating law as sovereign command and the upholding of law by ordinary citizens without the "artificial reason" of Coke and Hale.[45] That is, Hobbes's support of the common law practice of jury trial is closer than Berman supposes to his own position that conscience is embedded within the law, and thus conscience should not be understood solely as justifying opposition to law.

The artificial reason of common lawyers that Berman defends is akin to the cultivated conscience of Schulweis, whose enlightened skepticism about conscience not being innate in all human beings seems to run counter to Berman's Protestant conscience. However, both men believed in living traditions that connect the present to the past and enlighten paths to the future. Both think the world is enriched by moral and legal judgments enabling life to flourish, rather than simply "Xeroxing" Scripture, Magna Carta, or the US Constitution as the grounds of a judgment. The judgments of conscience, like legal judgments, are not free floating but are intelligent interpretations of what is given to judgment by the tradition one inhabits and the changing circumstances in which one finds oneself.

Perhaps we should think of the cultivation of conscience as akin to jurisprudential skill and jurors' duties as akin to Bayle's innate conscience in all human beings. The juror's duty is not to make an instinctive judgment for the prosecution or the defense, not to rush to judgment, but to diligently search for the truth from the available evidence, to listen to the judge's summation of the case and to one's fellow jurors with whom one disagrees, and then make one's verdict. Jurors do not have the legal training, and their verdicts, like the verdicts of conscience, can err. Judges may overturn a jury verdict of guilty if they think insufficient evidence from the prosecution did

[45] Edward G. Andrew, *Conscience and Its Critics: Protestant Conscience, Enlightened Reason, and Modern Subjectivity* (Toronto: University of Toronto Press, 2001).

not warrant the verdict, but they may not overturn a jury verdict of not guilty.

## CONCLUSION: CONSCIENCE AND EQUALITY

Now what is the contemporary relevance of Bayle's affirmation of the rights of conscience and Locke's skepticism about claims of conscience? Schulweis demonstrated that advocacy of the rights of conscience is not a Protestant monopoly and Berman clarified how Bayle could uphold both the rights of conscience and the rule of law. A question that remains is: What has conscience to do with contemporary intuitions of human equality?

Religions teach us that human beings are all equal in the eyes of God. That does not mean that we are equally intelligent, have equal aesthetic sensibilities, equal craft, technical, or commercial skills. The greatest of secular thinkers established human equality on different grounds. Hobbes thought humans are equal in what matters most, the ability to kill one another, and hence all are equally vulnerable to the worst of all evils, a premature and violent death. Locke's *Two Treatises of Government* asserted the equality of human beings but did not provide the grounds of that assertion. Locke's skepticism about conscience impairs our ability to provide a secular basis for human equality. Religion holds that God judges humans on the basis of their moral conduct and that it is our moral choices – not our tasteful consumer choices – that decide our eternal destiny. In secular terms, our judgments of conscience are constitutive of who we are – more so than our intellectual capacity or our aesthetic sensibility. If the Hobbesian argument that we are equally vulnerable to premature and violent death is insufficient to ground our claim to human equality, an alternative claim to equality is that our moral choices are most constitutive of personal identity and that we have an equal propensity to follow our inner compass or lose our way. Pierre Bayle's understanding of the rights of conscience provides an enlightened alternative to Locke's political theology.

Jean-Jacques Rousseau overturned the political theories of hierarchy based on differential intelligence for a politics of equality based on human will and conscience. In his *Discourse on the Arts and the Sciences*, Rousseau attacked the idea that cultivation in the arts and sciences would produce virtuous citizens and morally attractive human beings. He concluded his *Discourse* with a paean to conscience as "the sublime science of simple souls," which he later elaborated in *Émile*'s "The Profession of Faith of the Savoyard Vicar" and other writings. Rousseau's moral and political populism has become dominant in our times, characterized by attacks on elites and a supposedly "elitist" press that separates fact from opinion. Our current moral populism is facilitated by new social media, which enable viewers to reinforce their political prejudices without weighing evidence or considering facts that may conflict with their presuppositions. The postmodern turn against enlightenment that seems to authorize any opinion as equally valid would have no support from Bayle. Bayle's rights of erroneous conscience do not warrant moral populism. Rights of conscience entail conscientious duties. Moral judgment is not prejudice (pre-judgment) or unwillingness to consider the evidence or the facts of the case, any more than it would authorize Bertrande Guerre to claim a tall, handsome hunk as her husband, Martin. Conscience requires a diligent and sincere pursuit of truth. Bayle's Protestant conscience was enlightened by a scholar's patience, akin to the duty of judges and jurors to make judgments on the basis of the evidence available to them.

Duties of conscience are similar to the duties of jurors but are also quite different. Jurors judge for others; conscience judges for oneself. Conscience does not sit in judgment on others; it does not dictate that all human beings should be vegetarian; it dictates that eating flesh is wrong for oneself, and it may dictate that one should try to persuade others of the benefits of a vegetarian diet. Conscience does not judge whether another should neglect the care of an infirm parent to serve in the military; it judges the particular circumstances where one's self or soul is confronted with the conflicting claims of patriotic and familial obligations. Conscience individuates judgments of right and wrong; it puts one's whole self on the line, unlike judgments of self-interest. Conscience stakes one's all (one's immortal soul or personal integrity) on one's judgment.

## RECOMMENDED READING


Andrew, Edward G. *Conscience and Its Critics: Protestant Conscience, Enlightened Reason, and Modern Subjectivity*. Toronto: University of Toronto Press, 2001.

Beiner, Ronald S. *Civil Religion: A Dialogue in the History of Political Philosophy*. Cambridge: Cambridge University Press, 2011.

Berman, Harold J. *Law and Revolution: The Formation of the Western Legal Tradition*. Cambridge, MA: Harvard University Press, 1983.

*Law and Revolution II: The Impact of the Protestant Reformations on the Western Legal Tradition*. Cambridge, MA: Harvard University Press, 2003.

Curran, Charles E., ed. *Conscience*. New York, NY: Paulist Press, 2004.

King, Martin Luther Jr. *The Trumpet of Conscience*. New York, NY: Harper and Row, 1968.
Schulweis, Harold M. *Conscience: The Duty to Obey and the Duty to Disobey*. Woodstock, VT: Jewish Lights, 2008.
Strohm, Paul. *Conscience: A Very Short Introduction*. Oxford: Oxford University Press, 2011.
Witte, John Jr. *The Reformation of Rights: Law, Religion, and Human Rights in Early Modern Calvinism*. Cambridge: Cambridge University Press, 2007.
Witte, John Jr. and Frank S. Alexander, eds. *Christianity and Law: An Introduction*. Cambridge: Cambridge University Press, 2008.

# 10

# Freedom of Conscience and Its Right to Constitutional Protection

## *The Contribution of Roger Williams*[*]

DAVID LITTLE

### INTRODUCTION

Leo Pfeffer, one of the United States' foremost authors, scholars, and jurists on the subject of church-state relations and religious freedom, wrote these words concerning Roger Williams:

> In [the colony of] Rhode Island [which Williams established in 1636] ... religious liberty was not a practice forced on an unwilling leader by an accident of history, but an ideal founded on the concept which a century and a half later was to achieve its fullest expression in the American Constitution – the concept of the mutual independence of religion and government.
>
> Williams's pamphlet, *The Bloody Tenent of Persecution, for Cause of Conscience* [1644] ... is an epocal milestone in the history of religious freedom and the separation of church and state. Along with *Jefferson's Act for Establishing Religious Freedom* [1786] and Madison's *Memorial and Remonstrance* [1784], and the First Amendment [to the US Constitution, 1789], it stands as one of the cornerstones of the American experiment.[1]

Pfeffer's evaluation of the contribution of Roger Williams to the "American experiment" is largely accurate, as is the implication that in regard to religious freedom, Williams is the forerunner of Jefferson and Madison.[2] At the same

[*] This is a substantially revised version of a chapter, "Constitutional Protection of the Freedom of Conscience in Colonial America: The Rhode Island and Pennsylvania Experiments," in *Christianity and Freedom, Volume I: Historical Perspectives*, eds., Timothy Samuel Shah and Allen D. Hertzke (New York, NY: Cambridge University Press, 2016), 235–63.

[1] Leo Pfeffer, "Freedom and/or Separation: The Constitutional Dilemma of the First Amendment," *Minnesota Law Review* 64 (1980): 561.

[2] See Martha C. Nussbaum, *Liberty of Conscience: In Defense of American's Tradition of Religious Equality* (New York, NY: Basic Books, 2008), ch. 2 for a discussion of Williams's contribution to the right of religious freedom in America.

time, while Pfeffer's judgment finally seems to be gaining acceptance, such acceptance did not come easily. Sampling the record of misunderstanding that has for too long obscured Williams's place in American history helps us to see that.

There is little disagreement over the general outlines of Williams's life. Though the birth records were destroyed in a church fire, it is known that he was born of middle-class parents in London, England, probably in 1603. Although, as an infant, Williams was baptized into the Anglican church, and, as a young man, studied for the Anglican clergy at Cambridge University, he early came under the influence of Calvinist theology in one of its more radical Puritan forms, a movement called "Separatism."[3]

But Separatism, at least as practiced in New England, did not meet his expectations. Williams spoke of a "restless unsatisfiedness of my soul,"[4] which, having driven him from England to the New World, where he arrived in 1631, thereafter drove him from church to church, in a relentless spiritual quest. First abandoning the Church of England and later the Separatists, he temporarily identified with the Baptists, until he finally withdrew from religious communion altogether, believing that "Christians had lost their church, and there was no present way to recover it"[5] until the Second Coming of Christ.

Williams's restless quest had decided political consequences. He refused to withhold or modify his sharp criticisms of church and government in Massachusetts Bay, and by 1635 was, as a result, officially banished. From there he found his way to what became the colony of Rhode Island, where he managed to establish "the first commonwealth in modern history to make religious liberty ... a cardinal principle of its corporate existence and to maintain the separation of church and state on these grounds."[6] After an

3 Rejecting the rituals and practices of the established Church of England, some Separatists went so far as to object to any kind of state enforcement of religious belief and practice as a fundamental violation of the doctrine of freedom of conscience, which, they believed, was central to Christian faith. By 1631, when Williams had decided to emigrate to the newly created colony of Massachusetts Bay in North America, he was himself a committed Separatist. In these details of Williams's life, as in other matters, I am indebted to the excellent book by James Calvin Davis, *The Moral Theology of Roger Williams* (Louisville, KY: Westminster John Knox, 2004).

4 Edward Gaustad, *Liberty of Conscience: Roger Williams in America* (Grand Rapids, MI: Eerdmans, 1991), 90.

5 Edmund S. Morgan, *Roger Williams: The Church and the State* (New York, NY: Harcourt Brace & World, 1967), 53.

6 Sydney E. Ahlstrom, *A Religious History of the American People* (New Haven, CT: Yale University Press, 1972), 172.

eventful and varied life as a politician, statesman, publicist, trader, public debater, and family man, he died there around the year of 1683.

But if the outlines of Williams's life are generally agreed upon, what is to be made of that life, and how it is to be interpreted, is not. On that question, the opinions of historians have varied widely and wildly. One view is that Williams was a "Christian freethinker," more interested in society and politics than in theology. In that spirit, Williams has been described as the "Tom Paine of the seventeenth century," whose "interest in international affairs and his defense of a principle of liberty were grounded in his concern for the welfare and integrity of the individual."[7] On another view, Williams should be seen as a "transcendental mystic," with strong attachments to Emerson, or Unitarianism, or Romanticism.[8] One very distinguished American colonial historian, by his own testimony, needed two tries to get Roger Williams right. In his first account, he characterized Williams as something of a crackpot, committed to "an irresponsible pursuit of individual holiness" whom "the [Massachusetts Bay] colony was better off without." But as he read and reread Williams, he admitted he had badly misjudged the man and thereupon set about to provide a more satisfactory account.[9] Finally, others have interpreted later developments in Williams's life, such as his attacks on Quakers or his withdrawal from religious communion, as signs that he was reversing his earlier liberal commitments or that he was changing his beliefs in face of some sort of religious crisis.

There is strong evidence that these interpretations are largely in error. Few historical figures, for several reasons, have been as consistently and seriously misrepresented as Williams. There is, to be sure, the complexity and originality of his thought (together, no doubt, with its density and prolixity!), plus the rich variety of his undertakings and activities and the intricacies of his personality. However, the primary reason for the misunderstanding is the failure to appreciate that Williams is best characterized as a Puritan theologian in the Calvinist tradition. Familiarity with Calvinism in all its complexity is indispensable for understanding the thought world out of which Williams's principles of religious and political liberty emerged.[10]

7 Davis, *Moral Theology of Roger Williams*, 10.

8 LeRoy Moore, "Roger Williams and the Historian," *Church History* 32 (December 1963): 442ff.

9 Edmund S. Morgan wrote these different accounts in *The Puritan Dilemma: The Story of John Winthrop* (Boston, MA: Little, Brown, 1958), 132–33, and then in the foreword to *Roger Williams: The Church and the State* (New York, NY: Harcourt, Brace & World, 1976).

10 See David Little, "Roger Williams and the Puritan Background of the Establishment Clause" in *Essays in Religion and Human Rights: Ground to Stand On* (New York, NY: Cambridge University Press, 2015), 256–68.

## ROGER WILLIAMS AND THE FREEDOM OF CONSCIENCE

It is now clear that an important source of modern constitutionalism, including, eventually, the protection of freedom of conscience and other rights, were the colonial covenants and compacts established by Anglo-American Puritans in the seventeenth century[11] on the basis of their Calvinist heritage.[12] Whatever their other differences, American Puritans "in their towns and congregations" were of one mind that "the crucial feature of all covenants" is "a people's willing consent," that "covenant [is thus an] instrument and expression of popular decision-making."[13]

According to a leading authority, the Charter of Massachusetts Bay of 1629 "was not strictly a popular constitution, because it was in form and legal effect a royal grant, but in its practical operation after the transfer, it approximated a popular constitution more closely than any other instrument of government in actual use up to that time in America or elsewhere in modern times."[14] The Puritan authorities went well beyond the original wording, claiming that their charter permitted an astounding degree of political independence. As early as 1641, they refused help from the English Parliament because the colony might "then be subject to all such laws as [the Parliament] should make or at least such as [it] might impose upon us."[15] When in 1646 the authorities were criticized for considering themselves "rather a free state than a colony or corporation of England," they agreed! Parliament might have authority in England, but "the highest authority here is in [our legislature], *both by our charter and by our own positive laws .... [O]ur allegiance binds us not to the laws of England any longer than we live in England,*"[16] an interpretation applying to the charters and compacts of the other colonies, as well. Though the colonials were slow to admit it, it was not a large step to the eventual replacement of the authority of the English crown, as well as of Parliament, with the will of "the people" who inhabited the colonies.[17]

11 Donald S. Lutz, *Origins of American Constitutionalism* (Baton Rouge, LA: Louisiana State University Press, 1988).
12 See David Little, "Religion, Peace, and the Origins of Nationalism," in *Essays in Religion and Human Rights: Ground to Stand On* (New York, NY: Cambridge University Press, 2015), 223–36.
13 David D. Hall, *A Reforming People: Puritanism and the Transformation of Public Life* (New York, NY: Alfred A. Knopf, 2011), 157.
14 C. H. McIlwain, *Constitutionalism and Its Changing World* (Cambridge: Cambridge University Press, 1939), 241.
15 From *Winthrop's Journal* cited in McIlwain, *Constitutionalism and Its Changing World*, 234.
16 Ibid., 235 (emphasis added).
17 Lutz, *Origins of American Constitutionalism*, 37.

A critical part of these early constitutions were the declarations of rights that were included. The Body of Liberties, adopted by the Massachusetts Bay legislature in 1641, amounted to an exceptionally lengthy list of fundamental rights.[18] Though it incorporated provisions from English statutes and precedents, it went well beyond them. It redefined and restructured the traditional rights of English subjects in the light of Puritan Christianity, adding modified portions of biblical law, and some "daring rights proposals"[19] from left-wing English Puritan pamphleteers. The document opens, significantly, by referring to "such liberties, immunities, and privileges" that "humanity, civility, and Christianity call for as due to every man in his place and proportion without impeachment or infringement," highlighting the several grounds, religious *and* natural, which rights were believed to rest on.[20]

But however central to constitution-making was the protection of individual rights, colonial Puritans disagreed sharply among themselves over the precise basis and scope of those protections, especially in regard to freedom of conscience. A key reason for the expulsion of Roger Williams from Massachusetts Bay and for the consequent founding of the Rhode Island colony in 1636 was his radical dissent from what he regarded as the overly narrow and deeply mistaken interpretation of freedom of conscience enforced in Massachusetts Bay at the time.

One part of the Body of Liberties that generated a particularly strong division of opinion were the rights pertaining to religious belief and practice, namely, Section 95, Articles 1 through 11, identified as "A Declaration of the Liberties the Lord Jesus hath given to the Churches." According to these articles, all members of the colony have "full liberty" to practice religion according to conscience, though only so long as they "be orthodox in judgment," and, "every church has full liberty to elect church officers," "provided they be able, pious and orthodox."

This was the basis of what John Cotton, a prominent clergyman in the colony, referred to as the "theocratic" character of Massachusetts Bay, namely, a state governed by officials regarded as divinely guided.[21] Cotton and other

[18] Edmund S. Morgan, *Puritan Political Ideas, 1558–1794* (Indianapolis, IN: Bobbs-Merrill, 1965), 171–97.

[19] John Witte, Jr., *Reformation of Rights: Law, Religion, and Human Rights in Early Modern Calvinism* (New York, NY: Cambridge University Press, 2007), 280.

[20] Morgan, *Puritan Political Ideas*, 172–73. I have modernized and here and there "translated" some of the archaic words and forms of speech in the Body of Liberties, and in some of the subsequent citations from Puritan writings.

[21] Cotton actually uses the term to describe what in his mind is "the best form of government in the commonwealth, as well as the church," in Morgan, *Puritan Political Ideas*, 163.

leaders believed that church and state should not be "confounded," so that magistrates were precluded from holding church office and church officials from holding civil office. At the same time, he and his associates affirmed with equal resolution that only church members might vote in civil elections, that churches and clergymen should receive direct public support through taxes and other donations, and that religious beliefs and practices be extensively and severely regulated by laws covering blasphemy, irreverence, profanity, idolatry, and "schismatic" activity

Almost from the start, Roger Williams (1603–83?) opposed the laws establishing religion in Massachusetts Bay. He claimed that the authority of the civil government extends not to spiritual matters but only "to conserve the civil peace of people, so far as concerns their bodies and goods."[22] For making this claim, along with challenging the right of the English crown to native American lands, disparaging the red cross at the center of the English flag, and rejecting the requirement that unbelievers take oaths in court, he was indicted in late 1635, convicted as charged, and condemned to return to England for punishment after the new year. However, he eluded the authorities and, with the help of Narragansett Indians he had befriended earlier, found his way in early 1636 to the territory that, under his leadership, would ultimately become the Rhode Island and Providence Plantation.

In 1643, Williams acquired a minimal patent for the towns of Providence, Portsmouth, and Newport from Parliament, which by 1647 was expanded into a fuller constitutional document that "gives us power to govern ourselves and such others as come among us, and [to establish] such a form of civil government as by the voluntary consent, etc., shall be found most suitable to our estate and condition." In words less hesitant than the sentiments found in Massachusetts Bay, the document specifies without apology or reservation that the form of government will be "democraticall," which is to say, "a government held by the free and voluntary consent of all, or the greater part of the free inhabitants," assuring "each man's peaceable and quiet enjoyment of his lawful right and liberty." Then it continues in language largely reminiscent of the 1629 Charter of Massachusetts Bay and 1641 Body of Liberties to outline a representative political system together with legal institutions carefully regulated by due process, including extensive rights and liberties against arbitrary injury, trial, imprisonment, loss of property, and so on.[23]

[22] Ibid., 200.

[23] *1647 Acts and Orders of Rhode Island*, Online Library of Liberty (Indianapolis, IN: Liberty Fund, Inc.), oll.libertyfund.org/pages/1647-acts-and-orders-rhode-island.

Where the Rhode Island and Providence colony differed most sharply from Massachusetts Bay and other colonies was in the treatment of religion. The Charter of 1644 and the Civil Code of 1647 were essentially secular documents, since, unlike contemporaneous charters in other colonies, no mention is made of any special religious privileges. Then the Rhode Island and Providence Plantation Charter of 1663, a document serving "effectively as [a] colonial constitution and as [a] state constitution as well,"[24] that Williams and his associate, John Clarke, acquired from King Charles II, explicitly enshrined an expansive right of freedom of conscience. It commended the aspirations of the colonists "to hold forth a lively experiment, that *a most flourishing civil state may stand and best be maintained* ... *with the full liberty in religious concernments* ... *and* ... *in the free exercise and enjoyment of all* ... *civil and religious rights*." (italics added). In a radical departure from Massachusetts Bay's traditional and circumscribed understanding of "full liberty," it then expressed a radically modern conception articulated in language that anticipated Jefferson's Statute of Religious Freedom of 1786:

> No person within said colony, at any time hereafter, shall be [in] any wise molested, punished, disquieted, or called into question, for any difference of opinion in matters of religion, and do not actually disturb the civil peace ... but that all and every person and persons may ... freely and fully have and enjoy ... their own judgments and consciences in matters of religious concernments ... they behaving themselves peaceably and quietly.[25]

"The trouble with welcoming everyone to a haven of religious liberty was that, sooner or later, everyone came." Baptists, Quakers, Jews, Congregationalists, Anglicans, along with many others "seeking only to escape religion, not to embrace it,"[26] and even those "who turn atheistical and irreligious"[27] – they all came. The result was by no means always harmonious. Not only were there no precedents for managing such an array of divergent religions, early Rhode Island had to contend with a distracted British Parliament, duplicitous and predatory neighboring colonies, and special, often venal, interests that were daunting challenges for anyone.

[24] Lutz, *Origins of American Constitutionalism*, 49.
[25] Charter of Rhode Island and Providence Plantations – July 15, 1663, Lillian Goldman Law Library, avalon.law.yale,edu/17th_century/ri04.asp1.
[26] Gaustad, *Liberty of Conscience*, 175–76.
[27] Roger Williams, "The Hireling Ministry None of Christ's," in *Complete Writings of Roger Williams* (New York, NY: Russell & Russell, 1963), 7:181. Citations from Williams are modernized for easier understanding.

In coping with these realities, Williams never surrendered his unrelenting assault on the idea of the legal establishment of religion, whether in its many historical guises or in the form it took in England, before, during, or after the Puritan Revolution, or in the various colonial versions Williams knew firsthand.

The titles of Williams's two best-known works, *The Bloody Tenent* (1644) and *The Bloody Tenent Yet More Bloody* (1652), epitomize what is for him the essential problem. The legal enforcement of religion, according to which people are punished for their conscientious convictions, opposes all that is right and holy, and, in addition, gives rise to violence and bloodshed. Williams finally rested his case on the age-old distinction between conscience and government that lay deep within the Christian tradition and was developed in various ways by his Calvinist forbears.

Calvin himself called attention to a sharp distinction between two forums or tribunals, the "internal forum" (conscience), and the "external forum" (civil authority).[28] The first concerns personal, inward deliberation regarding fundamental belief and practice that is regulated by "spiritual power," and the second concerns "external" or public deliberation regarding "outward behavior" – the needs of "the present life," such as food, clothing, and the laws of social cooperation – that are regulated by the "power of the sword."[29]

Calvin said as much in his commentary on the thirteenth chapter of the Letter to the Romans, although he dramatically reversed himself later in life, calling upon government to enforce both tables of the Decalogue.[30] As much as anything, this antinomy in Calvin's thought came to signify the basic division between Williams and many of his fellow colonists. Williams embraced the first part, the liberal side, of Calvin's thought, and wholeheartedly rejected the second, while Massachusetts Bay affirmed and implemented the second part by playing down, if not entirely discarding, the first.

For Williams, there could be no two ways about it. Experience, natural reason, and religion all ultimately point the same way: the law of the sword – the indispensable instrument of the "external forum" – is not all-powerful. It must defer to and protect the law of the spirit – the law of reason, will, and emotion that governs the "internal forum."

"A most lamentably true experience of all the ages," wrote Williams, "is that persecution for the cause of conscience" is a "lance that has pierced the veins

[28] John Calvin, *Institutes of the Christian Religion*, ed. John T. McNeill, trans. Ford Battles, 2 vols. (Philadelphia, PA: Westminster Press, 1960), 3.19.15, pp. 847–48; 4.10.5.

[29] Ibid., 3.19.15.

[30] Ibid., 4.20.2.

of kings and kingdoms, of saints and sinners, and filled the streams with their blood."[31] Efforts by the external forum to coerce "the natural conscience and reason of all men"[32] may appear effective in the short term but will eventually fail. Whenever such interference seems to prevail it is because superior force succeeds temporarily in quieting opposition, though it cannot on its own elicit inward consent nor ever completely eliminate potential resistance.

Beyond the lessons of experience, attempting to coerce conscience is to make a grievous mistake about how the mind works. Above all, it is to neglect the fault between physical force and conscience. This ought to be self-evident as a matter of natural reason. If one is attempting to regulate what Calvin called the "outward behavior" of human beings – to prevent them from taking what does not belong to them or maiming or killing others to their own advantage – "cannons ... bullets, powder, muskets, swords, [and] pikes ... are weapons effectual and [proportional]."[33] Such weapons are appropriate because without them physical harm or injury would occur. They are required for and capable of restraining action considered morally and legally illicit, and they may, if necessary, be effectively applied without or against the consent of the offender. It is precisely because the behavior in question is "outward" that it is under the jurisdiction of the "external forum," whose essential function is the regulation of legitimately administered physical force.

But things are different with the internal forum. "Stocks, whips, prisons, swords, gibbets, stakes" have no effect on the conscience[34] because it is characterized by inward consent based on a conviction of truth and right, something physical force, in and of itself, cannot produce. Belief depends on reasons consisting of arguments and evidence, and the threat of force, as in a case of robbery or rape, is not a reason in the proper sense because it lacks justification. Thus, the only "weapons" suitably employed in the internal forum are "spiritual," namely, appeals and arguments subject to common rational standards whose object is consensual or heartfelt agreement. Using force against conscience is a fundamental violation of the nature of conscience itself.[35]

[31] Williams, *Complete Writings*, 3:182.

[32] Ibid., 4:443.

[33] Ibid., 3:148.

[34] Ibid., 3:148–49. I have omitted passing references Williams makes to God's role in changing consciences since it is incidental to the more general conceptual point Williams affirms here and elsewhere concerning the implied distinction between reasons and causes we call attention to in the text.

[35] For Williams's agreement with Calvin, see Williams, *Complete Writings*, 3:153; for his disagreement with him, see 3:223.

In a number of important passages, Williams elaborates his understanding of the nature of conscience and its right to protection.

> Conscience (in Greek [*synderesis*], Latin [*conscientia*], and English) signifies a knowing together, a reflection or looking back on a man's mind or spirit upon itself.[36]
>
> The natural truth or light is received internally by a natural or moral understanding – civil and moral light sorts and agrees with those moral and civil convictions of natural light ... [they are received] by an internal faculty ... a receptive faculty within[,] willing to receive but only with regard to natural and moral understanding.[37]
>
> Remember that that thing which we call conscience is of such a nature ... that ... although it be groundless, false, and deluded [with respect to religious matters], yet it is not by any arguments or torments easily removed ... I speak of conscience, a persuasion fixed in the mind and heart of man, which forces him to judge ... and to do so with respect to God [and] his worship. The conscience is found in all mankind, more or less.[38]
>
> The best religion is a torment to the soul and conscience that is forced against its own free love and choice to embrace and observe it. And therefore there ought to be no forcing, but the soul and mind and conscience of man – that is, indeed the man [himself] – ought to be left free.[39]
>
> Straining of men's conscience by civil power ... cause men to play the hypocrite and dissemble in their religion.... [It] so weakens and defiles [the conscience] that it loses its strength and the very nature of a common honest conscience.[40]
>
> Soul oppression [involves] yokes where [people are] forced to receive doctrine and pray ... wracking their souls, bodies, and purses.... [A] great load may be made up by parcels and particulars, as well as by in mass or bulk ... and the backs of some men ... may be broke, by a withdrawing from them some civil privileges and rights, which are their due as well as afflicting them in their purses, or flesh upon their backs.[41]
>
> Forcing of a woman that is a violent act of uncleanness upon her body against her will we count as rape: by proportion that is spiritual or soul rape [that is] a forcing of the conscience of any person to acts of worship.[42]

36 Cited in James Calvin Davis, ed., *On Religious Liberty: Selections from the Works of Roger Williams* (Cambridge, MA: Belknap Press of Harvard University Press, 2008), 268.

37 Williams, "George Fox Digg'd Out of His Burrows," in *Complete Writings*, 5:370–71.

38 Williams, "Bloody Tenent Yet More Bloody," in *Complete Writings*, 4:508–9.

39 Ibid., 4:439–40.

40 Ibid., 4:209.

41 Ibid., 4:527–28, 414.

42 Ibid., 4:325.

> The bloody tenent of persecution for cause of conscience [is] a notorious and common pirate that takes and robs, that [burns] and sinks the spiritual ships, the consciences of men.[43]

Drawing on passages such as these, religious ethicist and human rights scholar Sumner B. Twiss has brilliantly summarized the main features of Williams's concept of conscience and its right to freedom as a natural right,[44] which may be paraphrased briefly as follows: Conscience is a natural inborn human capacity to determine fundamental convictions regarding moral and religious truth that, in turn, define personal identity and integrity, and manifest themselves in private and public behavior. These convictions are subject to change based on argument, evidence, and personal experience, but not because of coercion, which may affect outward behavior but not basic beliefs. Coerced behavior contrary to fundamental convictions causes a revolting sense of self-betrayal or the betrayal of solemn bonds to others and if long engaged in, can destroy personal identity and integrity. The widespread practice in Williams's time of punishing religious convictions – whether by taxation, deprival of civil standing and livelihood, imprisonment, torture, or death – was, he thought, premised on the mistaken assumption that core convictions can be attacked forcibly without damage to the person. On the contrary, punishing religious convictions is analogous to the crimes of rape and piracy, with rape a severe violation of an individual's physical integrity, and piracy of a group's material security. Violating the right of the freedom of conscience is equally heinous, perhaps more so.[45]

We should add that by explicitly linking violations of conscience or fundamental personal integrity with violations of physical or material integrity, like rape and piracy, Williams considers the natural right to freedom of conscience to be closely related to the natural right of self-defense. The right of self-defense may be defined as "the moral right to use reasonable or defensive force for the purpose of defending one's own life or the lives of others against a threat of arbitrary force," where "arbitrary force" means (at a minimum) "the deliberate infliction of death, impairment, severe pain/suffering, and/or material destruction for self-serving or manifestly unfounded reasons," and "reasonable or defensive force" means force necessary, proportional, and likely

43 Ibid., 4:5.

44 Sumner B. Twiss, "Roger Williams and the Right to Freedom of Conscience and Religion As a Natural Right," in *Religion and Public Policy: Human Rights, Conflict, and Ethics*, eds. Sumner B. Twiss, Marian Gh. Simion, and Rodney L. Petersen (New York, NY: Cambridge University Press, 2015), 45–76.

45 Ibid., 58–59.

successful in providing defense.[46] The crucial implication is that the right to freedom of conscience is one aspect – an aspect of the highest priority – of the right of self-defense, since surrendering one's deepest convictions and loyalties is to surrender one's very personhood. As such, the right is urgently worthy of forceful protection, along with other rights designed to protect against physical or material violations.

As morally compelling as the right of self-defense is, it poses a serious conundrum, of which natural rights thinkers, like Williams, were well aware. If everyone has a right to defend oneself against arbitrary force, then everyone has a right to take the law into one's own hands. Each person is his or her own judge, jury, and police officer, all wrapped up together, thus severely reducing the chances for impartial justice and raising the probability, ironically, of a very high incidence of arbitrary force. The solution, according to the natural rights tradition, is to establish and give consent to a constitutional government having as its primary purpose protecting the basic rights of citizens; in Williams's words, "the rights of a civil society ought justly to be preserved by a civil state."[47] A legitimate government, according to Williams, depends on representative institutions dedicated to the impartial making, adjudicating, and executing of laws aimed at guaranteeing the basic rights of citizens, especially the right of self-defense, which includes the right of freedom of conscience.[48]

Quite predictably, given the natural rights rationale just reviewed, Williams leaves no doubt about the source of legitimacy of earthly governments and their authority for using force. The "power, might, and authority" of government, he declared, "is not religious, Christian, etc., but natural, humane, and civil."[49] He hammered this point home in a three-day debate with Quakers in Newport in 1672. His charge that Quakerism leads to "arbitrary government" was met with the claim that Quakers, on the contrary, favor just government, one mark of which is the refusal to use force.

> I replied[, said Williams,] that [my opponent] mistook me[. By] arbitrary government, I did not intend a government ruling by force (for there could

[46] Author's definitions. See Little, *Essays in Religion and Human Rights*, 2.

[47] Williams, "Bloody Tenent Yet More Bloody," in *Complete Writings*, 4:74.

[48] See Twiss, "Roger Williams and the Right to Freedom of Conscience," 64–71 for an excellent discussion of Williams's notion of consensual government as the proper system for guaranteeing the right of freedom of conscience. To be precise, a legitimate government protects the right of self-defense, (1) by regulating it – e.g., passing laws restricting the use of guns and (2) by largely taking over the responsibility of defending citizens against arbitrary force through the rule of law.

[49] Williams, "Bloody Tenent of Persecution," 3:398.

> be no government in the world without the sword), but "arbitrary"... from *arbitrum*, which signified will or pleasure. And so my argument was that [for] persons immediately speaking from God, it was impertinent and profane to clog and encumber them with laws, [since] the voice of God proceeded out of their mouth.[50]

For Williams, there are two serious defects with the Quaker theory of government. One is the mistaken belief that a well-ordered government can completely renounce force. The other is that basing civil law on divine authority amounts to acting outside the law, or arbitrarily, precisely because political authority is not religious, but "natural, humane, and civil." Giving religious justification for the laws and policies of government is to give reasons that are "manifestly unfounded."

We should also add that the right to freedom of conscience, as well as other natural rights, was not for Williams without limit. Just as force may not be inflicted for self-serving reasons, such as personal benefit or gratification, so it may not be inflicted for even the most conscientiously held religious reasons. Williams harshly condemned "many priests and sects" in places like Mexico who imposed as part of their "horrid worship" the "sacrificing yearly [of] many thousands [of] infants to their bloody deities," and he included in his condemnation "one of the very kings of Judah" who "fell into the bloody pit" and "offer[ed] up ... children through the fire to Molech."[51]

More controversially, he condoned the right of rulers to constrain freedom of conscience in the interests of "chastity, humanity, etc." For example, he praised the Emperor of Rome for censuring Ovid because of that "wanton book of his, *De Arte amandi*, as a spark to immodesty and uncleanness."[52] And while, consistent with his policy of religious tolerance, "no Quaker was ever fined or whipped or burned or hanged" in Rhode Island for their beliefs or practices "on grounds of religious convictions alone,"[53] Williams nevertheless permitted some "moderate restraint" of Quakers in curbing behavior that, he felt, posed a threat to public order and safety. "Doubtless," he wrote, "it is the duty of the civil sword to cut off the incivilities of our times, as the monstrous hair of women, up[on] the heads of some men."[54] He also believed the Quaker practice of addressing authorities with the informal "thou," violated

[50] From Williams, "George Fox Digg'd Out His Burrowes," in *On Religious Liberty*, ed. Davis, 265 (italics added).

[51] Williams, "The Examiner Defended," in *Complete Writings*, 7:243.

[52] Ibid.

[53] Gaustad, *Liberty of Conscience*, 178.

[54] Williams, "The Examiner Defended," 7:243.

respect for superiors guaranteed by the fifth commandment, and he went so far as to favor restraining expressions of contempt for authority.[55] Other Quaker actions, such as excessive fasting, bodily quakings, and public nudity could equally be restrained because they were liable, he thought, to cause violence or prompt "fiery persecutions" by people opposed to such practices.[56] By suggesting debatable limitations like these, Williams entered a gray area of ongoing dispute right up to the present over which actions constitute actual threats to public order and safety.

When it came to limitations in the public interest on the exercise of natural rights in other ways, Williams was, again, probably not as permissive as might be expected. He answered the objection of some citizens of the Providence Plantation to a requirement of compulsory military service by alluding to the responsibilities of a ship's captain. As a general rule, the captain has no right to tell the crew and passengers what they should believe or how they should manifest the dictates of conscience, unless the public order or the material welfare of others is threatened. However, if the ship comes under attack, the captain is within his authority to command all hands to rally to the ship's defense. This, he implies, is a simple matter of the necessary protection of the outward bodies and goods of the people on board and is thus a consistent application of the basic principles of constitutional authority.[57]

His argument appears to run against a provision exempting conscientious objection from military service adopted by Rhode Island authorities in 1673 (the first of such colonial laws), after Williams was out of office. It is possible that those whom Williams was addressing were opposed not just to conscription but to the legitimacy of civil authority itself, in which case he was simply putting forward a general defense of civil government. However, it is also possible that in cases of conflict between an individual's conscientious objection to fighting and the people's compelling need to defend the common good, Williams decided in favor of the latter. If so, he was not as liberal as some of his fellow citizens proved to be.

Williams supplemented his natural rights argument with an appeal to natural justice or equity.[58] As Calvin had taught, the concept of equity, something "God has engraved upon the [human mind]," consists of two rules: "That everyone's rights should be safely preserved," and that everyone

55 Ibid., 5:58–62, 306–8; 7:179–80.

56 W. Clark Gilpin, *The Millenarian Piety of Roger Williams* (Chicago, IL: University of Chicago Press, 1979), 169.

57 Timothy L. Hall, *Separation of Church and State: Roger Williams and Religious Liberty* (Chicago, IL: University of Chicago Press, 1998), 46.

58 See Twiss, "Roger Williams and Freedom of Conscience," 53–56.

"be beneficent to neighbors" and "helpful to the necessities of others," relieving indigence with abundance.[59] The natural moral disposition toward both justice and benevolence is what makes civil community possible.

> Frequent experience in all parts of the world tells us that many thousands [of people] are far more peaceable subjects, more loving and helpful neighbors, and more true and fair dealers in civil interaction than many who account themselves to be the only religious people in the world.[60]
>
> [T]here is a moral virtue, fidelity, ability, and honesty which other men (beside church members) are, by good nature and education, by good laws and good examples, nourished and trained up in – [so] that civil places of trust and credit need not be monopolized into the hands of church members ... and all others deprived of their natural and civil rights and liberties.[61]

This innate moral capacity, however subject to corruption and distortion, is a crucial feature, for Williams, of the "natural, humane, and civil" authority upon which political society rests. Because that capacity exists – in tension, to be sure, with countervailing human impulses – Christians and other religious groups may confidently surrender their ill-founded ambition to take charge of earthly government, believing that peace and order across the world depend on them alone.

It would, however, be a serious mistake to conclude Williams left things at that. Along with references to experience and natural reason, he added extensive appeals to Christian Scripture, doctrine, and history. In one place, he writes that in shedding "the blood of so many hundred thousand of poor servants [of Jesus] by the civil powers of the world, pretending [thereby] to suppress blasphemies, heresies, idolatries, superstition, etc.," the persecutors of conscience are "lamentably guilty" of spilling the "most precious blood" of Jesus himself.[62] The decisive transgression took place

> when Constantine broke the bounds of this his own and God's edict, and [drew] the sword of civil power in suppressing other consciences for the [sake of] establishing the Christian [church.] [T]hen began the great mystery of the churches' sleep, [by which] the gardens of Christ's churches turned into the wilderness of National Religion, and the world (under Constantine's dominion) into the most unchristian Christendom ....There never was any

[59] John Calvin, *Epistles of Paul the Apostle to the Romans and to the Thessalonians*, trans. Ross Mackenzie (Grand Rapids, MI: Eerdmans, 1976), 420 (discussing 2 Thess. 3:12).

[60] Williams, "Bloody Tenent Yet More Bloody," 4:238.

[61] Ibid., 4:365.

[62] Ibid., 4:494.

> National Religion good in this world but one [namely, ancient Israel], and since the desolation of that nation, there shall never be any National Religion good again.[63]

This passage makes clear that Williams's famous image of the "wall of separation" between "the garden" and "the wilderness" does not mean, as Mark deWolfe Howe claimed,[64] that the wilderness is the civil state from which the "the gardens of Christ's churches" must be walled off pure and undefiled and with which the churches must have nothing whatsoever to do. Howe asserts erroneously that Williams favored a wall between the garden and the wilderness "not because he was fearful that without such a barrier the arm of the church would extend its reach. It was, rather, the dread of worldly corruptions which might consume the churches if sturdy fences against the wilderness [of the civil state] were not maintained."[65]

On the contrary, the wilderness Williams fears is the condition created by an established religion where *both* church *and* state are mutually degraded and corrupted by failing to observe the critical distinction between the inward and outward forums. A state where there is no establishment – where conscience is free to exercise itself as it should – is, to be sure, a place in which "the gardens of Christ's churches" can exist as intended; but it is also a place in which the state can perform its duties as intended, as well. It is such circumstances that exhibit the desirable degree of consonance and harmony between religious and civil organizations, with each fulfilling its proper vocation.

Williams occasionally argued that Scripture and history prove that "although the ... church and the civil kingdom or government [properly understood] be not inconsistent, but ... may stand together, yet they are independent,"[66] such that a political order may exist peacefully either without the presence of the church or alongside churches that are divided from each other, so long as those divisions do not disrupt the affairs of state.[67]

But while it is undoubtedly possible for secular regimes to organize themselves in peace and prosperity without Christian assistance, the proper

63 Ibid., 4:442. The reference to "ancient Israel" as the one exception to the Nonestablishment Principle underscores Williams's belief that the close interconnection of the religious and civil communities evident in the Old Testament was provisionally authorized by God "until Christ came." That arrangement was, as Williams says often, "a Nonesuch," or something never to be repeated.

64 Mark deWolfe Howe, *The Garden and the Wilderness* (Chicago, IL: University of Chicago Press, 1965).

65 Ibid., 6.

66 Williams, "Bloody Tenent of Persecution," 3:224–25.

67 Ibid., 3:355.

Christian approach adds a significant layer of support and encouragement for a well-ordered constitutional system dedicated to the disestablishment of religion and the protection of natural rights, including freedom of conscience. In short, the world needs all the help it can get in disabusing itself of the distortions of "national religion" and in thereby recovering its preexisting capacities for common civil and moral goodness. The Christian message, properly preached and practiced, may be of considerable auxiliary assistance. "Now that [the state] is under Christ, when all nations are merely civil," civil justice, having merely "a material nature," is aimed solely at the protection of outward behavior and cannot "extend to matters of the spirit and soul."[68] It is emphatically the disestablished state that "will be found to agree most punctually with the rules of the best politician that ever the world saw, the King of kings and Lord of lords."[69]

Of special salience in understanding how Williams's arguments for freedom of conscience based on experience, reason, and religion converged in practice was his attitude toward the Native Americans of his time, and particularly the Narragansett Indians, who dwelt in the region that would be occupied in part by the Rhode Island colony. Above all, Williams manifested a deep respect and sympathy for them, not least because they welcomed and provided for him after he was banished by the Massachusetts Bay authorities for his subversive opinions. One of those opinions – that "we [English settlers] have not our land by patent from the King, but that the natives are the true owners of it, and that we ought to repent of such a receiving by patent"[70] – became a key provision of the Rhode Island Charter, declaring that "that it shall not be lawful to or for the rest of the colonies to invade or molest the native Indians."[71]

In his remarkable study of the language and mores of the Narragansetts, *A Key into the Language of America: A Help to the Language of the Natives in That Part of America Called New England*,[72] Williams opposed the idea of most of the settlers that Native Americans had no concept of property.

[68] Williams, "Bloody Tenent," cited in Perry Miller, *Roger Williams, His Contribution to the American Tradition* (New York, NY: Atheneum, 1962), 133 (italics added). I confess I have reconstructed this passage, thereby (I hope) clarifying its meaning.

[69] Williams, "Bloody Tenent of Persecution," 3:178.

[70] Cited in Irwin H. Polishook, ed., *Roger Williams, John Cotton and Religious Freedom: A Controversy in New and Old England* (Englewood Cliffs, NJ: Prentice Hall, 1967), 47.

[71] Cited in Martha Nussbaum, *The New Religious Intolerance: Overcoming the Politics of Fear in an Anxious Age* (Cambridge, MA: Belknap Press of Harvard University Press, 2012), 152.

[72] Roger Williams, *A Key into the Language of America: A Help to the Language of the Natives in That Part of America Called New England* (Bedford, MA: Applewood Books, 1936), first published in England in 1643.

He contended, on the contrary, that "the natives are very exact and punctual in the bounds of their lands, belonging to this prince or people ... notwithstanding a sinful opinion amongst many that Christians have a right to heathen lands."[73] Accordingly, he developed a sterling reputation with the Narragansetts as a fair and honorable partner in all land transactions, as well as in his extended dealings with them over the years as proprietor of a trading post. He was especially close friends with two Narragansett chiefs, Massosoit and Canonicus, who came to think of him as a Sachim, or native leader, like them.

Beyond that, Williams believed steadfastly that Native Americans have a right to their own government.

> It cannot be denied ... that their civil and earthly governments be as lawful and true as any governments in the world, and therefore consequently their governors are keepers of the church, or both tables, if any church of Christ should arise or be amongst them. And therefore ... if Christ has entrusted and charged the civil power with his church, they must judge according to their Indian or American consciences, for other consciences it cannot be supposed they should have.[74]

Given Williams's general theory of conscience, including the limits he enumerates against violations of both tables of the Decalogue, he no doubt means that Native American governments, along with all other temporal governments, should be held accountable to common standards of justice and equity. If a Christian church were to be found under their jurisdiction, Native Americans, like everyone else, would be responsible to uphold the natural rights of all, including the right to freedom of conscience, as well as the other obligations that follow from an idea of authority that is "natural, humane, and civil." But assuming all that, Williams's primary point here is to defend the sovereignty of Native American governments and their right to carry out without interference political and legal functions as regards religious bodies and other matters according "to their Indian or American consciences."

Notably, he assures his readers that native consciences can be trusted. Despite the fact that he often sharply disagrees with Native American religious beliefs and practices (as he did with many of the religious groups he welcomed to Rhode Island), he admired their tolerant spirit. "They have," he says, "a modest religious persuasion not to disturb any man, either [among]

[73] Ibid., 95.
[74] Cited in Davis, *On Religious Liberty*, 133.

themselves [or the] English, Dutch, or any [others] in their conscience and worship."[75] "The very Indians" "abhor" the idea of compelling people to do things they should decide for themselves, such as commanding "an unwilling spouse ... into a forced bed."[76] Moreover, such solicitude is part of a broader pattern of persistent benevolence. "If any stranger come in, they presently give him to eat of what they have; many a time, and at all times of the night (as I have fallen in travel upon their houses) when nothing has been ready, have themselves and their wives, risen to prepare me some refreshing."[77]

In fact, Native Americans frequently outshone the colonists in the practice of basic human decency. "If nature's sons both wild and tame, humane and courteous be: How ill becomes it sons of God to want humanity?" Accordingly, Williams warns the colonists against presumptions of cultural and moral superiority: "Boast not, proud English, of thy birth and blood, Thy brother Indian is by birth as good. Of one blood God made him and thee and all, as wise, as fair, as strong, as personal."[78]

Williams opposed attempts to convert the Native Americans to Christianity for several reasons. One was the evidence of moral and spiritual inferiority of the Christian colonists. To win Native Americans to perverted expressions of Christian faith and action would do them no favor. Another reason was the conviction, informed by his millenarianism, that since Christ's second coming had been postponed, it is best to wait until "Zion and Jerusalem be rebuilt and reestablished before the law and word of life be sent forth to the rest of the nations of the world, who have not heard of Christ."[79]

But a very prominent reason, predictably, was that the colonists, given their abysmal record of predatory abuse, could not be trusted to respect the consciences of Native Americans. "If the reports [by historians] be true, what monstrous and most inhumane conversions [colonialists in many parts of the world] have made, baptizing thousands, yea ten thousands of poor natives, sometimes by wiles and subtle devices, sometimes by force compelling them to submit to that which they understood not, neither before nor after ... their monstrous Christenings of them."[80]

75 Williams, "A Key into the Language of America," in *Complete Writings*, 1:153.

76 Williams, "A Brief Discourse Concerning That Name, Commonly Given to the Indians," in *Complete Writings*, 7:38.

77 Williams, "A Key into the Language of America,"1:46.

78 Ibid., 1:39, 81.

79 Williams, "A Brief Discourse Concerning That Name, Heathen, Commonly Given to the Indians," 7:40.

80 Ibid., 7:36.

## CONCLUSION

With the help of recent scholarship, we have confirmed an important conclusion drawn a century ago by the Austrian legal scholar, Georg Jellinek.[81] It is not to eighteenth-century figures, whether French or American, that we must look to find the early theoretical foundations of the constitutional protection of freedom of conscience but to a colonial Puritan of the seventeenth century, Roger Williams. Employing ingenious arguments based on experience, natural reason, and religion, he inspired and guided "the first commonwealth in modern history" to provide constitutional protection for such a broadly inclusive right to religious freedom.[82] The experiment was not without its serious difficulties and shortcomings, and the Rhode Island colony would fall far below Williams's original standards during the eighteenth and nineteenth centuries. Still, there is no gainsaying the continuing allure of his contribution, both in theory and practice.

## RECOMMENDED READING

Byrd, James P. Jr. *The Challenges of Roger Williams: Religious Liberty, Violent Persecution, and the Bible*. Macon, GA: Mercer University Press, 2002.

Davis, James Calvin. *Moral Theology of Roger Williams: Christian Conviction and Public Ethics*. Louisville, KY: Westminster John Knox, 2004.

ed. *On Religious Liberty: Selections from the Works of Roger Williams* Cambridge, MA: Belknap Press of Harvard University Press, 2008.

Gaustad, Edward. *Liberty of Conscience: Roger Williams in America*. Grand Rapids, MI: Eerdmans, 1991.

Gilpin, W. Clark. *Millenarian Piety of Roger Williams*. Chicago, IL: University of Chicago Press, 1979.

Hall, Timothy L. *Separation of Church and State: Roger Williams and Religious Liberty*. Chicago, IL: University of Chicago Press, 1998.

Lutz, Donald S. *Origins of American Constitutionalism*. Baton Rouge, LA: Louisiana State University Press, 1988.

McIlwain, C. H. *Constitutionalism and Its Changing World*. Cambridge: Cambridge University Press, 1939.

Miller, Perry. *Roger Williams, His Contribution to the American Tradition*. New York, NY: Atheneum, 1962.

Miller, William Lee. *The First Freedom: America's Foundation in Religious Freedom*. Washington, DC: Georgetown University Press, 2003.

[81] Georg Jellinek, *The Declaration of the Rights of Man and of Citizens: A Contribution to Constitutional History* (Westport, CT: Hyperion Press, 1979), 77, first published in German in 1895.

[82] See n. 6.

Morgan, Edmund S. *Roger Williams: The Church and the State*. New York, NY: Harcourt Brace & World, 1967.
Nussbaum, Martha C. *Liberty of Conscience: In Defense of American's Tradition of Religious Equality*. New York, NY: Basic Books, 2008.
Pfeffer, Leo. "Freedom and/or Separation: The Constitutional Dilemma of the First Amendment," *Minnesota Law Review* 64, no. 3 (1980): 561–84.
Polishook, Irwin H., ed. *Roger Williams, John Cotton and Religious Freedom: A Controversy in New and Old England*. Englewood Cliffs, NJ: Prentice Hall, 1967.
Twiss, Sumner B. "Roger Williams and Freedom of Conscience and Religion As a Natural Right." In *Religion and Public Policy: Human Rights, Conflict, and Ethics*, edited by Sumner B. Twiss, Marian Gh. Simion, and Rodney L. Petersen, 45–76. New York, NY: Cambridge University Press, 2015.
Wilken, Robert Louis. *Liberty in the Things of God: The Christian Origins of Religious Freedom*. New Haven, CT: Yale University Press, 2019.
Winslow, Ola Elizabeth. *Master Roger Williams: A Biography*. New York, NY: Macmillan, 1957.

## 11

# Jonathan Edwards on Conscience

MICHAEL MCCLYMOND

What the American theologian and philosopher Jonathan Edwards (1703–58) wrote on conscience was original in content and orderly in argumentation. Scattered through the seventy-three-volume critical edition of Edwards's writings are discussions of this theme. The term itself appears around 1,800 times.[1] As a Christian thinker, Edwards was primarily concerned with conscience as a human faculty or function in its relation to God – the "conviction of conscience" as he termed it – rather than conscience in daily decision-making. Occasionally, he commented on so-called matters of conscience and the ecclesiastical question of what the Christian church should or should not do to bind its members to definite standards of belief and practice. This was a traditional Protestant theme in which Calvinist-Puritan thinkers took exception in the name of gospel liberty to what they viewed as Roman Catholic legalism. Nonetheless, the main line of development in Edwards's treatment of conscience moved in a different direction and was shaped by his twofold identity. Edwards was both an inheritor of Calvinist-Puritan theology and an eighteenth-century philosophical innovator engaged with the moral sense and benevolist theories of such Enlightenment thinkers as Lord Shaftesbury (Anthony Ashley Cooper, 3rd Earl of Shaftesbury; 1671–1713) and Francis Hutcheson (1694–1746).

Among the salient features in Edwards's approach to conscience was a distinction – but not separation – between what Edwards called "natural conscience" and what one might call supernatural or Holy Spirit–enabled

[1] All citations of primary texts herein are to the 73-volume critical edition, Jonathan Edwards, *The Works of Jonathan Edwards*, vols. 1–26 (1957–2008) (New Haven, CT: Yale University Press); and vols. 27–73 (New Haven, CT: Jonathan Edwards Center at Yale University) (hereafter, WJE). All 73 volumes may be accessed at edwards.yale.edu. Citations will follow the traditional style of: WJE volume number:page number.

conscience. It is intriguing to see that Edwards – known for attaching distinctive names to his own key concepts (e.g., "excellency," "consent," "sense of the heart") – did not in this case introduce any neologism to denote the human conscience in its Spirit-enabled operations. Though the distinction between natural and Spirit-enabled conscience appears in dozens if not hundreds of passages, the two phenomena are denoted with the single term "conscience." In this way, Edwards highlighted the integrity rather than disparity of nature and grace, and so his writings accord with the famous dictum of Thomas Aquinas that *gratia non tollit sed perficit naturam* ("grace does not destroy nature but perfects it"). He writes:

> The way of the Spirit's working, when it does convince men, is by enlightening natural conscience. The Spirit does not work by giving a testimony, but by assisting natural conscience to do its work. Natural conscience is the instrument in the hand of God, to accuse, condemn, terrify, and to urge to duty. The Spirit of God leads men into the consideration of their danger, and makes them to be affected therewith.[2]

Edwards' basic position was thus that the Holy Spirit works in and through natural conscience, actualizing or enhancing something that already exists within human nature.

Alongside this harmonious understanding of nature and grace was another aspect in Edwards's theology, pulling in a different direction. Like earlier Puritan authors, and Catholic Augustinians (e.g., Jansenists), Edwards presumed that human nature had been corrupted by human sin. Human nature, as fallen, stood under God's just condemnation. Salvation came by grace, and not by nature alone. Salvation from a state of corrupted nature required conversion and rebirth by the power of God's Spirit and not mere moral self-improvement. Yet fallen human beings, in self-serving fashion, could knowingly or unwittingly counterfeit the operations of grace and conversion to produce insincere and hypocritical manifestations of religion. What Edwards shared with earlier Puritan authors – and in contrast to eighteenth-century Enlightenment thinkers – was a preoccupation with identifying the marks of genuine and sincere religion in contrast to specious and hypocritical piety. Like earlier Puritans, he presumed that spiritual experiences must not be taken at face value but ought rather to be interrogated. This led toward introspection and the self-questioning and sometimes self-lacerating Puritan conscience. Edwards's life-long quest to distinguish true from false religion sets the context for understanding his teaching on conscience.

[2] Edwards, WJE 2:156.

In summary, one may identify a *unitive motif* in Edwards's idea of natural conscience in its functioning both apart from and in accord with the Holy Spirit, and a *differential motif* in Edwards's effort to demarcate true religion from its simulacra. This tension largely mirrors a contrast between the two ethical traditions to which Edwards was equally indebted, viz., seventeenth-century Puritanism and eighteenth-century moral sense philosophy, to which we now turn.

## THE PURITAN AND ENLIGHTENMENT BACKGROUND IN EDWARDS'S THOUGHT

In seventeenth-century New England Puritanism, most authors held that God usually prepares a person for conversion by a series of steps, using means of grace such as preaching and prayer and progressing through such steps as knowledge of the law, conviction of sin, striving for grace, false assurance, disappointment, and finally saving faith. This "morphology of conversion" went back to Puritan divines William Perkins (1558–1602) and William Ames (1576–1633) but was redeployed in response to the 1636–38 antinomian crisis involving Anne Hutchinson (1591–1643) and others who taught that conversion comes apart from human activity or the use of the means of grace.[3] Puritan theologians wanted to emphasize the role of the law in showing spiritual seekers that they do not measure up to God's standards and so need a savior. They also typically distinguished the steps leading up to conversion, warning that following them does not guarantee conversion, and that there is a difference between the human efforts of preparation for the grace of conversion and the gift of God's grace itself.[4]

In interpreting Scripture, Edwards followed Puritan authors by stressing the preparatory function of the law in ancient Israel and also in Christians' experience. He commented that God "first revealed the law with thunders and lightnings from Mount Sinai before the full revelation of his grace by Jesus Christ." So too it was "with particular persons": "God first awakens them to a sense of his awe-inspiring justice and displeasure toward sin before giving them a "sense of his grace."[5] A fear of punishment accompanies this awareness of God's justice: "'Tis much according to God's way of dealing, that the sinner

[3] On the "morphology of conversion," see Edmund S. Morgan, *Visible Saints* (New York, NY: New York University Press, 1963), 66–70.

[4] Ibid., 68–69.

[5] Edwards, WJE 13:412.

should first be terrified with a sense of his danger before God manifests his favor."[6] God's customary manner in preparing people for grace involves a threefold process. A person sees his or her "danger of eternal misery," which Edwards terms "conviction," and then in the stage known as "humiliation" someone gains ability "to see the absolute necessity of a savior," and only after that, in "conversion," "see[s] the sufficiency and excellency of the Savior that is offered."[7] The minister's pastoral task was to discern when genuine conversion had taken place and to distinguish such genuine conversion from merely natural or transient feelings that might soon dissipate and leave behind no residue of solid faith. To the diagnosis of parishioners' spiritual state, the Puritan minister applied all the care and diligence that today's cardiac specialist might devote to the ascertainment of heart arrhythmia, tachycardia, or pericarditis. In the words of the American religious historian, Brooks Holifield, for the Puritan minister "the most dangerous pastoral temptation ... [was] to offer premature comfort to persons under conviction, thereby producing complacency at exactly the wrong moment."[8]

Edwards maintained the "preparationist" perspective of his New England forbears, that is, the idea that those who were under conviction of sins but not yet converted by grace needed to make vigorous use of the means of grace in order to press forward toward conversion. "We advise persons under convictions," he wrote, "to be earnest and violent for the kingdom of heaven ... watchful, laborious, and earnest, in the whole work of religion." His sermon on Jacob's wrestling with the angel had as its thesis: "The way to obtain the blessing of God is not to let God go except he bless us."[9] But Edwards was impatient with teachings about the pre-conversion process that were overly formulaic or that implied that a sequence of experiences had necessarily to follow one another in a fixed order. The Apostle Paul, he argued, received God's saving grace without first experiencing any conviction of his own sins (Acts 9), and the crowds on the Day of Pentecost (Acts 2) were likewise recipients of saving grace without being "explicitly convinced" of their own

6 Ibid., 13:283.

7 Ibid., 13:385, 398, 400.

8 E. Brooks Holifield, A *History of Pastoral Care in America: From Salvation to Self-realization* (Nashville, TN: Abingdon Press, 1983), 90–91: "He filled the pastoral office, helping to interpret the experiences of his parishioners, lending aid in decisions involving 'cases of conscience,' as they were called." Cf. John Smith, "Editor's Introduction," in WJE 2:4.

9 Edwards, WJE 16:91, 22:542. On Edwards's preparationism, see John Gerstner, *Steps to Salvation: The Evangelistic Message of Jonathan Edwards* (Philadelphia, PA: Westminster Press, 1960); and John Gerstner and Jonathan Neil Gerstner, "Edwardsean Preparation for Salvation," *Westminster Theological Journal* 42 (1979): 5–71.

status as sinners. Edwards's own experience departed from the stereotypical Puritan pattern. His "turns of weeping and crying" over his own sins came many years after his conversion and not prior to it.[10] Edwards's greatest innovation – contrary to his reputation as a hellfire preacher – may have been precisely in the diminished role that he assigned to fear and terror as a spiritual motivator, in contrast with his Puritan predecessors. He saw the motivation for conversion as an *attraction* to God's beauty much more than a *repulsion* from divine judgment or punishment.

The eighteenth-century intellectual world was dominated by an idea later termed "benevolism" – the notion that human beings are naturally benevolent because of an inherent altruism or "moral sense." For his part, Edwards was convinced from biblical teaching as well as from general experience that human nature had been corrupted by sin and so that the optimism of benevolism was misplaced. As a philosopher, Edwards sought to use the very premises and arguments of benevolism to stand it on its head. His *Nature of True Virtue*, written near the end of his life (though published much later), reflected two aims: to show that the "moral sense" was simply the old-fashioned conscience in disguise and to make his own idea of holiness as benevolence toward God "a philosophically credible notion in the forums of enlightenment."[11] He accepted the benevolists' assumption that general benevolence (i.e., directed toward all persons) was the summit of virtue, but he argued that their moral sense was reducible to natural conscience together with expanded forms of self-love (e.g., love for spouse, family, friends, tribe, nation) that *all fell short of general benevolence*. As Norman Fiering expressed Edwards's view: "True virtue stands against the parochiality of the world, the comforting alliances of like souls and common blood."[12] He affirmed the benevolists' consensus that virtue was "something beautiful" but insisted that their notions of beauty, based on symmetry and harmony, were only "secondary" shadows of what he called "primary beauty," which consisted in the "consent" or "union" of spiritual beings to one another and of all spiritual beings to God himself.[13]

Edwards's *Nature of True Virtue* has for its thesis the proposition that true virtue "most essentially consists in benevolence to being."[14] Because the concept of "being" – as Edwards understood it – not only included God but

[10] Edwards, WJE 23:86–87, 13:398, 16:803.

[11] Norman Fiering, *Jonathan Edwards's Moral Thought and Its British Context* (Chapel Hill, NC: University of North Carolina Press, 1981), 106.

[12] Ibid., 196.

[13] Edwards, WJE 8:561–65.

[14] Ibid., 8:540.

placed God at the center of all reality (as "Being in general"), there could be no bona fide moral philosophy of benevolism that excluded God from his rightful role as the preeminent focus of all human benevolence. While the eighteenth-century philosophers sought to extricate morality from religion, Edwards in contrast sought to bind them together again. Francis Hutcheson had stipulated that people become moral when they apprehend and approve of goodness and beauty. Edwards employed Hutcheson's ethical framework but adapted it for his own purposes, claiming that moral apprehension and moral approval required the new "sense of the heart" that comes only with the perception of God's own "excellency" that occurs in religious conversion. Because of original sin, the natural mind cannot see God's moral beauty through its own unaided powers. Moreover, goodness and beauty do not exist apart from God, as Hutcheson intimated, but they are aspects of God's own character. Thus, the virtue that regenerate persons (i.e., those who have received saving grace from God) see and approve is *God's* virtue. Human moral goodness might be understood as a "participation" in God's own moral goodness. Edwards goes so far as to say that human consent to moral goodness is a finite image or analogy of the consent between God the Father and God the Son.

Edwards in *Nature of True Virtue* presented an encompassing picture of human moral life. In a work that never quotes the Bible and was clearly intended for readers who did not share his theological vision, Edwards explained that all human beings share certain common moral goals or aspirations. The unregenerate (i.e., those who have not received God's saving grace) do not approve of these goals for the same reasons that the regenerate do, but both nonetheless approve of the same moral ends. While only the regenerate are able to see the true beauty of general benevolence, both regenerate and unregenerate alike perceive that general benevolence is grounded in natural uniformity, equality, and justice. This shared perception is possible because nearly all human beings share the same general sense of moral good and evil, otherwise known as conscience, engraved by God the Creator on all consciences alike. Following biblical and Puritan precedents, Edwards held that an individual's conscience might be seared through repeated acts of grievous sin and so become deadened and devoid even of common notions of good and evil. Such instances were, though, for Edwards, exceptional rather than normative.

Edwards argued in *Nature of True Virtue* that human beings share aesthetic perception and an appreciation of many sorts of physical and spiritual beauty. Such shared perception carries moral meaning even though it falls short of the perception of what Edwards called "primary beauty" and which consists in consent to universal being. Furthermore, nearly all human beings share in certain elementary religious knowledge (e.g., the awareness of God's existence and beneficent providence) and also instinctual kind affections such as pity or compassion and familial love.[15] The natural awareness of good and evil is ineluctably linked to some notion of deserved rewards or punishments. This, for Edwards, is the origin of the instinct for justice, and its pervasiveness in human life is apparent when one examines the laws and customs of various nations. The well-known phenomenon of patriotism falls short of true benevolence and reveals itself in Edwards's analysis to be a form of enlarged self-interest. Nonetheless, patriotism draws the individual beyond the limits of private self-interest, evokes noble sacrifices for some larger good, and so displays at least some analogy to benevolence to being in general. Such shared experiences led Edwards to conclude that every person held a place within the structure of being and was obliged to acknowledge this and to give "cordial consent" to it by seeking its highest good. This means that one had to love the "Being of beings" or "Being in general" (understood to be God) and all other beings in the cosmos.[16]

## NATURAL CONSCIENCE, TRUE RELIGION, AND "THE SENSE OF THE HEART"

For Edwards, conscience was a natural disposition, arising from self-love, that is "uneasy in a consciousness of being inconsistent" with itself. We feel unease when we do to others what we would object to, and what would make us angry, if done to us. Likewise, we feel unease in neglecting to do for others what we think they ought to do for us in comparable circumstances. In other words, God has implanted into all human beings an awareness of something like the Golden Rule. Edwards functions not with a Kantian principle of *universalizability*, as expressed in Kant's categorical imperative, but rather a principle of *reversibility*, whereby moral reasoning is based on an empathetic imagining of oneself in the other person's shoes. The principle of reversibility also functions in another way, as one imagines oneself as having opportunity (i.e., in becoming another person) to act in certain ways (i.e., helpful or harmful) toward one's own self. Edwards writes: "There is also an approbation of conscience of the conduct of others towards ourselves. As when we are blamed, condemned, or punished by them, and are conscious to ourselves that if we were in their case, and they in ours, we should in like manner

[15] Ibid., 8:50–56, 134–36.
[16] Ibid., 8:620.

blame, condemn, and punish them."[17] In addition to the conscience, God gives to every person an aesthetic "sense of desert" that recognizes "a natural agreement, proportion, and harmony" that exists between doing wrong and receiving resentment or punishment, and "between loving and being loved . . . showing kindness and being rewarded." Human conscience is not equivalent to true virtue or "benevolence to being in general." Yet if a natural person's understanding is enlightened and his or her prejudices are removed, the conscience "concurs with the law of God . . . and joins its voice with it in every article."[18]

Natural conscience can thus fall short of true virtue and yet approve of true virtue, though without any delight in or vision of God's beauty. Edwards suggested that God ordered natural conscience in this way for two reasons: for the good order and preservation of society and to provide an image (in the conscience's consent to aesthetic proportion) of the mutual consent and union between the Father and the Son. Natural conscience approves of benevolence toward God because it is aware of our need to repay the Creator who gave us life. Yet natural conscience does not taste the sweetness of such benevolence toward God. Related closely to conscience is the natural sense of justice – a sense that God gives to all human beings through creation. This too is rooted in the aesthetic perception of "a natural agreement and adaptedness of things that have relation to one another." Human beings naturally understand that "he which from his will *does* evil to others should *receive* evil from the will of others, or from the will of him whose business it is to take care of the injured," and also that "he that loves [should have] the proper returns of love." Most of our moral duties, Edwards believed, "partake in the nature of justice" – the duties of children and parents, spouses and neighbors to one another, and human beings to God and Christ. Justice is among those virtues that comprise "the beauty of order in society" in which people fulfill their differing social roles. Such beautiful order is "not of a different kind from the regularity of a beautiful building, or piece of skilled architecture," for they all exhibit "the united tendency of thoughts, ideas, and particular volitions, to one general purpose." Those who are regenerate, or "with a truly virtuous taste" will especially relish justice because of its conformity to the principle of general benevolence.[19]

Conscience has the obvious function in Edwards of bringing someone to awareness of wrongdoing. Both unregenerate and regenerate persons experience

[17] Ibid., 8:590.
[18] Ibid., 8:589, 593; 42:594–95.
[19] Ibid., 8:568, 571–72, 573–74 (emphasis in original).

such awareness or conviction. Both can be moved to moral action by a stirring sermon or earnest exhortation. Yet the sense of moral urgency among unregenerate persons occur "only [by] the assistance of natural principles."[20] Their moral nature, common to all persons, is excited by the knowledge of their wrong and by a sense of obligation. "But special grace causes the faculties to do that that [sic] they do not by nature," wrote Edwards. It imparts to the soul new things "that are above nature," such as love for God. These are not mere fleeting impulses but a permanent habit that "lays ... a foundation for a continued course of exercises" of love. In this way "saving grace" differs "not only in degree, but in nature and kind from common grace, or anything that is ever found in natural men." While "common grace" may impart temporary influences and illuminations of the Holy Spirit, it does not communicate the Spirit in his own "proper nature," as in regenerate persons.[21]

Edwards used the phrase "sense of the heart" (and sometimes "new sense") to highlight the way in which the Holy Spirit – or sometimes a "divine and supernatural light" – communicated to the individual regenerate person "a true sense of the divine excellency of the things revealed in the Word of God and a conviction of the truth and reality of them."[22] This "sense of the heart" was never known or experienced at second hand or as an observer, but only at first hand and as a participant. It is a "spiritual illumination" in which persons become "inwardly sensible of the divine excellency, giving a new spiritual sense, [or] a new sense of [the] heart, a new spiritual relish."[23]

One of Edwards's most famous analogies to illustrate this point was as follows:

> There is a difference between having a rational judgment that honey is sweet, and having a sense of its sweetness. A man may have the former that knows not how honey tastes; but a man can't have the latter, unless he has an idea of the taste of the honey in his mind. So there is a difference between believing that a person is beautiful, and having a sense of his beauty. The former may be obtained by hearsay, but the latter only by seeing the countenance.[24]

Edwards compared the "sense of the heart" to Locke's "new simple idea."[25] Those who lacked the new sense would not be able to understand someone else's explanation of it – just as a person born blind would not be able to understand the differences between colors.

20 Ibid., 21:153, 155.
21 Ibid., 18:230–32, 498; 11:94.
22 Ibid., 17:410–13.
23 Ibid., 25:303–4.
24 Ibid., 17:414.
25 Ibid., 2:205.

## CONSCIENCE IN ITS NATURE AND FUNCTIONS

In Edwards's conception, the human conscience was intrinsically connected to notions of reward and punishment. He writes: "Men's natural conscience naturally ... suggests a relation between their crimes and punishment."[26] In *Freedom of the Will*, Edwards connects human moral agency with "praise and blame, approbation and remorse of conscience" – a phrase suggesting that conscience has the basic function of praising or blaming the individual in question.[27] Edwards judges that the link between conscience and punishment is universal in human history: "All nations have this sense of the propriety of punishing men for faults."[28] As an illustration, Edwards cites Cicero: "So great is the power of conscience, that those, who have committed any fault, live in perpetual fear of punishment."[29] One might distinguish the awareness of *right* and *wrong* from that of *rewards* and *punishments* and both of these from the concepts of *rewardability* and *punishability*. A pained or guilty conscience is not itself punishment but rather an awareness that punishment is due or merited by a certain evil action. Like the later philosopher Immanuel Kant, Edwards asserted that someone's awareness of having done moral wrong included within it a sense of *punishability* – that is, of being justly subject to punishment.

Ancient peoples throughout the world generally held that God or the gods were agents of retribution, visiting punishments on the guilty and conferring rewards on the righteous. For Edwards, the awareness of a powerful and even fear-inducing God – such as the Bible depicts on Mount Sinai, in the giving of the Ten Commandments (Exod. 19) – enlivens the human mind to apprehend the punishability of evil acts and the rewardability of good acts. Edwards writes: "The awful and terrible greatness of God ... assists conscience the more strongly and fully to suggest the relation that there is between their sins and punishment, and assists it to intimate a relation or proportion between their sins and a very great punishment. That is the proper work of conscience, to suggest a relation between sin and punishment, or sin's desert of punishment. If there be anything at all of conscience in a natural man, there is something of this."[30]

For Edwards, the conscience is connected either with "pain" or "disquiet," or else with "peace" or "tranquility," based on the decision either to act in

26 Ibid., 13:509.
27 Ibid., 1:464.
28 Ibid., 21:429.
29 Ibid., 23:214; citing Cicero, *Pro Milone*.
30 Ibid., 13:511.

accord with or in discord with one's own moral perception. He speaks of "remorse of conscience," and of "conscience" as consisting in "pain inflicted on the person in whom this moral evil is."[31]

When conscience is in "pain," then the "natural inclination" – that is, to approve or disapprove of certain actions in oneself or another – is thereby "contradicted." "Uneasiness" or "disquiet" is the inevitable reflex of someone's violation of their own "natural inclination."[32] Such moral uneasiness occurs in the life of believers no less than in the life of nonbelievers, and "when true Christians are in an ill frame, guilt lies on the conscience; which will bring fear, and so prevent the peace and joy of an assured hope."[33]

Paul Ramsey interpreted Edwards's discussion of the conscience's moral disquiet versus moral tranquility as implying an ethic of "self-union," "consistency with self," or "integrity."[34] Conversely, "when there is no sense of any such dissent from being in general, there is no contradiction to the natural inclination . . . and then there is peace of conscience."[35] Regarding peaceful conscience he writes: "Take notice when we are in the best frames, meditating on divine excellence, our idea of that tranquility and peace which seems to be overspread and cast abroad upon the whole earth and universe naturally dissolves itself into the idea of a general love and delight, everywhere diffused. Conscience is that sense the mind has of this consent."[36] This seems a picture of heaven on earth – tranquility, consent, and love expressed by all intelligent beings and toward all intelligent beings, including God as the ultimate giver and recipient of such love.

Depending on individual moral choices, someone's conscience over time may become more "tender" and sensitive to moral wrong, or else "stupefied" and unfeeling. Edwards judged that the youthful David Brainerd fell into the former category: "How tender was his conscience! ... How strict his care and watchfulness against sin!"[37] Conversely, it is "that higher degree of

31 Ibid., 1:458; 1:358.
32 Ibid., 1:50.
33 Ibid., 2:195.
34 Paul Ramsey, "Editor's Introduction," in WJE 8:42.
35 Edwards, WJE 6:366, Misc. 232, on the misery of the damned, develops the same ideas.
36 Ibid., 6:365. Brainerd himself wrote: "Oh, how blessed a thing is it to enjoy peace of conscience! But how dreadful is a want of inward peace and composure of soul!" Ibid., 7:440.
37 Ibid., 5:507. Brainerd commended those Natives Americans whom he viewed as having a "tender" conscience: "I was refreshed to see the tenderness of conscience manifest in some of them, one instance of which I cannot but take notice of. Perceiving one of them very sorrowful in the morning, I inquired into the cause of her sorrow, and found the difficulty was she had been angry with her child the evening before and was now exercised with fears." Ibid., 7:313.

wickedness, which causeth stupidity of conscience," when "conscience has been stupefied by frequent violations."[38] Because "some men . . . will go on in sin against clearer light and stronger convictions of conscience," their culpability will also be greater than that of other people.[39] The greater one's sense of moral right or wrongness in any situation, the greater one's obligation to follow moral sense.

Conscience, on Edwards's view, is not an infallible guide but may be erroneous. The case of David Brainerd (whose diary Edwards published posthumously) is instructive. Edwards regarded this young missionary among Native Americans in the wilds of Pennsylvania as a sincere, earnest, and self-denying believer who was nonetheless mistaken in believing that he needed to adopt an ascetic lifestyle (involving fasting, vigils, exposure to cold, etc.) even as he was plainly becoming more and more sickly. Edwards commented that "his enfeebled spirits cast on fuel to fire his sickness," and added, "had not a friend of his convinced him of his erroneous conscience misleading him at that time, he had murdered his body out of conscience to save his soul and to preserve his grace."[40] After abjuring his excessively strict regimen, Brainerd later succumbed to tuberculosis – a victim of his own over-scrupulous conscience.

## CONSCIENCE IN RELATION TO SUPERNATURAL GRACE AND THE HOLY SPIRIT

As noted above, Edwards in his ethical writings was concerned to define both the extent and the limits of natural conscience. He writes that "even in a graceless state, men do have a moral conscience by which they can devise a reasonably decent mode of life, but such virtues as attach to this natural morality never rise to the heights of a true virtue."[41]

One of the challenging ideas arising within Edwards's reflection on the "natural man" is his claim that such persons may receive assistance by the Holy Spirit in perceiving right and wrong, yet without receiving the regenerating or saving grace of the Holy Spirit: "The Spirit of God may operate and produce effects upon the minds of natural men that have no grace, as he does when he assists natural conscience and convictions."[42] The natural man in

[38] Ibid., 8:615, cf. 18:436.
[39] Ibid., 8:597.
[40] Ibid., 7:429.
[41] Ibid., 3:36.
[42] Ibid., 21:192.

such a case is *neither regenerated, nor devoid of the Spirit's work in giving moral illumination and insight in some measure*. In light of this passage, the line in Edwards's theology between the natural and the supernatural is not as clear as one might have imagined. Even a natural person, on realizing that she owes all that she has to God, may perceive the obligation of loving God supremely – "yielding all to God, as we receive all from God."[43] Nonetheless, such an acquiescence by a natural person to the justice of loving God will not involve any genuine perception of the beauty of loving God: "A natural man has no sense of the beauty and amiableness of virtue and the turpitude and odiousness of vice."[44] Here we see the double-sidedness of Edwards's position, affirming the value of natural conscience yet delimiting its sphere of operation.

Edwards's distinction between natural conscience and Spirit-guided conscience appears in his parallel distinction between legal and evangelical humiliation. "In a legal humiliation, the conscience is convinced," he writes, "but because there is no spiritual understanding the will is not bowed, nor the inclination altered: this is done only in evangelical humiliation."[45] Such legal humiliation does not in itself engender conversion, because it does not bring a change of inclination that affects and transforms the whole self. Someone may turn away from sin by being repelled from it, and yet this state would not be tantamount to a gracious conversion of the self, as Edwards explains: "There is a twofold weanedness from the world. One is having the heart beat off or forced off from the world by affliction, and especially by spiritual distresses and disquietudes of conscience that the world can't quiet. This may be in men ... natural men. The other is a having the heart drawn off by being shown something better, whereby the heart is really turned from it."[46] In "evangelical humiliation," the human self does not merely turn from sin but sees something of the loveliness and excellence of Christ as a Savior and so turns in faith, gratitude, and hopefulness toward him. Edwards judged that religious fear might arise not from the Holy Spirit but from natural causes such as "melancholic passions rising only from mere imaginations, strongly conceived in the brain ... on a sudden, like lightning into a house."[47] Such sudden terrors might fall into Edwards's category of legal humiliation but would not be an instance of evangelical humiliation.

[43] Edwards, as quoted in Ramsey, "Editor's Introduction," WJE 8:45.
[44] Edwards, WJE 17:153.
[45] Ibid., 2:312.
[46] Ibid., 8:337.
[47] Ibid., 2:157.

In connection with the Great Awakening of 1740–42, Edwards became concerned with various forms of false religion that he saw among his parishioners and their effects on the conscience. Certain persons in the midst of the religious revivals had unusual and paranormal experiences that Edwards later came to judge unfavorably: "Some indeed under great terrors of conscience have had impressions on their imaginations; and also under the power of spiritual discoveries, they have had livelily impressed ideas of Christ shedding his blood for sinners, his blood running from his veins, and of Christ in his glory in heaven and such like things."[48] Such powerful experiences led some persons to put their trust in their own experiences rather than God or Christ: "What blindness and deceit, what self-flattery, self-exaltation and self-confidence reigns there ... when once conscience is blinded, and convictions killed, with false, high affections ... fed up and prompted by false joys and comforts, excited by some pleasing imaginations impressed by Satan, transforming himself into an angel of light."[49] Edwards contrasted true and false penitence: "A true penitent is like a burnt child, that dreads the fire. Whereas on the contrary, he that has had a counterfeit repentance, and false comforts and joys, is like iron that has been suddenly heated and quenched; it becomes much harder than before. A false conversion puts an end to convictions of conscience."[50] Genuine conversion is brought about by a continued sensitivity to one's sin and an awareness of one's own fallibility.

Edwards had a surprising amount to say about Satan as an agent in the religious revival, misleading people with false religious experiences: "For though convictions of conscience do often cause terror; yet they don't consist in it; and terrors do often arise from other causes." For "the devil, if permitted, can terrify men as well as the Spirit of God: 'tis a work natural to him, and he has many ways of doing it, in a manner tending to no good. He may exceedingly affright persons, by impressing on them many external images and ideas, of a countenance frowning, a sword drawn, black clouds of vengeance, words of an awful doom pronounced."[51]

## CONSCIENCE IN RELATION TO GOD, CHRIST'S ATONEMENT, AND THE FINAL JUDGMENT

The human awareness of being in the wrong, argues Edwards, *involves a correlative sense that God is in the right*. This line of reasoning leads him into

[48] Ibid., 16:56.
[49] Ibid., 2:172.
[50] Ibid., 2:364.
[51] Ibid., 2:156.

some psychological musings. Those who – despite being morally in the wrong – seek to justify themselves, end up blaming God, who is the inevitable point of reference in all such efforts at self-exoneration. People blame God, or blame their situation, to deflect attention from their own guilt. Such persons "secretly charge him [i.e., God] with all the blame."[52] He adds that "if the law of God be preached in its strictness . . . [then] they justify themselves with their inability; and the design and end of the law . . . to fit them for Christ, is defeated."[53] Nonetheless, there are evildoers who recognize God's justice in condemning them, "they give some kind of consent to it," though "many times it don't [sic] continue."[54]

An original feature in Edwards's account of conscience lies in the way in which he connects it with Christ's atonement. As Edwards views it, believing in Christ's atonement implies repenting from sin: "Our accepting such sufferings as an atonement for our sin implies a heart fully repenting of and renouncing sin, for it implies . . . a conviction that we deserve so great a punishment and . . . [a] hatred of the sin punished."[55] Trust in Christ's atonement absolves the sinner's guilty conscience: "Faith is that which removes guilt of conscience. Guilt of conscience is the sense of the connection between sin and punishment . . ..The mind is under the weight of guilt as long [as] it has a sense of its being bound to punishment."[56] Elsewhere, Edwards highlights the practices of sacrifice – including human sacrifice – among ancient peoples to confirm his point: "If they [i.e., sacrifices] were voluntarily taken up and practiced by men, there is an indication of mind and conscience, that some deference must be paid to divine justice; and that, to such a degree, that they were sometimes ready . . . to sacrifice the fruit of their body [i.e., their own children], for the sin of their soul."[57]

The eschatological aspect of Edwards's reflection on conscience is one of his original contributions. The damned, for him, in some sense recognize God's justice in condemning them and yet fail to see the goodness, glory, and beauty of God in doing so. In Edwards's thinking, the Last Judgment provides a limiting case in the functioning of human conscience. "The conscience of an awakened sinner" at the present time is an anticipation of the future judgment: "The same discoveries are in some measure given in the conscience of an awakened sinner in this world, which will be given more fully

52 Ibid., 1:467.
53 Ibid., 1:468.
54 Ibid., 2:158.
55 Ibid., 20:510.
56 Ibid., 21:428.
57 Ibid., 23:158.

in the consciences of sinners at the Day of Judgment. The same kind of sight or apprehension of God, in a lesser degree, makes awakened sinners in this world, sensible of the dreadful guilt of sin."[58] This means that "God sits enthroned in the conscience, as at the last day, he will sit enthroned in the clouds of heaven; the sinner is arraigned, as it were, at God's bar; and God appears in his awful greatness, as a just and holy, sin-hating and sin-revenging God, as he will then."[59] Even those finally separated from God in hell may well agree with God in his exercises of justice: "It cannot be denied that natural men are capable of a conviction of their desert of hell, and that a man's conscience may be convinced of it without a sight of God's glory ... as doubtless their consciences will echo to the sentence of the judge and will condemn them."[60]

It is striking to see how often Edwards appeals to the scenario of the Last Judgment in his effort to explain the functioning of conscience at the present time: "In the perfect light of that day ... God will reprove them, and set their sins in order before them; their consciences will be greatly awakened and convinced, their mouths will be stopped, all stupidity of conscience will be at an end, and conscience will have its full exercise: and therefore their consciences will approve the dreadful sentence of the Judge against them."[61] Edwards compares God's future action to that of the human judge who not only declares but explains the verdict he passes: "'Tis proper for a judge when he condemns a criminal to endeavor so to set his guilt before him as to convince his conscience of the justice of the sentence. This the Almighty will do effectually."[62] Again he comments: "In another world, the eyes and mouth of conscience will be fully opened. God will hereafter make wicked men to see and know these things, which now they industriously hide their eyes from ... [and] their conscience will condemn them only, and not God."[63] Regarding Satan and the demons, Edwards writes something akin to what he says regarding the human damned: "The devils know their hatred of God is unreasonable: they have a full condemnation of it in their conscience; but yet their hearts don't disrelish it and loath it: if they did, it [i.e., hatred of God] would have no place in their hearts."[64]

58 Ibid., 2:277.
59 Ibid., 25:621.
60 Ibid., 17:153.
61 Ibid., 8:597.
62 Edwards, as cited in Ramsey, "Editor's Introduction," WJE 8:48.
63 Edwards, WJE 25:619–20.
64 Ibid., 21:317–18.

## CONCLUSION: ON EDWARDSEAN AND KANTIAN CONSCIENCE

Views concerning human conscience, argues philosopher Allen W. Wood, may be distinguished into *moral knowledge theories*, *motivation theories*, and *reflection theories*. The first notion implies that conscience "tells someone what to do," and, in religious thinkers, may carry the idea that the voice of conscience is the voice of God. The second idea suggests that there are "prickings" or "proddings" from conscience that urge persons to do the right thing and causes them to feel uneasy if they do not. The third perspective means that conscience involves a way of deliberating over one's course of action.[65]

Edwards's many-sided reflections on conscience in his writings generally fall into the first and second categories. It is telling – and congruent with Edwards's philosophical anthropology – that he draws no sharp distinction between *moral knowledge* of the rightness or wrongness of one's own actions and the *affective response* that arises as a kind of immediate reflex. The one who does wrong experiences "pain" or "disquiet" of conscience, just as the one who does right has "peace" or "tranquility," in recognition of one's own inconsistency or consistency with oneself. Given the Puritan background of Edwards's thought, and his involvement in religious revival, it is not surprising that he has more to say regarding "disquiet" of conscience than its converse. In revivalist Christianity, it is the unhappy conscience that causes sinners to seek after God's mercy in Christ.

Immanuel Kant is known for interpreting morality in terms of "universalizability" – famously embodied in his categorical imperative. In Edwards's ethical thinking, the key test is not "universalibility" but rather "reversibility," or putting oneself in someone else's place. This fits with the Golden Rule ("do unto others ..."; Mt. 7:12), and it is an approach to conscience that seems more congruent with everyday moral reasoning than Kant's high-flying question regarding an application of moral rules to "all rational beings."[66] In ethical decision-making, most people do not concern themselves with "all rational beings" but rather the question of "what if I were in the other person's shoes"? Moreover, in another point of contrast to Kant, Edwards erects his

65 Allen W. Wood, "Conscience," in *Kantian Ethics* (Cambridge: Cambridge University Press, 2008), 182–92, esp. 182. Wood claims that "Kant's conception of conscience is a motivation theory set in the context of a reflection theory." Ibid., 183.

66 Kant writes: "The question is therefore this: is it a necessary law *for all rational beings* always to appraise their actions in accordance with such maxims as they themselves to will to serve as universal laws?" Immanuel Kant, *Groundwork of the Metaphysics of Morals* (Cambridge: Cambridge University Press, 1998), 35 (emphasis in original).

ethical theory on the foundation of such human phenomena as spousal and parental love, patriotism, and pity or compassion. Edwards sees moral duty as congruent with natural inclinations, while Kant for the most part does not. This gives Edwards's theory of conscience a much more embodied character than that of Kant.[67]

A striking contrast between Edwards and Kant lies in the former's conceptualization of the influence of the Holy Spirit on the human conscience. Not only does Kant not refer to the Holy Spirit (or anything analogous to it) within his ethical theory, but arguably Kant's notion of autonomy would exclude all ideas of an extra-human or transcendent agent that causes or enables human moral awareness. This might imply *heteronomy* rather than *autonomy*, and violate Kant's foundational understanding that "the rational being's will" functions "as author or legislator of the moral law" – not only receiving the moral law but also giving the law to itself.[68] The precise way in which Edwards conceived the Holy Spirit as engaging and enlivening the human conscience is an underdeveloped theme in the secondary literature. Yet that the Spirit somehow affects the conscience is not in doubt in Edwards's account.

One of the most original aspects of Edwards's account of conscience is his focus on an *eschatological dimension* – that the person smitten with a sense of sinfulness anticipates God's final verdict upon himself at the time of the Last Judgment. The Holy Spirit, in this sense, evokes in the human mind a foreshadowing of God's future action. Clearly Edwards's reflections on the demons and the damned in the Last Judgment extend his discussion of conscience far beyond the sphere of daily life. This is a reflection of Edwards's reliance on sacred Scripture, and the belief – evident through his writings – that the dictates of the natural conscience are always consistent with divine grace and with subjective experience as engendered through the Holy Spirit.

## RECOMMENDED READING

Cochran, Elizabeth Agnew. *Receptive Human Virtues: A New Reading of Jonathan Edwards's Ethics*. University Park, PA: Pennsylvania State University Press, 2011.

Danaher, William J. Jr. *The Trinitarian Ethics of Jonathan Edwards*. Louisville, KY: Westminster John Knox, 2004.

67 Wood argues that Kant's ethical theory is not quite so antithetical to human inclinations, emotions, and sympathies as is generally imagined. Wood, *Kantian Ethics*, xi–xiii, though it is clear that Kant did not found his idea of ethical right and wrong upon such inclinations, in the way that Edwards did in the *Nature of True Virtue*.

68 Wood, "Autonomy," in *Kantian Ethics*, 106.

Edwards, Jonathan. *Ethical Writings: The Works of Jonathan Edwards*, vol. 8, edited by Paul Ramsey. New Haven, CT: Yale University Press, 1989.
*The Works of Jonathan Edwards*, 73 vols. New Haven, CT: Yale University Press, vols. 1–26; and New Haven, CT: Jonathan Edwards Center at Yale University, vols. 27–73. All 73 volumes may be accessed at edwards.yale.edu.
Fiering, Norman. *Jonathan Edwards's Moral Thought and Its British Context*. Chapel Hill, NC: University of North Carolina Press, 1981.
Gerstner, John. *Steps to Salvation: The Evangelistic Message of Jonathan Edwards*. Philadelphia, PA: Westminster Press, 1960.
McClymond, Michael J., and Gerald R. McDermott. "True Virtue, Christian Love, and Ethical Theory." In *The Theology of Jonathan Edwards*, 528–48. New York, NY: Oxford University Press, 2012.
Ramsey, "Editor's Introduction." In *Ethical Writings: The Works of Jonathan Edwards*, edited by Paul Ramsey, vol. 8, 1–121. New Haven, CT: Yale University Press, 1989.
Spohn, William C. "Religion and Morality in the Thought of Jonathan Edwards," PhD dissertation, University of Chicago, 1978.
Wilson, Stephen A. *Virtue Reformed: Rereading Jonathan Edwards's Ethics*. Leiden: Brill, 2005.

# 12

# Obeying God Rather Than Men

## *Uneasy Evangelicals, Conscience, and Politics*

MICAH WATSON

"We've been doing this for over twenty years, so we've had several requests that my conscience just couldn't allow me to print." This is how print shop owner Blaine Adamson answered a question about the various requests he had turned down over the course of operating his business in Lexington, Kentucky. Adamson turned down messages with profanity as well as violence, a church youth group request for a shirt featuring Jesus along with a bucket of chicken, and a pastor's order for a plain black t-shirt with the white words stating, "Homosexuality is sin." About the last item, Adamson said that "my conscience didn't feel good printing that message just that way. It felt wrong."[1]

Adamson had an arrangement with another print shop that would take any orders he could not, in good conscience, accept, and for many years this allowed his would-be customers to get the product they wanted while also respecting Adamson's religious scruples. It was not until Adamson declined to print a shirt for Lexington's LGBT Pride week in 2013 that things became more complicated. The Lexington Human Rights Commission (LHRC) determined that Adamson's refusal to make the shirts was not based on an objection to the message but on the sexual identity of the disappointed customers. Not surprisingly, Adamson saw things differently. Noting that his business has always served and often employed gay customers and workers, Adamson distinguished between the status of the people and the content of the message printed on the shirts. His decision to turn down the Pride Week T-shirt no more committed him to animus against gays than his decision not to print the Jesus-and-bucket-of-chicken shirt means he discriminates against Christians. He took the LHRC to court and won and then won again after the

[1] "Justice for Jack," video from a panel at the Heritage Foundation on September 6, 2017, www.heritage.org/religious-liberty/event/justice-jack-free-speech-and-religious-liberty-the-supreme-court.

LHRC appealed. At the time of this writing, the case is pending before the Kentucky Supreme Court.

Adamson is an evangelical Christian who attends a nondenominational church. He is one of several evangelicals in recent years who have had to reckon with the consequences of following the dictates of their conscience in a political and legal culture that is struggling to work out the tension between religious liberty and LGBT equality. Baronelle Stutzman was sued for declining to provide floral arrangements for a same-sex wedding in Washington State. Aaron and Melissa Klein shut down their bakery after the state of Oregon fined them $135,000 for refusing to provide a same-sex wedding cake. In 2015, the city of Atlanta dismissed its fire chief, Kelvin Cochran, for writing a book on his own time because he included standard Christian teaching about sexuality, a message deemed discriminatory. Jack Phillips is another baker who was sued in Colorado for refusing to participate in a same-sex wedding. Carl and Angel Larsen run a video and film company in Minnesota but have run afoul of a state law that requires artists to give "equal time" to stories about same-sex weddings in addition to traditional weddings. Jon and Elaine Huguenin of New Mexico saw their photography business shut down because they declined to shoot a same-sex wedding in 2006.

The people involved in these cases found themselves in trouble with the law because they followed the dictates of their consciences. It is perhaps no accident that the vast majority of business owners being sued or penalized for holding to their religious convictions are evangelical Christians.[2] By honoring their consciences even at the risk of their livelihoods, Adamson, Phillips, Stutzman, and the rest are, whether they know it or not, inheritors of an evangelical tradition that has long prioritized the important role of conscience in the lives of individual Christians and the body politic. In the pages that follow, we will sketch out the part that conscience has played in the evangelical tradition, from the historical origins of evangelicalism to the challenges faced by contemporary evangelicals. Such a sketch requires wading first into the definitional quagmire involved in determining the identity of evangelicals such that we can speak intelligibly of an evangelical tradition. Once we have a working definition, we can meaningfully describe what evangelicals have meant, and still mean, by conscience.

[2] This is not to say that everyone in similar straits is evangelical. Stephen Tennes is a Michigan apple farmer and Roman Catholic who has been prohibited from participating in East Lansing's farmers' market because his farm does not host same-sex weddings. Emily Monacelli. "Farmer Banned at City Market over Gay Marriage Stance Has Day in Court," *MLive*, September 13, 2017, www.mlive.com/news/kalamazoo/index.ssf/2017/09/country_mill_farms_hearing.html.10f"/>.

## WHO ARE EVANGELICALS?

Defining evangelicalism is as difficult as it is unavoidable if one wants to understand American politics and religion. The difficulties are not hard to describe. Unlike other Christian denominations or traditions, there is no official membership roll of evangelicals. There is no equivalent to the Magisterium of the Roman Catholic Church, which can determine the authoritative evangelical teaching on this doctrine or that moral controversy. There is no official source of evangelical teaching on conscience, nor a formal history to consult as there would be, for example, for the Church of England. It's not surprising then that some scholars reject or strongly question evangelicalism as a useful conceptual tool altogether; one leading scholar of American evangelicalism, historian Nathan Hatch, has gone so far as to say that "there is no such thing as Evangelicalism," and another religious historian, D. G. Hart, writes that the term "evangelicals" is a "constructed ideal without any substance."[3]

Moreover, since the 2016 presidential election, the term evangelical carries with it not only inherent conceptual difficulties but, for many, normative baggage as well. Recently, Princeton University's student group for evangelicals – founded in 1937 – changed its name from Princeton Evangelical Fellowship to Princeton Christian Fellowship. The leadership of the group found that "evangelical" no longer connotated anything about their theological convictions but instead identified them as religious supporters of President Trump.[4] Baylor historian Thomas Kidd explains why he will still use the term historically but admits it is no longer helpful as a religious description given the many different, conflicting, and unwelcome meanings it conveys.[5]

Nevertheless, according to the Pew Forum on Religion and Public Life and its comprehensive U.S. Religious Landscape Survey, evangelicals make up more than a quarter of the American adult population,[6] or about sixty

3 Nathan Hatch, "Response to Carl F. H. Henry," in *Evangelical Affirmations*, eds. Kenneth S. Kantzer and Carl F. H. Henry (Grand Rapids, MI: Zondervan, 1990), 97. Hart is quoted in Corwin E. Smidt, *American Evangelicals Today* (Lanham, MD: Rowman & Littlefield, 2013), 1.

4 Rebecca Ngu, "Princeton Christian Fellowship Ditches the Label 'Evangelical'," *The Daily Princetonian*, October 1, 2017, www.dailyprincetonian.com/article/2017/10/princeton-christian-fellowship-ditches-the-label-evangelical.

5 Thomas Kidd, "Is the Term 'Evangelical' Redeemable?," *The Gospel Coalition*, September 8, 2017, blogs.thegospelcoalition.org/evangelical-history/2017/09/08/is-the-term-evangelical-redeemable/.

6 Pew Forum on Religion & Public Life, *U.S. Religious Landscape Survey* (Washington, DC: Pew Research Center, 2014), www.pewforum.org/religious-landscape-study/; see also Daniel

million people. However daunting the conceptual challenges of defining the boundaries of evangelicalism, and however unpopular it may currently be, the term points to a demographic reality so significant that scholars who wish to speak about the American political and religious landscape simply must engage with the phenomenon known, or perhaps someday formerly known, as evangelicalism.

One might be tempted to despair of definitions and paraphrase former Supreme Court justice Potter Stewart in saying that we cannot define evangelicals but we know them when we see them.[7] But this would be a mistake. Several scholars acknowledge the conceptual difficulties but have found fruitful ways to describe evangelicals and employ social scientific tools to operationalize those definitions and offer revealing data and explanations.[8] Perhaps the most famous definitional approach to evangelicalism is British scholar David Bebbington's "four emphases" description. "Emphases" is particularly apt, as the theological content of these characteristics is not alien to Christianity more broadly; it is simply that evangelicals put particular stress on the centrality of these beliefs. Following Bebbington's formulation, they are:

(1) Conversionism: a belief in the importance of conversion, often expressed with "born again" language.
(2) Biblicism: a belief that Scripture is the highest authority for spiritual and moral truth.
(3) Activism: the belief that believers should take their faith into the "real world" through both evangelism and service.
(4) Crucicentrism: a focus on the work done by Christ's death to make possible reconciliation with God.[9]

Sociologist and president of evangelical Gordon College Michael Lindsay omits crucicentrism altogether and helpfully adds to our understanding of conversionism in writing that the crucial element is not so much a

Cox and Robert P. Jones, "Additional Evidence of White Protestant Decline," *Public Religion Research Institute*, September 11, 2017, www.prri.org/spotlight/additional-evidence-white-evangelical-protestant-decline/.

7 *Jacobellis* v. *Ohio*, 378 U.S. 184 (1964).

8 Stephen Monsma, "What Is an Evangelical? And Does It Matter?," *Christian Scholar's Review* XLVI, no. 4 (2017): 323–40. See also Corwin E. Smidt, *American Evangelicals Today* (Lanham, MD: Rowman & Littlefield, 2013).

9 See David Bebbington, *Evangelicalism in Modern Britain: A History from the 1730s to the 1980s* (London: Unwin Hyman, 1989), 1–17. This account also draws from my chapter "C.S. Lewis As Natural Law Evangelist: Evangelical Political Thought and the People in the Pew," in *Natural Law and Evangelical Political Thought*, eds. Jesse Covington, Bryan McGraw, and Micah Watson (Lanham, MD: Lexington Books, 2013).

before-and-after experience but an emphasis on a personal relationship with Jesus. Former Calvin College and Notre Dame historian George Marsden adds a fifth characteristic, "transdenominationalism," an unwieldy term describing evangelicals' willingness to work with other evangelical denominations as part of the same family. While scholars will continue to debate about these definitions, these four emphases are – with Lindsay's addendum to conversionism, and Marsden's transdenominationalism – part of a good working definition.

But only a part. A helpful recent introduction to this definitional debate is a short essay by the late Pepperdine and Calvin College political scientist Stephen Monsma, which clearly and accessibly lays out the various approaches, including the emphases listed above. Monsma critiques several approaches before defending his own formulation, which describes three historical moments critical to the evangelical religious tradition. The three eras that inform both the *content* of evangelical belief and practice and the living *tradition* that modern day evangelicals have inherited are (1) The Protestant Reformation and its aftermath, (2) the revival movements of the eighteenth and nineteenth centuries, most prominently the First and Second Great Awakenings, and the twentieth- century emergence of evangelicalism as distinct from mainline Protestantism, on the one hand, and fundamentalism, on the other.[10]

These historical eras are critical because evangelicalism is a living tradition with a past and an inheritance, not just a list of beliefs. Monsma concludes that evangelicalism is a branch of Protestantism characterized by

(1) belief in the traditional, historic, orthodox Christian beliefs as found in the New Testament and articulated and reemphasized in the Protestant Reformation and in twentieth-century defenses of historic, orthodox Christianity, and
(2) a personal, heartfelt, life-changing commitment in accepting those beliefs.

The virtue of considering Monsma's historical moment approach combined with the previous emphases is that it allows us to speak of modern evangelicals and their forbears without needing to trace an evangelical movement back to biblical times. That is, one can speak of the crucial role that Martin Luther, Roger Williams, and Jonathan Edwards played in making an evangelical branch of Protestantism possible without claiming they are of the same exact genus as the modern evangelical. This applies to evangelical politics and the

[10] Though, to be sure, the links between fundamentalism and evangelicalism are much stronger than between evangelicalism and mainline Protestantism.

claims of conscience as well, for if these historical moments are the sources of what is now evangelicalism, then how conscience was understood and applied in the political controversies and climate of those times will also inform the contemporary evangelical approach to politics and conscience.[11]

## WHAT IS THE EVANGELICAL CONSCIENCE?

While all Christians value the Bible, evangelical Protestants are particularly committed to Scripture as the "norming norm" and the most trustworthy source of God's will. Given that "biblicism" is one of the defining characteristics of evangelicalism, evangelicals will start with Scripture in determining what conscience is. In his entry on conscience in *Baker's Dictionary of Evangelical Ethics*, theologian Clark Pinnock explains that the Hebrew Scriptures do not have a word for conscience but nevertheless refer to the concept several times.[12] The New Testament Greek word for conscience is *suneidesis*, rendered *conscientia* in the Latin, from which we derive our English spelling. Pinnock chronicles the various mentions of conscience both explicit and implicit. While Jesus seems to reference the idea in Matthew 6:22–23 in describing the eyes as the lamp of the body, most appearances of the term come from the Apostle Paul. Paul claims a clean conscience before the public authorities in Acts 24 and notes that one's conscience may be good or bad depending on how one has lived.[13] He explains that the Gentiles' conscience "bears witness" to the moral quality of their conduct in the famous natural law proof text of Romans 2:14–15 and also provides an extended pastoral discussion of conscience and its diversity in the stronger/weaker brother discussion in 1 Corinthians 8–10 and Romans 14.

What exactly is the conscience then, according to how evangelicals read the Scriptures? Pinnock describes it as "an inner witness to moral responsibility, the inherent human capacity to distinguish between good and evil." Though not a card-carrying evangelical himself, C. S. Lewis offers a helpful definition that captures something implicit in the biblical account of conscience. Speaking to the Oxford Pacifist Society in 1940, Lewis described conscience as more than a faculty but rather "the whole man engaged in a particular

[11] Monsma understands evangelicalism as a religious movement as including black Protestants, yet the political experience of black and white evangelicals is so different that for the sake of continuity and space "evangelicals" here will mean "white evangelicals." The role of conscience in the African-American evangelical tradition deserves its own treatment.

[12] Clark H. Pinnock, "Conscience," in *Baker's Dictionary of Christian Ethics*, ed. Carl F. H. Henry (Grand Rapids, MI: Baker Book House, 1981), 126–27.

[13] 1 Timothy 1:5; 4:2; Hebrews 10:2, 22; 13:18; 2 Timothy 1:3; 4:2; Titus 1:15.

subject matter." The conscience means both "the pressure a man feels upon his will to do what he thinks is right" as well as "his judgment as to what the content of right and wrong are." In the first sense, conscience must always be obeyed, as Paul teaches in Romans 14. But in the second sense, conscience can be mistaken, and thus we have a perpetual obligation to inform our consciences with moral truth. Thus, Paul can write of our having a good or bad conscience and the searing or breaking of our consciences (1 Tim. 4:2). If we thought of conscience as simply a faculty that delivers moral data infallibly, moral education would be pointless, as would the countless exhortations in Scripture to learn God's law and standards.

In layman's terms, then, the conscience informs or simply is our judgment of what is right and wrong *and* that interior sense of obligation that urges us to act accordingly. This understanding connects the biblical and historic treatment of conscience with the language used by modern day bakers and florists to describe why they take the stands they do. Yet this definition, important as it is, does not fully capture the significance of conscience for the evangelical Christian. While one's conscience is always operative, only when it is tested can one gauge its true value. No one speaks of feeling convicted to follow one's conscience when everyone agrees on the issue and there is no cost or risk involved. We admire those who follow the dictates of their consciences – who do the right thing – when doing so is difficult and success far from guaranteed. Thus Christians (but not only Christians) remember Joshua's proclamation that "As for me and my house, we will serve the Lord" (Josh. 24:15, ESV). They remember the three young Jewish men in the book of Daniel who braved the furnace rather than bow to an idol (Dan. 3) and Peter and the Apostles' reply to the authorities who commanded them to stop preaching: "We must obey God rather than men" (Acts 5:29). Even if apocryphal, Martin Luther's "Here I stand, I can do no other" resonates for evangelical Protestants much as Thomas More's heroic example inspires Roman Catholics. Evangelical Christians, in particular, admire figures like William Wilberforce, Dietrich Bonhoeffer, and Martin Luther King Jr., men whose convictions led them to take severe risks and pay significant costs.[14]

What do the stands of Joshua, Peter and the Apostles, and Wilberforce, Bonhoeffer, and King have in common beyond the moral vision informing their convictions? It is not just the potential cost of taking a stand but the proximate cause of the cost: conflict with political authority.

14 Of course, Christians do not have a monopoly on exemplars of conscience. Socrates is one obvious example.

## THE DNA OF EVANGELICAL POLITICS AND CONSCIENCE

The potential for conflict between political authority and individual conscience or conviction is as old as politics itself. Aristotle reminds us that we can only expect as much exactitude from a subject as the subject allows, and human behavior is so variegated that it is simply impossible for written rules and laws to anticipate and regulate every possible interaction. Most legal systems thus have procedures that allow for discretionary judgment as to how the rules apply to particular cases that defy easy interpretation by existing law. To put it perhaps too simply, any legal system describes three categories of behavior: first, those actions required of all citizens or some (e.g., taxes); secondly, a category of prohibited actions (e.g., murder); and third, the largest category comprising the vast number of human actions that are not required nor prohibited. Courts are frequently tasked with deciding cases that straddle the boundaries of those categories, and scruples of conscience often motivate the actors in those cases.[15]

A thorough treatment of evangelicals and conscience in their politics would cover how conscience was understood and practiced in society and law throughout the three historical periods that Monsma identified as forming the modern-day evangelical tradition. That is, on the religious plane one would need to dive into the theological and political histories of the Reformation and its aftermath, the Great Awakenings and religious fervor of the eighteenth and nineteenth centuries, and the fundamentalist-modernist controversies of the late nineteenth and early twentieth centuries. Politically, one would look at the legislative and judicial records corresponding to each of these periods. Such a treatment of course is on the scale of libraries, not books nor chapters in books. It would need to cover the religio-political aftermath of the Reformation in several countries, the American political experiment from colonial days to the antebellum era, and roughly the last 120 years or so of evangelical Protestant involvement in American politics.

It is an understatement to note, however, that there exists serious scholarly work in all these areas and a wealth of primary and secondary sources for scholars and laypersons alike to investigate further. The concept of conscience

[15] Though it is not always the case in the legal realm that "conscience" necessarily means a tension with the law. University of Chicago law professor Richard H. Helmholz describes the English courts of conscience that understood conscience as what is morally obligatory and thus coinciding with the duty to obey the law as written. Richard Helmholz, "Conscience and the English Courts Between 1500 and 1800," in *Law and Religion: The Legal Teachings of the Protestant and Catholic Reformations*, eds. Wim Decock, Jordan Ballor, Michael Germann, and Laurent Waelkens (Göttingen: Vandenhoeck & Reprecht, 2014), 91–106.

played a crucial role, in particular, in the Reformation era and the Great Awakenings, both politically and religiously. Indeed, it is something of an artificial academic construct to separate the theological from the political, as we see in the titles and content of several seminal works on this matter: a volume of collected essays in German and English *Conscience in the Legal Teachings of the Protestant and Catholic Reformations*, the American Founding scholars Daniel Dreisbach and Mark David Hall's edited volume, *The Sacred Rights of Conscience: Selected Readings on Religious Liberty and Church-State Relations in the American Founding*, and the seminal two-volume collection edited by political scientist Ellis Sandoz, *Political Sermons of the American Founding Era, 1730–1805*.[16]

These works and a host of others document the importance of conscience, its connection to religious freedom, and how the strength and diversity of religious convictions contributed to a convoluted but progressive evolution of political forms and structures that would eventually culminate in the American political experiment in limited government and religious liberty. Before moving too quickly to the modern era we should note three crucial lessons from the post-Reformation period and the eighteenth and nineteenth centuries. The first is the powerful connection between conscience and inward assurance of salvation, the second is the link between conscience and outward acts of charity and justice, and the third is the near identification of evangelicalism with American religion and politics.

We find evidence of the first lesson in the writings of the Puritan English Reformed theology of the 1600s, the same Puritan tradition that flourished on both sides of the Atlantic and played an undeniable role in the story that American evangelicals tell about themselves. The renowned Reformation scholar Richard A. Muller chronicles the ubiquitous presence of conscience in the theological pamphlets of several notable figures, such as William Perkins, John Downham, and John Bunyan, who were working out the relationship between God's sovereign action in salvation with human will and response.[17] Believing that all true Christians were saved by God's unconditional decree and not by anything they had done, the English Puritans nevertheless searched for assurance of their salvation; they found it in their

[16] Daniel L. Dreisbach and Mark David Hall, eds., *The Sacred Rights of Conscience: Selected Readings on Religious Liberty and Church-State Relations in the American Founding* (Indianapolis, IN: Liberty Fund, 2009); Ellis Sandoz, ed., *Political Sermons of the American Founding Era, 1730–1805*, 2 vols. (Indianapolis, IN: Liberty Fund, 1998).

[17] Richard A. Muller, "Covenant and Conscience in English Reformed Theology: Three Variations on a 17th Century Theme," *Westminster Theological Journal* 42, no. 2 (Spring 1980): 308–34.

struggles with conscience. If someone has been saved, then God will awaken one's conscience to a particular moral failing or unworthy habit. Those who truly belonged to the covenant of grace would then look upon struggles of conscience as assurance of their own salvation, for if they were not saved, they would not be bothered by a guilty conscience.

This understanding was significant not only because of the importance of conscience for knowledge of one's salvation but also because the doctrine did not stop with personal introspection. Christians were called out into the world to do battle with God's enemies as a means not merely of salvific assurance but also godly obedience. Muller observes that this development "marks the accomplishment of an intellectual transition from an inward exercise of conscience for the sake of assurance to an active assault by means of the cases of conscience on the foes of God's election." This external application of our wrestling with conscience leads to the second lesson.

What does an assault on the foes of God's election look like when translated into the context of 1800s America? It means getting involved in the world and its problems and taking the truths of God's word and applying them to social and spiritual ills. Here we find the root of the "activism" emphasis characteristic of modern evangelicals. It is hard to imagine a contemporary equivalent to the sheer social energy unleashed in the wake of the religious revivals that swept across the country. An assurance of salvation and a personal relationship with Jesus characterized tens of thousands of "decisions" made in tents and churches, but these decisions were not merely private or individualistic. Evangelical leaders organized and directed these energies toward ends both spiritual and tangible. Historian Mark Noll notes the influence of figures like Lyman Beecher, father of Harriet Beecher Stowe author of *Uncle Tom's Cabin*, who founded scores of voluntary societies such as the American Board for Foreign Missions in 1810, the American Bible Society in 1816, the American Sunday School Society in 1824, the American Tract Society in 1825, and the American Education Society, American Society for the Promotion of Temperance, and American Home Missionary Society in 1826.[18] Political scientist Corwin Smidt describing the mind-boggling proliferation of these voluntary societies, noting that Massachusetts alone witnessed the creation of 350 such societies between 1810 and 1830.[19]

[18] Mark A. Noll, *A History of Christianity in the United States and Canada* (Grand Rapids, MI: Eerdmans, 1992), 169.

[19] Smidt, *American Evangelicals Today*, 23, citing James Moorhead, "The Erosion of Postmillennialism in American Religious Thought, 1865–1925," *Church History* 53 (March 1984): 61–77.

These groups continued their work through the 1800s, promoting causes that may appear to the modern reader as falling into two categories: secular and religious. Thus, there were scores of societies promoting missions, Bible reading, and Sunday school, but also societies organized to protect young ladies newly arrived in big cities, advocate for abolition, promote women's suffrage, and fight the scourge of alcoholism and related poverty. It would be an anachronism, however, to read back into the mindset of evangelicals then (and now) a division between church and "secular" social causes. Whereas conscience in post-Reformation England was more associated with an interior assurance of salvation, salvation and conscience for these American evangelicals meant external application of the fruits of their salvation. Newly minted Christians were "saved for service" – a popular phrase at the time – and that service included any and all of these causes as ways to serve God and neighbor inside and outside of the church.

The connection to the role of conscience and its place in the DNA of evangelicalism from the nineteenth-century revival era seems clear. Christians are saved not only for themselves but for serving others. Not only that, but such service acted as "salt and light" in the larger culture and is absolutely crucial for preserving the health of the church broadly understood[20] and society at large. Historians later referred to this massive movement as the "Evangelical United Front," which Smidt describes as united not in theological particulars per se but rather in the "creation of a certain kind of America" made possible by "a united front socially for the purposes of eliminating evil everywhere."[21] Mark Noll observes that this campaign was not merely social but also strongly influenced the political parties and practices of the day. There is very little about partisan political rallies then (and now) that cannot be linked back to religious revivals and camp meetings. It is to this connection between politics and religion and American evangelical identity that we now turn.

"The line between religion and politics has always been a thin one in America," Noll writes. "In the heyday of 'Evangelical America,' it was virtually nonexistent."[22] Such was the seamless connection between evangelicals as Christians and evangelicals as Americans that when New York City "took over the Protestant Public School Society in 1842," it was no hostile secular

20 The cooperation between members of different denominations in these voluntary societies offer supports Marsden's "transdenominationalism."

21 Smidt, *American Evangelicals Today*, 24.

22 Noll, *A History of Christianity in the United States and Canada*, 243.

appropriation but a natural "triumph for a kind of nondenominational Protestantism."[23] Noll writes that prior to the Civil War, "Evangelicalism held sway across almost the entire ecclesiastical landscape," such that non-evangelical traditions showed evidence of being influenced by evangelical practices and dispositions. Noll concludes that evangelicalism "was America's public theology from the Revolution to the Civil War."[24]

While we might draw several conclusions from the close confluence of evangelical spirituality and social activism, on the one hand, and the rather seamless fusion between American and evangelical Christian identity, on the other, three ideas stand out, in particular, regarding understanding evangelicals and the role of conscience. The first is that evangelicals strongly identified themselves as inheritors of a combined spiritual and political tradition. The job of the Christian was to follow her conscience in sharing the gospel and combatting social ills in society, and evangelicals, in particular, took this to heart. The job of the government was at the very least to protect the background conditions favorable for such benevolence, if not to undertake the actual role itself, as we saw with New York City taking over the Protestant schools. This is a rather powerful example of how much things have changed, considering how many contemporary evangelicals would view the politics and educational philosophy of New York City. The evangelicals who came of age during Noll's "Evangelical America" era were raised by those who simply equated American religion and American politics with evangelical Protestantism.[25]

Second, and as a result, evangelicals not surprisingly looked back upon the American Founding as uniquely their own. This is not to say that the American Founding generation itself was entirely evangelical, of course. While Reformed Protestantism had a strong presence in the Founding generation, if Monsma and Smidt and Noll are correct, we don't really have the birth of what we now think of as evangelicalism until after the Great Awakenings. Nevertheless, evangelicals then and evangelicals now have a strong affinity with the American political tradition, perhaps rivaled only by the Latter-day Saints.[26] This identification with the Founding and American politics helps explain the ongoing sense that many contemporary evangelicals

[23] Smidt, *American Evangelicals Today*, 24.

[24] Noll, *A History of Christianity in the United States and Canada*, 241–42.

[25] Evangelicals drew on their faith to fight slavery and defend it. An "Evangelical America" also made things rather difficult, to put it mildly, for Roman Catholics and others non-majority believers at the time.

[26] That evangelicals remain strongly committed to the American political tradition is seen in several polls, e.g., Lauren Markoe, "Evangelicals Top Religious Patriotism; Believe in

have had that they are "losing" their culture. If the first few generations of evangelicals saw their faith tradition and American politics and culture as more or less seamless, then the last 120 years or so have marked a diminution of influence and power.[27]

Third, and finally, the evangelical identification with the Founding generation has significant import for our topic given that generation's remarkable focus on the importance of conscience and government's role in protecting it. The conventional story about the first settlers of what became the American colonies, sailing across the Atlantic for their own religious freedom, is as undeniable a part of the American (and thus evangelical) story even if it is incomplete. The diversity of religious groups and sects in the colonies and then the states made conscience protection a practical necessity even for many unpersuaded of the principled case for it.

Conscience or one of its derivates shows up throughout the many sermons collected by Ellis Sandoz in his two-volume collection.[28] The historical record of the importance of conscience is replete with debates not as to its importance, which was a given, but on how to protect it. As Daniel Dreisbach and Mark David Hall write in their introduction to the *Sacred Rights of Conscience*, one key debate between James Madison and George Mason centered around whether Virginia's Declaration of Rights should use the language of religious *toleration* or religious *liberty*. The problem with toleration is it presents a posture of governmental permission toward a given religious practice, belief, or community. Madison argued that this approach did not do enough to protect freedom of conscience, and thus religious liberty must be enshrined because it puts the emphasis on the citizens and their rights rather than what the government allows or tolerates. Instead of Mason's language that "all Men shou'd enjoy the fullest Toleration in the Exercise of Religion," Madison wrote that "all men are equally entitled to the full and free exercise of [religion] accord[in]g to the dictates of Conscience." It was Madison's approach that won the day in Virginia's Statute for Establishing Religious Freedom and then in the First Amendment of the Constitution, and thus became the default view of the American experiment in ordered liberty.[29] This all-too-brief account of course leaves out much. The important takeaway for understanding evangelicals then and now, however, is that both their

American Exceptionalism, Poll," *Huffington Post*, July 4, 2013, www.huffingtonpost.com/2013/07/04/religious-patriotism-_n_3545537.html.

[27] As we will see, this has significant consequences for how conscience plays out today.

[28] See n. 15.

[29] Dreisbach and Hall, eds. *The Sacred Rights of Conscience*, xxviii–xxxi.

religious scriptures and their political scriptures – so to speak – assured them that consciences are of paramount importance, something to be cultivated and obeyed religiously and enshrined and protected politically.

## EVANGELICALS AND CONSCIENCE TODAY

The story of evangelicals in the twentieth century and up to the present moment is a story of the cultural and political ground shifting beneath their feet. One need only consider one of the most significant social movements of the early twentieth century – Prohibition and the passage of the 18th Amendment – and contrast that with the advent of same-sex marriage with the Supreme Court's 2015 decision in *Obergefell* v. *Hodges*. Prohibition is impossible to imagine without the groundwork laid by decades of evangelicals involved in Temperance Societies. While *Obergefell* as a Supreme Court decision does not convey the same sort of political achievement that an actual constitutional amendment does, it did seem to deliver a knockout blow to the cultural and religious political resistance to same-sex marriage. Imagine trying to make a persuasive case to contemporary evangelicals to enlist in a campaign to pass a constitutional amendment to outlaw alcoholic beverages. Imagine if one could go back in time and explain to early twentieth-century evangelicals that in roughly one hundred years men could marry men and women could marry women and the state will consider businesses who decline to provide services for such weddings as akin to whites-only hotels and restaurants and prosecute accordingly. The shift has been seismic in scope and revolutionary in nature.

The conventional story about the decline of evangelical influence is that the rise of biblical higher criticism, Darwinian evolution and industrialization at the end of the nineteenth century undermined the dominant Protestant hegemony.[30] Rather than a triumphant exercise of political and cultural muscle and influence, Prohibition was instead a last gasp of the previous paradigm as emphasized by the Scopes Monkey Trial of 1925. Traditionalist Protestants retreated from the culture into a defensive posture

30 This conventional story has been challenged in some of its details, primarily the extent to which fundamentalism really was an integral component of evangelicalism. Justin Taylor summarizes the relatively recent work of David Bebbington, Barry Hankins, and Michael Hamilton on this score, as well as a response from George Marsden. Justin Taylor, "How Historians Are Quietly Rewriting the Typical Story of American Fundamentalism and Evangelicalism," *The Gospel Coalition*, Oct. 20, 2017, www.thegospelcoalition.org/blogs/evangelical-history/historians-quietly-rewriting-typical-story-american-fundamentalism-evangelicalism/.

of fundamentalism that sought to preserve theological doctrine, while progressive Protestants flourished in mainline denominations and continued to preach the social gospel in the public square.

Modern evangelicalism emerges from the protective cocoon of fundamentalism, the story continues, with several key events in the 1940s and 1950s. Theologian Carl F. H. Henry published a book with a noteworthy name, *The Uneasy Conscience of Modern Fundamentalism* in 1947, the same year that Fuller Seminary was founded, where Henry served as an original faculty member.[31] Henry argued that the separation of traditional orthodox Christian doctrine (the concerns of fundamentalists) from socio-political concerns about poverty and moral issues (the concerns of mainline Protestants) was a scandal to be repudiated. Evangelicals should engage the world, and Henry's program, Fuller President Emeritus Richard Mouw notes, set an agenda for Fuller. In addition to Fuller Seminary, Henry was also the first editor of *Christianity Today*, first published in 1956 and an important outreach and outlet for evangelical engagement ever since. Finally, the Billy Graham crusades began in 1947 and continued at a steady pace in the 1950s and 1960s and beyond. It is hard to overstate Graham's impact on evangelicals or on American Christianity generally. Smidt writes that "perhaps no other person had more of an effect on twentieth-century Christianity."[32] Nathan Hatch and Michael Hamilton describe two ways Graham's network of parachurch ministries furthered evangelicalism's "transdenominationalism." First, this ecumenical approach brought many fundamentalists into a larger world of Christian social and political cooperation, and second, it made it easier for such Christians to agree with Graham's "cautiously progressive positions on . . . issues like civil rights, poverty, and the nuclear arms race."[33] If Carl Henry's *Uneasy Conscience* was the intellectual blueprint for a re-engaged evangelicalism, Billy Graham provided the permission by his charismatic example and inspiration.

The second half of the twentieth century witnessed an explosion of evangelical involvement in the public square, beginning most notably with the birth of the pro-life movement in the 1970s and then morphing into various

[31] Richard Mouw, "The Evangelical Conscience, Still Uneasy 70 Years Later," *The Gospel Coalition*, November 4, 2016, www.thegospelcoalition.org/article/the-evangelical-conscience-still-uneasy-70-years-later.

[32] Smidt, *American Evangelicals Today*, 36.

[33] Ibid., quoting Nathan Hatch and Michael Hamilton, "Taking the Measure of the Evangelical Resurgence, 1942–1992," in *Reckoning with the Past: Historical Essays on American Evangelicalism from the Institute for the Study of American Evangelicals*, ed. D. G. Hart (Grand Rapids, MI: Baker Books, 1995), 395–412.

coalitions and alliances in the 1980s and 1990s.[34] What is remarkable about the years between Henry and Graham's laying the groundwork for evangelicalism's resurgence as a cultural and political force is how quickly the focus changed. It has largely shifted from positively advocating for various positions – school prayer, pro-life policy, traditional sexual norms – that would apply to society at large, to attempts to carve out or preserve spaces for traditionally minded Americans to maintain their beliefs and follow the dictates of their consciences at home and in their churches and places of business. While evangelicals did not abandon attempts to reform society, they increasingly looked for the state to simply leave them alone. Critics would perhaps frame this differently, describing this "carving out" as an example of special pleading, an effort to be exempt from the norms and practices of the larger society.

In the mid-twentieth century, modern evangelicals sought to follow their conscience into the public square in two complementary ways. First, they advocated for public policies that reflected their normative positions. Second, they continued the legacy of their nineteenth-century predecessors by participating in civil society directly through charitable groups such as crisis pregnancy centers and soup kitchens. In the last two decades, the political efforts to establish policy on a broad level have largely failed,[35] and so the political battle is not so much over what the policy will be but what *New York Times* columnist Ross Douthat refers to as the "terms of surrender" for those who lost in the culture wars.[36] Will American law and policy allow for evangelicals and other religious Americans to dissent from the prevailing sexual paradigm in their personal and professional lives? Or will the template follow the example of race and the civil rights movement, in which unrepentant racists were, by official policy and cultural stigma, relegated to the margins of society?

This brings us back full circle to the florists, bakers, photographers, and others with whom we started. As we have seen, the evangelical faith that animates Jack Phillips, Baronelle Stutzman, Kevin Cochran, Blaine Adamson, and all the others, has deeper roots and resources than one might have guessed given the last few decades of evangelicalism and the 2016 presidential election. Evangelicals believe that the roots of their convictions and

[34] Not everything was related to the public square or the culture wars. Since the Evangelicals made conscience-based decisions that were not high-profile but nevertheless were counter-cultural and contrary to normal business practices. The practice of Hobby Lobby and Chick-Fil-A to close their stores on Sundays provides a good example. I am grateful for Mark David Hall for this insight.

[35] With the exceptions of slow but steady progress in pro-life policy.

[36] Ross Douthat, "The Terms of Our Surrender," *New York Times*, March 1, 2014, www.nytimes.com/2014/03/02/opinion/sunday/the-terms-of-our-surrender.html.

the demands of their consciences go back to the Bible itself. They can draw not only from the historical and theological legacy of Christianity broadly, but also the particular doctrines, practices, and examples of the Reformation and its aftermath, the Great Awakenings and American revival movement, and the emergence of modern evangelicalism in the mid-twentieth century. They have long admired those figures like Wilberforce, Bonhoeffer, and King who stood by their convictions and followed their consciences even when, or especially when, the world seemed completely opposed. They have been "saved for service," or as Paul writes in Ephesians 2:10, they are "God's handiwork, created in Christ Jesus to do good works, which God prepared in advance." They are to obey God rather than men. Predicting what will happen in the next chapter for American evangelicals is a foolhardy venture given the utterly unpredictable changes of the last few decades. Nevertheless, it is hard to imagine the future of the American religious, cultural, and political landscape without a vibrant presence of evangelical Christians attempting, imperfectly to be sure, to follow their consciences in serving God and neighbor.

## RECOMMENDED READING

Budziszewski, J., and David L. Weeks. *Evangelicals in the Public Square: Four Formative Voices on Political Thought and Action*. Grand Rapids, MI: Baker Academic, 2006.

Decock, Wim, Jordan Ballor, Michael Germann, and Laurent Waelkens, eds. *Law and Religion: The Legal Teachings of the Protestant and Catholic Reformations*. Göttingen: Vandenhoeck & Reprecht, 2014.

Dreisbach, Daniel L., and Mark David Hall, eds. *The Sacred Rights of Conscience: Selected Readings on Religious Liberty and Church-State Relations in the American Founding*. Indianapolis, IN: Liberty Fund, 2009.

Hall, Mark David. "Religious Accommodations and the Common Good." *The Heritage Foundation: Backgrounder* 3058, October 26, 2015.

Hart, D.G., ed., *Reckoning with the Past: Historical Essays on American Evangelicalism from the Institute for the Study of American Evangelicals*. Grand Rapids, MI: Baker Books, 1995.

Henry, Carl F. H. *The Uneasy Conscience of Modern Fundamentalism*. Grand Rapids, MI: Eerdmans, 2003.

Monsma, Stephen V. "What Is an Evangelical? And Does It Matter?" *Christian Scholar's Review* XLVI, no. 4 (Summer 2017): 323–40.

Muller, Richard A. "Covenant and Conscience in English Reformed Theology: Three Variations on a 17th Century Theme." *Westminster Theological Journal* 42, no. 2 (Spring 1980): 308–34.

Noll, Mark A. *The Work We Have to Do: A History of Protestants in America*. Oxford: Oxford University Press, 2002.

Sandoz, Ellis, ed. *Political Sermons of the American Founding Era: 1730–1805*, 2 vols. Indianapolis, IN: Liberty Fund, 2000.

Shields, Jon A. *The Democratic Virtues of the Christian Right*. Princeton, NJ: Princeton University Press, 2009.

Sider, Ronald J. *The Scandal of Evangelical Politics: Why Are Christians Missing the Chance to Really Change the World?* Grand Rapids, MI: Baker Books, 2008.

Smidt, Corwin E. *American Evangelicals Today*. Lanham, MD: Rowman & Littlefield, 2013.

Witte, John Jr., and Joel A. Nichols. *Religion and the American Constitutional Experiment*, 4th ed. New York, NY: Oxford University Press, 2016.

13

# Mormonism and Conscience

ROSALYNDE WELCH AND NATHAN B. OMAN

## INTRODUCTION

While Mormons occasionally invoke the idea of conscience, it has played at best a muted role in Mormon thought and experience. To organize our account of conscience in Mormonism, we frame our definition around two separate but related functions. First, conscience can refer to a subjective moral sense that gives one access to moral truths about right and wrong; call this the epistemic function. Second, it can be used as a source of subjective moral authority, in which the integrity of individual morality is asserted against a collective source of moral authority like the church or the state; call this the moral-practical function. While traces of both conceptions of conscience can be found within Mormon discourse and practice, Mormon theology and experience have mitigated against both the epistemic and the practical claims of conscience.

Mormonism is not without conceptual resources for thinking about the tensions between individual moral choice and the claims of collective authority. However, Mormonism primarily addresses these concerns using language and concepts other than conscience, notably personal revelation, communal integrity, and a divine immanence known as the light of Christ. In comparison to other Christian traditions, the Mormon approach to conscience-based conflicts between individual and collective authority is unusually communal and deferential to claims of religious and secular authority. This is particularly true of the limited authority of Mormon private conscience vis-à-vis internal ecclesiastical authority. Nevertheless, particularly when it comes to civil legal authority, Mormon experience and theology provides some resources for religious conscience to challenge the claims of the law.

The low profile of conscience in Mormon thought is best grasped in the context of the idea's development in Protestantism, the religious environment within which Mormonism originated and the theological tradition from which it often departs. Since its first full Christian formulation in the writings of Thomas Aquinas, the idea of conscience has acquired a wide range of meanings as a consequence of changing religious and political uses. Practical moral judgment, psychological introspection, moral inhibition, and subjective antinomianism all inform the word's use. In this chapter, we draw on these diverse meanings as they touch on the concept's development in Mormon thought, but we will focus primarily on conscience as an arbiter of competing claims of authority. Our interest is not in the morality of human freedom or the limits of institutional authority per se. Rather, in exploring conscience in Mormonism we are inquiring into *a subjective way of producing authority*.

This chapter will first examine the idea of conscience in Western thought with an emphasis on how it claims subjective epistemic and moral authority. We will then explore how conscience is worked out in Mormon thought in relation to ecclesiastical and public authority. Ultimately, we will conclude that the claims of conscience within Mormonism are muted. Mormons do have an idea of subjective epistemic authority, but it is limited. They have very little idea of subjective moral authority. Rather, they tend to mediate the claims of authority using other ideas, such as personal revelation, stewardships, free agency, and the importance of ecclesiastical independence with respect to state authority.

## CONSCIENCE IN WESTERN THOUGHT

What follows is not an exhaustive review of the development of Protestant conscience; rather, we focus on the epistemic and moral functions of conscience, in order to better characterize the unique contours of Mormon thinking about conscience. During the modern period, conscience evolved from a practical disposition of the soul witnessing divine and natural law to a subjective source of binding subjective moral direction.[1] As C. S. Lewis put it, "*conscience*, so to speak, passed from the witness-box to the bench and even to

1 Of course, any account of the religious and political development of conscience must acknowledge historical complexity. No simple trajectory, whether intellectual history of the early modern passage from scholasticism to Enlightenment self-awareness or a triumphal narrative of the emergence of sovereign individuality, does justice to the development of a category as contested as private conscience. As an arena of conflict between notions of public and private, spiritual and temporal, law and anarchy, equality and pluralism, the social function of conscience has shifted over time. For recent scholarly reckoning with the complexity of conscience in the early modern period, see Harald E. Braun and Edward Vallance, "Introduction," *Renaissance Studies* 23, no. 4 (2009): 413–22.

the legislator's throne."[2] A brief account of this process provides a useful background for understanding Mormon approaches to the idea of conscience and how they diverge from other traditions.

The ideological transformation of conscience in the modern West opens with Thomas Aquinas's definition of conscience. The scholastic formulation, drawing on biblical and classical accounts of morality, divided conscience into two parts: *synderesis*, an internal disposition toward natural law that inherently inclines to general principles of moral good, and *conscientia*, the application of these general principles to one's personal situation and the exercise of practical judgment to allow or prohibit particular acts.[3] Two tensions present in the Thomistic formulation proved salient in subsequent Protestant and Mormon iterations of the concept. First, *synderesis* as a "storehouse" of natural law is a universal and permanent disposition of every human soul, Christian or pagan, and never errs in exposing the soul to the good; whereas *conscientia* is a subjective faculty of cognition and thus capable of error in understanding the situation, applying the law, or drawing a conclusion. For Aquinas, "one should not act contrary to conscience, even in the case of erroneous reason."[4] For later thinkers, the contradictions implicit in the authority of erroneous conscience became a confounding locus of debate. Second, one can discern in the Thomistic distinction between *synderesis* and *conscientia* the kernel of the conceptual chasm that emerged between, on one hand, negative, inhibitory, rule-oriented conscience, hitched to the objective content of natural law, and, on the other, positive, action-oriented, subjective conscience, empowered to legitimize private choice against external claims.

The antinomian character of conscience engaged the Protestant religious mind. Conscience stood both inside (as *synderesis*) and outside (as *conscientia*) systems of law, sometimes as subservient enforcer of law and sometimes as magisterial judge of law itself. For Luther, "conscience represented an antinomian rupture with the Thomistic tradition of natural and divine law."[5] Protestant thinkers wished to bolster conscience as the source of binding moral precept; yet, in doing so, the authority of conscience inevitably collided

2 C. S. Lewis, *Studies in Words*, 2nd ed. (New York, NY: Cambridge University Press, 2013), 191.

3 Thomistic conscience has been well explored in secondary literature. See, e.g., Edward G. Andrew, *Conscience and Its Critics: Protestant Conscience, Enlightenment Reason, and Modern Subjectivity* (Toronto: University of Toronto Press, 2001); Richard J. Regan, *The American Constitution and Religion* (Washington, DC: Catholic University of America Press, 2013).

4 Regan, *The American Constitution and Religion*, 245.

5 Andrew, *Conscience and Its Critics*, 20.

with the authority of the Bible, and the anarchic energies of antinomianism were released.[6] One historian has observed that "In the sixteenth century the most persistent and determined law-breakers were the godly who – like twentieth century conscientious objectors in wartime – claimed to be obeying a higher authority [conscience] than that of the state."[7] The Bible could be marshalled to check the excesses of conscience, both by supplying *synderesis* with the content of divine law and by disciplining its antinomian energies, as a standard against which erroneous conscience may be refuted. Yet even as Luther attempted to evade unbridled subjectivism by grounding conscience in the Bible, his teachings privileged individual interpretation over the authority of the church to declare the meaning of the canon. The uncertainty surrounding the status of the inviolable yet fallible conscience thus persisted in all post-Reformation treatments of the subject. Indeed, Mormon notions of conscience may be understood to respond to this dilemma by siding against the antinomianism of subjective conscience and with ecclesiastical authority assuming the authority of the Bible.

The antinomian energies of Protestant conscience stood opposite another approach, in which conscience acts not as moral legislator but moral prosecutor, accusing the soul, discouraging unlawful acts, and punishing with guilt and shame. Conscience resides in the heart as a kind of demiurge presaging the final judgment of God. Influential Puritan sage William Perkins wrote that conscience is "a little God sitting in the middle of men's hearts."[8] The influence of this prosecuting "little God" was twofold: first, it raised the subjective status of conscience above community and canon, as the highest human authority under God; second, it reduced private conscience to an internal enforcer of external authority, limiting its effects to self-censorship.[9] This second function is evident in Hamlet's famous lines, "Thus conscience does make cowards of us all;" or, as Shakespeare's Richard III puts it more pointedly, "For Conscience is a word that Cowards use, / Devis'd at first to keep the strong in awe." Both impulses – to elevate the subjective status of conscience and to reduce its function to internal law enforcement – decisively

6 See James Calvin Davis, "William Ames's Calvinist Ambiguity over Freedom of Conscience," *The Journal of Religious Ethics* 33, no. 2 (2005): 333–55.

7 Christopher Hill, *Liberty against the Law: Some Seventeenth-Century Controversies* (London: Viking Adult, 1996), 181. Cited in Andrew, *Conscience and Its Critics*, 26.

8 Mika Ojakangas, *The Voice of Conscience: A Political Genealogy of Western Ethical Experience* (New York, NY: Bloomsbury Academic, 2015), 84, quoting William Perkins, *Discourse of Conscience* (Cambridge: John Legate, 1596), 9.

9 See Camille Wells Slights, "Notaries, Sponges, and Looking-Glasses: Conscience in Early Modern England," *English Literary Renaissance* 28, no. 2 (1998): 231–46.

shifted the locus of moral authority to the individual's interior world. The subjectivity of conscience proved to be an enduring feature of the idea as deployed to broker the religious and political dilemmas of the Reformation and the emergence of religious pluralism. Just as it eschews the antinomian conscience, Mormonism largely abandons the self-accusing internal conscience, outsourcing to community norms the functions of encouraging good and penalizing bad behavior.

The subjectivity of early modern ideas of conscience was important in English debates over public and private authority. The Elizabethan religious settlement required public participation in the state religion but allowed a degree of private dissent. Elizabeth I's mythic statement, "I would not open windows into men's souls," suggests one compromise between public and private authority: a public space under the public authority of church and state and a private space under the private authority of conscience. Ideas of conscience internalized and "privatized" moral deliberation, encouraging practices of exhaustive self-examination and personal self-fashioning. The private dictates of conscience were practiced in the private spaces of the prayer closet or, more dangerously, the priest hole, a secret harbor for outlaw Catholic priests in recusant homes. Yet boundaries between public and private had to be negotiated. Elizabethan Catholic recusants and Puritan radicals, including and especially women assessing their place in the private sphere, enlisted conscience to enlarge its frontier. In one sense, the public/private compromise contained conscience, depriving it of public authority; in another sense, conscience burnished the cultural prestige of subjective experience and encouraged individuals and groups to expand the jurisdiction of private authority. As one scholar has noted "the individual and the collective intersect in the conscience."[10] While discussions of conscience tend to portray the conscientious individual alone against the world, the protection of "private" conscience was often claimed by collective members of minority religious groups, rather than by isolated individuals. Private conscience could thus be deployed as a shield for group religious practice against the authority of a hostile state, rather than as a celebration of subjective individualism. It is this corporate sense of private conscience that most directly informs the Mormon discourse of conscience, such as it is.

In the societies of early modern Europe, the fragmentation of the church threatened to fragment the political unity of the state. Hobbes and Locke proposed radically different solutions to this challenge. The American republic,

[10] Ibid., 231.

with no national established church, sided with Locke, whose vision of distinct, limited domains for government and religion informs the First Amendment. Government's domain is the safety of person and property in this world; religion's domain is private conviction relating to the next. Like the Elizabethan settlement, the Lockean settlement neutralizes the antinomian energies of religious conscience by confining it to a separate sphere of private opinion. Thus, Locke "restricted the operation of conscience, at least for the most part, to negative judgments of reason from religious premises that were only opinion. In this respect, he was a forerunner not only of the modern Western settlement in favor of religious tolerance, but of modern subjectivist interpretations of conscience, as well."[11] Yet conscience rarely limits its dictates to beliefs and private opinions; since its first Thomistic formulation, it has also entailed practical judgment that directly influences behavior. America's religious diversity adds a further dimension: a structural division between public and private matters may function in the context of Reformed religion, which heavily privileges private personal experience over communal and ritual observance but makes little sense for religions that require external markers of membership. Like other compromises based on non-overlapping jurisdictions, the American settlement invites negotiation and contest over the boundaries between this world and the next, between behavior and belief, and between the authority of Congress and the authority of conscience.

From this historical account, we distill two conceptual categories that will organize our treatment of Mormon conscience. First, the *epistemic* authority of conscience is grounded in its putative witness of some concept of the good, variously conceived as natural law, divine law, communal norms, or private felt conviction. From the beginning, theorists of conscience have struggled to identify and defend the precise content of *synderesis*; in a pluralistic society committed to egalitarianism, the task may be impossible. Jocelyn Maclure and Charles Taylor argue that the epistemic privilege of conscience originates in the state's "recognition of the limits of rationality, its inability to decide the questions of ultimate meaning of existence and the nature of human fulfillment in a decisive way."[12] Epistemic pluralism mediated through private conscience is thus a mechanism to accommodate ideals of both social diversity and social equality.

Second, we observe the *moral* authority of conscience as a privileged subjective faculty, that is, its status as a "little God" within the soul issuing

[11] Regan, *The American Constitution and Religion*, 256.

[12] Jocelyn Maclure and Charles Taylor, *Secularism and Freedom of Conscience*, trans. Jane Marie Todd (Cambridge, MA: Harvard University Press, 2011), 10.

binding mandates that overrule the external authorities of state or ecclesia. The possibility that conscience may err does not meaningfully vitiate this moral authority: while in theory conscience may be substantively mistaken, external authorities can offer no objective basis on which to determine its error. Thus, conscience provides a compelling moral reason for action independent of its epistemic authority, and its internal moral authority overrules external injunctions. The moral authority of the conscience resides near the center of the modern (Protestant) self. To violate the dictates of conscience is to threaten the coherence of the self. As we have seen, the anarchic potential of conscience has been a persistent anxiety for Christian Anglo-American thinkers and several mechanisms for its containment have emerged. Given the ideological parameters under which the modern conscience has developed, there is no easy, uncontestable solution to such quandaries. It seems that the ultimate force of conscience lies in its appeal to our deepest will. As William Earle puts it, the dictates of conscience "are neither correct nor incorrect, but affirmed or rejected."[13]

## CONSCIENCE IN MORMON THOUGHT

While Latter-day Saints occasionally use the word conscience in their sermons and writings, it plays a limited role in Mormon thought.[14] When it comes to moral epistemology, Mormons tend to speak in terms of personal revelation from God rather than innate moral faculties such as *synderesis* and *conscientia*. The primacy of divine revelation in Mormon thought is reinforced by the fact that for Latter-day Saints the paradigmatic case of revelation is not transcendental union, as in the mystical traditions of Christianity, Judaism, and Islam, but what one Mormon writer has labeled "dialogic revelation," which places emphasis on the propositional content of religious experience and the discrete personhood of God.[15] In this framework, conscience tends to be identified with revelation of the Holy Spirit, understood as a distinct personified being, rather than with an inherent moral faculty. Furthermore, the need to contain the antinomian tendencies of personal revelation resulted early on in

[13] William Earle, "Some Paradoxes of Private Conscience As a Political Guide," *Ethics* 80, no. 4 (1970): 312.

[14] For example, the term "conscience" appears repeatedly in section 134 of the Doctrine and Covenants, which is discussed below. See *The Doctrine and Covenants of the Church of Jesus Christ of Latter-day Saints* (Salt Lake City, UT: The Church of Jesus Christ of Latter-day Saints, 1989), section 134, 2–4 (hereafter D&C).

[15] See Terryl Givens, *By the Hand of Mormon: The American Scripture That Launched a New World Religion* (New York, NY: Oxford University Press, 2003), 209–39.

Mormon history in a series of concepts that severely limit its ability to act as a basis for challenging either ecclesiastical or political authorities. The absence of a well-developed conception of conscience in Mormon thought, however, does not mean that the tradition is without resources to limit the claims of legal authority. It does mean that Latter-day Saints have tended to invoke ideas such as the special moral status of human freedom or the importance of communal independence and integrity rather than the moral sovereignty of subjective conscience.

## *Conscience and Epistemic Authority*

The development of Christian conscience may be imagined in broad terms as a relocation from the confessional box of Catholicism to the private prayer closet of Protestantism, transforming along the way from a largely epistemic function that testifies of right and wrong action, to a morally authorizing function that elevates private judgment in relation to other kinds of authority. Mormonism does not fit neatly on this historical-ideological spectrum from Catholic to Protestant. Broadly, Mormonism rebuffs the antinomian subjective moral authority of conscience, while it recognizes in limited ways the epistemic functions of *synderesis*.

The idea of conscience as an internal witness of right and wrong that accuses the soul of wrongdoing and provokes guilt as a spur to repentance is present, albeit sparingly, in Mormon scripture. The Book of Mormon speaks in several passages of "remorse of conscience" as the consequence of knowingly breaking the commandments of God.[16] Like the scholastic notion of *synderesis*, the Book of Mormon emphasizes humanity's knowledge of divine law and the punishment that is justly affixed to transgression. Divine law emanates from a heavenly source and must be made available to the human mind to guide its actions. Conscience is a minor vector of that knowledge, and preaching and communal norms are the primary means of transmitting divine law and encouraging obedience in Mormon scripture and practice. Mormonism imposes strict behavioral requirements on its adherents, and it is rather surprising that Latter-day Saints rely so little on the language of conscience to enforce those requirements internally. Mormon teaching tends instead to appeal to the relational force of communal and sacramental covenants to encourage obedience. When serious transgression occurs, the consequences are mediated through ecclesiastical discipline and curtailment of

[16] Alma 29:5, 42:18.

communal worship participation, rather than through the torments of conscience. The idea of conscience as a teacher and deputy of divine law appears infrequently and plays a minor role in Mormon teachings.

An analogue in Mormon theology for the idea of conscience as an epistemic authority is what Latter-day Saints call "the light of Christ."[17] The Book of Mormon contains a passage stating, "Wherefore, I beseech you, brethren, that you should search diligently in the light of Christ that you may know good from evil; and if you will lay hold upon every good thing, and condemn it not, you certainly will be a child of Christ."[18] As it developed in Mormon theology, the light of Christ became identified with a universal infusion of divine revelation that gives to all people the ability to discern right and wrong. It thus represents a universally available manifestation of the Holy Spirit. As Brigham Young insisted:

> I do not believe for one moment that there has been a man or woman upon the face of the earth … who has not been enlightened, instructed, and taught by the revelations of Jesus Christ …. [I] am far from believing that the children of men have been deprived of the privilege of receiving the spirit of the Lord to teach them right from wrong.[19]

Other Mormon leaders and theologians have identified the light of Christ with human conscience. A widely used twentieth-century theological reference declares, "every man has a conscience and knows more or less when he does wrong, and the Spirit guides him if he will hearken to its whisperings."[20] More recently, a prominent Mormon leader has written, "Conscience affirms the reality of the Spirit of Christ in man. It affirms, as well, the reality of good and evil, of justice, mercy, honor, courage, faith, love and virtue, as well as the necessary opposites – hatred, greed brutality, jealousy."[21]

The light of Christ, however, differs from Protestant ideas of conscience in ways that tend to diminish claims to subjective moral authority. Where some Protestants saw conscience as a "little God" at the center of the self, endowing personal moral judgment with an inviolable status, Mormons understand the light of Christ quite differently.[22] First, the light of Christ is not linked in

[17] See C. Kent Dunford, "Light of Christ," in *The Encyclopedia of Mormonism*, ed. Daniel H. Ludlow (New York, NY: Macmillan, 1992).

[18] Moroni 7:19.

[19] Brigham Young, *Discourses of Brigham Young*, ed. John A. Widtsoe (Salt Lake City, UT: Deseret Book, 1983), 32.

[20] Joseph Fielding Smith, *Doctrines of Salvation: Complete Three-Volume Work*, ed. Bruce R. McConkie (Salt Lake City, UT: Bookcraft, 1999), 38.

[21] Boyd K. Packer, "The Light of Christ," *Ensign* (April 2005), www.lds.org/ensign/2005/04/the-light-of-christ?lang=eng.

[22] Perkins, *Discourse of Conscience*, 9. See n. 8.

Mormon theology with a conception of the self that emphasizes its subjective moral sovereignty or the overriding importance of personal moral commitments. For Latter-day Saints, human freedom is seen primarily in terms of a moral test, in which human beings either choose to follow God or to reject him. Human freedom is thus given a high moral status, but not because it is tied to a thick conception of moral self-authorship or personal authenticity. Thus, the light of Christ comes from beyond the self as a moral demand imposed on the individual by God, even if the individual does not believe in God or recognize his or her moral intuitions as divine revelation.

Second, while the moral sense that every person gains through the light of Christ is a species of divine revelation, it is not the only form of personal revelation. Indeed, within Mormonism's revelation-centric theology, there is a hierarchy of revelatory forms that are mediated in part through the institutional authority of the church. Thus, while the light of Christ is universally available, Mormons also believe in what they call the "gift of the Holy Ghost,"[23] which is a special spiritual gift available only to those who covenant with God through baptism. It promises the "constant companionship of the Holy Spirit" to those who are worthy, a companionship that is, in some not fully specified sense, superior to the light of Christ. This hierarchy of moral guidance resembles in some ways Protestant attempts to negotiate questions of universality and confessional exclusiveness. Some Protestant thinkers acknowledge the universal influence of "natural conscience" or *synderesis* but privilege the Christian conscience that has been nourished by biblical precept.[24] The Bible, and one's interpretation thereof, prioritizes various claims and forms of conscience. Mormonism's solution to these questions departs in an important respect, substituting ecclesiastical authority for individual interpretive authority. Crucially, in Mormon practice one receives the gift of the Holy Ghost through a ritual – or "ordinance" in Latter-day Saint parlance – that must be administered through "the laying on of hands" by someone holding the Mormon priesthood. The effect is to link personal revelation to the disciplining force of the church's claims to exclusive priestly authority.

Finally, the scope of the authority of personal revelation received through the gift of the Holy Ghost or the light of Christ is limited by the concept of "stewardship."[25] The concept of stewardship is in some respects analogous to,

[23] See Bruce Douglas Porter, "Gift of the Holy Ghost," in *The Encyclopedia of Mormonism*, ed. Daniel H. Ludlow (New York, NY: Macmillan, 1992).

[24] See discussion in Davis, "Calvinist Ambiguity," 342.

[25] See J. Lynn England, "Stewardship," in *The Encyclopedia of Mormonism*, ed. Daniel H. Ludlow (New York, NY: Macmillan, 1992).

though ultimately distinct from, the notion of separate secular and religious spheres often deployed to manage the antinomian impulses of Protestant conscience against the authority of the state. For Mormons, stewardship is a circumscribed realm of responsibility entrusted to an individual by God. The idea can be employed in an institutional or ecclesiastical sense. With an almost entirely lay ministry, most Mormons are given some ecclesiastical role – known as a "calling" – such as leading a congregation, teaching in the church, or perhaps serving for a time as a missionary. These roles are stewardships. However, the idea can be applied more loosely to personal roles. Hence, for example, Latter-day Saints mothers and fathers speak of having a stewardship over their families. One is entitled to revelation for one's own stewardships, but not for the stewardships of others. Furthermore, those within the ecclesiastical hierarchy can have stewardship "over the church" in their area, giving their revelation primacy in church government over the revelation of others. For this reason, Mormon stewardships are seldom subject to the contest and negotiation that characterize Protestant attempts to sequester conscience within a circumscribed sphere. Thus, when the light of Christ is seen within the broader economy of Mormon revelation, it yields a distinctly anemic conception of individual conscience. The subjective moral sovereignty of the self is subordinated to the revelatory authority of God and the ecclesiastical ideas and structures that order the potentially antinomian potential of personal revelation. This limited epistemic authority is coupled with limited practical authority against the claims of both church and state.

## *Conscience and Ecclesiastical Authority*

Mormonism is a highly institutionalized and hierarchical religion. The Church of Jesus Christ of Latter-day Saints is a tightly integrated ecclesiastical polity. In contrast to the decentralized, congregational structure that is most common in American Protestantism, every Mormon congregation is nested in a hierarchical ecclesiastical structure with ascending priesthood authorities. One can analogize the Mormon church to the Catholic hierarchy, but in practice the Mormon church is far more tightly integrated and disciplined than the Catholic church, which tolerates a fairly wide range of regional variation in teaching and practices. Mormonism is far more centralized and unified.

At the apex of the ecclesiastical structure are the church's presiding councils, the Quorum of the Twelve Apostles and the First Presidency, whose members are accepted by Latter-day Saints as "prophets, seers, and revelators." These leaders not only have a great deal of practical administrative authority, they also make strong claims to priestly and revelatory authority. Mormon theology insists that the performance of certain ordinances is a necessary component of salvation and such ordinances can only be performed by those holding proper priesthood authority. The high Mormon hierarchy claims the exclusive authority to direct the use of that priesthood. Additionally, Mormonism's open canon means that the hierarchy always has the ability to add additional scripture, something however, that has happened rarely since 1844. Of greater practical significance, the hierarchy claims the ability to receive less formalized divine guidance on behalf of the church as a whole. Mormon leaders frequently make claims to moral and ecclesiastical authority, and one of the persistent issues in Latter-day Saint experience has been the extent to which concepts of private conscience and personal revelation may be legitimately invoked against the authority of the church and its hierarchy.

Paradoxically, the hierarchical nature of the Mormon church exists alongside a theology that celebrates personal revelation and the ability of each individual to receive very specific divine instructions. From the very beginning, the idea of dialogic revelation meant that Latter-day Saints expected personal revelation to deliver more than simply moral discernment. It could contain detailed and specific commandments that went well beyond any subjective capacity to discern right from wrong.

The necessity of reconciling the competing claims of individual revelation and hierarchical and communal authority appeared early in Mormon history. Joseph Smith launched the Mormon movement with the publication of the Book of Mormon, which declared among other things that in the last days the faithful were to gather and build up the New Jerusalem somewhere on the American continent.[26] The question arose of where the city of Zion was to be built. One of Smith's associates, Hiram Page, declared that he had received a revelation declaring the location of the New Jerusalem.[27] Many of the members of the infant church initially accepted Page's revelations as authoritative, and the issue threatened to split the community. Events came to a head at the church's second general conference. Smith responded to Page's claims

[26] See 3 Ne. 16; 3 Ne. 21:24; Ether 13:4–8. For the role of the Book of Mormon in the earliest LDS theologies, see Grant Underwood, "The Earliest Reference Guides to the Book of Mormon: Windows into the Past," *Journal of Mormon History* 12 (1985): 69–89; Grant Underwood, "Book of Mormon Usage in Early LDS Theology," *Dialogue: A Journal of Mormon Thought*, 17, no.3 (Autumn 1984): 35–74.

[27] The incident is recounted in Richard L. Bushman, *Joseph Smith and the Beginnings of Mormonism* (Urbana, IL: University of Illinois Press, 1985), 167–68; Bruce G. Stewart, "Hiram Page: An Historical and Sociological Analysis of An Early Mormon Prototype," master's thesis, Brigham Young University, 1987, 112–43.

to authority by an appeal to the recently adopted "Articles and Covenants" – a constitutional document for the church – based on biblical arguments and a new revelation declaring, "[N]o one shall be appointed to receive revelations and commandments in this church excepting my servant Joseph Smith, Jun., for he receiveth them even as Moses."[28] The conference sided with Smith, declaring "Brother Joseph Smith Jr. was appointed by the voice of the Conference to receive and write Revelations & Commandments for this Church."[29] This settlement has largely held through Mormon history: each individual is entitled to revelation for themselves, but personal revelation cannot be invoked against the authority of the church and its leaders.

From the time of Hiram Page to the present, Mormonism has periodically struggled with the schismatic tendencies inherent in the claims of revelation. At various times, charismatic figures have arisen claiming authority based on some special revelation.[30] Generally, Mormon leaders and theologians have responded with the limiting strategies outlined above, strategies that are widely accepted by Latter-day Saints. The result is a religious discourse that abounds with stories and discussions of divine instructions on the details of individual lives while at the same time sharply limiting the ability of such personal religious experiences to claim any broader moral authority over others or against the religious authority of the ecclesiastical hierarchy. Likewise, dissenters in Mormon history have occasionally invoked the idea of personal revelation and conscience against the authority of the church.[31] However, such claims have more often than not been met with suspicion and hostility by both rank-and-file Latter-day Saints and the church hierarchy. LDS theology offers relatively few resources for articulating such claims against communal authority in terms of Mormon concepts. Thus, when dissenters and others have used the language of conscience or individual rights in asserting their claims against

[28] D&C 28:2.

[29] Donald Cannon and Lyndon W. Cook, eds., *Far West Record: Minutes of the Church of Jesus Christ of Latter-day Saints, 1830–1844* (Salt Lake City, UT: Deseret Book Co., 1983), 3.

[30] The most dramatic example of this tendency is the persistence of polygamy among "Mormon fundamentalists" after the Church of Jesus Christ of Latter-day Saints abandoned polygamy around the turn of the twentieth century and began systematically excommunicating those who continued to practice polygamy. The result has been a profusion of charismatic polygamist leaders founding new Mormon sects. See generally Newell G. Bringhurst and Craig L. Foster, eds., *The Persistence of Polygamy, Vol. 3, Fundamentalist Mormon Polygamy from 1890 to the Present* (Independence, MO: John Whitmer Books, 2015); B. Carmon Hardy, *Solemn Covenant: The Mormon Polygamous Passage* (Urbana, IL: University of Illinois Press, 1992).

[31] See generally Roger D. Launius and Linda Thatcher, eds., *Differing Visions: Dissenters in Mormon History* (Urbana, IL: University of Illinois Press, 1994).

the authority of the church, they are generally seen by other Latter-day Saints as rejecting Mormon theology rather than elaborating it.

## *Conscience and Public Authority*

If anything, Mormonism is even more hostile to claims that personal revelation or subjective conscience justifies disobeying the law. Latter-day Saints insist that they have a religious duty to obey the law. Here again, Mormonism sides decisively against radical Protestantism by discounting the moral status of personal conviction relative to the moral status of civil law. The Mormon position seems to hearken back to an earlier Pauline notion of conscience as an internalized deputy of the divine authority that ordains government: "Let every soul submit itself to the higher powers. For there is no power but of God, and the powers that be are ordained of God .... Therefore it is necessary that ye be subject, not only for punishment, but also for conscience sake."[32] Yet Mormons almost never cite these verses. Rather, scriptural support for the Mormon duty to obey the law comes from two texts authored in the 1830s and 1840s and added to the Mormon canon. Early Mormonism operated in a millenarian world in which the end times were assumed to be imminent. Accordingly, the Latter-day Saints were to build up Zion, a New Jerusalem that was to be located in Jackson County, Missouri at the extreme western edge of American settlement in the 1830s. This was to be an independent Mormon polity with its own laws that would await the imminent second coming of Jesus Christ. "[V]erily I say unto you that in time ye shall have no king nor ruler, for I will be your king and watch over you ... ye shall have no laws but my laws when I come, for I am your lawgiver," the Lord declares in one of Joseph Smith's earliest revelations.[33] However, in part because of this frontal assault on the secular state's monopoly over legal authority, mobs drove the Saints first from Jackson County and then from Missouri. In the face of these reverses, Mormon revelations and theology turned toward secular law as a bulwark for the Saints against the extralegal violence of their persecutors.[34]

32 Romans 13:1, 5 (KJV).

33 D&C 38:22. For a discussion of the conception of divine law contained in this and other early revelations, see Nathan B. Oman, "'I Will Give unto You My Law': Section 42 As a Legal Text and the Paradoxes of Divine Law," in *Embracing the Law: Reading Doctrine and Covenants 42*, eds. Jeremiah John and Joseph M. Spencer (Provo, UT: Neal A. Maxwell Institute for Religious Scholarship, 2017); Mark Ashurst-McGee, "Zion Rising: Joseph Smith's Early Social and Political Thought," PhD thesis, Arizona State University, 2008, 207–49.

34 See Mark Ashurst-McGee, "Zion in America: The Origins of Mormon Constitutionalism," *Journal of Mormon History* 38, no. 3 (2012): 90–101.

During the course of the nineteenth century, Mormons never fully abandoned their dream of a sovereign Zion and secular law proved an imperfect protection at best for the Saints.[35] The key Mormon texts on legal authority, however, emerged from this turn toward secular law.

The first is a document entitled "Of Governments and Laws in General."[36] It was written in the 1830s and states:

> We believe that governments were instituted of God for the benefit of man; and that he holds men accountable for their acts in relation to them, both in making laws and administering them, for the good and safety of society.[37]

It went on to insist that "We believe that all men are bound to sustain and uphold the respective governments in which they reside."[38] The statement was formally included in the Mormon canon in the 1835 edition of the *Doctrine & Covenants* and has remained part of Mormon scripture to the present.[39] The second text comes from a statement of Mormon beliefs entitled the "Articles of Faith," published by Joseph Smith in 1842. The twelfth of these articles states, "We believe in being subject to kings, presidents, rulers, and magistrates, in obeying, honoring, and sustain the law."[40]

Neither of these texts claims a revelatory provenance. The first was likely written by one of Joseph Smith's close associates and presents a theology of the state that is largely indistinguishable from contemporary republican and Protestant ideas.[41] The Articles of Faith were prepared as part of a letter to a newspaper editor and drew extensively on early Mormon pamphlets.[42]

35 See, e.g., Dallin Oaks, *Carthage Conspiracy: The Trial of the Accused Assassins of Joseph Smith* (Urbana, IL: University of Illinois Press, 1975) (recounting the murder of Joseph Smith and the law's anemic efforts to punish his murderers and protect his followers).

36 For a brief summary of the background to the statement, see Steven Craig Harper, *Making Sense of the Doctrine & Covenants: A Guided Tour through Modern Revelations* (Salt Lake City, UT: Deseret Book, 2008), 493–94.

37 D&C 134:1.

38 Ibid., 134:5.

39 It is canonized as section 134 of the current edition of the Doctrine and Covenants.

40 Articles of Faith 12.

41 See Rodney K. Smith, "James Madison, John Witherspoon, and Oliver Cowdery: The First Amendment and the 134th Section of the Doctrine and Covenants," *Brigham Young University Law Review* 2003, no. 3 (2003): 891–940.

42 See Karen Lynn Davidson et al., eds., *Histories: 1832–1844*, The Joseph Smith Papers (Salt Lake City, UT: The Church Historian's Press, 2012), 489–91. Compare Orson Pratt, *A Interesting Account of Several Remarkable Visions, and the Late Discovery of Ancient American Records* (Edinburgh: Ballantyne and Hughes, 1840), 24. For a detailed discussion of the relationship between the Articles of Faith and Pratt's pamphlet, see Breck England, *The Life and Thought of Orson Pratt* (Salt Lake City, UT: University of Utah Press, 1985), 67–71. Interestingly, however, the twelfth article of faith does not have an analogue in Pratt's earlier pamphlet.

Nevertheless, they have emerged as the key texts supporting a Mormon duty to obey the law. With the exception of their stronghold in the Intermountain West of the United States, Latter-day Saints are always a tiny minority of the societies in which they live. Accordingly, Mormon leaders have insisted on the duty of legal obedience as a way of making the community as small a target as possible.

The most dramatic example of this dynamic can be seen in the case of Helmuth Hubener, a young German Mormon who was executed by the Gestapo during World War II for writing and distributing anti-Nazi pamphlets.[43] Among modern Germans, Hubener is remembered as one of the heroic handful of "good Germans" who resisted Nazi tyranny. However, his official treatment by the LDS Church has been more ambivalent. Frightened of becoming an object of the Nazis' wrath, Hubener's local ecclesiastical leaders immediately excommunicated him from the church for failing to "honor, obey, and sustain the law." While his story has been repeatedly told by various Latter-day Saint writers as an example of moral courage, it has seldom been mentioned in official church publications, and that only recently. This is no doubt because his act of resistance endangered the church and his co-religionists, and Mormons in other repressive regimes who followed his example could place their religious community in danger. In the twentieth century, in particular, Mormon allegiance to the law has been a key part of the church's efforts to avoid the hostility of suspicious foreign governments worried about Latter-day Saints fomenting political unrest.[44]

Despite this tradition, Mormonism does have resources for challenging secular authority. It has seldom done this, however, in the name of individual conscience. The most dramatic example of Mormon resistance to the law came in the nineteenth-century battles over the practice of polygamy.[45] Joseph Smith secretly introduced "plural marriage" toward the end of his life as a restoration of the ancient practices of the biblical patriarchs. After his death, the church publicly proclaimed the practice in 1852 and Congress responded

43 For a discussion of the relationship between Hubener and modern Mormon theologies of legal authority, see Frederick Mark Gedicks, "The Embarrassing Section 134," *Brigham Young University Law Review* 2003, no. 3 (2003): 959–63. Interestingly, however, the modern church has formally eradicated the effect of Hubener's excommunication. Mormons believe that it is possible for living people to posthumously perform ordinances on behalf of the dead. Accordingly, the First Presidency of the church has "restored the blessings" of Hubener, which constitutes a posthumous reversal of his excommunication. See ibid., 959, n. 9.

44 See Nathan B. Oman, "International Legal Experience and the Mormon Theology of the State, 1945–2012," *Iowa Law Review* 100, no. 2 (January 2015): 715–50.

45 See Sarah Barringer Gordon, *The Mormon Question: Polygamy and Constitutional Conflict in Nineteenth-Century America* (Chapel Hill, NC: University of North Carolina Press, 2002).

with the Morrill Anti-Bigamy Act of 1862, which criminalized polygamy in Mormon Utah. Latter-day Saints, however, refused to comply with the law. They first challenged the constitutionality of the Morrill Act in the US Supreme Court on free exercise grounds.[46] When that appeal failed, they simply refused to obey the law. Congress responded with ever more punitive legislation, which the Mormons challenged in the Supreme Court, generally unsuccessfully.[47] Eventually, the federal government pursued a policy of mass incarceration of Mormon polygamists, revoked the right of Mormon women to vote, disenfranchised Mormon polygamists, and moved to confiscate Mormon temples and other assets. Faced with institutional annihilation and permanent political disenfranchisement, Mormon church president Wilford Woodruff officially abandoned polygamy in 1890, beginning the torturous process that resulted in the early twentieth century with the church's full embrace of monogamy. Thus, for roughly four decades, Mormons actively resisted federal law.

To be sure, in their prolonged battle with the federal government, the Mormons at times invoked the language of conscience before the Supreme Court, and incarcerated Mormon polygamists referred to themselves as "prisoners for conscience sake."[48] However, Mormons never justified their resistance to federal law primarily in terms of the moral sovereignty of their subjective conscience. The challenge to the law's authority did not come from within the subjective self but rather from allegiance to what Mormons regarded as God's revelations and the community of the saints. In this sense,

[46] See *Reynolds* v. *United States*, 98 U.S. 145 (1879) (upholding the constitutionality of the Morrill Act).

[47] See, e.g., *Murphy* v. *Ramsey*, 114 U.S. 15 (1885) (upholding the disenfranchisement of polygamists); *United States* v. *Cannon*, 116 U.S. 55 (1885) (adopting a relaxed definition of unlawful cohabitation in order to facilitate prosecution of Mormon polygamists); *In re Snow*, 120 U.S. 274 (1882) (defining the scope of unlawful cohabitation charges against Mormon polygamists); *The Late Corporation of the Church of Jesus Christ of Latter-day Saints* v. *United States*, 136 U.S. 1(1890) (upholding the disenfranchisement of the Mormon church and the federal government's confiscation of its property). In addition to the federal government, local governments also moved against the Mormons. The Idaho territorial legislature adopted a law that disenfranchised all Mormons – monogamous and polygamous. The law was upheld by the US Supreme Court. See *Davis* v. *Beason*, 133 U.S. 333 (1890). See Edwin B. Firmage, "Free Exercise of Religion in Nineteenth Century America: The Mormon Cases," *Journal of Law and Religion* 7, no. 2 (January 1, 1989): 281–313, doi.org/10.2307/1051123 (summarizing the Mormon cases); Orma Linford, "The Mormons and the Law: The Polygamy Cases, Part I," *Utah Law Review* 9, no. 2 (1964): 308–71 (same); Orma Linford, "The Mormons and the Law: The Polygamy Cases, Part II," *Utah Law Review* 9, no. 3 (1965): 543–92 (same).

[48] See, e.g., George Ticknor Curtis, *A Plea for Religious Liberty and the Rights of Conscience* (Washington, DC: Gibson Bros, Printers and Bookbinders, 1886); Bruce A. Van Orden, *Prisoner for Conscience' Sake: The Life of George Reynolds* (Salt Lake City, UT: Deseret Book Co., 1992).

the Mormon appeal to conscience, to the extent it existed, was akin to the Catholic recusant approach to confessional solidarity in early modern England, which invoked private conscience to legitimize the illegal practice of Roman religion in the face of hostile government action rather than to elevate personal moral authority vis-à-vis the Catholic magisterium. For example, in an elaborate 1882 letter issued by the First Presidency on how Mormons were to respond to the anti-polygamy Edmund's Act, the word conscience does not appear, while there are appeals to revelation, prophecy, and loyalty to Zion.[49] Alternatively, Mormons argued that religious persecution resulted in unwarranted violence and suffering. Hence, in replying to a defense of the anti-polygamy laws by Vice President Schulyer Colfax, Mormon leader John Taylor likened the federal government's actions to the persecutions of Hugenots, Waldenses, and Albigenses.[50] Tellingly, in rehearsing the stories of Protestant martyrdom, Taylor did not invoke Protestant ideas of conscience but dwelt on the material suffering generated by religious persecution. Mormons also insisted that the authority of the Constitution, properly understood, trumped the decisions of Congress. Revelations published by Joseph Smith during the Mormon turn to secular law insisted that the Constitution was the result of divine inspiration, and in resisting congressional enactments Mormons could thus insist that they were being true to their religious duty to honor, sustain, and obey the higher law of the Constitution.[51] This infused Mormons' constitutional arguments with a religious significance. For example, when George Q. Cannon, a member of the First Presidency and the political mastermind of Mormon resistance, penned an elaborate response to the Supreme Court's defense of the constitutionality of the Morrill Act, he declared "[N]ot the least of the considerations which prompt me to this review, is that I desire that all the people of my faith may know that we have not been deceived in our ideas respecting the Constitution and our rights under it."[52] In short, the subjective moral authority of individual conscience played virtually no real role in how Mormons conceptualized their resistance to federal anti-polygamy laws.

49 See John Taylor, George Q. Cannon, and Joseph F. Smith, *An Address to the Members of the Church of Jesus Christ of Latter-day Saints* (Salt Lake City, UT: n.p., 1882).

50 John Taylor and Schulyer Colfax, *The Mormon Question* (Salt Lake City, UT: Deseret News, 1870), 8–9.

51 See D&C 98:5–6; 101:77, 80; 109:54. See also Ashurst-McGee, "Zion in America" (discussing the historical background for these additions to Mormon scripture).

52 George Q. Cannon, *A Review of the Decision of the Supreme Court of the United States, in the Case of George Reynolds vs. The United States* (Salt Lake City, UT: Deseret News Printing and Publishing Establishment, 1879), 6.

The muted role of conscience can be seen in the role of Mormonism in the development of free exercise law during the post-Civil-rights era in the United States. The LDS Church's most prominent intervention in those debates came in *Corporation of the Presiding Bishop* v. *Amos*.[53] In that case, the church successfully defended the exemption of religious institutions from the anti-discrimination rules of Title VII from an Establishment Clause attack, arguing that such an exemption was necessary for religious communities to define their own rules of membership. The church has successfully defended the same position before the European Court of Human Rights.[54] As scholars have noted, "The connecting thread [in Mormon concerns with religious freedom] is the right of religious organizations to autonomy in their affairs."[55] In this concern can be seen the echoes of the earliest Mormon theology of law, which imagined the creation of Zion as an independent polity with its own laws awaiting the imminent second coming. While modern Mormonism has abandoned immediate apocalyptic expectations and any effort to create an independent Mormon commonwealth, Zion remains a potent idea within Mormon thought. Hence the emphasis on the integrity and independence of religious communities. It is a vision of religious challenges to legal authority in which the claims of individual conscience play almost no role. At most, the language of conscience is deployed – as it was by religious dissenters in Tudor and Stuart England – to defend the claims of minority religious communities against the state.

## CONCLUSION

The idea of conscience developed from scholastic moral philosophy and was honed in the debates of the Protestant Reformation. What emerged were conceptions of conscience that granted enormous epistemic and practical authority to the subjectivity of the self. In its starkest form, conscience suggests that the brute fact of moral conviction can claim a certain kind of moral authority. Mormonism has proven largely hostile to such claims. Its moral epistemology centers on the idea of personal revelation from God but controls against the antinomian possibilities of such revelation through a robust notion of religious hierarchy and delineated personal stewardships. In this vision,

[53] 483 U.S. 327 (1987).

[54] See *Obst* v. *Germany*, Application No. 425/03 (December 23, 2010) (European Court of Human Rights).

[55] Cole Durham and Nathan B. Oman, "A Century of Mormon Theory and Practice in Church-State Relations: Constancy Amidst Change" November 7, 2006, p. 28, papers.ssrn.com/sol3/papers.cfm?abstract_id=942567.

conscience is seen as at best a rudimentary form of personal revelation. The result is that there is very little space within Mormonism for the claims of conscience against ecclesiastical authority. For largely historical reasons rooted in their experience as an often-persecuted religious minority, Mormons have developed a theological discourse that tends to emphasize a religious requirement of obedience to secular law. However, Mormon history is replete with examples of Mormon challenges to legal authority. Latter-day Saints have generally not rooted the legitimacy of such challenges in the subjective authority of the individual conscience. Rather, Mormonism has tended to emphasize the claims of communal solidarity and independence when challenging legal authority, a stance that is rooted in some of the earliest and most basic structures of Mormon thought. Mormonism has only blessed resistance to the law when the integrity of Zion – conceptualized as the institutional church and the Mormon community – have demanded it, and Mormon efforts to limit the reach of the law through efforts such as constitutional litigation and lobbying have tended to focus on the claims of religious institutions and communities rather than the claims of subjective conscience.

## RECOMMENDED READING

Aquinas, Thomas. *Summa Theologiae* I Q79 a12.

Cannon, George Q. *A Review of the Decision of the Supreme Court of the United States, in the Case of Geo. Reynolds vs. the United States*. Salt Lake City, UT: Deseret News Printing and Publishing Establishment, 1879.

*The Doctrine and Covenants of the Church of Jesus Christ of Latter-day Saints*. Section 134. Salt Lake City, UT: The Church of Jesus Christ of Latter-day Saints, 1989.

Dunford, C. Kent. "Light of Christ." In *The Encyclopedia of Mormonism*, edited by Daniel H. Ludlow, 835. New York, NY: Macmillan, 1992.

Gedicks, Frederick Mark. "The 'Embarrassing' Section 134." *BYU Law Review* 2003, no. 3 (2003): 959–72.

Givens, Terryl L. "The Book of Mormon and Dialogic Revelation." *Journal of Book of Mormon Studies* 10, no. 2 (2001): 16–27.

Oman, Nathan B. "International Legal Experience and the Mormon Theology of the State, 1945–2012." *Iowa Law Review* 100, no. 2 (2015): 715–50.

Pulsipher, J. David. "'Prepared to Abide the Penalty': Latter-day Saints and Civil Disobedience." *Journal of Mormon History* 39, no. 3 (2013): 131–62.

Smith, Rodney K. "James Madison, John Witherspoon, and Oliver Cowdery: The First Amendment and the 134th Section of the Doctrine and Covenants." *BYU Law Review* 2003, no. 3 (2003): 291–340.

Welch, Rosalynde Frandsen. "Latter-day Saint Conscience." *Element: The Journal of the Society for Mormon Philosophy and Theology* 2, no. 1 (Spring 2006): 49–57.

# 14

# Culture and Conscience in the Thought of Joseph Ratzinger, Pope Benedict XVI*

PETER J. CASARELLA

## INTRODUCTION

Is conscience an "organ" of the human person, written on the heart of every person, or "an expression of the absolute value of the subjective self?"[1] The former allows for the condemnation of a great deal of unjust social *and* religious practices and, simultaneously, the discovery of a seat of wisdom planted in humanity by God. Cardinal Newman famously and provocatively toasted this view of conscience and accorded it a priority higher than that of obedience to the Pope. The latter view opens the door to a God who remains forever silent within the moral realm, not to mention "the canonizing of relativism."[2] Joseph Cardinal Ratzinger, later Pope Benedict XVI and now Pope Emeritus, notes that both views have been touted as the valid interpretation of St. Paul's espousal in Romans 2:14–15 of a conscience bearing witness by virtue of a law written into the hearts of all persons. In arguing for the relevance of the former, more ancient concept as opposed to the latter, modern one, he acknowledges the presence of "pagan saints" who are found "everywhere and in every age."[3] Moreover, he is the first to caution for genuine Christian humility before using the pre-modern wisdom as a moral battle axe: "What God makes of the poor broken pieces of our attempts at

* This chapter represents an edited version of an essay appearing in: Peter Casarella, "Culture and Conscience in the Thought of Joseph Ratzinger/Pope Benedict XVI," in *Explorations in the Theology of Benedict XVI*, ed. John C. Cavadini (Notre Dame, IN: University of Notre Dame Press, 2012), 63–86.

[1] This introductory paragraph follows very closely Joseph Ratzinger, *Truth and Tolerance: Christian Belief and World Religions* (San Francisco, CA: Ignatius Press, 2004), 206–7.

[2] Ibid., 206.

[3] Ibid., 207.

good, at approaching him, remains his secret, which we ought not to presume to try to work out."[4]

Joseph Ratzinger/Pope Benedict reflected frequently and over half a century on the relationship between Christianity and the laws of conscience. This chapter attempts to gather together those timely reflections as they unfolded with a great deal of consistency. The first section looks at the problem of culture as an ethical challenge and a challenge for ethics, in order to lay the groundwork for contextualizing Ratzinger's response thereto. The second section lays out the main lines of Ratzinger's idea of conscience. The final sections highlight the distinctive approach that he took to the act of witnessing in conscience to personal and social violations of conscience in order to show how closely intertwined the cultural and ethical projects are to one another. In sum, in Ratzinger's view, there is no theology of conscience without a theology of culture and vice versa.

## CULTURE: THE DYNAMIC OF ADVENT

In his study of the philosophy of culture, Joseph Ratzinger likens the dynamic within culture to the phenomenon of Advent, or broadly speaking, the anticipated future arrival of some truth that orients a people, such as the anticipated birth of Christ. This comment derives from Theodor Haecker's study of Virgil, much esteemed by Ratzinger. Haecker was an ardent opponent of fascism in Germany, who earned fame for his translations of Kierkegaard and Newman. Father D. Vincent Twomey SVD, in his fine book on Pope Benedict, rightly suggests its wider applicability to Pope Benedict's theology of culture.[5] Accordingly, the fullest sense of progress within a culture is progress made toward the revelation of a Redeemer. Progress here is defined in unsecular terms. Ratzinger questions notions of social progress that have become untethered from belief in God and ties real progress to a challenging and self-critical process of intercultural dialogue.

For Ratzinger, all cultures are in some fashion religious. Most reach a crisis when agents of social change submit the religious element to critical inquiry. Ratzinger counters the Enlightenment model of criticism, namely, that of gradual emancipation from self-imposed tutelage and the undue influence of religious institutions, without ignoring its potential benefits. The idea that religion and culture are separate spheres, he says, is an invention of relatively

4 Ibid.

5 Vincent Twomey SVD, *Pope Benedict XVI: The Conscience of Our Age* (San Francisco, CA: Ignatius Press, 2007), 132.

modern European vintage. This secularizing norm does not prevail in other cultures and in other periods.[6] Ratzinger defines culture as "the social form of expression, as it has grown up in history, of those experiences and evaluations that have left their mark on a community and have shaped it."[7] Cultural agents are not solely occupied with religious questions, but these questions occupy a central place: "Indeed, the very heart of the great cultures is that they interpret the world by setting in order their relationship to Divinity."[8] Some cultures – Ratzinger terms these entities "cosmic/static cultures" – do not valorize the historical dimension. The cosmic cultures reveal the universe as a mystery and point out that death and rebirth are paths for human existence. The cultural paths of Judaism and Christianity are, by contrast, historical paths. Without the historical dimension, cosmic cultures are not well positioned to deal with change.

Renewal and change are valuable processes in cultural development. The meeting of cultures, he states, is "the healing Pasch for a culture, which through an apparent death comes to new life and becomes then for the first time truly itself."[9] The phenomenon of Advent presupposes that there are agents of change within the dynamic of a culture that advocate radical change based upon the religious wisdom of the community. Ratzinger himself mentions the struggle to achieve racial equality in the United States as an example of a religiously based social transformation.[10] Although this connection is not made explicit, he appears to be speaking in a phenomenological key about the "prophetic radicalism" of the Old Testament.[11] For example, he cites Jonah's prophetism as an example of religious progress, since Jonah is able to warn the heathens of Nineveh of God's destruction of their city. "They know in their inmost hearts," writes Ratzinger, "that he exists, the one God, and they recognize the voice of that God in the preaching of the foreign prophet."[12] The modern critiques of religion by Dietrich Bonhoeffer and Karl Barth (and

6 Ratzinger, *Truth and Tolerance*, 59.

7 Ibid., 60.

8 Ibid., 61.

9 Ibid., 63.

10 Joseph Ratzinger, "The Church's Teaching – Authority – Faith – Morals," in *Principles of Christian Morality*, eds. Heinz Schürmann, Joseph Cardinal Ratzinger, and Hans Urs von Balthasar (San Francisco, CA: Ignatius Press, 1986), 47.

11 This term is used to refer to an aspect of the Old Testament that is taken up by Jesus. See Benedict XVI, *Jesus of Nazareth*, I:122–27. For a thoughtful Muslim contemporary on Christian prophecy as treated by Benedict XVI, see Mona Siddiqui, "'Searching for the Face of the Lord': Hope or Heresy?," in *The Pope and Jesus of Nazareth: Christ, Scripture, and the Truth*, eds. Adrian Pabst and Angus Paddison (London: SCM Press, 2009), 247–61.

12 Ratzinger, *Truth and Tolerance*, 99.

even in a certain way by Ludwig Feuerbach and Karl Marx) all carry some vestige of this radicalism.[13] In sum, historical cultures are never static but have a great capacity to endure over time because they are constantly subjected to further tests of allegiance to their ultimate source of Being. Cultural progress here is tied to a firm belief in a Creator.

Violence can ensue when cultures come into conflict with one another. Here we encounter what appears at first glance as one of Ratzinger's signature criticisms of contemporary Catholic theology. He relativizes the centrality of "inculturation" as a way of speaking about how cultures come into contact with one another. He prefers to speak about "the meeting of cultures" or "interculturality." His basic concern is again to lay bare the unacknowledged impact of secularism on the interpretation of religious experience:

> For "inculturation" presupposes that, as it were, a culturally naked faith is transferred into a culture that is indifferent from the religious point of view, so that two agents that were hitherto alien to each other meet and now engage in a synthesis together. But this depiction is first of all artificial and unreal, because there is no such thing as a culture-free faith and because – outside of modern technical civilization – there is no such thing as religion-free culture.[14]

In other words, only in a fairly secularized context might one assume that a culture is a fixed body of unreligious beliefs that includes a certain number of separate or at least separable religious beliefs. According to the secularized view as defined by Ratzinger, inculturation would then consist in the adaptation of those elements of the religious beliefs that are not in accord with the other values of that culture. But since religious belief is, mutatis mutandis, the very foundation of *every* culture, the surgical model of cultural adaptation never works in practice. When one tries to extract all religion from the culture (or vice versa), one is left with a cadaver. The living bond between religion and culture is much more complex and organic.

The Advent dynamic is a way to speak about the progression of cultures "toward the Logos of God, who became flesh in Jesus Christ."[15] In that sense, its theological presuppositions are clear. But Advent also refers to the capacity

[13] Ibid., 65–66.
[14] Ibid., 64.
[15] Ibid., 193–97. This entire discussion is an unfolding of the notion of truth in John Paul II's encyclical Faith and Reason, *Fides et ratio* (1998), especially in the light of accusation that the Pope had adopted a fundamentalist view of religion and culture. See *Fides et ratio*, September 14, 1998, especially secs. 28–35. For the Latin text of the encyclical, see *Acta Apostolica Sedis* 91 (1999), 5–88.

of any culture – Christian or non-Christian – to remain open to an *encounter* with another culture without sacrificing *either* its religious foundation *or* the necessary stance of openness. This definition speaks volumes. It is more easily illuminated by broadening one's examination of the thought of Joseph Ratzinger/Pope Benedict XVI to consider his category of interpersonal encounter. This is a carefully defined leitmotif in Ratzinger's thinking.[16] Advent is a cross-cultural, interpersonal reality that obtains in some measure before, during, and after the historical advent of Christian faith:

> A successful transformation is explained by the potential universality of all cultures made concrete in a given culture's assimilation of the other and its own internal transformation. Such a procedure can even lead to the resolution of the latent alienation of man from truth and himself, which a culture may harbor.[17]

Over time, historical cultures remain rooted in their beliefs in a transcendent Source but become more purified and more open to challenges to their own potentially universal scope. This openness derives from the fact that all cultures have a common experience with human nature. No culture has a monopoly on human nature, and every culture can learn something new about human nature through its interaction with other cultures. Ratzinger's resolute commitment to intercultural dialogue is nurtured by his confidence in the ability of our contemporaries to recover the lost language of human nature.

## CONSCIENCE IN OUR AGE

The link between human nature and the need for dialogue brings us to the question of conscience. This link has been a concern of Joseph Ratzinger since the early stages of his own intellectual formation. For example, he tells the story from his days as a young academic of meeting a fellow professor, a skeptic about Christian morality, who claimed that Hitler and members of the

16 I treat this theme in my "Searching for the Face of the Lord in Ratzinger's Jesus of Nazareth," in *The Pope and Jesus of Nazareth: Christ, Scripture, and the Truth*, eds. Adrian Pabst and Angus Paddison (London: SCM Press, 2009), 83–93. Emery De Gaál notes that Ratzinger's 1959 inaugural lecture concluded with this citation from Richard of St. Victor: "Quaerite faciem eius semper" ("seek always his countenance"). Emery De Gaál, *The Theology of Pope Benedict XVI: The Christocentric Shift* (New York, NY: Palgrave MacMillan, 2010), 76.

17 Joseph Ratzinger, "Christ, Faith, and the Challenge of Cultures," Address to the Presidents of the Asian Bishops' Conference in Hong Kong (March 2–5, 1993), www.vatican.va/roman_curia/congregations/cfaith/incontri/rc_con_cfaith_19930303_hong-kong-ratzinger_en.html.). Cf. Ratzinger, *Truth and Tolerance*, 63 for a nearly identical statement.

Nazi SS would have their actions automatically justified in heaven on account of the inherently subjective nature of an erroneous conscience. "Since they followed their (albeit) mistaken consciences," he reports his colleague as saying, "one would have to recognize their conduct as moral and, as a result, should not doubt their eternal salvation."[18] That troubling experience led him to the Catholic psychologist Albert Görres, who had written about how feelings of guilt are objective constituents of the human constitution. "All men need guilt feelings," states Görres.[19] Ratzinger is thus concerned that conscience has been treated reductively and rightly worries about the consequences of such a reductivism:

> The identification of conscience with superficial consciousness, the reduction of man to his subjectivity, does not liberate, but enslaves. It makes us totally dependent on the prevailing opinions, and debases these with every passing day.[20]

At its root, the problem of conscience is not different from that of culture. In both cases, the central issue is the avoidance of the question of truth. An erroneous conscience is self-justifying only in a world in which truth has been shunted to the side.

In his 1991 address at the annual workshop of the National Catholic Bioethics Center on "Conscience and Truth," Ratzinger faces this problem in two ways: in terms of paradigmatic witnesses to the truth of conscience and in terms of a new presentation of the basic structure of conscience. In that address, he develops an initial approach "of example and narrative" by re-reading two figures: Newman and Socrates.

Ratzinger was introduced to Newman by Theodor Haecker, by his teacher Gottlieb Söhngen, and also by a German writer named Alfred Läpple, who returned from an English war prison in 1946 to serve as a prefect to young seminarians and even before the war had started a dissertation on Newman's theology of conscience.[21] The key to the mature Ratzinger's reading of

[18] Joseph Ratzinger, "Conscience and Truth," Keynote address of the Tenth Bishops' Workshop of the National Catholic Bioethics Center, on the general topic of "Catholic Conscience: Foundation and Formation," in Ratzinger, *On Conscience*, 21.

[19] A. Görres, "Schuld und Schuldgefühhle," in *International Katholische Zeitschrift "Communio* 13 (1984): 434, as cited in Ratzinger, *On Conscience*, 18, n. 3.

[20] Ratzinger, *On Conscience*, 21.

[21] Joseph Ratzinger, *Milestones, Memoirs 1927–1977* (San Francisco, CA: Ignatius Press, 1998), 43. Tracy Rowland reports: "As Alfred Laepple once remarked, when he and Ratzinger were seminarians, Newman was their hero." Tracey Rowland, "The Influence of John Henry Newman on Benedict XVI," *ABC Religion and Ethics*, September 16, 2010, www.abc.net.au/religion/articles/2010/09/16/3013343.htm.

Newman, which he reprised again on the occasion of the beatification, is the way in which Newman's understanding of conscience is "diametrically opposed" to a metaphysical division of the world into an objective realm of scientific experiment and a subjective realm of morals. Newman submitted himself and his conscience to a path of obedience to the truth. This path involves siding neither with the modern advocates of scientism nor with the modern advocates of subjectivism. It involves training one's attention on the objective demands of an interior truth. Ratzinger is by his own admission trying to draw out the Augustinian in Newman:[22]

> Conscience for Newman does not mean that the subject is the standard vis-à-vis the claims of authority in a truthless world, a world that lives with a compromise between the claims of the subject and the claims of the social order. Much more than that, conscience signifies the perceptible and demanding presence of the voice of truth in the subject himself. It is the overcoming of mere subjectivity in the encounter of the inferiority of man with the truth from *God*. The verse Newman composed in 1833 in Sicily is characteristic: "I loved to choose and see my path; but now lead thou me on!"[23]

Newman heals the rift between subjective and objective truth by appealing to his own neo-Augustinian phenomenology of graced inwardness. Accordingly, we must turn inward to resolve our moral dilemmas, but in that introspective move we confront something other than the mere shell of subjectivity. Ratzinger maintains that conscience is given as "an organ, not an oracle," in the words of Robert Spaemann.[24]

Having established the graced nature of inward moral certitude, it might seem like a step backward to present as the second guide a pagan author such as Socrates. But that is not at all the case for Ratzinger, who draws here heavily from Romano Guardini's *The Death of Socrates*. Ratzinger equates "the final meaning of the Socratic search" with "the profoundest element in the witness of the martyrs." Ratzinger recognizes that the serene acceptance of death by

[22] On this point, see Ratzinger, *On Conscience*, 24, as well as his "Presentation by His Eminence Cardinal Joseph Ratzinger on the Occasion of the First Centenary of the Death of Cardinal John Henry Newman," Congregation for the Doctrine of the Faith, April 28, 1990, www.vatican.va/roman_curia/congregations/cfaith/documents/rc_con_cfaith_doc_19900428_ratzinger-newman_en.html.

[23] Ratzinger, *On Conscience*, 25, citing from Newman's famous poem, "Lead Kindly Light," in John Henry Newman, *Verses on Various Occasions* (London: Longmans, 1888). The italics are in the original.

[24] Joseph Ratzinger, "Bishops, Theologians, and Morality," in *On Conscience*, 61, citing Robert Spaemann, *Moralische Grundbegriffe* (Munich: Beck, 1982), 81.

Socrates stands in stark contrast to Jesus' cup of wrath.[25] The figure of Socrates represents not just Stoic resolve but rather our capacity as citizens to make an argument for the sake of the *polis*. Socratic reasoning in this view aims at the truth in the face of a Sophist's counterargument that we set the standards for ourselves. Ratzinger recognizes that some Catholic moralists have appropriated Socrates for their own purposes, that is, in order to rationalize the positive content of the biblical message. Socrates nonetheless remains for Ratzinger the nearly universal paradigm of conscientious political martyrdom.[26]

Two distinct dimensions of Ratzinger's general theory of conscience converge in this portrait of Socrates. Socrates is a political liberator because he recognized that truth transcends formal labels such as conservative, reactionary, fundamentalist, progressive, or revolutionary.[27] His engagement in argument is not for the sake of displaying his virtuosity as a rhetorician or any other mode of technical mastery. His sacrifice is made for the love of justice and to show the emptiness of judgments made on the basis of "a pure formalism." Socrates represents an unmodern prelude to Kant's categorical imperative. His witness shows the limits of political justice in Periclean Athens (or potentially of any political community), but as public testimony, it speaks certainly as persuasively as Kantian universalism to humanity's given capacity to seek truth. If there is a transcultural *exemplum* of conscience transcending any particularity, it would have to retain the Socratic feature of maintaining a connatural affinity with a truth not of one's own making.

Ratzinger also highlights the tragic and paradoxical character of Socrates' quest.[28] Socrates engages Euthyphro on piety while knowing that he himself is a man condemned for impiety. The judgment that piety cannot be what is pleasing to the gods becomes through Socrates' midwifery a recognition that the gods are at war in a very worldly fashion. The implicit pantheism is firmly established by Socratic interchange but is taken by Ratzinger as a "renunciation" of the radical Mosaic distinction between God and world. Herein lies Socrates' Advent-like greatness: he can educate mankind to a worldliness that remains in itself a tragic blessing. He is the pre-Christian prophet of the grandeur and misery of human progress. "What God makes of the poor broken pieces of our attempts at good, at approaching him, remains his secret, which

[25] See Joseph Ratzinger, *Eschatology: Death and Eternal Life*, 2nd ed. (Washington, DC: Catholic University of America Press, 2007), 72–79.

[26] For his reservations about how Socratic rationalism can enter into a Catholic context in an uncritical fashion, see Joseph Ratzinger, "The Church's Teaching Authority – Faith – Morals," in *Principles of Christian Morality*, 52, n. 2.

[27] Ratzinger, *On Conscience*, 28–29.

[28] Ratzinger, *Truth and Tolerance*, 221–22.

we ought not to presume to try to work out," writes Ratzinger.[29] Both of Ratzinger's guides testify to the value and limits of the breadth of reason. Conscience is a rational organ whose form of rationality is inherently self-limiting.

On this basis Ratzinger proceeds to develop a general theory of conscience. Drawing upon the clues provided by Newman and Socrates, he seeks out ways to build "bridges between subject and object."[30] The medieval scholastic tradition distinguished between two levels of conscience: *synderesis* and *conscientia*. St. Bonaventure, for example, reviews the prevailing distinctions between the two terms and concludes that *synderesis* names the natural potentiality and conscience a disposition.[31] Ratzinger upholds the general scholastic distinction although he seems to prefer in his own articulation of *conscientia* the more finely articulated view of St. Thomas. The general distinction Ratzinger himself makes is between an ontological level and a level of judgment. He can follow St. Thomas in noting that in the *actus* of *conscientia*, what he labels "an event in execution," one is bound to follow one's conscience even if it is erroneous. But he notes that there is nothing here that leads to a "canonization of subjectivism" (in either a modern or in a neo-Abelardian sense).[32] St. Thomas thus invalidates the subjectivist claim that the binding character of an erroneous conscience can unbind the sinner from all guilt. The fault here lies rather (and here the formulation comes from Ratzinger) "in the neglect of my being [one] that made me deaf to the internal promptings of the truth."[33]

Ratzinger maintains that "many of the unacceptable theses regarding conscience are the result of neglecting either the difference or the connection" between the ontological level of conscience and conscience as an act of judgment.[34] On this basic point, his concept of conscience upholds the scholastic tradition. He then introduces an innovation, one that he offers to clarify the sometimes imprecise mode of expression in the standard account.

29 Ibid., 207.

30 Ratzinger, *On Conscience*, 34.

31 He writes: "'*Synderesis*' names the natural potentiality, as it is naturally adapted [to us], whereas '*conscientia*' names a disposition which is not just natural but also acquired; and that nature is always, in itself, rightly moved, whereas what is acquired may fall under rightness or under deviance. Hence, although *synderesis* always exists rightly, *conscientia* may be right or mistaken." St. Bonaventure, *Commentary on Peter Lombard's Book of Judgments*, 2.29, as found in Timothy C. Potts, *Conscience in Medieval Philosophy* (Cambridge: Cambridge University Press, 1980), 121.

32 On this see, Ratzinger, *On Conscience*, 80, n. 19.

33 Ibid., 38.

34 Ibid., 30.

*Synderesis*, he suggests, can be better expressed by means of the Platonic category of *anamnesis* or what we might today call "memory of the origin." The Bonaventurian distinction between natural potency and an acquired disposition is thus replaced by a more Thomistic distinction, one between an *inner ontology* that is repugnant to evil and attracted to good and an *act* that recognizes the good, bears witness to it, and then makes a judgment based upon the particularities of the situation.[35] The ontological foundation of conscience is thus, in his words, "the fact that something like an original memory of the good and true (they are identical) has been implanted in us."[36]

I cannot enter here into a comparison of Ratzinger's new language with the whole of the scholastic tradition, but I would just note that the terminological shift coheres remarkably well with more general features of Ratzinger's thinking about the origins and destiny of the human person. In his *Eschatology*, a text he first published in 1977, there is similarly an original theory of a dialogical relationship between the creature made in the image and likeness of God and the divine Trinitarian communion.[37] The theory of the immortality of the soul is in this way treated as an original Christian inheritance via a reading of Augustine on *memoria* time.[38] In his 1985 catechesis *In the Beginning*, Cardinal Ratzinger also recovers the lost doctrine of the original human dependency on God.[39] Seen in this light, the foundation of moral conscience is a preexisting capacity for dialogue with the very source of one's Being, with the openness to Love that is revealed in the flesh of the person of the first born of all creation. The innate moral sense is akin to St. Basil's notion regarding "the spark of divine love that had been hidden in us" or, even better, to St. Augustine's, when he said: "We could never judge that one thing is better than another, if a basic understanding of the good had not already been instilled in us."[40] This inner sense is the condition for the possibility of acting in good conscience but by itself has no "retrievable contents."[41] Because of its universal scope, the link between a memory of the good implanted in a creature and the creature's responsiveness in and through

[35] For a modern reformulation of the Bonaventurian doctrine, which takes it as peculiarly Franciscan and an ultimately unconvincing form of modern intuitionism, see Potts, *Conscience in Medieval Philosophy*, 32–44.

[36] Ratzinger, *On Conscience*, 32.

[37] Joseph Ratzinger, *Eschatology: Death and Eternal Life*, 150–53.

[38] For a commentary that highlights this feature, see De Gaál, *The Theology of Pope Benedict XVI*, 280–84.

[39] Joseph Ratzinger, *In the Beginning: A Catholic Understanding of the Story of Creation and the Fall* (Grand Rapids, MI: Eerdmans, 1995), 79–100.

[40] Ratzinger, *On Conscience*, 32, citing *De Trinitate*, VIII, 3 (4), PL 42, 949.

[41] Ibid.

the activity of conscience is a safeguard against relativism. The givenness of conscience cannot be erased by an erroneous conscience. The givenness of conscience is a form of being a dependent creature that likewise transcends what is given to conscience by a particular culture.

Sometimes an emphasis by theologians on the doctrine of conscience is taken to be individualistic. Ratzinger is rightly concerned to counter this not uncommon objection. His starting point is well grounded in recent Catholic social teaching. *The Compendium of the Social Doctrine of the Church* says that the Church's social doctrine is "theological-moral" because it is found at the crossroads where Christian life and conscience come into contact with the real world.[42] The term "political conscience" is also used in the *Compendium*.[43] Ratzinger has likewise become known as an ardent advocate of the Church's social teaching, especially since the promulgation of *Caritas in Veritate* (2009).[44]

The precise issue here is more specific than just the affirmation of teachings about social justice. The question is, rather, this: "How, if at all, does Ratzinger/Pope Benedict connect a coherent vision of society with the general formation of conscience?" If we take his 1984 keynote address to the National Catholic Bioethics Center as the point of departure, we see that the formation of conscience is indeed a thoroughly social process. At the same time, he circumscribes certain false conceptions of a social conscience. His basic concern remains the rift between objective thinking and subjective morality. Given that conscience must steer clear of both objectivism and subjectivism, Ratzinger then addresses the questions of how the will of God and the community can each serve as sources of morality. His presentation of the role of social processes is dialectical. In general, he follows Spaemann's model that conscience can be likened to the learning of a language, since language acquisition also involves a complementarity of internalized and externalized processes.[45]

I will highlight three elements in Ratzinger's dialectics of social consciousness. First, a society informed by the truth of the Christian message must break down existing social boundaries and present itself as a new entity in the world. This is the root meaning of catholicity, he notes, and as such it continues to have meaning for us even today. This new form of ecclesial

[42] Pontifical Council for Justice and Peace, *Compendium of the Social Doctrine of the Church*, www.vatican.va/roman_curia/pontifical_councils/justpeace/documents/rc_pc_justpeace_doc_20060526_compendio-dott-soc_en.html, sec. 73.

[43] Ibid., sec. 531.

[44] Benedict XVI, *Caritas in Veritate* (Charity in Truth), encyclical letter, www.vatican.va/content/benedict-xvi/en/encyclicals/documents/hf_ben-xvi_enc_20090629_caritas-in-veritate.html.

[45] Joseph Ratzinger, "Bishops, Theologians, and Morality," in *On Conscience*, 61–62.

solidarity was dramatically represented in the martyrs of the early Church, but that quality of newness cuts across all generations. Catholicism cannot degenerate into a club based upon national, ethnic, or ideological allegiances without sacrificing its pledge of allegiance to evangelical newness. Second, the unconditional nature of God's will is a constant for social formation. The modern turn to the subject may have made it more difficult to articulate a mission from God, but it remains a legitimate basis for both authentic moral formation and the self-reflexive process of overcoming ethnocentrism and idolatry. Nominalism (the treatment of the will as antithetical to the demands of reason) and deism (a Christianity that has become blind to the active and unconditional will of God) are but two sides of one coin in this regard.[46] The will of God allows a believer to form her or his conscience in such a way as not to rely exclusively on experience and custom. In a secular landscape, this form of liberation is desperately needed. The will of God awakens conscience to its own transcendent calling. Social consciousness comes into play precisely where the awakening to transcendence is taking place. The community is the "we" that constitutes the proximate source of moral knowledge for individuals in diverse contexts and with diverse compositions. Third, the process of authentically interpreting divine revelation for the sake of communal formation points to the role of the Church. The scaffolding for social consciousness thus consists in recognizing the new place of the Christian community in the world, seeing the analogical import of the communion with the divine will, and promoting processes of inclusive incorporation that incarnate this vision. All formation of conscience is social even though some forms of social consciousness can be driven by the norms of a secular ideology that distorts our receptivity to God's will. The formation of an individual conscience focused only on private self-improvement would by the same token be a further expansion of the dictatorship of relativism. Ratzinger recognizes that this account is nothing more than an ideal construct and offers in the rest of the 1984 address specifics on the role of bishops and magisterium in its implementation. I have focused on how he articulates the phenomenology of Christian social existence to show that he has coherently expressed the reasonability of a Christian social conscience.

[46] Ratzinger's most famous and forceful rejection of nominalism is found in the address delivered at the University of Regensburg on September 12, 2006. See "Faith, Reason and the University: Memories and Reflections," Lecture of the Holy Father at the University of Regensburg, September 12, 2006, www.vatican.va/content/benedict-xvi/en/speeches/2006/september/documents/hf_ben-xvi_spe_20060912_university-regensburg.html.

Where does grace fit into Ratzinger's account of conscience? Part of Ratzinger's genius, I would submit, is his ability to step back from the standard approaches to a theology of conscience in order to consider anew the dynamics of nature and grace. Before commenting on this question, I would note that the general question here had been a main concern of the young scholar who gave his 1959 Inaugural Lecture in Bonn on the topic: "The God of Faith and the God of the Philosophers: A Contribution to the Problem of Natural Theology." I also want to highlight a little known and still untranslated Ratzinger lecture delivered in 1961 and published in *Miscellanea Medievalia* in 1963. It concerns how St. Bonaventure sought to clarify the question posed by Henri de Lubac regarding the role of the supernatural in Catholic theology. Whereas de Lubac, in his 1946 study *Surnaturel Études historiques*, had claimed that the independence of nature from grace originated after St. Thomas Aquinas with the freeing of the category of the supernatural from the natural desire to see God according to his essence, Ratzinger shows that a similar tendency is already making itself visible in the works of the Seraphic Doctor (what he terms die beginnende Verselbstständigung der Metaphysik bei Bonaventura, "the beginnings of an autonomy of metaphysics in the work of Bonaventure"). The thesis itself verifies that Ratzinger was no restorationist in his early studies of the tradition. On the contrary, he was in the wake of Henri de Lubac's impetus exploring the roots of the problem of modernity as it was evinced in medieval authors. Regarding Bonaventure's doctrine of conscience, the thirty-four-year-old theologian states:

> "*et hoc ius est, quod dictat recta ratio*" ("and in this case right is what is prescribed according to correct reason"). If one adds to that [statement of Gratian] Bonaventure's statement in his doctrine of conscience, namely, that truth is *naturaliter impressa* ("implanted by nature") in the heart of man, there is thus practically speaking an authentically metaphysical doctrine of natural law and correspondingly an authentically metaphysical concept of nature, that in and for itself can give way to an autonomous realm (*Eigenbereich*) of philosophical thinking .... The metaphysical concept of nature consequently remains subject to historical, which in terms of our question means theological, illumination.[47]

It would be a mistake to read too much into this early historical research, but the points of connection to what came later are nonetheless clear. From an

[47] Joseph Ratzinger, "Der Wortgebrauch von Natura und die beginnende Verselbständigung der Metaphysik bei Bonaventura," in *Miscellanea Medievalia*, vol. 2, *Metaphysik im Mittelalter* (Berlin: DeGruyter, 1963), 493.

early stage, Ratzinger was curious about the possibility and limits of a rational conscience as that tradition developed in the course of the Christian experience through the ages. In the case of this essay, Ratzinger showed only a passing interest in the mechanics of conscience. He intimated in 1961 that perhaps even Bonaventure was willy-nilly a transitional figure on the way to modern developments. He was already then focused squarely on the problematic separation of an autonomous realm of abstract reason from the guidance of nature's own claims and from the salvific balm of grace.

Ratzinger believes with the whole of the Catholic tradition that the Word of God, the gifts of the Holy Spirit, the witness or advice of others, and the *magisterium* of the Church all contribute to the formation of conscience.[48] But he is also able to unfold the dynamics of graced inwardness through an indirect method. In his essay "Conscience and Truth," he cites the conclusion of Aeschylus' *Oresteia* and a comment made by von Balthasar about the implicit theology of the tragedian: "Calming grace always assists in the establishing of justice, not the old graceless justices of the *Erinyes* period, but that which is full of grace."[49] Aeschylus provides a clue as to how natural reason can confront the Socratic paradox regarding the plethora of gods. Orestes' guilt for matricide is a result of his obedience to the will of Apollo and the *simultaneous* claim made on his conscience by the Furies. But the final scene in which the Furies are miraculously transformed into spirits of reconciliation points toward the advent of a personal redeemer who can expiate by bearing human suffering. Once again, we witness the centrality of the Advent dynamic.

Christian revelation is ultimately about such a freeing of conscience, that is, a new and non-innocent openness to a washing away of guilt. Revelation surpasses the natural expectations of reason without violating or subtracting from what reason can see on its own accord. In 1975, Ratzinger turns to the pre-Constantinian experience of claiming the name of Christian and writes:

> Here the link we found in the Ten Commandments between the concept of God and the moral idea is repeated at a most sublime and exacting level in the Christian context: the name "Christian" implies fellowship with Christ, and hence the readiness to take upon oneself martyrdom in the cause of goodness. Christianity is a conspiracy to promote the good; the theological and moral aspects are fused inseparably, both in the word itself and deeper, in the basic concept of what Christian reality is.[50]

[48] Cf. *The Catechism of the Catholic Church*, sec. 1785.

[49] Ratzinger, "Conscience and Truth," in *On Conscience*, 40.

[50] Joseph Ratzinger, "The Church's Teaching: Authority, Faith, Morals," in *Principles of Christian Morality*, 61.

By taking the name "Christian" one is already submitting to a moral vision of reality. But that claim does not make the moral experience of being Christian purely deontological. The experience of grace among the followers of Christ is one in which there is a palpable offer of communion with God through a recognition in faith of the power of the cross to heal sins. This can be a real liberation: "The yoke of truth became 'easy' (Matt. 11:30) when the Truth came, loved us, and consumed our guilt in the fire of his love."[51] This is a distinctively Christian idea. Prior to Christianity, Ratzinger writes, purification could involve either the external expiation of animal sacrifices or ritual actions aimed at a more noetic and disembodied flight into the realm of pure Ideas. Nineteenth-century Christianity, he continues, reduced purity to the sexual sphere and thereby reverted to the pre-Christian suspicion of the body. Drawing upon Saint John's Gospel, Ratzinger sees Christian purification as primarily being incorporated into Christ's body, "being pervaded by his presence."[52]

## WITNESSING TO TRUTH

Pope Benedict maintains that a good conscience is directed to the truth. But how can the truth of a good conscience be disseminated in our day, viz., in the wake of relativism's dictatorship? In his "Letter to Artists," Pope Benedict recalls the vital connection between beauty and truth:

> Indeed, an essential function of genuine beauty, as emphasized by Plato, is that it gives man a healthy "shock," it draws him out of himself, wrenches him away from resignation and from being content with the humdrum – it even makes him suffer, piercing him like a dart, but in so doing it "reawakens" him, opening afresh the eyes of his heart and mind, giving him wings, carrying him aloft.[53]

The overcoming of moralism flows through the path of beauty. This vision extends beyond the artist as such. It applies to the neo-Augustinian form of rhetoric that Joseph Ratzinger forged as a bishop and as bishop of Rome. The fruits of conscience should not be articulated in an abstract, overly technical fashion. "Morality requires not the specialist but the witness," states Ratzinger.[54] Witness in our contemporary idiom can have an overly juridical

[51] Ratzinger, *On Conscience*, 41.

[52] Benedict XVI, *Jesus of Nazareth, II, Holy Week: From the Entrance into Jerusalem to the Resurrection* (San Francisco, CA: Ignatius Press, 2011), 60–61.

[53] Benedict XVI, "Meeting with Artists: Address of His Holiness Benedict XVI," November 21, 2009, www.vatican.va/content/benedict-xvi/en/speeches/2009/november/documents/hf_ben-xvi_spe_20091121_artisti.html.

[54] Joseph Ratzinger, "Bishops, Theologians, and Morality," in *On Conscience*, 69.

sense, a narrowing that loses the link to beauty. Witness here means a witness to the natural beauty of conscience. The connection to beauty and its contemplation also establishes the fundamental difference between genuine witnessing and modern attempts at a renewed biblical "orthopraxy."[55]

Pope Benedict speaks of witnessing to the truth in order to paint a broad canvas of how conscience and culture can be renewed in our times. A few examples will suffice to illustrate his vision of the authentic power and beauty of conscience. The first is hardly known outside of German circles, namely, the poet Reinhold Schneider (1903–58). His witness is not easily encapsulated. Hans Urs von Balthasar produced two versions of a biography.[56] Resistance fighters in Nazi Germany carried his sonnets to the front lines as a source of hope; he himself openly opposed rearmament after Germany's defeat. Ratzinger's most important essay on this topic, "Das Gewissen in der Zeit" (literally "Conscience in Time," signifying both "in the tradition that has been handed on to us" and "as a temporal process"), was published when he was a Professor in Regensburg and appeared in the German edition of *Communio* in the first year of its existence.[57] It reiterates his well-known skepticism regarding Jesus as a social revolutionary.[58] The heart of the essay is, however, a meditation on the legacy of Schneider and, in particular, the political import of a free conscience as developed in Schneider's influential novel about Bartolomé de las Casas. Ratzinger highlights four acts of conscience, three from the historical novel and one based upon a contemporary conversation. The first is the testimony of a fictional Indian girl bereft of power and political ambition who in Schneider's work convinces the Spanish conqueror to see for the first time the depth of suffering of the indigenous. The second is the prophetic figure of Las Casas, who petitioned the Spanish Crown with only partial success to

55 Cf. Ratzinger, *Truth and Tolerance*, 94–95, 123–26, 129–30, and Ratzinger, "The Church's Teaching, Authority – Faith – Morals," in *Principles of Christian Morality*, 47–73, on the proper understanding of the relationship of orthopraxy to orthodoxy. This critique is not solely or even principally a rebuke of academic positions. It is also a way to question "the gray pragmatism at work in the everyday life of the Church."

56 Hans Urs von Balthasar, *Reinhold Schneider: Sein Werk und Sein Weg* (Cologne: Bei Jakob Hegner, 1953), and *Nochmals Reinhold Schneider* (Einsiedeln: Johannes, 1991). The second version was published in English as *Tragedy under Grace: Reinhold Schneider and the Experience of the West* (San Francisco, CA: Ignatius Press, 1997).

57 Joseph Ratzinger, "Conscience in Its Time," in *Church, Ecumenism and Politics* (New York, NY: The Crossroad Publishing Company, 1988), 165–79. The original can be found as "Das Gewissen in der Zeit: Ein Vortrag vor der Reinhold-Schneider Gesellschaft," *Internationale katholische Zeitschrift Communio* 1 (1972): 432–42.

58 For example, Ratzinger writes: "The growth of freedom that mankind owes to the martyrs is infinitely greater than that which it could be given by revolutionaries." See "Conscience in Its Time," 174.

recognize Indians as creatures of God and candidates for baptism. The third is the young emperor Charles V. He agrees to meet Bartolomé with a copy of *The Imitation of Christ* on his desk and must then and there decide how to wield power in the light of the friar's extraordinary request. The fourth is Charles DeGaulle, a man haunted by the colonialist legacy of Napoleon who in André Malraux's sympathetic account melancholically resigns himself to Algerian independence as a self-limiting choice for the soul of France. In each case, Professor Ratzinger's point is that Christians do not gain power by revolutions: "Power attains greatness when it lets itself be moved by conscience." He no doubt wrote the essay to provoke those on the Catholic left who had tired of the language of conscience and advocated in its place structural social change. But even here, Ratzinger's polemical rejoinder is notable for its balance. Christianity must struggle against totalitarianism (Hitler openly denied the free exercise of conscience, he recalls) and other ideologies that limit the freedom of conscience precisely in order to make space for the free play of justice. The shocking claim of the cross of Christ is that the testimony of a powerless witness can make possible in a radical way the self-imposition of limits on the conscience of the powerful.

Another testimony is Pope Benedict's address to the Latin American bishops at Aparecida on May 13, 2007, an event at which he was accompanied and assisted by Cardinal Jorge Mario Bergoglio of Buenos Aires (now Pope Francis). There he spoke, twenty-four years after the publication of the first document from the Congregation of the Doctrine of the Faith on social liberation, and made this bold proclamation:

> The Church is the advocate of justice and of the poor, precisely because she does not identify with politicians nor with partisan interests. Only by remaining independent can she teach the great criteria and inalienable values, guide consciences and offer a life choice that goes beyond the political sphere. To form consciences, to be the advocate of justice and truth, to educate in individual and political virtues: that is the fundamental vocation of the Church in this area.[59]

This call of conscience is directed toward the transformation of individual, social, economic, and political structures. Conscience is moved by its own co-natural affinity with the truth. The Christian admirer of Socrates rehearses in the same address his critique of ideologies that proffer social utopias in the

[59] Benedict XVI, "Address of His Holiness Benedict XVI to the Inaugural Session of the 5th General Conference of the Bishops of Latin America and the Caribbean," May 13, 2007, sec. 4, www.vatican.va/content/benedict-xvi/en/speeches/2007/may/documents/hf_ben-xvi_spe_20070513_conference-aparecida.html.

place of an openness to transcendence. The Church must take its distance from and examine critically the courts of opinion that render their judgments based upon beliefs in gods who do not save. The purpose of this self-distancing from ideology is *not* disengagement or privatization. On the contrary, the taking of a distance allows the disciple of Christ to commit to a new form of life, to focus on the face of Christ in the wounded innocence of the poor. Guided by an informed conscience and nurtured by the sacraments, integral human liberation becomes a new possibility for humanity. In this sense, Benedict's doctrine of conscience strengthens through its renewed moral clarity the preferential option for the poor.

To this litany, I would add only the Holy Father's testimony to two quite different instantiations of the modern *polis*, the German Reichstag[60] and the Cuban people assembled in the "Plaza de la Revolución" in Havana.[61] In the former address, he offered the "listening heart" of King Solomon as a renewed path for modern juridical reason, as his thoughts regarding that which establishes in our day the foundations of a free state of law (in his native tongue, "einige Gedanken über die Grundlagen des freiheitlichen Rechtsstaats"). Even the environmental movement, he wagered, gives us the opportunity to listen to the language of nature and respond accordingly. Positivist reason is compared to a bunker with no windows. "Is it really pointless to wonder," he asks his fellow Germans, "whether the objective reason that manifests itself in nature does not presuppose a creative reason, a *Creator Spiritus*?" In his Cuban homily, he reiterated: "The personal encounter with the one who is Truth in person compels us to share this treasure with others, especially by our witness." As a final reflection on the Gospel, he offered the example of a patriot and thinker much revered by the Cubans, Fr. Félix Varela:

> Father Varela offers us a path to a true transformation of society: to form virtuous men and women in order to forge a worthy and free nation, for this transformation depends on the spiritual, in as much as "there is no authentic fatherland without virtue" [*Letters to Elpidio*, Letter 6, Madrid 1836, 220]. Cuba and the world need change, but this will occur only if each one is in a position to seek the truth and chooses the way of love, sowing reconciliation and fraternity.[62]

60 Benedict XVI, "Address of His Holiness Benedict XVI at the Reichstag Building, Berlin," September 22, 2011, www.vatican.va/holy_father/benedict_xvi/speeches/2011/september/documents/hf_ben-xvi_spe_20110922_reichstag-berlin_en.html.

61 Benedict XVI, "Homily of His Holiness Benedict XVI at the Plaza de la Revolución José Martí, Havana, Cuba," March 28, 2012, www.vatican.va/holy_father/benedict_xvi/homilies/2012/documents/hf_ben-xvi_hom_20120328_la-habana_en.html.

62 Ibid.

The wisdom of Solomonic listening and Varela's search for transformative virtue are both testimonies to a truth about human nature that has largely been forgotten in the West. By invoking them in these very distinct and particular contexts, the Holy Father's words remain provocative, timely, and universal.

## CONCLUSION: CONSCIENCE AND CULTURE

Conscience is an attribute of human nature that in its universal, quasi-Socratic scope serves as a beacon to all cultures. At the same time, a Christian conscience needs to confront itself and other moral systems in culturally specific situations to guarantee that its truthfulness stands at the service of human nature in all of its conflicting variations. Living out this challenge can yield tragic results, as we see in the cases of those who die for their conscience. Interculturality in this account is part and parcel of the path, for such a truth-driven encounter is a potent antidote to the dictatorship of relativism.

The full interior connection between culture and conscience can be found in Benedict's retrieval of the Pauline notion of *logike latreia* (Rom. 12:1, "spiritual worship").[63] Pope Benedict offers as his paraphrase: "wordlike" sacrifice, an embodied and thus culturally meaningful offering to God offered as self-expression of the whole of the human person. Paul is exhorting us to see that when Christian living is offered in the one Body and in the one living Christ, then it becomes its own kind of Eucharist for the world.[64]

## RECOMMENDED READING

Casarella, Peter. "*Martyria*: Witnessing, Interculturality, and Secularism." In *Witnessing: Prophecy, Politics, and Wisdom*, edited by Maria Clara Bingemer and Peter Casarella, 99–111. Maryknoll, NY: Orbis, 2014.

Cavadini, John, ed. *Explorations in the Theology of Benedict XVI*. Notre Dame, IN: University of Notre Dame Press, 2012.

De Gaál, Emery. *The Theology of Pope Benedict XVI: The Christocentric Shift*. New York, NY: Palgrave Macmillan, 2010.

Ratzinger, Joseph (Pope Benedict XVI). "Conscience in Its Time." In *Church, Ecumenism and Politics*. New York, NY: The Crossroad Publishing Company, 1988, 165–79.

*Eschatology: Death and Eternal Life*, 2nd English ed. Washington, DC: The Catholic University of America Press, 2000.

*On Conscience: Two Essays*. San Francisco, CA: Ignatius Press, 2007.

[63] The entire verse reads: "I urge you therefore, brothers, by the mercies of God, to offer your bodies as a living sacrifice, holy and pleasing to God, your spiritual worship."

[64] Joseph Ratzinger, *Pilgrim Fellowship of Faith* (San Francisco, CA: Ignatius Press, 2005), 114–18.

*The Unity of the Nations: A Vision of the Church Fathers*. Washington, DC: The Catholic University of America Press, 2015.
*Truth and Tolerance: Christian Belief and World Religions*. San Francisco, CA: Ignatius, 2004.
*Values in a Time of Upheaval*. San Francisco, CA: Ignatius, 2006.
Rowland, Tracy. *Ratzinger's Faith: The Theology of Pope Benedict XVI*. Oxford: Oxford University Press, 2008.
Spaemann, Robert. *Basic Moral Concepts*. London and New York, NY: Routledge, 1988.
Twomey, Vincent, SVD. *Pope Benedict XVI: The Conscience of Our Age*. San Francisco, CA: Ignatius Press, 2007.
Varela, Félix. *Letters to Elpidio*, edited by Felipe J. Estévez. Mahwah, NJ: Paulist, 1989.

# PART III

# Applied Topics in Law and Conscience

# 15

# Liberty of Conscience, Free Exercise of Religion, and the US Constitution

NATHAN S. CHAPMAN

One of the enduring questions of American religious freedom is the extent to which it protects, and ought to protect, nonreligious conscientious objectors. The Religion Clauses of the United States Constitution focus, of course, on religion: "Congress shall make no law respecting an establishment of *religion*, or prohibiting the free exercise thereof." Yet members of the founding generation referred to freedom of "religion" and "conscience" interchangeably. To what extent did they intend for the First Amendment to protect nonreligious conscience? Today, many political theorists believe that "liberty of conscience" should extend to all deep and comprehensive beliefs, including those that are not religious. Recent polls show that a growing number of Americans self-identify as having no religious preference. Is religious liberty simply irrelevant for these Americans, or should courts interpret religious accommodation laws broadly to protect their moral commitments? Even more, does the Constitution require courts to do so?

The United States Supreme Court has developed a number of interrelated doctrines governing the scope of religious and nonreligious conscience rights. While the Court has consistently maintained that the Free Exercise Clause protects only religious exercise, it has interpreted "religion" generously to include a variety of nontraditional beliefs and practices. Moreover, the Court has interpreted other provisions of the First Amendment to protect specific rights of conscience, whether based on religion or not.

This chapter explains the complicated conceptual and doctrinal relationship between religious liberty and freedom of conscience in American law. The first Section ("Ways to Conceive of Religion and Conscience") provides a conceptual overview. Over time, religious liberty advocates have built their arguments on different conceptions of religion, conscience, and the relationship between them. Grasping those conceptual changes is important for understanding and assessing current law. The second

Section ("Free Exercise of Religion in Supreme Court Doctrine") explores the Supreme Court's approach to religious accommodations. The court has consistently interpreted the concept of religion generously while maintaining that most religious accommodations need not extend to nonreligious conscientious objectors. At the same time, as the third Section ("Conscience Rights under American Law") explains, American law protects some specific rights of conscience, whether based on religion or not. A number of conscientious objector statutes expressly extend to nonreligious objectors, and the Supreme Court's free speech, free press, and free association doctrines protect core exercises of nonreligious conscience. The final Section ("Does the Constitution Require Religious Accommodation Laws to Protect Nonreligious Conscience?") addresses the most persistent question about liberty of conscience in American law: Does the Constitution require statutory provisions that expressly protect religious exercise to extend to nonreligious conscience as well?

## WAYS TO CONCEIVE OF RELIGION AND CONSCIENCE

This section explores the ways that Americans have conceived of religion, conscience, and the relationship between them. Each conception has a different implication for the meaning of "liberty of conscience" and "free exercise of religion." The classical liberal conceptions of religion and conscience were overlapping but distinct: religion was the duty one owes to God, and conscience was an internal faculty that creates and applies moral rules based on a number of influences, including religion. Though founding-era Americans generally shared these conceptions of religion and conscience, the evidence strongly suggests that when they argued for liberty of conscience, they were almost always making a case for religious liberty, not for freedom of moral choice more broadly. Contemporary liberal theory has a different notion of liberty of conscience. It is the freedom to honor one's fundamental moral and philosophical commitments, whether religious or not. According to this view, fairness demands extending laws that protect "religious" exercise to protect equally important nonreligious commitments.

### *Classical Liberal Conceptions of Religion and Conscience*

American jurists exploring the history of religious liberty in the United States encounter a thicket of references to freedom of conscience, religious liberty, and free exercise of religion. The Virginia Declaration of Rights (1776) is exemplary. Section 16 describes "Religion" as "the duty which we owe to our

Creator, and the manner of discharging it," and declares that "all men are equally entitled to the free exercise of religion, according to the dictates of conscience."[1] A compromise born of legislative debates between Patrick Henry and James Madison, the provision leaves little doubt about the meaning of religion. Altogether, the provision suggests a view of religious liberty rooted in Protestant and Enlightenment conceptions of salvation, individual responsibility, and the social contract.

During a controversy over a proposed bill that would have taxed Virginians to support Christian ministers, James Madison elaborated on these themes. He began by quoting the definition of "religion" in the Declaration of Rights and its assertion that "the Manner of discharging it, can be directed only by reason and conviction, not by force or violence." "[T]he duty . . . to render to the Creator such homage, and such only, as he believes to be acceptable to him" implies an "unalienable right" "toward man." This duty "is precedent both in order of time and degree of obligation, to the claims of Civil Society." "[E]very man who becomes a member of any particular Civil Society, [must] do it with a saving of his allegiance to the Universal Sovereign." As a result, "Religion is wholly exempt from [Civil Society's] cognizance."[2]

This account of religion, and the free exercise of religion it implies, nicely summarizes the view of earlier Enlightenment advocates for religious liberty, especially John Locke. The conception is at once theological and political. It assumes that religion describes a relationship between a Creator and human beings that is constituted at least in part by duty. And, consistent with modern liberal conceptions of the human, it emphasizes the responsibility and corresponding capacity of individual human beings to ascertain the scope of that duty. For Madison, the implications of this view of religious duty for political theory depend on a further supposition that the government derives its authority and legitimacy only from the consent of the governed. Because no one entering into the social contract could have alienated a prior duty to the Creator, he argues, civil society cannot legitimately interfere with that duty.

This argument for religious liberty has implications for its scope. The freedom to comply with one's duties to the Creator appears to be absolute. Furthermore, the liberty's denominational coverage is not as sectarian as it may appear at first glance: it would presumably extend beyond Protestantism

1 George Mason, *Declaration of Rights* (1776), Personal Papers, Collection (Richmond, VA: Library of Virginia), sec. 16, accession 21512.

2 James Madison, "Memorial and Remonstrance against Religious Assessments," in *The Papers of James Madison*, ed. William T. Hutchinson et al. (Chicago, IL: University of Chicago Press, 1973), 8:298–304.

to the practice of any religious tradition with a theology of human duty to the divine, including some with which Madison was certainly familiar, such as Catholicism, Judaism, and Islam. On the other hand, religion-as-duty-to-the-Creator probably would not extend to beliefs and practices that many now consider to be religious but that do not depend on a theology of duty, or, indeed, that may not involve a notion of the divine at all. As we shall see, modern American courts have tended to extend the freedom of religious exercise to a wide array of beliefs and practices, not only to those based on a theology of duty. Nevertheless, Madison's definition of religion and its implication for religious liberty remain important. The conception, consonant with John Locke's, continues to animate liberal theories of religious liberty, even when those theories reject its underlying theological suppositions and argue that religious liberty should be extended to nonreligious conscience.

In classical liberal thought, "conscience" and "religion" were distinct, yet overlapping concepts. Conscience was widely understood to be an internal faculty that makes and applies moral rules. John Locke articulated this view in his *Essay on Human Understanding*.[3] Locke argued that moral principles are not innate; they "require Reasoning and Discourse, and some Exercise of the Mind, to discover the certainty of their Truth."[4] Many "come to assent to several Moral Rules, and be convinced of their Obligation" "by the same way that they come to the knowledge of other things": "*Perswasion*."[5] People receive "moral rules" through "Education, Company, and Customs of their Country." Moral rules, once received through social life, "will serve to set Conscience on work, which is nothing else, but our own Opinion or Judgment of the Moral Rectitude or Pravity of our own Actions."[6]

Locke here articulates a notion of conscience that is unmoored from religion per se. Conscience operates as a judge in cases calling for the application of moral rules. One may arrive at those rules through social life and through reasoning, including reasoning about religious doctrine and experience. But the source of those rules is inherently external.

Western moral traditions have elaborated on this conception in a variety of ways. Most importantly, perhaps, the Catholic Church has developed a nuanced theological account of conscience that builds on the core notion of conscience as an internal moral judge. Relying largely on the thought of

3 John Locke, *An Essay concerning Human Understanding*, ed. Peter H. Nidditch (Oxford: Oxford University Press, 1975).

4 Ibid., 66.

5 Ibid.

6 Ibid.

Thomas Aquinas, the Catholic Catechism explains that conscience is a faculty that "includes the perception of the principles of morality (*synderesis*); their application in the given circumstances by practical discernment of reasons and goods; and finally judgment about concrete acts yet to be performed or already performed."[7] Even more, the Catechism holds that conscience is a place of intimacy with the divine, and thus a source of moral truth. Conscience is "a law inscribed by God . . . man's most secrete core and his sanctuary. There he is alone with God whose voice echoes in his depths."[8] Though conscience is a source of moral truth, the Catholic tradition maintains that it is fallible; it needs moral formation through "the Word of God," "the Lord's Cross," "the gifts of the Holy Spirit," "the witness or advice of others," and "the authoritative teaching of the Church."[9] In many regards, the Catholic notion of conscience merges the classical liberal notions of conscience and religion.

### *Liberty of Conscience at the Founding: Conscience As a Subset of Religious Exercise*

The members of the founding generation inherited the Lockean view that the duties of religion and the operation of conscience were overlapping but distinct conceptions.[10] Yet when they argued for "liberty of conscience" and "freedom of religious exercise," they used the terms interchangeably. They almost always meant the freedom to seek and follow God according to one's conscience.[11]

The colonial charter of Massachusetts Bay (1691) was typical of the charters in the century that followed it: "There shall be a liberty of Conscience allowed in the Worship of God to all Christians (Except Papists)."[12] Nearly a

7 *Catechism of the Catholic Church* (New York, NY: Doubleday, 2012), sec. 1780.

8 Ibid., sec. 1776 (quoting Paul VI, *Gaudium et Spes* (Pastoral Constitution on the Church in the Modern World), encyclical letter [1965]).

9 Ibid., sec. 1784.

10 See Nathan S. Chapman, "Disentangling Conscience and Religion," *Illinois Law Review* (2013): 1457–1501.

11 Ibid., 1464–71; Michael McConnell, "The Origins and Historical Understanding of Free Exercise of Religion," *Harvard Law Review* 103 (1990): 1493; William Lee Miller, *The First Liberty: Religion and the American Republic* (Washington, DC: Georgetown University Press, 1985), 112–23.

12 "Charter of Massachusetts Bar" (1691), in *The Federal and State Constitutions, Colonial Charters, and Other Organic Laws of the States, Territories and Colonies Now or Heretofore Forming the United States of America, ed. Francis Newton Thorpe* (Washington, DC: Government Printing Office, 1909), 3:1870, 1881.

hundred years later, the North Carolina Constitution spoke in terms that nearly all of the early state constitutions echoed. "[A]ll men have a natural and inalienable right to worship Almighty God according to dictates of their own consciences"[13]

Americans of all political and theological persuasions employed this notion of liberty of conscience. In a sermon delivered in 1774, Samuel Sherwood declared that "I desire that every man may think and judge for himself in religion, and enjoy all the sacred rights and liberties of conscience in full."[14] President Washington wrote to the Society of Quakers that "[t]he liberty enjoyed by the people of these States, of worshipping Almighty God agreeably to their own consciences, is not only among the choicest of their blessings, but also of their rights."[15] Even a political and theological radical like Thomas Paine maintained this orthodox understanding of the rights of conscience: "Man worships not himself, but his Maker; and the liberty of conscience which he claims, is not for the service of *himself*, but of his God."[16]

This notion of liberty of conscience was in the background as the First Congress drafted the Bill of Rights. The First Amendment, as enacted, prohibits Congress from making a "law respecting an establishment of religion, or prohibiting the free exercise thereof." When James Madison proposed the Bill of Rights, he included several provisions that would have also protected rights of conscience. The provision that became part of the First Amendment, as well as one directed at the states, would have protected the "equal rights of conscience."[17] The limited historical evidence about the drafting and discussion of these proposals does not fully explain how these "equal rights of conscience" provisions would have been different, if at all, from the one meant to protect the free exercise of religion. Some scholars suggest that Madison may have meant for the conscience provisions to guarantee "the same safeguard of conscience to the non-Christian and

13 N.C. Const. art. XIX (Dec. 18, 1776), in *Constitutions and Charters*, 5:2787, 2788. See also Chapman, "Disentangling," 1466–67.

14 Samuel Sherwood, "Scriptural Instructions to Civil Rulers" (1774), in *Political Sermons of the Founding Era, 1730–1805*, ed. Ellis Sandoz (Indianapolis, IN: Liberty Fund, 1998), 1:373, 380.

15 "Letter from George Washington to the Religious Society Called Quakers" (Oct. 1789), in *George Washington on Religious Liberty and Mutual Understanding: Selections from Washington's Letters*, ed. Edward F. Humphrey (Washington, DC: n.p., 1932), 11.

16 Thomas Paine, *The Rights of Man: Being an Answer to Mr. Burke's Attack on the French Revolution* (1791), reprinted in *Selected Writings of Thomas Paine*, eds. Ian Shapiro and Jane E. Calvert (New Haven, CT: Yale University Press, 2014), 172, 213.

17 *Annals of Congress* (1789), 450–51. See also Carl Esbeck, "Uses and Abuses of Textualism and Originalism in Establishment Clause Interpretation," *Utah Law Review* (2011): 531–35.

nonreligious" as to Christians.[18] Indeed, this may have been one reason they failed: the framers may have been concerned that it would extend to non-religious conscience, a notion that was not widely popular.[19] Consistent with the general usage of "rights of conscience" to refer to religious liberty, I submit that Madison used "equal rights of conscience" to emphasize political and legal equality among *religious* groups. If that was indeed the purpose of the "equal rights of conscience" language, it might explain why the language failed. At the federal level, an equality provision was redundant. The No Religious Test Clause of Article IV, the Establishment Clause, and the Free Exercise Clause together enforced a commitment that the federal government would not play religious favorites. As for the conscience right that would have applied against the states, many in Congress likely perceived it as a threat to state establishments, some of which did in fact give preferential treatment to members of particular religious groups. Ultimately, most agree that the founding generation likely understood the First Amendment as enacted to embody whatever Madison meant by "equal rights of conscience," and now that provision applies not only to the federal government, but also to the states.[20]

The congressional debates about another proposed constitutional amendment also seem to reinforce the notion that the framers understood conscience rights as a subset of religious freedom. The provision that would become the Second Amendment, which provides that "the right of the people to keep and bear arms, shall not be infringed," originally included what we would now call a conscience clause. It would have exempted from "military service" any "person religiously scrupulous of bearing arms." The debates about the provision mostly had to do with whether a religious accommodation from compelled militia service should be required by federal law or left up to the states.[21] But the proposed accommodation for those who are "religiously scrupulous" strongly suggests that the framers were operating with a thoroughly conventional understanding of which sorts of conscientious objections could plausibly be accommodated by law. Liberty of conscience was the freedom to exercise religion, defined by Madison as the duty to "render to the Creator such homage, and such only, as [one] believes to be acceptable to him."

18 Esbeck, "Uses and Abuses," 535.

19 Ibid.

20 *Cantwell* v. *Connecticut*, 310 U.S. 296 (1940) (applying the Free Exercise Clause to the states by means of the Due Process Clause of the 14th Amendment).

21 *Annals of Congress* (1789), 778–80, 796.

*Liberty of Conscience in Liberal Theory: Religion As a Subset of Conscience*

Modern political philosophy operates with a conception of conscience that appears to be very broad – coextensive with the broadest concepts of religion, in fact – but unfortunately it remains largely unarticulated. Nonetheless, on the basis of this notion of conscience, many contemporary scholars argue for a version of liberty of conscience that is both extremely wide and very thin.

The principal spokesman for this conception was the philosopher John Rawls. In *Political Liberalism*, Rawls adapted the tradition of liberal political theory to the intellectual rigor of modern analytical philosophy and to the practical realities of modern pluralistic liberal democracies.[22] Rawls maintained that liberty of conscience is the freedom to "honor" "fundamental religious, moral, and philosophical interests."[23] Rawls's examples are mostly drawn from the history of struggles for religious toleration, but he also argued that liberty of conscience should extend to commitments to comprehensive philosophical systems such as Immanuel Kant's and David Hume's.[24]

In an important respect, Rawls believes that a modern pluralistic society should protect liberty of conscience for the same reason classical liberals like James Madison did: because "religious and moral obligations" are perceived by citizens to be "binding absolutely in the sense that one cannot qualify his fulfillment of them for the sake of greater means for promoting his other interests."[25] At the heart of Rawls's project is the empirical fact that modern liberal democracies, especially the United States, are composed of members who have "reasonable," "opposing and irreconcilable" doctrines that are "comprehensive" insofar as they "include conceptions of what is of value in human life, and ideals of personal character, as well as ideals of friendship and of familial and associational relationships, and much else that is to inform our conduct."[26] For Rawls, as for the classical liberal thinkers, this "irreconcilable latent conflict" admits of two possible resolutions: "Mortal conflict moderated only by circumstance and exhaustion, or equal liberty of conscience and

[22] John Rawls, *Political Liberalism: Expanded Edition* (New York, NY: Columbia University Press, 2011), 3–4.
[23] Ibid., 206.
[24] Rawls, "Introduction," in *Political Liberalism*, xxvii.
[25] John Rawls, *A Theory of Justice* (Cambridge, MA: Harvard University Press, 1971), 207. See also ibid., 214 ("Moral and religious freedom follows from the principle of equal liberty; and assuming the priority of this principle, the only ground for denying the equal liberties is to avoid an even greater injustice, an even greater loss of liberty.").
[26] Rawls, *Political Liberalism*, 13.

freedom of thought."[27] Liberty of conscience is "the fundamental basis to be accepted by all citizens as fair and regulative of the rivalry between doctrines." This is because no one who takes "religious, philosophical, or moral convictions of persons seriously" "would gamble" on whether their commitments would be shared by the political majority.[28]

Rawls presents an account of "conscience" that expressly encompasses not only religion, and not only personal moral judgments, but the totality of one's reasonable comprehensive commitments. Though this view of conscience implies a liberty of conscience that is remarkably generous, it would seem to go well beyond the text, and perhaps the purpose, of the First Amendment and many religious accommodation laws. This conception has influenced many religious liberal theorists and continues to shape academic discourse on the proper scope of religious liberty.[29]

## FREE EXERCISE OF RELIGION IN SUPREME COURT DOCTRINE

We now turn from concepts to doctrine. It was not until the mid-1940s that the Supreme Court began to regularly interpret and apply the Free Exercise Clause. Within several decades, the Court had discovered a potential tension between the demands of the Free Exercise and Establishment Clauses. The Establishment Clause prohibits the government from deciding religious questions. Doing so would require the government to engage in theological reasoning and would inevitably favor one religious viewpoint over another. However, the free exercise of religion is at least potentially in tension with the no-religious-question principle. Determining what counts as the "free exercise" of "religion" may require a theological judgment. A court could deploy the no-religious-question principle to interpret the Free Exercise Clause broadly to protect *any* deep conscientious commitment. Yet this would affect the meaning of the Establishment Clause, which prohibits the government from making a "law respecting an establishment of *religion*." If "religion" means "deep conscientious commitment" in the Free Exercise Clause, then the most natural reading would give it the same meaning for the Establishment Clause. Yet interpreting that Clause broadly to prohibit the government from making "a law respecting an establishment" of any

[27] Rawls, "Introduction," xxvi.

[28] Rawls, *Political Liberalism*, 311.

[29] See, e.g., Micah Schwartzman, "What if Religion Is Not Special?," *University of Chicago Law Review* 79 (2012): 1351–1427 (relying on Rawls's theory to argue that special protection for religion is not morally attractive).

important moral commitment would disable the government from implementing a host of mundane regulations.

Courts have consistently resolved this potential tension with two doctrinal features. First, the Supreme Court has maintained that the Free Exercise Clause extends only to religious exercise.[30] This comports with the language and history of the First Amendment. In recent cases, the Court has applied the Clause to protect religious organizations from governmental interference in their selection of a "minister" and to prohibit governments from discriminating against religious organizations who seek public benefits on equal terms with nonreligious groups.[31] Never has the Court extended the Free Exercise Clause to nonreligious beliefs or conduct.

Second, courts have minimized the potential tension between the Establishment and Free Exercise Clauses by interpreting "religion" broadly to encompass beliefs and practices that play a similar role in the lives of adherents as those played by well-known western religious traditions. Courts have developed a variety of tests to define the exercise of "religion."[32] Sometimes they reason by analogy to well-known religions, asking whether the conduct at issue is like a practice such as participating in a Christian sacrament.[33] One leading case suggested a multi-factor test for determining whether the claimant's conduct was religious. In *Mulnak* v. *Yogi*, several New Jersey public high schools offered a class on the "Science of Creative Intelligence Transcendental Meditation," using a textbook written by the founder of "the Science of Creative Intelligence," and teaching meditation and mantra as a way to connect with the "pure creative intelligence" that is the basis of all life.[34] Plaintiffs argued that the course violated the Establishment Clause. The state maintained that the material and practices (including a "Puja chant") were entirely secular. The court was therefore obligated to determine whether the Science of Creative Intelligence, and the practices taught in the course, amounted to a "religion" for purposes of the First Amendment. Judge Adams, writing in a concurring opinion, suggested that

[30] See, e.g., *Frazee* v. *Ill. Dep't of Employment Sec.*, 489 U.S. 829 (1989); *Thomas* v. *Review Board*, 450 U.S. 707 (1981); *Wisconsin* v. *Yoder*, 406 U.S. 205 (1972).

[31] *Hosanna-Tabor Evangelical Lutheran Church and School* v. *EEOC*, 565 U.S. 171 (2012) (holding that the Free Exercise and Establishment Clauses together require an accommodation); *Trinity Lutheran Church of Columbia, Inc.* v. *Comer*, 137 S. Ct. 2012 (June 26, 2017).

[32] See *Friedman* v. *Southern California Permanente Medical Group*, 102 Cal. App. 4th 39 (2002).

[33] See Kent Greenawalt, "Religion As a Concept in Constitutional Law," *California Law Review* 72 (1984): 753–816.

[34] See 592 F.2d 197 (3d Cir. 1979) (per curiam).

modern notions of religion require courts to look beyond Madison's definition of religion to inquire whether the beliefs and practices at issue have three indicia of sociological understandings of religion: (1) are the beliefs about "ultimate concerns," (2) are they "comprehensive," and (3) are there "any formal, external, or surface signs that may be analogized to accepted religions"?[35]

Though the Supreme Court has never purported to define "religion" under the First Amendment, it has never suggested that the Clause should be read narrowly, either. Indeed, as we will see, the Court has sometimes interpreted religious accommodation statutes broadly to encompass non-theistic commitments.[36] This suggests that the Court would likely embrace the lower courts' generous understanding of religion, even though it is unlikely to extend the Free Exercise Clause to nonreligious beliefs and practices.

Before considering how American law protects rights of conscience, whether religious or not, it is important to remember that the free exercise of religion protects religious beliefs and practices that do not necessarily arise from religious *conscience*. Many people participate in religious practices out of solidarity with a community, to maintain a tradition, or to explore religious truth. Such practices may not be accompanied by theological commitments and may not be required by conscience. But they are all exercises of religion protected by the Free Exercise Clause.

## CONSCIENCE RIGHTS UNDER AMERICAN LAW

As we have seen, the Supreme Court has consistently held that the Free Exercise Clause protects only the free exercise of religion. What about nonreligious conscience? The founders focused on protecting religious exercise, but many theorists today believe there is no good reason to privilege religion over similarly deep and comprehensive moral and philosophical commitments. In some important respects, modern American law reflects this impulse. Several First Amendment doctrines protect core exercises of nonreligious conscience. Also, a number of state and federal religious accommodation statutes expressly accommodate nonreligious moral objectors.

35 Ibid., 200 (Adams, J., concurring in the judgment).

36 See *United States* v. *Seeger*, 380 U.S. 163 (1965) (interpreting the selective service religious exemption broadly to protect someone who professed a "religious" belief against war but who was agnostic about the existence of God); *Welsh* v. *United States*, 398 U.S. 333 (1970) (interpreting the selective service religious exemption broadly for one who asserted that his conscientious objection was entirely secular).

In the 1940s, the Supreme Court began to develop several important First Amendment doctrines in a series of cases involving Jehovah's Witnesses. The Witnesses were a relatively new religious group that boldly preached an austere and anti-nationalist brand of Christianity, and many Americans responded with suspicion and, in some instances, outright oppression. One of the intriguing aspects of the Jehovah's Witnesses cases was that the Supreme Court decided them under a variety of different provisions of the First Amendment, not only the Religion Clauses.[37] The Court found that the Witnesses' various methods of proselytizing and adhering to the demands of their faith were also protected under the Speech Clause and the Press Clause.[38] By doing so, the Court expanded the reach of those rights beyond religious exercise to any form of speech, publication, and association.[39]

Perhaps the most important of these rights is the right against compelled governmental speech. The Jehovah's Witnesses objected on religious grounds to participating in the flag salute and the pledge of allegiance to the United States. In a 1940 case, the Supreme Court held that public schools could compel students to participate in the salute despite their religious objections.[40] Only three years later, after an outbreak of violence against Jehovah's Witnesses for their perceived lack of patriotism, and after the United States had entered the war against the Nazis, the Supreme Court shifted course. In one of the Court's most rhetorically stirring opinions, Justice Jackson explained the importance of individual freedom against compelled governmental speech: "If there is any fixed star in our constitutional constellation, it is that no official, high or petty, can prescribe what shall be orthodox in politics, nationalism, religion, or other matters of opinion or force citizens to confess by word or act their faith therein."[41] The Court solidified this important protection of individual conscience in a case where a Jehovah's Witness objected to displaying the New Hampshire state motto of "Live Free or Die"

37 See *Cantwell* v. *Connecticut*, 310 U.S. 296 (1940) (holding that a municipal law forbidding the distribution of religious literature before obtaining a certificate from an official violated the Free Exercise Clause).

38 See *Martin* v. *City of Struthers*, 319 U.S. 141 (1943) (holding that a municipal ordinance forbidding persons from knocking on the door or ringing the doorbell of a residence to distribute literature violated the Speech and Press Clauses of the First Amendment); *Lovell* v. *City of Griffin*, 303 U.S. 444 (1938) (holding that a municipal rule forbidding the distribution of literature of any kind without prior permission of the city manager was an impermissible prior restraint under the Press Clause).

39 See generally Shawn Francis Peters, *Judging Jehovah's Witnesses: Religious Persecution and the Dawn of the Civil Revolution* (Lawrence, KS: University Press of Kansas, 2002).

40 *Minersville School District* v. *Gobitis*, 310 U.S. 586 (1940).

41 *West Virginia State Board of Education* v. *Barnette*, 319 U.S. 624 (1943).

on his license plate.[42] The right to be free from coerced speech is one of the core rights under the First Amendment, and it extends to any speech, whether religious, political, or ideological.

The Supreme Court has likewise extended the right to associate with others who share a mutual conviction beyond the free exercise of religion to any group formed on the basis of politics or ideology. The Court has held that groups like the Boy Scouts of America may ensure that their members share their ideals, even if that means discriminating on the basis of sexual orientation.[43] Like the freedom from compelled speech, this right protects conscientious conduct whether based on religion or not.

In addition to these important First Amendment rights, US law often protects nonreligious conscience through statutory accommodations. Many statutes that accommodate religious objectors likewise expressly accommodate those who object on moral or philosophical grounds. This is especially the case for statutes that accommodate those who have a moral objection to killing. For example, a number of statutes that authorize physicians to engage in abortion, physician-assisted suicide, or capital punishment provide an exemption for those with a religious or other moral objection.[44] Though US law does not expressly exempt nonreligious conscience to the extent that it accommodates religious exercise, the law nevertheless provides a number of specific constitutional and legislative protections for those with nonreligious conscientious objections to coerced speech, association, or morally grave conduct.

## DOES THE CONSTITUTION REQUIRE RELIGIOUS ACCOMMODATION LAWS TO PROTECT NONRELIGIOUS CONSCIENCE?

In some ways, the most difficult question of liberty of conscience in modern American law is the extent to which the Constitution, or perhaps morality more generally, requires religious accommodations to extend to nonreligious conscientious objectors. On the one hand, liberal theorists argue that there is no moral difference between religion and similar nonreligious comprehensive commitments, and the Supreme Court has, on rare occasions, suggested that statutory religious accommodations should extend to nonreligious objectors. On the other, the Supreme Court has consistently held that there is no constitutional requirement that the Free Exercise Clause or religious

[42] *Wooley* v. *Maynard*, 430 U.S. 705 (1977).
[43] *Boy Scouts of America* v. *Dale*, 530 U.S. 640 (2000).
[44] See, e.g., Chapman, "Disentangling," 1459–60, nn. 8–11.

accommodation statutes extend to nonreligious moral commitments. Ultimately, the answer turns on one's view of democratic legitimacy and political morality.

As we have seen, liberal theorists maintain that "liberty of conscience" rightfully encompasses not only religiously inspired conduct but also conduct that is inspired by equally deep and comprehensive moral beliefs. John Rawls, who first developed the theory in depth, pointed to the work of David Hume and Immanuel Kant as examples of moral or philosophical systems that would be akin to religious beliefs. In some ways, the argument of Rawlsians for equal treatment of nonreligious commitments is circular. Nonreligious commitments that are *similar to* or that are in all important respects *the same as* religious commitments should enjoy equal rights. This assertion depends upon a prior evaluation of what makes a religious belief or practice worth protecting and the ways in which a particular nonreligious belief or practice are equivalent. Given the courts' generous interpretation of religious exercise, perhaps conscientious objections based on comprehensive doctrines, as described by Rawls, are little different. Indeed, perhaps courts today would consider such objections to be forms of religious exercise.

At the same time, a person may maintain a moral objection to obeying a particular law and likewise insist that the objection is not religious. There are relatively few examples of this in US legal history, but they are important. The United States conscripted soldiers to fight in the war in Vietnam. The draft regulations permitted alternative service for those who objected to war in any form on the basis of their religious training and belief, including their belief in a Supreme Being. The Supreme Court decided two cases that pushed the boundaries of this accommodation. The first involved an objector who claimed to be "religious," putting that term in quotes, but who disclaimed belief in a Supreme Being. The Supreme Court interpreted the statutory accommodation broadly to extend to him.[45] The second involved a draftee who affirmatively disclaimed that his conscientious objection was based on religion. A majority of the Supreme Court agreed that he was entitled to the statutory exemption. A plurality of the Court simply interpreted the statute to extend to him. Justice Harlan, casting the deciding vote, argued that the statute could not plausibly be read to extend to him. Instead, he said, the Establishment Clause forbade giving an accommodation for religiously-inspired objectors but not for nonreligious objectors like the claimant.[46] The dissenters agreed with Harlan that the statute could not

[45] *United States* v. *Seeger*, 380 U.S. 163 (1965).
[46] *Welsh* v. *United States*, 398 U.S. 333 (1970).

be read to extend to the claimant, but they could not agree that the Constitution required extending the accommodation beyond what Congress expressly allowed. The case illustrates the variety of views that courts may take on whether to extend a religious accommodation to a nonreligious objector.

Outside of war, it is unclear that the Supreme Court would require religious accommodations to extend to nonreligious claimants. It is useful to distinguish between two scenarios. In the first, a religious claimant seeks an accommodation under the Free Exercise Clause or a statute that specifically accommodates religious exercise. The government, or perhaps a third party, challenges the accommodation on the ground that the text of the provision does not extend to a similarly situated nonreligious claimant. The argument is that it is unfair or unconstitutional to give religious claimants a special accommodation. Courts have mostly rejected this argument. As the Supreme Court has said, "[w]here … government acts with the proper purpose of lifting a regulation that burdens the exercise of religion, we see no reason to require that the exemption come packaged with benefits to secular entities."[47] Indeed, the Court has consistently enforced a variety of statutes that alleviate substantial burdens on religious exercise imposed by federal and state law.[48]

There has been one exception. The Court invalidated a law that exempted a limited number of religious publications from sales tax. The majority agreed that the law violated the Establishment Clause because it subsidized the dissemination of religious teaching. So far, the reach of the case has been limited to its unusual facts, which expressly tied tax breaks to the sale of periodicals "that consist wholly of writings promulgating the teaching" of a religious faith and "books that consist wholly of writings sacred to a religious faith."[49] Otherwise, courts have not invalidated a religious accommodation statute on the ground that it did not extend to nonreligious objectors.[50]

47 *Corporation of Presiding Bishop of Church of Jesus Christ of Latter-day Saints* v. *Amos*, 483 U.S. 327, 338 (1987).

48 See *Gonzales* v. *O Centro Espírita Beneficente União do Vegetal*, et al., 546 U.S. 418 (2006) (applying the Religious Freedom Restoration Act to provide a religious accommodation from federal drug law); *Cutter* v. *Wilkinson*, 544 U.S. 709 (2005) (upholding the Religious Land Use and Institutionalized Persons Act against an Establishment Clause challenge).

49 *Texas Monthly, Inc.* v. *Bullock*, 489 U.S. 1, 5 (1989).

50 The Supreme Court has also invalidated a statute that required all corporations to allow any employee to take off on the employee's Sabbath. The Court reasoned that the statute had no exceptions, applied to only one form of religious exercise, and placed unusual burdens on employers and other employees. *Estate of Thornton* v. *Caldor, Inc.*, 472 U.S. 703 (1985).

A second scenario is when a nonreligious objector claims protection under a statutory accommodation that, by its terms, extends only to religious objectors. In this case, the claimant argues that the Establishment Clause, the Equal Protection Clause of the Fourteenth Amendment (in a case against a state), or the Due Process Clause of the Fifth Amendment (in a case against the federal government) requires extending the statutory accommodation to a similarly situated nonreligious claimant. These cases are rare. As illustrated by the conscientious objector decisions above, a court facing such a challenge has several options. One is to invalidate the law. In the conscientious objector case, this option was not even raised. As discussed above, the Supreme Court has rarely invalidated a religious accommodation law on the ground that it promotes religion and only when the law subsidized the dissemination of a certain kind of religious speech.

Another option is to read "religion" broadly to extend to the claimant's conduct. The problem with this approach, as Justice Harlan pointed out, is that it may do violence to the statute, depending on its text. Furthermore, for claimants who expressly disclaim religion, holding that their commitments are in fact religious, even to grant their request, does not take their claim seriously.

A third option is to hold that the accommodation is valid, but it extends only to religious exercise. This option seems to have support in Free Exercise Clause jurisprudence. As discussed above, the Supreme Court has consistently held that the Free Exercise Clause extends only to religious exercise. But this does not fully answer the charge that the statute at issue may be constitutionally suspect on the ground that it does not extend to comparable nonreligious objectors. The statute presumably provides more protection for religious exercise than the Free Exercise Clause does. If not, the two provisions would be redundant (and the statute would be valid). So, a statute that provides more protection than the Free Exercise Clause may, at least in theory, be subject to constitutional objections that do not apply to that clause. The Free Exercise Clause therefore does not answer the more specific question about whether the Constitution requires *this* religious accommodation to extend to nonreligious objectors. Again, there are few precedents to guide a court's analysis, partly because there are so few nonreligious objectors who assert an accommodation claim under a statute designed to protect religious exercise.

The final option is Justice Harlan's: extend the accommodation to the nonreligious objector because the Constitution does not permit the government to accommodate a religious but not a nonreligious objector. This rests on a premise, stated or assumed, that there is no meaningful distinction between a conscientious objection based on religious beliefs and one based on nonreligious moral beliefs. This was the basis for a recent decision to extend the "religious organization" exemption from the Affordable Care Act "contraceptive mandate" to the nonreligious organization March for Life. Because the purpose of the exemption, based on the language of the regulation, was to accommodate conscientious objection to abortion, and March for Life conscientiously objects to abortion, there could be no reasonable basis to exclude the organization from the exemption simply because its objection was nonreligious.[51]

## CONCLUSION

Liberty of conscience is one of America's founding values, but its relationship to the First Amendment and other laws protecting the free exercise of religion has not always been clear. For the founding generation, the two were one and the same. Religious liberty was the freedom to follow God according to one's own judgment about God's demands. More recently, liberal theorists have emphasized the similarity between religion and other deep philosophical and moral commitments. American jurisprudence has navigated the complexity, ambiguity, and dynamism of the concepts "religion" and "conscience" by interpreting religious liberty provisions generously to protect a wide range of religious exercise and by extending narrower, but important, constitutional and statutory protection for moral objectors, whether their views are based on religion or not.

## RECOMMENDED READING

Chapman, Nathan S. "Disentangling Conscience and Religion." *University of Illinois Law Review* (2013): 1457–1501.

Greenawalt, Kent. "Religion As a Concept in Constitutional Law." *California Law Review* 72 (1984): 753–816.

Koppelman, Andrew. "Conscience, Volitional Necessity, and Religious Exemptions." *Legal Theory* 15, no. 3 (2009): 215–44.

Laycock, Douglas. "Religious Liberty As Liberty." *Journal of Contemporary Legal Issues* 7 (1996): 313–56.

Lund, Christopher C. "Religion Is Special Enough." *Virginia Law Review* 103 (2017): 481–524.

McConnell, Michael W. "The Origins and Historical Understanding of Free Exercise of Religion." *Harvard Law Review* 103 (1990): 1409–1517.

[51] See *March for Life* v. *Burwell*, 128 F. Supp. 3d 116 (D.D.C. 2015).

Miller, William Lee. *The First Liberty: America's Foundation in Religious Freedom.* Washington, DC: Georgetown University Press, 2013.
Rawls, John. *Political Liberalism: Expanded Edition.* New York, NY: Columbia University Press, 2011.
Schwartzman, Micah. "What if Religion Is Not Special?" *University of Chicago Law Review* 79 (2012): 1351–1427.
Smith, Steven D. "What Does Religion Have to Do with Freedom of Conscience?" *Colorado Law Review* 76 (2005): 911–40.

# 16

# Religious Conscience Protections in American State Constitutions

MICHAEL J. DEBOER

## INTRODUCTION

In 1833, two generations after the United States Constitution was approved, Justice Joseph Story of the Supreme Court of the United States described the American constitutional order regarding religious freedom and conscience protections in his influential three-volume *Commentaries on the Constitution of the United States*. He observed that "the whole power over the subject of religion is left exclusively to the state governments, to be acted upon according to their own sense of justice, and the state constitutions." The framers of the Constitution, he thought, had "deemed [it] advisable to exclude from the national government all power to act upon the subject" of religion, and thus they provided security against the contentious issue of religious establishments by "extirpating the power" from the federal government.[1]

In the constitutional order Story described, the rights of conscience were understood to be natural rights, and the obligations imposed by conscience had priority over the obligations imposed by civil government. Story reflected this understanding of the primacy of a person's conscience when he wrote: "The rights of conscience are, indeed, beyond the just reach of any human power. They are given by God, and cannot be encroached upon by human authority, without a criminal disobedience of the precepts of natural, as well as of revealed religion."[2] Story believed that civil government has a duty to foster religion among citizens, but he did not believe that this duty conflicted with conscience rights. In his view, government's duty to encourage religion is "a point wholly distinct from that of the right of private judgment in matters of religion, and of

[1] Joseph Story, *Commentaries on the Constitution of the United States* (Boston, MA: Hilliard, Gray and Co., 1833), 3:§1873.

[2] Ibid., 3:§1870.

the freedom of public worship according to the dictates of one's own conscience."[3] Pressing his point further, he reiterated that government's duty to encourage religion, even Christianity, is "very different from the right to force consciences of other men, or to punish them for worshipping God in the manner, which, they believe, their accountability to him requires."[4]

The constitutional order Story described in 1833 – namely, that the rights of conscience (involving beliefs and private judgment as well as public conduct such as worship) come from God and are beyond human power to control, that government should encourage religion but respect religious freedom, and that the matter of religion including ecclesiastical establishments is left exclusively to states under their constitutions and laws – largely remained intact for the first century and a half of the nation's history. It thus held sway from the 1770s and 1780s when the first state constitutions were adopted to the 1940s when the United States Supreme Court incorporated the establishment and free exercise provisions of the First Amendment, thereby making these two religion provisions applicable to states.[5] Consequently, for the first three quarters of our nation's history, the American states through their constitutions and laws determined issues such as the scope of religious conscience protections and ecclesiastical establishments.

This chapter tells the story of the development of the American state constitutional provisions that have protected religious conscience for over two and a quarter centuries. It delineates five periods of state constitution-making regarding religious conscience protections, highlights principal developments in each, and examines early textual formulations and conceptual frameworks that have been preserved in state constitutions. It concludes by describing the current status of these protections.

This chapter places emphasis on religious conscience. It does so, not because secular conscience is inconsequential, but because state constitutional texts link conscience rights to religion, religious freedom, and non-establishment of religion and because protection of secular conscience is a more recent development in American constitutional law. This chapter also highlights the emphasis state constitutional texts have placed on persons whose consciences have been the principal concern. Additionally, it draws attention to two key dimensions of religious life included within state religious conscience protections: (1) the belief dimension, which is indicated by terms

3 Ibid., 3:§1865.

4 Ibid., 3:§1870.

5 The significance of the incorporation doctrine in this story will be developed more fully later in this chapter.

such as belief, conscience, conviction, opinion, reason, sentiment, and understanding and (2) the conduct dimension, which is indicated by terms such as enjoy, exercise, practice, profess, and worship and by references to public worship and mode or manner of worship.

## A BRIEF SKETCH OF THE HISTORICAL AND ECCLESIASTICAL CONTEXTS

Religious conscience protections in American state constitutions developed against a background of Old World and New World establishments and religious dissent. In early modern Europe, there was a widely held belief that, in an organized civil society, a state must support an established religion by both prescribing a faith and proscribing other faiths, and consequently alliances were formed between state and church. According to that understanding, the supporting state and the established religion are mutually dependent, and each is equally necessary to the other. As a consequence, various nations in early modern Europe had Christian establishments: England had an Anglican establishment; France, Italy, Portugal, and Spain had Catholic establishments; Germany and Scandinavia had Lutheran establishments; and Germany, the Netherlands, Scotland, and Switzerland had Reformed establishments.

As European nations colonized the New World in the seventeenth and eighteenth centuries, they exported their Old World religious establishments. However, the authority of these establishments was challenged in the New World as they encountered religious pluralism and sustained resistance from religious dissenters who appealed to conscience. English Puritans were among those who set up New World religious establishments, but Puritan teachings regarding conscience and Puritan encounters with religious dissenters who invoked the authority of conscience challenged the authority of their establishments.

In the American story of religious conscience protections, Puritans are central figures. They understood conscience (from Latin *conscientia*, *con-* ["with"] *scientia* ["knowledge"]) to be a rational faculty that gives knowledge that is held in common with God and knowledge of a person's standing before God. Puritans were supremely concerned about knowing, serving, and glorifying God, and conscience was "the mental organ in men through which God brought his word to bear on them."[6] For Puritans, conscience was God's witness and judge in the soul, advising regarding duties owed to God and others. Accordingly, when rightly instructed by Scripture, it is capable of

6 J. I. Packer, *A Quest for Godliness: The Puritan Vision of the Christian Life* (Wheaton, IL: Crossway Books, 1990), 107.

making correct judgments regarding the rightness and the wrongness of particular actions. Additionally, because God speaks his will through conscience, conscience is authoritative and requires fidelity. In time, the *Westminster Confession of Faith* (1647) and the *Savoy Declaration of Faith and Order* (1658) would articulate the Reformed and Puritan understanding: "God alone is Lord of the conscience" and has "left it free from the doctrines and commandments of men" that are "in any thing, contrary to His Word." Puritans thus taught that true liberty of conscience is necessary for genuine belief and faithful obedience.

Puritan dissenters to the Church of England brought these teachings to Plymouth Colony (established in 1620) and Massachusetts Bay Colony (established in 1628), but the colonial leaders there followed a more restrictive understanding of liberty of conscience. Conflicts over theological teachings and liberty of conscience soon arose with two early religious dissenters, Anne Hutchinson (1591–1643) and Roger Williams (1603–83), and both were banished from Massachusetts Bay Colony. Williams traveled south and established a settlement that would become Providence Plantation and later Rhode Island. He became an early advocate of "soul liberty" and conscience, which he defined as "a persuasion fixed in the mind and heart of a man which enforceth him to judge ... and to do so and so, with respect to God, his worship, &c." In 1663, he secured a royal charter for Rhode Island Colony that accorded religious liberty to its inhabitants, a first in the New World. As a consequence, Rhode Island became a haven for religious conscience.

Other colonies also became havens for religious conscience but some for only a period of time. For instance, Maryland Colony was founded in 1632 by Roman Catholic proprietor George Calvert and his son Cecil Calvert as a haven for Catholics suffering persecution in England. In 1649, the Maryland Assembly passed an Act Concerning Religion that protected persons in the "free exercise" of religion. However, later in the seventeenth century, the Church of England was established in Maryland, and Maryland ceased providing a haven for religious dissenters and Catholics.

Pennsylvania Colony was founded in 1681 when William Penn (1644–1718), a Quaker who grew up among English Puritans, was granted a charter. Quakers (the Religious Society of Friends) believed that an individual's conscience is authoritative on moral issues and that they should not participate in war or take oaths. As a religious outsider, Penn suffered persecution in England for his beliefs, and he became a prominent advocate of liberty of conscience, which he understood to mean "liberty of the mind, in believing or disbelieving this or that principle or doctrine" and the ability to engage in religious exercise "in a visible way of worship, upon our believing it to be indispensably required at our hands, that if we neglect it for fear or favour of any mortal man, we sin, and incur divine wrath." The constitution and laws that Penn wrote to govern Pennsylvania afforded religious freedom protection to residents who met specified conditions. Delaware Colony was governed as part of Pennsylvania until 1701, when Penn granted a charter to its inhabitants and it gained an independent legislature. Like Pennsylvania's founding legal documents, Delaware's charter provided for freedom of conscience, and Delaware too became a haven for religious conscience.

The colonies of Carolina and New Jersey, founded by proprietors in 1663 and 1664, respectively, were governed by legal documents that provided religious conscience protections similar to those afforded in Rhode Island's charter. In Carolina, the *Fundamental Constitutions of Carolina* was adopted in 1669, and it provided a modest degree of religious freedom. The English philosopher John Locke, a friend of Penn who likewise grew up amid English Puritan influences and advocated religious toleration, played a key role in drafting the *Fundamental Constitutions*, which, contrary to his wishes, provided for an Anglican establishment in Carolina. Regrettably, by early in the eighteenth century, Carolina and its Anglican establishment became increasingly intolerant.

During the colonial period, Delaware, Pennsylvania, and Rhode Island (and, for shorter periods of time, Carolina and Maryland) thus provided protective havens for religious conscience, and religious pluralism emerged there and attracted Catholics, Jews, and Protestants of all types, including Lutherans and Huguenots, Quakers and Mennonites, Moravians and Pietists. Significantly, Delaware, Pennsylvania, and Rhode Island never had religious establishments. Likewise, New Jersey and most of New York never had established churches, and robust religious pluralism was found in each. By contrast, Connecticut, Massachusetts, and New Hampshire (as well as the independent territories of Maine and Vermont) had Puritan congregational establishments, and Georgia, Maryland, North Carolina, South Carolina, and Virginia (as well as four counties constituting New York City) had Anglican establishments.

In the 1730s and 1740s, a spiritual movement (the First Great Awakening) occurred in New England and the Middle Colonies, which broadened the challenges posed to ecclesiastical establishments by religious dissenters and religious pluralism. The revivals occurred among descendants of the Reformed branch of the Magisterial Reformation and descendants of the English Reformation, but outsider groups such as Baptists and Methodists saw great increases in their numbers. This growth among groups outside the dominant traditions in Europe (Anglican,

Lutheran, Reformed, and Roman Catholic), together with the burgeoning religious pluralism in colonial America, further eroded the authority of ecclesiastical establishments.

The story of Baptists in America highlights the growing stature of religious conscience and the eroding authority of ecclesiastical establishments in eighteenth-century America. Baptists had long been outsiders and dissenters, and their theological beliefs, coupled with their experience of religious persecution, made them fierce advocates of conscience rights. Isaac Backus (1724–1806), a Baptist minister in Massachusetts who was profoundly influenced by two key figures of the Great Awakening (Jonathan Edwards and George Whitfield), rediscovered the work of Roger Williams. In 1773, on the eve of the American Revolution, he wrote *An Appeal to the Public for Religious Liberty*, seeking to show how "our religious rights are encroached upon in this land." In building his case, he distinguished church and state as two kinds of government in the world that are distinct in nature. The church "is armed with light and truth, to pull down the strong holds of iniquity, and to gain souls to Christ, and into his church, to be governed by his rules therein." In contrast, the state "is armed with the sword to guard the peace, and the civil rights of all persons and societies, and to punish those who violate the same." For Backus, conscience was sacred: every person has a duty, "by the law of Christ," "to judge for himself, concerning the circumstantials as well as the essentials, of religion, and to act according to the full persuasion of his own mind." Furthermore, "in religion each one has an equal right to judge for himself[,] for we must all appear before the judgment seat of Christ."

Six years later, in 1779, when the people of Massachusetts were in the process of drafting a state constitution, Backus was consulted regarding his views on rights, and he wrote *A Declaration of the Rights, of the Inhabitants of the State of Massachusetts-Bay*. He proposed an article protecting religious conscience that included two sentences. The first emphasized liberty of conscience:

> As God is the only worthy object of all religious worship, and nothing can be true religion but a voluntary obedience unto his revealed will, of which each rational soul has an equal right to judge for itself, every person has an unalienable right to act in all religious affairs according to the full persuasion of his own mind, where others are not injured thereby.

The second sentence emphasized civil government's lack of jurisdiction in matters of religion and its responsibility to protect religious persons and institutions from interference:

> [C]ivil rulers are so far from having any right to empower any person or persons, to judge for others in such affairs, and to enforce their judgments with the sword, that their power ought to be exerted to protect all persons and societies, within their jurisdiction from being injured or interrupted in the free enjoyment of this right, under any pretense whatsoever.

Thus, for Backus, religious freedom was an inalienable right, and true religion could only be practiced voluntarily by a conscience free to listen for the transcendent word and make its own judgments in response to the divine sovereign. Consequently, civil government was without power to judge in religious matters and should use its power to safeguard the enjoyment of religious conscience.

The state bills of rights and constitutions approved in the 1770s and 1780s were developed against this background of religious establishments (especially Puritan establishments in New England and Anglican establishments in the Middle and Southern Colonies), religious pluralism (in New Jersey and New York), religious havens (in Delaware, Pennsylvania, and Rhode Island), and antecedent documents that protected religious conscience. The eighteenth-century revivalist movement and the Enlightenment influence heightened the desire for religious conscience protections, and the late eighteenth-century state constitutions were the principal means of guaranteeing liberty of conscience.

## THE FIRST PERIOD OF STATE CONSTITUTION-MAKING

During the first period of state constitution-making concerning religious conscience protections (from 1776 to 1791), states adopted bills of rights and constitutions that provided the first written constitutional protections of religious conscience in the new nation. And then, after most of the original states had adopted their bills of rights and constitutions, religions provisions were adopted in the United States Constitution and the First Amendment.

### *Virginia's First Steps toward Religious Conscience Protections*

During the American Revolution, Virginia broke new ground regarding religious conscience protections when the Virginia Convention adopted a Declaration of Rights on June 12, 1776. Article XVI of that Declaration stated:

> [R]eligion, or the duty which we owe to our Creator, and the manner of discharging it, can be directed only by reason and conviction, not by force or

> violence; and therefore all men are equally entitled to the free exercise of religion, according to the dictates of conscience; and . . . it is the mutual duty of all to practi[c]e Christian forbearance, love, and charity toward each other.

Soon thereafter, on June 29, 1776, the delegates separately approved the Virginia Constitution.[7] It included a religious test provision rendering all ministers of the gospel "incapable of being elected members" of specified governmental bodies.

These documents and the circumstances surrounding their development provide several insights regarding the treatment of religion, freedom of conscience, and ecclesiastical establishments in state constitutions. First, convention delegates adopted language drafted principally by George Mason that understood religion in terms of both a person's duty to God and a person's way of discharging that duty. For them, religion entailed a person's relationship to God, which included obligations that must be discharged.

Second, the delegates recognized the belief and conduct dimensions of religious life when they declared that people can properly discharge the duties they owe to God only when they have the freedom to act as their reason and conviction direct or, in other words, as their consciences dictate. Consequently, for the delegates, people cannot discharge their duties to God when their beliefs or actions are directed by others using force or violence. Additionally, although the delegates' conception of conscience may have been broad enough to include nonreligious convictions, the text situated conscience in the context of the free exercise of religion and the duties owed to God.

Third, the delegates recognized religious freedom as a right. Mason initially proposed language stating that "all Men should enjoy the fullest Toleration in the Exercise of Religion, according to the Dictates of Conscience," which implied that religious exercise is a privilege. So framed, civil government would be encouraged to allow and tolerate religious exercise, but it could nevertheless punish and restrain it when a person, under color of religion, disturbs the peace, happiness, or safety of society. The delegates, however, under the influence of James Madison, departed from Mason's proposal and embraced language conveying a more robust understanding of religious freedom as a right. The language they adopted emphasized the equal entitlement of all persons "to the free exercise of religion, according to the dictates of conscience." This language suggested that both establishment Anglicans and dissenter Baptists in

7 New Hampshire and South Carolina adopted constitutions on January 5, 1776, and March 26, 1776, respectively, but neither constitution included a bill of rights.

Virginia should equally and rightfully enjoy freedom to believe and act based upon their beliefs.

Nearly a decade later in *A Memorial and Remonstrance against Religious Assessments* (1785), Madison provided additional insight into the nature of the right they had recognized. He wrote:

> The Religion . . . of every man must be left to the conviction and conscience of every man; and it is the right of every man to exercise it as these may dictate. This right is in its nature an unalienable right. It is unalienable, because the opinions of men, depending only on the evidence contemplated by their own minds[,] cannot follow the dictates of other men: It is unalienable also, because what is here a right towards men, is a duty toward the Creator. It is the duty of every man to render to the Creator such homage and such only as he believes to be acceptable to him.

Madison also there noted that the right originates as a "gift of nature" and that "'the equal right of every citizen to the free exercise of his Religion according to the dictates of conscience' is held by the same tenure with all our other rights."

Fourth, although the delegates adopted language recognizing the equal right of all persons to act based upon their beliefs, the constitutional text they adopted stopped short of disestablishing the Anglican Church. Indeed, these constitutional documents neither expressly established nor disestablished religion, and thus Virginia's then existing ecclesiastical establishment remained unaffected. Additionally, Virginia's religious test provision precluded all Christian ministers (including ministers from established churches) from holding specified offices, which reflected a persistence of an Old World understanding. Nevertheless, the religious test provision did not mandate that public officeholders be professing Christians.

### *Patterns in Other States*

After Virginia took these first steps and established the first state constitutional pattern of religious conscience protections, other states followed with bills of rights and constitutions of their own. And, during this first period of state constitution-making, most of the original states adopted constitutions. As these states developed their own provisions, the framers found counsel in European and colonial experience with ecclesiastical establishments, religious persecution, and religious dissenters, and they (at times) adopted and (at other times) adapted the verbal formulations of antecedent documents, Virginia's constitutional documents, and other state constitutions.

Among these constitutions, several patterns of religious conscience protections differing from Virginia's emerged. A second pattern emerged in Maryland's Declaration of Rights and Constitution (1776), Georgia's Constitution (1777), Massachusetts's Declaration of Rights and Constitution (1780), and New Hampshire's Bill of Rights and Constitution (1784). This pattern recognized religious freedom as a right, retained elements of ecclesiastical establishments, and imposed religious tests.

For instance, the Massachusetts Constitution, authored primarily by John Adams who (consistent with his Puritan upbringing) strongly favored public encouragement of religion and virtue, recognized "the right as well as the duty of all men in society, publicly, and at stated seasons," to "worship the Supreme Being, the great creator and preserver of the universe." The belief and conduct dimensions of religious life are evident in the declaration that no person "shall be hurt, molested, or restrained, in his person, liberty, or estate, for worshipping God in the manner and season most agreeable to the dictates of his own conscience; or for his religious profession or sentiments." The right was nevertheless conditioned on persons not "disturb[ing] the public peace, or obstruct[ing] others in their religious worship."

Consistent with Massachusetts's Puritan establishment past, the constitution recognized that the people have "a right to invest their legislature with power to authorize and require, and the legislature shall, from time to time, authorize and require" local government or religious societies "to make suitable provision, at their own expense, for the institution of the public worship of God, and for the support and maintenance of public [P]rotestant teachers of piety, religion and morality, in all cases where such provision shall not be made voluntarily." It, nevertheless, recognized that monies paid to support public worship and public teachers "shall, if [the person who pays] require[s] it, be uniformly applied to the support of the public teacher or teachers of his own religious" denomination. Additionally, it stated that Christian denominations that "demean[] themselves peaceably, and as good subjects," "shall be equally under the protection of the law" and that "no subordination of any one sect or denomination to another shall ever be established by law." The constitution required that persons selected to specified public offices declare that they "believe the [C]hristian religion, and have a firm persuasion of its truth."

South Carolina's Constitution (1778) offered a third pattern. It declared the "Christian Protestant religion" "the [state's] established religion." It granted "tolerat[ion]" to "all persons and religious societies who acknowledge" one God and "a future state of rewards and punishments" and who affirm "that God is publicly to be worshipped." Christian Protestant denominations that "demean[ed] themselves peaceably and faithfully" were to "enjoy equal religious and civil privileges." Additionally, the constitution rendered any "minister of the gospel or public preacher of any religious persuasion" ineligible to serve in specified public offices. Under this constitution, only Protestants were eligible to be state legislators.

A fourth pattern is evident in New Jersey's Constitution (1776). This constitution recognized the belief and conduct dimensions of religious life, but it framed the worship of God as a "privilege," stating that "no person shall ever . . . be deprived of the inestimable privilege of worshipping Almighty God in a manner agreeable to the dictates of his own conscience." It provided that no person shall "be compelled to attend any place of worship" or "obliged to pay tithes, taxes, or any other rates" to support churches, places of worship, or ministers "contrary to what he believes to be right, or has deliberately or voluntarily engaged himself to perform." It declared that Protestant inhabitants shall not "be denied the enjoyment of any civil right, merely on account of [their] religious principles." Reflecting New Jersey's non-establishment colonial past, this constitution expressly prohibited an ecclesiastical establishment, declaring that "there shall be no establishment of any religious sect . . . in preference to another." Nevertheless, it imposed a religious test for select offices, prescribing that all professing Protestants who "demean themselves peaceably" "shall be capable of being elected" into specified offices.

Delaware's Declaration of Rights and Constitution (1776), North Carolina's Declaration of Rights and Constitution (1776), and New York's Constitution (1777) established a fifth pattern. This pattern protected the right to worship or the free exercise of religion, which protection extended to the belief and conduct dimensions of religious life. It also expressly prohibited any ecclesiastical establishment or expressly disestablished religion, but it imposed a religious test.

For instance, the New York Constitution declared that "the free exercise and enjoyment of religious profession and worship, without discrimination or preference, shall forever hereafter be allowed, within this State, to all mankind." Referencing the free exercise right recognized in the same provision, the New York Constitution continued: "The liberty of conscience, hereby granted, shall not be so construed as to excuse acts of licentiousness, or justify practices inconsistent with the peace and safety of this State." As this text shows, the delegates understood "liberty of conscience" and "free exercise" of religion as interchangeable expressions. This provision also highlighted the threats to liberty that the constitution was meant to counteract: "civil tyranny" and "spiritual oppression and intolerance wherewith the bigotry and ambition of weak and wicked priests and princes have scourged mankind." It abrogated and rejected as "repugnant to this constitution" all parts of the common law and statutes that "may be construed to establish or maintain any particular denomination of Christians or their ministers," thereby eliminating the Anglican establishment in four metropolitan counties. Additionally, it declared gospel ministers ineligible to hold any civil or military office.

A sixth pattern emerged in Pennsylvania's Declaration of Rights and Constitution (1776). In recognizing religious freedom as a right that includes the belief and conduct dimensions, the declaration stated that "all men have a natural and unalienable right to worship Almighty God according to the dictates of their own consciences and understanding." It prohibited compulsion of any person to "attend any religious worship, or erect or support any place of worship, or maintain any ministry, contrary to, or against, his own free will or consent." It barred any person who acknowledges God's existence from being "deprived or abridged of any civil right as a citizen, on account of his religious sentiments or peculiar mode of religious worship," and it prohibited any authority or power from interfering with or controlling "the right of conscience in the free exercise of religious worship." These documents did not expressly prohibit an ecclesiastical establishment, but the state had no established church during the colonial period. Nevertheless, the constitution required members of the House of Representatives to declare belief in "one God, the creator and governor of the universe, the rewarder of the good and the punisher of the wicked" and to acknowledge "the Scriptures of the Old and New Testament to be given by Divine inspiration." It prohibited any other religious test for any civil officer or magistrate.

### *Additional Religious Conscience-Protecting Provisions*

Some state constitutions also extended religious conscience protections to persons opposed to bearing arms or swearing oaths. For instance, Pennsylvania's Declaration of Rights stated that no person "who is conscientiously scrupulous of bearing arms, [shall] be justly compelled thereto." The New York Constitution included a similar provision, but it specifically identified Quakers as a group that objected on religious conscience grounds to bearing arms and joining the militia.

As for oaths, Delaware's Constitution required those assuming specified public offices to take an oath or, alternatively, an affirmation "if conscientiously scrupulous of taking an oath." Maryland's Declaration of Rights directed that "the manner of administering an oath to any person, ought to be such, as those of the religious persuasion, profession, or denomination, of which such person is one, generally esteem the most effectual confirmation, by the attestation of the Divine Being." It specifically identified Quakers, Dunkers, and Mennonites as persons "holding it unlawful to take an oath," and it directed that they "ought to be allowed to make their solemn affirmation" in an accommodated manner and that their affirmation then be accepted. South Carolina's Constitution provided that "every inhabitant ... when called to make an appeal to God as a witness to truth, shall be permitted to do it in that way which is most agreeable to the dictates of his own conscience."

### *Religion Provisions in the United States Constitution and the First Amendment*

After eleven of the first thirteen states had adopted their own constitutions, the United States Constitution and the federal Bill of Rights were ratified, and they included several provisions that correspond to religion and conscience provisions in state constitutions. First, the United States Constitution, which was ratified on June 21, 1788, and went into effect on March 4, 1789, included a provision barring any religious test "as a Qualification to any Office or public Trust under the United States." Second, like several state constitutions, the United States Constitution required both federal and state legislative, executive, and judicial officials to swear an oath or make an affirmation to support the Constitution.

Third, and most importantly, the First Amendment, which was submitted to the states for ratification on September 25, 1789, and adopted on December 15, 1791, along with nine other amendments, included a religious freedom provision stating that "Congress shall make no law respecting an establishment of religion, or prohibiting the free exercise thereof." This provision had two distinct but interrelated aspects. By forbidding Congress from making any law respecting an establishment of religion (the Establishment Clause), the First Amendment barred Congress both from establishing a national church and, at that time, from interfering with any state ecclesiastical establishment. Additionally, by proscribing Congress making any law prohibiting the free exercise of religion (the Free Exercise Clause), the First Amendment extended protection to the belief and conduct dimensions of religious life.[8]

The approval of the First Amendment was the culmination of a sustained effort by James Madison to protect religious conscience at the state level and

[8] The Supreme Court has displayed some interpretive inconsistency regarding the Free Exercise Clause's protection of both belief and conduct. Compare *Cantwell* v. *Connecticut*, 310 U.S. 296, 303 (1940) with *Reynolds* v. *United States*, 98 U.S. 145 (1878).

the federal level. Madison, a Virginian, had advocated recognizing religious freedom as a right in Virginia's Declaration of Rights. In 1785, he wrote his influential *A Memorial and Remonstrance against Religious Assessments* and introduced Jefferson's bill establishing religious freedom in the Virginia legislature, which passed in 1786. Madison had initially proposed a different version of what became the First Amendment, which read: "The civil rights of none shall be abridged on account of religious belief or worship, nor shall any national religion be established, nor shall the full and equal rights of conscience be in any manner, or on any pretext, infringed." He had also proposed an amendment prohibiting states from infringing the equal rights of conscience, but it did not receive congressional approval. Consequently, the First Amendment left the issue of religious conscience protections in the states to the states.

Madison's proposals for federal conscience protections reflected a robust vision of conscience rights, but they also reflected the vision of other defenders of religious conscience such as Baptist minister John Leland (1754–1841), a Massachusetts native who moved to Virginia and experienced religious persecution and other deleterious effects of ecclesiastical establishments in both states. Leland personally appealed to Madison for federal religious freedom protection. In Leland's view, without a constitutional defense, religious liberty was "not Sufficiently Secured," and it was "Very Dangerous leaving religious Liberty" at the mercy of a majority of Congress. Madison's efforts for conscience protections were mostly successful as the final version of the First Amendment's religion provision included key features of his initial proposal, but his proposal prohibiting state infringement of conscience rights was rejected.

As the first period of state constitution-making came to an end in 1791, the American constitutional order regarding religion was in place. Under the United States Constitution, the national government lacked power to act on religion. That subject, including the scope of religious conscience protections and state ecclesiastical establishments, was a matter for the states to address under their constitutions and laws, as Justice Story explained in his *Commentaries*. About half of the original thirteen states maintained some form of religious establishment in 1791, but Virginia had recently enacted Jefferson's religious freedom bill, thereby ending its Anglican establishment and setting an example other states would follow in ensuing decades.

Several observations may be made about religious conscience protections in the first state constitutions. First, the drafters used interchangeably terms such as rights of conscience, liberty of conscience, free exercise of religion, entitlement to the free exercise of religion, right to worship, and religious liberty, which demonstrates that they associated conscience rights with religion and that, in protecting religious conscience, they sought to safeguard both freedom of belief and freedom of belief-inspired conduct. Second, although different patterns can be identified among state constitutions and although language varied, the texts and the related histories reveal considerable borrowing as drafters adapted verbal formulations from other declarations of rights and constitutions and from antecedent documents. This was evident in 1791 when Vermont became the fourteenth state to join the United States. The religious conscience provisions of its constitution, originally approved in 1777, included language similar to that found in other state constitutions, such as its recognition of the "natural and unalienable right to worship Almighty God, according to the dictates of their own consciences and understanding."

## THE SECOND AND THIRD PERIODS OF STATE CONSTITUTION-MAKING

The second and third periods of state constitution-making extend over nearly one hundred and fifty years. During these two periods, religious conscience protections similar to those recognized in state constitutions during the first period were adopted in the constitutions of more than thirty states that joined the United States. Additionally, conscience rights gained increased standing during the Second Great Awakening that unfolded during the second period and continued to yield effects in the third period.

### *The Second Period*

The second period (from 1792 to the early 1830s) was critical for extending and making permanent religious conscience protections recognized during the first period. Several important developments are observable in this period.

First, ten states joined the United States: Kentucky (1792); Tennessee (1796); Ohio (1803); Louisiana (1812); Indiana (1816); Mississippi (1817); Illinois (1818); Alabama (1819); Maine (1820); and Missouri (1821). Most of these states included religious conscience protections in their constitutions, and the new state provisions reflected the language and patterns developed in the first period. Indiana's Constitution and Illinois's Constitution illustrate well the protections afforded. Both recognized a "natural and indefeasible right to worship Almighty God" "according to the dictates of their own consciences." Both prohibited state-compelled church attendance, government support of any place of worship, and public maintenance of any ministry, barred human authority controlling or interfering with conscience rights, and proscribed any preference being given by law to any religious society or mode of worship. Both also forbade any religious test as a qualification for office.

Second, Connecticut, New Hampshire, and Massachusetts, three of the original thirteen states, ended their state-sponsored religious establishments. These states had maintained aspects of their Congregational establishments from the colonial period. But then, in 1818, Connecticut adopted its first constitution, guaranteeing that all persons "shall forever be free" to exercise and enjoy "religious profession and worship, without discrimination" and prohibiting civil government giving by law a preference "to any [C]hristian sect or mode of worship." One year later, New Hampshire ended its religious establishment when it passed a toleration act stopping religious taxation. In 1833, Massachusetts took a similar step toward broader conscience protections when it amended its constitution and ended religious taxes. In doing this, Massachusetts became the final American state to disestablish religion.

Although these three states had maintained elements of ecclesiastical establishments for roughly half a century after the first state constitutions were adopted, spirited advocacy in favor of robust religious conscience protections and against religious establishments was present all along in these New England states. Again, Baptist minister Leland was a key figure. In 1791, he authored *The Rights of Conscience Inalienable*, a tract in which he appealed to New Englanders to allow enjoyment of "the full liberty of conscience,"[9] which he understood to be a right, not a privilege granted by government. In his view, civil government wrongfully restrains this right when it maintains a religious establishment, imposes religious tests for office, and requires religious dissenters to obtain certificates exempting them from church attendance. In addition to recognizing the belief and conduct dimensions of religious liberty, he was resolute in arguing that liberty of conscience requires civil government to recognize limits on its authority:

> Government has no more to do with the religious opinions of men, than it has with the principles of mathematics. Let every man speak freely without fear, maintain the principles that he believes, worship according to his own faith, either one God, three Gods, no God, or twenty Gods; and let government protect him in so doing, i.e., see that he meets with no personal abuse, or loss of property, for his religious opinions. Instead of discouraging him with proscriptions, fines, confiscations or death, let him be encouraged, as a free man, to bring forth his arguments and maintain his points with all

9 Consistent with other contemporaneous definitions, Leland defined conscience as "a court of judicature which the Almighty has erected in every human breast: a *censor morum* [a censor of morals] over all his conduct."

> boldness; then, if his doctrine is false, it will be confuted, and if it is true, (though ever so novel,) let others credit it.

Because defenders of religious conscience like Leland persisted in challenging laws and institutions that threatened full enjoyment of conscience rights, ecclesiastical establishments became historical relics in America, and with religious disestablishment in these three states, constitutionally recognized protections of religious conscience and constitutionally mandated non-establishment of religion became permanent realities.

Third, during roughly this same period, a series of popular revival movements (known collectively as the Second Great Awakening) swept through various parts of the new nation, including New England, the mid-Atlantic, the South, and the expanding frontier, and these movements highlighted the increasing prominence of conscience rights. During this awakening, many people came into the Christian faith. And as during the First Great Awakening, two upstart groups (Baptists and Methodists) experienced dramatic growth. As they grew, their past outsider status evaporated. Indeed, by the middle of the nineteenth century, they became dominant expressions of Protestant Christianity in America. Additionally, various new religious groups were formed, such as the African Methodist Episcopal Church, the Christian/Restoration Movement, and the Church of Jesus Christ of Latter-day Saints (Mormons). The theological themes that emerged in the Second Great Awakening differed considerably from the Reformed theological themes that predominated in the First. They included: the common person, the individual conscience, and the human will; egalitarianism and democracy; and distrust of clerical authority, church traditions, theological education, and creedal systems. These themes were expressed and exhibited in camp meetings on the American frontier where large groups of people gathered for successive days of evangelistic preaching, spiritual renewal, and social interaction.

By 1833, the Second Great Awakening was winding down, but the effects of the movement on the American religious landscape would endure. This awakening, together with the First Great Awakening and the American Revolution, had created an environment in which religious conscience was honored, religious pluralism multiplied, and religious outsiders and dissenters moved from the margins to the mainstream. Again, Baptists reflected this new reality. This formerly outsider group, which had championed religious conscience in colonial and Revolutionary America, flourished in this new environment, and their beliefs in soul freedom, soul competency, and freedom of conscience resonated with the spirit of freedom and democracy spreading across the new American republic.

By the end of the second period, more states had recognized constitutional protections for religious conscience, and ecclesiastical establishments were no more in America. Additionally, revival movements had deepened regard for religious conscience and broadened religious pluralism. Thus, by the end of the second period, the faint early morning light of religious freedom that had appeared on the horizon in the sixteenth and seventeenth centuries had grown into bright midday sunshine as the last remnants of Old World religious establishments in America ceased and religious conscience protections became the state constitutional norm.

### *The Third Period*

During the third period (from the mid-1830s to the 1920s), several key developments occurred concerning state constitutional protections of religious conscience. First, twenty-four more states joined the United States: Arkansas (1836); Michigan (1837); Florida and Texas (1845); Iowa (1846); Wisconsin (1848); California (1850); Minnesota (1858); Oregon (1859); Kansas (1861); West Virginia (1863); Nevada (1864); Nebraska (1867); Colorado (1876); North Dakota, South Dakota, Montana, and Washington (1889); Idaho and Wyoming (1890); Utah (1896); Oklahoma (1907); and New Mexico and Arizona (1912). These states followed the same path as those that had afforded religious conscience protections in their constitutions during the second period and adopted provisions with language patterned after state constitutions adopted in the first and second periods.

Washington's Constitution and Arizona's Constitution are illustrative. The Washington Constitution declared that "[a]bsolute freedom of conscience in all matters of religious sentiment, belief, and worship, shall be guaranteed to every individual, and no one shall be molested or disturbed in person, or property, on account of religion." Arizona's Constitution secured "[p]erfect toleration of religion sentiment" to every inhabitant and guaranteed that no inhabitant would "ever be molested in person or property on account of his or her mode of religious worship, or lack of the same." Both constitutions stated that the "liberty of conscience" secured therein was qualified so as not to "excuse acts of licentiousness" or "justify practices inconsistent with" public peace and safety. Both prohibited appropriation of public money or property "to any religious worship, exercise, or instruction" or "the support of any religious establishment." And both prohibited any religious test for public office and barred any witness or juror being rendered incompetent on account of religious beliefs. Both directed that oaths or affirmations be administered in a mode that is "most consistent with and binding upon the conscience of the person to whom" they are administered. Additionally, Washington's Constitution mandated that persons "having conscientious scruples against bearing arms" not be compelled to serve in the militia, provided they pay an equivalent for the exemption.

Second, Rhode Island, one of the original states, ratified its first constitution in 1842. Up until then, Rhode Island was governed under the royal charter that Roger Williams secured in 1663. That charter had granted inhabitants religious conscience protections that made the colony a haven for religious dissenters and fostered an environment in which religious pluralism and religious freedom could flourish. In the preamble to their new constitution, the people expressed gratitude to God for "the civil and religious liberty" they enjoyed. In declaring their religious conscience rights, they recognized that God had "created the mind free" and that "a principal object" of their ancestors was "to hold forth a lively experiment, that a flourishing civil state may stand, and be best maintained, with full liberty in religious concernments." The constitution prohibited compulsory church attendance or support for "any religious worship, place, or ministry." It declared that no person could be "restrained" or "molested" "in his body or goods," "disqualified from holding" public office, or made to "suffer" "on account of his religious belief." Recognizing the belief and conduct dimensions of religious life, it stated that every person has a right to "be free to worship God according to the dictates of his own conscience, and to profess and by argument to maintain his opinion in matters of religion." Those holding select offices were made to take an oath or make an affirmation.

Third, some states adopted new constitutions that modified or expanded religious conscience protections afforded in earlier adopted constitutions. For instance, in 1851, Indiana approved its second constitution, which enlarged religious conscience protections. It stated that people "shall be secured in the natural right to worship Almighty God, according to the dictates of their own consciences," thereby placing a duty on government to secure this right. In recognizing the right to worship and prohibiting any law "control[ling] the free exercise and enjoyment of religious opinions, or interfer[ing] with the rights of conscience," it acknowledged the belief and conduct dimensions of religious life. It barred any preference being "given, by law, to any creed, religious society, or mode of worship" and any compulsion "to attend, erect, or support, any place of worship, or to maintain any ministry." In addition to prohibiting any religious test for office, it prohibited any money being "drawn from the treasury, for the benefit of any religious or theological institution" and any person being "rendered incompetent as a witness" because of religious opinions. It directed that oaths or affirmations be administered in a mode consistent with the consciences of the persons to whom they are administered, and it exempted from service in the militia persons "conscientiously opposed to bearing arms" but required an equivalent payment for exemption.

Similarly, in 1868, North Carolina adopted a new constitution, and in its preamble, the people expressed gratitude to God for "the existence of [their] civil, political and religious liberties." The framers added the following language to the provision of its 1776 Declaration of Rights that recognized the natural and inalienable right to worship God according to the dictates of conscience: "No human authority can, in any case whatever, control or interfere with the rights of conscience." Although this provision (and similar provisions in other state constitutions) may protect secular conscience in addition to religious conscience, the earliest occurrences of this provision in Delaware's Declaration of Rights (1776) and Vermont's Constitution (1777) expressly linked "the rights of conscience" to "the free exercise of religious worship."

Also in 1868, Louisiana adopted a new constitution, which was its first to include a formal bill of rights. Like other state constitutions, it recognized that every person possesses a "natural right to worship God according to the dictates of his conscience." Additionally, it prohibited any religious test for office.

Fourth, during this period, federal pressure was placed on some states (primarily Western states) to adopt religiously discriminatory constitutional provisions. This development came about after Maine Representative James G. Blaine proposed an amendment to the United States Constitution in 1875. It would have prohibited "money raised by taxation in any State for the support of public schools, or derived from any fund therefor, nor any public lands devoted thereto," ever being "under the control of any religious sect" and "any money so raised, or lands so devoted," being "divided between religious sects or denominations." This proposal came at President Ulysses S. Grant's suggestion that states maintain free public schools and prohibit public school funding being used to benefit or aid any religious sect or denomination. Viewed more broadly, however, the proposal was a calculated response to mid-nineteenth century Catholic immigration and Catholic efforts to obtain public funding for their schools and other institutions, and it reflected anti-Catholic animus, which had become commonplace in mid-to-late nineteenth century America. Both houses of Congress considered the proposal in 1876, but it did not receive the requisite votes to pass.

Although the Blaine proposal failed, Congress required some states entering the union after 1876 to incorporate the substance of the proposal in their state constitutions. For instance, in 1889, Congress passed an enabling act to bring Montana into the union, and it required Montana to adopt language in its state constitution keeping its public school system free from sectarian control. The people of Montana approved a constitution that included such a provision with language patterned after Colorado's Constitution (1876) and California's Constitution (1879). Montana's provision prohibited direct or indirect appropriations, payments from public funds, or grants of lands or other property "in aid of any church, or for any sectarian purpose, or to aid in the support of any school, academy, seminary, college, university, or other literary, scientific institution, controlled in whole or in part by any church, sect or denomination whatever."

The inclusion of such provisions in state constitutions represented a departure from the decades-long trend in favor of religious conscience protections. However, some state constitutions included provisions that similarly prohibited state money being appropriated for the benefit of religious institutions, but these provisions did not originate in anti-Catholic animus or stem from Blaine's proposal. For instance, in a recent case interpreting the provision of Indiana's Constitution that bars money being "drawn from the treasury, for the benefit of any religious or theological institution," the Indiana Supreme Court observed that "anti-Catholic and anti-immigrant biases may not have significantly influenced Indiana's 1851 constitution," because Catholic and immigrant populations did not arrive and the forces advancing these views did not become politically significant in Indiana until years later.[10]

By the end of the third period, more states had adopted constitutions that included provisions recognizing conscience rights and affording religious conscience protections. The rights recognized in these provisions included the belief and conduct dimensions of religious life. And, throughout this period, states continued to exercise exclusive authority over the subject of religion, consistent with the American constitutional order Justice Story had described. However, when federal pressure was placed on some states to adopt religiously discriminatory state constitutional provisions reflecting the anti-Catholic bias of the failed Blaine amendment, the general trend in favor of state constitutional protection of religious conscience was disrupted.

[10] *Embry* v. *O'Bannon*, 798 N.E.2d 157, 164 (Ind. 2003).

## THE FOURTH PERIOD AND FEDERAL CONSTITUTIONAL OVERSHADOWING

During the fourth period (from the 1920s to the mid-1970s), federal constitutional rights and jurisprudence came to overshadow state constitutional protections. This overshadowing stemmed, in significant part, from the United States Supreme Court's development of the incorporation doctrine. Originally, the federal Bill of Rights applied only to the federal government. However, in the twentieth century, the Court made select provisions of the federal Bill of Rights applicable to the states through the Due Process Clause of the Fourteenth Amendment to the United States Constitution. The rights incorporated were those fundamental principles of liberty and justice that the Court deemed "implicit in the concept of ordered liberty" and deeply "rooted in the traditions and conscience of our people."[11] Over time, most but not all of the rights recognized in the federal Bill of Rights have been incorporated. And once this doctrine was coupled with an activist judicial philosophy in the middle of the twentieth century, federal constitutional rights moved to the center of the American constitutional stage, and state constitutional rights moved to the perimeter.

Among the rights selectively incorporated were the First Amendment's religious freedom rights. Thus, in 1940, in *Cantwell* v. *Connecticut*, the Court incorporated the free exercise provision and recognized that the free exercise right includes freedom to both believe and act.[12] In 1943, in another case, the Court reaffirmed the paramount importance of the First Amendment's free exercise and speech protections when it wrote: "If there is any fixed star in our constitutional constellation, it is that no official, high or petty, can prescribe what shall be orthodox in politics, nationalism, religion, or other matters of opinion, or force citizens to confess by word or act their faith therein." It added that "the purpose of the First Amendment" is to "reserve from all official control" "the sphere of intellect and spirit."[13] In 1947, in *Everson* v. *Board of Education*, the Court incorporated the federal religious establishment provision. It observed that this provision prohibits federal, state, and local governments from, among other things, setting up a church, passing laws that aid religions or prefer one religion over another, forcing a person to go to or remain away from church, forcing a person to profess belief or

[11] *Palko* v. *Connecticut*, 302 U.S. 319, 325 (1937).
[12] *Cantwell* v. *Connecticut*, 310 U.S. 296, 303 (1940).
[13] *W. Va. State Board of Education.* v. *Barnette*, 319 U.S. 624, 642 (1943).

disbelief in any religion, passing a tax to support religious activities or institutions, or participating in the affairs of any religious organizations.[14]

Having incorporated federal free exercise and establishment protections in the 1940s, the Court interpreted and applied the federal provisions during the ensuing decades, especially during the Warren Court period (1953–69) and a portion of the Burger Court period (1969–86). Thus, in 1961, in *Torcaso* v. *Watkins*, the Court invalidated the Maryland Constitution's religious test provision, which barred from public office persons who refuse to declare belief in God. The Court determined that civil government may not force any person to profess belief or disbelief in any religion.[15] In 1963, in *Sherbert* v. *Verner*, the Court held that the federal free exercise provision required a state to demonstrate a compelling interest to deny unemployment benefits and thereby burden a person's religious exercise regarding Sabbath observance.[16] In 1972, in *Wisconsin* v. *Yoder*, the Court held that a state law requiring Amish children to remain in school until a specified age violated the federal free exercise provision because the requirement unduly burdened the practice of religion and was not justified by a compelling government interest.[17] In 1971, in *Lemon* v. *Kurtzman*, the Court held that the statutorily created programs of two states that benefited religious schools violated both federal religion provisions and fostered excessive entanglement of government with religion.[18]

During this same period, the Court also signaled that its understanding of conscience protections extends beyond religious conscience. In 1970, in *Welsh* v. *United States*, it determined that a federal statutory exemption from military service, which applied to any person "who, by reason of religious training and belief, is conscientiously opposed to participation in war,"[19] violated the establishment provision. The Court remedied the violation by extending the exemption beyond the traditional religious basis for conscientious objector status and deeming it to "exempt[] from military service all those whose consciences, spurred by deeply held moral, ethical, or religious beliefs, would give them no rest or peace if they allowed themselves to become a part of an instrument of war."[20]

[14] *Everson* v. *Board of Education*, 330 U.S. 1, 15–16 (1947).
[15] *Torcaso* v. *Watkins*, 367 U.S. 488 (1961).
[16] *Sherbert* v. *Verner*, 374 U.S. 398 (1963).
[17] *Wisconsin* v. *Yoder*, 406 U.S. 205 (1972).
[18] *Lemon* v. *Kurtzman*, 403 U.S. 602 (1971).
[19] Section 6(j) of the Universal Military Training Service Act is currently codified at 50 U.S.C. § 3806(j).
[20] *Welsh* v. *United States*, 398 U.S. 333, 344 (1970). See also *United States* v. *Seeger*, 380 U.S. 163 (1965).

Following these developments in federal constitutional jurisprudence, federal constitutional standards came to overshadow state religious conscience protections, and this was evident in at least three significant respects. First, during the fourth period, two states joined the United States – Alaska (1959), and Hawaii (1959) – and both adopted constitutions that included religious freedom provisions nearly verbatim with the federal religion provisions. These state provisions stated that no law shall be "made" (Alaska) or "enacted" (Hawaii) "respecting an establishment of religion, or prohibiting the free exercise thereof." Absent were the distinct verbal formulations adopted in state constitutions in the first three periods, such as the right to worship according to the dictates of conscience, the bar on any person being molested or restrained on account of religious persuasion, the freedom from compulsion to attend or support, and the prohibition against interference with conscience rights.

Second, some states adopted new constitutions with provisions that paralleled the federal provisions. For instance, in 1968, Florida approved its sixth constitution and adopted language that echoed the federal language rather than the language of its 1885 constitution. Its 1968 constitution stated that "[t]here shall be no law respecting the establishment of religion or prohibiting or penalizing the free exercise thereof." Similarly, in 1974, California amended the primary religion provision of its constitution to add the following: "The Legislature shall make no law respecting an establishment of religion."

In 1974, Louisiana adopted a new constitution with language that followed the federal provisions and barred laws respecting an establishment of religion and prohibiting the free exercise of religion. It thus departed from language in its prior state constitutions that echoed language in other state constitutions. Its 1974 constitution added a new provision barring religious and other forms of discrimination in access to public areas and public accommodations. At the same time, it eliminated language included in its 1921 constitution that, like the failed Blaine Amendment, barred public moneys being paid, "directly or indirectly, in aid of any church, sect or denomination of religion."

Third, some state supreme courts adopted a lockstep interpretive approach to state constitutional provisions, including religious conscience provisions. Accordingly, rather than independently analyzing state constitutional provisions, these courts embraced the Supreme Court's interpretation of counterpart provisions of the federal constitution. For instance, the Michigan Supreme Court determined that the four-sentence state religious freedom provision, which includes several different aspects and employs language markedly different from the federal provisions, is nevertheless "subject to similar interpretation" as the First Amendment.[21] Likewise, the Illinois Supreme Court determined that the Illinois Constitution's religious establishment restrictions have an identical meaning as the First Amendment, even though the language differs considerably.[22]

By the end of the fourth period, the Supreme Court's incorporation of the First Amendment's religion provisions and its application of these provisions to the states brought about a fundamental change in the American constitutional order regarding religion. No longer was religion a subject, as Justice Story observed more than a century earlier, "left exclusively to the state governments, to be acted upon according to their own sense of justice, and the state constitutions."[23] Instead, the United States Constitution's religion provisions and the Court's First Amendment jurisprudence would play a more dominant role at the state and local levels, and the state religious conscience provisions would often be overlooked or interpreted to have the same meanings as the federal provisions.

## THE FIFTH PERIOD AND A RENAISSANCE OF STATE CONSTITUTION-MAKING

During the fifth period (from the late 1970s to the present), several significant developments occurred with state religious conscience protections. First, state constitutional protections began to receive renewed attention as the "new judicial federalism" movement emerged in the late 1970s. This movement has been understood to be a response to the apparent reluctance of the Burger Court (1969–86) and the Rehnquist Court (1986–2005) to give expansive recognition to federal constitutional rights, and it received early encouragement from Justice William J. Brennan Jr., who served on the Warren, Burger, and Rehnquist Courts and called upon state courts to rediscover their state constitutions.[24] This movement has inspired state judges to refocus on state constitutions to secure rights not protected under the United States Constitution, and during this period, state constitutional law has reclaimed its standing as an essential component of American constitutionalism.

21 Advisory Opinion re Constitutionality of PA 1970, No. 100, 180 N.W.2d 265, 274 (Mich. 1970).

22 *People ex rel. Klinger* v. *Howlett*, 305 N.E.2d 129, 130 (Ill. 1973). See also *Illinois* v. *Falbe*, 727 N.E.2d. 200, 207 (Ill. 2000).

23 Story, *Commentaries on the Constitution*, 3:§1873.

24 William J. Brennan Jr., "State Constitutions and the Protection of Individual Rights," *Harvard Law Review* 90 (1977): 489–504; William J. Brennan Jr., "The Bill of Rights and the States: The Revival of State Constitutions as Guardians of Individual Rights," *New York University Law Review* 59 (1986): 535–53.

This movement has had an impact on state religious conscience protections. For instance, the Colorado Supreme Court has expressed a desire to be "mindful [of] the specific 'text and purpose' of our state constitutional provision," even while consulting First Amendment jurisprudence and recognizing that "the federal and state constitutional provisions embody similar values."[25] Additionally, a body of legal scholarship has developed as attention has returned to state religious conscience protections.[26] Nevertheless, other state courts have continued to follow the lockstep approach or have otherwise not independently examined their state constitutional provisions.[27]

Second, the United States Supreme Court issued a decision in *Employment Division* v. *Smith* (1990) that helped to increase attention to state religious conscience protections. The Court determined that a neutral and generally applicable law that advances a legitimate government interest may burden religious exercise without violating the First Amendment. Consequently, after *Smith*, the First Amendment's free exercise provision no longer requires government regulation to satisfy the strict scrutiny standard, except in limited circumstances.[28] The United States Congress responded by passing (virtually unanimously) the Religious Freedom Restoration Act of 1993 (RFRA), which was signed by President Bill Clinton.[29] This federal act bars the federal government from substantially burdening religious exercise except when it meets the strict scrutiny standard.

Third, since the Supreme Court issued its *Smith* decision, some state courts have followed *Smith*, interpreting state religion provisions in lockstep,[30] but others have not. Many state courts have determined that religious conscience rights receive greater protection under state constitutions and state laws than is afforded under the First Amendment. Indeed, a number of state supreme courts have interpreted religious conscience provisions in state constitutions to require a strict scrutiny test.[31] For instance, the Ohio Supreme Court determined that the religious freedom protection afforded by its state constitution

[25] *Conrad* v. *City and County of Denver*, 656 P.2d 662, 670–71 (Colo. 1983).

[26] Kent Greenawalt, "The Concept of Religion in State Constitutions," *Campbell Law Review* 8 (1986): 437–47; G. Alan Tarr, "Religion under State Constitutions," *Annals of the American Academy of Political and Social Sciences* 496 (1988): 65–75.

[27] See, e.g., *Vermont* v. *Chambers*, 477 A.2d 110, 112 (Vt. 1984).

[28] *Employment Division* v. *Smith*, 494 U.S. 872 (1990).

[29] Religious Freedom Restoration Act, 42 U.S.C. §§2000bb–2000bb-4 (1993).

[30] See, e.g., *Meltebeke* v. *Bureau of Labor and Industries*, 903 P.2d 351, 361–62 (Or. 1995).

[31] See, e.g., *Swanner* v. *Anchorage Equal Rights Commission*, 874 P.2d 274 (Alas. 1994); *Hunt* v. *Hunt*, 648 A.2d 843, 853 (Vt. 1994); *Open Door Baptist Church* v. *Clark County*, 995 P.2d 33 (Wash. 2000).

was broader than the federal protection and required a different test than *Smith*.[32]

Particularly instructive are developments in Massachusetts, one of the original states, which has retained elements of its 1780 constitution in its current constitution. Four years after the *Smith* decision, the Massachusetts Supreme Judicial Court interpreted a religious freedom provision included in a 1917 amendment to its constitution. The court determined that this provision, which includes language that parallels the federal free exercise provision, requires a standard similar to that specified in the federal RFRA, not the First Amendment. Under the Massachusetts standard, courts evaluate whether a government action "substantially burdens [the] free exercise of religion, and, if it does, whether the Commonwealth has shown that it has an interest sufficiently compelling to justify that burden."[33] The court subsequently determined that, although government may infringe religiously inspired conduct when it satisfies the compelling interest test, "[r]eligious beliefs – what a person thinks, what faith he holds in his heart and mind – are indeed protected absolutely" from governmental interference.[34] The court has also explained that "the scope of protection" afforded by the Massachusetts religious freedom amendment "is greater than that afforded by the United States Constitution."[35]

State legislatures also responded to *Smith* and other developments. Twenty states have now passed state religious freedom statutes, with many patterned after the federal RFRA. Additionally, in 1999, Alabama approved a religious freedom amendment to its constitution. This amendment supplements the religious freedom provisions of its 1901 constitution and protects religious conscience under the strict scrutiny standard. Thus, Alabama's Constitution now includes layered protection under its older provisions and its newer strict scrutiny provisions.

Fourth, some state supreme courts have adopted standards distinct from the *Smith* test and the strict scrutiny test. For instance, the Indiana Supreme Court determined that the framers of the Indiana Constitution did not merely copy or paraphrase the First Amendment but instead adopted seven separate religion provisions. Consequently, the court explained, Indiana's religious freedom and conscience provisions should not "be equated with" the federal counterpart provisions, and federal jurisprudence does not "govern[] the

[32] *Humphrey* v. *Lane*, 728 N.E.2d 1039, 1045 (Ohio 1999).
[33] *Attorney General* v. *Desilets*, 636 N.E.2d 233, 236 (Mass. 1994).
[34] *Society of Jesus of New England* v. *Massachusetts*, 808 N.E.2d 272, 284 (Mass. 2004).
[35] *Rasheed* v. *Commissioner of Correction*, 845 N.E.2d 296, 302 (Mass. 2006).

interpretation of [Indiana's] guarantees."[36] The court concluded that Indiana government actors may not materially burden core values embodied in the religious conscience provisions.[37]

Fifth, Florida and Oklahoma recently considered repealing their Blaine Amendment–styled state constitutional provisions that ban use of public funds to support sectarian schools, but these proposals failed to pass. However, such provisions are likely to face proposals to amend or repeal in the years ahead because of recent attention given to the discriminatory history associated with these provisions and because of the Supreme Court's recent decisions in *Espinoza* v. *Montana Department of Revenue* and *Trinity Lutheran Church of Columbia, Inc.* v. *Comer*. In these cases, the Court determined that Montana and Missouri unlawfully discriminated against religious schools in violation of the First Amendment when they relied on their Blaine Amendment–styled, no-aid provisions to exclude religious schools and families from public programs because of their religious status.[38]

Sixth, over the last few decades, bakers, employers, florists, lessors, pharmacists, photographers, and others have claimed religious conscience and other constitutional protections in the face of laws barring discrimination or mandating provision of services in situations they find objectionable on religious conscience grounds. In some of these cases, courts have considered the application of religious conscience protections in state constitutions. For instance, in Colorado, a cake shop owner who objected on religious grounds to creating a same-sex wedding cake was charged with discrimination and found to be in violation. In declining the baker's conscience claim, a Colorado appellate court followed federal free exercise precedent in interpreting Colorado's religious freedom provision, determined that the anti-discrimination act is a neutral law of general applicability and refused to apply a heightened scrutiny standard.[39] Similarly, in Washington, the state supreme court upheld a lower court ruling that a flower shop owner who objected on religious grounds to providing flowers for a same-sex wedding violated state anti-discrimination law. The court determined that the florist's claim under the state religious conscience provision, which guarantees to every person "[a]bsolute freedom of conscience in all matters of religious sentiment, belief and worship," failed because, even if a heightened scrutiny standard applies, the anti-discrimination law is a neutral health and safety regulation serving the

36 *City Chapel Evangelical Free, Inc.* v. *City of South Bend*, 744 N.E.2d 443, 446 (Ind. 2001).
37 Ibid., 450.
38 *Trinity Lutheran Church of Columbia, Inc.* v. *Comer*, 137 S. Ct. 2012 (2017).
39 *Craig* v. *Masterpiece Cakeshop, Inc.*, 370 P.3d 272 (Colo. Ct. App. 2015).

broad societal purpose of "eradicating barriers to the equal treatment of all citizens in the commercial marketplace."[40]

The fifth period of state constitution-making has brought both expansions and restrictions of religious conscience protections. The new judicial federalism movement has inspired a refocusing on state constitutional provisions, including religious conscience provisions, and many state courts and legislatures have reengaged with the important matter of religious conscience protections under state law. And even though states now operate in a constitutional context in which the federal constitution's religion provisions overshadow state protections, this fifth period has shown that states can, through their constitutions and laws, provide greater protections than those afforded by the federal Constitution.

## CONCLUSION

Since the eighteenth century when the first state constitutions were written, some aspects of religious conscience protections in state constitutions have remained the same, but others have undergone change. One aspect that has remained unchanged is the understanding of freedom of religious conscience as a right, not a privilege. Nevertheless, today some advocate a narrow conception of religious conscience protections that safeguards only private belief but not the conduct dimension of religious life. If that narrow conception were to control, exercises of religious conscience, which necessarily extend beyond the belief dimension, would receive limited protection and face government regulation that interferes with personal conduct and restrains social institutions.

Another aspect that remains unchanged is the threat to religious conscience posed by orthodoxies and establishments. In the sixteenth, seventeenth, and eighteenth centuries, tests of theological orthodoxy, religious establishments, and alliances between political and religious authorities threatened religious conscience, and religious dissenters, theological outsiders, and other defenders of conscience were persecuted for their beliefs and their belief-inspired conduct. Today, religious conscience is threatened less by theological orthodoxies and ecclesiastical establishments than by newly formed ideological orthodoxies that constitute new cultural and social establishments. And when civil government enforces these newly developed orthodoxies and supports these new establishments with coercive power, the threats to religious

[40] *Washington* v. *Arlene's Flowers, Inc.*, 389 P.3d 543, 566 (Wash. 2017).

conscience become as real as those posed by theological orthodoxies and ecclesiastical establishments in earlier eras. Consequently, constitutionally based protections of religious conscience are needed now as much as they were then.

Among the significant changes since the first period of state constitution-making is the complete end to ecclesiastical establishments in America. This change occurred at the state level through changes in law made in response to arguments supporting conscience rights. It also came about as a consequence of a broadened religious pluralism and an altered religious landscape that emerged after two periods of spiritual awakening and a revolutionary war that promised expansive freedom.

Another significant change is the prominent role federal law now plays in the matter of religion. For three quarters of our nation's history, the power over the subject of religion rested exclusively with the states, as Story noted in his *Commentaries*. But, with the incorporation of the establishment and free exercise provisions of the First Amendment, federal constitutional law came to predominate, eclipsing the force of state constitutional provisions. Nevertheless, with the revitalization of state constitutional law over the last several decades, the constitutional promise that Americans can freely believe and freely act as they judge right based upon their deeply held beliefs comes closer to fulfillment. And now, robust state religious conscience protections joined together with federal religious freedom protections can provide two layers of security for conscience against the threats that civil governments continue to pose.

## RECOMMENDED READING


Adams, Arlin M., and Charles J. Emmerich. *A Nation Dedicated to Religious Liberty: The Constitutional Heritage of the Religion Clauses*. Philadelphia, PA: University of Pennsylvania Press, 1990.

Antieau, Chester James, Phillip Mark Carroll, and Thomas Carroll Burke. *Religion under the State Constitutions*. Brooklyn, NY: Central Book Company, 1965.

Carmella, Angela C. "State Constitutional Protection of Religious Exercise: An Emerging Post-Smith Jurisprudence." *Brigham Young University Law Review* (1993): 275–325.

Cobb, Sanford H. *The Rise of Religious Liberty in America: A History*. New York, NY: The MacMillan Company, 1902.

Curry, Thomas J. *The First Freedoms: Church and State in America to the Passage of the First Amendment*. New York, NY: Oxford University Press, 1986.

Dreisbach, Daniel L., and Mark David Hall, eds. *The Sacred Rights of Conscience: Selected Readings on Religious Liberty and Church-State Relations in the American Founding*. Indianapolis, IN: Liberty Fund, Inc., 2009.

Feldman, Noah. "The Intellectual Origins of the Establishment Clause." *New York University Law Review* 77 (2002): 346–428.
Gunn, T. Jeremy, and John Witte Jr., eds. *No Establishment of Religion: America's Original Contribution to Religious Liberty*. New York, NY: Oxford University Press, 2012.
Hamburger, Philip. *Separation of Church and State*. Cambridge, MA: Harvard University Press, 2002.
Kurland, Philip B., and Ralph Lerner, eds. *The Founders' Constitution*, vol. 5. Chicago, IL: University of Chicago Press, 1987.
Linton, Paul Benjamin. "Religious Freedom Claims and Defenses under State Constitutions." *University of St. Thomas Journal of Law & Policy* 7 (2013): 103–91.
McConnell, Michael W. "The Origins and Historical Understanding of Free Exercise of Religion." *Harvard Law Review* 102 (1990): 1409–1517.
Miller, William Lee. *The First Liberty: America's Foundation in Religious Freedom*, expanded and updated ed. Washington, DC: Georgetown University Press, 2003.
Witte, John Jr., and Joel A. Nichols. *Religion and the American Constitutional Experiment*, 4th ed. New York, NY: Oxford University Press, 2016.

# 17

# Forced Conformity or Accommodation?

## *Reconciling Conscience and Difference in a Pluralistic Democracy*

MARK RIENZI

### INTRODUCTION

Liberal democracies tend to value two principles that can sometimes conflict: majority rule and religious diversity. In a democracy, members of the political community have generally agreed to be governed by the rules and requirements the majority enacts into law. Yet a society with true religious liberty will almost always produce religious diversity, as free people will inevitably reach varying beliefs about deeply important personal questions such as religion. That religious diversity will sometimes come into conflict with the will of the majority. In particular, some members of the political community may exercise their religious liberty to arrive at religious beliefs and practices that are incompatible with a legal obligation imposed by the majority. These religious minorities will not be able to conform their conduct to the majority's rules without violating their religious beliefs.

These conflicts tend to arise when the majority lawfully imposes a requirement that members of the political community must engage in, or refrain from, particular conduct. The classic example is a military draft in which the majority deems it necessary to require a defined subset of the community (such as all healthy males of a certain age) to bear arms. If the community includes some members who are religiously opposed to fighting in the military (either as a general matter or to a particular war) then a conflict must be resolved: Does the majority's rule control? Or should an exception be made for the religious objector?

Similar conflicts can occur in relation to other legal requirements, ranging from requirements for jury service in a death penalty case, obligations to take certain oaths or pledges, regulations of the medical profession, requirements related to school, mandatory appearance or dress codes in certain jobs, or regulations of the consumption of alcohol, the use of drugs, or the preparation of food. Where religious diversity exists, such requirements may conflict with obligations that some members of the political community view as matters of religious conscience.

In a pluralistic democracy, these conflicts are most common, and most acute, where they concern the practices of religious minorities, although sometimes they concern majority religions holding beliefs not accepted by a majority of lawmakers. Still, members of the majority are particularly unlikely to face government-imposed obligations that conflict with their conscience, precisely because the government operates by majority rule. It is the minorities who are most likely to have religious commitments that are either rejected or ignored by the majority.

How should a liberal and pluralistic society respond to such conflicts between lawfully enacted majority will and the conscience of religious believers who cannot comply with the law? The American experience presents two starkly different answers: forced conformity or accommodation. At times, American law has taken what might be called a "majority rules" approach, in which religious believers simply must accept the fact that, as minorities, they will at times be forced to conform their conduct to laws that require them to violate their religion. Alternatively, at other times, American law has taken what might be called an "accommodationist" approach, in which room is provided for people to live out varying religious beliefs, and the government is only permitted to force a violation of religion in narrow circumstances. Generally speaking, when courts embrace the majority rules approach, they tend to do so out of concern that an accommodationist approach would create anarchy or unfair preference, with every person a law unto himself or herself.

Although the United States has embraced different approaches at different times and for different issues, the overall arc of American law has been toward accommodation. That arc has not always been consistent – at times our governments have sought to exclude or even exterminate members of unpopular religions, as happened with the Mormons in the mid-1800s. And even today, our laws in some respects can lean toward forced conformity. But the overall story of the American experience with religious diversity is one of increasing accommodation.

That pattern of increasing accommodation reveals two simple truths about dealing with conscience in a pluralistic democracy. First, the common objection to the accommodationist approach – namely, that it will produce anarchy – turns out to be baseless. In many areas of life, and in many jurisdictions, we have now lived for decades with accommodationist approaches that allow broad protection for conscience but do not produce anarchy or anything like it. Second, experience shows that accommodating acts of conscience by people with minority beliefs and practices actually tends to be beneficial for the broader society. Our society is strongest when we can reap the benefits of all members of our diverse community contributing to society; and we suffer tangible losses when we exclude religious people and organizations.

In the end, it turns out that the proper response to the question is not particularly close: a liberal pluralistic society should respond to religious differences with an accommodationist approach that allows religious minorities to live out their beliefs in peace.

## TWO CONFLICTING APPROACHES

Before exploring these two different approaches in practice, it is useful to try to consider how each responds to conflicts between majority-imposed laws and minority religious conscience. In their own ways, each approach relies on values inherent in pluralistic democracies, but with different points of emphasis. And each has roots in the earliest experiences of European settlers in the New World.

### *Majority Rules Approach*

One response to conflicts between the law and conscience is to say that the fundamental principles of popular sovereignty, majority rule, and equal treatment require that religious minorities be forced to comply with the same majority-imposed laws that apply to everyone else. On this view, democratic "might makes right," so to speak: those who have the votes get to decide what behaviors are required or forbidden, and those who disagree with the majority's judgment must either conform their conduct or suffer the consequences. Minorities are of course permitted, like anyone else, to participate in the democratic process. But if and when they lose any particular fight in that process, their obligation is to obey the law just like everyone else or to face the punishment or exclusion that follows from refusal to obey. We can call this the "majority rules" approach to conflicts between conscience and the law.

### *Accommodationist Approach*

An alternative approach to conflicts between law and conscience would provide greater protection for religious minorities seeking to live according to their deeply held religious beliefs, even in the face of a contrary requirement imposed by the majority. Under this view, the last election or latest legislative vote is not necessarily the final word where compliance with the law would require someone to violate her conscience. Rather, even when the majority has spoken as a general matter, room is left for accommodating the conscience of religious minorities who cannot comply with a government-imposed requirement. Under this view, the government is only permitted to force someone to violate her conscience when it has a particularly strong reason for doing so and where less restrictive alternatives would fail to achieve some particularly important government goal. We can call this an "accommodationist" approach to conscience. Religious minorities do not always win under this approach; but the government is always forced at least to provide a strong justification before requiring a violation of conscience.

## HISTORICAL UNDERPINNINGS

From the arrival of the first European settlers, the question of how to deal with religious differences has been at the heart of the American experience. Many of the first European settlers had been persecuted religious minorities in Europe and came to the New World specifically in search of a place where they would be free to live their lives according to their own religious values. Having witnessed the sometimes horrific consequences of religious conflict in sixteenth- and seventeenth-century Europe, some of these settlers arrived with an explicit commitment to creating a religiously tolerant society in which at least the two dominant European religious groups of the time (Protestants and Catholics) could live together in harmony. Still others, like the members of the Virginia Company who settled at Jamestown, arrived with a charter from the crown to spread Christianity in the New World.

The resulting policies and practices were uneven. In New England, the Puritan pilgrims succeeded in finding a place where they themselves would be permitted to exercise their own religion without a hostile government punishing them for doing so. But the Puritans quickly demonstrated a somewhat limited commitment to religious liberty: *Puritans* were free to live out and profess their faith, but members of other minority faiths, including the Quakers, were to be whipped and expelled from the colony and into the wilderness. To be sure, the Puritans established a new society that was democratic; but they clearly followed the "majority rules" approach to dealing with religious differences.[1]

[1] See Kevin Hasson, *The Right to Be Wrong: Ending the Culture War over Religion in America* (San Francisco, CA: Encounter Books, 2005).

The experience in Maryland was slightly better, at least at the outset. There, the colony itself was established by a mix of Catholic and Protestant settlers who arrived together in 1634. Lord Baltimore (a Catholic) had been granted Maryland by King Charles I (a Protestant). The settlers had left a Europe in which Catholics and Protestants were often at war. But Lord Baltimore envisioned a society in which people of different faiths could coexist in peace. That approach was eventually codified in Maryland's "Toleration Act" in 1649, which guaranteed religious freedom to both Protestants and Catholics. For the time, this was a remarkably accommodationist approach (though the law was still quite hostile to non-Christians).[2]

Unfortunately, as with the Pilgrims in Massachusetts, the temptation to punish religious differences soon reared its head in Maryland. Within a few years, the Toleration Act was repealed, then later reinstated and repealed again shortly after the Glorious Revolution of 1689.[3] Eventually, Maryland enacted laws that punished those who failed to conform to the Church of England. Catholics could not vote or hold office for several generations; non-Christians were not permitted to hold office until 1826.[4] As with the Pilgrims, an initial impulse toward religious liberty and accommodation had devolved into the majority rules approach, in which religious minorities had to either conform to the will of the majority or suffer the consequences.

## THREE EXAMPLES OF HOW WE PROGRESSED TOWARD ACCOMMODATION

Thankfully, our early history of overt religious discrimination has largely faded away. There of course have been exceptions, such as the Mormon extermination orders and banishment to the Utah territory in the 1800s,[5] or even current disputes about whether the federal government has instituted a "Muslim ban" or not.[6] But in the main, the religious conscience question in the United States has become not whether we will allow members of

[2] Maryland Toleration Act (September 21, 1649), www.avalon.law.yale.edu/18th_century/maryland_toleration.asp.

[3] Kenneth Lasson, "Free Exercise in the Free State: Maryland's Role in Religious Liberty and the First Amendment," *Journal of Church and State* 31, no. 3 (1989): 419, 435.

[4] Edward Eitches, "Maryland's 'Jew Bill'," *American Jewish Historical Quarterly* 60, no. 3 (1971): 258–79.

[5] Governor Boggs's Extermination Order (October 27, 1838), Missouri Secretary of State, www.sos.mo.gov/archives/resources/findingaids/miscMormonRecords/eo.

[6] Luke Goodrich, "No Anti-Muslim Bias at Supreme Court: Constitution, Argued Properly, Protects All Religions," *The Hill*, April 5, 2019, www.thehill.com/opinion/judiciary/437575-no-anti-muslim-bias-at-supreme-court-constitution-argued-properly-protects.

various religions to live here but how the law should react when there is a conflict between minority religious conscience and efforts by the majority to enforce conformity on a particular issue.

In that respect, across a variety of issues and times, American history has shown a general trend toward accommodating religious differences. Below are three examples of areas in which we have, in different ways, moved toward an accommodationist approach: forced recitation of the pledge of allegiance, forced military service, and forced participation in medical care.

### *Forced Recital of the Pledge of Allegiance*

Perhaps the most abrupt juxtaposition of the majority rules approach and the accommodationist approach can be seen in the Supreme Court opinions dealing with whether children can be forced to say the Pledge of Allegiance. Indeed, in a somewhat dizzying pair of World War II–era cases, the Supreme Court in rapid succession both aggressively embraced the notion of forced conformity and then turned around and aggressively endorsed a constitutional requirement of accommodation.

Both cases involved Jehovah's Witness children who objected to saluting the American flag as a matter of conscience. Many Jehovah's Witnesses believed that saluting or pledging allegiance to the flag offends God, because it amounts to worship of a graven image.[7] In Nazi Germany, Hitler's government had persecuted Jehovah's Witnesses for their refusal to perform the Nazi salute, fly Nazi flags in their homes, or otherwise signal obedience to the temporal authorities. Tens of thousands of Witnesses were imprisoned in concentration camps for these behaviors. Many were forced to recant their religious beliefs; some were tortured and some died in the camps.[8]

Both out of solidarity with their persecuted coreligionists in Europe and from a belief that saluting the flag offends God, many Jehovah's Witnesses in the United States began refusing to say the pledge of allegiance in the 1930s.[9] The Witnesses were already viewed with suspicion and dislike in many places due to their public proselytizing, and they were viewed as unpatriotic for their act of conscience in refusing to pledge allegiance. When Jehovah's Witness

7 *West Virginia Bd. of Education* v. *Barnette*, 319 U.S. 624, 629–30 (1943).

8 Christine E. King, "Jehovah's Witnesses under Nazism," in *A Mosaic of Victims: Non-Jews Persecuted and Murdered by the Nazis*, ed. Michael Berenbaum (New York, NY: New York University Press, 1990), 188–93.

9 Jehovah's Witnesses, "Flag Salute, Voting, and Civilian Service (Appendix)," in *Keep Yourselves in God's Love* (Warwick, NY: Watch Tower Bible and Tract Society of Pennsylvania, 2016), 214–15, www.jw.org/en/library/books/gods-love/.

children refused to say the pledge, they were often expelled from school. Sometimes, teachers physically forced their arms into what was then a stiff-arm Nazi-style salute to the flag.[10] Some Witnesses were tarred and feathered, paraded through town, and forced to drink castor oil; others lost their jobs or had their businesses boycotted.[11]

### *Gobitis* and Forced Conformity

In 1940, the Supreme Court heard the case of *Minersville School District* v. *Gobitis*.[12] The Gobitis children had, on grounds of religious conscience, refused to salute the flag. Initially, the school district did not have any rule for punishing children who refused to pledge allegiance to the flag. But in response to the refusal of the Gobitis children, the school board quickly enacted a rule allowing for the expulsion of children who would not conform. The Gobitis family sued, arguing that the school board had violated the children's rights under the First Amendment by forcing them to violate their conscience.

The Court began its opinion by noting that the conflict between liberty of conscience and government authority was particularly sensitive – balancing the "liberty of conscience" with government authority is a "grave responsibility" and the "severest test" for the judiciary.[13] The Court explained that religious conscience – "the affirmative pursuit of one's convictions about the ultimate mystery of the universe and man's relation to it" – is "beyond the reach of law."[14] But the Court explained that sometimes the religious conscience of one person "may bring his conception of religious duty into conflict with the secular interests of his fellow-men."[15] In that circumstance, society must "reconcile two rights in order to prevent either from destroying the other."[16]

The way to reconcile those two rights, according to the *Gobitis* Court, is to say that the will of the majority wins, regardless of the protections of the First Amendment or the importance of conscience, and regardless of whatever

[10] Such incidents still occur to Jehovah's Witnesses and other children who refuse to salute the flag. See Carol Kuruvilla, "Florida Teacher Suspended after Forcing Jehovah's Witness Student to Say Pledge of Allegiance," *New York Daily News*, November 16, 2013.

[11] The American Civil Liberties Union (ACLU), *The Persecution of Jehovah's Witnesses: The Record of Violence against a Religious Organization Unparalleled in America since the Attack on the Mormons* (New York, NY: American Civil Liberties Union, 1941), 6–21.

[12] *Minersville School Dist.* v. *Gobitis*, 310 U.S. 586 (1940).

[13] Ibid., 591.

[14] Ibid., 593.

[15] Ibid.

[16] Ibid., 594.

"leeway should be given to the claims of religious faith."[17] The Court explained that "[c]onscientious scruples have not, in the course of the long struggle for religious toleration, relieved the individual from obedience to a general law not aimed at the promotion or restriction of religious beliefs."[18] In other words, while the Court might allow conscience to defeat majority will if the point of the law was to advance or punish religious beliefs, it did not think conscience could be acceptable grounds for disobedience to a law enacted for less targeted purposes. In that circumstance, the majority's will must win, because "[t]he mere possession of religious convictions which contradict the relevant concerns of a political society" cannot relieve the citizen from the obligation to conform to the will of the majority.[19]

As the Court saw it, religious conscience must yield where the majority has deemed a required action "essential to secure and maintain that orderly, tranquil, and free society without which religious toleration itself is unattainable."[20] The Court viewed "[n]ational unity" as "the basis of national security" and thought the legislative majority had the "right to select the appropriate means" for instilling national unity.[21] The Court felt itself obligated to defer to the choices of the democratically elected school board majority, even when it forced a violation of religious conscience.

In this sense, *Gobitis* can be seen as the ultimate forced conformity or majority rules case. It is not that the Court thinks religious conscience is unimportant or that it is not allowing a serious burden to be imposed on Jehovah's Witness children. It is just that the Court views deference to the majority's power to enact laws of general applicability to be more important. The Gobitis children therefore received no special protection for their act of conscience, and they would either have to recite the pledge as required by the majority or be expelled from school.

The public reaction to the *Gobitis* decision was strong. In some respects, the public viewed the decision as allowing "open season on Jehovah's Witnesses," with hundreds of attacks. Mobs assaulted Jehovah's Witnesses, burned down their places of worship, boycotted their businesses, and destroyed their property. In the conflict between religious conscience and the majority, *Gobitis* seemed to embolden the majority's belief that it could and should punish dissenters, even outside the parameters of the law.[22]

[17] Ibid.
[18] Ibid.
[19] Ibid., 594–95.
[20] Ibid., 595.
[21] Ibid.
[22] ACLU, *Persecution of Jehovah's Witnesses*, 6–21.

**_Barnette_'s Turn toward Accommodation**

Just three years after *Gobitis*, the Supreme Court accepted another chance to address the issue of conscience in another forced pledge of allegiance case, *West Virginia Board of Education* v. *Barnette*.[23]

Like *Gobitis*, *Barnette* involved a Jehovah's Witness child who refused to pledge allegiance to the flag. Emboldened by the Court's denial of conscience rights in *Gobitis*, West Virginia had enacted a statute that required every student and teacher in the state to recite the pledge and deemed any failure to do so punishable "insubordination."[24] Students who refused were expelled from school and forbidden by law to be readmitted unless they complied. Expelled students were also treated as "unlawfully absent" and therefore "delinquent" and eligible to be sent "to reformatories maintained for criminally inclined juveniles."[25] Their parents could be prosecuted and face fines and prison.

Unlike *Gobitis*, however, the *Barnette* Court took a much more accommodationist approach to the conscientious objection of the Jehovah's Witness children. *Gobitis*, in embracing a forced conformity approach, had taken the view that the political majority should decide how best to instill patriotism in citizens. *Barnette*, by contrast, recognized that the "very purpose of a Bill of Rights" was to place certain subjects "beyond the reach of majorities and officials" and enshrine them as "legal principles to be applied by the courts."[26] Rather than letting bare majority rule control, *Barnette* emphasized that "fundamental rights may not be submitted to a vote; they depend on the outcome of no elections."[27]

*Barnette* emphasized that its conclusions did not rest on a finding that the pledge or patriotism were unimportant. Instead, it emphasized that the "freedom to differ is not limited to things that do not matter much" because "[t]hat would be a mere shadow of freedom."[28] Rather, the freedom of conscience must extend to the "right to differ as to things that touch the heart of the existing order."[29] Government officials – even those elected by or acting at the command of majorities – cannot "prescribe what shall be orthodox in politics, nationalism, religion, or other matters of opinion or force citizens to confess by word or act their faith therein."[30]

[23] Barnette, 319 U.S. at 624.
[24] Ibid., 629.
[25] Ibid.
[26] Ibid., 638.
[27] Ibid.
[28] Ibid., 642.
[29] Ibid.
[30] Ibid.

In these respects, *Barnette* adopted a highly accommodationist approach to conscience claims. The Court understood the entire purpose of the First Amendment – and its protections for speech, religion, and assembly – to be to ensure that these subjects were *not* controllable by the majority, but instead were fundamental rights beyond the reach of everyday politics.

### *Forced Military Service*

The rapid about-face and embrace of accommodationism in the pledge cases can be contrasted with a much slower and more incremental march toward accommodation on the question of compulsory military service.

From the nation's founding, our military has needed to deal with the question of citizens who were religiously opposed to bearing arms. In 1789, George Washington wrote to a Quaker correspondent:

> I assure you very explicitly, that in my opinion the conscientious scruples of all men should be treated with great delicacy . . . it is my wish and desire, that the laws may always be extensively accommodated to them, as a due regard to the protection and essential interests of the nation may justify and permit.[31]

Consistent with Washington's sentiment, the nation's history of military draft laws shows an evolving effort to find ways to accommodate at least some individuals who raise conscience-based objections to military service. This protection has never been complete or absolute. But the overall arc of this history shows a long-standing effort to protect conscientious objectors to military service, with steadily broader protections being introduced over time.[32]

Many early American state constitutions and conscription statutes contained conscience-protection clauses for at least some religious objectors.[33] These protections varied: many were limited to members of particular religious denominations, and many required objectors to pay a fee considered "equivalent" to personal service in the military.[34] While many colonial and

31 George Washington, "George Washington to the Religious Society Called Quakers (October 1789)," in *George Washington on Religious Liberty and Mutual Understanding*, ed. Edward Frank Humphrey (New York, NY: National Conference of Jews and Christians, 1932), 11.

32 The history presented in this subsection is distilled from my longer article, Mark L. Rienzi, "The Constitutional Right Not to Kill," *Emory Law Journal* 62, no. 1 (2012): 121.

33 See Claire Marblestone, "A Matter of Conscience: *United States v. Seeger* and the Supreme Court's Historical Failure to Define Conscientious Objector Status under the First Amendment," *Hastings Constitutional Law Quarterly* 38, no. 1 (2010): 204, n.18.

34 Pennsylvania, Delaware, New Hampshire, Vermont, and New York had constitutional provisions granting exemptions from conscription laws for conscientious objectors. See

state governments protected a right of conscientious objection to military service, efforts to expressly include such a provision in the Federal Constitution failed. Early drafts of the Second Amendment stated that "no person religiously scrupulous shall be compelled to bear arms."[35] While this proposed amendment was approved by the required two-thirds supermajority in the House, the Senate rejected this language, and our current Second Amendment is silent on the issue.[36]

The development of federal conscientious objector laws began with the Civil War. As the Supreme Court explained in *United States* v. *Seeger*, the Federal Militia Act of 1862 left control of conscription primarily to the states.[37] However, pursuant to General Order No. 99, later enacted as the Federal Conscription Act of 1863, the federal government struck "from the conscription list those who were exempted by the States."[38] The federal system also "established a commutation or substitution system fashioned from earlier state enactments."[39] This reliance on state conscientious objector laws ended with the Federal Conscription Act of 1863. At that point "the Federal Government occupied the field entirely."[40] In the 1864 Draft Act, the federal government directly "extended exemptions to those conscientious objectors who were members of religious denominations opposed to the bearing of arms and who were prohibited from doing so by the articles of faith of their denominations."[41]

To be sure, the protections for conscience during the Civil War era did not exempt objectors from aiding the war effort entirely. The Draft Act instead provided that bona fide conscientious objectors would "be assigned by the Secretary of War to duty in the hospitals, or to the care of freedmen."[42]

generally Ellis M. West, "The Right to Religion-Based Exemptions in Early America: The Case of Conscientious Objectors to Conscription," *Journal of Law and Religion* 10, no. 2 (1994): 375.

35 Joseph Gales, ed., *Annals of Congress*, vol. 1 (1789–91) (Washington, DC: Gales and Seaton 1834): 779.

36 Vincent Phillip Muñoz provides a detailed overview of the treatment of conscience language during Congress's consideration of the Second Amendment. Vincent Phillip Muñoz, "The Original Meaning of the Free Exercise Clause: The Evidence from the First Congress," *Harvard Journal of Law and Public Policy* 31, no. 3 (2008): 1109–19.

37 *United States* v. *Seeger*, 380 U.S. 163, 170 (1965).

38 Ibid.

39 Ibid.

40 Ibid.

41 Ibid. In the same year, the Confederate government extended similar protections for conscientious objectors.

42 Draft Act of 1864, chap. 13, § 17, 13 Stat. 6, 9, repealing Act of March 3, 1863, chap. 75, § 2, 12 Stat. 73, which did not contain a conscientious objector provision.

A conscientious objector could obtain relief from military service altogether only if he agreed to pay the government a fee that would assist wounded soldiers.[43]

When the federal government instituted a draft again in World War I, the provisions governing conscientious objectors largely tracked the 1864 Draft Act, which was tied to membership in particular denominations that opposed military service. In World War I, however, the law encountered criticism for not accommodating "individual objectors," that is, those without ties to an organized religion. President Woodrow Wilson accordingly issued an Executive Order that guided the Act's implementation to apply equally to "other conscientious scruples" along with religious objectors.[44]

The expansion of conscientious objection to include individual objectors who were not part of a peace church prompted the military to establish a board of inquiry that set out to determine the sincerity of the objector's beliefs.[45] The newfound standing for individual conscience objections not based on formal religious teaching presented a "troublesome problem" to board members.[46] Such objectors relied on their own interpretation of the Bible, or certain biblical passages – placing the reasonableness and consistency of their conscientious objection at issue.[47]

In the modern era (from World War II to the present), the Selective Service Act allowed an individual to base a conscientious objection on "religious training and belief," which the Act defined as "an individual's belief in a relation to a Supreme Being involving duties superior to those arising from any human relation, but does not include essentially political, sociological, or philosophical views or a merely personal moral code."[48] The Act required that the objector be "conscientiously opposed to participation in war in any form."[49] Over time, the Court interpreted the Selective Service Act of 1940 to broaden the definition of "religious training and belief."[50]

43 Ibid.

44 President Wilson's Executive Order of March 20, 1918 is reprinted in Walter Guest Kellogg, *The Conscientious Objector* (New York, NY: Boni and Liveright, 1919), 17–21.

45 Kellogg notes various factors considered to determine if an individual objector was entitled to an exemption, including whether he was "in appearance and bearing an honest man." Ibid., 28–29.

46 Ibid., 29.

47 Ibid.

48 Selective Service Act of 1948, chap. 625, 62 Stat. 604, 612–13 (amending the Selective Training and Service Act of 1940, chap. 720, 54 Stat. 885 [expired March 31, 1947]).

49 Ibid.

50 See Alfred J. Sciarrino and Kenneth L. Deutsch, "Conscientious Objection to War: Heroes to Human Shields," *Brigham Young University Journal of Public Law* 18, no. 1 (2003): 86–87.

For example, in *United States* v. *Seeger*, the Court considered Congress's choice to "deliberately broaden[]" the scope of objections by allowing individuals to reference a "Supreme Being" rather than "God" as their source of objection in the Selective Service Act.[51] After reviewing the statutory developments under the Act, the Court stated a broad test for conscientious objection, which includes not only religious objections but also moral and ethical objections: A sincere and meaningful belief that occupies in the life of its possessor a place parallel to that filled by the God of those admittedly qualifying for the exemption comes within the statutory definition. The Seeger Court recognized that the exemption provision needed to "deal[] with the beliefs of different individuals who will articulate them in a multitude of ways,"[52] and focused its test simply on the sincerity of the individual's conscientious objection.[53]

Even this broadened approach to conscientious objection remains focused on individuals who are opposed to participating in any war, as opposed to those who are opposed to participating in a particular war.[54] This leaves certain people who have conscientious objections to participation in particular wars – for example, someone who subscribes to "just war theory," which condemns some, but not other, wars – without protection.[55] This approach to conscientious objection remains the rule today, even within our all-volunteer military in which soldiers arrive without being drafted.[56]

### *Forced Participation in Abortion*

Unlike either the abrupt about-face and embrace of the accommodationist approach in the pledge context, or the long, slow, but steady development and expansion of conscience rights in the military context, accommodation for conscience rights related to abortion has remained remarkably strong from the start. Even before the Supreme Court established a constitutional right to

51 380 U.S. 163, 175 (1965).
52 Ibid., 184.
53 See ibid., 185.
54 See *Gillette* v. *United States*, 401 U.S. 437, 443 (1971) (holding that the Selective Service Act would be "strain[ed]" to be applied to objectors who are only opposed to a specific war, such as the Vietnam Conflict, and that the objection status applies to those opposed to "participation in all war" generally).
55 See, e.g., ibid., 439–41.
56 See U.S. Dep't of Def., Instruction No. 1300.06 (May 5, 2007), www.dtic.mil/whs/directives/corres/pdf/130006p.pdf.

abortion in *Roe* v. *Wade*, states that permitted abortion had established laws to protect conscientious objectors from forced participation in abortions.[57]

That trend of protecting conscientious objectors to abortions continued and dramatically expanded in the aftermath of *Roe*. Today, virtually every state in the country has some sort of statute protecting individuals and, in many cases, entities who refuse to participate in providing abortions. Some states expressly limit this protection to the practice of abortion, which is treated specially. Other states protect conscience for other procedures as well.

At the federal level, Congress likewise took almost immediate action after *Roe* to protect physicians and hospitals from being forced to perform abortions. In particular, as part of legislation known as the Church Amendment, Congress clarified that recipients of certain federal funds were not required to provide abortions and that those facilities may not be required to perform or participate in, or refer to any source for, any medical procedure that results in artificial insemination, sterilization, or termination of pregnancy.[58] In the years since *Roe*, Congress has enacted additional laws designed to protect healthcare workers who refuse to participate in abortions. For example, in 1996, Congress amended the Public Health Service Act to prohibit "[a]bortion-related discrimination in governmental activities regarding training and licensing of physicians."[59] In particular, the law prevents governments from discriminating against healthcare providers who refuse to provide a range of abortion-related services and protects doctors, medical students, and health training programs.[60] This protects refusals to participate in abortion or abortion-related services for any reason, and it is not limited to religious objections. Likewise, in 2005, Congress enacted the Weldon Amendment, designed to strip federal funding from any institution that forces an individual to participate in an abortion against his or her will.[61]

Thus, in a variety of ways, and at both the state and federal levels, legislators acted quickly, decisively, and at times nearly unanimously to protect conscience rights in the wake of *Roe*. These protections take a strongly accommodationist approach, and stand firmly against the notion that a majority rules or forced conformity approach could be appropriate on the question of abortion.

57 The history presented in this subsection is distilled from my longer article, Mark L. Rienzi, "The Constitutional Right Not to Participate in Abortions: Roe, Casey, and the Fourteenth Amendment Rights of Healthcare Providers," *Notre Dame L. Review* 87 (2011): 1.

58 Church Amendments, 42 U.S.C. § 300a-7.

59 Public Health Service Act § 245, 42 U.S.C. § 238n (1996).

60 Ibid.

61 Weldon Amendment, Consolidated Appropriations Act, Pub. L. No. 110-161, § 508(d), 121 Stat. 1844, 2209 (2007).

## CONSCIENCE AND DIFFERENCE: SOME LESSONS FROM THE AMERICAN EXPERIENCE WITH RELIGIOUS DIVERSITY

The American experience in dealing with claims of conscience related to the Pledge of Allegiance, military service, and abortion demonstrates that it is possible for a liberal and pluralistic democracy to find ways to allow room for individuals and organizations to exercise conscience, even when that conscience is opposed to the majority and the current legal regime. The conscience rights described above have not created anarchy, and they have not undermined our overall democratic approach to governance.

These experiences can be, and in fact have been, generalized to broadly cover other types of religious objections. For a time, the Supreme Court adopted an accommodationist approach to claims asserted under the Free Exercise Clause, only allowing the government to force someone to violate religious conscience if the government had a very strong need to do so.[62] As a matter of constitutional interpretation, the Court abandoned this approach in the 1990 case of *Employment Division* v. *Smith*. There, the Court rejected the notion that the First Amendment requires religious exemptions, arguing that "[a]ny society adopting such a system would be courting anarchy."[63]

The Court was well aware of the consequences of rejecting an accommodationist approach and leaving religious minorities to fend for themselves in the political process. In particular, the Court explained that it believed that religious minorities would be least likely to have their rights protected but found such a result a necessary aspect of life in a democracy.[64] But the Court thought that this "unavoidable consequence of democratic government" was preferable "to a system in which each conscience is a law unto itself."[65]

Ironically, when the Supreme Court took this majority rules approach, it was the democratically elected legislature that decided to impose a more accommodationist (and less majority-friendly) approach. That reaction has provided us with decades of experience that have now proven, beyond any serious challenge, that an accommodationist approach does not create anarchy.

62 See, e.g., *Sherbert* v. *Verner*, 374 U.S. 398 (1963).
63 *Employment Div., Dep't of Human Res. of Oregon* v. *Smith*, 494 U.S. 872, 888 (1990).
64 Ibid., 890 ("It may fairly be said that leaving accommodation to the political process will place at a relative disadvantage those religious practices that are not widely engaged in.").
65 Ibid.

That experience has been provided under the 1993 Religious Freedom Restoration Act, or RFRA.[66] RFRA was enacted by Congress, and signed by President Clinton, in direct response to the *Smith* decision. Soon thereafter, more than half of the states have adopted similar statutes[67] or interpreted their constitutional religious freedom provisions to apply essentially the same conscience-protective test that RFRA applies to federal laws. Under RFRA, the government is required to take an accommodationist approach to religious differences – the majority cannot force the minority to violate his or her religious beliefs absent a compelling need to do so and no other less restrictive way to achieve its goals.

Our experience in the quarter century since RFRA's enactment now proves broadly the lesson of our specific conscience examples discussed in this chapter: the accommodationist approach does not produce anarchy. Indeed, it turns out that RFRA laws are most often used by religious minorities[68] and tend to be under-enforced.[69] And because they are only applicable in some states but not others, we can tell that they don't create anarchy, because citizens frequently cross from RFRA to non-RFRA states without ever realizing that one allows for broad religious exemptions and the other does not.[70]

Ultimately, these experiences pose an insuperable challenge to those who would argue for a forced conformity approach, whereby citizens must yield to the will of the majority, regardless of their conscience. As a normative matter, liberal societies should only force citizens to violate their deeply held beliefs when it is strictly necessary. And we now know from experience that our society can and does frequently protect individual conscience in a wide range of circumstances, without either causing anarchy or threatening the general principle of majority rule.

66 The Religious Freedom Restoration Act of 1993, Pub. L. No. 103-141, 107 Stat. 1488 (1993).

67 National Conference of State Legislatures "State Religious Freedom Restoration Acts," May 4, 2017, www.ncsl.org/research/civil-and-criminal-justice/state-rfra-statutes.aspx.

68 Luke W. Goodrich and Rachel Busick, "Sex, Drugs, and Eagle Feathers: An Empirical Study of Federal Religious Freedom Cases," *Seton Hall Law Review* 48 (2018): 353.

69 See Christopher C. Lund, "RFRA, State RFRAs, and Religious Minorities," *San Diego Law Review* 53, no. 1 (2016).

70 Mark L. Rienzi, "The Case for Religious Exemptions – Whether Religion Is Special or Not," review of *Why Tolerate Religion?*, by Brian Leiter and *Defending American Religious Neutrality*, by Andrew Koppelman, *Harvard Law Review* 127, no. 5 (March 2014): 1395, 1415. There this point is made:

> The problem with this argument is that we have now had enough experience under religious exemption regimes to know that they do not create anarchy .... No serious claim can be made that these systems have produced anarchy or anything like it. Indeed, it is far more likely that none of us even notices when we travel from an exemption state to a nonexemption state and back.

The accommodationist approach also brings an additional benefit. If we pursued a majority rules approach as to matters of conscience, what we would eventually achieve is the banishment of people of good conscience who cannot comply with a particular demand, whether it be assisting with capital punishment, performing an abortion, or serving in the military. We know, for example, that the American College of Obstetricians and Gynecologists estimates that we will have a shortage of 9,000 OB-GYNs by 2030. Expelling large portions of that profession because they will not perform abortions will result in less healthcare for everyone.[71] The same is true for closing Catholic hospitals for refusing to participate in assisted suicides or abortions, or forcing religious pharmacists to close stores because they will not sell emergency contraception. Our society is better and stronger when we can obtain the contributions of all these people and organizations, even if they cannot provide every service every time it is requested. We would be weaker and poorer if we used the law to force conformity or exit.

## CONCLUSION

The case for an accommodationist approach to religious difference is supported by history, required by federal law under RFRA, and necessary to our survival as a liberal and pluralistic democracy. The accommodationist view is both practical and just. It allows us to order our society and to protect the fundamental rights of minorities. It creates not anarchy but a system in which people with different beliefs can live together in social harmony. If we are serious about valuing religious liberty, we must also learn to live with the religious diversity that liberty produces, rather than trying to use the sheer power of the majority to punish that diversity and force conformity.

## RECOMMENDED READING

Anderson, Ryan T., John Corvino, and Sherif Girgis. *Debating Religious Liberty and Discrimination*. New York, NY: Oxford University Press, 2017.

Barringer Gordon, Sarah. *The Mormon Question: Polygamy and Constitutional Conflict in Nineteenth-Century America*. Chapel Hill, NC: University of North Carolina Press, 2002.

[71] In one recent poll, more than 90 percent of healthcare providers said they would leave the profession if forced to violate their religion. See Paul Strand, "Gender Surgery? Abortion? Doctors & Nurses Say 'They'll Quit' if Forced to Violate Their Beliefs," Christian Broadcasting Network, September 18, 2019, www1.cbn.com/cbnnews/us/2019/september/many-doctors-and-nurses-say-theyll-quit-if-compelled-to-do-medical-procedures-they-morally-oppose.

Goodrich, Luke. *Free to Believe: The Battle over Religious Liberty in America*. NewYork, NY: Multnomah, 2019.
George, Robert. *Conscience and Its Enemies: Confronting the Dogmas of Liberal Secularism*. Wilmington, DE: Intercollegiate Studies Institute Books, 2016.
Hamburger, Philip. *Separation of Church and State*. Cambridge, MA: Harvard University Press, 2004.
Hasson, Kevin Seamus. *The Right to Be Wrong*. San Francisco, CA: Encounter Books, 2005.
Lasson, Kenneth. "Free Exercise in the Free State: Maryland's Role in Religious Liberty and the First Amendment." *Journal of Church and State* 31 (1989): 419–49.
McConnell, Michael. "Why Is Religious Liberty the 'First Freedom'?" *Cardozo Law Review* 21, no. 4 (February 2000): 1243–65.
Paul VI. *Nostra Aetate* (Declaration on the Relation of the Church to Non-Christian Religions). October 29, 1965.
Paulsen, Michael Stokes, and Luke Paulsen. *The Constitution: An Introduction*. New York, NY: Basic Books, 2015.
Rienzi, Mark L. "The Case for Religious Exemptions – Whether Religion Is Special or Not." Review of *Why Tolerate Religion?*, by Brian Leiter and *Defending American Religious Neutrality*, by Andrew Koppelman. *Harvard Law Review* 127, no. 5 (2014): 1395–1418.
Wardle, Lynn D. "Protection of Health-Care Providers' Rights of Conscience in American Law: Present, Past, and Future." *Ave Maria Law Review* 9, no. 1 (2011): 1–46.
Washington, George. Letter to the Hebrew Congregation in Newport, Rhode Island, August 18, 1790. In *The Papers of George Washington*, edited by W. W Abbot, et al., 6:285. Charlottesville, VA: University of Virginia Press, 1987.
West, John G. *The Politics of Revelation and Reason: Religion and Civic Life in the New Nation*. Lawrence, KS: University Press of Kansas, 1996.
Wilken, Robert Louis. *Liberty in the Things of God: The Christian Origins of Religious Freedom*. New Haven, CT: Yale University Press, 2019.

# 18

# Christian Conscience and Sexual Expression Rights

HELEN M. ALVARÉ

## INTRODUCTION

One of the most notable developments concerning Christian conscience in the late twentieth and early twenty-first centuries is the frequency and intensity with which Christian conscience claims clash with newly articulated rights of sexual expression. When I speak of sexual expression, I am referring to the definition from a leading contemporary account of sexual practices: "Any mutually voluntary activity with another person that involves genital contact and sexual excitement or arousal."[1] I am also referring to persons' publicly expressed sexual orientations and their subjective beliefs about sexual identity, as well as to acts and practices shaping or manifesting sexual behaviors. These include contraception and abortion, which separate sex from pregnancy or childbirth and promise to reduce the weight and "risks" of sex, and non-marital cohabitation and same-sex marriage, which publicly manifest sexual relationships.

The collision between sexual expression and Christian conscience is particularly characteristic of the West – Europe and the United States – and of parts of Oceania (especially New Zealand and Australia). I claim that it is a relatively new phenomenon because laws and social mores about sex were more or less overlapping with Christian convictions prior to the mid-twentieth century. Furthermore, prior to this time, other types of disagreements between Christians and the state assumed greater prominence. These concerned conscientious objections to, inter alia: military service, some forms of compulsory education of children, public expressions of religion, oath swearing, holy day observances, and the use of banned or restricted substances in religious

[1] Edward O. Laumann et al., *The Social Organization of Sexuality: Sexual Practices in the United States*, rev. ed. (Chicago, IL: University of Chicago Press, 2000), 67.

services. These clashes are still with us today but regularly overshadowed by conflicts involving rights of sexual expression.

Demands for conscience exemptions to laws supporting sexual expression first emerged prominently around the 1970s when abortion became a legal right and closely associated in the public mind with the movement for women's equality. Immediately, many medical personnel and institutions and some health insurers asked to be recused from cooperating with abortion.

Conscience objections were later raised to housing nondiscrimination laws protecting unmarried cohabitants. Most recently, Christians and others have demanded exemptions in connection with laws adding "sexual orientation" and "gender identity" to nondiscrimination laws, legalizing same-sex marriage, and instituting protections and benefits for transgender persons.

Sexual expression norms do not play a small role in Christianity. From the beginning of Christianity, Christians' practices of virginity, chastity, marital fidelity and permanence, and their rejection of abortion, same-sex relations, and exposing newborn children to die, stood out against a backdrop of contrary Greco-Roman practices.[2] Christianity understands its prescriptions concerning sex not as extrinsic disciplines unrelated to the core of faith, but rather as respect for God's creation and as crucial signposts and glimpses reflecting core aspects of the faith: how God intends human beings to know and understand His love, how human beings are made in God's "image and likeness," and how human beings are to love God and one another.[3] Christian norms about abortion are additionally tied to the sacred command never to kill.

For their part, supporters of the newer sexual expression norms understand these as tightly bound up with human beings' identity and dignity. Painting with a broad brush, whereas even sixty years ago it would have been common to think about permitted or forbidden sexual acts or interests, today – as described by philosopher Michel Foucault and law professor Chai Feldblum[4] – there is a strong inclination to think of sexual acts as an

[2] See Kyle Harper, *From Shame to Sin: The Christian Transformation of Sexual Morality in Late Antiquity* (Cambridge, MA: Harvard University Press, 2013).

[3] See N. T. Wright, "From Genesis to Revelation: An Anglican Perspective," in *Not Just Good but Beautiful: The Complementary Relationship between Man and Woman*, eds. Steven Lopes and Helen Alvaré (Walden, NY: Plough Publishing, 2015).

[4] Michel Foucault, "Right of Death and Power over Life," in *The History of Sexuality, Volume I: An Introduction*, trans. Robert Hurley (New York, NY: Penguin Books, 1978), 133–59, 156; Chai R. Feldblum, "Moral Conflict and Conflicting Liberties," in *Same-Sex Marriage and Religious Liberty: Emerging Conflicts*, eds. Douglas Laycock, Anthony R. Picarello Jr., and Robin Fretwell Wilson (Lanham, MD: The Becket Fund for Religious Liberty and Rowman & Littlefield, 2008).

important part of a person's very self-definition and membership in a community. For this reason and others discussed below, many laws and movements and institutions valorize sex – that is, credit it with achieving profound human goods such as dignity, freedom, equality, and identity. Opposition to any form of sexual expression is consequently regularly interpreted as antipathy to *persons*.

Given the importance of sexual expression to supporters of the new norms *and* to Christians it is not surprising that there are so many conflicts between Christian conscience and laws and cultural forces that not only permit but valorize same-sex relations, free choice of sexual identity, and sex unlinked to marriage or children by means of contraception and abortion. It is worth remarking, too, that the exponential growth in government regulation in all of the countries discussed here[5] puts the state and Christian conscience more often on a collision course in the arena of sexual expression.

More than a few features of the current conflicts between Christian conscience and state power respecting sexual expression are common across all of these countries. In order accurately but briefly to address the most important, this chapter will do the following: first, it will describe the types of sexual expression laws and regulations that have arisen over approximately the last sixty years. Second, it will sketch the leading cultural ideas and movements interacting with the law and valorizing sexual expression over roughly the same time period. Third, it will summarize Christian doctrine about sexual expression sufficiently for the purpose of highlighting the most significant points of disagreement. Fourth, it will suggest some of the common questions and legal features of this clash across regions. And fifth, it will conclude, with several thoughts about matters likely to influence the future shape and intensity of the clash between Christian conscience and sexual expression rights.

## SEXUAL EXPRESSION LAWS AND POLICIES

On its face, it would seem that sexual expression is a matter of private behavior, not public law. It concerns personal choices about sexual partners and acts. It also concerns: whether or not to separate sex from procreation or

[5] See Philip Hamburger, *Is Administrative Law Unlawful?* (Chicago, IL: University of Chicago Press, 2015); Giandomenico Majone, "The Rise of the Regulatory State in Europe," *West European Politics* 17, no. 3 (1994): 77–101; Regulation Taskforce, Commonwealth of Australia, "Rethinking Regulation: Report of the Taskforce on Reducing Regulatory Burdens on Business – Report to the Prime Minister and the Treasurer," 2006.

childbirth, via contraception or abortion; whether to hold oneself out as a person of a particular sexual orientation and/or of the opposite biological sex; and whether to seek medical intervention to transform gender identity.

Yet, today, sexual expression is frequently the subject of public laws and policies. Corporations and other public institutions and figures also adopt and communicate positions on sexual expression.

On reflection, it is not difficult to detect public dimensions of sexual decisions and behaviors. In the past – in the name of states' "police powers" encompassing "health, safety, welfare and morals" – states banned or limited contraception, abortion, adultery, nonmarital sex ("fornication"), cohabitation between unmarried partners, and sexual acts between persons of the same sex. Laws were also designed to discourage "illegitimacy" – as nonmarital birth was then called – and divorce.[6] Many of these laws had mixed motives, ranging from upholding shared morality, to defending unborn life, to avoiding state expenditures on nonmarital children. Some likely also had the purpose of avoiding children's suffering – financially, emotionally, and otherwise – although there did not exist fifty years ago even a fraction of the voluminous literature available today concerning the relationships between family structure and children's well-being.

Generally speaking, during this earlier period, corporations, the media, the entertainment industry, and the academy, alongside Christian churches, supported the perspectives manifested in these laws and policies.[7]

Today, sexual expression is a public matter for different reasons. Foremost among them is that legal rights to sexual expression – including virtually every sexual expression previously banned or limited, excluding adultery – are closely associated with currently ascendant values of equality, freedom, and individual dignity.[8]

Public laws concerning sexual expression initially had a libertarian cast. These involved overthrowing prior bans and permitting citizens – often in the name of privacy or personal health – legal access to contraception, abortion, cohabitation, homosexual relations, and most recently, state-recognized same-sex marriage.

But the laws and policies that followed were far less libertarian. In the name of allowing fellow citizens to exercise their sexual expression rights, many demanded cooperation from individual citizens or institutions. And as noted above, the state closely linked these rights with the vindication of

6 See Robert E. Rodes Jr., *On Law and Chastity* (Durham, NC: Carolina Academic Press, 2006).

7 Ibid.

8 Roger Trigg, *Equality, Freedom & Religion* (Oxford: Oxford University Press, 2013); Helen M. Alvaré, "Religious Freedom versus Sexual Expression: A Guide," *Journal of Law & Religion* 30 (2015): 475–95.

extraordinarily important social values. Consequently, religious conscientious objectors were quickly labeled bigots or retrograde.

It is impossible within the confines of one chapter to provide an exhaustive or exact chronological listing of all of the laws in the West and Oceania overturning prior norms and embracing new forms of sexual expression. It is possible, however, to offer a general timeline of the law's movement toward more, and more coercive, sexual expression laws.

Beginning in the second half of the twentieth century, many countries that had banned or limited the sale and use of contraception lifted those bans, first for married and later for single persons. Soon after, abortion was legalized, albeit some countries continue to impose limits, for example, in terms of gestational weeks or the circumstances leading to the pregnancy. Over time, laws banning adultery, non-marital cohabitation, and fornication were increasingly unenforced, selectively enforced, or overturned. Laws concerning homosexual relations proceeded similarly.[9]

In the last decades of the twentieth century, governments ceased characterizing legal rights to contraception and abortion strictly as health or anti-poverty measures and began framing them as tools to achieve women's equal rights. Over time, contraception and abortion mandates were inserted into more insurance plans, health care and training protocols, and government grants and aid programs. Questions immediately arose concerning the ability of medical personnel or schools or hospitals to recuse themselves from the practice or training of contraception and abortion, whether insurance suppliers could refuse to insure for contraception or abortion, and the conscience rights concerning sexual expression of private entities receiving government grants or contracts.

During the later twentieth and early twenty-first centuries, some housing and employment nondiscrimination laws began including "marital status" (alongside more traditional categories of race, sex, religion, etc.) to the set of specially protected categories. Some jurisdictions interpreted marital status to foreclose discrimination against non-marital cohabiters. Some objecting landowners and employers won disputes on the grounds of religious conscience, and some lost.[10]

[9] See Joanne Sweeny, "Undead Statutes: The Rise, Fall and Continuing Uses of Adultery and Fornication Criminal Laws," *Loyola University of Chicago Law Journal* 46 (2014): 127–73; For a history of legislation concerning homosexual relations in the United States and Europe, see *Lawrence* v. *Texas*, 539 U.S. 558, 569–73 (2003).

[10] See Courtney G. Joslin, "Marital Status Discrimination 2.0," *Boston University Law Review* 95 (2015): 805–31; Helen M. Alvaré, "Is This Any Way to Make Civil Rights Law? Judicial Extension of 'Marital Status' Nondiscrimination to Protect Cohabitants," *Georgetown Journal of Law and Public Policy* 17 (2019): 247–86.

Laws banning homosexual relations began to disappear from the jurisdictions under consideration from the later 1970s through the early twenty-first century.[11] Later – and often in the name of privacy, dignity, and equality – homosexual relations became a legally protected right. In some places, sexual orientation and sometimes gender identity joined the ranks of statuses specially protected against housing, employment, or commercial vendor discrimination. Eventually, many nations in Europe as well as the in the United States and New Zealand formally recognized same-sex marriage. These developments led to myriad conscientious objections by churches, wedding vendors, marriage-license clerks, and other involved state officials. They also led to conscience claims by religious employers in connection with decisions about employment of, or benefits for, homosexual persons who had entered same-sex marriages. Adoption agencies and assisted reproduction clinics asserted conscience objections to providing children to same-sex couples. In some jurisdictions, clergy found themselves asserting religious conscience claims against the application of "hate speech" laws interpreted to punish or enjoin preaching about homosexual relationships.[12] Like abortion and contraception, matters concerning sexual orientation, gender-identity, and same-sex marriage also began to affect Christians' eligibility to partner with governments to carry out various social programs.

The most current sexual expression controversy concerns transgenderism: an individual's conviction that his or her actual sex is the opposite of the biologically manifested sex. Coming quickly after the legal and social controversy about same-sex marriage, transgender activism was immediately cast in similar terms: as a fight about equality and dignity. Like abortion and same-sex relations, the transgender question is today part of debates about the scope of nondiscrimination laws, doctors' willingness to perform transgender surgery, health insurance coverage mandates, and the ability of religious groups to receive governmental grants and contracts.

A few additional examples illustrate the breadth of social arenas affected by sexual expression rights. There are disputes over whether same-sex pairs may adopt or foster children through Christian agencies and over whether Christians who conscientiously oppose same-sex pairing may adopt or foster children.[13] There are disputes over whether charities opposed to same-sex

[11] See n. 9.

[12] Lee Duigon, "Canadian 'Human Rights' Commissions Bear Down on Christian Clergymen," *Chalcedon*, September 25, 2008, chalcedon.edu/resources/articles/canadian-human-rights-commissions-bear-down-on-christian-clergymen; Todd Starnes, "City of Houston Demands Pastors Turn Over Sermons," *Fox News*, October 14, 2014, www.foxnews.com/opinion/2014/10/14/city-houston-demands-pastors-turn-over-sermons.html.

[13] See Tim Ross, "Foster Parent Ban: 'No Place in the Law for Christianity,' High Court rules," *The Telegraph* (UK), February 28, 2011 (reporting that the High Court ruled that Christians

marriage or abortion or contraception may obtain licenses to operate in a particular jurisdiction and whether they are entitled to tax exemptions like other nonprofits. There are disputes over what school curricula must say about sexual expression and about parents' rights to absent their children from particular lessons. At schools receiving state money, there are disputes about whether self-organized student groups disagreeing with current sexual norms are entitled to the same rights and benefits as groups that agree.

In short, governments are the source of a growing list of rights and benefits, grants and licenses, bans and mandates. By virtue of more and more governments' taking a side in contemporary sexual expression disputes, the numbers and types of clashes with Christian conscientious objectors has grown exponentially.

Governments have not moved in this direction in a vacuum. Laws and policies interacted with prominent ideas and movements favorably disposed to sexual expression rights. This dynamic is not subject to precise empirical measurement but is best grasped by reviewing these ideas and movements through the writings of leading twentieth and twenty-first century philosophers, sociologists, economists, and historians.

## CULTURE AND SEXUAL EXPRESSION[14]

More than a few ideas and movements influenced the rise of sexual expression rights. Sometimes law took the lead in recognizing them, and sometimes an idea or movement did so. Below, I summarize several of the most prominent.

### *The Individual*

The modern "turn toward the self" quite likely supported the rise of a preoccupation with sexual expression divorced from children and marriage. This notion holds that finding and becoming oneself is an important task and a source of progress.[15] It tends toward taking one's subjective opinion as the

opposed to homosexual practices may not foster children), www.telegraph.co.uk/news/religion/8353496/Foster-parent-ban-no-place-in-the-law-for-Christianity-High-Court-rules.html; Laurie Goodstein, "Bishops Say Rules on Gay Parents Limit Freedom of Religion," *The New York Times*, December 28, 2011, www.nytimes.com/2011/12/29/us/for-bishops-a-battle-over-whose-rights-prevail.html.

14 Portions of this section are drawn from Helen M. Alvaré, *Putting Children's Interests First in U.S. Family Law and Policy: With Power Comes Responsibility* (Cambridge: Cambridge University Press, 2017), 50–57.

15 Steven Seidman, *Romantic Longings: Love in America, 1830–1980* (New York, NY: Routledge, 1993), 72.

only important or even the final word on a subject, possibly combined with a willingness to allow other people to do likewise.[16] In the words of philosopher Charles Taylor, this turn rendered the self less "porous," and more disengaged from everything but its own mind. The purposes and meanings of things are believed to arise within the person.[17] Sociologist Pitirim Sorokin (founder of Harvard University's Department of Sociology), argued as early as 1956 that this turn had influenced people's thinking about sex: the individual was coming to "regard[] himself as law giver and judge entitled to juggle all moral and legal standards."[18]

The most articulate explanation of the re-making of sex as a subjective, meaning-making enterprise is provided by sociologist Anthony Giddens in his landmark 1992 book, *The Transformation of Intimacy*. There, Giddens introduced the notion of "plastic sex": sex with subjectively moldable meaning, unmoored from its physical structures, in particular, its link with procreation. He connected its development with the introduction of modern contraception and assisted reproductive technologies. Once sex is severed from reproduction, he argued, it is severed from kinship and from "the generations." Its meaning is reduced to pleasure. Sexuality then becomes "a property of the individual," a tool for forging self-identity and for forming relationships that may or may not last.[19]

Another aspect of individualism involves the decline of the role of the transcendent. Formerly, the divine was understood to be the author of all creation, including the body, which was therefore a "given," as distinguished from something one constructed for oneself. One looked to the body for norms for oneself and the community. Today, belief in the transcendent has declined, and the "givenness" of creation, including the body, is more easily a matter for personal interpretation. The body becomes more of a resource, an object of investigation, manipulation, improvement, or even mining. The person seems self-made. The meanings and purposes of even organic things – such as the functioning of the human body, the existence of two sexes, the link between sex and procreation – point neither to the transcendent nor to behavioral norms. The body's givenness is an obstacle to human desires. Even marriage itself, with its

[16] Charles Taylor, *A Secular Age* (Cambridge, MA: Belknap Press of Harvard University Press, 2007), 38.

[17] Ibid.

[18] Pitirim A. Sorokin, *The American Sex Revolution* (Boston, MA: Porter Sargent, 1956), 88.

[19] Anthony Giddens, *The Transformation of Intimacy: Sexuality, Love, and Eroticism in Modern Societies* (Redwood City, CA: Stanford University Press, 1992), 2, 27, 112, 121, 144, 156, 167, 174, 175, 178–80.

usual or expected structure, becomes a problem, because it has been handed down, which seems a threat to self-expression. Stigma arising out of any sexual choice likewise becomes problematic.

### *Happiness*

Another cultural idea that enjoyed growing popularity in the later twentieth and early twenty-first centuries concerns the centrality of sexual happiness. Charles Taylor writes that while the notion of a human right to happiness had been historically conditioned by shared ethics concerning good citizenship, self-rule, and sexual morality, these limits were set aside after World War I, especially regarding sexual mores. In Taylor's view, the modern "triumph of the therapeutic"[20] is a closely related phenomenon. Traditional ideas about morality are rather subordinated to the imperative of personal fulfillment and becoming our "authentic selves."[21]

Margaret Sanger, Planned Parenthood's founder, picked up the theme of sexual freedom as happiness, in making arguments for birth control. She predicted that sex unlinked with children would make a husband for his wife "a veritable god – worthy of her profoundest worship," and could provide "spiritual illumination" to "light up the holy path to an earthly paradise."[22] Later feminists – Betty Friedan in her *Feminine Mystique* and Simone de Beauvoir in *The Second Sex* – also predicted significant, positive transformations of male/female relations when sex was separated from children.[23]

The right to happiness was also applied to the sexual context by the German scholar who invented the term "the sexual revolution." In his book *Die Sexuelle Revolution*, Freudian disciple Wilhelm Reich wrote that the "core of life's happiness is sexual happiness."[24]

[20] See Phillip Rieff, *The Triumph of the Therapeutic: Uses of Faith after Freud* (London: Chatto & Windus, 1966).

[21] Taylor, *A Secular Age*, 485–93, 507–8, 618–20.

[22] Margaret Sanger, *Happiness in Marriage* (Garden City, NY: Blue Ribbon Books, 1940), 121, 126, 271.

[23] Betty Friedan, *The Feminine Mystique* (New York, NY: W.W. Norton & Co., 1963), 86; Simone de Beauvoir, *The Second Sex*, ed. and trans. H. M. Parshley (New York, NY: Vintage Books, 1989), 724–31.

[24] Wilhelm Reich, *The Sexual Revolution: Toward a Self-Regulating Character Structure*, trans. Therese Pol (New York, NY: Farrar, Straus and Giroux, 1945), 88.

### *Sex As Revolutionary*

Another idea that gained power beginning in the twentieth century is the notion that sexual license is itself a tool for overthrowing traditional and repressive authority. This is often expressed by lawmakers and interest groups who believe that personal and social freedom is gained by women and LGBT persons by means of contraception or abortion or same-sex marriage. A surprising number and diversity of thinkers have explored it.

Hebrew University sociologist Eva Illouz speculates that the idea of socially forbidden sexual expression originated with popular stories about taboo or star-crossed love, stories in which love is irruptive, and has the potential to undermine authority and cross social lines.[25]

Early twentieth-century journalist and social critic Walter Lippman noted the tendency in the 1920s to associate overthrowing traditional sexual mores with women's empowerment.[26] Charles Taylor describes the emergence of the belief that persons formerly cast out of polite society on the grounds of their sexual conduct – or anyone repressed by bourgeois conventions – could be liberated by transgressive sex because it brought the person in touch with and linked mind and body, reason and feeling. It was a reaction against old taboos and the double standard, which evaluated men's and women's sexual behavior according to different yardsticks.[27]

American literature professor Robert Oscar Lopez identifies historical signs of the belief that transgressive sex is revolutionary, highlighting the growing use and acceptance of pornography, the use of women's bodies in advertising, and literature such as *The Crucible*, which "reinforced the association in Americans' minds between sexually judgmental Puritans and their penchant for political persecution." [28]

### *A Reduced Valuation of Children*

Beginning especially in the 1960s, fears of a "population bomb" cast a long shadow on the value of children, especially in poorer societies. At the same

[25] Eva Illouz, *Consuming the Romantic Utopia: Love and the Cultural Contradictions of Capitalism* (Berkeley, CA: The University of California Press, 1997), 8.

[26] Walter Lippmann, A *Preface to Morals* (New York, NY: The Macmillan Company, 1929), 290–307.

[27] Taylor, A *Secular Age*, 616.

[28] Robert Oscar Lopez, "Civil Rights and the Sexual Revolution Need a Divorce," *The Federalist*, April 19, 2016, www.thefederalist.com/2016/04/19/civil-rights-and-the-sexual-revolution-need-a-divorce.

time, with the rise of a feminist consciousness, children were portrayed as hindrances to women's growing education and employment opportunities. By this time too, due to the decline of the family farm and child labor, children were rarely contributing to a household's income; they were consumers not producers.

### *Technology*

There is a very powerful modern notion that what is stated or offered as scientifically based is objectively true and even absolutely necessary to achieve progress. This is sometimes referred to as the "technological imperative." When technology offers sex unlinked to children, therefore, it is presumed to constitute progress. This helps to explain how the pill and later contraceptives became robustly linked with the cause of women's freedom.

On a practical level, the "technology shock"[29] of the pill, combined with new educational and economic opportunities for women, are linked by more than a few economists and sociologists with important changes in the markets for sex and marriage that make nonmarital sexual expression more common and less stigmatized. In bare economic terms, the narrative proposes that women became increasingly self-supporting at the same time that contraception and abortion seemed to eradicate the risks of sex. Women no longer needed to abide by the terms of the old exchange: her granting sex for a promise of his support. It became less consequential to say "yes" to an otherwise attractive offer for sex, which began to occur more often outside the search for a marriage partner and even regularly became the price of having a relationship with a man. Marriage was delayed. "Shotgun marriage" disappeared. Nonmarital sex skyrocketed and thus also non-marital pregnancies and abortion. Eventually the stigma earlier attached to these began to fade.[30]

### *Sex and Materialism*

More than a few scholars have explored the twentieth century's predilection to conceive of sex and its positive effects as a consumer item.

[29] See George Akerlof, Janet L. Yellen, and Michael L. Katz, "An Analysis of Out-of-Wedlock Childbearing in the United States," *The Quarterly Journal of Economics* 111 (1996): 277–317, 294.

[30] Ibid. See also Mark Regnerus, *Cheap Sex: The Transformation of Men, Marriage, and Monogamy* (Oxford: Oxford University Press, 2017).

Generally, they propose that the norm of capitalist materialism – of consuming as pleasure and self-expression and self-fulfillment – has invaded the sexual arena. Sexual acts are reframed *as* consuming. Sex is used to *sell* consumption of other objects. Consuming certain things becomes sexy. Professor Illouz points out that this idea overlaps with the idea of transgressive sex as freedom, and affirms a "consumerist idiom of postmodern culture . . . promising transgression through the consuming of leisure and Nature."[31]

### *The Spread of Movements and Ideas Favoring Sexual Expression*

Some strands of feminism and the gay rights movements relied upon more than a few of the above ideas – in combination with effective legal and cultural strategies directed toward lawmakers and social influencers – to achieve victories in both spheres on behalf of the sexual expression laws and mores that today pressure Christian conscience.

These ideas became prominent in all forms of entertainment and social media. They pour into societies – "images tumbling across screens" – all day and all night for years on end.[32] They also emerged dominant in institutions of higher learning. Quite recently, even corporations have begun to lend their voices to the support of sexual expression in law and culture. This is happening in the United States, in Europe, and in Oceania by means of advertising, social media, employment policies, and donations to political campaigns. Huge multinational corporations wielding outsized cultural and economic power give citizens the impression that the larger society has reached a consensus about the meanings and value of sexual expression.[33]

## CHRISTIANITY AND SEXUAL EXPRESSION

Christian beliefs about marriage are understood by many as nothing more than a list of prohibitions on behaviors that are today accepted as natural and

[31] Illouz, *Consuming the Romantic Utopia*, 8–10.

[32] Glynn Harrison, *A Better Story: God, Sex & Human Flourishing* (London: InterVarsity Press, 2016), 57.

[33] See, e.g., Judith Ireland, "Corporate Giants Join Push for Same-Sex Marriage," *The Sydney Morning Herald*, March 31, 2015, www.smh.com.au/federal-politics/political-news/corporate-giants-join-push-for-samesex-marriage-20150331-1mbuq3.html; Google Ireland, "Google Supports Marriage Equality #ProudToLove," *YouTube*, May 11, 2015, www.youtube.com/watch?v=EuaDPZINJc4.

healthy. In the words of Pope Benedict XVI, they are understood as "blow[ing] the whistle just when the joy which is the Creator's gift offers us a happiness which is itself a certain foretaste of the Divine."[34] The true state of affairs is more profound, and is described below.

Arguably, various Christian denominations did not take the trouble until the later twentieth century to fully explain Christian beliefs in a form accessible to a wide audience. Like other institutions, churches assumed a continuation of the long-standing and traditional consensus on sexual mores. Today, however, a variety of Christian scholars are publishing accounts of Christian teachings in terms of currently cherished values and hopes.[35]

While it is impossible to thoroughly depict here all Christian denominations' teachings on sexual expression – and some denominations within the Anglican, Lutheran, Methodist, and Presbyterian traditions, for example, are revising their positions – it is possible here to set forth some of the most basic elements of long-standing Christian beliefs about sex, marriage, parenting, and abortion. These will suffice to illustrate the conflict with current laws and mores on sexual expression.

Some parts of these teachings are derived from Scripture, some from the writings of early Christian scholars, and some were developed by theologians and defended consistently by Christianity throughout many hundreds or thousands of years. Within the Roman Catholic tradition especially, some are also derived from the natural law, which is defined by the Catechism to mean the law "written and engraved in the soul of each and every man, because it is human reason ordaining him to do good and forbidding him to sin."[36] Speaking quite generally then, and highlighting differences with contemporary stances, Christian teachings about sexual expression are as follows:

By contrast with the view that a person's biological sex is of no moral significance, the book of Genesis holds that there is divine significance in God's having made two sexes and ordaining a procreative, one-flesh relationship between them. This is held to be part of God's manifestation of his own image and likeness in the world. Furthermore, that the one-flesh union is the source of human life is received as an unmistakable sign of God's special

[34] Benedict XVI, *Deus Caritas Est*, encyclical letter, December 25, 2005, sec. 3.

[35] See, e.g., Harrison, *A Better Story*; John Paul II, *Man and Woman He Created Them: A Theology of the Body*, trans. Michael Waldstein (Boston, MA: Pauline Books and Media, 2006); Russell Moore, *Onward: Engaging the Culture without Losing the Gospel* (Nashville, TN: B & H Publishing Group, 2015).

[36] *The Catechism of the Catholic Church* (Vatican City: Libreria Editrice Vaticana, 1994), sec. 1954, citing Leo XIII, *Libertas praestantissimum*, encyclical letter, June 20, 1888, sec. 597.

blessing of this union; God has allowed the man and the woman, in an act of love, to participate in human creation alongside God.

By contrast with the view that contraception is a source of progress and equality for women, Roman Catholics hold that contraception severs the completeness of the male-female union as God designed it. It also reduces the meaning of sex below God's plans for it, in a manner easily leading to the subjugation of women, the objectification of women's bodies, the demeaning of sex, the retreat from marriage, and the disvaluing of children.[37]

By contrast with the position that nonmarital sexual relations are unproblematic or even good, Christianity – particularly by means of the Bible's frequent analogizing of marriage to humans' relationship with God – holds that the permanent, faithful, fruitful union of marriage is the only place wherein human beings' one-flesh union provides them a privileged glimpse of God's love for us, and of human beings', ideally, for one another. Thus, St. Paul writes to the Ephesians that marriage between a man and a woman is a "great mystery, but I speak in reference to Christ and the Church." (Eph. 5:32).

By contrast with support for same-sex relations or marriage, Christianity holds that there is something uniquely important about the complementarity and procreativity of male/female relations and marriage; these not only create new life but image God's permanent, faithful, fruitful love for us.[38] They establish a structure by which children can be known and loved and cared for by their parents. To equate same- and opposite-sex marriage would be to deny the importance of new life and the weight of children's interests in their kin.

Despite the positive nature of these Christian teachings on their face and their attention to respecting creation and promoting lasting love and respect for women and children, today they are often classified as bigotry. This is not only due to various denominations' prior failure to communicate ancient teachings in new language, but also to their suffering declines in prestige, membership, and vocations coincident with the rise of sexual expression rights. Speaking broadly, some of the following factors are at play. There is a general impression that rapid gains for science render religion less relevant, powerful, and explanatory. Christian teachings and

[37] See Paul VI, *Humanae Vitae*, encyclical letter, July 25, 1968; Francis, *Amoris Laetitia*, post-synodal apostolic exhortation, April 8, 2016, sec. 68.

[38] See, e.g., Wright, "From Genesis to Revelation: An Anglican Perspective," and Jean Laffitte, "The Sacramental Reality of Human Love: A Catholic Perspective," in *Not Just Good but Beautiful: The Complementary Relationship between Man and Woman*, eds. Steven Lopes and Helen Alvaré (Walden, NY: Plough Publishing, 2015), 75–78, 90–92, 95–96.

practices concerning the rights of women (in connection with ordination and otherwise) are deemed retrograde. Christian teachings on sex are characterized as blind adherence to tradition, or even evidence of antipathy to women and gay persons. Christian religions are charged with using a person's sexual behavior as a sole or shorthand test of who is in the "bark of salvation." And the sexual abuse scandal, particularly in the Roman Catholic Church, spotlighted clerical hypocrisy about sex and vastly reduced the church's credibility.

## COMMON FEATURES OF THE LEGAL AND CULTURAL CLASH

Strong Christian convictions about the meaning and value of sexual expression clash weekly, if not daily, with the contemporary embrace of free sexual expression as a core human right. Even across widely dispersed regions of the world, there are some common procedural and substantive features of this clash. They are not only shaping present outcomes but likely to shape future resolutions as well.

### *Deciding Whether Religious Conscience Is Burdened*

Depending upon the kind and degree of cooperation a sexual expression law demands of conscientious objectors, some courts and sexual expression advocates are asking whether a law genuinely burdens religious conscience and who should get to decide. This was a prominent feature of the lawsuits over the 2012 US regulation requiring many religious institutions to insure employees for free contraception and early abortifacients. The government insisted that the *state* – not believers – should be able to judge whether or not religious employers are burdened by the requirement to enable the government to attach free birth control to their insurance plan at no cost to the employer.[39] Religions and US courts, however, remain generally opposed to allowing the state to evaluate religious doctrines and believers' consciences.

### *The Prominence of the Nondiscrimination Framework*

While in Europe, movements to attain legal protection for sexual expression often proceed under the banner of "privacy" – because of the privacy

[39] See *Zubik* v. *Burwell*, Supreme Court of the United States No. 14-1418 (2016), Oral Argument, Official Transcript, 45–46, 49–50.

provisions of the European Convention on Human Rights[40] – sexual expression activists also often rely upon the categories of nondiscrimination or equality to achieve legal and popular progress for their interests. Today, equality is arguably the most stirring rallying cry due to its association with the powerful claims of the civil rights and feminist movements of the later twentieth century. The equality banner also allows sexual expression interest groups to portray conscientious objectors as bigots.

The campaign for same-sex marriage employed the most straightforward pitch for equality, referring to its goal as "marriage equality." Activists on behalf of government-funded contraception and legal abortion also argue that both are necessary to ensure equality between men and women, given that women alone get pregnant and give birth, and, far more often than men, act as single parents. Contraception and abortion ensure that women and men can both take part in sex without one party experiencing a pregnancy or a childbirth, which could interrupt plans for education and employment.

### *Dignitary Harm*

Supporters of sexual expression rights regularly highlight the dignitary harm they experience when, for example, a conscientiously objecting vendor refuses to serve their wedding or an employer fires them for disapproved sexual behavior. Supporters of religious conscience respond that their dignity is also on the line because dignity is a "two way street."[41] They argue that citizens enjoy rights of speech, association, and religious exercise that regularly and inevitably will lead to disagreements and potential feelings of trampled dignity; in other words, they reply that the law cannot salve all hurt feelings.

### *Status or Conduct?*

Antidiscrimination laws forbid exclusion from, for example, housing or employment or services, based upon certain protected statuses, including race,

[40] See, e.g., *Case of Stübing* v. *Germany* (European Court of Human Rights, Fifth Section) App. No. 43547/08, April 12, 2012. Here the court held that protection for private life includes a person's sexual life.

[41] See Jeremiah A. Ho, "Find Out What It Means to Me: The Politics of Respect and Dignity in Sexual Orientation Antidiscrimination," *Utah Law Review* (2017): 463–530; Eric Rassbach and Hannah Smith, "Symposium: Shotgun Wedding? Forcing Religious Vendors to Participate in Wedding Ceremonies," *SCOTUSblog: Supreme Court of the United States Blog,* September 14, 2017, www.scotusblog.com/2017/09/symposium-shotgun-wedding-forcing-religious-vendors-participate-wedding-ceremonies/.

sex, marital status, and sometimes sexual orientation. Wedding vendors refusing to participate (with, e.g., flowers or photography) in a same-sex wedding or employers rejecting candidates on the basis of their same-sex marriage or cohabitation, claim that they are not discriminating based on a person's *status*. Rather, they claim to be responding to another's *conduct* (cohabiting or marrying) and – in the case of same-sex weddings – on the basis of a vendor's *right not to participate* in a ceremony violating conscience. They also rely on legal protections of private speech and/or expression. Vendors and employers often buttress their claims with evidence of past employment of, or service to, gays or single persons. In the United States, in particular, there is a decided trend among courts to conflate status and conduct; that is, courts conclude that the practical or disproportionate effect of a conscientious objector's behavior is to disadvantage women or gay *people*, even if that was not the objector's past practice or current intention.

### *Emotionality v. Empiricism*

Logical and empirical arguments do not have their finest hour in the clash between sexual expression and religious conscience. Questions amenable to reasonable investigation are sometimes not taken up at all, or if they are, do not figure prominently in the popular or legal debate. Even credible research questioning the wisdom of a new sexual expression right, as well as the researchers behind it, are more often pilloried than engaged.

### *The Place of Children*

Children's well-being is importantly affected by adults' sexual expression choices because a child's family structure – a crucial element of well-being – is begun at sex. Yet the effects of adults' sexual expression upon children are very little consulted as a basis for legal and social decision-making. This is best articulated by the late University of Chicago theologian Don Browning, who referred to children's interests as set at the "back door" of the law while adults' interests and desires are set at the "front door."[42] Not a few prominent scholars have lamented the insufficient attention paid to the dynamic Browning articulates: that only *adults*' interests have attained the status of a right, linked to equality and freedom. It becomes difficult or impossible therefore for

[42] Don S. Browning, "Modern Law and Christian Jurisprudence on Marriage and Family," *Emory Law Journal* 58 (2008): 35–36.

conscientious objectors to succeed – politically or popularly – on the basis of arguments framed in terms of children's well-being.

## WHAT THE FUTURE MAY HOLD

The future of the clash between Christian conscience and sexual expression rights will depend upon the trajectory of many features of the current debate and likely also some factors we cannot anticipate. In addition to the continuing influence exerted by the legal and cultural events and ideas described above, here are some additional factors that may affect the future of the clash between sexual expression rights and Christian conscience.

Tending toward a decline in the power of sexual expression rights are the following factors. First, promoters of these rights have sometimes exhibited aggressive behavior toward religious individuals and institutions. They engage in ad hominem attacks and use the power of the law to coerce religious believers to cooperate with or participate in practices like abortion or same-sex marriage. Quite famously, a same-sex marriage advocate threatened to "firebomb" a pizzeria in the United States for its conscientious objection to serving a (theoretical) same-sex wedding.[43] Such behavior may lead to a backlash against sexual expression rights. This is already evident in developing countries, where leaders (along with Pope Francis) have denounced attempts at "ideological colonization" of their societies by wealthier Western nations wielding a broad notion of sexual expression rights.[44]

Second, a growing scholarly and popular literature reveals some downsides – especially among vulnerable populations – to the new sexual expression rights. Women, for example, regularly report dissatisfaction with the "markets" for sex, dating and marriage shaped largely by the unlinking of sex from marriage from children.[45] As noted above too, there is also growing evidence that children's family structure is strongly associated with their economic,

[43] Shekhar Bhatia, "Exclusive: 'If a Child of Mine Was Gay I Would Love Them, but I Still Wouldn't Go to the Wedding.' Defiant Indiana Pizza Parlor Owners Who Won't Cater Gay Receptions REOPEN Store Tomorrow, Buoyed by Donations of $842,000," *The Daily Mail* (UK), April 7, 2015, www.dailymail.co.uk/news/article-3028925/If-child-gay-love-wouldn-t-wedding-Defiant-Indiana-pizza-parlor-owners-won-t-cater-gay-reception-REOPEN-store-today-buoyed-donations-842-000.html.

[44] Joshua J. McElwee, "Francis Warns against 'Ideological Colonization' of Family, Reaffirms Contraception Ban," *The National Catholic Reporter*, January 16, 2015, www.ncronline.org/news/vatican/francis-warns-against-ideological-colonization-family-reaffirms-contraception-ban.

[45] See, e.g., Peggy Orenstein, *Girls and Sex: Navigating the Complicated New Landscape* (New York, NY: Harper Collins, 2016); Laura Sessions Stepp, *Unhooked: How Young Women Pursue Sex, Delay Love and Lose at Both* (New York, NY: Riverhead Books, 2007); and Kathleen A.

emotional, educational, and familial outcomes; children are disadvantaged by the absence of stably married parents. Family structure differences are also robustly associated with large and growing gaps between racial groups and between those with high versus low educational attainment. These are increasingly unpalatable to supporters of equality and freedom.

Tending toward an expansion of sexual expression rights is the continuing ascendancy of the value of equality in every leading social institution, paired with successful messaging linking equality with sexual expression freedoms. Furthermore, the memory of diminished legal and social rights for sexual minorities is still very much alive. Public debate about the scope of freedom for sexual expression is also driven importantly by emotion, and sexual expression interest groups have excelled at telling an emotionally engaging story about the populations involved.[46] Finally, the case for sexual expression rights would be strengthened if evidence emerges linking these rights with improved physical, emotional, or social health for adherents.

Tending toward diminished tolerance of Christian conscience, there is, first, the fact that in all the regions discussed, the state is increasingly sponsoring the social services once dominated by Christian providers and employers. This could mean reduced concern to preserve the existence of religious charities demanding conscientious objections. Second, in addition to the Catholic Church's clerical sex abuse scandal, there exists continuing ill will – even disbelief – regarding the sexual teachings of many Christian churches. And the growing ranks of those who embrace sexual practices at odds with Christian teaching very likely means less religious affiliation and practice in the future.

Third, as religious affiliation and practice shrink for many Christian churches and religion becomes less salient in the lives of a growing cohort of people, it seems possible that more and more religious authorities will be tempted to make their peace with new patterns of sexual expression. Perhaps they will do this by finding ways to alter doctrine or pastoral practices, or just by ceasing to assert conscientious objections. Christian churches refusing to alter their teachings could then experience additional pressure.

Tending toward growing tolerance of Christian conscience is the possibility that various Christian denominations will make greater efforts to incorporate their teachings about sex into larger, positive proposals about truth, dignity, freedom and happiness. They may move away from older language about

Bogle, *Hooking Up: Sex, Dating and Relationships on Campus* (New York, NY: New York University Press, 2008).

46 See Harrison, *A Better Story*.

rules or shame and work to draw out the rationality, positivity, and fairness of their proposals, as well as to better communicate sexual teachings as part of God's larger and loving plan for human beings. As noted above, publications moving in this direction are already appearing.

Christian denominations might also decide to strengthen their case for conscientious objection by moving beyond strictly legal arguments about their rights of conscience or religious freedom and rather better engage empirical arguments about the effects of sexual expression rights on society, particularly on the most vulnerable. These fact-based arguments might stress the emerging literature about the losses suffered by women, children, and the poor when sex is reduced in meaning, when marriage becomes a luxury item for the privileged, and when children are separated from their parents. They might also engage the growing literature about how religious and more privileged persons are disproportionately reaping the benefits of the sexual mores Christianity embraces, while the nonreligious and the poor are suffering a disproportionate share of the negative effects of exercising the new sexual expression rights.[47]

## CONCLUSION

It would be a mistake – the fallacy of the present – to conclude with certainty that sexual expression rights will continue to pose the biggest challenge to Christian conscience for the foreseeable future. At the same time, there is little doubt that the manner in which Christians and defenders of such rights conduct themselves, and the arguments that win the day, will exert important and lasting effects upon the future scope of freedom of conscience.

## RECOMMENDED READING

Alvaré, Helen. *Putting Children's Interests First in U.S. Family Law and Policy: With Power Comes Responsibility*. Cambridge: Cambridge University Press, 2017.

Corvino, John, Ryan Anderson, and Sherif Gergis. *Debating Religious Liberty and Discrimination*. Oxford: Oxford University Press, 2017.

Freitas, Donna. *Sex and the Soul: Juggling Sexuality, Spirituality, Romance, and Religion on America's College Campuses*. Oxford: Oxford University Press, 2015.

Giddens, Anthony. *The Transformation of Intimacy: Sexuality, Love, and Eroticism in Modern Societies*. Redwood City, CA: Stanford University Press, 1993.

[47] Brookings Institution and American Enterprise Institute Working Group on Poverty and Opportunity, "Opportunity, Responsibility and Security: A Consensus Plan for Reducing Poverty and Restoring the American Dream (2015)," www.brookings.edu/wp-content/uploads/2016/07/Full-Report.pdf. (2016): 30–41.

Harrison, Glynn. *A Better Story: God, Sex & Human Flourishing*. London: InterVarsity Press, 2016.
Illouz, Eva. *Why Love Hurts: A Sociological Explanation*. Cambridge: Polity Press, 2012.
John Paul II. *Man and Woman He Created Them: A Theology of the Body*, translated by Michael Waldstein. Boston, MA: Pauline Books & Media, 2006.
Laycock, Douglas. "Religious Liberty and the Culture Wars." *University of Illinois Law Review* (2014): 839–40.
Laycock, Douglas, Anthony Picarello, and Robin Fretwell Wilson, eds. *Same-Sex Marriage and Religious Liberty: Emerging Conflicts*. Lantham, MD: Rowman & Littlefield, 2008.
Regnerus, Mark. *Cheap Sex: The Transformation of Men, Marriage, and Monogamy*. Oxford: Oxford University Press, 2017.
Seidman, Steven. *Romantic Longings: Love in America 1830–1980*. New York, NY: Routledge, 1991.
Trigg, Roger. *Equality, Freedom & Religion*. Oxford: Oxford University Press, 2012.
Wilson, Robin Fretwell, ed. *The Contested Place of Religion in Family Law*. Cambridge: Cambridge University Press, 2018.
Wojtyla, Karol. *Love & Responsibility*. San Francisco, CA: Ignatius Press, 1993.

# 19

# Conscience and the Roman Catholic "Just War" Tradition

JOSEPH E. CAPIZZI

## INTRODUCTION

The Christian just war approach presumes an understanding of conscience formed by the acceptance of the use of force in the pursuit of peace but that places that pursuit of peace within a much broader framework than the modern nation-state. Though the Christian conscience justifies in some circumstances the use of even lethal force to defend peace, no nation-state can embody the fullness of peace toward which all humans strive. Thus, every state's common good draws upon the interrelationship of political common goods expressed in other states, in the emerging international political community, and in international law. In other words, every Christian who pursues peace does so knowing that she may need to make a specific judgment against the state of which she is a citizen when the peace it seeks imperils the peace of a greater human good. Thus, the just war approach makes space for judgments of conscience *against* what we might typically think of as "reasons of state."

Christian reflection on the morality of war has contributed to the specification and development of the Christian conception of "conscience." Once Christians began to argue that peace could be pursued even by the uses of force associated with war-making, they began as well to describe those circumstances under which Christians, in faith, would have to say "no" to their states' demands. Christian teaching on "conscience" sharpened and developed in contact with its teaching on the morality of war. This chapter will first describe the biblical and theological foundations of the "politics" that grounds the just war approach. Then it will consider the place of just war thinking within the wider Roman Catholic teaching about conscience. Finally, it will survey and criticize the legal and moral grounds of the American exemption granted only to citizens opposed to all wars, as distinguished from citizens opposed only to wars they deem unjust.

## PEACEMAKING AND THE USE OF FORCE

In the Gospel of John, as he is preparing them for his departure, Jesus says to his disciples, "Peace I leave with you, my peace I give you not as the world gives, do I give to you. Let not your heart be troubled, nor let it be fearful" (John 14:27). A few simple words of farewell, and yet the implications are clear: the promise of peace Jesus has bestowed on his disciples in his person, "not as the world gives" peace, but alone as He, the Christ, can bring peace. Jesus promises a peace that admits of no anxiety, no fear. Christ's peace thus operates as a power against the forces of the world that will attempt to prevail against men and women of faith. The forces of disorder will persist; indeed, the world brings disorder and Jesus promises no relief from the disorder of human society. Seeking peace as the conclusion of human disorder is to seek the wrong peace. His words suggest as much: to tell his disciples not to be troubled or fearful acknowledges that trouble and fear are reasonable responses to the human condition. The peace some mistakenly seek is on those terms, and they will be frustrated as such peace is possible only through Christ.

That peace given by Christ serves to measure such worldly justice as any political order might attain; that peace provides less a goal than a rebuke: such peace as men and women cobble together pales in comparison to that given by Christ. The Christian conception of peace – not given as the world gives – frees the Christian from false association of peace with the order brought about by this or that earthly city, in Augustine's term. The constant human temptation is to judge the political order too important, as more important than any temporal good could bear. Absent the transcendent perspective of peace given by Christ, earthly peace becomes a substitute for which anything might be sacrificed, including theoretically any neighbor, any enemy, any *one* who appears potentially to inhibit that peace's coming into being. The irony of the just war account is not that it licenses the subordination of anything to earthly peace but that it begins with the peace given by Christ and proclaims that only in the context of this peace does any sacrifice make sense at all. Thus, Paul Ramsey wrote, "modern secular man is unable any longer to look into the heart of the tragic ambiguity of all earthly sacrifice, the meagerness of every political achievement and the transience of the common good men serve by means of political power."[1] Absent the context of a peace guaranteed

1 Paul Ramsey, "The Uses of Power," in *The Just War: Force and Political Responsibility* (Lanham, MD: Rowman & Littlefield, 2002), 17.

by Christ, we are tempted to guarantee earthly peace by force or by guile, by anything contributing to our peace, including the sacrifice of the innocent. But, of course, not only will such sacrifices fail to guarantee that which cannot be given in time, but everything will be sacrificed in its pursuit, ensuring that our failure will be barbarous. There are many examples of nation-states sacrificing innocents in the name of peace, including the US decision to use atomic weapons on Japanese cities in the Second World War. Many Catholics protested that decision, including prominent Catholics like Fulton Sheen and Elizabeth Anscombe. John Courtney Murray SJ said that barbarous decision was made possible by a "thickening mood of savage violence."[2]

The Christian community witnesses to the peace given by Christ in different ways, including those bearing witness by their renunciation of violence. Many Christians have, in conscience, committed themselves to that witness, and many pacifist and non-violent approaches to conflict resolution and peacemaking have emerged over time attempting to give communal expression to the peace given by Christ. At the Second Vatican Council, the Council Fathers requested that governments make legal provisions "for the case of those who for reasons of conscience refuse to bear arms, provided, however, that they accept some other form of service to the human community."[3]

But the dominant witness to that peace given by Christ, both historically and currently, remains some variant of the "just war" approach. The approach recognizes, on the one hand, the occasional need to oppose violence by means of the use of force, and on the other hand, the complementary need *not always* to use force against violence, even violence that may pose catastrophic threats against one's state or people. In other words, the just war approach acknowledges limitations on violence's justifications, and indeed, the entire rationale of the just war approach helps discern when those limitations have been reached and the ways by which Christians may witness the peace given by Christ.

According to this approach, the right to wage war derives from the nature and function of political authority, which God has given to promote political goods such as order, justice, and community. Among the means God

[2] John Courtney Murray SJ, "Remarks on the Moral Problem of War," *Theological Studies* 20, no. 1 (1959): 54.

[3] Second Vatican Council, *Gaudium et Spes* (The Pastoral Constitution on the Church in the Modern World), December 7, 1965, sec. 77.

entrusts to the state for serving these ends is the sword. The use of force in the service of legitimate political objectives is an obligation and right of the state derived from God's divine institution and made necessary by the reality of sin. This is a view attested in Scripture already with God's institution of the death penalty as part of the Noahic covenant (Gen. 9) and reiterated most famously in Romans 13. The just war tradition is a framework of moral reflection that emerges from the Christian theory of the state. Because political authority has been ordained to the service of political goods, and because the exercise of political authority involves the use of force, the practice of war must be an extension of the legitimate exercise of political authority. As with all acts of political authority, the use of force must be placed in the service of ends such as order, justice, community, or the common good. In other words, the just war approach locates war within the larger practice of political authority.

Conceiving just war as derivative of political authority means insisting that war remain an extension, and not an abrogation, of politics. That is, the just war approach seeks to limit resort to and the conduct of war by bringing war into a clear relationship with the legitimate aims of politics. The resort to military conflict is not a qualitative leap beyond the other uses of force typical of the state, including for instance law enforcement and the exercise of judgment and punishment. Asserting continuity between conduct prior to war and conduct during war means that the goals and standards of conduct acceptable prior to war obtain during war: for example, reprisals are forbidden and non-combatants must be protected from direct harms.

Moreover, that war be placed in the service of political objectives requires that the course of war be continually reassessed with reference to the political goals that use of force pursues. Once any political strategy has been adopted, a temptation arises to view the strategy itself as the aim of politics: politicians seek to justify the strategy and conform all relevant information to its justification. In circumstances involving the use of force, war can assume its own logic and dictate new political objectives, rather than serve them. By reconnecting war to statecraft, the just war approach insists on constant interplay between politics, the strategies adopted in their pursuit, and the attainment of the goal of peace, which understands the contending parties as potential members of the ensuing community for which that peace becomes a goal.

The intention of a just war is always witness to, and pursuit of, peace. As the United States Catholic Bishops have said, the just intention of any war is the "pursuit of peace and reconciliation, including avoiding unnecessarily destructive acts or imposing unreasonable conditions (e.g., unconditional surrender)."[4] Peace justifies and guides the instrument of force, even in war. Peace, however, is a principle of order, and order in international politics is the result of the organization of power. Therefore, peace itself depends on the responsible exercise of statecraft.

The just war account, then, assumes a conscience ordered to peace. This means that, for a Christian, the decision to participate in war should never, in conscience or otherwise, depart from a conscience committed to peace. The moral norms and virtues developed by the Christian over the course of his or her life remain in place. When drawn upon in the service of peace they guide all his or her actions; departing from them in any way would be a failure not only of service to that peace, but of conscience as well.

The just war approach understands the use of force as an instrument in the service of legitimate political goods pursued by actual political communities. Force cannot, therefore, be used to pursue just any political objectives or political objectives that could be secured only by the adoption of illicit means; the approach therefore rules out uses of force in the pursuit of vengeance, reprisals, and those necessarily reliant upon a suspension of moral rules. In this last case, for instance, though political theorist Michael Walzer makes a powerful case for the suspension of the prohibition against direct targeting of noncombatants in "supreme emergency" situations, the Catholic church (and other just war approaches) disagree: in such cases, national self-defense would have to be foregone. The prohibition on direct targeting of noncombatants is absolute, much as philosopher G. E. M. Anscombe argued in her essay, "Mr. Truman's Degree."[5]

In addition to imposing limits on the moral conduct of war, the Christian witness to peace imposes conditions, or limits, on the scope of any nation-state. Political communities like nation-states are historic and spatial realities that instantiate real goods for human beings. But they are limited historically and spatially: they come and go, they grow and diminish, they become more or less distorted in their service of genuine goods. From the Christian perspective, they all are judged by a genuine communal good that exceeds them: the good of the human family created by a good God. All legitimate politics

[4] National Conference of Catholic Bishops, *The Challenge of Peace: God's Promise and Our Response* (1983), sec. 95, www.usccb.org/upload/challenge-peace-gods-promise-our-response-1983.pdf.

[5] Elizabeth Anscombe, "Mr. Truman's Degree," in *Collected Philosophical Papers*, vol. 3, *Ethics, Religion and Politics* (Minneapolis, MN: University of Minnesota Press, 1981), 51–71. For Walzer's argument on the "supreme emergency," see Michael Walzer, *Just and Unjust Wars: A Moral Argument with Historical Illustrations* (New York, NY: Basic Books, 2015), 250–67.

therefore drives toward a common good open to greater inclusivity. National communities can be genuinely good, but they are good to the extent they serve people and not just their own citizens. The goods of citizens are bound up with the goods of citizens of other nations and ultimately of the human community. Thus, Pope John XXIII wrote, "We must bear in mind that of its very nature civil authority exists, not to confine men within the frontiers of their own nations, but primarily to protect the common good of the State, which certainly cannot be divorced from the common good of the entire human family."[6] The common good of any political community connects to the goods of other political communities and the good of the entire human family.

Peace, then, is the goal and measure of political authority. The just war account rejects the ethos "my country, right or wrong," which philosopher and literary critic G. K. Chesterton called "obvious nonsense."[7] Right or wrong depends not on the assertion of political authority, but on the standard of peace that authority serves. When activities of political authority depart from that goal, both the individual and subordinate social communities are compelled to push against those activities, to demand their retraction or their reform. The Church as a community reserves the right to "pass moral judgment in those matters which regard public order when the fundamental rights of a person or the salvation of souls require it."[8] The judgments of political authority are, then, moral judgments that retain their force only to the extent they express the true and the good: "A regime which governs solely or mainly by means of threats and intimidation or promises of reward, provides men with no effective incentive to work for the common good. And even if it did, it would certainly be offensive to the dignity of free and rational human beings. Authority is before all else a moral force."[9] For this reason, the appeal of rulers should be to the individual conscience, to the duty that every man has of voluntarily contributing to the common good. "Hence, representatives of the State have no power to bind men in conscience, unless their own authority is tied to God's authority, and is a participation in it."[10]

All of this should inform the conscience of the Christian as she or he thinks about legitimate uses of force. There are political goods the pursuit of which will involve harms brought against others. Sometimes, those goods justify war

6 Pope John XXIII, *Pacem in Terris* (Peace on Earth), encyclical letter, April 11, 1963, sec. 98.
7 G. K. Chesterton, *Collected Works*, vol. 29 (San Francisco, CA: Ignatius, 1988), 44.
8 *Gaudium et Spes*, sec. 76.
9 *Pacem in Terris*, sec. 48.
10 Ibid., sec. 49.

in their defense or pursuit, but even war must abide the moral law. The move to war is not a move from peace and morality to violence and immorality; instead, war can be an expression of the conscience ordered toward peace, guided by morality, open always to the conversion of self and neighbor from opposed wills to wills joined in communion and ordered toward peace.

## THE PERSONAL AND COMMUNAL ASPECTS OF CONSCIENCE

According to the *Catechism of the Catholic Church*, conscience is "a judgment of reason whereby the human person recognizes the moral quality of a concrete act that he is going to perform, is in the process of performing, or has already completed. In all he says and does, man is obliged to follow faithfully what he knows to be just and right. It is by the judgment of his conscience that man perceives and recognizes the prescriptions of the divine law."[11] Conscience, then, involves the exercise of practical reason: a situation is confronted, a judgment is made about its moral resolution, and then this judgment is carried out.

Because related to reason, conscience is highly esteemed. Conscience is the locus of a conversation between the person and God, where he or she "hears" God's voice and which itself "speaks" to him or her the directives of action. Conscience so understood can describe a division or fragmentation of the self: the self "hears" conscience speaking the dictates of reason it apprehends to a will awaiting instruction. The fragmentation of the self into speaking, hearing, instructing, and receiving parts finds reflection in an interplay between doubt and certitude. On the one hand, the drama of the process – speaking, hearing, instructing, receiving – suggests lack of certainty regarding action, as the subject discerns an appropriate course of action. On the other hand, the final result suggests an authoritative command to be obeyed as certain, internally dogmatic, and invulnerable to external questioning. The result is our contemporary notion of conscience as the giver of law to the person obliged to obey the conscience's commands. Conscience is a "law of the mind." As such, the person "must not be forced to act contrary to his conscience. Nor must he be prevented from acting according to his conscience, especially in religious matters."[12]

The relationship of conscience as giver of commands to an obedient moral subject evokes our experiences of individuals facing external "crises

[11] *Catechism of the Catholic Church*, 2nd ed. (Vatican City: Libreria Editrice Vaticana, 2000), sec. 1778 (hereafter cited as CCC).

[12] CCC, sec. 1782.

of conscience," when someone or some institution looks to them to follow commands that those individuals find contrary to their conscientious judgments. The second of these, in other words, suggests we have external crises of conscience parallel to internal crises of conscience. In other words, the simultaneous existence of internal and external crises of conscience reveals the simultaneously personal and communal nature of the individual conscience.

Though personal in the ways described, conscience is never separated from the community but arises and is formed within a community of truth-seeking women and men. The *Catechism* calls the word of God the "light of the path" of conscience;[13] Christians believe that our consciences are illumined in their reflection on truth by God's word, a word itself transmitted to us within community, by a shared language and tradition of interpretation, and therefore bound to the community giving witness to that word. So, while conscience is intimately personal – again, where a person listens to God – the capacity to hear God is formed by constant, prayerful engagement with a community to which that person is accountable. An overemphasis on the personal aspect of conscience could lead us into a false perception of the freedom of conscience from communal accountability, but the *Catechism* guards against that, emphasizing the prior need of conscience formation: "The education of conscience is indispensable for human beings who are subjected to negative influences and tempted by sin to prefer their own judgment and to reject authoritative teachings."[14]

The attitude of the Christian tradition toward "conscience" can be displayed in certain historical examples of crisis, at least two of which are well known to many, and both of which show the personal and communal aspects of conscience. One is that of Thomas More, the great British saint known for his execution by King Henry VIII for refusing to sign the Succession to the Crown Act of 1534. In Robert Bolt's play, *A Man for All Seasons*, More, pressured by the Duke of Norfolk, to "come with us, for fellowship," replies, "And when we stand before God, and you are sent to Paradise for doing according to your conscience, and I am damned for not doing according to mine, will you come with me, for fellowship?" Two points jump at us from the brief dialogue: first is the Duke's appeal to community: More should relent and stand with the Duke, the representative of the community of which he and More are a part. More's intransigence, the Duke suggests, breaks their fellowship. Of second note is that for Bolt's More it is not the rectitude of his

[13] Ibid., sec. 1785.

[14] Ibid., sec. 1783.

or Norfolk's judgment that is at issue but their respective commitments to their consciences. If in conscience Norfolk believes he must sign, then sign he must; just as More must refuse to sign in obedience to his conscience. Failure to obey conscience, and not the accuracy of their respective moral judgments, sentences them to eternal damnation or bliss. Conscience speaks, anticipating a moral subject willing and able to carry out its commands. Failure to obey conscience's judgment convicts the moral subject, not the rightness or wrongness of the act itself.

A less famous but equally worthy account is that of the Austrian martyr, Franz Jägerstätter.[15] Jägerstätter, the only opponent in his village of the German *Anschluss*, refused to serve in the Wehrmacht under Hitler. His refusal led to the accusation he had undermined military morale, for which he was tried, convicted, and executed on August 9, 1943. Jägerstätter's situation was akin to More's: he knew execution would be the consequence of abiding his conscientious judgment against military service. Despite communal isolation, including direct appeals from family members and a local priest, Jägerstätter stood fast. In 2007, Pope Benedict XVI declared him a martyr, and in October of the same year he was beatified in Linz. More and Jägerstätter are among the many women and men who witness to both the challenge and power of minority conscience: each stood virtually alone against the pressure to conform their views to that of the majority. Each chose the sacrifice of his life over the sacrifice of his conscience in the face of such pressure. Each has become a powerful symbol of conscientious objection in the face of political power.

The pressure in conscience cases like these and the many others we see today expresses itself in at least two ways. First is the pressure stemming from the common desire to conform or fit in. In a different context, St. Augustine in Book I of *The City of God* refers to this pressure to conform, to avoid correcting or challenging others' behavior, because "we wish to avoid enmities which might impede or injure us in respect of some temporal thing which either our greed desires to obtain or our infirmity fears to lose."[16] That desire to fit in is a sign of weakness and rooted in the ways individuals are first members of communities of accountability; these "weak men," Augustine writes, are "men who live a married life; who have, or wish to have, children; and who

[15] The most important account of Jägerstätter remains Gordon C. Zahn, *In Solitary Witness: The Life and Death of Franz Jägerstätter* (New York, NY: Holt, Rinehart & Winston, 1964).

[16] Augustine, *The City of God against the Pagans*, trans. and ed. R. W. Dyson (Cambridge: Cambridge University, 1998), 1.9.13.

have houses and families ... [they are] afraid to lose these things."[17] They are, that is, afraid to lose their loved ones, their social standing. More and Jägerstätter were implored to think of the social consequences of their stances. But of course, that loss – should it occur – is only momentary. Conscience, the tradition reminds us, may be witnessed to by individuals standing alone, ostracized from their communities, but this is not because they stand *against* their communities, but *for* them. Though cast as betrayals, the conscientious claim of a More or a Jägerstätter says that the community fails to see what a conscience well formed by that community should see, often as in these cases because the community is thinking about the moral question too parochially and without reference to the bearing of the moral question on the entirety of the community to which any individual member witnesses. Jägerstätter's refusal to serve in Hitler's army represented his judgment that the human family should renounce the evil he saw before him. His judgment did not represent mere opinion but the application of a law spoken to him about the moral impossibility of squaring service in the Wehrmacht with the pursuit of peace to which all are called. In their failure to see as he did, his peers separated themselves from their community and that community's singular representative, Jägerstätter. Men and women like Jägerstätter and More speak for the community against those other members whom history will judge to have failed in their moral judgment. Ultimately, the passage of time will vindicate witnesses of rightly formed conscience and the judgment of communities returned to their moral senses.

Because history alone sometimes vindicates such men and women against their communities, a second source of pressure is the acknowledgment of the possibility of error in conscientious judgment. The *Catechism of the Catholic Church* recognizes the complexity of conscience formation, the many variables combining to educate and form consciences, and the possibility and even likelihood of at least occasional error. "Standing apart," then, is not merely an instance of holding ground in the face of social isolation but also and always implicates the feature of questioning and doubt: Where my friends, coworkers, and even family have judged differently, is this a case in which I may be in error? The addition of this human element only deepens our respect for men like More and Jägerstätter, counseled by friends and family just to give in, to allow the excuse of doubt to free them from captivity to conscience. Cranmer asks More if "the matter is capable of question?" More replies, "Certainly," to which Cranmer responds – as any of us might,

[17] Ibid., 1.9.14.

"But that you owe obedience to your King is not capable of question. So weigh a doubt against a certainty and sign."[18] Conviction in conscience does not evaporate doubt; instead, Bolt's play exhibits how conviction and doubt coexist. We can begin to see, then, the moral and intellectual difficulties associated with conscience formation and adherence, especially in those cases where the passage of time becomes necessary to vindicate the individual conscience against the mistaken judgment of the community in which the conscience was formed.

## CONSCIENCE AND MILITARY SERVICE IN THE UNITED STATES

The relationship of personal and communal aspects of conscience does not map perfectly onto US law governed by the Military Selective Service Act (MSSA), the act that governs the mustering of the forces necessary to the defense of the United States and that specifies in section 3806j exemptions for those "conscientiously opposed to war."[19] On the one hand, the law esteems individual conscience when expressing a comprehensive judgment against war, even though no community need be spoken for or represented by that conscience. Merely to express the conscientious personal conviction against all war qualifies one for exemption according to the MSSA. On the other hand, even when speaking on behalf of identifiable faith communities with centuries-old traditions of reflection, consciences speaking for judgments against particular wars are not esteemed and protected. The Act protects only conscientious objectors (CO), and not those whose objections are to particular wars (selective conscientious objectors, SCO). To be clear: Franz Jägerstätter falls into that second category. His objection was not to war in general but to serving on behalf of Nazi Germany.

Much of the case law surrounding objection to military service arose in the context of conscription of young men into the military, a practice that traces back to the Civil War, through the World Wars, Korea, and Vietnam, and ended in 1973. Since 1980, the United States Selective Service System has required that "male citizens of the United States and other male persons residing in the United States"[20] between the ages of eighteen and twenty-five register with the system designed to "maintain a system that ... rapidly provides personnel in a fair and equitable manner while managing an

[18] Robert Bolt, *A Man for All Seasons* (New York, NY: Vintage, 1990), 133.
[19] 50 U.S.C.A. §3806 (1994).
[20] Proclamation 7275, 65 Fed. Reg. 9199 (Feb. 22, 2000).

alternative service program for conscientious objectors."[21] As we see from this description, provision for CO is built right into the Selective Service System; to SCO, however, no mention is made.

United States law (in the MSSA) and the Department of Defense Instruction (DDI) define CO at length. The DDI 1300.06 "Conscientious Objectors" states, "Consistent with the national policy to recognize the claims of authentic conscientious objectors in the Military Services," approval of conscientious objector status will be extended to any individual:

(a) Who is conscientiously opposed to participation in war in any form;
(b) Whose opposition is based on a moral, ethical, or religious belief;
(c) Whose position is firm, fixed, sincere, and deeply held.[22]

The DDI expands on the "moral, ethical, and religious" nature of this commitment, emphasizing the religious quality of the foundation of the objection: "A Service member's objection may be founded on religious training or belief; it may also be based on personal beliefs that are purely moral or ethical in source or content and occupy to the Service member a place parallel to that filled by more traditional religious convictions."

The DDI then specifies the ways to determine the integrity with which the foundational beliefs supporting a firm objection to war is expressed in the applicant's life. The Instruction looks at the applicant's personal history, including his participation in activities associated with those foundational beliefs, and testimonies supporting the evidence. The goal of the evaluation is to determine the totality of the applicant's life and the integrity of the categorical objection to war, without prejudicial regard for the applicant's "belief system" from the reviewing authority. The evaluation seeks to establish the applicant's objection is not of a political nature: he does not disagree with or object to this war but to all war. The burden of proof lies entirely with the applicant, who must show both that the objection to war is grounded in his fundamental beliefs and that his objection is categorical. In the distant past, the objector had to root his objection in belief in God or, later, a Supreme Being.[23] Today, as the language indicates, the objection need only be grounded ("fixed, sincere, deeply held") and not necessarily express a commitment arising out of communal, religious, formation.

[21] Selective Service System, Statement of Mission, www.sss.gov.

[22] US Department of Defense, "Conscientious Objectors," in *The Department of Defense Instruction* 1300.06, July 12, 2017, www.hsdl.org/?abstract&did=802711 (hereafter cited as *DoD Instruction*).

[23] See Joseph E. Capizzi, "Selective Conscientious Objection in the United States," *Journal of Church and State* 38, no. 2 (Spring 1996): 339–64, 342.

The CO provisions of the SSA comport well with both the theoretical and practical implications of US liberal democracy. We anticipate and even cherish that our conception of freedom extends to people of good will and deep religious or religious-like commitment who, drawing on that commitment, find themselves incapable of serving in the military even in times of national emergency. Conscientious objection is as old as the country's involvement in warfare.[24] It was recognized on the state level in colonial times, when most exemptions from "drafts" (localized call-ups during the Revolution) were granted to Quakers, Mennonites, and Brethren. Three states proposed amendments to the Constitution calling for CO recognition. The state constitution of New York stated the exemption in very specific terms: "That all such of the inhabitants of this State being of the people called Quakers as, from scruples of conscience, may be averse to the bearing of arms, be there from excused by the Legislature."[25] Recognition of CO status, then, is part of the American civic tradition.

A tradition nearly as old excludes selective conscientious objectors from this provision. Selective conscientious objectors are those persons acknowledging the permissibility of some uses of force and their willingness to participate. They stand ready to help defend the common good, even by participating in the use of force, in those conflicts that follow the moral law. They admit, however, that sometimes their government might err in its judgment and call its people to conflicts in which they could not participate. From the perspective of US law, should they establish that their opposition to *this* war arises from a conscience formed by equivalent "moral, ethical, or religious beliefs," they would nonetheless fail to show foundations opposing "participation in war in any form." The discriminating character of a "selective" objection excludes it from possible exemption under the statute; according to the law, being selective essentially erases the "conscientious" character of the objection. This view is clear in the majority opinion in *U.S.* v. *MacIntosh*.[26]

Douglas MacIntosh was a Canadian Baptist professor teaching at Yale University who sought and was denied US citizenship. Citizenship required an oath of fidelity to the United States with an explicit pledge to defend the

[24] See Robert T. Miller and Ronald B. Flowers, *Toward Benevolent Neutrality: Church, State, and the Supreme Court* (Waco, TX: Markham, 1992), 104–9.

[25] F. N. Thorpe, *The Federal and State Constitutions, Colonial Charters and Other Organic Laws of the States, Territories, and Colonies Now or Heretofore Forming the United States of America* (Washington, DC: Government Printing Office, 1909), vol. 5., quoted in Michael Walzer, *Obligations: Essays on Disobedience, War, and Citizenship* (Cambridge, MA: Harvard University Press, 1970), 125.

[26] *U.S.* v. *Macintosh*, 283 U.S. 605 (1931).

United States by force of arms if necessary. MacIntosh refused. Employing Chestertonian language, MacIntosh told the court, "I do not undertake to support 'my country, right or wrong' in any dispute which may arise."[27] Of course, MacIntosh was not objecting to any particular war; he merely asserted the right of conscience described above: those in political authority may err in their moral judgments, even regarding war. The Court recognized and rejected the implication of MacIntosh's refusal:

> When he speaks of putting his allegiance to the will of God above his allegiance to the government, it is evident, in the light of his entire statement, that he means to make *his own interpretation* of the will of God the decisive test which shall conclude the government and stay its hand. We are a Christian people according to one another the equal right of religious freedom, and acknowledging with reverence and the duty of obedience to the will of God. But, also, we are a nation with the duty to survive; a nation whose Constitution contemplates war as well as peace; whose government must go forward on the assumption, and safely proceed upon no other, that unqualified allegiance to the nation and submission and obedience to the laws of the land, as well those made for war as those made for peace, are not inconsistent with the will of God.[28]

"Unqualified allegiance" is the key phrase in the passage and resonates in later SCO cases. "Unqualified" contradicts "selective." All US case law follows the reasoning in *MacIntosh* and identifies "selective" conscientious objection as contrary to unqualified allegiance to the state. Yet, the just war account and the examples of More and Jägerstätter confirm that deep conscientious commitment to a moral position is compatible with a *qualified* willingness to serve in the armed forces and that unqualified allegiance to the state is not guaranteed by either general conscientious objection to war or by a general willingness to serve. Further, the decision refuses to acknowledge that at least in some cases the particular objection to war stems not from an individual's "own interpretation of the will of God," but instead – as in the Catholic case–from readily available and communally accountable moral principles found in the Catholic theological tradition.

Over time, however, CO and SCO case law in the United States moved the basis of conscientious exemption from service away from explicit grounding in religious formation, revealed typically in membership in a "peace church." Conscientious objection to a *particular* war would not meet the criteria for

[27] Ibid., 618.
[28] Ibid., 625.

standing under the MSSA, no matter how central such claims might be to a faith community like Catholicism, which views participation in some wars as potentially murderous. Instead of explicit religious appeal, the depth of the applicant's commitment would be measured solely by whether the objection to war was general. If not, the application would fail. Evidence of this shift comes from the two most significant SCO cases: *Gillette* v. *United States*,[29] and its companion case, *Negre* v. *Larsen*.[30]

Guy Gillette was convicted of failure to report for induction into the armed services. He argued that he should have been classified as a conscientious objector and thus exempted from such service. Gillette maintained that though not religious, his "humanist" convictions led him to oppose the war in Vietnam. He maintained he would be willing to serve his country in a war of national defense, or a peace-keeping effort sponsored by the United Nations, but that the war in Vietnam was unjust and he therefore could not conscientiously serve in it. His counsel made three arguments on his behalf: challenging first the vagueness of the wording of the statute; second, that as stated it violated the Establishment Clause of the First Amendment; and finally, that it violated the Free Exercise Clause of that Amendment.

According to the first line of Gillette's defense, the wording in §6(j) of the 1967 Military SSA was vague enough to cover selective objectors.[31] The pertinent passage stipulates that "Nothing contained in this title ... shall be construed to require any person to be subject to combatant training and service in the armed forces of the United States who, by reason of religious training and belief, is conscientiously opposed to participation in war in any form."[32] His counsel argued that the phrase "in any form" was vague enough to cover either the absolute rejection of all wars by modifying "war," or it could refer to an absolute rejection of service in a particular war by modifying "participation." The Court rejected this argument; Congress's intent, the Court concluded, was to exempt only those with unqualified objection to war. The Court noted that the statute itself provided that a conscientious objector be assigned to noncombatant service unless opposed to such service, thus carving out other forms of participation for those objecting to war.

29 *Gillette* v. *United States*, 401 U.S. 437 (1971).

30 *Negre* v. *Larsen*, 394 U.S. 968 (1969).

31 See Kent Greenawalt, "All or Nothing at All: The Defeat of Selective Conscientious Objection," *The Supreme Court Review* (1971): 31–94; and Andrew J. Haile, "Reconsidering Selective Conscientious Objection," *University of Richmond Law Review* 52 (2018): 831–86, especially 857–61.

32 81 Stat. 100, 104 (1967).

After rejecting Gillette's statutory claim, the Court rejected his two constitutional claims. Gillette contended that the wording of the statute favors one class of religious objection and therefore violates the prohibition against the establishment of religion. The line of argument is as follows: regardless of whether conscientious objector status is a right guaranteed by the Constitution, if the exemption is granted to one class of objectors, it must be extended to other objectors as well. If the exemption were not granted to both classes of objectors (general and selective), the exemption would discriminate against and burden those religions and religious beliefs that lead to SCO, an argument made explicitly in *U.S.* v. *McFadden*.[33] The Court interpreted the argument as a challenge to the Establishment Clause and responded in two ways.

First, the Court admitted that article (6)j has a de facto discriminatory effect but denied that one could thus conclude that the article works an establishment of religion. Second, according to the Court, the appropriate test for determining whether the exemption is valid is whether government neutrality is ensured; a discriminatory classification may be acceptable if resulting from neutral, secular reasons. The government's action must be "secular in purpose, even-handed in operation, and neutral in primary impact."[34] According to Justice Marshall, "there is no occasion to consider the claim that when Congress grants a benefit expressly to the adherents of one *religion*, courts must either nullify the grant or somehow extend the benefit to cover all religions." A privilege extended to one group does not show "establishment." Indeed, the statute does not name any religious groups and identifies no denomination for special treatment. In the Court's opinion, Justice Marshall stated that "a virtually limitless variety of beliefs are subsumable under the rubric, 'objection to a particular war.'"[35] Therefore, a distinction of some kind is required. In support of this, the Court cited a variety of reasons that the distinction the statute made was neutral. For example, there is the pragmatic hopelessness of converting a sincere objector into an effective fighting man, as well as the government's interest in maintaining a fair system of determining who should serve when not all serve. Congress's intent, according to the Court, in distinguishing general and selective objectors was to ensure that draft boards could differentiate the sincere objector from the insincere one. It

[33] *United States* v. *McFadden*, 309 F. Supp. 502, 506 (1970): "The statute in question clearly discriminates between those who are opposed to all wars on religious grounds and those who are opposed to particular wars on religious grounds. In effect, this discriminates between the so-called 'Peace Churches' and other religions such as the Catholic Church."

[34] *Gillette*, 401 U.S. at 450 (1971).

[35] Ibid., 455.

would be too difficult to discriminate between a sincere selective conscientious objector and an insincere selective conscientious objector. The Court states that it "does not bespeak an establishing of religion for Congress to forgo the enterprise of distinguishing those whose dissent has some conscientious basis from those who simply dissent."[36]

Kent Greenawalt has shown, however, that "the arguments for granting an exemption apply almost as powerfully for genuine selective conscientious objectors to participation as for general objectors." He wrote, "There are some selective objectors whose conscientious and religious feelings are as intensely opposed to participation in a war as those of the average general objector, the basic harm in coercing them against conscience is as great, and such coercion is as likely to embitter them."[37] Certainly, the examples of More and Jägerstätter comport with Greenawalt's suggestion: conscientious opposition to *this* war can arise from such deep commitment that the objector would willingly sacrifice even his or her life rather than contravene that commitment. Many Catholics objecting to specific wars draw upon the examples of More and Jägerstätter, the former a man eager to serve his king and country up until he was asked to swear an oath contrary to his faith, the latter a man who refused to take a loyalty oath to Hitler but volunteered to serve in the medical corps. Much conscientious activity is "selective," if only in the sense of drawing important distinctions between activity judged permissible or impermissible within the roles in which people find themselves. The nature of the objection as *conscientious* is equivalent, and the harm of coercing the objector to perform something contrary to that objection would be equivalent as well.

Much more common than objections to fighting in wars are the routine cases of servicemen and -women facing conscientious challenges in their ordinary roles as servicemen and -women. While we are accustomed to portraits of conscience relying upon heroic stances of historic significance – including such diverse figures as Martin Luther, St. Thomas More, and Martin Luther King Jr. – conscientious expression is more frequently mundane than singular and heroic. Powerful witnesses of individual resolve in the face of communal coercion do not exhaust the fullness of conscientious behavior. Rather, even the soldier *following* her orders is no less conscientious than the one "in conscience" disobeying hers.

Some deny the moral agency of soldiers and regard them as mere instruments of military strategy. Military structure and discipline contributes to this regard: the military anticipates neither criticism nor complaint, nor even

36 Ibid., 457.
37 Greenawalt, "All or Nothing at All," 48.

hesitation, in the completion of orders duly communicated. Paragraph 509b of the United States *Law of Land Warfare* states that, "obedience to lawful military orders is the duty of every member of the armed forces; [members of the armed forces] cannot be expected, in conditions of war discipline, to weigh scrupulously the legal merits of orders received."[38] Because they are not expected to "weigh scrupulously" the merits of orders received, the impression arises that soldiers forfeit agency by virtue of the command structure. Superiors command; inferiors act.

And yet, neither morality nor law regard soldiers as mere instruments, as agents without rationality. Instead, morality and the law require and expect them to exercise agency in following commands. If they carry out unlawful commands, soldiers will be held responsible. Gary D. Solis writes, "Obedience to orders . . . has been the most frequent defense raised by soldiers charged with their violation . . .. It rarely is a successful defense."[39] So, while servicemen and women give due deference to orders as bearing the presumption of their legality, they nonetheless must be prepared to disobey, in conscience, orders that contravene moral law. Put in the same language as above, soldiers have a right to expect their orders to serve justice; they have a right, Solis states, "to presume the lawfulness of orders they receive."[40] Servicemen and women are never automatons but always rational beings. Even when the suggestion comes from those in the military, the view that they are not conflates the specific constraints under which moral agency in the military (and any hierarchical organization) operates, with the utter disappearance of moral agency altogether. The great codifier of military law, Francis Lieber, recognized instead that "[m]en who take up arms against one another in public war do not cease on this account to be moral beings, responsible to one another and to God."[41] Every order followed, and every order disobeyed, involves an act of practical reasoning on the part of the soldier. Every day, in other words, servicemen and women make "acts of conscience" throughout the world in the service of peace.

[38] Department of the Army, *FM 27-10, The Law of Land Warfare* (Washington, DC: Government Printing Office, 1956), 509b.

[39] Gary D. Solis, *The Law of Armed Conflict: International Humanitarian Law in War* (Cambridge: Cambridge University Press, 2010), 374.

[40] Ibid., 381. The "presumption" subordinates extend to superiors finds antecedents in the theological tradition. The great Spanish theologian, Francisco de Vitoria wrote that subjects "may lawfully go to war trusting the judgment of their superiors." Francisco de Vitoria, "On the Law of War," ques. 2, art. 2, sec. 3, in *Francisco de Vitoria: Political Writings*, eds. Anthony Pagden and Jeremy Lawrence (Cambridge: Cambridge University, 2010), 308.

[41] Francis Lieber, *General Order no. 100, Instructions for the Government of the Armies of the United States in the Field*, art. 15, www.avalon.law.yale.edu/19th_century/lieber.asp/.

## CONCLUSION

We have seen a positive Christian posture toward the use of force given certain conditions. The use of force, up to and including force in war, can be an apt expression of one's love for neighbor and not merely a concession to "how things are," or to choosing the lesser evil. We have seen as well that this posture toward peace is part of a much larger Christian disposition toward life in community and, therefore, toward neighbors and potential neighbors appearing in the guise of the enemy. The implication of this last point bears upon our understanding of the role of conscience in questions of war and peace, as too often conscience is understood only, or merely, as the intervention in crisis situations of one's own moral reflection on some question, as though conscience is the axe behind glass waiting to be broken in cases of emergency.

The Christian tradition sees the conscience as corporately formed and corporately accountable. What this has meant and continues to mean is that the person is constantly aware of his or her status before God and in relationship with his or her fellow citizens. Conscience is animated constantly, reflecting on the requirements of justice (the virtue capturing this relationship of individuals to God and others), in terms of his or her role in society. All women and men are responsible for assessing the moral implications of action and inaction, regardless of their status as subordinates, and even when they extend to superior authorities' presumptions of legitimacy. Sometimes the immorality of an action, including a war, can be so powerful, "even citizens and subjects of the lower class may not," Vitoria wrote, "use ignorance as an excuse for serving as soldiers."[42]

As a political community of women and men committed to respect of conscience, the United States strives to respect the conscience of those who might be forced to participate in something to which they object. In the realm of the use of force, where that participation would be an activity perceived as murderous, and thus the harm great, US law and practice has carved out space respecting the conscientious objection to war in any form. But whether the objection is to all wars or particular wars, forcing a person to participate in a war he perceives as unjust forces them to participate in murderous activity; the substantive harm to the person is the same. The time has come to carve out a little more space for those women and men who, ready to serve their nation even up to the use of force in the service of peace, nonetheless recognize that the peace to which they witness and which they serve, judges all nations, and sometimes by the light of their faith, their nation may be judged in the wrong.

[42] Vitoria, "On the Law of War," 308.

## RECOMMENDED READING

Anscombe, G. E. M. "Mr. Truman's Degree." In *Collected Philosophical Papers*, vol. 3, *Ethics, Religion and Politics*, 51–71. Minneapolis, MN: University of Minnesota Press, 1981.

Augustine. *The City of God against the Pagans*, translated and edited by R. W. Dyson. Cambridge: Cambridge University Press, 1998.

Capizzi, Joseph E. *Politics, Justice, and War: Christian Governance and the Ethics of Warfare*. Oxford: Oxford University Press, 2015.

*Gillette* v. *United States*, 401 U.S. 437 (1971).

Greenawalt, Kent. "All or Nothing at All: The Defeat of Selective Conscientious Objection." *The Supreme Court Review* (1971): 31–94.

Johnson, James Turner. *Just War Tradition and the Restraint of War*. Princeton, NJ: Princeton University Press, 1981.

Murray, John Courtney SJ. "Remarks on the Moral Problem of War." *Theological Studies* 20, no. 1 (1959): 40–61.

National Conference of Catholic Bishops. *The Challenge of Peace: God's Promise and Our Response* (1983). www.usccb.org/upload/challenge-peace-gods-promise-our-response-1983.pdf.

*Negre* v. *Larsen*, 394 U.S. 968 (1969).

O'Donovan, Oliver. *Just War Revisited*. Cambridge: Cambridge University Press, 2003.

Pope John XXIII. *Pacem in Terris* (Peace on Earth), encyclical letter (1963).

Ramsey, Paul. "The Uses of Power." In *The Just War: Force and Political Responsibility*, 3–18. Lanham, MD: Rowman & Littlefield, 2002.

Solis, Gary D. *The Law of Armed Conflict: International Humanitarian Law in War*. Cambridge: Cambridge University Press, 2010.

*United States* v. *McFadden*, 309 F. Supp. 502, 506 (1970).

Walzer, Michael. *Just and Unjust Wars: A Moral Argument with Historical Illustrations*. New York, NY: Basic Books, 2015.

Zahn, Gordon. *In Solitary Witness: The Life and Death of Franz Jägerstätter*. New York, NY: Holt, Rinehart & Winston, 1964.

# 20

# Institutional Conscience, Corporate Persons, and *Hobby Lobby*

CHRISTOPHER TOLLEFSEN

## INTRODUCTION

That the rights of conscience of an individual are to be respected by the laws of a democratic polity, and that forced violations of conscience are to be avoided, is as near a commonplace of our constitutional and legal history as can be imagined. James Madison is representative: "Conscience is the most sacred of all property; other property depending in part on positive law, the exercise of that, being a natural and unalienable right."[1]

Of course, there have been controversies about almost every aspect of the commonplace: What *is* an act or judgment of conscience? What does it mean to respect or violate it? When may or must the norm of respect for conscience be overruled? Yet most parties to these controversies take for granted that there *is* such a reality as conscience and that it has *some* importance, such that the law must take cognizance of that reality.

That convergence of opinion has lately disappeared and the very idea of conscience may be said to be in a crisis. Two prominent forms of doubt are responsible for the erosion of the sense of respect once accorded to conscience. The first concerns what conscience *is*. Is conscience one's best judgment about what the moral *truth* is, or is it merely a subjective preference, with little real authority? The second concerns the value of conscience; is conscience in need of respect because of its close connection to the important goods of integrity, religion, and community? Or is the importance of conscience at best only a means to keeping one's hands clean and at worst an excuse for imposing one's moral preferences on others?[2]

[1] James Madison, "Property," *National Gazette*, March 29, 1792, www.press-pubs.uchicago.edu/founders/documents/v1ch16s23.html.

[2] See, e.g., Julian Savulescu, "Conscientious Objection in Medicine," *BMJ: British Medical Journal* 332 (2006): 294–97.

This skepticism about conscience is matched, and perhaps exceeded, by skepticism concerning *institutional* conscience. The grounds for this skepticism track the skepticism concerning conscience as such. For, first, just as there is skepticism over what (individual) conscience *is*, so there also are questions about whether an institution may properly be said to have a conscience at all. Can an institution, such as a business, act or fail to act conscientiously? If so, which institutions, and why? And, second, just as there are doubts about the value or importance of individual conscience, so are skeptical doubts extended to the normative question of whether institutional conscience, if it exists, demands the same kind of respect that individual conscience does. Does conscience in its institutional incarnation have the same value that it is alleged to have for individuals?[3]

In recent years, these questions have received special attention in the context of bioethical controversies over medical professionalism.[4] Skepticism about individual conscience has played a role in arguments against affording accommodations to those who, for religious or other reasons, refuse to perform or assist in abortions, dispense emergency contraceptives, or assist in a patient's death. Skepticism about institutional conscience has likewise played a role in arguments over religiously affiliated health care institutions. May Catholic hospitals, for example, be said to have a conscience and, if so, must it be accorded respect? Or is it rather the case that attributions of conscience and rights of conscience to institutions in the health care setting always come with costs, whether to the adequacy of care for patients or to the individual freedoms of those working in the institutions?

These questions about institutional conscience converge, I believe, with the recent consideration by the Supreme Court of the question of corporate personhood. This question arose in the context of the Court's ruling concerning the Patient Protection and Affordable Care Act's (ACA) "contraceptive mandate," in *Burwell* v. *Hobby Lobby Stores, Inc.*[5] There the Court addressed the issue of whether closely held corporations should be considered "persons" under the Religious Freedom Restoration Act of 1993 (RFRA) and whether as persons they could engage in an exercise of religion as a matter of law. If so,

[3] Both kinds of doubt may be seen in Spencer L. Durland, "The Case against Institutional Conscience," *Notre Dame Law Review* 86 (2011): 1655–86.

[4] See, most recently, Ronit Y. Stahl and Ezekiel Emanuel, "Physicians, Not Conscripts – Conscientious Objection in Health Care," *New England Journal of Medicine* 376 (2017): 1380–85.

[5] 134 S. Ct. 2751 (2014), together with No. 13-356, *Conestoga Wood Specialties Corp. et al.* v. *Burwell, Secretary of Health and Human Services, et al.*

they could be entitled to the protections offered by RFRA.[6] The Court answered both questions affirmatively, and its full answer addressed the two kinds of objections we have just seen.

We could identify the first objection as ontological, regarding both the agency and intellection of such corporate persons: Are they capable of *acting* in a way that could be construed as an exercise of religion? And are they capable of having sincere beliefs, including the kinds of beliefs that are constitutive of judgments of conscience? The second kind of question we should see as normative, asking, in effect, whether the exercise of religion can be something *of value* for a corporation, and even to society, and thus something worthy of protection by means of the law.

Although the Court did not frame its inquiry in terms of the notion of "institutional conscience," it is clear that it asked the same questions of corporate persons that it is necessary to ask about institutional conscience: "Is there such a thing," and "is this reality valuable?" As we will see, the answers to these questions given by the Court in its treatment of corporate personhood are precisely the sorts of answers that vindicate the existence of institutional conscience, pointing, as they do, to the capacity of a group subject to make commitments and act conscientiously on those commitments. The same is true of the Court's answers to the value question.

Accordingly, in this chapter, I will look at the issue of institutional conscience through the lens of the Court's treatment of corporate persons in *Hobby Lobby*. If the issues of corporate persons and institutional conscience are really as close as I claim, then the soundness of the Court's treatment of the one should shape our understanding of the other. We should thus see *Hobby Lobby* as having implications for the questions of institutional conscience that currently vex bioethics.

Of course, the claim that corporations can be said to be persons, or that institutions may be said to have a conscience, is of limited importance if *individual* conscience is ontologically or normatively suspect. For individuals must be seen as the paradigm cases of persons who exercise judgments of conscience; if those judgments are merely disguised expressions of preference, or if the value of conscience is minimal, the same is surely true of institutional conscience. Thus, while the nature and value of institutional conscience are my primary focus in this chapter, nevertheless, I will briefly identify what individual conscience is, and why it should be considered of importance.

[6] Pub. L. No. 103-141, 107 Stat. 1488 (November 16, 1993), codified at 42 U.S.C. § 2000bb through 42 U.S.C. § 2000bb-4.

I will then describe the current argument in bioethics about *institutional* conscience, followed by a brief account of the background of the *Hobby Lobby* case. Thereafter, I'll look closely at the Court's treatment of corporate personhood and the religious exercise of such persons, extending the Court's argument as necessary to answer affirmatively our two leading questions: whether there can be such a reality as the corporate exercise of religion and whether that reality should be recognized as valuable. Finally, I return to the question of institutional conscience, particularly for religiously affiliated hospitals.

## THE NATURE AND VALUE OF CONSCIENCE

A judgment of conscience is, in the paradigm case, a person's final determination of what is permitted, not permitted, or obligatory in some circumstance or other. What faculty is responsible for these judgments? The traditional view is articulated by St. Thomas: it is *practical reason* that knows the first principles of the moral law; and *practical reason* that applies those principles to situations and circumstances so as to lead to moral judgment. Thus, the faculty that is responsible for particular judgments of conscience, as well as the more general normative judgments presupposed by conscience, is reason.[7]

As noted earlier, the idea that individual conscience should be protected has been relatively uncontroversial until recently. But now, in medicine, an important trend in thinking about medical professionalism holds that it is part of the professional ethic for doctors and other healthcare professionals to provide their patients all the services that the law makes available. When a physician does not believe herself able in conscience to do so, it is often said that she should "find another profession."[8] Conflicts of this sort arise over the issues of abortion, sterilization, physician-assisted suicide, and, more recently, the treatment of gender dysphoria.

Such objections can be treated by addressing the value question about conscience. For laws protecting physician conscience protect at least two important goods: integrity and religion. Integrity is the good of having an integrated practical character, in which judgment, choice, action, and emotion are all unified. While that unity can be minimally achieved in a wicked person whose character is oriented to what is bad, nevertheless, like all basic goods, the good of integrity is realized more fully when it is realized in morally

7 St. Thomas Aquinas, *Summa Theologiae (S.T.)*, I-I, q. 79, aa. 12, 13.

8 Savulescu, "Conscientious Objection in Medicine," 294.

upright ways. But integrity is a basic good that is to be protected not just in oneself but in others.

Thus, laws and practices that require acts of persons contrary to their integrity do a wrong to those persons if there is not adequate reason for requiring those acts.[9] *Of course* persons may be thwarted from pursuing wicked plans even if they pursue them with integrity; but in general, human persons should be given the practical opportunity to live out their lives without significant threats to the integrity of their practical character.

The same is true of the good of religion. Agents who see their lives and character as shaped by religious commitments and concerns should, when possible, be given the practical space necessary for them to be able to do so. *Of course* suicide bombers are to be thwarted, even when they act from religious reasons; but there exist many other circumstances where agents should not be stopped from acting on the basis of religious convictions.

Both goods are obviously implicated in the decisions of many physicians and other health care professionals who refuse to participate in the killing of unborn human beings, or to assist in patient suicides, or who refuse to aid in the mutilation of healthy bodies, or to prescribe medications whose purposes are, they believe, contrary both to health and morality. The integrity and religious commitments of such health care practitioners thus ought to be protected to the extent possible, barring serious reasons not to.

## THE DEBATE ABOUT INSTITUTIONAL CONSCIENCE IN BIOETHICS

Not only individual but also institutional conscience is protected by the earliest and most important piece of federal legislation concerning conscience, the 1973 Church Amendments.[10] Sponsored by Senator Frank Church, the amendments state that neither individuals nor institutions in receipt of federal funds can be required to perform abortions or sterilizations, "if doing so would be contrary to the provider's religious beliefs or moral convictions." Individuals are protected against reprisals by their institutions if they refuse to perform abortions; but likewise, institutions are protected from government reprisals. Receipt of federal money cannot be conditioned, for example, on a Catholic hospital's willingness to perform abortions or sterilization procedures. The subsequent Weldon

9 See the discussion by Anderson and Girgis in John Corvino, Ryan Anderson, and Sherif Girgis, *Debating Religious Liberty and Discrimination* (New York, NY: Oxford University Press, 2017).

10 42 U.S. Code § 300a-7.

Amendment also protects health care institutions, and not only individuals, against discrimination.[11]

Despite such protections, there is skepticism about institutional conscience. Bioethicist Mark Wicclair articulates the case against institutional conscience:

> [I]nstitutions are not living, conscious organisms. They lack awareness and do not have the capacity to think, form intentions, or feel good or bad. Moreover, in contrast to health care professionals, institutions cannot *experience* the effects of a loss of moral integrity, and they cannot *experience* guilt or *suffer* from injury to their identity.[12]

Although Wicclair goes on to acknowledge that there *are* some similarities and analogies between individuals and institutions, nevertheless, his claims here identify one important source of doubt about institutional conscience: institutions are not the sorts of things that can exercise conscience, for they cannot think, intend, or feel. The objection raised here is thus within the "ontological" sphere of the debate.

Spencer Durland, a lawyer, likewise raises ontological objections:

> Institutional conscience is fundamentally different from individual conscience . . .. Legal fiction aside, a hospital is not a person; it is a physical structure within which providers give medical care. It does not perform procedures or counsel patients. It does not take lunch hours or vacations. And it does not have a conscience.[13]

Like Wicclair, Durland objects that institutions are not the sort of thing that can have a conscience; Durland's objections appear primarily rooted in the inability of an institution to *act*: "It does not perform procedures or counsel patients."

Durland also makes a moral argument against institutional conscience: treating institutions as having a conscience contributes to the breakdown of medical professionalism similar to that which an overemphasis on patient autonomy creates. When the norm of medicine is "the patient decides, and the physician obeys," then physicians lose their own autonomy and are treated as mere vendors. But the extension of conscience protection to institutions likewise works against physician autonomy, for physicians now can make no claim either against the demands of patients *or* the demands of the institution.

[11] See 83 Fed. Reg. 3880.

[12] Mark R. Wicclair, *Conscientious Objection in Healthcare: An Ethical Analysis* (New York, NY: Cambridge University Press, 2011), 148.

[13] Durland, "The Case against Institutional Conscience," 1659.

As Durland notes, "By permitting a Catholic hospital to dictate the treatments a physician may prescribe, a Catholic healthcare institution's "conscience" takes primacy over the physician's clinical morality."[14] Thus, if "institutional conscience" is acknowledged as real and valuable, this comes at a cost to individual conscience.

As ethicist Elliott Louis Bedford has noted, a number of Catholic authors have defended the idea of institutional conscience.[15] Bioethicist Kevin Wildes, for example, holds that an institution's conscience must be understood in terms of its mission; thus, institutional conscience and institutional integrity are closely related concepts, for both concepts are related to the existence of a mission. An institution has integrity to the extent that its actions serve its mission; it makes judgments of conscience to the extent that it determines what it should do in relation to its mission.[16]

The question of institutional conscience has significant consequences for public policy and law. If institutional conscience is either unreal or valueless, then it will not be available to religious hospitals to seek accommodations or exemptions from laws that require them to, for example, provide health care services that are forbidden by the moral standards of their religious denominations. In particular, such hospitals might worry that they will be required to provide contraceptive services, abortion, sex-reassignment surgery, physician-assisted suicide, or euthanasia, despite their membership in religions that teach the immorality of such acts. Moreover, religious hospitals might, without the protection afforded to institutional conscience, be prohibited from terminating the employment of their workers who act in ways contrary to the mission of the institution – by providing abortions as a side job, for example, or even in the hospital itself. Without robust protections for institutional conscience, these hospitals might find themselves compelled in conscience to close.

Since the purpose of this chapter is primarily to investigate the question of institutional conscience through the lens of the treatment of corporate persons in the *Hobby Lobby* case, I postpone for now my own treatment of institutional conscience in bioethics. I turn instead to the ACA and the difficulties its contraceptive mandate created for the owners of Hobby Lobby, Mardel, and Conestoga Wood.

14 Ibid., 280.

15 See Elliot Louis Bedford, "The Concept of Institutional Conscience," *National Catholic Bioethics Quarterly* 12 (2012): 409–20.

16 Kevin Wildes, "Institutional Identity, Integrity, and Conscience," *Kennedy Institute of Ethics Journal* 7 (1993): 413–19.

## THE ACA AND HOBBY LOBBY

The ACA was passed in 2010 and contained a requirement that certain forms of preventive care for women be provided in all insurance packages (for companies above a certain size) with no cost sharing. Eventually, in collaboration with the Institute of Medicine, the Department of Health and Human Services (HHS) determined that "preventive services" for women should be understood to include all Food and Drug Administration (FDA) approved contraceptives, including "Ella" and "Plan B," both forms of "emergency" contraception, and the IUD, a long-term contraceptive device.[17] HHS admitted that these last three could work on some occasions by making it impossible for an embryo to implant in the uterine lining.[18] Some thus call them abortifacients.

It was on this ground that the contraceptive mandate was challenged by Hobby Lobby Stores, Mardel Christian and Education, and Conestoga Wood Specialities. All are closely held, for-profit companies. Hobby Lobby is a crafts company, owned by the Green family; Mardel is a spin-off company that sells religious books. Conestoga Wood manufactures furniture and is owned by the Hahn family. The members of both families are practicing Christians and believe they have an obligation to run their businesses in accordance with the principles of their faith. Accordingly, in both cases, the companies objected to the mandate's inclusion of contraceptives that may result in the demise of a human embryo. Believing that abortion is an unjust taking of human life and morally impermissible, both companies argued that providing abortifacients would be contrary to the conscience of their owners and would violate their religion. However, refusal to provide insurance meeting the contraceptive mandate's requirements would generate extremely high fines: for Hobby Lobby, about $475 million per year, for example. They therefore brought suit under RFRA.

Passed by Congress in response to the Supreme Court's decision in *Employment Division, Department of Human Resources of Oregon* v. *Smith*,[19] RFRA restored the pre-*Smith* balancing test of the *Sherbert* v. *Verner*[20] era, which was far more protective of religious freedom. *Smith*

[17] See Health Resources and Services Administration (HRSA), "Women's Preventive Services Guidelines," www.hrsa.gov/womens-guidelines/index.html#2.

[18] See *Burwell*, 134 S. Ct. at 2755 (The Department of Health and Human Services acknowledged that the drugs and devices to which Hobby Lobby objected "may result in the destruction of an embryo.").

[19] 494 U.S. 872 (1990).

[20] 374 U.S. 398 (1963).

permitted the government to burden religious freedom with "neutral" laws of "general applicability," on a mere showing that the law at issue was rationally related to a legitimate state interest. *Sherbert*, by contrast, held that a law that imposes a substantial burden on religious exercise must serve a compelling state interest by the least restrictive means possible. Congress passed RFRA in 1993, intending it to apply to both federal and state legislation. A subsequent ruling by the Supreme Court struck down RFRA as applied to states but upheld it as applied to federal legislation.[21]

An important feature of the holding in *Hobby Lobby* concerned exemptions and accommodations already provided to other companies and institutions. Regulations implementing the "preventive health care" portion of the ACA exempted from the mandate only religious institutions that met very stringent criteria. Other religious institutions – such as schools, hospitals and charities – were only given an "accommodation," not an exemption. They were required to sign a waiver opting out of purchasing contraceptive coverage in their insurance plans. Signing the waiver would then trigger a requirement on the insurance companies to themselves provide free contraceptive coverage to employees at the relevant institutions. HHS reasoned that such a requirement would cost the insurance companies no extra money, assuming that widespread contraceptive use would preclude health care costs associated with unplanned pregnancies. Corporations like Hobby Lobby and Conestoga Wood were not protected by either an exemption or an accommodation.

The *Hobby Lobby* Court accepted that the mandate created a substantial burden in the form of a forced choice between high fines and the violation of conscience. The Court assumed without deciding the Obama Administration's claim that it had a compelling interest in the contraceptive mandate; but it also held that since a less restrictive means existed for ensuring widespread contraceptive availability, even in dissenting institutions – in the form of the "accommodation" – RFRA required extension of the accommodation to Hobby Lobby and Conestoga Wood.

## "PERSON" AND "RELIGIOUS EXERCISE" IN *HOBBY LOBBY*

A central question of *Hobby Lobby* concerns whether Hobby Lobby and Conestoga Wood can even petition for relief under RFRA: Can corporations count as persons for this purpose? The Court begins its treatment of this issue by noting that,

[21] *City of Boerne* v. *Flores*, 521 U.S. 507 (1997).

> RFRA prohibits the "Government [from] substantially burden[ing] a person's exercise of religion even if the burden results from a rule of general applicability" unless the Government "demonstrates that application of the burden to the person – (1) is in furtherance of a compelling governmental interest; and (2) is the least restrictive means of furthering that compelling governmental interest." 42 U. S. C. §§2000bb–1(a), (b) (emphasis added). The first question that we must address is whether this provision applies to regulations that govern the activities of for-profit corporations like Hobby Lobby, Conestoga Wood, and Mardel.[22]

The Court's initial consideration of this question is primarily concerned with whether or not Congress intended to include such corporations. In her *Hobby Lobby* dissent, although Justice Ginsburg challenged Justice Alito's claims about RFRA and Congress on this question, I am less concerned here with this question of legislative intent, than with what we could call the philosophical questions concerning the ontology (the question of being) and axiology (the question of value) of corporate personhood and, ultimately, of institutional conscience. Accordingly, in what follows, I will address the Court's handling of the questions of agency and intellect of corporate persons and then the value of corporate personhood (reversing the order of the Court's discussion). I will then indicate how the Court's treatment of these issues bears on the question of institutional conscience.

The Court begins its treatment of the agency and intellect questions by acknowledging a clear truth: "Corporations, 'separate and apart from' the human beings who own, run, and are employed by them, cannot do anything at all."[23] This is in response to an objection against considering corporations as persons that was raised by the Third Circuit Court of Appeals. As the Court implies, while true, this is beside the point; no one who considers corporations persons for the purposes of protecting their actions holds the obviously false belief that those actions are performed by the corporate persons *independently* of the individual persons who make them up. Rather, what defenders of corporate personhood believe is that the actions, intentions, and judgments of corporations are not entirely reducible to a mere aggregate of the individual acts of those members.

Instead, the acts of a corporation are the acts of what the philosopher Margaret Gilbert calls a "plural subject."[24] When a plural subject acts, its

22 *Burwell*, 134 S. Ct. at 2767.

23 Ibid., 2768.

24 See, e.g., Margaret Gilbert, *Sociality and Responsibility: New Essays in Plural Subject Theory* (Lanham, MD: Rowman & Littlefield, 1999).

act cannot simply be identified with the sum of the individual acts of its members; for they act *together* in a way that an aggregative view fails to recognize. Thus, a "corporation's act," such as the act of Hobby Lobby, though clearly dependent upon the acts of its members, is not simply identical to the sum of those acts.

What appears to be necessary for such acts, and for the intentions and beliefs that underlie them, is what Gilbert calls a "joint commitment."[25] There exists a plural subject only when the individuals that comprise that subject are *jointly committed* to realizing some psychological state, such as a belief or intention, together. Thus, it is not enough that two persons each form an intention to go to the movies; those two persons must jointly commit to intend *together* to go to the movies. Similarly, a corporation's acting as a plural subject, as a corporate person, in other words, requires that at least the relevant members jointly commit to acting together, with regard to some subject matter or in some particular way, and so on.

This is why the initial treatment of the Green and Hahn businesses in *Hobby Lobby* is so important: it makes clear that in fact both families had jointly committed not simply to act for a minimal set of business purposes together but to act together in a particular manner prescribed or governed by Christian beliefs. As the *Hobby Lobby* Court noted concerning the Green family,

> Hobby Lobby's statement of purpose *commits* [my emphasis] the Greens to "[h]onoring the Lord in all [they] do by operating the company in a manner consistent with Biblical principles." App. in No. 13–354, pp. 134–35 (complaint). Each family member has signed a pledge to run the businesses in accordance with the family's religious beliefs and to use the family assets to support Christian ministries.[26]

This commitment is not simply a commitment that *each* of the Greens will operate in accordance with biblical principles but that *the Greens* will together, and more specifically, that *the company* will. Hobby Lobby thus appears on the surface to be a plural, or group subject. This is not sufficient for considering something to be a *corporate* subject, of course, for the group must operate under the corporate form. But both Hobby Lobby and Conestoga clearly operate in that manner; so they seem not merely to be group subjects but corporate subjects and so plausibly corporate persons insofar as that term is used to identify a legally relevant set of group subjects.

[25] Ibid., 3.

[26] *Burwell*, 134 S. Ct. at 2766.

Understanding Hobby Lobby and Conestoga Wood as group subjects is essential for understanding the Court's responses to the principal argument of HHS, that Hobby Lobby and Conestoga Wood cannot exercise religion. The reason for this exclusion cannot be the corporate form as such, for HHS acknowledged that non-profit corporations *could* act with religious purpose and thus exercise religion so as to be protected by RFRA. Moreover, HHS acknowledged that protection of non-profit corporations' exercise of religion is important and valuable because thereby the religious exercise of their members is benefited. I will return to this point below. But the Court points out that this leaves only the for-profit nature of Hobby Lobby as providing an explanation for why Hobby Lobby cannot exercise religion.

The Court again notes the nature of the ontological issue: the exercise of religion requires "not only belief and profession but the performance of (or abstention from) physical acts' that are 'engaged in for religious reasons.'"[27] And the Court answers that "[b]usiness practices that are compelled or limited by the tenets of a religious doctrine fall comfortably within that definition."[28] This answer must be read in light of the earlier discussion of the Green's statement of purpose and what that statement *commits* the business to. Were it the case that the commitment was only to sell a good product and make money, then product sales and making money would be the primary forms of "performance" such a company would engage in, and its corporate beliefs would largely be limited to those relevant to these acts. But the Green's statement of purpose clearly indicates an enlarged set of purposes for which the joint subject is to exist: to act in accordance with Christian beliefs and biblical principles, to support Christian ministries, and the like; Conestoga Wood has similar guiding principles.

In a footnote, the Court responds to the principal dissent, by Justice Ginsburg, who writes, "[f]or-profit corporations are different from religious nonprofits in that they use labor to make a profit, rather than to perpetuate the religious values shared by a community of believers."[29] This objection fails, however. As a for-profit corporation, it is obvious that the actions available to the corporation as a group subject will include moneymaking. But having profit as one motivation, and one justifying purpose for the social commitment to act together, does not rule out the possibility of *other* motives and justifying purposes, and both the Greens and the Hahns clearly have these, in the form of their religious commitments. Thus, if not-for-profit corporations can act for

[27] Ibid., 2770.
[28] Ibid.
[29] *Burwell*, 134 S. Ct. at 2797, (Ginsburg, J., dissenting).

religious reasons in virtue of their joint commitment so to act, then so can for-profit corporations, if they too exist in part because of a joint commitment to act for such reasons.

By the same token, companies that do not exist as a result of such commitments should not be thought of as engaged in an exercise of religion. The guiding principles accepted by the Court in thinking through the ontological issue of corporate persons thus come with limits. So, while it is not unreasonable to see even nonreligious, for-profit companies that are not held closely to act for *some* purposes that transcend simply making money – such as environmental purposes, or social causes – it would be unreasonable to expect large, diversely held corporations to exercise religion and thus unreasonable to worry that a rash of RFRA cases will find their way to the Court as a result of large, not closely held, for-profit businesses.

Similar considerations guide the Court's treatment of whether it is possible to ascertain the sincerity of a corporation's beliefs. A reasonable understanding of a corporation's beliefs follows the same lines as the understanding of its actions: its corporate beliefs, which belong to it as a group subject, are those that it has jointly committed to holding together as its beliefs. This makes it unlikely that a very disparate group of persons, all holding individually different, or no, religious beliefs, would, in incorporating, jointly commit to hold some set of religious beliefs. As the Court notes, "the idea that unrelated shareholders – including institutional investors with their own set of stakeholders – would agree to run a corporation under the same religious beliefs seems improbable."[30] Indeed. But it is, on the one hand, quite likely that such persons can jointly commit to act for the sake of profit or some other relatively thin goal; and, on the other hand, quite likely that a small, religiously homogeneous group of persons *could* jointly commit to certain beliefs and adequately communicate those beliefs to others. In fact, the Court pointed out in *Hobby Lobby* that no one had disputed the sincerity of the beliefs under discussion.

Finally, the Court raises a question about the possibility of disagreement within a corporate subject or person. Such phenomena raise no serious ontological problems about the existence of group beliefs (or actions), and, where corporations are concerned, there are legal procedures for the resolution of such conflicts in light of a company's governing structures.

The Court has thus effectively made the case for the ontological status of corporate persons. If we take the most serious objections to such persons to

[30] *Burwell*, 134 S. Ct. at 2774.

be the inability of groups, corporations, or for-profit corporations to believe or act, then the case against such persons is weak. The owners of Hobby Lobby and Conestoga Wood, in particular, seem to have made the appropriate kinds of joint commitments that make group action and belief possible. Since the relevant groups in these cases are incorporated, the relevant group actions and beliefs are corporate actions and beliefs; and this gives us license to speak of corporate actions and persons insofar as "person" reasonably designates the category of being whose actions and beliefs, inter alia, should be protected.

There remains, however, the question of value. Granting that corporations can be persons and even persons of the sort that can exercise religion, what good is to be gained by acknowledging and protecting their status as persons in cases involving the exercise of religion? The Court answers:

> Congress provided protection for people like the Hahns and Greens by employing a familiar legal fiction: It included corporations within RFRA's definition of "persons." But it is important to keep in mind that the purpose of this fiction is to provide protection for human beings. A corporation is simply a form of organization used by human beings to achieve desired ends. An established body of law specifies the rights and obligations of the people (including shareholders, officers, and employees) who are associated with a corporation in one way or another. When rights, whether constitutional or statutory, are extended to corporations, the purpose is to protect the rights of these people.[31]

There are several points to make about this. First, although I have argued in the previous discussion that the Court rightly, though implicitly, identifies Hobby Lobby and Conestoga Wood as group subjects, which can be the subjects of both belief and action, nevertheless, the Court at the same time recognizes, again rightly, that "person" cannot be said *in the same way* of these corporations as it is said of individual human beings. In the paradigm case of personhood, persons are, in Boethius's famous phrase, "individual substances of a rational nature." Human beings, for example, are persons, for they are individual living beings of a species, homo sapiens, which has rationality as one of its attributes. But neither Hobby Lobby, nor Conestoga Wood, nor any other corporation, is an individual substance of this sort; rather corporations are artifacts, entities that are the product of human construction and fail to have the independence and ontological primacy that substances have. Thus, they are called "persons" only in an analogous sense, a sense that takes its

[31] *Burwell*, 134 S. Ct. at 2768.

meaning from resemblance to the paradigm case in certain obvious and important respects. Hence corporate personhood can be identified as a legal fiction without evacuating the ontological account of corporate personhood of significance and indeed, without obscuring the fact that even within the class of "corporate persons," there will be varying degrees to which these persons resemble paradigm-case persons.

The second, and more important point, concerns the value claims made by the Court. Why is the legal fiction of corporate personhood important, and why are corporations in need of protection? The legal answer is this: protecting such corporations is a way of protecting human beings. And the reason that this is so returns us to the ontological claims. As the Court states, "A corporation is simply a form of organization used by human beings to achieve desired ends." That is to say, individuals engage in collective action through joint acts of will in order to achieve certain ends that cannot otherwise be achieved, or that cannot be as well achieved, in the absence of joint beliefs and intentions.

The Court's point here, suitably expanded, encompasses considerations such as these: many joint subjects of collective belief and action are engaged in cooperative endeavors, seeking to achieve together what individually is beyond the reach of the various agents. Joint action contributes to efficiency and success. Moreover, in seeking to achieve these ends cooperatively, such agents may take the *joint* achievement of their ends as itself something valuable: their cooperative engagement is itself a realization of the basic human good of friendship and sociality. Were human agents to achieve all their other apparent ends in the absence of cooperative joint action, still, an important good would go missing. Thus, as John Finnis notes, "institutions and other associations are worth calling personal primarily because they enable individual human people to pursue shared purposes, fruitfully, and in association with others."[32]

So, the joint action of the Green and Hahn families not only contributes to the specific purposes they seek, purposes both mercantile and religious, but also to their supervening purpose of achieving their purposes *together*, as members of a family and of a religious community. The corporate form is not the only way in which the Hahns or the Greens could act as joint subjects, but it is a particularly suitable one insofar as they seek to extend their familial and religious unity into the work domain of their lives.

[32] John Finnis, "Persons and Their Associations," in *Collected Essays: Volume II, Intention and Identity* (Oxford: Oxford University Press, 2011), 92–99.

What would be the case were institutions recognized as for-profit corporations excluded from religious liberty and free exercise consideration? The Court raises the problem:

> According to HHS, however, if these merchants chose to incorporate their businesses – without in any way changing the size or nature of their businesses – they would forfeit all RFRA (and free-exercise) rights. HHS would put these merchants to a difficult choice: either give up the right to seek judicial protection of their religious liberty or forgo the benefits, available to their competitors, of operating as corporations.[33]

The Court recognizes such a forced choice as unjust, putting *persons* at a disadvantage in virtue of their decision to pursue important goods collectively; such persons would give up their rights to religious liberty in choosing to incorporate for business purposes. Such a scenario would additionally be insufficiently attentive to the social aspect of the human good, to the way in which pursuing goods socially is both advantageous for the individual good and constitutive of the good of friendship. By creating disincentives to social action, the law, were it to refuse to acknowledge corporate persons, would dissuade persons from acting in ways truly to their advantage.

This last point goes to the heart of what is implied in the Court's claims in regard to the value question. "The purpose of the fiction is the protection of human beings," calls to mind the claim of Justinian's *Digest*: "all law is made for the sake of human beings."[34] The protection of corporate persons thus is in keeping with the purpose of the law precisely to the extent that such protection serves the overall function of law, the protection of human beings, the paradigm cases of personhood.

## THE IMPLICATIONS OF *HOBBY LOBBY* FOR INSTITUTIONAL CONSCIENCE

I turn now in this concluding section to the relevance of the *Hobby Lobby* case to the question of institutional conscience. It is my claim that the Court's treatment of corporate personhood sheds light on this question; and by now, I hope that this claim is fairly obviously true. For in its

[33] *Burwell*, 134 S. Ct. at 2767.

[34] Justinian, *Digest*, 1.5.2, as quoted by John Finnis in "The Priority of Persons," in *Collected Essays: Volume II, Intention and Identity* (Oxford: Oxford University Press, 2011), 19–35, 19. The translation is Finnis's.

treatment of the ontology of corporate persons, the Court implicitly addresses skepticism both about the ontological state and the value of institutional conscience.

How can institutions be considered to have a conscience or to act conscientiously? Consider a hospital, and then a Catholic hospital, respectively. The hospital is an institution, the founders and leadership of which jointly commit to providing a particular range of health-related services – many requiring a specialized technical knowledge to perform – to those in need. This joint commitment establishes the institution as a joint subject of certain kinds of actions. When the hospital rejects certain forms of treatment as not conducive to health and so does not offer them, or when it requires that its employees perform certain procedures when requested, then the hospital can be said to act on the basis of its judgments and indeed, to act conscientiously. Of course, as with corporate persons, the ways in which conscience is attributed to a hospital are only analogous to the way in which individuals are said to have a conscience and to act conscientiously. But speaking of the conscience of a hospital is not just a roundabout way of talking about what all the individuals in a hospital think or do; it is a way of talking about what the hospital is committed to.

Similarly, when we consider the value question, we see that treating a hospital as a subject of institutional conscience is of value to those individuals who have jointly committed to the shared purposes that give the hospital's existence point and meaning. As with other groups, the hospital allows many people to do what they could not do individually, and it allows them to pursue those purposes together, in community with one another. And thus a hospital can be expected to have limits to the extent to which it can accommodate the conscience of those members who cannot, for their own conscientious reasons, act in the ways to which the hospital is committed. There are good reasons for a hospital, for example, that provides abortions to grant an accommodation for nurses or physicians who will not participate in those abortions; their judgments are made in good faith, are health-related, and concern matters on which there is legitimate contestation within the medical profession. But similarly, there are good reasons for thinking that a hospital may refuse to accommodate employees whose conscientious judgments involve invidious discrimination: employees who refuse to serve women, or ethnic, religious, or sexual minorities, for example.

When we turn to consider a specifically Catholic hospital, we can see that what the institution is committed to – what its founders and leaders have jointly committed to – is typically much more robust than what, say, a for-profit hospital is committed to. For a Catholic hospital's commitments include joint commitments of its leadership that the hospital carry out its work as part of an apostolate, furthering the mission of the Church in the world and a commitment to do so in ways that follow and witness to the moral teachings of the Catholic Church. The concrete implications of those teachings for medicine are (partially) identified by the Ethical and Religious Directives[35] in accordance with which all Catholic health care institutions are expected to abide. Thus, a Catholic health care institution will typically have a more robust institutional conscience than a non-sectarian for-profit hospital.

By the same token, protecting that institution's conscience will protect the ability of its members to pursue more robust and far-reaching commitments than will be typical in a for-profit hospital. The Catholic hospital is an institutional locus for the pursuit not just of health but also of religion and religious community. Without the protection of such an institution, therefore, the ability of human persons to pursue the most fundamental aspects of their own well-being will be deeply compromised.

This is why the objection that religious institutions should not be able to make claims of conscience against their employees who wish to act in ways contrary to their institutions' commitments is ill-conceived. The objection claims to be asserting the supremacy of individuals over institutions, and at this level of generality, the objection is rooted in truth. Institutions exist for individuals, not individuals for institutions. But not all the goods of individuals are possible without group action, much of which is facilitated by the existence of institutions; so if individuals are systematically privileged against institutions, then the good of individuals will itself be damaged. Where the institutions are of a robustly moral or religious nature in particular, there will be fairly stringent limits to the extent that those within the institution may claim exemption from the governing mission to which the institution is committed.

To summarize: while conscience is predicated of an institution only by way of analogy to the paradigm case of individual conscience, nevertheless, institutional conscience is a valuable reality worthy of protection. This, it seems to me, is the clear implication of the consideration in *Hobby Lobby* of the question of corporate personhood. In an age of skepticism about even individual conscience, the Court's judgment there should be seen as a touchstone for reasoned analysis of the yet more controversial issue of institutional conscience.

35 United States Conference of Catholic Bishops, *Ethical and Religious Directives for Catholic Health Care Services*, 5th ed., November 17, 2009, www.usccb.org/issues-and-action/human-life-and-dignity/health-care/upload/Ethical-Religious-Directives-Catholic-Health-Care-Services-fifth-edition-2009.pdf.

## RECOMMENDED READING

Bedford, Elliott Louis. "The Concept of Institutional Conscience." *National Catholic Bioethics Quarterly* 12 (2012): 409–20.

Corvino, John, Ryan T. Anderson, and Sherif Gergis. *Debating Religious Liberty and Discrimination.* New York, NY: Oxford University Press, 2017.

Durland, Spencer L. "The Case against Institutional Conscience." *Notre Dame Law Review* 86 (2011): 1655–86.

Finnis, John. "Persons and Their Associations." In *Collected Essays: Volume II, Intention and Identity*, 92–99. Oxford: Oxford University Press, 2011.

"The Priority of Persons." In *Collected Essays: Volume II, Intention and Identity*, 19–35. Oxford: Oxford University Press, 2011.

Gilbert, Margaret. *Sociality and Responsibility: New Essays in Plural Subject Theory.* Lanham, MD: Rowman & Littlefield, 1999.

Kaczor, Christopher. "Conscientious Objection and Health Care: A Reply to Bernard Dickens." *Christian Bioethics* 18 (2012): 59–71.

Savulescu, Julien. "Conscientious Objection in Medicine." *BMJ: British Medical Journal* 332 (2006): 294–97.

Sulmasy, Daniel, P. "Institutional Conscience and Moral Pluralism in Healthcare." *New Theology Review* 10 (1997): 5–21.

Tollefsen, Christopher O. "Conscience, Religion, and State." *American Journal of Jurisprudence* 54 (2009): 93–116.

"The Philosophical and Theological Roots of Institutional Conscience." In *The Conscience of the Institution*, edited by Helen M. Alvaré, 28–46. Notre Dame, IN: St. Augustine's Press, 2014.

Wicclair, Mark R. *Conscientious Objection in Healthcare: An Ethical Analysis.* New York, NY: Cambridge University Press, 2011.

Wildes, Kevin. "Institutional Identity, Integrity, and Conscience." *Kennedy Institute of Ethics Journal* 7 (1993): 413–19.

# 21

# Religion, Conscience, and the Law

## *Reasons, Bases, and Limits for Exemptions*

R. KENT GREENAWALT

My aim in this chapter is to explore a wide range of factors that bear on a desirable relation between US law and citizens' sentiments of religious conscience. As with many important subjects, it is difficult to avoid simplification of what is at stake, and my main objective here is to counter that to the extent that I can. I do express my views about some specific topics. Since I have written about many of these in past years, and convincing readers is not the main objective of this piece, I do not go into most of these matters in great depth. I concentrate on exemptions.

Here is a summary of the factors that I explore. On the matter of conscience, what constitutes a sense of "conscience"? When are those senses "religious," and how do religious people develop them? (Since the law is not going to treat "Christian conscience" differently from that of other religions, I focus on the broader category.) What aspects of our lives does "conscience" cover; is how we treat others a basic element? How far are nonreligious bases of conscience distinguishable from religious ones?

Among the important practical questions are these. When it comes to the law, how far can we accept generalizations that should apply to liberal democracies broadly? How far are desirable practical conclusions dependent on the composition of a particular society and its stage of cultural history? In our society, and others, should the law treat religious conscience more or less favorably than nonreligious conscience, and does that depend significantly on the particular topic? To what extent should the law provide exemptions for those who see compliance with the law as violating their conscience, and when, if ever, should these be limited to religious conscience? A somewhat different related issue I shall not explore in this chapter is whether officials and citizens should rely on "public reasons," not religious convictions, in making and supporting conclusions about what the law should do.[1]

On many of the questions I address, I believe it is very difficult to draw certain lines, whether in theory, or about what real people are capable of doing and what others are in a position to assess about what various people do and perceive. Since the law generally involves definite borders that apply to whether acts are protected or not, these complications profoundly affect how far legal standards should attempt to do what might be ideal in some theoretical sense. Trying to come to terms with this obstacle is an important factor in my practical suggestions. Another major theme is that we deeply need to respect others and recognize that many of our fellow citizens are bound to disagree with our own appraisals of subjects for which a dispositive rational answer is absent. These ideas bear significantly on what should be forbidden and on how far exemptions should be granted from some legal duties. I do not delve into how far various exemptions should be legislated specifically, rest on generally worded statutes, or be seen to rest on constitutional rights.[2]

## RELIGIOUS CONSCIENCE AND SOME FUZZY EDGES

If a person believes that an act would be morally wrong or morally required, her conscience may tell her what she should refrain from doing or actually perform. When one's basis is religious conviction, her grounds are religious conscience. Atheists and agnostics can also have senses of conscience. Two key questions about various matters are whether conscience should be treated differently from other moral sentiments and whether religious conscience or broader sentiments should be treated differently from nonreligious conscience.

The boundaries of conscience are a central element here, especially about what the law should do. For individuals, how far does conscience embrace what they believe they should do morally? I think it is fair to say that it covers convictions of considerable strength. Notably, a person will be troubled by possibly acting contrary to what her conscience tells her to do. If a restaurant purchaser considers it morally relevant how large a tip she should leave for a waiter who is poorer and receiving only a modest wage, she is unlikely to feel

[1] My most recent writing on this is in *When Free Exercise and Nonestablisment Conflict* (Cambridge, MA: Harvard University Press, 2017), 201–45, a much briefer exploration than in earlier work.

[2] These matters are covered in my book *Exemptions: Necessary, Justified or Misguided?* (Cambridge, MA: Harvard University Press, 2016).

that it would violate her conscience if she leaves only 15 percent instead of a morally preferable 20 percent. On the other hand, a person's conscience may well tell her it is fundamentally wrong to lie to family members and close friends.

For many people, perhaps nearly everyone, it may be hard to say exactly how far their moral sentiments amount to feelings of conscience. Just how powerful these sentiments must be to amount to "conscience" is vague,[3] and even those who grasp the basic concept may have different senses of what is covered. Especially with respect to subjects in which no one is inviting or proposing that a person act against a moral conviction, she may not even have a sharp sense of her strength of sentiment. Matters become yet more complicated if one person must decide whether the sentiments of another amount to conscience. All this suggests that this is not an easy line for the law itself to draw. I do not mean to claim that this is never appropriate. The draft law exemption for those who were conscientious objectors to military participation would be an example of sensible coverage. And one might think the categorization is desirable even for many other matters. For some of these, it may be hard to imagine a person objecting unless his objection amounts to conscience. For other subjects, one may understand that the actual coverage will be broader or more than a bit uncertain, or both, but that nevertheless this is a healthy way to frame a privilege. These concerns are key to many modern issues about exemptions, a topic to which we shall return.

The line between religious and nonreligious conscience is also vague. Of course, many clear instances lie on one side or the other. If a person is relying completely on church doctrine or how she believes God responded to a prayer, her conviction is religious. If the only influence is a nonreligious moral assessment, the basis is nonreligious. But what if what she was once taught was God's will in Sunday school, she now believes is supported fully by rational analysis, and she gives little thought to the religious premises? What if she clearly believes a position is definitely supported on both religious and nonreligious bases, but she is unsure how far her conclusions are influenced by each? If the law treats religious convictions in a special way, individuals and officials may need somehow to decide where these borderline instances fall.

It helps here to be clear about the various ways religious conscience can develop and why it might be significant for the law whether a conscientious objection is religious or nonreligious. Crucial for various bases of religious conscience are these: the force of what are taken to be sacred texts; statements

3 My approach to all of this is summarized in "Religious Toleration and Claims of Conscience," *Journal of Contemporary Legal Issues* 21 (2013): 449–86.

by those with authority in religious organizations; communications with others who share overall convictions and membership (this can happen among Quakers in the Society of Friends in which no one has special authority); individual assessments based on what one understands as religious premises, whether these are very general or quite specific elements of a faith; and internal feelings that one understands as a divine response to prayer.

For many conclusions along these lines, people may not be able to separate completely how far they are relying on religious premises and nonreligious analysis. One obvious aspect we can often disregard is the place of causal effects as compared with present assumptions. How far is someone's present nonreligious analysis affected by what he was taught as religious truth at an early age? That could actually have an influence even if he has now become an atheist or agnostic. What someone else has long believed is true on nonreligious grounds could affect various ways in what he understands a religion to which he has become a member.

The extent to which, within religious denominations, various aspects of religious truth are seen as tied to general premises of reason has varied significantly throughout history, and this continues. Within Christianity, some evangelical Protestants see religious understanding as highly special. Even if certain conclusions fit with ordinary reason, their religious truth is not really dependent on that. Roman Catholic assumptions about "natural law" are different. Just how that is to be seen has varied throughout history, but what I believe is the dominant claim now is that what is presented as natural law is convincing according to ordinary reason.[4] This claim is thought to cover even specific religious conclusions, such as the inappropriateness of using contraceptives, which are at odds with what most people now assume and believe is supported by ordinary reason.[5]

What does this tell us about the convictions of a Roman Catholic whose conscience tells her she should comply with an aspect of stated natural law, such as the inappropriateness of abortion, since life begins at conception? She may see that conclusion as strongly support by historic church doctrines *and* by nonreligious reason. This could be an example of a kind of combination of

[4] See, e.g., Jean Porter, *Natural and Divine Law: Reclaiming the Tradition for Christian Ethics* (Grand Rapids, MI: Eerdmans, 1999), 29–30. Porter describes the Catholic version of natural law: "Because moral norms are grounded in human nature, which is the same everywhere, they are accessible to all reasonable men and women without the necessity of revelation."

[5] Pew Research Center, "Where the Public Stands on Religious Liberty vs. Nondiscrimination," *Pew Research Center: Religion and Public Life*, September 28, 2016 (finding that "just 4% say contraception is morally wrong"), www.pewforum.org/2016/09/28/where-the-public-stands-on-religious-liberty-vs-nondiscrimination/.

religious and nonreligious conscience; this is especially likely for Catholics given that their authoritative source on abortion relies first upon scientific findings and rational analysis, and only secondarily on Scripture and Tradition.[6] For many people, the combination can be more intricate. Take someone who was raised as a Catholic and continues to be a member. She is aware of the church's position on abortion before she reads the natural law analysis in an authoritative text. After her reading, she is persuaded by the nonreligious argument. But we outsiders will ask "why is she persuaded?" If she has long been a member, she would certainly not want to conclude that ordinary reason is opposed or inconclusive on a topic for which church leaders consistently claim it provides a clear answer. Also, she may see the church leaders as genuinely expert on this subject. Those assumptions could well influence her own independent analysis if she undertakes that. They could also lead to a kind of deferment to experts, not unlike the way most of us believe climate change is a threat because so many experts conclude that.[7] When we put all of this together, how should one characterize the convictions of a Catholic who believes that premises of natural law are supported by nonreligious reason?

## THE RANGE OF CONSCIENCE AND HOW THOSE COMPLEXITIES AFFECT DESIRABLE LAW

What does conscience cover, and how is that relevant for thought about the law? Most obviously, conscience covers acts that we may or may not do. My conscience may tell me I should not lie to my children and that I should spend cooperative time with them. It is interesting here that if I am strongly attracted to do something and don't see it as any sacrifice, I don't *feel* this is a matter of conscience, even if I do believe doing it is supported by powerful moral bases.

Obviously, a central aspect of conscience is how we treat other people. This can affect not only what positive acts we should perform but also how much we should leave to their freedom of choice. Thus, my conscience may tell me that individuals generally, including my children, should be able to decide what profession to pursue, and not imposed upon by myself in this regard.

[6] Sacred Congregation for the Doctrine of the Faith, *Declaration on Procured Abortion*, 1974, www.vatican.va/roman_curia/congregations/cfaith/documbents/rc_con_cfaith_doc_19741118_declaration-abortion_en.html.

[7] Lydia Saad, "Global Warming Concern at Three-Decade High in U.S.," *Gallup*, March 14, 2017, www.news.gallup.com/poll/206030/global-warming-concern-three-decade-high.aspx.

Beyond this, someone's conscience may tell him what he should impose upon others. As a principal of a school, a woman's conscience may tell her that she should insist that all her teachers show genuine respect for students.

These realities bear on what the law should do. If most members of a society believe as a matter of conscience, they should not perform a certain act, that is a powerful basis not to require it. If a significant percentage have that feeling, that is a reason to create an exception even if a general requirement makes sense. This is now a crucial issue about nondiscrimination laws regarding same-sex marriage, a subject to which we will return.

A difficult question is whether convictions of conscience can bear on what one believes should be legally prohibited. The answer is "yes" although the connection is less direct. If a person's conscience tells him that abortion is deeply wrong morally, he may possibly support a law that prohibits it. In this sense, one's conscience can affect what he thinks should be the laws affecting what others are required to do or forbidden from doing.

For both exemptions and basic reasons for legal requirements, does it matter whether the relevant grounds of conscience are religious or not? This has long been an issue about various exemptions, including military service. Obviously, one factor is how far nonreligious conscience seems plausible in context. We will explore this issue below in the context of several current controversies.

## EXEMPTIONS: HOW THE PARTICULAR CONTEXT MATTERS?

In this exploration of exemptions, I address how a number of general questions bear on the desirable resolution of various concrete subjects, including the present controversy about acceptance of the right of same-sex marriage. Among the basic issues are these: Should an exemption from a particular legal duty be created? If so, how far should it extend? Is it defensible, and even desirable, to treat religious conscience specially? We shall look at the traditional military draft exemption, at some excuses from laws dealing with protection of animals and ingestion of substances, at performance of abortions, and at the treatment of those engaged in same-sex marriage. At various points I do indicate my own positions on debatable subjects without attempting to defend them in any detail.

A vital overall position is that tolerance for others is a crucial element of liberal democracy, especially one that is as open to people of various backgrounds and convictions, as is the United States. We have had a regrettable development in recent years of leaders and citizens powerfully rejecting the views of others as completely unwarranted and reprehensible. Whether we can return generally to more balanced, thoughtful approaches is highly uncertain, but doing so would reduce polarization within our country. In any event, I strongly believe such attitudes are badly needed to have in our society when the scope of exemptions is considered. This can affect both their general desirability and specific range.

A central aspect of my treatment of draft exemptions and those that relate to treatment of animals and the ingestion of substances is to respond to one-sided claims about whether religious convictions should be treated specially. Some believe it is always appropriate, or at least acceptable, to give religion a special concession here. Some others believe that is always wrong. I see both positions as misguided. For some matters it is appropriate; for others it is not.

I want to note here a general complication I will address in connection with certain subjects. A legal exemption is, of course, a legal privilege not to perform. But formally this is not the only way that the government and others may react to claims of conscience against ordinary standards of performing duties. One obvious response is simply to eliminate the duty, giving everyone the freedom not to perform. A variation of this does not eliminate the duty but allows anyone to perform either it or an alternative task. Another option is that rather than having a formal exemption, the law may leave it to officials or others in charge of performance to exercise their discretion not to require it. Such discretion may be exercised on an individual basis, as when despite my general duty as a Deputy to review criminal cases, the Solicitor General excused me from reviewing a brief that defended a position I thought was gravely unjust. In other circumstances, leading officials may announce a policy in advance, so that those who consider taking a position will realize what they will not have to do. Whether formally announced or not, the practice in many states of not requiring government lawyers to work on capital punishment cases if they object to that practice, effectively works in this way, benefitting both those with that conviction and allowing the hiring of a broader range of well-qualified lawyers.

## *Draft Exemptions*[8]

In respect of specific subjects, exemptions from a military draft have existed throughout United States history, starting with the Revolutionary War for independence, in which the composition of the military was originally within the individual colonies, rather than a created national government. Just how

[8] A fuller account is found in my work, *Exemptions*, 23–46.

inclusive such a draft should be has been at certain stages of the country's history a serious issue. For most of that history, the privilege did depend upon religious convictions, a requirement that the modern Supreme Court managed to effectively terminate by giving an implausibly broad reading to a statutory definition.[9]

Pacifism has been a conviction of some Christians throughout Christian history, and it has been an important element of some groups, such as the Quakers. In some early states, one had to be a member of such a group in order to qualify, and in some one had to pay compensation, in order to receive an exemption.[10] The requirement of group membership was also contained in the Civil War Draft Act of 1864 and the World War I Draft Act.[11] Although group membership may make it easier to decide who qualifies, we can identify powerful objections to that limit in terms of the values of free exercise and nonestablishment. Suppose a man belongs to another denomination, such as Methodism, and happens to develop pacifist convictions. If the law is cast with a group requirement, he may have a temptation simply to leave his group and join the Quakers if he wants to avoid the draft. There is also the problem that not all genuine Quakers are pacifists. A member who is not may nevertheless choose to seek the exemption to avoid military service.

According to the 1940 Selective Training and Service Act, which is still formally intact, applying now to a military person who becomes a pacifist while in service, coverage was broadened to someone who "by reason of religious training and belief, is conscientiously opposed to participation in war in any form."[12] Our courts of appeals divided on what qualified, and Congress in 1948 responded against a more inclusive sense of religion by specifying that one needed belief in a Supreme Being and in duties superior to those arising from any human relation. It specified that neither beliefs arising essentially from "political, sociological, or philosophical views," or from a "merely personal moral code" qualified.[13] After Congress's amendment, which clearly required a traditional kind of religious view, the courts of appeals again came up with somewhat different constructions. Some of these cases reached the Supreme Court, which, in *Seeger* v. *United States*[14] and *Welsh* v. *United States*,[15] effectively disregarded what the legislators

9 Ibid., 26–30; The broadest reading was in *Welsh* v. *United States*, 398 U.S. 333 (1970).
10 Ibid., 25.
11 13 Stat. 9 (1864); 40 Stat. 76 (1917).
12 54 Stat. 885.
13 Selective Service Act of 1948, 62 Stat. 604 § 6(j).
14 380 U.S. 163 (1965).
15 398 U.S. 333 (1970).

had tried to do and instead made the presence of typical religious convictions unnecessary. In *Welsh*, decided in 1970, the applicant had actually struck the word "religious" from his application and referred to "reading in the fields of sociology and history," objecting that "the military complex wastes both human and material resources" and "fosters disregard for … human needs and ends."[16] Eight Justices were sitting. They divided four to four on whether the statutory language covered Welsh. The four who said "yes" clearly were not construing the language in either an ordinary sense or in terms of what Congress aimed to do. Justice Harlan, one of the Justices who read the language normally, still voted in favor of Welsh. His basis was that because it would be unconstitutional to preclude genuine nonreligious pacifists, the coverage should be extended rather than the statute itself made invalid.[17] Perhaps influenced slightly by the fact that I had clerked for Justice Harlan some years earlier, I then found, and now find, this approach convincing.

Whether one accepts Justice Harlan's constitutional conclusion, the reasons for equal treatment are these. For the military exemption, draft boards interviewed those who claimed the pacifist exemption and explored their convictions in some depth. It is unfortunate if a genuine pacifist is put in jail for refusing to serve, and if he does submit to the draft, he may risk indirectly causing harm to other colleagues by failing to fire his weapon at the enemy. As a matter of what is desirable, this is an area in which exemptions are best not limited to religious claims.

A different issue about draft exemptions I shall just mention is whether a selective objector, someone strongly offended by a particular military conflict, should be excused from participation. The reasons not to require people to act against conscience are present, but countervailing concerns are far from trivial. When the country is involved in various military endeavors, a person may object to one but not others; and over time, our involvement and practices often change. Individuals may find it harder to assess when their basic disagreements with government policy amount to an objection in conscience, and draft boards would find this review often difficult. Although on balance I think some form of excuse would be desirable, and should not be available only to religious objectors, the balance of considerations is much more difficult than it is with pacifists.

16 Ibid., 341–42.
17 Ibid., 344–54.

### *Killing Animals and Ingesting Substances*

The factors that bear on whether exemptions should be limited to religious claimants can arise in other contexts, but it does not follow that such a line is always misguided. One such example is the way animals to be eaten are killed. Many states have laws that prescribe techniques that are seen as less painful for the animals.[18] Within the Orthodox Jewish religion, members are supposed to eat only kosher food; kosher standards indicate how animals are to be killed and these often do not quite fit the modern legal requirements.[19] Given that the killing pain is not excessive, it makes perfect sense to create an exception so that the Orthodox Jewish will still be able to eat this meat. Here it is hard to imagine a genuine nonreligious conviction that one must kill animals in a way that fails to meet requirements set to protect the animals in a minor way. Thus, limiting an exemption to religious bases is appropriate here.

The ingestion of substances is similar, although it produces further complexities in how an exemption is cast. Suppose it is decided, as once was true in various states, that the drinking of alcohol can be so harmful it should be forbidden.[20] Over time, the ingestion of various drugs, including peyote, has been made criminal.[21]

Within the Roman Catholic Church, the drinking of wine – conceived to be the blood of Jesus – has been considered a crucial part of Communion, given what Jesus did at the Last Supper. Many Protestant denominations consider the use of wine as desirable, although grape juice may be an acceptable substitute. We have two strong reasons for an exemption. This use of wine is very important to Catholics and some other Christians and this amount of wine does not cause actual harm, although it is conceivable that someone who takes a sip at a church service may want to go home and drink more. A similar worship ground reaches the use of peyote in Native American services, although that does produce a hallucinatory state similar to what someone might prefer on a nonreligious basis.[22] With both alcohol and peyote, it is hard to conceive nonreligious

18 See Jeff Welty, "Humane Slaughter Laws," *Law & Contemporary Problems* 70 no. 1 (Winter 2007): 189–90, n.100 (collecting state laws regarding humane slaughter and noting that a slight majority of states have them).

19 See, e.g., ibid., 177–78.

20 See Kenneth M. Murchison, "Prohibition and the Fourth Amendment: A New Look at Some Old Cases," *Journal of Criminal Law & Criminology* 73, no. 2 (1982): 473–74.

21 See Lisa N. Sacco, *Drug Enforcement in the United States: History, Policy, and Trends* (Washington, DC: Congressional Research Service, 2014), 4.

22 *Employment Div., Dep't of Human Res. of Oregon v. Smith*, 494 U.S. 872, 874 (1990).

convictions that one must be able to ingest them, not only based on desire but on what is fundamentally required.

With these substances, a different but related question is how broad an exemption should be. This problem is closely related to how difficult it may be to figure out if someone genuinely qualifies. An honest claimant may somehow misconceive what is needed or how his individual feeling fits the requirement; and, especially if actual review is absent, some of those who want to ingest a substance may be glad to state a conviction that is not genuine. Also, if the amount given in group worship is limited, an exemption that extends to individual use could effectively eliminate any genuine restraint on the amount ingested. When those various factors are considered, it becomes evident why a sensible exemption here should probably be limited to worship gatherings, not reaching every individual who claims that religion supports his or her use at home or with friends. A crucial point here is that with a great many actual or conceivable exemptions, it is fundamental whether a possible line is workable. This reality should be recognized by those who would like to be exempted as well as by those who must draw the lines that become part of the law.

### *Practice of Abortion*

The practice of abortion involves a number of important considerations about exemptions, including whether it makes sense to draw the line at religious conscience. I shall start with some general observations and then sketch their implications.

Whether abortion is an appropriate procedure depends on the status of a fetus and the rights or privileges of women to determine whether to have children and what happens within their bodies. For most of American history, abortions generally were illegal, but the Supreme Court in the notable case of *Roe* v. *Wade* decided in 1973[23] women have a constitutional right to an abortion up to the time of viability. Even after that, the Court has said that no state may prohibit an abortion needed for a woman's "health," conceived broadly to include psychological, familial or financial distress.[24] *Roe* v. *Wade* overrode the laws of most states and was highly controversial. The basic objection was, and is, that even an early fetus counts as a human being who deserves protection. Needless to say, the plausibility, the source, and the

[23] 410 U.S. 113 (1973).
[24] *Doe* v. *Bolton*, 410 U.S. 179, 192. (1973).

degree of acceptance of this view bears on what exemptions from involvement in abortions should be granted.

I want to start with a position about which many will disagree. On two related elements, I do not believe that rational nonreligious reasons provide an answer, although many Americans do. One element is when the embryo or fetus first has an intrinsic status deserving at least a degree of protection (some see this question as tied to the presence of the human genome in the zygote, others do not). The other element is whether at that point it warrants protection as great as that for newborn babies or the appropriate degree of protection increases over time. One aspect that matters for a possible exemption is how widespread and plausible is the view that the deserved protection is great enough to cast doubt on the morality of abortion. Is such a view almost certainly based on religion?

With abortion, the relation of law and exemptions is more extensive than excusing people from direct legal duties. Two questions that are about direct legal duties but involve organizations are whether hospitals should provide abortions and whether on any basis those that must generally provide needed medical help may be excused from performing abortions. A key question about abortions that is different is whether individuals who work in hospitals should be excused from a service the hospital generally provides. Within a short time after *Roe* v. *Wade*, Congress enacted a law that when federal support was involved for hospitals and other medical facilities, they could not require that their employees "perform or assist" with abortions if their objection rests on "religious belief or moral conviction."[25]

Here are four basic questions. Is an exemption for religious conscience warranted here? Should it be extended to nonreligious convictions? Does "assist" constitute a sensible border of coverage? Should there be an exception for special circumstances?

The answer to the first question is easy and not complex. Over time many Christian sects, notably including Roman Catholicism, have taught that life deserving protection, based on scientific, rational, and religious reasons, does begin at conception and that abortion is not appropriate. These convictions undoubtedly were a substantial explanation of why abortion was forbidden. Although some believers may not find things so simple, many will see abortion as the intentional taking of human life. The argument that people should not have to directly perform what they see as really a kind of murder is very strong. Especially if I am right that rational analysis does not really tell us when full

[25] 42 U.S.C. §300a-7 (1973).

protection is warranted, giving this exemption for religious believers is called for.

We can perceive strong reasons to include nonreligious convictions. If rationality does not really tell us when life-deserving protection begins, some people's nonreligious sense may intuitively fit with the traditional Christian view. Some of these may think rational thought tells them when life begins. The argument is strong that they should not be required to do what they take as fundamentally wrong.

The boundary of coverage at "assist" seems sensible, if undeniably a bit vague at the edges. If a doctor need not perform an abortion, a crucial nurse should not have to hand the key instruments to a doctor who is performing one. One the other hand, various hospital workers, such as those who admit patients or have general responsibilities should not be able to directly deny help to a woman who is to receive an abortion or refuse to provide a service, such as cleaning rooms, that will provide a kind of indirect benefit to any patient.

Federal law does not provide any explicit qualification to the privilege not to perform or assist, but a number of state statutes do, and courts may read in a qualification even if it is not set out. The important situation here is when a woman for reasons of her own survival or health badly needs an abortion at a particular time and others are not available to provide it. Although some employees might feel that even in these extreme circumstances a fetus should not be destroyed, I believe that if no alternative is available, requiring their help to save the woman is appropriate.

### *Contraceptives and Insurance*

When one turns to contraceptives some questions are similar to those about abortions, especially when it comes to those that can work after the moment of conception. Should pharmacies be able to decline to provide those, and should companies be able to refuse to have their insurance provisions cover them?[26]

I shall say just a few words about the more straightforward issue. If those running a pharmacy genuinely object to providing them, they have a basis to claim an exemption. After all, their customers can get them elsewhere.

[26] See Guttmacher Institute, "State Policies in Brief: Emergency Contraception," *Guttmacher Institute: State Laws and Policies*, October 1, 2019, www.guttmacher.org/state-policy/explore/emergency-contraception.

A counterargument is that people tend to rely on one pharmacy, and in certain locations there may be only one. If people seek a standard drug and it is refused, they may end up doing without it. Given that we are not talking here about individual involvement, and those running a pharmacy are not really seeking to assist all uses of their drugs, I believe that limiting any exemption to religious convictions makes sense. In contrast with the draft example, no one is going to closely review the strength of a conviction.

A more complex issue arises over insurance coverage of contraception. Should a company that provides insurance for employees be able to refuse to cover contraceptives? This is a large controversy in US law, following a regulation adopted in 2012 forcing most religiously connected institutions – though not churches themselves or religious orders – to provide insurance coverage of both contraceptives and of drugs and devices that may act to shed an already-formed embryo.[27] Two critical questions about such a mandate are how the law should understand a "substantial burden" on religious conscience, and how the law should be treating indirect kinds of involvement. One approach is that "substantial burden" rests on the sentiments of the claimant. In terms of our lives, this makes some sense, but if the government is not in a position to review sentiments carefully, this comes very close to eliminating the requirement. All a claimant will need to do is to assent that his objection is based on deep convictions. That is troubling.

This problem relates somewhat to the question of an objector's degree of involvement. Providing insurance does not really encourage someone to do whatever is covered, and it represents a very thin causal relation to what someone decides to do with his life. In this context, we can compare companies paying wages and people paying taxes. A company that provides a salary may have that money spent for all sorts of things of which it may disapprove. Insurance coverage does not seem all that different. When we pay taxes, we understand that these will aid general financing, some of which may go to practices to which we strongly object. People have not been given a right to refuse to pay taxes, and providing insurance does not seem much more direct in affecting the choices those receiving coverage make. Putting all this together, I believe the arguments are strong both that "substantial burden" should depend significantly on more general perceptions and that objections

[27] Patient Protection and Affordable Care Act of 2010 (ACA), 124 Stat. 119 (2010); Group Health Plans and Health Insurance Issuers: Relating to Coverage of Preventive Services Under the Patient Protection and Affordable Care Act, 76 Fed. Reg. 46, 626 (August 3, 2011); Religious Exemptions and Accommodations for Coverage of Certain Preventive Services Under the Affordable Care Act, 82 Fed. Reg. 47792 (2017).

to insurance coverage, whether religious or not, should not lead to rights of nonperformance.

### *Same-Sex Marriage*

The most controversial questions about exemptions now concern same-sex marriage. Genuine competing concerns are in play and these make it difficult to say what makes the most sense, a problem not assisted by the intolerance many of those in competing positions have for each other. I shall begin with a brief sketch of how the basic right came into being.

For most of human history, including that of the United States, marriage has been seen as closely tied to the creation and raising of children. Given that only sexual intercourse between a man and a woman could generate a child, and that men and women were viewed quite differently in what their lives were about, marriage was seen as obviously involving a member of each gender. This understanding was supported by religious views, including those of Christianity, which also perceived homosexual behavior as morally wrong. Even for some believers who thought all sexual relations outside of marriage were wrong, homosexual ones were seen as unnatural in a way not true about unmarried sex between men and women.[28] For most of American history, homosexual behavior was formally criminal, although actual prosecutions were rare.[29]

Within the last few decades, many states repealed such laws and the Supreme Court declared that punishing such behavior was unconstitutional. Some states extended a right to marry to gay couples, and in the notable 2015 decision of *Obergefell* v. *Hodges*[30] the Supreme Court ruled, 5–4, that such marriage was constitutionally protected under the Due Process and Equal Protection clauses. This was obviously an evolutionary approach about a specific practice, since at the time of the Bill of Rights and post–Civil War Fourteenth Amendment no one would have seen that marriage as protected; but Justice Kennedy's majority opinion urged that the framers intended that the clauses be construed in light of developing views about actual values. Given the significance of marriage for the liberty of individuals and the

[28] See, e.g., Gallup, "Gay and Lesbian Rights," *Gallup in Depth: Topics A to Z*, 2017, www.news.gallup.com/poll/1651/gay-lesbian-rights.aspx (showing that some respondents opposed gay marriage because they felt it was "[u]nnatural/[a]gainst the laws of nature").

[29] See ibid. See also, e.g., *Lawrence* v. *Texas*, 539 U.S. 558, 569 (2003) (observing that "[l]aws prohibiting sodomy do not seem to have been enforced against consenting adults acting in private").

[30] 135 S. Ct. 2584 (2015).

importance of marriage for various rights for which equality is a concern, a constitutional protection was held warranted.

Where does this leave us in respect to exemptions? Some opponents have argued that if a basic right to equal treatment is created it is obviously wrong to allow private citizens to treat people unequally. For most of our history, however, private firms and individuals were essentially free to favor some people over others on any bases they chose. What countered this freedom were not basic constitutional rights but antidiscrimination statutes, which became common in the twentieth century. And notably most of these laws have included various exceptions, such as for renters who live close to rooms they rent.[31]

Thus, the central question about exemptions regarding same-sex marriage is whether they are an appropriate qualification of antidiscrimination statutes. Within some states, there may be political considerations of what qualifications are needed to get such a statute passed, but my focus here is on what should be seen as warranted, not what may or may not be a necessary compromise to achieve adoption.

When one thinks about whether an exemption from equal service is called for, it helps to begin by looking at the arguments for each side. In this era, nearly all gay-married partners are bound to see themselves as not having a fundamental defect that has led to their choice. They will want others to respect them and afford them equal treatment, and they will definitely prefer not to be rejected because of their status. Under modern notions, they will almost certainly see these feelings as natural and supported by the assumption that in a liberal democracy people have an equal status. They could also see their views as supported by a correct religious view, but that is unlikely to be their main source of reliance.

What of those who have a moral objection to gay marriage? For most of them, religious convictions will figure importantly. Some may rely directly on church doctrine or biblical passages. Others, having been taught the religious position, may think it is supported by nonreligious analysis of the nature of human beings, family life, and the way children are mainly created and ideally raised. Only recently has human creation become possible outside of sexual intercourse between men and women. Some people, perhaps influenced by religious traditions but no longer believers, may have a strong objection now based solely on what they see as sensible human interactions, but I would guess that the percentage of objectors in this category is very small.

[31] See, e.g., Fair Housing Act, 42 U.S.C. § 3603(b)(2) (1994).

How should each side regard the contrary view? It was widely believed in the past and is still now thought by some that homosexual inclinations are based on misguided contacts or psychological defects. Many more persons think today than in earlier generations that homosexuality is primarily the natural inclination with which some people are born.[32] Given this reality, the moral evaluation made by same-sex married partners should not seem surprising or unreasonable to them. What of the reverse? Given the long history of the Christian tradition and the similar outlooks of most other religions, given the historical limit of marriage to those of opposite genders, and given the comprehensible views why that is called for by the creation and raising of children, strong proponents of gay marriage should recognize that the fact that some religious and nonreligious groups and individuals see gay marriage as wrong is not surprising and does not itself show that all these people are irrational and prejudiced.

This is a clear example of why mutual tolerance is called for, a mutual recognition that those with opposing views have a plausible basis and are not necessarily unreasonable people.

If an exemption is to be granted, how broad should it be, and should it be limited to those with religious convictions? Roughly speaking, we can distinguish direct participation in the marriage, versus indirect connections involving services, such as hotel reservations and food sales, made once the couple is married. As with abortion, if someone strongly believes an act is deeply wrong, we have a good reason not to require that he perform or assist it. Given free exercise law, churches themselves almost certainly do not have to perform same-sex marriages, and a substantial reason exists not to insist on individuals participating if doing so violates their religious conscience.

What about later services? Giving those to gay partners is only an indirect relation to the marriage itself. I think it is crucial here to think about what services are broadly given to those who have acted wrongly. Very few companies and individuals will deny services to people who once committed serious crimes, who are engaged in sexual intercourse outside of marriage, who have remarried without what is seen as a proper cancellation of a prior marriage, or who are known to have had abortions. If this is so typical, should it be right to refuse these services to same-sex married partners? Unless one thinks any negative treatment of homosexuals is alright, it is hard to defend

[32] David Masci, "Americans Are Still Divided on Why People Are Gay," Pew Research Center Facttank, March 6, 2015, www.pewresearch.org/fact-tank/2015/03/06/americans-are-still-divided-on-why-people-are-gay/ (noting that in a 2013 poll, "[t]he percentage of all Americans who believe[d] that people are born gay or lesbian ha[d] roughly doubled [to 41%] . . . since 1985.").

Lund, Christopher. "Religion Is Special Enough," *Virginia Law Review* 103 (May 2017): 481–524.
McConnell, Michael W. "Accommodation of Religion: An Update and a Response to the Critics." *George Washington Law Review* 60 (1992): 642–85.
"The Problem of Singling Out Religion." *DePaul Law Review* 50, no. 1 (Fall 2000): 1–47.
Schwartzman, Micah. "What if Religion Is Not Special?" *The University of Chicago Law Review* 79, no. 4 (Fall 2012): 1351–1427.
Schwartzman, Micah, Nelson Tebbe, and Richard Schragger. "The Costs of Conscience." *Kentucky Law Journal* 106, no. 4 (2017–18): 781–812.
*Seeger* v. *U.S.*, 380 U.S. 163 (1965).
*Welsh* v. *U.S.*, 398 U.S. 333 (1970).

Lund, Christopher. "Religion Is Special Enough," *Virginia Law Review* 103 (May 2017): 481–524.
McConnell, Michael W. "Accommodation of Religion: An Update and a Response to the Critics." *George Washington Law Review* 60 (1992): 642–85.
"The Problem of Singling Out Religion." *DePaul Law Review* 50, no. 1 (Fall 2000): 1–47.
Schwartzman, Micah. "What if Religion Is Not Special?" *The University of Chicago Law Review* 79, no. 4 (Fall 2012): 1351–1427.
Schwartzman, Micah, Nelson Tebbe, and Richard Schragger. "The Costs of Conscience." *Kentucky Law Journal* 106, no. 4 (2017–18): 781–812.
*Seeger* v. *U.S.*, 380 U.S. 163 (1965).
*Welsh* v. *U.S.*, 398 U.S. 333 (1970).

# Index

importance of marriage for various rights for which equality is a concern, a constitutional protection was held warranted.

Where does this leave us in respect to exemptions? Some opponents have argued that if a basic right to equal treatment is created it is obviously wrong to allow private citizens to treat people unequally. For most of our history, however, private firms and individuals were essentially free to favor some people over others on any bases they chose. What countered this freedom were not basic constitutional rights but antidiscrimination statutes, which became common in the twentieth century. And notably most of these laws have included various exceptions, such as for renters who live close to rooms they rent.[31]

Thus, the central question about exemptions regarding same-sex marriage is whether they are an appropriate qualification of antidiscrimination statutes. Within some states, there may be political considerations of what qualifications are needed to get such a statute passed, but my focus here is on what should be seen as warranted, not what may or may not be a necessary compromise to achieve adoption.

When one thinks about whether an exemption from equal service is called for, it helps to begin by looking at the arguments for each side. In this era, nearly all gay-married partners are bound to see themselves as not having a fundamental defect that has led to their choice. They will want others to respect them and afford them equal treatment, and they will definitely prefer not to be rejected because of their status. Under modern notions, they will almost certainly see these feelings as natural and supported by the assumption that in a liberal democracy people have an equal status. They could also see their views as supported by a correct religious view, but that is unlikely to be their main source of reliance.

What of those who have a moral objection to gay marriage? For most of them, religious convictions will figure importantly. Some may rely directly on church doctrine or biblical passages. Others, having been taught the religious position, may think it is supported by nonreligious analysis of the nature of human beings, family life, and the way children are mainly created and ideally raised. Only recently has human creation become possible outside of sexual intercourse between men and women. Some people, perhaps influenced by religious traditions but no longer believers, may have a strong objection now based solely on what they see as sensible human interactions, but I would guess that the percentage of objectors in this category is very small.

31 See, e.g., Fair Housing Act, 42 U.S.C. § 3603(b)(2) (1994).

How should each side regard the contrary view? It was widely believed in the past and is still now thought by some that homosexual inclinations are based on misguided contacts or psychological defects. Many more persons think today than in earlier generations that homosexuality is primarily the natural inclination with which some people are born.[32] Given this reality, the moral evaluation made by same-sex married partners should not seem surprising or unreasonable to them. What of the reverse? Given the long history of the Christian tradition and the similar outlooks of most other religions, given the historical limit of marriage to those of opposite genders, and given the comprehensible views why that is called for by the creation and raising of children, strong proponents of gay marriage should recognize that the fact that some religious and nonreligious groups and individuals see gay marriage as wrong is not surprising and does not itself show that all these people are irrational and prejudiced.

This is a clear example of why mutual tolerance is called for, a mutual recognition that those with opposing views have a plausible basis and are not necessarily unreasonable people.

If an exemption is to be granted, how broad should it be, and should it be limited to those with religious convictions? Roughly speaking, we can distinguish direct participation in the marriage, versus indirect connections involving services, such as hotel reservations and food sales, made once the couple is married. As with abortion, if someone strongly believes an act is deeply wrong, we have a good reason not to require that he perform or assist it. Given free exercise law, churches themselves almost certainly do not have to perform same-sex marriages, and a substantial reason exists not to insist on individuals participating if doing so violates their religious conscience.

What about later services? Giving those to gay partners is only an indirect relation to the marriage itself. I think it is crucial here to think about what services are broadly given to those who have acted wrongly. Very few companies and individuals will deny services to people who once committed serious crimes, who are engaged in sexual intercourse outside of marriage, who have remarried without what is seen as a proper cancellation of a prior marriage, or who are known to have had abortions. If this is so typical, should it be right to refuse these services to same-sex married partners? Unless one thinks any negative treatment of homosexuals is alright, it is hard to defend

[32] David Masci, "Americans Are Still Divided on Why People Are Gay," Pew Research Center Facttank, March 6, 2015, www.pewresearch.org/fact-tank/2015/03/06/americans-are-still-divided-on-why-people-are-gay/ (noting that in a 2013 poll, "[t]he percentage of all Americans who believe[d] that people are born gay or lesbian ha[d] roughly doubled [to 41%] . . . since 1985.").

these special refusals of treatment for those married couples when one does not refuse others who have done what one thinks is wrong. This leads me to conclude that an exemption here should be limited to direct participation. Exactly what constitutes such participation is not simple, but to take two cases, the second of which the Supreme Court is now considering, I believe that being the main photographer of a wedding is direct participation but the baking of a cake used for the wedding celebration is not. If you are the key photographer of a wedding taking photos that will last for generations, that is fairly direct involvement. If all you do is provide a cake of the sort available to all couples with no special message, that is much less direct.

I shall briefly mention one special activity after the marriage that is more direct involvement. That is deciding whether it is relevant for adoption that a same-sex couple has applied for a child. Given that adoption agencies can consider matters such as age and income that would not be permitted in many other contexts, and given that someone who approves of same-sex marriage may still believe that for many children having at least one parent of the same gender, and perhaps parents of both genders, is desirable, I think it would be wrong to require adoption agencies to afford absolutely equal treatment here. But I believe they should not be able to simply exclude same-sex couples, especially since it is possible that no mixed-sex couple applies for a child or that a particular same-sex couple has many positive qualities.

When it comes to a basic exemption, if that is genuinely limited to direct participation, I would not favor a limit to religion. Someone who feels it is fundamentally wrong to do that should be excused. However, given the reasons against extending the exemption, which include concerns that people will make false claims to satisfy prejudiced constituents or to promote political objectives, I believe that if, contrary to my position or because it is needed politically, the exemption is extended more broadly, it would make sense to require religious conscience for contact beyond direct participation.

## CONCLUSION

This chapter illustrates some general truths about human categorizations and how they affect desirable law and also explores more specific issues about warranted exemptions from general law duties and duties imposed by private enterprises.

The general truth is that many categorizations are vague with uncertain edges. That is true about both "conscience" and "religious convictions." This reality is not a serious problem for ordinary human understanding and discourse, but vagueness can be a problem for legal standards designed to control behavior. This can affect how exemptions from legal duties should be framed.

When it comes to questions about specific exemptions, a point of central importance is that we all need to understand that various views about some crucial subjects are not unusual, that we should not condemn all those who disagree with us, and we should often accommodate to their convictions and their needs. Regrettably, our culture has moved in recent years to more unqualified condemnation of those who hold opposing opinions. For exemptions, we need understanding of why the law does what it does, such as promoting the genuine equality of same-sex couples; but we also need tolerance of those with a traditional religious sense of homosexual relations. A degree of mutual understanding and sympathy can help promote desirable exemptions and their limits, including whether a line should or should not be drawn at religion and how strong relevant convictions that behavior is wrong need to be.

## RECOMMENDED READING

*Employment Division, Dept. of Human Resources of Oregon* v. *Smith*, 494 U.S. 872 (1990).

Gedicks, Frederick Mark. "An Unfirm Foundation: The Regrettable Indefensibility of Religious Exemptions." *University of Arkansas at Little Rock Law Journal* 20 (1998): 555–74.

Greenawalt, Kent. *When Free Exercise and Nonestablisment Conflict*. Cambridge, MA: Harvard University Press, 2017.

*Exemptions: Necessary, Justified or Misguided?* Cambridge, MA: Harvard University Press, 2016.

"Religious Toleration and Claims of Conscience." *Journal of Contemporary Legal Issues* 21 (2013): 449–86.

Hamilton, Marci A., and Lana Seligsohn. "Religion Governed by the Rule of Law." *Human Rights* 39, no. 2 (Jan. 2013): 7, 10.

Koppelman, Andrew. "You Can't Hurry Love: Why Antidiscrimination Protections for Gay People Should Have Religious Exemptions." *Brooklyn Law Review* 72, no. 1 (Fall 2006): 125–46.

Laycock, Douglas. "Regulatory Exemptions of Religious Behavior and the Original Understanding of the Establishment Clause." *Notre Dame Law Review* 81, no. 5 (June 2006): 1793–1842.

*Religious Liberty*, 5 vols. Grand Rapids, MI: Eerdmans, 2018.

Laycock, Douglas, Anthony R. Picarello Jr., and Robin Fretwell Wilson, eds. *Same-Sex Marriage and Religious Liberty: Emerging Conflicts*. Lanham, MD: Rowman & Littlefield, 2008.